volume I

CUR

volume I

JOHN CURTIN'S WAR

JOHN EDWARDS

VIKING
an imprint of
PENGUIN BOOKS

VIKING

UK | USA | Canada | Ireland | Australia
India | New Zealand | South Africa | China

Penguin Books is part of the Penguin Random House group of companies
whose addresses can be found at global.penguinrandomhouse.com.

Penguin
Random House
Australia

First published by Penguin Random House Australia, 2017

1 3 5 7 9 10 8 6 4 2

Cover design by Louisa Maggio © Penguin Random House Australia
Image credits: Texture by Shutterstock / binik; Paper texture by Shutterstock / autsawin uttisin;
John Curtin courtesy of Getty Images and the Bettman Collection; back cover image courtesy
of the John Curtin Prime Ministerial Library.
Text design by Midland Typesetters, Australia
Typeset in 12/16 pt Adobe Garamond by Midland Typesetters, Australia
Colour separation by Splitting Image Colour Studio, Clayton, Victoria
Printed and bound in Australia by Griffin Press, an accredited ISO AS/NZS 14001 Environmental
Management Systems printer.

National Library of Australia
Cataloguing-in-Publication data:

Edwards, John, author
John Curtin's War / John Edwards
9780670073474 (hardback)

penguin.com.au

MIX
Paper from
responsible sources
FSC® C009448
www.fsc.org

Contents

	7 October 1941	ix
1	The Trans	1
2	The life that thrills	11
3	A new beginning	27
4	Capitalism is collapsing	33
5	Perth again	49
6	Labor leadership	60
7	The men who matter	65
8	Curtin's Australia	78
9	Leader	103
10	Defending the Empire	119
11	Menzies to power	138
12	Menzies versus Curtin	148
13	War in Europe	154
14	Australia defenceless	173

15   Knife edge   192

16   Curtin warns of war in the Pacific   212

17   Preparing for government   234

18   Curtin to power   244

19   Curtin Forms His Government   270

20   Early decisions, and caucus crisis   287

21   It has come   317

22   Turning to America Curtin appeals to Roosevelt and Churchill   343

23   AIF for the Pacific War   367

24   Resistance collapses in Malaya, Rabaul is invaded, and Curtin makes an ill-timed visit to Perth   381

25   Fall of Singapore Bringing the AIF Home   410

26   The threat of Japanese invasion   429

27   Australia imperilled   446

Endnotes   455

Bibliography   485

Acknowledgements   495

Index   499

For Deborah, and for Alex, Clara, Daisy and Harry — and for V J Carroll, the greatest Australian newspaper editor of his generation. He was my mentor in journalism, as he has been for so many.

7 OCTOBER 1941

In the group photograph of the new ministry taken on the morning of 7 October 1941 twenty men in suits are arranged in two rows, one row sitting and one standing. John Curtin is in front, sitting next to the Governor-General, Lord Gowrie. Curtin's hands are folded, right over left. He has thinning grey hair and wears spectacles. In this photo he cannot hide the cast in his left eye by looking down or turning side-on to the camera. He wears a white shirt and a dark three-piece suit with a high waistcoat. In the breast pocket of his suit there is a folded triangle of white handkerchief. It is a black and white photograph but we know Curtin is in his good blue suit, not only because it is the one he usually wears on formal occasions but also because he has only three, and this is neither the brown nor the blue with the white pencil stripe. He wears his black shoes, not the brown. Of his six ties he has chosen one that is plain and dark.

In this photograph of Curtin a few moments after his swearing-in as Prime Minister and Minister for Defence Co-ordination we cannot see what he is, but we can see what he is not. In his expression there is no grandeur, no easy command, no triumph. He looks, as always, ill at ease, as though caught in a conversation from which he hopes soon to excuse himself. Those who know him well will remember his sincerity, his intelligence, his reserve. They will not recall him as an imposing man, like his political opponent Bob Menzies. He is, as one of his secretaries, Hazel Craig, would say, 'a very, very normal nice human being'. He is also an adroit and accomplished politician, unusually free of vanity or illusion. He is often underestimated, which does not trouble him at all. It was only later, long after this photograph was taken, long after he was buried among the pines and gums at Karrakatta, that Artie Fadden would remember him as the greatest leader of his time in politics, and Harold Cox, an unsentimental reporter who had seen many prime ministers come and go would say of Curtin that he was the biggest figure in Australian politics since the colonies federated in 1901. Curtin did not look like a great man, Bob Menzies would one day write, though 'he undoubtedly became one'.[1]

It is now four days since the two independents in the House of Representatives joined Labor in voting down Arthur Fadden's coalition government. Fadden had been prime minister only since the end of August, following the rebellion within the United Australia Party that forced Menzies' resignation as prime minister. Curtin is Australia's third prime minister in six weeks. He leads the the first federal Labor[2] government in a decade. He is fifty-six years old and it is the first time in his life he has held ministerial office. Ten years ago Curtin was so frequently drunk his colleagues referred to him as 'Poor John'. He has been sober for the last six years, but he is not a healthy man. Patches of his skin are sometimes red and inflamed with psoriasis. He has spent many days in the last month lying on his bed at the Hotel Kurrajong, tormented by neuritis. Already he has heart disease. In the less than four years of life he has remaining he will do things that even now, posing for this ceremonial photo and already impatient to be driven back to Parliament House to chair his first Cabinet meeting at noon, he does not intend or expect or even imagine. Curtin himself will find that he cannot undo what he has done, though he will try.

Curtin had announced the new ministry on Monday night after a caucus ballot on Monday morning that took three hours and seven successive ballots. Sworn in moments before, the new ministers pose in front of the fluted columns of the portico of Yarralumla, not long ago the home of Scottish settlers who farmed sheep on the high Monaro plains. Of the nineteen other men in the photograph, men who are to write themselves into the Australian story over the remainder of the decade, one whose company Curtin finds congenial is Gowrie. Canberra in 1941 has a population of only 9000 people. Curtin hates flying and the journey home by train takes four days, first to Melbourne, then Adelaide, then across the Nullarbor Plain to Kalgoorlie and then to Perth. When Parliament is sitting he mostly stays in Canberra while his wife, Elsie, takes care of the family and the cottage in the Perth beachside suburb of Cottesloe. Some weekends, after writing to Elsie from his room at the Kurrajong, Curtin visits Gowrie and his wife for tea. Gowrie is sixty-nine and won his Victoria Cross fighting the Dervishes in the Sudan Campaign at the end of the nineteenth century. At the time Curtin was a sixteen-year-old messenger boy in a Melbourne club. Blue-eyed, pink-cheeked, white-haired and usually dressed in a superbly tailored pinstripe suit, Gowrie is an English gentleman. His father was a baron, his mother's father an earl. He pronounces 'coming' as 'comin' – there are no 'gs' to his 'ings'.[3] It is an unlikely friendship, one that will deepen during the next few years. In six weeks' time Curtin will visit Yarralumla to share with Gowrie the first of what will be many deep griefs as prime minister: the sinking of the light cruiser HMAS *Sydney* with its entire crew of 645 sailors. Gowrie respects Curtin but he would very much prefer that Menzies was still prime minister, perhaps in an all-party government like Britain's. He plans to write to the Secretary of State for Dominion Affairs, Viscount Cranborne, suggesting a seat be found for Menzies in the House of Commons. Churchill will adroitly respond to this unwelcome request by telling Cranborne that the brilliant Menzies is much too valuable where he is.

On the other side of Gowrie, Deputy Leader of the Labor Party Frank Forde looks unexpectedly glum. This is perhaps because he wanted to be Treasurer in the new government and Curtin has instead made him Minister for the Army, or perhaps because he remembers that but for one vote in the Labor Party caucus six years earlier (and that exercised as a proxy on behalf of a caucus member who if present might well have voted for Forde), Forde would be prime minister and Curtin might instead be Minister for the Army. Steady, loyal and reliable, Forde is a good deputy. Next to him is the Attorney-General and Minister for External Affairs, Bert Evatt. Even in the still photograph Evatt seems to bustle with impatience. He is accustomed to ceremonial photographs. Immensely intelligent and hard-working, he has been a successful barrister and a High Court judge. Soon, Roosevelt and Churchill will be amused by his many peculiarities. Curtin values Evatt's brilliance but distrusts his common sense. For most of the past year he has been fighting with Evatt over political tactics. Even now he rightly suspects that Evatt believes the Curtin Government will not last long, and will soon be succeeded by an all-party government in which Evatt hopes to have a prominent place. Curtin knows that Gowrie also believes this, as do the leaders of the United Australia Party and the Country Party. He knows they may well be right.

Treasurer Ben Chifley sits beside Curtin, glancing away from the camera. He has been back in federal Parliament for only a year, but already Curtin thinks of him as his closest lieutenant. They have been political allies for more than a decade. They first met in Canberra during Jim Scullin's Labor Government, which was destroyed by the Great Depression. Chifley was defence minister in that government, a junior portfolio when there were only token defence forces and nothing to defend against. Curtin was then an unhappy backbencher, sometimes, as he said, borrowing a few pounds to go 'off on a scoot' with a drinking friend, but one who better understood the Depression than all but two or three federal politicians. Like Curtin, Chifley has learned steadfastness from frequent political failure.

They were allies in the fight against the populist demagogue, Jack Lang, in New South Wales, and his supporters in federal Parliament.

The leader of the Lang faction now sits with them in the front row of the ministerial photo – Jack Beasley has been back in the Labor Party only since March. Ten years ago he helped to finish off Scullin's Labor Government and force an election in which both Curtin and Chifley lost their seats. Though he moved their expulsion from the Labor Party in 1931, it was Curtin's first achievement as the Labor Party's federal leader to bring Beasley and his allies back into the party in March 1936. Lang ordered him out again in 1940 but Beasley has now returned. In appointing him Minister for Supply and Development, Curtin has given Beasley a big job. He hopes he will want to keep it. He knows that, despite his loyalty to Lang, Beasley is a conservative, thoughtful man and a good administrator. With Curtin's support he had topped the caucus ballot for election to the ministry. He carries great weight in caucus. Lang may be a spent force but Curtin wants to keep Beasley separated from his sometime ally, Eddie Ward, whom Curtin has been unable to prevent from winning a position in the ministry. Ward now stands in the back row, looking down at Curtin before him. His hair is swept back, his boxer's shoulders set. He is Curtin's enemy.

Menzies will later tell the United States Consul at lunch in Melbourne that the new ministers are 'scum – positive scum'.[4] Before his resignation in August he told his Cabinet colleagues that many Labor members were 'very dubiously British'. The key to understanding Australian Labor, he agreed with British Labour Leader Clem Attlee earlier this year, was the Irish influence.[5] In their suits and ties they do not look like radicals. For some of those looking at the camera on the portico at Yarralumla, the pleasure of being sworn in as new ministers on a fine spring morning in Canberra shines through. Australia is at war, so they also strive to be dignified and solemn. The ministers are still indignant that Australian troops have been pushed out of Greece and Crete with considerable loss. The British, they believe, failed to provide air cover. Without assurances of sufficient air power, Menzies should not have agreed to the use of Australian soldiers. Now they are concerned about Australian troops besieged in Tobruk, whom Fadden has been insisting Churchill relieve.

The British Prime Minister is already displeased. In the War Cabinet rooms under Whitehall, shielded by steel and concrete from haphazard night bombing by the Luftwaffe, Churchill can read on the great wall maps the shifting positions of the German, Italian and British armies in North Africa and the Middle East, the clash of Soviet and German armies on the Eastern Front, the dispositions of the British fleet in the North Sea and the Atlantic, the daily tally of merchant ships lost to German submarines, the RAF losses over Europe. On these maps, if it is there at all, Australia is way off to the right and well down. There are no pins, coloured wool threads or other markers there or nearby – there is no war in that part of the world. Churchill values the Australian troops in the Middle East, though he thinks their commander, Sir Thomas Blamey, a tactless man, and more a politician than a soldier. As for Australian political leaders, though he does not care for him Churchill recognises Menzies' ability. He thinks Australian politicians are otherwise a poor lot. He dislikes former Australian prime minister Stanley Bruce, now High Commissioner in London. He deplores Curtin's refusal to be part of a national government, like his. Churchill has never been to Australia, or for that matter east of India. Australia is far away and its leaders do not have the full picture. They do not know enough. Only at the centre, only at the very centre of the centre, do leaders know enough. Only he is there.

For the new government, 'there will be no half-heartedness' in prosecuting the war, Curtin will sternly tell a War Loan rally in Sydney that night. Even so, Australians do not let the war weigh on their spirits. Yesterday, a holiday, 80 000 people turned out for Derby Day at Sydney's Randwick Racecourse. Even the War Loan rally will be a good show. The Eastern Command Band will play as representatives of the Allies march to the platform in national dress. Gladys Moncrieff and Peter Dawson will sing.[6] Subscribers to the loan will be invited to write a message to Hitler on 18-pounder artillery shells.

The new ministers have read reports in the *Canberra Times* that morning of the progress of the new German drive against Moscow. Hitler promises the offensive will finally destroy what is left of the Soviet armies. Since invading the Soviet Union in June, German forces have captured 155 million hectares of Soviet territory and a population of 65 million. They have captured three million Soviet troops. Now German troops are besieging Leningrad and attacking Moscow. Hitler's new offensive against Moscow deploys two million German soldiers and 2000 tanks. A few days ago Hitler told the people of Berlin that the final battle of the war on the Eastern Front was beginning. If Hitler wins the battle for Moscow and destroys Soviet military power, if he is able to rule most of Europe from the Mediterranean to the Arctic, if he has reliable tributaries where he does not actually rule, how can Britain and its dominions stand against him?

But for now the war remains in the balance. The Russian winter is coming, and in any case the war is a long way away. It is a terrible war, but perhaps not as terrible as the previous one. In the Middle East Australian troops are fighting Germans and Italians in a war of tanks, trucks and aeroplanes rather than mud, trenches, barbed wire and machine guns. The casualties are correspondingly lighter than they were on the Western Front and the Dardanelles in the Great War. The Germans are hard but honourable warriors, as they were last time. The ministers do not know that in Europe the war is changing. They do not know that Hitler has now agreed that German Jews should be deported to the East. They do not know that last month the Germans ordered the murder of 33 771 Jews in a ravine at Babi Yar, on the outskirts of Kiev. Or that a few weeks ago 300 Jews and 600 Soviet prisoners of war were brought to Auschwitz and killed with prussic acid gas, a new technique in mass execution which might achieve the efficiency required for the much bigger task ahead.

The new ministers fear Japan but they trust the might of the British Empire and the United States. Earlier in the year he thought war with Japan likely, but now Curtin hopes the talks between the United States and Japan in Washington will be successful. Opinions differ. On the same day the new government is sworn in, the Combined Operational Intelligence Centre in Victoria Barracks, Melbourne, reports that Japan's preparations for war are 'considered almost complete'.[7] Of course, preparations for war do not necessarily mean war. In Manila the previous day[8] General Douglas MacArthur had told the visiting Australian representative, Sir Earle Page, that after five years of war with China and now threatened by the Soviet Union on the northern flank, Japan was already 'overextended' and 'facing a critical situation'. In Singapore the British are confident the Japanese will not move for months. Air Chief Marshal Sir Robert Brooke-Popham, the British Commander-in-Chief in the Far East, has told Curtin that the north-east monsoon makes naval operations off the east coast of Malaya almost impossible from November to March. When the Japanese do move, they are more likely to attack the Soviet Union than Malaya. In the Middle East the commander of Australia's divisions, Blamey, is confident the Japanese will not attack south. He thinks the 8th Division, now in Malaya, should be sent on to him in the Middle East, as promised.

Because of the war, important information is closely held. Already, some of the new ministers know a lot more than others. Those who know more have a quite different view of the world than colleagues who know less. Many of Curtin's colleagues are confident in the might of the British Empire and the great British naval base at Singapore. Japan would be very foolish to attack south when a British fleet, sailing from the Mediterranean to Singapore, could destroy the Japanese ships and cut off the Japanese invading forces. Curtin, Forde, Evatt and Beasley, members of the Advisory War Council, know otherwise. They know that while Britain is sending a few big ships into the Indian Ocean it will not send a powerful fleet to protect them. They know the military planners have now recognised that the defence of Malaya depends on planes rather than ships, and they also know that the British command in Singapore has less than a quarter of the fighters and bombers needed to repel an attack by Japan. Even so, Curtin has been assured by British military commanders that the combat effectiveness of the Japanese navy is below the standard of even the Italian navy. Japanese naval pilots, he has been told by the British military headquarters in Singapore, are poorly trained. The Japanese-manufactured Zero fighter plane is no match for the American-made Brewster Buffalo, now being provided to the British forces in Malaya.

Curtin, Beasley and Evatt know in a general way that the United States and Britain agree that if both Japan and the United States join the war, the United States will give priority to the war against Germany. They do not know – Menzies and Fadden did not know – important details of secret Washington talks between America and Britain earlier in the year on how they would fight a war against Japan and Germany. They do not know that while Churchill would welcome war with Japan because it would likely engage the Americans in a war against Germany as well, he is determined to prevent the Americans from committing resources to a Pacific war that might be used to fight Germany and Italy. They probably do not know that some Australian military leaders believe there is no point in Australia building a large home army to defend itself. If Japan enters the war and the United States does not, and if for any reason Britain is unable to send a superior fleet, their argument runs, Japan will bring Australia to terms by using sea power alone. If the United States is in, then a large home army is similarly unnecessary.

None of those posing on the steps of Yarralumla knows that two months ago Admiral Isoroku Yamamoto submitted to the Imperial Japanese Navy General Staff plans for a five-pronged Japanese Pacific offensive, nor that two days ago General Hideki Tōjō, the Minister for War and leader of the army party in the Japanese Government, called a meeting of his allies in his office in Tokyo, and decided the Emperor must be persuaded to approve the attack.[9] Even now preparations are being made so that next month the Japanese attack fleet under Vice Admiral Nagumo Chūichi can leave its home waters and sail in complete radio silence, shielded by foggy weather in the North Pacific, towards a position 443 kilometres north of Hawaii. They do not know that in eight weeks Curtin will be woken by his press secretary in his room in the Victoria Palace Hotel in Melbourne to be told that Japanese planes were attacking the United States fleet in Pearl Harbor, or that a little later he will be told that Australian bombers had already attacked Japanese transports landing troops on the east coast of Malaya, and sunk the first Japanese ship lost to hostile fire in the new war. They do not know that a few days later the newest and most formidable battleship in the British fleet, HMS *Prince of Wales*, sent to the Far East to deter Japan from war, will be sunk off the east coast of Malaya by Japanese dive bombers as it attempts to oppose more landings. Or that, despite their superior numbers, Australians and other British Empire troops will be forced down the Malay Peninsula by Japanese troops, that in five months the great British naval base in Singapore will surrender to Japan, and that the survivors of Australia's 8th Division will be marched into Japanese prison camps. They do not know that Japanese troops will soon invade the Netherlands East Indies, land in New Guinea, and bomb Australian towns. They do not know that in a few months their generals will tell Curtin that Japan was at liberty to attempt to invade Australia 'if it so desired' and Australia must prepare to resist. Churchill himself does not know that within a few months he will no longer be at the centre of the centre, which will move from 10 Downing Street and his map room under Whitehall, to the Oval Office and to a more modest map room, one modelled on Churchill's, in Franklin Roosevelt's White House.

Like Curtin, most of the men who have just been sworn in as ministers in His Majesty's Commonwealth Government were born at the end of the last century, when Victoria was Queen and Empress. Few remember anything abundant, easy or prosperous in their lives. They were born too late to enjoy the great Australian boom based on fine wool, gold discoveries, a flood of new settlers, and rising land prices. They grew up in the 1890s, when that forty-year boom had turned to a decade-long bust. Things picked up for a while, but then there was the Great War and the slump after it. They could remember the 1920s as not being too bad, before the world tumbled into the Great Depression. Australia is now well out of the Depression, but into another war. These new ministers have never known a prolonged period of peaceful prosperity. After a lifetime of work, of deep slumps and slow recoveries, their generation is not much better off in 1941 than their mothers and fathers were in 1890.

As professional politicians, their careers have been dismally unsuccessful. Their party started well, forming the first national labour government in the world in 1904 and holding office for more than a third of the time in the first sixteen years after Australia was created in 1901. But Labor then split over conscription for the Great War. After thirteen years in opposition it won office in 1929, losing it two years later in another rancorous split which kept it out of office for another decade. Two years of office in the last quarter-century. Fifteen of the nineteen Cabinet members in the photograph have never been ministers. Labor has been sworn into office this morning, but for how long, and with what constraints?

The new ministers looking at the camera wonder how long it will take them to learn the business of their departments. They want to see preference for union members strictly enforced. They think soldiers' pay and old age pensions should be increased, that the rich should pay more for the war. They think the economic arrangements in Australia are unsatisfactory, though without a Labor majority in either of the Parliament's two chambers they realise there may not be much they can do about them. They believe that Australia should remain white and British. They think of themselves as Australians but also as

Britishers in the South Seas, as a self-governing dominion, part of a vast Empire which includes India, Burma, Malaya and Hong Kong. They do not know that the war will destroy the Empire as surely as it destroys Hitler and Tōjō. They do not know that while they are British, their children will not be. They do not know that Australia, so remote from the centre of British civilisation, will soon find itself in quite another world, one in which it is not at all remote. They do not know that they are about to discover who they are, and what Australia will become.

Sitting at the centre and front of the group this very, very normal, nice human being is now in a world that is not at all nice or normal, and many of the people he will deal with – Blamey, MacArthur, Churchill, Roosevelt, his own colleagues Evatt and Ward, let alone the actual enemy – are anything but nice or normal.

Chapter 1

The Trans

On a Monday evening in March six years earlier, Labor member for Fremantle in the House of Representatives John Curtin could have been found on the Great Western Express platform of Perth railway station, beginning his journey to Canberra for the first sitting day of federal Parliament in 1935.[1]

As a child of the 1880s, of the great age of railway construction in Australia, there was something about more modern forms of transit he could not gladly embrace. In 1935 the airline services between Perth and the eastern states were not frequent or comfortable, but even when possible he didn't care to fly. Much later, in wartime, when he had no choice but to travel by flying boat across the Atlantic from the east coast of the United States to Ireland and back, Curtin would gloomily tell his secretary he placed his only hopes of making the crossing in the skill of the pilot, the rotation of the earth, and God Almighty.

They were so unusual for Curtin that an aeroplane flight could be discussed for years after. In a moment of poor judgement during the 1943 election campaign he would be persuaded by the Royal Australian Air Force and his own press secretary, Don Rodgers, to fly from Adelaide to Perth in a Lancaster bomber then touring Australia to drum up air crew recruits. The only concession to civilian travel in the configuration of the unpressurised and unpadded bomber,

Curtin's party discovered, was that the bombs had been removed. The deafening roar made conversation impossible. Curtin himself was given the navigator's seat behind the pilot, where he could look out and see the desert beneath. His staff were accommodated on two steel benches around the bomb bay, sitting between struts, their backs curved into the fuselage. Most of the RAAF crew promptly went to the back of the plane, unrolled sleeping bags and dozed off. The flight over the sea after leaving Adelaide was pleasant enough, Curtin's secretaries Gladys Joyce and Hazel Craig remembered, but when they reached the Nullarbor it was not so good. Fulfilling his mission to attract attention and admiration, their pilot, well-known war hero Peter Isaacson, roared low over little towns. It seemed to Craig that he wiggled his wings at every rabbit he saw on the Nullarbor. Around the bomb bay Curtin's staff began to feel very sick, Joyce vomiting into brown paper envelopes she had thoughtfully brought along. Even the WAAF officer vomited.

On and on they flew, Isaacson jerking the plane down to buzz tiny settlements, cheerfully ascending again with a departing roar, the staff in a nauseous delirium, the full brown paper envelopes spilling around them. Landing in Kalgoorlie, Joyce was taken to hospital semi-comatose and was later helped onto a train for Perth. She would spend the week there in hospital. The others flew on to Perth, landing at last at the Pearce air force base and stumbling out of the plane to a lunch that began with a greasy soup. Half a century later Joyce and Craig, then in their eighties, would still remember the flight with Isaacson and marvel they ever flew again.

Up front, Curtin claimed to enjoy the scenery. He was not sick, he told Joyce later, though he came pretty close. Feeling sick was the least of his anxieties about planes. The flying boat trips across the Atlantic to visit Churchill, another in the United States to visit Roosevelt, and the Lancaster bomber trip from Adelaide to Perth were among the very few flights Curtin ever took, not counting the final one when the biscuit bomber carrying his coffin flew low over Parliament House, dipped its wings, and banked west for the long flight home to Perth. And even then, Curtin past caring, his body stowed on the bomber, his wife Elsie watching the plane's ascent would think of how nervous Dad had always been of flying.[2]

Curtin was not alone in his anxiety about flying. After all, his was the first generation for which air travel had become possible. Evatt did not care for flying. His insistence on having planes double-checked for defects before take-off was well attested, though it is difficult to credit the widely circulated story that he insisted on carrying fishing lines to sustain the party if forced to land on a Pacific atoll. The fabled General MacArthur was likewise said not to care for flying, though for him it was sometimes unavoidable. Even as he was hunted by the surrounding Japanese, MacArthur refused as unsafe the first plane sent to rescue him from the Philippines.[3] Escaping on a somewhat better plane sent to replace the first, he left it in Alice Springs and thereafter travelled by train and car all the way to Adelaide, across to Melbourne, and on to Canberra.

Nor was the worry entirely unfounded. Everyone had a story about a crash, or a near miss. Menzies as prime minister lost three ministers and the Chief of the Army in a 1940 plane crash near Canberra. It was said it happened after the plane pulled out of its landing approach and commenced a second circuit. When Menzies' DC-3 was descending into Melbourne airport during the election campaign a few weeks later, the pilot suddenly aborted the approach, advanced the throttle to full power and banked sharply. Sitting next to him, reporter Harold Cox noticed Menzies lying back, his eyes closed, fingers tensed, knuckles white. 'Well, we're doing a second circuit too, Prime Minister!' Cox shouted gaily over the engine's roar.[4]

As early as the 1919 Labor Conference in Perth, Curtin had advocated Australia equip itself with planes that could drop explosives on invading ships, but he himself didn't care for the new machines. If there was a sea between him and his destination, he preferred to sail rather than fly. He sailed from Melbourne to Perth to take up his new job as editor of the *Westralian Worker* in 1917. He later sailed to Europe as a delegate to the International Labour Organization in Geneva. When first elected to Parliament in 1928 he sailed from Perth to the eastern states, his family with him. He was so accustomed to the voyage from Melbourne across the Bass Strait to Tasmania, where the love of his life, Elsie Needham, had lived with her family before their marriage, that as Opposition leader during the 1937 election campaign he would insist on sailing there on the 13-knot SS *Wollongbar*[5], a fifteen-hour voyage he spent reading detective stories while the accompanying reporters uneasily watched the notoriously changeable weather. Bothered by the menace of German and Japanese submarines, Curtin sometimes found even sea travel disturbing. His famously hard-working wartime defence official, Fred Shedden, concealed a catty side from his boss, but opened up in his private diary. Sailing the Pacific to the United States with Curtin, he recorded that Curtin answered the lifeboat drill siren so promptly that he was often first to reach his designated boat, anxiously looking back for his slower fellow passengers. (Nor was that worry entirely unfounded. The *Wollongbar* would be torpedoed by a Japanese submarine in April 1942.)

He used them when necessary but Curtin did not care for cars either. He never learned to drive and did not wish to. Later, when prime minister, he came to trust his driver Ray Tracey – and not only to drive a car. Tracey was a punter, followed the form guide closely, and could discuss horses with Curtin with a depth of knowledge matched only by the Parliament House barber, Cec Bainbrigge. Tracey also played a good game of billiards with Curtin when the Prime Minister returned to the official residence, the Lodge, after a long day of meetings. Tracey took care of the fowls at the Lodge, and was said to be able to coax Curtin out of his occasional black depressions. He had driven mules and trucks on the Western Front during the Great War, and returned home to find himself driving Australian prime ministers. He had driven Billy Hughes, Stanley Bruce, Jim Scullin,

Joe Lyons, Earle Page, Bob Menzies and Artie Fadden before driving
Curtin, though his relationship to those others was only as a driver
rather than, as to Curtin, a companion of his solitude.

Tracey would be there at the beginning, the last few months of
1941, driving the new prime minister from Parliament House to the
Lodge, and sometimes to War Cabinet meetings at Victoria Barracks
in Melbourne. He would be there at the end, on the evening of
4 July 1945, visiting Curtin in his bedroom in the Lodge at around
ten o'clock, six hours before he died. 'How are you, Ray?' Curtin
would whisper. 'I've had a pretty tough day today.'[6] So confident was
Curtin in Tracey's ability that he was untroubled or at least stoical
when Tracey, driving Curtin to a critical Cabinet meeting, rushed him
in the official Cadillac, the graceful vehicle disfigured by a charcoal-
burning gas apparatus, from Sydney to Canberra in what Tracey later
claimed to be three and a quarter hours, and once from Canberra to
Melbourne in six hours and forty minutes – times that would even
half a century later, on better roads with better cars, be thought quite
quick.[7] Perhaps Tracey embellished. Curtin's trust in Tracey's driving
was merely an aspect of his overall comfort in Tracey's company.

For an Opposition politician paid twenty pounds a week, a car
would in any case have been an unusual ostentation. At home in
Cottesloe (one day to be among Australia's most expensive suburbs,
but then a scattered settlement of single-storey bungalows on sandy
blocks) he and Elsie and the two kids lived well enough but did not
yet have a refrigerator or an indoor toilet, let alone a car.

Even later, as Prime Minister and Minister for Defence, when the
whole of the Royal Australian Air Force might be thought of as his to
command, he preferred to travel to Perth by train – though by then,
instead of the first-class sleeper berth he was entitled to as a member
of federal Parliament, he could take the entire Prince of Wales
carriage with office space, private bathroom and two bedrooms.
(Strolling beside the track during the engine's frequent stops for fuel
and water, he would startle the soldiers who filled the carriages and

sometimes the cattle cars with his genial inquiries. 'Young Syd Gray, I thought you were up north somewhere!' he called to one delighted private he met while breakfasting at the railway station in Adelaide, later inviting him to the Prince of Wales saloon car for sandwiches and a beer[8], and agreeing to attend his wedding a few days hence.) As secretary of the Timber Workers Union he had travelled much of Victoria by train, often at night to save on hotels. A few years later he would so far as possible crisscross Australia by train, speaking at five or ten meetings by day in his first federal election as Opposition leader, catching another train to the next town, the next electorate, again speaking five or ten times, sleeping in country pubs when not sleeping in the train and this time companioned by Don Rodgers, his new press man on loan from the *Labour Daily*. Rodgers found it an interesting but tiring campaign, memorably so when in one town Curtin's rest was so disturbed by the roaring of a nearby circus lion he woke Rodgers and talked and smoked through the night and into the dawn.

So on a Monday evening early in March 1935 Curtin would be at Perth railway station with his suitcase, dressed as he always was for train travel in a well-cut wool suit, his tie carefully knotted to place the dimple in the centre under the knot just so, his high-cut waistcoat buttoned, his watch chain with its Australian Journalists Association badge across his waistcoat, his black shoes polished. He wore a smart, narrow-brimmed hat or perhaps the bowler he sometimes affected. He smoked Craven A cigarettes, using a holder. He took them from their red package with its black cat motif, or perhaps from the silver cigarette case he had been given when he resigned as editor of the *Westralian Worker* to enter Parliament. He carried a good-quality wool overcoat, either the blue or more commonly the tweed.[9] In his case he had probably tucked his dressing-gown, and the old grey travelling rug he bought for his travel to Geneva twelve years earlier and had taken everywhere since.[10] He wore the flat rim, round eye, white gold spectacles he always wore, his Perth optometrist so far sharing his unchanging preference that decades later he would write a letter of indignant protest when the clay spectacles were removed from a clay bust of Curtin, rightly arguing that he was far more recognisable with his spectacles than without.[11]

Boarding the train and settling into his first-class sleeper carriage, he was polite and courteous but a little distant from the other Western Australian politicians returning to Canberra. They could not be offended. They knew that Curtin was never cheerful or communicative on the first leg of the trip, that starting out he felt keenly his separation from Elsie and the two children, from the comfortable round of meetings in Trades Hall and the Labor Party offices, and that it would take him until Kalgoorlie to reconcile himself to another couple of months away from them and begin thinking about the session ahead.[12]

Even after Curtin had settled into the journey his fellow travellers could sense there was something about him that resisted easy fellowship. An obscure federal politician from the most remote state in the federation, a member of a party that could muster fewer than a quarter of the seventy-five members in the House of Representatives, a man now aged fifty who after thirty years in politics had never been an elected leader of his party or a minister in its governments, respected as a good speaker and a fluent writer but not as a dominating politician with a loyal following, there was for all that something about Curtin his friends and opponents respected. It was his intelligence, his earnestness, his knowledge of his weaknesses, his silences, his distance. He had some kind of moral authority, difficult to define but undeniably there. He was also, some of his old Perth acquaintances would remember, a 'queer' man. 'You'd meet Jack Curtin in the street,' an old Perth acquaintance recalled, 'you'd be talking to him and all of a sudden he'd walk away.'[13] It did not make Curtin an easy companion. He was genial and unassuming, but distant.

Belching smoke and coal cinders from its steam locomotive the Great Western pulled out from the station, gathering speed as it began its long journey east to the goldfields of Kalgoorlie. Leaving Perth they passed through scrubland and small farms. Sometimes, rounding a bend, Curtin could see in the locomotive headlight kangaroos bounding away from the track. Later the conductor would convert the leather bench in his first-class car into two bunks. Curtin would dip into his considerable collection of Clarence E. Mulford's Hopalong Cassidy westerns – perhaps *Trail Dust*, published only the previous year – and turn in, feeling as he drifted into sleep the rising gradient as the train left the Avon Valley and climbed into the hills and then the vast black spaces of the wheat belt.

Woken by the conductor with tea and two biscuits the following morning, Curtin had showered and shaved by the time the Great Western stopped at Southern Cross soon after eight. While the locomotive took on coal and water, railway workers coupled to the train a dining car and a kitchen, already smelling pleasantly of frying bacon and eggs. Cheered by a breakfast served on starched white tablecloths with heavy polished cutlery, by the amiability of the men's first-class club car with its leather chairs and card tables, by now reconciling himself to the return to Canberra, Curtin began to fall in with the familiar rhythms of the train. He could smoke, yarn to colleagues in the club car, play bridge, read another western. Hopalong was shabby and disreputable, at least before the success of the film versions encouraged Mulford to rewrite the earlier novels to conform to the more heroic character depicted on screen. Shabby or shining, Hopalong helped the weak against the strong.

They travelled on in the bright morning light through drier, well-wooded country that in spring would be carpeted with brilliant wildflowers. In the early afternoon of Tuesday, seventeen hours after they left Perth, they reached the goldmining town of Kalgoorlie. There Curtin and the other passengers travelling through to the eastern states took down their suitcases, left the Great Western, and moved across the platform to board the Trans-Australian train running on the Commonwealth's railway line to Port Augusta in South Australia. Built as part of the bargain to bring Western Australia into the federation, the rails of the 1700-kilometre Commonwealth line were set a little wider than the Western Australian line they had been on. A train traveller between Perth and Brisbane encountered five changes in gauge. As Curtin had reflected five years earlier, Australia became 'a nation politically before becoming a nation economically'.[14]

By the early evening of Tuesday[15] Curtin was travelling across a granite plateau, well timbered with salmon gums and sandalwood and fields of white everlasting daisies, until after 270 kilometres the eucalypts abruptly stopped and they entered limestone plains of black oak, mulga and myall before reaching the Nullarbor itself. Stopping occasionally for water and coal they travelled on through Tuesday night, awaking on Wednesday morning to find themselves in the saltbush and bluebush of the Nullarbor Plain. Air-conditioning would come to the Trans-Australian Railway the following year but in 1935 Curtin and his fellow travellers relied on fans and open windows. The average temperature across the Nullarbor in early March was around 30 degrees. Some days it was in the low forties. Exactly every 30 kilometres they passed a railway fettlers' settlement of exactly six houses, each with exactly three rooms and a corrugated iron roof.

In its entire length the Trans-Australian track did not cross a single permanent stream of water. There were no kangaroos or wallabies on the treeless limestone plains, the bed of an ancient sea. There were dingoes living in the caves, and plenty of rabbits. Sometimes they would see a flock of plain turkeys lift off and fly away as the train approached. Overhead eagles circled, looking for rabbits. White owls hunted by night.[16] Stretching their legs during the stops for water and coal, the travellers crunched fossils of sea creatures underfoot.

By and by they reached the beginning of 500 kilometres of precisely straight track through low scrub and rock of the vast plain between the Great Australian Bight to the south and the Great Sandy Desert to the north. The sun rose from the track in front at dawn, and set in the evening on the track behind. During the cloudless days Curtin could see the circle of the plain around him from horizon to horizon.

In the brilliant nights he could see through the right-hand windows the points of the Southern Cross in the sky over the Great Australian Bight, and through the upper corner of the left-hand windows the constellation of Orion and the blaze of the Pleiades over the Great Sandy Desert.

Tiny stations rolled by – Parkeston, Golden Ridge, Karouie, Zanthus, Naretha, Haig. On and on they travelled, passing during the night a small stone cairn marking their passage from Western Australia to South Australia, through to the eastern edge of the Nullarbor and the beginning of the short gums of the mallee scrub, then the sand hills marking the eastern edge of the limestone plains, then the granite country with its vast salt lakes.

On and on, through Immarna, Barton, Wynbring, then Tarcoola, Wilgena, Kingoonya, 174 Miles, station after station until night fell and the passengers again slept through the blackness of the scrub to reach Port Augusta at 5 a.m. Thursday – a night, a day, another night, another day and another night after Curtin had left Perth, and still only in Port Augusta, with a lot of South Australia, all of Victoria and a good part of New South Wales yet to go before reaching the town of Goulburn, where he could change again for the final 100 kilometres to Canberra. Now nonchalant about vast distances, Curtin would tell Elsie he thought of Port Augusta as practically 'a suburb of Perth'.[17] If he went straight through from Perth to Canberra and his room at the Kurrajong Hotel the journey would take five nights and four days, on six different trains, with five changes of gauge.

Curtin had crossed the Nullarbor perhaps twenty times since he had moved from Melbourne to Perth eighteen years earlier. Dry and treeless, it was also clean, simple and vast. Strolling beside the track in the baking heat, Curtin could smell the faint dry fragrance of the saltbush and mallee eucalypt scrub. It was what it was, as it had been for millions of years. The ancient seas had drained off their bed and in time some twisted shrubs, the saltbush, a few animals and birds, had found it was enough.

CHAPTER 2

THE LIFE THAT THRILLS

(1)

Later that year it would all change for Curtin, but if he reflected on his first half-century as the Trans was crossing the Nullarbor in early 1935 he could only conclude that his political career was a flop. Looking around the first-class club car at his fellow politicians also travelling on the Trans through to the eastern states, Curtin had much to ponder.

Travelling several days together, sharing the news telegrams, taking meals together, reading and yarning in the club car, strolling together by the side of the track, the Trans passengers made a community. All but one of the Western Australian federal politicians who might also have joined Curtin in the first-class club car in Perth for the journey to the opening of the new session in Canberra – all six senators from the state and three other members of the House of Representatives – were from the United Australia Party or the Country Party and supported the government of Prime Minister Joe Lyons. Their mood was buoyant. In his 1935 New Year message Lyons had congratulated his fellow countrymen on their sacrifices in the 'economic crisis', through which they had 'won a position which was the envy of the world'. The Great Depression, which had seen a fifth of Australian workers unemployed,[1] was ending – and Lyons claimed the credit.

The small space and the long journey encouraged civility, despite
political differences. Even so, Curtin would be pleased if the train was
joined in Kalgoorlie by the local federal member, Albert Green, the
only other Labor Party member of federal Parliament from Western
Australia in 1935. Green was commonly known as 'Texas', a nickname
that had once referenced early travels in America and in time become
so fixed in his identity that in newspaper photographs his wife was
identified as 'Mrs Texas Green'. Sixteen years older than Curtin, Green
had held the federal seat of Kalgoorlie since 1922. In Jim Scullin's short-
lived federal Labor Government during the Depression, Green had
been Minister for Defence and later Postmaster-General and Minister
for Works and Railways. Green's seniority in Western Australia was
an obstacle to Curtin when he ran unsuccessfully for the Scullin
Government ministry in 1929, but despite this past inconvenience
their relationship was now cordial. Later that year Green would be
one of two colleagues who first encouraged Curtin to run for the
leadership of the party.

Sometimes Curtin would find a more difficult figure than Green
among the travelling politicians. It would not happen on all Curtin's
train journeys across the Nullarbor because Western Australia's senior
federal politician actually resided in Melbourne rather than Perth, but
every now and then Senator Sir George Pearce, then sixty-five, would
be in the first-class smoking car, his pipe clenched in his teeth, his
bridge hand held close, his mild brown eyes searching his partners',
his expression entirely neutral. Pearce was a man of consequence.
Even the transcontinental railway they were travelling on existed
because of Pearce, who had insisted the Commonwealth pay this price
for Western Australia's inclusion in the new nation. Calm, measured,
orderly in all things, Pearce played a bad hand as skilfully as a good one.
He had twice helped to split the Labor Party, once from government
(and as a Labor minister) and once from opposition. There had been
forty-three Labor members of Parliament left when Prime Minister
Billy Hughes, Pearce and their followers walked out of the party

room in the split over conscription for overseas service in 1916. In 1935, four years after Scullin's government split in the Depression, a split encouraged by Pearce's obduracy as Leader of the Opposition in the Senate, there were just twenty-one. During the conscription split Pearce had Curtin gaoled. After the second split Curtin lost his seat in the House. In a long journey across the Nullarbor, these incidents were best overlooked.

A carpenter by trade, Pearce had first risen to political power in Western Australia's trade union movement and the Labor Party. A senator for Western Australia since the Senate was created in 1901 and at first a Labor representative, Pearce was now Joe Lyons' Minister for External Affairs. To Pearce, this was no great distinction. His great achievements, his most enduring interests, were not in foreign policy, and particularly not in Australian foreign policy at a time when the nation maintained no embassies other than in London, had no information other than that provided by London (and the newspapers), and found it difficult to come to any view other than London's. Pearce's abiding interest was in ships, planes, armies, weapons and war. He had been Minister for Defence in Andrew Fisher's Labor governments before and during the Great War, Defence Minister in the Hughes Labor Government which followed Fisher's, and Defence Minister (and the trusted, crafty lieutenant of his leader) in the Hughes Nationalist Government which followed the Hughes Labor Government. He had been happy enough to serve Prime Minister Bruce as a close political adviser and as Minister for Home and Territories and Vice-President of the Executive Council, but he was happier still when Prime Minister Lyons brought him back as Minister for Defence. Forced out two years later by public indignation over the woeful inefficiency of his department – a scandal in which he not only refused responsibility, but joined in the general indignation – he had nonetheless so deeply put his stamp on the Australian armed forces and Australian defence strategy as the nation's longest-serving Defence Minister that even now he

overshadowed his successor. Pearce could claim to have built the
Australian navy and the air force, introduced compulsory military
service, founded training schools for the air force, the army and the
navy, and created small arms and military clothing factories. So far
as he could he had selected the higher officers, and influenced the
higher strategy and command arrangements.[2]

He had also selected the enemy. Japan's victory in its war with
Russia in 1905, four years after the Australian colonies federated and
Pearce was elected to the Senate, convinced him. Australia's enemy
would be Japan.

Compared to Pearce, Curtin had achieved nothing. And Texas
Green had after all been a minister and had held his seat with good
majorities, achievements Curtin could not claim. True, he had won
back his seat of Fremantle in the House of Representatives in 1934
and he had been elected by his colleagues to the executive of the
parliamentary party. He drank less. He was admired by his colleagues
as a forceful and well-informed speaker, as a politician who had
consistently opposed the Premiers' Plan to remedy the Depression,
and now as a peacemaker doing the most anyone could to find a
compromise between Labor's federal leader, Jim Scullin, and former
premier of New South Wales, Jack Lang, who controlled much of
the party in New South Wales and was extending his influence
in Victoria and South Australia. Curtin could say, too, that he was
happily married, that he loved his eighteen-year-old daughter Elsie,
and his fourteen-year-old son John, and that he had acquired in a
lifetime's reading and experience a reasonable stock of understanding
and reflection. He was respected for his honesty, his seriousness of
purpose and selflessness by his colleagues on his own side of the
House, and by those who knew him on the other side. He smoked too
much, he still had episodes of black depression and painful headaches,
but he could say he was happy – or at least contented.

But he could not say that his political achievements fulfilled
his early ambitions. He could not say that he had realised the high

hopes that his friends and mentors held for him when he appeared, eager, empty and zealous, from the slums of inner Melbourne a few years before the six colonies federated to form the Commonwealth of Australia.

The child of Irish immigrants, Curtin was born in 1885 in Creswick, Victoria. Like so many other immigrants, Curtin's father, John, had been attracted to Australia by its wealth and freedom.[3] When John Curtin left Ireland in 1873, Australian workers were the best paid in the world. When he arrived there, Melbourne had overtaken Sydney as Australia's biggest city, and for decades it would remain the leading centre of industry and finance. By 1878 he had joined the Victorian Artillery Corps[4], leaving it the following year to join the Victorian police as a constable. After four years of service he was posted to Creswick, a goldmining town in regional Victoria.

By the time the young John Curtin was five, his father invalided out of the police service and the family moving on from Creswick, the first great golden age of Australian prosperity was ending. His political career, almost his entire life, would be spent in a country less hopeful, less successful, less prosperous than it had been in the four decades from 1850 to 1890. Melbourne real estate prices and rural land prices, driven by reckless lending, had risen to a giddy peak from which they would soon collapse. British capital had been supporting the expansion of Australia. When the Argentine Government defaulted on payments to British lenders in 1890, the crisis threatened to bring down the British banking system. The Bank of England stepped in, but in the financial panic lending to Australia dropped sharply. Land prices in Australia crashed, leaving borrowers unable to repay loans. From the peak in 1889 to the trough eight years later the value of output fell by nearly one-third[5], a deeper and longer fall than the Great Depression forty years later.[6]

Unable to meet depositors' demands, banks began to close their doors. Bank failures deepened the slump, implanting in newly forming labour parties a conviction that fixing the banking system was a top priority. In the platforms of the colonial labour parties, nationalisation of banking or at least state control was an early and fond objective. Through the decade infant unions fought back as employers cut wages on the waterfront, in mines and shearing sheds. The unions were beaten. Defeated in the workplace, they looked to political labour parties in the legislatures to strengthen their arm.

By the time Curtin left school, the worst of the depression of the 1890s was over but recovery was slow and uncertain. His father managing one luckless hotel after another, the family slipped into poverty. Curtin later recalled his childhood as 'bread without butter and tea without milk'. The family moved from one small, bare and crowded cottage to another, usually in the inner Melbourne suburb of Brunswick.[7] Curtin shared a bed with his brother. When he got his first job, and for many years after, he continued to live at home, his wages sustaining the family.

The slump of the 1890s, the years of Curtin's childhood and adolescence, would reverberate through Australia's subsequent history and Curtin's political career. It inspired the federation movement. When Federation came in 1901, constitutional powers over immigration, banking, tariffs and industrial disputes were bestowed on the new Commonwealth partly or wholly in response to the shock of the slump. Four decades later, and as prime minister, Curtin and his colleagues would still be influenced by it.

Curtin had left school at fourteen, a boy of no particular promise. He was a fair cricketer and footballer, interests he would keep all his life. He found work as a copyboy for *The Age*, as a junior in a print shop, a page in a Melbourne club. But the boy was hungry for something, for some greater thing. It was not the Catholic faith of his parents. It was later said he played a cornet in a Salvation Army band for two years[8]; if he did, the Salvation Army was not it either. His true calling, as he discovered in the conflict in Melbourne between the broken unions and the struggling employers, was the red revolution. At first it was the Sunday morning study circle run by the Labor member for the state seat of Brunswick, Frank Anstey, a man Curtin would later say had more influence on him than any other. Twenty years older than Curtin, English-born Anstey had run away to sea at age eleven, before settling in Melbourne and beginning his political career. Anstey drank too much and swore colourfully[9], habits Curtin would acquire. Slumps were caused by the manipulations of bankers, Anstey believed, a conviction that had great influence on his protégé. Jews were responsible, Anstey thought – a conviction Curtin does not seem to have shared. Anstey and others led Curtin to the Victorian Socialist Party, founded by the English trade unionist and socialist Tom Mann in a mission to the colonies to spread the word.

In the VSP the young Curtin, the child of barely literate immigrants, met clever people with great purposes and public ambitions, who could write and speak winningly in ways that explained the world and commanded adherence to their cause. His discovery of politics changed his life. He met on fraternal terms men and women of greater ability and reach, of wider sweep, than he had ever known among his friends and family, his schoolteachers, his supervisors and employers. He met men and women equal to great political causes. For unemployment, for poverty, for all the economic evils he saw around him in the Melbourne slums, they had remedies.

Mann was in Australia for seven years, from 1902 to 1909. Curtin was seventeen when he arrived in Melbourne. With Ben Tillett, Mann had been leader of the 1889 London dockers' strike. A powerful speaker, writer, agitator and organiser, Mann was one of the great figures in the world of English-speaking working class politics. So was Tillett, who visited Australia in 1897–98 and again in 1907–08. Curtin would have been too young to have met him on the first visit, but by the second visit, when he had become close to Mann, he would have seen a lot of Tillett.[10] There were English trade unions long before Mann and Tillett, but they were mostly craft unions based on skilled trades. Mann and Tillett organised the unskilled – the dockworkers, miners and seamen. Both men were superb orators. It was said that

Tillett could get his audience to weep, and Mann could get them to fight.[11] Like Curtin, like most people, they had left school young. What they knew they had found out for themselves.

Curtin's discovery of politics, of the qualities of political leaders whom he admired and who sought his adherence, who encouraged and taught him to write and to speak and persuade others, was the most astonishing experience of his life. He discovered it, and it discovered him – it discovered his intelligence, his curiosity, his thirst for understanding, his capacity to instruct and persuade. By his early twenties Curtin had been remade. The things he now believed in, his enjoyment in wide reading, in poetry and novels as well as socialist political economy tracts, in the English humanist tradition, were Mann's. Mann gave him, Curtin later wrote, 'a veritable education'.[12] His greatness, Curtin told Mann's farewell dinner in the upstairs dining room of the Rubira Cafe in Bourke Street in 1909, 'consisted in ever keeping in view the big thing, and yet not being negligent of the small things'.[13]

The big thing for Mann never changed. The work of the Socialist Party 'must be primarily EDUCATIONAL' he wrote in *The Socialist* published on Christmas Eve, 1909, as he prepared to return to Britain, the block letters emphasising his faith. (Curtin would one day tell an interjector in federal Parliament he did not believe in compulsory military training, or compulsory unionism, or in compulsory voting, but he did believe in compulsory education.[14]) During Mann's trial for sedition and unlawful assembly after a miners' strike in Broken Hill, Curtin wrote in a letter to a young friend that the socialist leader was that 'man of men' and that despite the 'wrong and nasty' things said by the newspapers, 'he and his good comrades are the purest and best among many who are indeed worthy'. All human progress, he wrote, 'has been won by men who have stood four-square to all the winds that blew – who, seeing the right, did daily maintain it.'[15]

Mann went home to Britain in time to be convicted for sedition after the Liverpool dock strike of 1910, to oppose the Great War in 1914, welcome the Russian Revolution in 1917, and help form the Communist Party of Great Britain in 1921. Too old to fight in the Spanish Civil War, he was delighted when the Tom Mann Centuria of the International Brigade was named to honour him. In the Labor caucus Curtin would one day move a resolution to congratulate Mann on his eightieth birthday.

Socialist politics converted, saved and remade Curtin in ways religion could not reach. For a spiritual interpretation of the world it substituted an economic one. Without the community of the Victorian Socialists he was, as he appeared to be, a hardware pricing clerk, living in a crowded Brunswick terrace, his small wage shared with his parents and siblings. With it, he was a member of a vast and international movement of people who shared convictions and ways of thinking, who sought the same goals, who circulated and discussed among themselves writings in economics and politics that explained how the world worked. They could change the world, perhaps soon. He was, he wrote, 'having the life that thrills'.[16] He found the 'sheltering tree' of friendship, his first romance, lifelong friends, in the Young Comrades Contingent of the Socialist Army of the VSP.[17] He went on picnics with other young socialists, played games with them. Remembering later his friend Frank Hyett[18] who died in the Spanish Flu epidemic of 1919, Curtin wrote of 'living again the old days. The Socialist Party in Collins Street; meetings here, there and everywhere; football and cricket matches; card games we played and all the little things and big things that have made up fifteen years of intimacies about almost everything, and which became part of ourselves as we grew from youth on.'[19]

'In my boyhood I had two heroes,' he wrote to one of them, Frank Anstey, in the bleak aftermath of the defeat of Scullin's government and the loss of his own seat of Fremantle in 1931. The other was Mann. 'They are still my shining stars and they twinkle for me their message as I grow older. Age is nothing to these white lights that have guarded my ship from the rocks of dismay.'[20]

Following Mann's example, politics would be Curtin's life. Leaving his job as an estimates clerk with the Titan Manufacturing Company in 1911, he took his first full-time political job as secretary of the Victorian Timber Workers Union.

He was confident that the world was changing, that there was a mighty revolution coming. 'We are at the point in the history of men where the centre of economic gravity is surely shifting to its final repository in the bosom of the toiling and teeming multitude,' Curtin wrote to his future father-in-law, a socialist and a former Methodist preacher, in June 1912. 'We are now able to do more than curse at tyranny and bewail injustice. We can, if we will, and there are enough of us willing, found the army of liberation, drill it, and set it in battle array. Oh, it is mighty work. Let us do it night and day and never stop.'[21]

Curtin soon realised that the flames of the red revolution would not be ignited among the workers of Melbourne. They wanted the eight-hour day and union recognition and higher wages and won them all and, with them, also the vote and the first Labour Party to hold office anywhere, and all without firing at the police, and without requiring the socialisation of production, distribution and exchange. The class war was real enough but it could be fought in the parliaments. Curtin's revolutionary socialist convictions would fade but what he became in those years in the VSP he remained. Through to the Great Depression, then his early leadership of the Labor Party, then through to his work on the full employment white paper in the months before he died, Curtin would continue to think that the peril of capitalism was that supply would outrun demand. Unless managed by government, destructive slumps were inevitable. He believed in education long after he had ceased to believe in the imminent collapse of capitalism. He remained a speaker, a writer, a persuader. The friends he found in the movement he kept. The political alliances he formed stuck. His first romances were in the movement, and his wife and her parents were attached to it.

(2)

Curtin had been so completely transformed that by 1910, aged twenty-five, his speeches attracted audiences, he could write a denunciation of capitalism drawing upon the latest socialist scholarship, and he was already reading widely in the poetry, history and novels of late nineteenth-century Britain. Soon, he was also in love. In 1912, the year after he began work for the Timber Workers Union, he met Elsie, the daughter of that Tasmanian socialist and preacher, Abraham Needham. Elsie redeemed him. Curtin was not a hard man. He did not have the energy and resilience, the indifference to personal attack, of other labour leaders. He was burdened by the sincerity of his convictions, and the failure of his hopes of red revolution. He spent time in pubs, drank too much, and when drunk talked excitedly and too much. Anstey worried about him, as did other older colleagues.

By age thirty Curtin disliked his life and wanted to change it. 'Because I love you better than all else in the world,' he wrote to Elsie in 1915, 'I am resolved to no longer mess around in a swirl of nothingness.' The swirl of nothingness was his job as secretary of the Timber Workers Union. He wanted to change the world but the timber workers did not. The management committee – 'the precious, small souled, sixpence chasing Management' – would not even pay for socialist literature. He was not the management type: 'the secretarial work of the Union called for day and night; here, there and everywhere and held me kind of bond slave to the unknown and unlooked for daily troubles of 4000 men.' Tired of the union demands, tired of his intermittent drunkenness, Curtin resigned. He told Elsie that 'this epochal step in my poor humdrum life has been taken because I love you so and would be worthy of you. You see, my heart, I cannot now and will not continue lotus eating, beer drinking between the arguments, travelling from office to mill, sleeping in trains and having the place where I profess to live know me best as a kind of periodical visitor.' He promised her 'my whole life, hopes for happiness, work and being to have, to hold, and to be in your service by word, deed and reflection, day in and out until time ends and nothing is.'[22]

Curtin wanted to stop beer drinking between the arguments, but he found it hard. He was, his friend from the VSP, trade union leader Vic Stout, later wrote, 'not overstrong' and had 'temporary lapses towards the bottle as a let out'. Curtin, Stout recalled, 'sometimes drank immoderately although spasmodically. He was not a regular heavy drinker like some of his associates but drank rather in bursts with long irregular intervals between drinking bouts of a few days duration.'[23] A prohibitionist, Stout could not approve.[24] The next year, in July 1916, Curtin was drying out in a clinic at Lara, near Geelong. 'Don't hate yourself, despise yourself, or be ashamed of yourself or ashamed to face others,' Frank Anstey wrote to him. 'There is no redemption that way.' Redemption was through political leadership, through the cause. 'John drunk was a damned nuisance, but he was even in that state a better man than thousands sober, and John sober is the Nestor of them all. Stand upright, proud of yourself, proud of the conquest that you are going to achieve and the good you will yet do.' Anstey wanted him to come out of the clinic as 'John' – and 'let Jack go with the booze.'[25]

(3)

He came out of the clinic to fall into the most tumultuous struggle of the young Australian Labor Party since its creation at the end of the previous century. On the Western Front the Allied and German armies struggled in the bloodbath of the Somme. On 1 July alone the British suffered 60 000 casualties. The Australian and New Zealand attacks at Pozières and Mouquet Farm later in July cost the Australians 23 000 casualties, with 6741 men killed. The Australians lost more men in six weeks of the Battle of the Somme than they had in eight months at Gallipoli. Visiting Britain and the French battlefields in

May and June, Labor Prime Minister Billy Hughes was convinced that conscription was now necessary to replace the dead and wounded in the all-volunteer Australian Imperial Force fighting in the trenches in France. Britain had introduced conscription in January 1916, Canada would legislate for conscription the following year, and Britain would attempt to impose conscription on Ireland in 1918. Labor in Australia had supported conscription for home defence but not for overseas service. Aware of the hostility of trade unions, left-wingers and the many Irish Catholics in the party, Hughes proposed a plebiscite to decide the question.

The national executive of the trade unions anti-conscription committee recruited Curtin to organise the campaign against conscription. Pro- and anti-conscriptionists were fiercely hostile and public interest intense. Curtin had never been engaged in a political struggle of such immediacy, intensity and size. On 4 October 1916, on the Yarra Bank in Melbourne, he spoke at an anti-conscription rally of 50 000 – a big crowd in a city of around one million residents. Ordered to register for military training, Curtin refused and went underground. 'I do not sleep in Brunswick & change my abode each night because we have to keep out of gaol in order to keep up the effort,' he wrote to Elsie in October 1916. 'I did not turn up as ordered by the proclamation & in addition there are the Lord only knows what other reasons they may fake to lay hold of me. Curiously enough they will not do anything publicly & so long as I dodge them at night I am safe enough.'[26]

Excited, imagining terrors, Curtin edged into hysteria. A revolution portended. 'All the keys are responsive to my control,' he hinted darkly to Elsie, 'particularly the industrial policy we contemplate if the referendum should be declared carried. A majority vote in favour will not make conscription acceptable to the unions & whatever happens the plebiscite is but an incident. If Hughes loses the referendum he proposes a coup de etat [sic] & if he wins we propose one.' Curtin's sensible side asserted itself, too. In the same letter he mentions the sacking of John Hilton, the pro-conscription editor of the Perth's Labor Party paper, the *Westralian Worker*. Jack might be imagining a coup. Needing a reliable income and steady work to be able to marry Elsie, John wanted Hilton's job in Perth.

The anti-conscription campaign won by a small margin.

Losing the national plebiscite they expected to win (and, Hughes thought, cow a hostile caucus majority into amending the existing legislation to extend conscription to overseas as well as home service), Hughes and his lieutenant, Senator George Pearce, designed the destruction of their opponents in the Labor caucus.

A little after 11 a.m. on 14 November 1916, almost three weeks after the first conscription plebiscite was narrowly defeated[27], Pearce and the ministers loyal to their leader walked in single file behind the short, slight, lively Hughes to the first-floor caucus room of Parliament House, Spring Street, Melbourne, where the federal Parliament then met. To reporters watching that morning the Prime Minister appeared, as ever, 'debonair', 'care free' and 'aggressively good humoured'.[28] The doors of the caucus room closed behind them, swung open two hours later for lunch, and closed again at 2 p.m. on the sixty-eight members of the caucus of the Federal Parliamentary Labor Party, one of the most successful labour parties in the world. It had governed the new nation for a third of its existence and either alone or in support of other governments had laid some of the foundations of the new Australian state: old age pensions, industrial arbitration, White Australia, tariffs, the armed forces. At 4.30 p.m.[29] the caucus doors swung open again and the tiny Prime Minister strode out, still carefree, still debonair, still good-humoured, leading twenty-four followers[30] and leaving behind forty-three members of a Labor Party crippled for a generation. Facing a motion of no confidence in his leadership, Hughes and his supporters had walked out before the vote.

Carrying the key of the Senate club room, Pearce walked ahead of Hughes and his other followers, unlocking the room for the first meeting of what they then declared to be the National Labor Party. In the new Hughes Government, which depended on the support of the Liberal Party, Pearce was again Minister for Defence, and second in Cabinet seniority to Hughes. Compared to the party it had been at eleven that morning, the party Hughes and Pearce left behind when they walked out of the party room was more Irish, more Catholic, more closely linked with trade unions, more isolationist, further to the left. It would not form another government for thirteen years, and then for only two years before shattering again and returning to opposition for another decade.

Within a month Curtin was arrested and imprisoned for failing to register for military training, an experience to which he responded not with the lofty detachment expected from the suffering righteous, but with something close to horror. After three days Pearce ordered his release.

(4)

By the end of 1916 Curtin was in the running for the editorship of the *Westralian Worker*, but the outcome was uncertain. He wrote to Elsie:

> I'm horribly lonely & I want you near me all the time. Maybe I'm down in the dumps today overmuch but I cannot help it. That beastly old jail has put its brand on me. I haven't the temperament not to still feel the narrowness of the cell & the damnation of its equipment. This week is a week of waiting. There is nothing to do except fool around . . . This year is nearly done. It has been a year I do not want to live again. And yet it has been a wonderful year. It proved how richly blessed I am to have not lost you as I deserved.[31]

There was another month to wait but on 31 January 1917, the board of the *Westralian Worker* voted five to one to appoint Curtin, from a list of twenty applicants,[32] after their first choice declined.[33] Two days later he telegraphed Elsie – 'Definitely appointed Editor'. His VSP friends held a big send-off in the Socialist Hall in Elizabeth Street.[34] *The Socialist* reported that Curtin was 'broken up' as they farewelled him at the wharf.[35] On 7 February he sailed from Melbourne for Fremantle on SS *Katoomba*. 'At the end,' Curtin wrote to Elsie the following day, 'I felt too much like crying to be comfortable. On the wharf were hundreds. All of them genuinely good and anxious I prosper.' The Tuesday night farewell at the Socialist Hall was 'a heart maker. Every part of the hall was crowded out and the usual speeches were served up.' Melbourne was 'a city I loved and pals I believed in and four walls that cradled my mental infancy. There are indeed holy places on the earth. That had to be one of them.'[36]

Adela Pankhurst – a daughter of the English feminist, a Melbourne resident and like Curtin a fierce campaigner against conscription – was also sailing to Fremantle. 'We talk a great deal,' reported Curtin. 'She is very industrious & reads and writes assiduously. There is no one else on ship that either of us knows – so I look after her.'[37] From the ship he wrote to the Western Australian Labor politician, Hugh Mahon, who had supported him for the editorship of the *Westralian Worker*. 'I shall do my best to vindicate your confidence . . . More than anything I shall strive to justify in that respect which has to do with my personal conduct.'[38] A year out of the alcoholism clinic, Curtin knew marriage and a new job in a distant city offered him a chance to remake himself.

CHAPTER 3

A NEW BEGINNING

(1)

In 1917, at age thirty-two, Curtin's life changed. He was in a new city, on the edge of the Indian Ocean and on the opposite side of the immense continent from Melbourne. He was soon married. He drank less. He and Elsie rented a house at West Leederville[1] and later a cottage near the sea at Cottesloe. They started a family. Their daughter, Elsie, was born in December 1917, and son, John, a little more than three years later. Curtin sent a quarter of his income to support his family in Melbourne[2], but even so had enough to get by. He worked industriously at the *Westralian Worker*, making it in the contemporary judgement one of the best Labor papers in the country. Supporting the anti-conscriptionists against the Hughes loyalists in a second conscription referendum in December 1917, he became a key figure in the Western Australian Labor Party. Hughes remained prime minister at the head of a new conservative party, the Nationalists, until he was edged out by Stanley Bruce in 1923. Bruce would be prime minister for nearly seven years. In Western Australia a state Labor government was more congenial. In time Curtin was elected president of the state branch of the Australian Journalists Association. He attended lectures on economics given by Professor Edward Shann at the University of Western Australia. He wrote articles on economics, foreign policy, poetry, novels, sports.

There were bleak times and furious local political battles but the twelve years of Curtin's thirties and early forties were also ones of obscurity, serenity and intellectual development. His own placidity corresponded to the global recovery between the end of the Great War and the beginning of the Great Depression. They were the years of the roaring twenties and the stock market boom, of international disarmament or at least of agreements on ship numbers and tonnages between the naval powers, of the German experiment with democracy. Japan developed its empire in Manchuria, Korea and Taiwan but did not much offend America or the European colonial powers in the Pacific. Under the surface the rise of fascist parties in Italy and then Germany, the shift to greater self-sufficiency in food production in Europe, American isolationism, Britain's return to the gold standard, German problems with reparations, discord in China, all portended problems. But the calamities of the next decade were not inevitable. It took the Great Depression to make them so, and there was nothing inevitable about that.

He was not in Parliament, but as editor of the *Westralian Worker*, as an eloquent speaker and forceful writer, Curtin became well known in the national Labor movement during the 1920s. His offices were in Stirling Street, Perth. The *Worker* was published each Friday, usually in eight pages and sometimes sixteen. The print run was four or five thousand.[3] He grew close to Alex McCallum, the Labor Party state secretary who had worked with Anstey to get Curtin the job.

He attended party conferences in other state capitals, was close to the parliamentary leadership in Western Australia, and kept in touch with trade union leaders. Arthur Calwell, later a party enemy, met him first in Melbourne in 1927 at the side entrance to the old Trades Hall council chamber. Curtin was there with Elsie, and young Elsie and John. Calwell noticed that he greeted people with 'comradely warmth' but thought (then, or later in retrospect) 'he seemed conscious of the fact that he was the beheld of all beholden'. He was not tall, but Calwell thought then and later he was a 'commanding figure' with 'qualities of leadership'. He had a 'strident voice' when speaking, and an unusual combination of reserve and assertion. 'Although he was rather shy he exuded confidence.' He never lost his 'natural shyness', Calwell recalled, and 'always remained sensitive and reserved'.[4]

Curtin loved Elsie. Apart or together, she was the rock. In his first big trip away, to London, Geneva and Paris in 1924, he was forlorn without her. As his ship neared Marseilles in June he wrote to her mother, who shared their home. 'I've seen many women since I left Fremantle,' he wrote, '& I bless you for having had a daughter who is a prize above rubies for any man . . . The more I reflect on the sweetness of the wife who was your little girl in the long ago, the stronger grows the affection I've always had for you and the dearer & nearer becomes in my heart the memory of what I know is most precious to you.' He signed it 'your loving son, Jack'.[5]

Curtin had acquired characteristic mannerisms. Pondering a point, he would rub his hand down his chin.[6] In his speeches Calwell noticed that 'when he was reaching his peroration, he would always pick up a pencil that he had left lying in front of him. He would raise the pencil gradually and, as he reached the end of his final smashing sentence, he would drop the pencil on the table.'[7] By 1928 he had been making speeches for more than twenty years, at a time when making a speech was the usual way a politician communicated to a mass audience. He had learned from Tom Mann and Ben Tillett, great speakers. Sixteen years later Canadian prime minister Mackenzie King would marvel at Curtin's ability to give a speech to a banquet of hundreds at the Guildhall in London or to a joint sitting of the two houses of the Canadian Parliament, without a note, without hesitation, without once stumbling for a word, his listeners rapt.

Curtin had begun as a young man studying radical socialist texts. In those texts, the economy and economic relations were the driving forces of politics. The political contest was between the owners of capital and their employees. The objective of political engagement was

to seize power and create a socialist economy. In his early twenties
Curtin and his fellow socialists were interested in unions and the
possibility that general strikes might be an alternative way of seizing
power, but Curtin was quite soon drawn into parliamentary politics.
His mentor, Frank Anstey, was a radical member of the Victorian
Legislative Assembly. Curtin himself first stood as the Labor candidate
for the Victorian federal seat of Balaclava in 1914, when he was twenty-
nine. He expected to lose, and did, but it marked his commitment to
parliamentary politics.

Though a socialist, Curtin was a firm supporter of White Australia
and had no hesitation in appealing to race prejudice when it was
useful to him. During the election campaign in 1917 Curtin told his
readers that the election would have 'deep significance' for the 'future
of the white race'. Hughes would dismantle the White Australia policy
and replace 'Anzacs with Chinese' while the 'white sons of Australian
mothers are fighting for the Empire on the blood-stained fields of
France'.[8] Visiting Geneva in 1924, he found the Japanese delegates
curious about Australia's racial exclusions. Curtin later said he had
prepared a note he gave to the Japanese 'giving the history of the White
Australia policy'. It arose, he explained, because of the 'ill treatment
of Kanakas brought to Queensland for the sugar industry and the
protests made by the British government against such treatment'.[9]
It was not, he would tell reporters decades later, 'a racial theory'.
He certainly sometimes spoke and wrote as if it was.

In principle he wanted the overthrow of capitalism. In practice,
in his first decade in Perth, he sought useful and attainable reforms.
Appointed on the recommendation of Labor premiers as a member
of the 1927–28 Royal Commission on Child Endowment or Family
Allowances, Curtin and his colleagues examined evidence of family
needs, other forms of government assistance, and the relationship
between wages and family income. After his years as an estimator for
Titan Manufacturing in Melbourne, Curtin was good at arithmetic.
The majority report of the Royal Commission found against child

endowment: it was expensive, and in any case the Commonwealth Court of Conciliation and Arbitration's basic wage was supposed to provide for children. Curtin and his colleague Mildred Muscio disagreed, submitting a minority report that found in favour of child endowment.

He moved on from the largely Marxist interpretations of his youth in the VSP to some familiarity with Keynes and other contemporary economists. Though Shann had once been a Fabian socialist, by the time Curtin attended his classes he taught that successful enterprise in Australia was being held back by high tariffs and economic regulation. Then and later Curtin continued to think demand could persistently fall short of supply, impossible in classical economics. And while most classical economists typically argued that money was merely a 'veil' over real economic activities, he continued to think that shortages of credit and financial crises could cause economic crises rather than merely result from them. Keynes had the same view.

In 1919 Curtin was badly defeated when he ran as the Labor candidate for the federal seat of Perth. The strain of the campaign while running the paper, the magnitude of the defeat, pushed him into months of gloom. His illness was diagnosed as neurasthenia, a term which at the time indicated symptoms of depression, fatigue and inability to concentrate. He rested in a country hotel, unable to work. 'It was a difficult time,' Elsie recalled:

> He veered between moods of high optimism and deep melancholy, as inexplicable as they were irregular. He would wake up in the morning at peace with the world and I'd start my household chores with a light heart. By lunchtime I would be treating him with the blend of sympathy and, 'come, now, things aren't as black as all that,' which I learnt through the long months was the best mixture. He'd seem to improve for a while and I'd think he was really better. Then he'd slip back into despondency again.

It was during that time, she thought, 'he trained himself to relax completely – shoes off, feet up and a rug over his legs'.[10]

(2)

Six years later he ran as the Labor candidate for the federal seat of Fremantle and chalked up his third loss in his third attempt to enter a parliament. He ran for Fremantle again in the general election in November 1928. Australia was already feeling the early effects of what would soon become the Great Depression. Curtin won the seat. His life was about to change again.

He and Elsie sailed from Fremantle in *Katoomba* on 12 January 1929, their cabin full of flowers, coloured streamers in their wake as the ship pulled away for the eastern states. In Canberra they stayed at the Wellington Hotel. Young Elsie and John went to school in nearby Telopea Park for a term.[11] When caucus met on 5 February, he was elected to its executive, a rare distinction for a new member. The following day he sat in the House of Representatives for the first time as a member. He was sworn in, with two other new Labor members, Ben Chifley and Jack Beasley, both from New South Wales.

Australia was already feeling the tug of a global tidal change. 'There is something wrong somewhere,' Prime Minister Stanley Bruce had vaguely remarked to the state premiers in May 1929.[12] Prices for Australian wheat, wool and meat were tumbling. Responding to the looming world slump, Bruce tried first to win greater power over unions and strikes. That legislation scuttled, Bruce instead sought to pull the Commonwealth out of industrial relations except for shipping and the waterfront. Defeated in the House, he sought a mandate from the people, dissolving the House and calling a general election for October. Bruce lost to Labor, led by James Scullin, in a landslide. Thirteen years after the conscription split which had turned Labor out of office, less than a year after Curtin had first won his seat in Parliament, Labor was back in government. Curtin's life was splendid with promise.

CHAPTER 4

CAPITALISM IS COLLAPSING

(1)

It was, instead, the bitterest and most futile time in his life. It very nearly destroyed his party, and left Curtin with an abiding consciousness of personal and political failure. For two calamitous years from the end of 1929 to the end of 1931 he was on the government backbench, watching in helpless frustration as his party, as the government he supported, tore itself apart under the delighted gaze of its political enemies.

Even as the votes were counted in Fremantle on the night of 12 October 1929, even as Bruce and three of his ministers saw with astonishment that they would not only lose government but lose their own seats as well, even as Jim Scullin prepared to form the first Labor government since the 1916 split, workers all over the country were being sacked from businesses that suddenly could no longer pay them, output was contracting, and foreign lenders began calling in their loans. Twelve days after Curtin was declared the winner in Fremantle, the sell-off in the United States share market abruptly deepened and the panic was on. Banks across America collapsed, throwing the United States into the Great Depression. 'Thousands of factories and plants have ceased operations' in America, Curtin told the House when it met after the election. There were 'a hundred and one causes contributing to the present industrial depression' but one cause in America stood out: banks had stopped lending.[1]

In his own electorate of Fremantle, he saw the sudden, vast increase in unemployment, the soup lines, the epidemics of scurvy and rickets.[2] Not far away ruined farmers walked off their properties and found tents in bush camps for the unemployed. When he was re-elected for Fremantle and Labor swept to government in 1929 a fifth of the trade unionists in his home state could not find work, and by 1932 nearly a third. In Canberra he saw his prime minister and party leader, Jim Scullin, and the Treasurer, Ted Theodore, perplexed by a slump that got worse and worse, the London creditors demanding their money while Sir George Pearce, by then Leader of the Opposition in the Senate, sat calmly in the other chamber across King's Hall, throwing his willing Opposition majority across the path of anything Scullin and his ministers wanted that might make a difference and needed the concurrence of the Senate.

Curtin saw it all, though not as he had hoped and expected from around the Cabinet table. He had been elected to the executive of caucus only nine months earlier, and had performed well in opposition. He would have expected to be elected to the ministry in the ballot on 22 October 1929. He had prepared meticulously. His name was on the ministerial ticket circulated by the Australian Workers' Union loyalists. It was also on the ticket circulated by the adherents of the New South Wales executive – the Lang group. Of the ten names on both tickets, only Curtin failed to get elected.[3] He had, he suspected, been blocked by the Deputy Leader and now Treasurer, Ted Theodore. 'Theodore walked down the caucus room when voting was about to take place and said "one Anstey in cabinet is enough",' Curtin later told Arthur Calwell.[4] For Theodore, the Lang group's support for Curtin might have been enough to annoy him. One Anstey was certainly enough and arguably one too many in Cabinet – though a wiser Theodore might have seen that with encouragement Curtin could be played against Anstey and become a useful ally in the struggle ahead.

Theodore vetoed him and so instead of seeing it from a seat at the Cabinet table, instead of sharing in the making of decisions, Curtin saw what he could of the Government's agony and perplexity from the caucus room and from the backbench. Or he saw it through the fog of tobacco smoke late at night and into the early hours of the morning in the snug 'cupboard' bar of the Kurrajong, Curtin smoking a Craven A in a holder, a beer in his hand, arguing excitedly, sometimes when he was drunk simply babbling, the reporters and politicians in the bar regretting his easy drunkenness, regretting that the pertinence and ferocity of his argument was spent on them, in the cosy bar, rather than the Cabinet table where it might have made a difference. Years later, when Curtin had become a distant, shy and sober man, weighed with the cares of government, with the peril of his country, reporters would remember his excitement, his candour, his drunken conviviality there in the little bar where politicians and reporters gossiped about the crisis which had seen Australia's income fall by a third, hundreds of thousands thrown out of work, and a Labor government rip itself to pieces.

Australia's problems, Curtin soon realised, were not those of America. Australian banks did not fail, as they had in the 1890s. The problem was the debt Australian governments owed to British lenders. Australia had emerged from the Great War deeply indebted to Britain, which financed Australian war spending. Australian governments, state and federal, then added to the debt year by year to finance the buildings of schools, hospitals, water, sewerage, electricity, roads, bridges, ports, railways and airports. By 1929 interest and dividend remittances to foreigners were equal to more than a quarter of Australian exports, compared to a little under a sixth a decade before.[5] By the time the Scullin Government came to office, the annual addition to the London debt of Australian governments was about equal to the interest commitments on their existing debt.[6] Australia borrowed to pay the interest on what it had borrowed.

At first it had seemed as if it might be another slowdown, like so many others. Confidence was what was needed. 'If we are blessed with good seasons our troubles will soon disappear, and we will commence a new era of progress and prosperity,' the new Treasurer cheerfully predicted in his first Budget statement.[7] But as the global Depression took hold Theodore found he could no longer borrow in London. The termination of new borrowing was all the more awkward because an unusually high proportion of the debt of the state and federal governments was soon due for repayment. It was not unemployment or the slump itself that suddenly magnified political conflict in Australia in the first year or two of the Depression.[8] It was this pressing need to either repay short-term debt or persuade London lenders to roll it over. It was a political struggle into which Curtin was drawn as soon as he returned to Canberra after the 1929 election.

The Scullin Government was able to raise tariffs against imports within six months of election. On remedies requiring legislation, Scullin was blocked by Pearce and the Opposition majority in the Senate. Conservative opposition was particularly strong against government attempts to wrest control of central banking from the Commonwealth Bank Board, led by Chairman Sir Robert Gibson. Scullin and Theodore wanted the bank to fund more of the government deficits. Gibson insisted on spending cuts and wage reduction as the price of Commonwealth Bank support. For Curtin, control over central banking, and the scope it would give for expanding lending and for funding government deficits, was the single most important issue in Parliament. 'No solution of the economic problem is possible without a radical change in the credit policy of the great banks,' he argued when speaking on the Central Reserve Bank Bill on 10 June 1930.[9] Australia's problems, he continued, 'are largely due to the determination of banks in concert with certain interests to deflate the price of labour and costs generally'.[10] It was an implausible analysis, but it was certainly true that the government-owned Commonwealth

Bank wanted deflation of costs and prices as a condition of lending money to the Government.

With London creditors demanding repayment of loans due, Gibson and his board insisting on stern measures to cut deficits, the economy sinking, the Senate refusing to agree to Scullin Government proposals, and a forthcoming inspection visit from Bank of England director Sir Otto Niemeyer arranged by Gibson, the Government was struggling. Whatever chance it may have had was then injured by two calamitous events. Theodore was forced to resign in July 1930 following findings against him by a Queensland royal commission inquiring into the allocation of mining leases in that state while Theodore was premier. The Government had been in office barely eight months. At roughly the same time Scullin decided to visit London to reassure lenders, a five-month absence during which the Labor Party and his government fell apart.

Though Curtin fought Theodore on policies, he had come to admire him. He was shocked by Theodore's resignation. 'It has been a week of sensation on sensation,' he wrote to Elsie on Wednesday, 9 July 1930, four days after the announcement of Theodore's resignation.[11] 'Last week I told you that Mrs Theodore had appeared greatly worried. Of course she knew more than I did. And on Friday, just as we – the works – were leaving for Sydney the mine beneath Theodore's feet exploded.' His resignation speech to the House 'made an extraordinary impression; there was complete silence; a packed House – benches & galleries – hung tensely on every word. And his composure, general restraint and command over himself was really wonderful.' Curtin thought that 'it is a tribute to his extraordinary talents that he conveyed to all of us the relief that he can completely vindicate himself'.

For all that, he told Elsie, the Budget completed by Theodore was 'a shocker':

Taxes galore to meet the deficit. If we are forced to the country within a year we are gone – that is the common belief.

No matter. But for the failure to attack the financial system
& deal constructively with the problem of unemployment
boldly I could justify all we have done. But on these two points
I am hopelessly outvoted by a combination of fear and folly.
And Theodore has been the chief figure in defeating me in the
party. Yet I do hope he is cleared at the finish.[12]

With Theodore out of the ministry, and the Bank of England's
Niemeyer saying budgets must be balanced, Curtin was gloomy. He
sympathised with Scullin. Walking with the Prime Minister on Friday,
1 August, not long before he left for London, he found Scullin 'has
troubles enough. Sir Otto Niemeyer is proving difficult; Theodore
wants a Federal Royal Commission; the revenue from Customs was
½ a million below expectations – & so on!'[13]

'And yet the obvious thing,' he told Elsie in a letter the following
day, 'an attack on banking control, a reduction in the interest rate
& the credit of the nation being made a monopoly of the nation, he
will not face. So I argued with him fruitlessly. The capitalist system is
breaking down.'[14]

Joining the rebels, Curtin moved in a caucus meeting the following
Wednesday 6 August that Joe Lyons, Acting Treasurer in Theodore's
stead, give caucus a full account of the nation's financial condition.[15]
The motion was lost.

At the insistence of Niemeyer and Gibson, on 18 August 1930
the Commonwealth Government and the state premiers made what
became known as the Melbourne Agreement. Scullin was ill. Deputy
Prime Minister James Fenton and Acting Treasurer Lyons represented
the Commonwealth. They agreed to balance their budgets, reduce
wages and welfare payments, and cancel projects. Scullin then left to
attend an Imperial Conference in London, reassure United Kingdom
lenders, and press the appointment of Sir Isaac Isaacs, Chief Justice of
the High Court, as the first Australian-born Governor-General. Other
Australian prime ministers before him had made extended visits to

Britain during the parliamentary recess. To absent himself from the seventh Imperial Conference might well offend not only Britain but the other dominion prime ministers as well. As it happened, it was a more than routine gathering because it approved the Statute of Westminster recognising the legal equality of the self-governing dominions. But in Scullin's circumstances it was a fateful decision, taken on the assumption that Parliament (and therefore caucus) would not need to meet again before his return. To implement the Melbourne Agreement, however, Parliament had to meet.

At the beginning of October 1930, Fenton, then Acting Prime Minister, and Lyons won Cabinet approval to a deficit reduction plan. Caucus would not be so amenable. When Jack Lang resoundingly won the New South Wales state election on 25 October with a campaign to reject the Melbourne Agreement, the split widened. His adherents in the federal caucus now formed the left of the party and Lyons the right, with Curtin, Anstey and others in the middle. Sometimes working through others and sometimes directly, Theodore pressed his own views. In a sequence of lively caucus meetings in November, the party began to disintegrate.

Two days after Lang's election victory, Lang loyalist Jack Beasley won caucus support for a motion to disagree with Niemeyer's proposals for reducing costs and tariffs.[16] The following day, and in this highly charged atmosphere, Lyons proposed his policy to caucus. Theodore promptly proposed another. His plan looked to more funding from the Commonwealth Bank, currency depreciation, and smaller spending cuts. In a sequence of furiously fought caucus meetings Lyons' deficit reduction proposal was resoundingly defeated, and Theodore's plan carried. But without the support of the Commonwealth Bank, without the support of Lyons as Treasurer, the policy could not be implemented.

With Anstey, Curtin moved to Theodore's left. In an angry caucus meeting on Thursday, 6 November, Curtin opposed a plan by Lyons to issue a new loan to repay one coming due. He successfully moved that the Commonwealth Bank board should be asked to pay out the loan coming due or Parliament should be asked to approve a rollover rather than pay out to local bondholders a loan coming due.[17] Curtin's successful amendment brought the Government to the brink of an open split. Fenton and Lyons said they would 'consider their position'. Lyons then cabled Scullin threatening resignation. Scullin replied that he thought the caucus proposal 'appalling', and Lyons decided to ignore it.

'I have just spent the morning with Anstey working out the situation,' Curtin wrote to Elsie. 'The press is in uproar. But I do not fear that. They always yell when a whole new course is planned.' As so often in times of stress, Curtin was unwell and evidently depressed. 'I am well comparatively,' he wrote, 'I sleep alright and will commence to eat ordinary food today . . . It is a rotten life.'[18]

On Wednesday, 12 November, Curtin declared his position in a speech to the House on the Government's financial statement. He rejected the belief that the Budget deficit had to be eliminated. There 'can be no budgetary equilibrium in Australia, either for the Commonwealth or the States,' he told the House, 'so long as 200 000 of our people are out of work and our industries are incapable of carrying on effectively.'

His argument was the same as Maynard Keynes would use in *The General Theory*. Governments would find that 'every step they take along the road of the Niemeyer plan makes it increasingly difficult for them to realize their financial expectations. Every reduction in wages, every rationing in employment, every diminution in the purchasing power of the community, reacts upon the taxpaying capacity, and as a result the revenues which have been forecast by the Treasurers, Commonwealth or States, have not been, and will not be, realized.'[19] He wanted the Budget balanced, but over five years, not one.

Because of the Senate's refusal to pass the necessary legislation, he pointed out 'this Government has no power over the monetary policy of Australia'.

The exchange rate of the Australian against the British pound was set by the banks. Curtin (and Theodore) wanted to remove the exchange rate from the control of banks and allow the currency to float: 'I would ask this Parliament to consider the undesirability of allowing the banks to peg the rate of exchange at whatever figure they care to choose.' The banks 'should be compelled to unpeg the exchange and allow it to operate naturally'.[20]

Orthodox economists such as Shann, by then a consultant to the Bank of New South Wales, prescribed a balanced budget, wage cuts and cuts to the interest rate paid to Australian holders of government debt. Unorthodox then, Curtin's alternative prescription of a floating exchange rate, an increase in the money supply and lower interest rates, a government budget deficit and other measures to stimulate demand would later become mainstream. Within a few years Keynes' theories would support the fiscal elements of Curtin's position. Many years later Milton Friedman's theories would support the monetary elements, particularly the floating exchange rate and increased money supply. Seen by their proponents as alternative remedies, they would in time be seen as Curtin saw them: as complementary.

Responding to one interjection he revealed to the House his distress about the economic direction of Fenton and Lyons. 'There are conservative governments everywhere,' he said. 'One of the most conservative is the present Federal Government.'[21]

Curtin persisted in using caucus to thwart the more orthodox approach of Fenton and Lyons. On 10 December 1930, and with Chifley as his seconder, he moved that the Government issue an economic statement prepared by Fenton, Lyons, Anstey, Theodore and Curtin. It was a direct move to wrest control from Lyons and Fenton, and it was carried by caucus.

Lyons meanwhile was energetically campaigning to encourage Australians to invest in a new bond to replace the one coming due. He staked his political survival on a successful conversion. Two days after caucus agreed to the committee with Theodore, Curtin and

Anstey as well as Lyons and Fenton, the loan conversion closed – oversubscribed. Lyons was triumphant. With Parliament adjourning for the Christmas break, the caucus battle was adjourned.

Returning from London early in January 1931, Scullin reinstated Theodore as Treasurer, the Queensland Government having failed to bring charges against him. Offended and at odds with Theodore's more radical policies, Fenton and Lyons resigned from the ministry early in February and soon began discussions with the Opposition Nationalists. It was nearly a year before it fell, but with the Beasley group splitting to the left and the Lyons group to the right, the Scullin Labor Government was already doomed.

When Lang instructed his supporters in the federal caucus to vote against Scullin Government measures to implement the Melbourne Agreement, Curtin supported Scullin. Despite his antipathy to the Melbourne Agreement, he insisted that federal caucus be free to make decisions on federal issues. At a special Labor Conference held towards the end of March 1931, Curtin moved expulsion of Lang's New South Wales branch. In this he split with Anstey, who was sympathetic to Lang, and found himself in close company with Lang's enemy, Theodore.

Theodore's plans to mitigate the slump with easier credit once again defeated in the Senate, Scullin and Theodore resumed discussions with the state premiers in late May. In early June they agreed on the Premiers' Plan for spending cuts, revenue increases, wage cuts and cuts to interest rates on government debt for Australian but not overseas lenders.[22] Australian banks devalued the currency, an action that for farmers cushioned the fall in international wheat, wool and meat prices when paid to them in Australian pounds.

Late in June 1931, the Labor Party federal executive decided that Labor members of Parliament should be free to vote for or against the Premiers' Plan.[23] That compromise meant it could pass the House with Opposition support. When it came his turn to speak on 24 June 1931, Curtin said he was 'opposed to the plan in its entirety' because it did not implement 'equality of sacrifice' as claimed. Labor Party endorsement of the plan would bring about the 'demoralisation of the Labour movement'. His speech was wide-ranging, but not entirely coherent. He opposed the plan not only because 'the variations of interest rates are contingent upon my acquiescence in the reduction of payments to old age, invalid, and war pensioners' but also because 'implicit in the plan is an abandonment of the whole conception of the Labour movement in regard to the reconstruction of society'. He said the plan 'leaves untouched the top-heavy political system of this country . . . in effect it says to me, "Go out and justify the taking of 2s. 6d. a week from the income of an old age pensioner", while at the same time it is proposed that we shall continue to maintain the panoply of six sovereign States, with six agents-general, six governors, and all the pomp and ceremony of thirteen chambers connected with the political mechanism of this country'.

The plan, Curtin said, abandoned the Labor policy of monetary reform, yet the 'difficulty is essentially a monetary one. This plan is, in essence, the plan of the party opposite.' He believed 'The Labour movement is faced, in connection with this plan, with what I recognise as a great crisis in its history and structure.' Three or four months ago, he recalled, he had said that Labor had to find ways to put its own plans into operation, 'or else permit its opponents to give effect to their programme'. Now the Government was stabbing its people in the back – an action 'of which even Brutus was incapable'. Theodore responded with a ruthless allusion to Curtin's drinking. 'The honourable member,' he interjected, 'is becoming drunk with his own rhetoric.'[24]

Curtin voted against the Premiers' Plan, which was carried by the Opposition.

After its long death struggle, the end of the Scullin Government was surprisingly peaceful. Curtin witnessed it from the backbench, probably with relief. After a long break, the House resumed sitting at 3 p.m. on Wednesday, 25 November 1931. Only *The Argus* that morning had a taste of the day's story. It reported the Prime Minister, Mr Scullin, had 'yesterday refused to dismiss lightly the threatened attack in the House of Representatives by the Lang Supporters'. Attacking Theodore, Beasley and his group demanded a royal commission into unemployment relief payments in New South Wales. Scullin refused. Within a few hours Scullin lost his majority in a vote of the House, and called an election.

(2)

Curtin was a minor figure in the drama, a footnote to the accounts of the time, completely overshadowed by Scullin, Theodore and Lyons. Even among the rebels he was overshadowed by Anstey – though he was not entirely without distinction. Saddening and infuriating, because all that he had been taught by Mann and Anstey, all he had excitedly discussed with his friends in the young comrades league, all that he had read and learned and said and written as a young man in the mighty work, all that he had predicted in his weekly pieces in the *Westralian Worker*, was, he thought, actually happening, actually coming true. Capitalism, as he wrote to Elsie, *was* collapsing. It really was. Capitalism was collapsing and there he was, after decades of predicting just this event, decades of saying that supply would outrun demand, that when it collapsed the burden would fall most heavily on the workers, now a Labor member of the Parliament, supporting a Labor government, someone who could speak and write thoughtfully, who had no hesitation in speaking on the economic themes impenetrable to many of his colleagues, not yet fifty and at what he thought was the height of his powers, someone whose entire life and training had been driving towards this exact point, encountering this exact problem, to deal with this exact difficulty. And yet he was finding that in this great world crisis he could do absolutely nothing except talk, drink, smoke, and argue with his caucus colleagues in the Government members party room or with reporters in the cupboard bar of the Kurrajong. Back on those benders, the one or two days of drinking, the occasional lapses that Vic Stout had seen in Melbourne, borrowing a few quid here and there to 'go off on a scoot' with a drinking companion, cadging a whisky from his friend Frank Green, the Clerk-Assistant of the House, diminishing himself in his colleagues' estimation when he most needed their votes to join the ministry.

Shaming himself. Even with Elsie and the children, he could not stop drinking. Travelling on the train from Melbourne to Canberra with his family, he drank. Young Elsie saw him drinking in the corridor from a silver flask, and told her mother. When he returned to his seat, his daughter recalled, her mother 'leant forward and flicked back his coat, took the flask and threw it out of the open window'. They'd missed their train the night before because of Curtin's drinking. The normally equable Elsie was fed up.[25] Don Rodgers did not know Curtin then, but later inquired. He concluded that Curtin 'was never a drunkard as such, or even an alcoholic. I think he was what's called a cheap drunk and because of the political turmoil of the time and the fact that his Party was headed for certain defeat, he was probably what might also be called a crying drunk.'[26]

Whatever he did later, whatever Chifley, Beasley, Scullin, would do later, if they ever had another chance to do something, would be done remembering those terrible years. It must not happen again. It would take Curtin, a perceptive reporter would write on the eve of the Pacific War – a conflict that would demand more of Curtin than ever the Depression asked of Scullin and Theodore and Lyons – more than a decade to recover the confidence in himself and his party crushed in the Depression.

The election called, the date announced, Curtin returned to Perth by train early in December.[27] He had no hope of winning. He would, as he said, 'go through the motions' of fighting for his seat.

He travelled to Melbourne, across to Adelaide, on to Port Augusta and again on to the Trans-Australian to Kalgoorlie, the sun now rising behind them in the morning and setting before them in the evening, the Southern Cross blazing over the Great Australian Bight to their left in the clear nights. Curtin was acccompanied in the club car by Senator Sir George Pearce, still sober, calm and quiet after two and half years of deftly blocking Scullin and Theodore, now returning on the same train to campaign for the new United Australia Party in Western Australia. Pearce had blocked a floor price for wheat, legislation to increase government control over the Commonwealth Bank and Theodore's plan to issue additional credit. He had worked closely with Sir Robert Gibson, chairman of the Commonwealth Bank, who adamantly fought the Scullin Government's plans for greater control over it. 'I cherish my confidences with the late Sir Robert Gibson,' Pearce would later write to a friend, 'and I am proud to know we were able to render each other material services of very great value to Australia.'[28] He had contributed all he could to prising Lyons away from Labor and into the arms of the Melbourne 'Young Nationalist' group led by the young Bob Menzies and his stockbroker friend, Stan Ricketson, who arranged for John Latham to hand the Opposition leadership to Lyons.

Pearce was there in the first-class club car, with Opposition colleagues Senators Bertie Johnston and William Carroll and three Opposition members of the House and also perhaps Texas Green, who had not long ago run along the railway platform in Canberra looking for Lyons' carriage as he began his journey to Melbourne for the meeting with Menzies and Ricketson. 'For God's sake, don't do it, Joe, don't do it!'[29] Green had shouted through Lyons' carriage window, his voice lost in the clatter of the train as it drew away. Curtin travelled back to Perth on the railway Pearce had caused to be constructed, for the election Pearce caused to occur, to a campaign both Pearce and Curtin knew would ravage Labor just as surely as the 1916 split, an earlier calamity in which Pearce had played his part and which had washed Curtin up in Perth to begin a new career – now, very probably, ending.

The election was held on 19 December 1931, six days before Christmas. Nationally, there was a 21 per cent swing against Labor. In the 75-seat House Labor lost thirty-two seats, including four to the Lang party in New South Wales. One of the losses was Curtin's seat of Fremantle.

(3)

From his election to federal Parliament in 1928 to his defeat a little more than three years later Curtin had made no important national decisions, implemented no policies, shaped no events. Yet those years of the Great Depression completely engaged him as no issue had since the campaign against conscription. He had wrestled with its causes and remedies, he had written and spoken about it at every opportunity, he had agitated in caucus and in the House for what he thought were better policies than those pursued by either his own party or by the Opposition. He wanted deficits reduced more slowly, the central bank to finance repayment of Australian currency debt to the extent markets were reluctant to roll it over, and he wanted a flexible and probably lower exchange rate. He saw that the Government could not either persuade the Commonwealth Bank to create more money, to lend more, or command it to do so. He saw that a determined Opposition commanding a majority in the Senate could readily thwart a government, no matter how large its majority in the House. He saw that state governments could effectively oppose federal government policies, and that they had the revenue and spending powers to do so. He would remember.

There was another important lesson yet to be learned. The capitalist system was not collapsing. Australia was one of the first countries to fall into the slump, but it was also one of the first out.

The wheat farmers weren't paid the promised floor price, but they did greatly increase output in expectation of it, and the huge harvest made a difference to Australia's foreign exchange balances. The depreciation of the currency helped farmers by increasing their returns in Australian pounds. It also helped manufacturers by increasing the price of competing foreign products in the Australian market. Unlike the United States, where the collapse of the banking system amplified and protracted the slump, the Australian financial system and Australian banks continued to function – one of the reasons Sir Robert Gibson was so highly regarded by Menzies, Pearce and their colleagues. By 1934 Australia was emerging from the Depression.

The politics of the Depression were also instructive for Curtin. At the height of the Depression a third of workers were unemployed, yet he could see that the Labor Party, the party of the trade unions and the working class, was not stronger for the distress of its constituency. On the contrary, it had again split, and lost government in a landslide. Out of a job, out of luck, but happy to be spending time at home in Cottesloe with his wife and growing children, Curtin had much to ponder.

CHAPTER 5

PERTH AGAIN

Defeated in Fremantle, the Labor Party shattered, Curtin seemed for a while uncertain of his direction. Three days after the federal election of 19 December 1931, he wrote to Henry Boote, editor of the AWU's *Australian Worker* in Sydney, seeking his help to find a job in the eastern states. 'We have gone to dusty death,' he told Boote.[1] The same day he wrote to Ted Theodore, who had also lost his seat. Curtin was now an almost unqualified admirer of the former Treasurer. He wrote that 'The Party was afraid both of you and your ideas. I was not. I supported both . . . each day I grew more and more to esteem your quiet courage and strength'. Referring perhaps to advice Theodore had given him about his conduct, Curtin wrote, 'You have been helpful to me in a very personal sense and I value it in a way that I need not express. I shall face the future mindful of what you would wish.'[2]

Theodore had perhaps cautioned Curtin about his drinking. He encouraged Curtin to believe he yet could be Labor leader. 'Your defeat is a sad personal misfortune,' he replied, 'for you could have done good work in Opposition and established your claims to the ultimate leadership of the Federal forces. I have long believed you are destined for great things, if you keep hold of yourself, and if that old hag, fate, is not too relentless.'[3] For his part, Curtin pressed Theodore to take the leadership of the party from Jim Scullin. He suggested the workers wanted 'some man to inspire them with hope and guidance.

I am not talking behind anyone's back when I say there is no one in Federal Parliament who fills the bill.'[4] Theodore was no longer interested. If the workers wanted hope and guidance, someone else would have to provide it.

Curtin's party was now a hapless minority in the federal Parliament. He didn't have a job or much of an income. He was no longer sought out by reporters or caucus colleagues. The phone in the hall of their home in Jarrad Street, Cottesloe, didn't ring as it had. In Western Australia, Phil Collier's Labor Government had been soundly defeated by Sir James Mitchell's National – Country Party coalition in April 1930. Curtin would not get state government assignments. By the end of 1931, when Curtin was again living at home in Cottesloe, Western Australia was deep into the Depression, and divided by a campaign for secession from the Federation. Western Australians objected to the high tariffs imposed to support industry in the eastern states. Wheat and the gold of Kalgoorlie would support a new independent nation in the west, they told each other.

Though his political education had begun in Victoria, Curtin acquired Western Australian sensibilities. Unlike most of his federal colleagues, he was not a proponent of high tariffs. Nor did he support an ever more dominant role for the Commonwealth – though in practice the changes he was to carry through as prime minister guaranteed increasing authority for Canberra. On secession, feeling ran strong. George Pearce led the local campaign against it, and was shouted down at noisy meetings. Visiting with her husband, the Prime Minister, in March 1933, Enid Lyons was pleased by the warmth of a reception by the Mayor. 'Why all this secessionist pother?' she remarked to Curtin, attending as a reporter. 'Everyone seems delighted to see us. We thought we would be torn limb from limb.' Curtin warned her not to trust Perth appearances. 'Here we affect a manly, breezy insincerity but don't let it mislead you,' he said. 'Wait for tonight!'[5] Speaking at the Theatre Royal that evening, Lyons struggled to make himself heard over raucous interjections and intermittent singing of 'Poor Old Joe'. Curtin opposed secession, but wisely ducked a leading role in opposing it.

Curtin got by, with the bits and pieces defeated politicians must contrive while they await their next chance. He was appointed publicity officer for the Perth Trades Hall Council. Labor paid for a column in the Perth newspapers, which Curtin wrote. He was paid three pounds (later raised to six) a week to write sporting news for the *Westralian Worker*. His son, John, at age eleven in closer touch with the names and careers of local sporting heroes, later said, 'I had to tell him what to write.' He gave race selections that others thought were 'pretty good' though Curtin said he didn't 'know the first thing about' horse racing.[6] He made stirring speeches, fighting the Communists on the left as earnestly as the Lyons Government on the right.

The time in Cottesloe wasn't so bad, or at least it turned out well. After three years in distant Canberra it was a chance to live again with the family, to see relatives and friends, to read and think. To Elsie as well as the children he was Dad. To him, Elsie was Nip. Curtin was followed about by Kip, the black kelpie. Kip had his own chair in the lounge room, near Curtin's, and was said by Elsie to be so smart that when the Curtins packed suitcases for a visit away the dog would feign illness to discourage them from going.

Curtin was fond of his daughter Elsie, now fifteen and thinking about what she would do when she left school. Elsie would write poetry, and came to enjoy parties. She had a strong but sometimes brittle personality, like her father's. She was worried by flying and riding in lifts. Like his dad, son John was a keen sportsman. John's characteristic expression, again like his father's, was a little anxious. They played cricket in the back yard, tennis in the front yard.

Built to their specifications in 1923, the home at 14 Jarrad Street was a comfortable, one-storey brick cottage of a style known as California Bungalow, with a garden at the front and a big yard at the back. The front door opened from a cool dark brick porch. John and Elsie's bedroom was to the left off the main hallway. The phone was in the hallway. Curtin refused to allow a chair by the phone, hoping to cut short young Elsie's conversations. She was already, the family agreed, quite 'social'. She failed to understand, her brother recalled, 'that the phone was for father at all times'. At the end of the hallway was the lounge room, with a library in an alcove and Curtin's favourite reading armchair. He worked at a desk there, among the books, Kip dozing on his chair nearby.

On the lounge room walls hung Abraham Needham's paintings of Cottesloe Beach, local bushland, the steam train running between Perth and Fremantle, yachts sailing off the coast. On Sunday mornings Grandmother Annie Needham listened to church services on the radio in her bedroom, off a corridor that led to the back door. The kitchen and dining room were on the other side of the corridor. The bathroom was at the back of the house, and behind it a laundry. Until the verandahs at the front of the house were enclosed to make extra bedrooms for the children, Curtin could stride through, smoking and thinking up speeches. In the yard there was a box tree, a grape trellis, a lemon tree, a fig tree and a clothesline. Wattle birds squawked in the box tree. Magpies, cockatoos, kookaburras and galahs visited. The flies were bad – there were always too many flies for a barbecue, John recalled. The toilet was behind a lattice at the bottom of the garden. It had been discussed for a decade but Jarrad Street was not scheduled to be sewered until 1936.[7] The house doors were never locked, and none of the family carried keys. 'Grandma was always there,' young John remembered, 'Grandma and the dog.'

A block away, the railway line from Fremantle to Perth crossed Jarrad Street. The long silences of the house were broken by warning bells at the crossing, then the puffing of the steam engine and the warning hoot of the train coming from Fremantle, followed by the screech of metal on metal as it stopped at the Cottesloe station on its way to Perth. Curtin rode it to Trades Hall, chatting to his fellow passengers.

He liked good clothes, especially hats.[8] For leisure wear he preferred cream jackets, cream pants and cream shirts – his 'planter' outfit, as it was known in the family.[9] Wearing cream pants and a cream shirt and a panama hat, he and Kip often walked west along Jarrad Street and across the golf course to the paths adjoining the Esplanade above Cottesloe Beach. It was a grander view than the cow paddocks and eucalypt scrub around Canberra. In the evening he would see banks of clouds lit by the sun setting over the Indian Ocean, and hear the chatter of parakeets bickering in the great pines along the Esplanade.

He swam in the sea. With binoculars slung over his shoulder, he attended race meetings most Saturdays. He grew zinnias in the garden, and played cricket with John. He and Elsie went often to the movies. He didn't care for dinner parties. Later he came to know Alec Reid, a state Treasury official who became Chancellor of the University of Western Australia. With Reid and his wife the Curtins would see movies, or a Gilbert and Sullivan light opera, or visit each other's homes for a meal.[10]

Curtin liked to sing, but wasn't gifted. His wife said she 'often heard him start off with Annie Laurie and turn her into Old Black Joe'.[11] Elsie played the piano for him. He 'liked light ballads, the older musical comedies, Gilbert and Sullivan – nothing too classical. But he didn't like jazz. Sometimes he'd sing. "Sweet Genevieve" was his favourite. I'd set him off, then I'd sing the contralto part. Before we'd gone very far "Dad" would be all over the place.'[12] Under the shower he sang an old song from his youth in Brunswick, *We are the boys of the Sydney Road, we are the men who are free*. He could get as far as the second line.[13]

Curtin had been slowly changing from the radical socialist he had still been when he first arrived in Perth, to a politician more interested in reform than revolution.[14] It had been evident for a while in his leading articles for the *Westralian Worker*. It was apparent, too, in the pieces he now wrote for local papers. They were often hotly hostile to capitalism, but more often concerned with how to make capitalism work rather than how to overthrow it. Experiences like the child endowment inquiry helped. So did the experience of the Scullin Government. After all, as Theodore pointed out, it had been deserted by Labor voters.

If he was becoming a little more conservative in politics, he remained then and later indifferent to religion. He and Elsie did not attend church. Neither of the children was baptised. 'When his children attended school and forms were required to be filled in with personal details,' his daughter wrote, Curtin 'usually put a dash against the word Religion.' The children's grandfather, Abraham Needham, had been a Methodist minister, but at the end even he had requested a non-denominational burial.[15]

Careful of his clothes, Curtin neglected his health. He smoked too much. He perhaps thought the holder he used minimised ill-effects. The family knew he was at home because of the smell of tobacco smoke. He took long walks with the dog but otherwise had little exercise. He rarely smiled straight into a camera. Noticed by strangers, who were not quite sure which way he was looking, the cast in his left eye didn't bother Curtin – though he preferred portrait photos from his right side. Later, President Roosevelt was said to have offered to have his eye fixed at the Bethesda Naval Hospital, an operation that would take a few hours: he could go in Saturday and be out Sunday afternoon. Curtin told him he had 'carried it for so many years he would let it go'.[16]

He probably still drank, sometimes perhaps too much, but it was now easier to control. His daughter said he gave up alcohol after the 1931 election.[17] Others said he had given it up earlier, and yet others that he gave it up later. His wife later wrote that he gave it up twice, once from around their marriage in 1917 until 1927, and then again after his defeat in 1931.[18] It was widely said he had pledged not to drink again when running for Labor leader. It is surely true he could not have been elected leader if he had still been the occasional drunk he was during the Scullin Government.

Elsie was a good housekeeper. She knew what things cost and what they could afford. Later she acquired blocks of land, reckoning on the district's future. The house was in her name. She bought land across the road intending it for their retirement home. 'We've never been rich but we've always got by,' she would tell the family. Elsie maintained certain standards of decorum. Even among relations she expected to be addressed as Mrs Curtin, and used like formality in return. Her clothes and young Elsie's (and later her granddaughters') were made by a dressmaker, just as Curtin's suits were made by a tailor. Unusually for the neighbourhood the dinner table had proper serviettes, her granddaughters later recalled, with serviette rings.[19] There was always bread on the table, and butter.

They did not have a refrigerator, still unusual except in wealthy households. A fridge could cost more than a car. To avoid mice and flies, Elsie kept fresh food in a wire mesh safe hung from the ceiling by a pulley. Her cooking was nutritious, if not extensive in range. Until young Elsie took over the cooking the family ate meatballs one night, pot roast the next, then lamb chops, and back again to meatballs. This was the food Curtin liked. His tastes were rigorously plain. He didn't care for crumbs on his chops, or batter on his fish, or gravy on meat.[20] Elsie did all the cooking and cleaning. Curtin may have been expected to perform the handyman's duties but notably lacked dexterity and competence. He could chop wood and set fires. Elsie wore her long hair pinned up. She had bad knees and with the passing years became dumpy. She wore enveloping flowery dresses. She chatted and joked and was much loved. Stories of Elsie's eccentric good humour were family jokes long before they startled Prime Minister Curtin's press secretary, Don Rodgers, and his principal public servant, Frederick Shedden. The family read more than most, and joked more than most.[21]

Perth people had a stronger sense of community than was common in the big eastern cities.[22] Politicians were expected to be approachable and without airs. Curtin would chat about sports at the barber's, or about gardening on the train to Perth. His much-remarked humility as prime minister was part of his temperament but also a Perth characteristic, in a nation where deference was anyway uncommon and grandeur usually comic.

His friends in the trade unions had arranged a small office he could use in Trades Hall, and gave him access to a secretary. He thought of himself as a journalist. He barracked for South Fremantle. He was still the leading thinker on economic issues in the local Labor Party. His sponsored column was notable for the vigour of its analysis. More often than not he wrote about the Depression, its causes and remedies. He had fallen out with Edward Shann over Shann's support for spending and wage cuts during the Depression and his consultancy with the Bank of New South Wales. Tom Mann's imprint was deeper. Speaking to a women's group in November 1932, Curtin said, 'We have to destroy capitalism and the only way to do that is to break the position it holds in the minds of the people' – much the same as he had shouted by the Yarra twenty years earlier. He read widely. Speaking to one group he recommended H G Wells (*The Outline of History*), J R Green (*A Short History of the English People*) and Thorold Rogers (*Six Centuries of Work and Wages: The History of English Labour*). He also recommended Shakespeare, poetry, novels and plays that gave 'an insight into the rise of human possibility'.[23]

Writing to Theodore on 30 September 1932, Curtin told him:

life has been good; I have a reasonable amount of leisure and browse at home with books and periodicals, and enjoying the time with Mrs Curtin and the kids – They are growing more rapidly than I thought. One of the nasty aspects of the Parliament was the confoundedly lengthy separations. Young John is nearly twelve, plays football in the school team, and he goes with me to the matches and assists me to follow the game, and sub-edits the blooming report before it goes in.[24]

Things brightened up in April 1933, fifteen months after Curtin had lost his seat and his income, when Mitchell was swept from office and Collier returned as a premier with a comfortable Labor majority. On the same day Western Australians voted nearly two to one for secession from the Federation, a vote that had no legal force and reflected as much as anything else the annoyance of Western Australians with low wheat prices, unemployment, and the high tariffs that protected manufacturing in the eastern states.[25] Later that year Collier appointed Mitchell Lieutenant-Governor, without consulting his party. He said it was a matter of 'royal prerogative', an argument Curtin would remember years later when as prime minister he appointed a brother of King George VI as Governor-General.

Collier appointed Curtin to the Metropolitan Milk Board. He also appointed him to chair a committee preparing Western Australia's submission to the new Commonwealth Grants Commission. The Commission was established in July 1933 to address the complaints of the smaller states against the revenue and spending advantages of the bigger and more closely settled states of Victoria and New South Wales. It was not least a response to the secession vote in Western Australia. Curtin's committee was required to estimate Western Australia's sources of revenue and its spending needs against those of the more populous states and formulate claims for a higher share of Commonwealth revenues than warranted by population. For Curtin it was another class in his political education. It was later reflected in his views on the respective roles of federal and state governments, and on the increasing importance of the Grants Commission as Commonwealth revenues swelled. After fifteen months in which the family savings were probably drawn down, it was helpful to have another job.

Whatever he might be doing to get by, Curtin was by now a professional politician. He kept his eye on the federal seat of Fremantle. Planning to retire at the next election, early in 1934 Frank Anstey encouraged Curtin to run for party preselection for his safe

Labor seat of Bourke in Melbourne. Curtin refused. If unsuccessful he would have damaged his standing in Fremantle. If successful he would have to move the whole family to Melbourne and find his way again in a Victorian Labor movement he had left sixteen years earlier. In Perth he now had a considerable political base. The Perth *Sunday Times* reported in February 1934 that he might contest Bourke, and then the leadership of the federal party.[26] Not a story Curtin would have planted, it demonstrated people other than Theodore thought Curtin had a chance at taking the federal leadership. Curtin rarely declared his political intentions and personal ambitions. He preferred the appearance of being dragged forward, a style which contributed to the illusion that he was a reluctant politician. He also liked to keep his party opponents in the dark. The following week the same paper carried a statement from Curtin denying that he would contest the Bourke preselection.

Curtin's plan was to run again for Fremantle. He would have calculated that another candidate would be unlikely to edge him out of Labor preselection, and it would not take much of a swing against the Lyons Government for Curtin to regain the seat. Curtin was close to Collier, who was struggling with an alcohol problem Curtin could well understand. He was closer still to Collier's deputy, Alex McCallum, who had supported him for the editorship of the *Westralian Worker*. Short, lame and caustic, McCallum was 'a museum of the classic Australian working-class antipathies', particularly towards the Chinese.[27] Curtin would not have much differed with his patron on this point. McCallum was now the member for the state electorate of South Fremantle, his political base. He could use his considerable influence in Fremantle on Curtin's behalf. No doubt that was one reason Curtin did not seek an alternative career after the 1931 loss, as Theodore had. Another, perhaps, was that he was better at politics than any alternative occupation which came readily to mind. In any case, there were not many jobs around. Even by the end of 1934, when Western Australia was coming out of the Depression, unemployment among trade unionists still stood at 16 per cent.[28] When Lyons called an election for 15 September 1934, Curtin stood again for Fremantle. After the rout of 1931 when Labor had lost thirty-two seats and the United Australia Party won a majority in its own right, Scullin made up a little ground. Labor gained four seats and the UAP and the Country Party together lost eight. One of the Labor gains was Curtin's seat of Fremantle.

On the other side of the country a brilliant young barrister and Victorian state politician, Robert Gordon Menzies, had won the safe UAP seat of Kooyong, left vacant when former Leader of the Opposition, John Latham, resigned to briefly return to the bar before his appointment as Chief Justice of the High Court.

CHAPTER 6

LABOR LEADERSHIP

Curtin was back. In the small caucus of 1934, he was now a veteran. Ted Theodore and Frank Anstey, to his mind the great figures in the Depression debates, and the two important currents of his own thinking, had both left Parliament. For Curtin there was now no model, no caucus member who was indisputably cleverer or a better orator or more usefully experienced than Curtin himself. Joe Lyons was now on the other side, as prime minister. The damage caused by the split in New South Wales was also apparent in the election. The federal party had eighteen seats in the House of Representatives. Lang Labor had nine. Without resolving the split in New South Wales, Labor could not win government. The Langites loathed Jim Scullin, and he them.

After election of party leaders at a caucus meeting on 22 October 1934, Curtin was elected one of three additional members of the caucus executive, along with Edward Holloway, known as Jack, from Victoria and Darby Riordan from Queensland.[1] A year later both would back him for the party leadership.

Scullin and Lyons were still fighting over their records, but both leaders were tiring. Lyons was visibly strained by three years in office. During 1935 Scullin was often at home or in hospital with influenza and then pneumonia. On 11 August he collapsed at Mass in St James', North Richmond.[2] He told his colleagues he had had enough. He formally resigned at a caucus meeting on 1 October.

There was little doubt among reporters that the party leadership ballot would be won by his loyal deputy, Queenslander Frank Forde, member for Capricornia. Curtin was not an obvious candidate to the press or outside the party, but had advantages in caucus. He had opposed the Premiers' Plan, which Scullin and Forde supported. He was from Perth, and while he had prominently supported the expulsion of Lang, he was not so inveterate an enemy of the Lang group that he could not be reconciled to them. On the contrary, he had played a useful part in unity discussions during the last few years. He was known as an occasional drunk, but also as a powerful speaker, with a mind that could grapple with difficult questions of economics and public finance.

Determined to stop Forde, the former secretary of the Victorian Trades Hall Council, Jack Holloway, a Melbourne member who had vehemently opposed the Premiers' Plan, urged Curtin to run for the leadership. Holloway had been like Curtin an acolyte to Tom Mann's and later secretary of the anti-conscription committee in Victoria at the time Curtin had been one of its most prominent organisers and speakers. He is said to have extracted from Curtin a promise to quit drinking, though this may have been merely a ploy to meet the single most pertinent objection to Curtin. Texas Green was also a keen supporter. With a few others they set about quietly unpicking Forde's apparently overwhelming majority.

Curtin and his supporters worked hard on the leadership ballot, invisibly. The *Cairns Post*, for example, reported on 19 September that Scullin would support Forde, who would be elected leader. As for Curtin, the paper reported that while he was 'a man of outstanding ability and great debating power', he was 'anything but a self seeker and he will probably prefer to line up loyally behind Mr Forde'. On the day of the ballot *The News* in Adelaide reported that Curtin was not expected to be a candidate.

All eighteen Labor members of the House and three senators in the Federal Parliamentary Labor Party voted in the leadership ballot, some by proxy.

Holloway and Curtin had worked closely together in preparing for the ballot. Curiously, however, the caucus minutes record that at the meeting to decide the leadership Holloway moved that the ballot be postponed until after the next round of unity talks, to be conducted by the Federal Executive. Curtin successfully opposed this motion. Holloway presumably wanted the Lang votes back in caucus to support Curtin against Forde, who had backed the Premiers' Plan. Even to Holloway, who organised for Curtin, the numbers must have looked uncertain. As he often would, Curtin followed his own tactical instincts. He was perhaps also signalling to caucus that he would not be beholden to the Lang group.

Curtin's victory by eleven votes to ten was certainly a surprise to the press. It was an even bigger surprise to Forde, who thought he had the leadership. Reporters had missed Holloway's careful preparations. According to *The Argus* the following day, 'Mr Curtin's nomination came as a last minute surprise to many members, as he did not indicate his intention to nominate until the ballot was called on.' It was a crafty tactic. 'Believing that he had been assured of victory,' *The Argus* reported, 'Mr Forde's supporters did not make a very thorough canvass, but Mr Curtin's supporters were most active.' Of the Victorian members, only Scullin voted for Forde. Holloway had detached the Victorian vote for Curtin, and added an unexpected Queensland vote.[3] The *Argus* reporter believed the Queensland vote for Forde was split by David 'Darby' Riordan, member for Kennedy, who died at age forty-eight a year later. Coming from the same area, Riordan was expected to support Forde. The *Sydney Morning Herald* reported that Riordan could not support someone who had supported the Premiers' Plan. Curtin's fiery speech in the House, the speech in which Theodore lashed him with the accusation that he was drunk on his own rhetoric, had won Curtin the party leadership four years later.

Despite the shock, both Curtin and Forde handled it with aplomb. Curtin said that he felt a deep sense of responsibility. Forde extended his heartiest congratulations. In a statement he avowed that he and Curtin were 'close personal friends'.

The following day the papers carried short accounts of Curtin, a figure hitherto little known to their readers. They judged that he was 'one of Labour's most effective speakers', and told their readers that he was 'a great admirer of Frank Anstey', who was evidently much better known. They recalled that Curtin had been 'closely associated with Tom Mann and Ben Tillett during their stay in Australia'. He had been secretary of the Victorian Timber Workers Union, editor of the *Westralian Worker*, and president of the Western Australian branch of the Australian Journalists Association. Beyond those bare facts, Curtin was an unknown. In an otherwise sensible and welcoming editorial, the *Sydney Morning Herald* told its readers that if Curtin had been in federal Parliament during the Scullin Government (he was) he would have been a minister (he wasn't), and that he had previously been a member of the Western Australian parliament (he wasn't).[4] About Curtin, eastern states reporters had much to learn.

On the wall of the Opposition party room were the photos of Curtin's six predecessors as leader of the Federal Parliamentary Labor Party. Chris Watson had been the first leader, and the first Labour prime minister not only in Australia but anywhere in the world. Then Andrew Fisher, who had been prime minister three times. The next was Billy Hughes. Hughes had been leader for only one year and one month before he walked out of the party room and formed a new government and shortly joined with his former Liberal opponents. That split had helped keep Labor out of power during the five years that Frank Tudor was leader and then the five years that the colourless Matthew Charlton led the party. Scullin had then taken the party to government, and contributed through poor decisions to what was probably anyway an inevitable defeat at the polls after little more than two years in office. He had stayed on for another

three and a half years, battling Lang in New South Wales and Lyons
in the federal Parliament. Now it was Curtin's turn to lead the Federal
Parliamentary Labor Party, a once powerful political force that for
nearly twenty years had failed at both government and opposition.
As the new Leader of the Opposition Curtin would have to establish
his authority, unify the party, and give it hope it could win power.

    He became leader just as the political struggle changed direction.
While the Australian economy was recovering from the Depression,
the world was sliding towards armed conflict. One had given rise to
the other. 'We are in a deranged world,' Curtin had remarked in the
House earlier in April 1935. 'All the portents are of evil' – and largely,
he thought, because of 'economic pressure'.

    Though it was ending in Australia, the Depression was changing
the world. Germany's economic distress had helped Hitler's rise to
power two years earlier. Tariff increases in response to the Depression
had hindered Japan's access to markets in Europe and America and
prompted its interest in creating an Asian empire. The long slump
had turned America inward. What would these changes mean for
Australia? Curtin could read the newspapers, and ponder. His grander
opponents on the government side could go and see for themselves.

Chapter 7

The men who matter

(1)

A few weeks before Curtin boarded that train in Perth for the new session of Parliament in Canberra, a younger and far more prominent and successful politician had left Sydney Harbour on a much longer journey. Tall and even at age forty a little stout, the Attorney-General and Industry Minister of the Commonwealth of Australia, Bob Menzies, was in cheerful spirits when he and his wife Pat boarded the 20 000-ton Orient Liner RMS *Otranto*[1], Captain L V James commanding, at Circular Quay on Wednesday, 19 February 1935. With its two raked funnels and graceful lines, *Otranto* was fast, comfortable and elegant. There was room enough in its cabins for 572 first-class passengers, and double that number of third-class passengers. They would be a month on board, sailing across the Indian Ocean to Colombo, then through the Red Sea and the Suez Canal to Port Said, and across the Mediterranean to Naples. There the Menzies would leave the ship and travel by train across Italy and France to Calais. From Calais they would cross the English Channel by ferry to Dover, and then board the train for London.

Like Curtin, Menzies came from rural Victoria. Born in 1894 in the town of Jeparit, he was the fourth of five children. His father was a storekeeper and a local politician. Both his parents were born in Australia. His father's family were from Scotland and his mother's from Cornwall. Unlike Curtin, Menzies was admired from infancy. A bright child, Robert topped a state scholarship exam when he was thirteen and later won scholarships to Melbourne's Wesley College and then Melbourne University. Intelligent, witty, hard-working and companionable, Menzies' progress as a child, adolescent and young man was always at the front rank.

Joining the bar, he read with the leading Melbourne barrister and future High Court chief justice, Owen Dixon. Menzies had become nationally known in 1920. Still only twenty-five, and only two years after his admission to the bar, he had won the Engineers' case in the High Court.[2] The ruling overturned two decades of High Court interpretations of the Constitution. It was a momentous decision – one that over ninety years later was still thought of as the most important decision on federal–state relations in the High Court's history. It permitted over the years a great expansion of Commonwealth authority compared to that allowed by earlier High Court rulings. As a member of the Nationalist Party Menzies had entered the upper house of the Victorian Parliament, the Legislative Council, in 1928, when he was aged thirty-three and already a celebrated barrister. By 1930 he had moved to the Legislative Assembly. By the time he resigned to enter federal politics, he was Attorney-General for the state of Victoria, Deputy Premier, and widely spoken of as the next premier.

At age forty he had been in federal Parliament for less than six months, but was already Attorney-General and Industry Minister in the Lyons Government and one of its most senior ministers. Within the United Australia Party only Sir George Pearce outranked him in ministerial seniority. Menzies was thus the second-ranking UAP member in the House, and Lyons' obvious successor. It was widely said that Lyons had promised Menzies he would resign before the next election and support Menzies to succeed him as leader of the UAP, and prime minister.

Though he was now a senior minister in the Commonwealth Government, until that day neither Menzies nor his wife had ever left Australia. Now he was to attend the Silver Jubilee of the reign of King George V. It was such a momentous experience he thought he might write a book about it. He had a title: 'Jubilee Pilgrim'. That would capture just the right combination of a visit to a hallowed place, and the contemporary note of the celebration of George V's 25-year reign. It would be a pleasure to write, and would also broaden his accomplishment. He would need to keep a diary and record his experiences.

The 'slow agony' of shipboard farewells by family and friends reached the 'oh well' stage by four-thirty in the afternoon, Menzies recorded good-humouredly in the first of his entries, and were then 'miserably prolonged' until six. Menzies was travelling with his colleagues, Prime Minister Joe Lyons[3] and the minister responsible for trade treaties, Sir Henry Gullett. There was work to do on the voyage. They had departmental briefs to read in preparation for negotiations with the British Government on a new meat agreement. They needed to discuss tactics for the conference of British Commonwealth prime ministers scheduled around the Jubilee celebrations. There was a cheerful holiday feel to the ship, however, and Menzies had time to read for pleasure. In the first few weeks he reread both *Macbeth* and *King Lear*, one play illustrating the perils of usurping power, the other of abdicating it.

Menzies sympathised with Lyons' evident fatigue with 'the necessities of social chatter', though he himself was just as evidently delighted and amused by shipboard life. 'The most abbreviated shorts on record appear on Miss D,' he recorded in his diary. Reclining in her deckchair, 'all legs and attendant swains', she asked Menzies what he thought of her shorts. 'Sorry,' he blandly replied, 'I hadn't noticed them.' For Pat's birthday on 2 March he threw a cocktail party for sixty fellow passengers, many of them presumably strangers two weeks earlier. Steaming north-west they crossed the equator, sweltering sleeplessly in their cabins. In Colombo, capital of the British colony of Ceylon, the Menzies were entertained by the Governor. From there they sailed to the British possession of Aden, and on to the British protectorate of Egypt and through the Suez Canal – jointly owned by Britain and France. Crossing the Mediterranean they reached Naples, the first time in the Menzies' lives that they were on land not part of the British Empire.

Arriving by ferry at Dover on 21 March, Menzies had his first sight of Britain, the country that both his grandfathers had left to join the Victorian gold rushes eighty years before. The white cliffs were on his right, and 'crowning them the Dover Castle'. Thirty years later, more than half of them as Prime Minister of Australia, Menzies would be offered the ancient title of Constable of Dover Castle by Queen Elizabeth, part of his demesne as Lord Warden of the Cinque Ports. 'At last we are in Britain,' he recorded, his mind 'abandoned to those reflections which can so strangely (unless you remember our traditions and our upbringing) move the souls of those who go "home" to a land they have never seen.' He could now see for himself the Britain he had imagined since childhood in the Victorian wheat district of the Wimmera, and visit those monuments he had learned about in history at school, and in studying common law at Melbourne University. By ten-thirty that night Menzies was alone in Trafalgar Square looking at a Wren church by starlight.

Material for 'Jubilee Pilgrim' accumulated. Visiting Westminster's Great Hall of William Rufus a few days later, Menzies recorded that he had stood where Warren Hastings had stood for his trial 150 years earlier. He thought of himself 'listening for the echo of the ringing tones of Burke's great denunciation'. Built by the Conqueror's son, he recalled, the hall was where 'Stafford was tried, where Charles I was tried'. Menzies enjoyed the pleasure of seeing something magnificent, storied, long cherished in his mind. In his school texts, history had been mostly English history.

The day after his March arrival in London he was given honorary membership of the Carlton Club, the Junior Carlton, and the

Athenaeum. A few days later he and Lyons met Prime Minister Ramsay MacDonald, a Great War pacifist Labour leader who had formed a government with the Conservatives when Labour split in the Depression. In these respects, Menzies may have noticed, MacDonald's history resembled Lyons'. MacDonald was both unwell and disliked by his Conservative colleagues; in June he would give way to Stanley Baldwin. (Menzies may also have noticed that something in Lyons was a lot harder than MacDonald. Lyons had already seen off Stanley Bruce, who had been disconcerted to find himself offered a very junior ministry when he returned to Parliament in 1931 after his humiliating defeat two years earlier. He gladly accepted the High Commissioner's job in London – for Bruce it was congenial, allowing him to bustle around London offering his views. Despite Lyons' evident amenability and gratitude for his assistance, Menzies was beginning to find the Prime Minister unexpectedly obtuse, including in his reluctance to specify the timing of his resignation in Menzies' favour.) At the meeting in the Cabinet Room at 10 Downing Street, MacDonald had to compete with 'Jubilee Pilgrim' for Menzies' attention. For the visiting Australian this was a 'great moment', with Robert Walpole 'looking down from the mantelpiece'. He reminded himself that 'Walpole, Chatham, Pitt, Disraeli, Gladstone, Asquith, Lloyd George' had presided over British governments in this room. 'If only walls could speak', he noted, his inspiration fading.

Menzies arrived in Britain six weeks before the climax of the visit, the Jubilee ceremony Lyons and he had come to witness. If 'Jubilee Pilgrim' was to be published, this would surely be its centrepiece. The Jubilee was marked on 6 May with a service in St Paul's Cathedral. Menzies attended 'in a Minister's uniform, with sword and cocked hat'. The Queen in procession was 'all poise and dignity'. Three days later he and Pat dined with King George V and Queen Mary at Buckingham Palace. The occasion was a little stiff. After dinner 'Pat and I have the honour of a talk with the Queen who, at a first meeting, does not talk easily'. His 'ten minutes with the King' were less stiff. The King 'talks readily and well and most informatively, and exchanges one or two Billy Hughes stories with me with obvious gusto'. All considered, 'A wonderful night, which we will never forget.'

Early in July Menzies and his wife were asked to tea with the Duke and Duchess of York. Prince Albert was the second son of King George V and Queen Mary. His childhood stammer lasted well into adult life (his address opening Australia's Parliament House in Canberra in 1927 was celebrated as the first major occasion on which he had been able to read an entire speech without stammering, or not much). He had knock knees, a duodenal ulcer, and graduated in the bottom of his class from the Royal Naval College. His wife, Elizabeth, Duchess of York, would survive him by half a century as Queen Mother to her elder daughter, Elizabeth II. Eighteen months after Menzies' visit Prince Albert would be crowned King of Great Britain and Northern Ireland, of the Dominions, and Emperor of India, taking the name King George VI.[4] The Duke and Duchess with their two daughters, Elizabeth and Margaret, lived at 145 Piccadilly. Menzies thought that 'The Duke has developed amazingly. Hardly a trace of his stammer remains; his voice is resonant and pleasant; his views well informed and clear-cut; his manner as easy as possible.' The family was 'as natural as possible. I distinctly heard Margaret Rose (aged 7) bullying Elizabeth outside the door!' He and Pat left, 'walking on air'.

Menzies was gathering plenty of good notes for 'Jubilee Pilgrim'. He would subtitle it: 'Being some account of the voyage of an Australian to Britain and Scotland and his sojourning there in the great year of 1935 when King George V came to his jubilee'.[5] Its motto would be a verse from Isaiah: 'Thine eyes shall see the King in his beauty: they shall behold the land that is very far off.'

He had long been interested in great world issues, but this was the first time in his life he could discuss them with the men who made the decisions. Helped by a welcoming British Government and the well-connected Australian High Commissioner and former prime minister, Bruce, Menzies was quickly introduced into the circles of what he called 'the men who matter'. He lunched in the House of Commons with Neville Chamberlain, then Chancellor of the Exchequer. Menzies had been told that Chamberlain was widely tipped to be the next prime minister. He found him 'most frank and attractive, without affectation, and clear mind'.

The issue on the minds of the men who mattered, Menzies found, was Germany. Hitler had been Chancellor for two years. Later in 1935, after the death of President Hindenburg, he would become Germany's Führer. He had ruthlessly crushed his opposition, and destroyed the left radicals in his own party. Germany had banned Jews from the public service and as business directors. Hitler had publicly disclosed during March that Germany now had an army of 300 000 men and an air force with 2500 planes, and was to introduce conscription to expand the army to over half a million.

German rearmament was a clear breach of the Treaty of Versailles. Britain had responded by announcing its own rearmament program on 11 March 1935, ten days before Menzies arrived at Dover. In June, Stanley Baldwin's government would sign an agreement permitting Germany a fleet three-tenths the size of the British navy. Under naval agreements, assuming they were adhered to, the German and Japanese fleets would be nearly equal to the British navy. Baldwin's policy was promoted as 'appeasement' of the reasonable claims of Germany. Hitler's ambition was still unclear. German leaders before Hitler had demanded a revision of the Versailles treaty, and it was Hitler's predecessor but one, Franz von Papen, who had ended reparation payments in 1932 at the height of the Depression. Over lunch Chamberlain told Menzies that the right approach to Germany was 'the concession of some power and self respect'. If Hitler was a sensible leader, Chamberlain's was a sensible view.

Chamberlain also had views about Japan, a rising power and a traditional ally of Britain. Despite vehement Australian objections,

Japan's possession of the Micronesian islands seized from Germany in
the Great War was recognised in the Versailles settlement. There were
now as many Japanese as Micronesians in the Micronesias. The lagoon
of the island of Truk was being developed to become the southern
forward operating base of the Japanese fleet, and Japan's biggest
naval base outside Japan. It was a little more than 1000 nautical
miles from Port Moresby, and two-thirds of the distance from Japan
to New Guinea. The previous year, 1934, Japan had announced that
it would withdraw from the 1922 and 1930 naval limitation treaties.
Chamberlain told Menzies that a 'friendly alliance with Japan' should
be pursued, which would have to involve recognition of Japan's
conquest of Manchuria and Manchukuo. Preoccupied by the threat of
war in Europe, already concerned that it would be unable to defend its
Asian possessions, Britain saw no point in annoying Japan.

Stimulated by the conversation with Chamberlain, Menzies
pondered the meaning of Hitler. 'Is he bona fide or not?' he asked
himself in his diary. 'Is he (as I suspect) a patriot who finds his
country suffering from a feeling of inferiority and servitude . . . and
is determined to restore her self-respect by as great a recapture of
military power as the other nations will permit, or is he a swashbuckler
who is preparing actually for an aggressive war?' It was a question
he would return to again and again over the next five years. On the
whole, he thought, 'the former seems to be the correct position'. If
so, Britain 'should exhaust every effort for a collective pact of security
to which Germany can be a self-respecting party'. Chamberlain was
right. Menzies was aware, however, of 'a definite fear of war here in a
few years'.

The most outspoken opposition to this view and to Chamberlain's
policies came from Winston Churchill, a backbencher widely held in
contempt by his fellow Conservatives. Menzies heard him in a House
of Commons debate on 2 May. The 'idol has feet of clay', Menzies
decided. His theme 'is a consistent repetition of "I told you so" and
first-class men usually don't indulge in this luxury'. His subsequent

talk with members of the House confirmed his impression that 'Winston has become an entertainer rather than a teacher'.

Menzies' warmth for Chamberlain's views was not checked by Churchill's speech, but a lunch with the Permanent Under-Secretary of the Foreign Office, Sir Robert Vansittart, on 17 May got him thinking. Vansittart was a hardliner on Hitler. Menzies recorded that Vansittart 'is convinced that Hitler is a megalomaniac'. Vansittart believed that 'Germany definitely looks towards war (in four or five years time)'. For Menzies it was 'a most illuminating two hours'. After a dinner at Oxford two days later Menzies seems to have swung right round. 'Germany is the real enemy of peace and must be made to understand that nobody will stand it!' he wrote indignantly in his diary.

A week later he also changed his mind about Churchill. Staying in the country with Maurice Hankey, the self-effacing but powerful Secretary to the Cabinet, they walked over to Chartwell, Winston Churchill's country home in Kent. They found Churchill bathing in a pool he had built himself on his 'beautiful property'. At tea Menzies found that 'Winston warms up slowly, and is just getting into top gear on the state of national defences and the impossibility of ever catching up to Germany in the air when we have to go.' Menzies was impressed, but unconvinced. 'My impression,' he recorded, 'is of a remarkable man who lives too well and lacks that philosophic mental self discipline which prevents a man from going to excesses of either mind or body. But an arresting person – and I have no delusions of grandeur in his presence!'

By early June, Menzies was troubled. 'Japan is gobbling up China. Mussolini is sabre rattling in Italy, announcing a clear intention to extend the Italian Empire into Abyssinia,' he noted of the newspapers on 10 June. He thought 'the peace of the world hangs on a rotten thread – the covenant' (of the League of Nations).

Visiting Canada and the United States towards the end of July, Menzies was unimpressed. Whatever concerns he had about the state of the world, he was quite sure North America could provide no remedy. While still in Britain he had noted in his diary that he disliked the Canadian accent, 'a harsh brand of American'. Canadians 'tend to irritate me almost intolerably'. In Washington early in August, perhaps troubled by the heat, he thought the debates in the Capitol 'beneath contempt'. Secretary of State, Cordell Hull, gave Menzies 'an impression of well meaning ineffectiveness'. Meeting President Franklin D Roosevelt, Menzies found him a 'charming man', who, though his 'infirmity compels him to receive you sitting, gives an impression of considerable physical vigour'. Roosevelt had 'a quick smile, a sense of humour, a belief that his policy is getting results, an obvious distaste for the commercial millionaire and a conviction that to destroy the hoarded wealth of the few will benefit the many. I got no impression that he was a clear and business-like thinker, but a very definite impression that he was honest and sincere, and with an instinctive feeling towards the British people and Dominions, which pleased me.' However affable, Roosevelt was unlikely to be around long. Menzies thought 'the opposition to Roosevelt is growing. I have not met one person who approved of his policies.' American politics proved hard to judge. The following year Roosevelt would carry every state in the Union except Maine and Vermont, winning 523 Electoral College votes to the eight for his opponent, Kansas Governor Alf Landon. He recorded the largest popular majority in United States presidential elections. Landon did not even carry Kansas.

Menzies adored the English. He did not care for North Americans.

One thing which impresses the mind is that we err if we regard Americans as our blood cousins. The majority of them are not Anglo-Saxon; their language is by no means identical; the appearance different; their ideas are cruder; their standards are lower; they engage in a nauseating mixture of sentiment ('Mother's Day') and dollar-chasing not palatable to the English mind; they have no consciousness of responsibility for the well being or security of the world; no sense of an Imperial destiny [except] collaring the world's trade and washing the hands of world responsibility.

Not surprisingly, he found 'the best Americans are pathetically conscious of this; they admire Great Britain and secretly envy her'.

Menzies returned to Australia with much to think about. Germany should be appeased, but Britain and its Empire must be better prepared for war. Japan should be conciliated, especially while there was a threat of war in Europe. The United States was not much interested in taking responsibility for the security of the world.

(2)

A month or so after Menzies returned from Britain and America and rejoined his colleagues on the government front bench of the House of Representatives, John Curtin was unexpectedly elected Leader of the Opposition. They would become friends so far as it was possible for political opponents to be friends, though in many respects Curtin and Menzies were political opposites. While Curtin in the federal Parliament argued against severe spending cuts and for extending the period over which the Budget deficits would be reduced, Menzies had taken a bedrock conservative position. The first aim, he had said in the Victorian Parliament, 'is public solvency. Public solvency does not depend upon some precarious balancing of the Budget for 1930/31. It depends on the balancing of the budget not only for this year but for years to come.'[6] He wanted wages and particularly wages of public servants cut, but not interest payments on public debt.

Speaking at a Pleasant Sunday Afternoon gathering at Wesley Church in Melbourne on Sunday, 3 May 1931, he had attacked the 'voice of the repudiationist', a voice his audience would understand to be Lang's. 'If Australia were going to get through her troubles by abating or abandoning traditional British standards of honesty, of justice, of fair play, of resolute endeavour,' Menzies sternly declared, 'it would be far better for Australia that every citizen within her boundaries should die of starvation during the next six months. To look for the easiest way out was about as traitorous a thing as any Australian could engage in at the present time.' *The Argus* reported that these remarks were greeted with loud applause[7], though even the Methodist congregation, severe and unbending as it might be, would hope not to starve to death, even to annoy Lang.

Like Curtin he was opposed to the Premiers' Plan, but for opposite reasons. Speaking in the Victorian Legislative Assembly on 14 July 1931 on legislation to implement the Premiers' Plan, Menzies had not objected to the proposed reduction in wages and salaries but he thought a reduction in interest payments was 'repudiation' of the obligation of contracts. He would vote against the Plan if it provided for 'repudiation'.[8]

While Curtin was agitating against Commonwealth Bank chairman Sir Robert Gibson, Menzies had been Gibson's legal adviser. When former acting treasurer Joe Lyons led the split which would later bring down the Scullin Government, Menzies was among the inner group of Melbourne Nationalists who negotiated with the Labor defector.

In the House, Menzies debated Curtin and his colleagues. Early in November 1934 he had disputed that public works could be 'a cure for unemployment', and criticised the 'easy theory that the present troubles of Australia or of the world are due to monetary factors'[9] – an argument Curtin pushed. Sharply different in their economic views, Curtin and Menzies would soon find differences on war and peace.

In asking him to move to federal politics, Lyons had encouraged Menzies to think he would soon step down in Menzies' favour. On reflection, Lyons found it his duty to remain. He did, however, give Menzies another step up. The deputy leadership of the United

Australia Party had been vacant since John Latham's resignation prior to the 1934 federal election. On Wednesday, 4 December 1935, two months after Curtin had won the leadership of the Labor Party, Lyons called for a party vote on the vacant position. Menzies won. His promotion to the deputy leadership of the party 'has been rapid', remarked *The Argus*. He had been a member of the House a little over a year, and half of that time had been spent visiting Britain. As gratifying as the deputy leadership may have been, Menzies still had every reason to believe Lyons would soon make way for him to become prime minister. In the House, Curtin sat at the table on the Speaker's left, opposite Lyons. Menzies sat on the government front bench behind Lyons, looking across at Curtin. Both wanted to sit in Lyons' chair.

For the next decade Curtin and Menzies would compete for the prime minister's chair. They would define Australia's political choices. Each aspired to lead the nation, a new European society in the South Seas, peopling a continent the size of the United States. Yet even in 1935 Australia was not as it had been when Curtin and Menzies were young. Their world was changing in ways far more dramatic and consequential than either of them would be well prepared to encounter.

Chapter 8

Curtin's Australia

(1)

In 1873 Curtin's father had emigrated from Ireland to what he thought of as a new land, a young country, one where vast areas were still unmapped, and where most European Australians were either immigrants like John and Kate Curtin, or the children of immigrants. By the time their son became Leader of the Opposition sixty-two years later, Australia was much changed.

Curtin and Menzies grew up in a country less hopeful than it had been in their parents' generation. With vast grazing lands for sheep, the discovery of gold and a rapidly increasing population, Australian wealth flourished in the first hundred years of European settlement. In 1890, the year of the great maritime strike, the average per capita income of the four million Australians was 40 per cent higher than that of Americans, nearly double the per capita income of Canadians, and one-fifth higher than the average per capita income of Britain.[1] Australia's fortunes then turned. The twenty years from 1890 to 1910, the years of Curtin's and then Menzies' childhood and youth, were more constrained, less abundant and successful, than the hundred years of European settlement in Australia that preceded them. Then there was the Great War, and the post-war recession. The fairly good years of the 1920s were terminated by the Great Depression.

Australians in 1935 were not better off than they had been in 1890 –
and by then they were less well-off than Americans.

Nor was it any longer a country of immigrants. In the first hundred
years of European settlement Australia had been a land of newcomers.
Spurred by the new pastoral land and then by easily mined gold in
the first half of the nineteenth century, migration to Australia had
been so high and the existing population so small that the number
of colonists could double in a decade. There were decades in which
Australia attracted more European migrants than Canada. People who
had been born elsewhere were a large chunk of the population, which
grew rapidly until the 1890s slump. In that decade nearly one in three
Australians had been born overseas.[2] Thereafter migration slowed.
The good and easily accessible pastoral land was taken up in sheep
runs and wheat farms. As the easy gold was exhausted, miners went
to other fields in other countries.[3] The Depression had intensified
the trend. During its course, more people emigrated from Australia
than migrated to it. By 1935 less than one in seven Australian residents
had been born overseas and a few years later it would be one in ten.[4]
In 1935 Australia was no longer – as it had been and would again
be – a country of immigrants. It would be another eighty years before
the share of Australians born overseas returned to the proportion it
had been in 1890.

Australians in 1935 were also older than they had been in the
nineteenth century, or would once again become in the late twentieth
century. The native-born population vastly exceeded the immigrant
population, and the birth rate of the native-born population was
slowing sharply. The Great War killed 60 000 young Australian men
and maimed many more, mostly before they could father children.
The birth rate had not recovered before the unemployment, poverty
and uncertainty of the Depression, a decade after the war ended,
caused marriages and child-bearing to be delayed. By 1935 the birth
rate was low. At the same time the death rate was falling as better
hygiene and medical advances reduced disease.

With fewer births and longer lives, the population was getting older. In 1871, nearly a hundred years after European settlement began, four out of ten Australian residents were aged fifteen or under. By 1933 less than three out of ten were aged fifteen or under.[5] At the same time the population aged sixty-five and over had increased, from under two in a hundred in 1871 to over six in a hundred in 1933.[6] The proportion of the population aged over sixty-five was markedly higher in 1933 than it would be in 2013, when public officials would gravely lament the 'ageing' of the Australian population. It will not be until 2030 that the proportion of Australians over sixty-five is expected to exceed the proportion it was when Curtin became Labor's federal leader and Menzies deputy to Lyons in the UAP.

It had never been diverse, but by 1935 the population was not only older than it had been and predominantly Australian-born, but also unusually homogeneous. European migrants to Australia had always been overwhelmingly from the British Isles, in striking contrast to migrants to the United States. Even before Federation Chinese migration had been restricted. After Federation the White Australia policy had been applied strictly and without apology or circumlocution. 'In pursuance of the "White Australia" policy', the official Year Book of the time forthrightly declared, 'the general practice is not to permit Asiatics or other coloured immigrants to enter Australia for the purpose of settling permanently.' Of the one-seventh of the population who were foreign-born in 1933, nearly four-fifths were born in the British Isles. Since the 1921 census the number born in Ireland had fallen by one-quarter, while the number born in Scotland had increased by more than a fifth and in Britain by nearly one-tenth. The number born in China had fallen by nearly half.

Almost all Australians who stated their religion in the 1933 census – and over four-fifths did – were Christians. Two-thirds were from major protestant denominations, mostly Church of England but also Presbyterian and Methodist. One-fifth of those who stated their religion were Catholics. The number of Buddhists, Confucians and Muslims had fallen since the 1921 census. There were just 1877 Muslims in Australia, and 23 553 Jews.

Australians still cherished stories of intrepid Europeans who had explored and mapped the country, and the settlers who had founded towns and cities, farmed the wilderness, pioneered the world's greatest wool industry and discovered gold. But the Australians for whose allegiance Curtin and Menzies would contest were settled in their ways. The 6 700 000 Australians in 1935 were now mostly native-born, older, and even more alike than before. Most Australians in 1935 could not think of themselves as prosperous or wealthy. They had seen worse times, and also better times.

(2)

Slowly, the economy was changing. In 1935, wool was still Australia's most important business and would remain so for decades to come. Australian wool supplied the looms of Britain, as America supplied their cotton. In the 1933 census Australia had 110 million sheep – far more than it would have in 2010. It had twice as many sheep as the United States or the Soviet Union. It produced twice as much wool as the United States, its nearest rival. Wool made up more than two-thirds of exports.

Many Australians still worked in the bush, but each year the proportion fell. By 1933 a little over one-sixth of the three million employees in Australia worked in agriculture. Helped by tariff increases and currency depreciation in the Depression, there were nearly as many in manufacturing. Most of the remainder – the majority of workers – worked in services such as commerce, finance, domestic service, transport and communications, public administration and the professions. Trade union membership was high.

Most of the services and manufacturing were in cities. Europe's population density was fifty times more than Australia's. Even in the wide open spaces of the United States, the population density was ten times Australia's.[7] But while Americans spread out, Australians gathered together. Compared to the United States, Australia had more desert and less rainfall, a smaller land area that could be used for growing crops, vast areas that could be used for beef and sheep grazing but not much else, and only one big internal river system that could support traffic more or less reliably year round. Australians congregated around the sea ports.

Stanley Bruce's government in the 1920s encouraged immigration to take up small farms. It didn't work. Its policy of extensive borrowing to support public works instead had the opposite effect of permitting the rapid expansion of population and amenity in the major cities. By the 1933 census nearly half the population lived in one of the six seaboard capital cities. One in six Australians lived in provincial cities and towns. Only a third of the population was still rural.[8] The metropolitan population was steadily increasing its share while the share of the provincial and rural population was steadily falling.[9] Because Australians were concentrated in cities, their cities were relatively large. With one-and-a-quarter million people, Sydney was the world's seventeenth-largest city; in the mid-1930s it was bigger than Los Angeles, Cairo, Calcutta or Bombay.[10] With one million people, Melbourne was smaller than São Paulo but bigger than Peking.

(3)

Curtin and Menzies contested the leadership of a nation still unformed. It was only thirty-five years since the six separate colonies had federated to become the Commonwealth of Australia, conferring on the Commonwealth certain specified powers such as defence and foreign affairs, leaving others for the colonies which now became states of a federation. So light was the Commonwealth's business in its early years that Australia's first prime minister, Edmund Barton, would sometimes conduct Cabinet meetings while cooking chops for his ministers' dinner. Even in 1935 the state governments of New South Wales and Victoria rivalled the Commonwealth in revenues, spending and political importance.

Yet the Australian federation in 1935 was already very different from the founders' intent, and it was still evolving. The Great War, in the opinion of contemporary writers, had permitted a vast and apparently irreversible expansion of Commonwealth powers. In 1920 Menzies had succeeded in overturning the High Court's doctrines of 'implied immunities' and 'reserved State powers' under which the bench had used an American precedent to confine the Commonwealth to those activities specifically assigned it in the Constitution. Six years later the Court rejected Menzies' arguments for the Victorian Government and confirmed that the Commonwealth could make specific purpose grants to the states for activities not included in the Constitution's list of Commonwealth responsibilities. The following year the states and the Commonwealth settled on a financial agreement and a Loan Council to coordinate borrowing. Pressed by London lenders and the Australian banks to cut spending and increase revenue, the Loan Council (and thus the Commonwealth Treasury) developed authority over the spending plans of the states and the Commonwealth. The exigencies of the Depression and of debt repayment also meant that the Commonwealth Bank, in its role as the central bank, acquired from the private banks control over the exchange rate of the Australian pound.

Its authority augmented, the Commonwealth by 1935 was emerging as a much stronger government than the colonies may have supposed or the founders intended at the time of Federation. But the Depression had shown that Australia's economic arrangements did not work well. In 1935, and for all the development of the Federation, for all the development of Commonwealth authority, Australia was still very far from possessing the means to exert national authority over the economy. The states still effectively controlled personal income tax. Their revenues from that source were two and half times the Commonwealth's, which relied on import tariffs and indirect taxes to support its spending. The central bank, such as it was, was beyond government influence or control and did not believe it had either the means or the responsibility to influence employment or mitigate booms and busts. The federal Treasury was an accounting and budgeting institution, exerting limited taxing and spending powers. When Lyons himself relinquished the Treasury portfolio in October 1935 he gave it to a minister of relatively junior rank, Richard Casey.

(4)

Though Australia in 1935 was emerging as an independent nation, its understanding of the world and its place in it was limited by its attachment to Britain and the British Empire. Unlike the governments of Canada and South Africa, the Lyons Government had not adopted the Statute of Westminster. Between Curtin and Menzies, the political contest would often be over Australia's unusual relationship to Britain.

In 1935 much of Curtin's everyday world was English-made. The wool of his suit would have been grown in Australia, but the cloth was woven in Britain. His shoes were probably made in Britain, his ties, the cotton for his shirts, his suitcase, his travelling blanket, his homburg hat. Even his Craven A 'Virginia' cigarettes ('made specially to prevent sore throats', declared the ads) were made in London. Other than the grand Cadillac he would one day use as prime minister, most of the cars he would be driven in would be manufactured in Britain. The trains he travelled in were made in Britain. If he could be persuaded to fly, it would probably be in an English-made plane.

Australians were 'British subjects'. The official view was that Australians were ethnically and culturally British, with a few differences that went rather to the advantage of the Australians. The European population 'is fundamentally British in race and nationality', a contemporary Year Book of the Commonwealth Statistician noted.

> The Australian people have the essential characteristics of their British ancestors, with perhaps some accentuation of the desire for freedom from restraint. The complete change in the climatic and social environment, the greater opportunity for an open-air life and the absence of the restricting convention of older countries are exerting a noticeable influence upon the physical characteristics and social instincts of the people.[11]

Yet while European Australians in 1935 were ethnically and culturally British, thought of themselves as British, and gave their loyalty to the King, they were also aware that they were not British like the English were British. They lived in a different part of the world. They were being shaped by a different history. Like the United States, the nation that Curtin and Menzies now aspired to lead was part of the New World, settled by Europeans after discovery by European navigators. Unlike the United States, religious passions played no part in Australia's settlement. It was settled in the late eighteenth century as a government colony where criminals might support themselves rather than live at public expense in British prisons. The first British settlers did not voyage to Australia voluntarily, or in pursuit of a freedom they were denied in Britain.

For much of its history this foundational fact obscured another, which was that the European settlement of Australia coincided with the Enlightenment. Adam Smith's *Wealth of Nations* was published twelve years before the first fleet of convicts and their guards went ashore at Port Jackson, the Constitution of the United States was written the year before, and the French Revolution began the year after.

In political struggles between early colonial governors and the officers of the colonial garrison, between free settlers and emancipated convicts, the land-owning gentry and the city tradesmen and shopkeepers, Catholic Irish and English Protestants, workers and bosses, Australians had established an early and enduring democracy. Property qualifications for voting were eliminated in Australia before Britain. Women voted in Australia before Britain or the United States. The Australian Labor Party was one of the first working-class parliamentary parties in the world, and one of the most successful.

The 1901 Federation and the Constitution then adopted were legislated by the British Parliament but were both entirely Australian projects, drawing as much on American as British political ideas. Australia shared with Britain respect for the rule of law, common law traditions, contract law and many aspects of criminal law. It shared representative government and the Cabinet system with an executive responsible to the legislature, and a revered but by convention powerless monarch as head of state.

Many characteristics of Australian government and politics, however, were foreign to the home country. Britain did not have a written constitution, or a federal system, or a high court to rule on constitutional issues. Australia's White Australia policy, industrial arbitration law, and high industrial tariffs were all characteristic of Australia but not of Britain. In some respects Australia and Britain were natural opposites. In Britain, 'free trade' and 'protection' referred to grain imports, with Tory landowners supporting protection and liberal manufacturers opposing it. In Australia the same term referred to imports of manufactures, with landowners generally against protection and manufacturers in favour. The English felt, with some justice, that Australia and the other dominions sought free entry for their agricultural produce in return for some preference for English manufactures in tariffs that were in any case much too high.

Over 150 years Australians had become unlike the British, with a different accent, different manners, a different class structure, a different organisation of government, and different political parties pursuing policies different from those in Britain. Australia did not have the very top and very bottom of English society. For all its variety, it had only the middle. There was no durable aristocracy, no peasantry, no culture of deference, and no great differences in accent to reliably identify class or region. Land was cheap and plentiful and capital readily available from London through the nineteenth century, while European labour was scarce. Farmers had been refused permission to import cheap indentured labourers.

Yet it was strange, Australia's relationship with Britain. Duplicated by New Zealand, it was otherwise unique. Because they were white, European and English-speaking in a region of brown people with their own languages, because they had never been at cross purposes with Britain, because a close relationship with a great naval power and a wealthy market suited their interests, they did not yet think of themselves as a separate culture, as Americans did by then. Irish Australians contested it but, much more than Canadians or South Africans, most Australians looked to Britain as home. Their flag adapted the British flag, their anthem was the English anthem, their monarch was the English monarch, their highest legal decisions could be and often were reviewed by the Judicial Committee of the Privy Council. They had no embassies other than to Britain, and consequently could effect no foreign policy different from Britain's. Their military chiefs were often British. When Scullin had insisted on selecting the Governor-General and appointed an Australian, his political opponents were appalled. It would be a decade and a half before another Australian was appointed. Loyalty to Britain was not imposed, not skilfully contrived by the British. It was freely offered. It would be 1948 before Australian law created Australian citizens as distinct from British subjects.

In creating their nation, the American settlers had at various times fought the Indians, the French, the British (twice), the Spanish, the Mexicans and each other. European Australians, by contrast, killed, expropriated, infected or simply pushed aside Aboriginal Australians, at little cost to themselves. They claimed and gradually occupied the entire continent untroubled by Aboriginal resistance, foreign intervention or civil conflict. Their military tradition was built in other countries, not in their own. In the Great War Australian troops had fought with heroism and endurance in Turkey, Palestine and France, under British command, against Britain's enemies, and half a world away from their homes. The memory of the brave defeat at Gallipoli was now a unifying legend, not because it declared Australia's particularity but because it warranted that British military traditions had been preserved in the new country, which could now claim a more respected voice in Empire councils.

Australians had never had to choose between their interests and Britain's. They fought no war of independence, because their development towards independence was assumed and unobstructed. Britain in the nineteenth century wanted no repeat of its humiliating defeat by colonial Americans, a military catastrophe all the more galling because the British soon knew victory over the American armies would have brought more troubles than the defeat, and sooner or later produced the same result. Australia would never be presumed upon in the same way. Lord Durham's 1839 report on rebellions in Canada had affirmed that the European settler colonies should be permitted to evolve towards self-government.

For its part, Australia had implicitly accepted the terms rejected by the Americans in 1778: local independence, no taxes imposed by London, no standing army, and British control over foreign policy.[12] The Australian colonies were the indulged children of British colonialism. After the first few decades of settlement there was no significant British army presence in Australia. There were no serious taxes or tributes to support Britain. From the 1850s, not much more than a half-century after European settlement and with a population still under one million, the colonies developed not only towards self-government but also towards a wider franchise – usually with support from London. When the squatters, pressing for title to vast holdings of Crown lands, resisted extension of the franchise, London usually supported the city dwellers. When the squatters wanted convict transportation continued as a source of cheap labour, then indentured workers from India and China, London usually (not always, and not at first) supported the city dwellers, rural workers and small farmers who wanted high wages and a society composed of people like themselves.

In the three and a half decades since Federation, Australia's formal independence from Britain had increased. In 1917 the British formally recognised that governors-general in Australia represented the Crown, but not the British Government – an important distinction. The British Government might on occasion advise an Australian government, but Australian governments advised the Crown and thus the governors-general.

Responding to pressure from Canada and South Africa (but not Australia) the Balfour Report considered at the 1926 Imperial Conference and then the 1931 Statute of Westminster declared the dominions to be 'autonomous Communities within the British Empire, equal in status, in no way subordinate to one another in any respect of their domestic or external affairs', united by a common allegiance to the Crown. Identifying themselves as British, Australians did not see the point of a formal separation. Once the Statute was adopted by a dominion, it released that dominion from restrictions on its power to enact legislation outside its territory, and the overriding force of existing British law.[13] Hindered by state government objections, and with no groundswell of public support, the Australian Parliament did not adopt the statute until Curtin and Evatt brought it forward in 1942. (New Zealand would not adopt the statute until after the Second World War.)

Australia in 1935 was bound to Britain by its almost wholly British and Irish ethnicity, its economic pattern – and also its fears. The English in South Africa were vastly outnumbered by the Afrikaners, and both were vastly outnumbered by the Bantu. Canada had a big French minority, and even New Zealand, for all its avid Britishness, had a formidable Maori minority. Australia's British identity was unmixed except for the Irish – and it was 1922 before southern Ireland ceased to be part of Britain. Released from the antagonisms of the old countries, Australians of English or Irish ethnicity got along after a generation or two. They often differed in religion but were united by a common language and skin colour, and by their antagonism to people with different languages, different-coloured skin, and unfamiliar faiths. Australia's strategic circumstances were also different. South Africa was unthreatened, other than from within. Canada could always depend on the United States for military protection – unless it was the United States itself, any power which threatened Canada also threatened its neighbour. Australians felt isolated as European settlers in the Asian region. Against the threat of Japan, Australia relied on the British fleet.

Curtin would one day recognise that Australian interests and British interests were sharply diverging, but his own political views were formed in the English socialist tradition, and influenced directly by two of its great English leaders: Mann and Tillett. His parents were Irish but Curtin was never an Irish nationalist, partly perhaps because he had left the Catholic faith. His most painstaking mentor, Frank Anstey, was English. Curtin read the British poets and novelists. The memories that stayed in his mind after his first visit to Britain were of the British Museum's Reading Room, the icon of free public inquiry, and the hard life of Welsh miners.[14] To Menzies, Britain was the men who mattered. To Curtin, Britain was the working-class socialist culture to which he belonged as a young man. No doubt he learned from his parents the Irish resentment against the English, the memory of Cromwell and the potato famine. Britain would never be 'home' to Curtin, as it was to Menzies. But he was not anti-English and, while recognising the difference in interests, would one day seek to strengthen the alliance with Britain.

(5)

There was Britain, and there was a greater thing, the Empire.

Australians in 1935 thought of their country as part of an immense empire, the most powerful the world had ever known. While Australians were a long way from their racial origins, they were not at all distant from the Empire. On the contrary, Australians lived close to the geographic centre of the British Empire, and in a far less threatening region than Europe or Britain itself. Britain was the major power in Asia. Many of the nearby countries were British possessions, administered by British officials, secured by armies commanded by British officers, protected by the mighty British navy, and linked by British commercial vessels and by postal, telegraph and telephone services patterned on the British model. The vast subcontinent of India was governed by the British. So were Ceylon, Burma, Singapore and Malaya. The British had concessions in China, and held Hong Kong as a Crown colony. The preponderance of the British Empire was in Asia. Perth was closer to its centre than London.

Australia was not isolated from European power, or in a hostile region. British friends or allies controlled most of the rest of Australia's region. The French held islands in the South Pacific, and all of Indo-China. The Dutch held the Netherlands East Indies. Australia itself held Papua and much of the rest of New Guinea. The United States held Hawaii and a number of islands, and it maintained military forces in the Philippines. The Mediterranean route from Britain to Asia and Australia was protected by the British colonies of Gibraltar, Malta and Cyprus, by British possession of Egypt and the Suez Canal, the Red Sea port of Aden, and naval bases at Ceylon and Singapore. The Cape route was protected by the Dominion of South Africa. In South-East Asia only Thailand was independent, and a minor power. Local war lords fought over feeble China, as did foreign powers.

The British Government reluctantly and partially empowered provincial Indian governments in 1935. In that year in the Netherlands

East Indies, nationalist leaders including Soekarno were in prison. In Canton, Ho Chi Minh and his Vietnamese communist colleagues held the first national conference of their party. The stirrings were there but only a very imaginative analyst in 1935 could detect them or see how completely and abruptly political power would shift in the region over the next decade. In 1935 there was only one Asian power capable of challenging the Europeans in Asia and the Pacific: Japan. But Japan had been Britain's ally, and in the opinion of British statesmen might well be so again. Otherwise, Australians imagined they lived in a tranquil part of the world. That, too, was changing, though not visibly to most Australians.

Australians still widely believed the Empire to be the most powerful force in the world, and thus they themselves shared this standing. But Britain had emerged from the Great War diminished and deeply in debt. It was no longer the acknowledged ruler of the seas. Under the 1922 Washington Naval Treaty the United States navy matched that of the British Empire. Japan was permitted three-fifths of the tonnage of Britain or the United States, but since it had only one sea to concern itself with instead of two or three, the agreement effectively recognised Japan as the dominant naval power in the western Pacific. After victory in the Great War, Britain had been free to deploy a bigger share of its military power in the Pacific and Indian oceans. But by 1935 Germany was once again a threat. Britain's leaders were becoming aware that the British navy might not be able to both protect the British Isles, and also protect Britain's empire in the east.

They would soon be allies in the Pacific, but in 1935 many Australians shared Menzies' distaste for the United States. It now possessed a stronger economy, a larger population, and greater capacity for military power than Britain. Though America had been a British ally in the Great War, by the 1930s it was a difficult relationship. Britain could not pay all of its war debts to the United States. As its population increased and diversified, Americans felt less kinship with Britain. The Depression was deeper and more persistent in the

United States than in Britain, and preoccupied Americans longer. In both countries defence spending had been sharply cut. Isolationists dominated the United States Senate – sufficiently so to keep the United States out of the League of Nations, though it had been created at President Woodrow Wilson's insistence. Even in China in the early 1930s the United States took second place to Britain, and Japan would soon place itself in front of both. The United States was not deeply involved in the affairs of Europe. There, Britain was a much more considerable force.

Australia still saw the world through British eyes. Though by 1935 Australia had been a member of the League of Nations for fifteen years, most of its relationships with other countries were still conducted through the British Foreign Office. Australia hoped to influence it, but foreign policy was decided in London, not Canberra. Nationalist Prime Minister Billy Hughes strikingly claimed to 'speak for 60 000 dead' at the Paris Peace Conference after the Great War, but a majority of his conservative Cabinet had opposed separate representation of the dominions at the conference.[15] By 1935 Canada had had a legation in Washington for over a decade, and France had an embassy in Ottawa. Australia had no foreign embassies or missions other than a High Commission in London and a few trade offices elsewhere. The British Government did not encourage Australia to seek separate representation in foreign countries. Later, when Australia decided to open embassies in Washington and Tokyo, Britain obstructed their establishment as long as it could. There should be only one Empire view on foreign policy, and it was best decided in Whitehall.

Though close to the centre of the Empire, though convinced of the Empire's might, though in a tranquil part of the world, Australians also felt both solitary and vulnerable. Curtin would describe it as a British outpost in the South Seas. Other than nearby and fraternal New Zealand, the nearest countries inhabited by Europeans were thousands of kilometres away and in a different hemisphere. Even through the Suez Canal by fast steamship, the voyage from Australia to Britain took more than a month. Racism and its companion, xenophobia, diminished Australia's imagination of itself. The ambition extended boldly out, then doubled back to the British Empire and London. Australian governments wanted London to do as they wished on issues of vital concern to Australia. They did not wish to act independently of London.

(6)

Taking up the Labor Party leadership in October 1935, Curtin could readily see that the threat of war was replacing unemployment as the great question of the day. Menzies, too, understood it clearly after his visit to London earlier in the year. Australia's defence policy in 1935, however, was much as it had been for decades. It was based on the Empire. If Imperial foreign policy was best decided in London, so too was Imperial defence policy. Australia possessed an army, a navy and an air force. By long-established agreement, however, the Australian navy would be put under British Admiralty command in time of war. The air force was tiny. After decades of spending cuts the army was small and poorly equipped. In training, doctrine, exchanges and strategy, Australian forces were part of the Empire's military forces. When Australian troops left to fight in the Middle East in 1940, the chiefs of staff of the Australian navy, army and air force were all British and officers of the British armed forces.

Australia's defence plan was quite simple. An enemy attacking Australia would have to come by sea, and Australia alone could not defend the country against a significant naval power such as Japan. Britain possessed what many Australians still believed to be the most powerful navy in the world. An invading force might reach Australia before the British navy could intervene, but it was surely impossible for an invader to sustain a force in Australia against intervention by the mighty British navy. It made sense to integrate Australian ships into the British navy in time of war. It also made sense for Australia to support Britain in distant theatres of war. After all, as Menzies asked, if Australia did not support Britain, why should Britain support Australia? Following this reasoning, Australia spent far more on the navy than on other defence forces.

From the Imperial defence doctrine developed in the second half of the nineteenth century came the Singapore strategy in the twentieth century.

Most of Britain's empire was east of Suez. To defend it and to secure Australia, the British navy required a major base in the region. As a base, Australia was too far south to be convenient for other British interests in the region. The major interest was India, then Burma and Ceylon, all British colonies. Further east there was Malaya, Singapore itself, and further north the British colony of Hong Kong and British concessions in China. It would probably not suit, but in any case Britain was precluded from building a base in the Pacific under a provision successfully sought by Japan in the 1922 Washington Naval Arms Limitations Treaty. A base in Western Australia might be useful in defending Australia. For British interests in the whole region, Singapore made more sense.

This was a sensible arrangement for Australia – so long as the British navy was, indeed, still the master of the seas, so long as it was configured to meet the kind of challenge a navy like Japan's would present, so long as a fleet superior to Japan's would be available when needed, and so long as the Singapore base was protected against attack from air and land as well as by sea. By 1935 none of those conditions could be guaranteed.

(7)

Even before it defeated Russia in 1905, Japan had been portrayed as a potential threat to Australia. Following a Japanese victory over

China in 1895, an Australian military exercise in Sydney was designed around the scenario of a Japanese attack on Sydney Harbour.[16] Japan's victory over Russia, a European power, was much more alarming.[17] Australian Prime Minister Alfred Deakin pointed out that Japan was 'the nearest of all the great foreign naval nations to Australia. Japan at her headquarters is, so to speak, next door, while the Mother Country is many streets away.'[18] The Australian representative on the Imperial General Staff in London reported back to the Australian army that a Japanese fleet steaming at a speed of 12 knots per hour would reach Australia in two weeks.[19] The year after Japan defeated Russia, Billy Hughes argued that Japan's presence demanded 'a bold and well defined plan of Australian defence' based on conscription.[20] Four years after the Japanese victory, Deakin's Defence Bill set up an Australian navy and an army based on compulsory military service. In 1911 the Fisher Labor Government, with George Pearce as Minister for Defence, created the Australian navy and introduced compulsory military service.

George Pearce's distrust of Japan was locked to his racism. Asians, he said in 1907, 'are people alien to us in race, religion and ideals' and 'we must shut our doors against races so foreign to us as the Asiatic races are'. The White Australia policy 'must have rifles behind it'. Pearce's whole political outlook was shaped by what he thought of as the threat from Japan. Racism continued to hinder Australia's thinking about Japan. Though Japan was a British ally in the Great War, Hughes overcame British objections at the Paris Peace Conference and blocked a resolution sought by Japan affirming national equality. It would be, Hughes argued, difficult to reconcile with the White Australia policy. In the Australian mind, racism and a military threat from Japan foolishly intermingled.

The British thought differently. In February 1902 Japan had become a formal ally, an alliance arising from their common concern with the expansion of Russia's eastern influence. When Japan rejected Russian ambitions in Manchuria and Korea, the

British Empire cheered. When Japan went to war with Russia the Australian newspapers, from the big city dailies to provincial papers, followed the struggle closely. But while Britain cheered, Australians were of two minds. 'Popular sympathy is on the side of the little Japs,' a commentator wrote in the Portland *Guardian* of 9 March 1904, but the 'Japanese statesmen have had the Northern Territory in their minds for some time'. They 'have frankly avowed so, and look askance at our White Australia Policy'. Little wonder 'Australian politicians have viewed with alarm the Anglo-Japanese Treaty'.

For a while, Australia sought to become more self-reliant. As Minister for Defence in the first and fragile Fisher Labor Government of 1908, Pearce joined Fisher in refusing to pay for a warship for Britain. London might be worried about Germany but he was worried about an opponent with 'darker skins than Germans'.[21] Deakin's intervening government concurred in its assessment of the danger of Japan and the need for home defence. Returning to office in the Fisher Labor Government of 1910, Pearce expanded an Australian army based on conscription.

Britain's alliance with Japan suited both partners. When war came in 1914 Japanese naval ships escorted Australian army volunteers to their training camps in the Middle East. As Defence Minister from September 1914, Pearce took over German New Guinea. He then formed a military force to take over German islands north of the equator. Over Australian protests, Britain instead agreed that Japan would occupy these islands. Abruptly, Australia's northern territorial limit and Japan's southern limit were only 458 kilometres apart.[22]

Victory over Germany left the British navy for a while better able to defend Britain's Far East possessions, if necessary. At the same time the experience of Australians fighting under British command and with British units on Gallipoli and the Western Front in the Great War strengthened Imperial ties and integrated Australian defence thinking more firmly into a conception of Imperial defence.

Even so, Japan's alliance with Britain bothered Pearce. It had taken control of Taiwan in 1894. It occupied Korea in 1910. It had steadily increased its influence in China and southern Manchuria. Pearce found allies in the Australian army. The head of Australian military intelligence, E L Piesse, warned in October 1918 that Japan was emulating the European powers in expanding its empire, and that it might well drive south towards Australia.[23] When Pearce convened a meeting of generals in 1920 to assess the army's needs, it was agreed that Japan was 'the only potential and probable enemy' for Australia. Australia was still 'peculiarly vulnerable to attack from Japan', especially over White Australia. They questioned whether the rest of the Empire would be 'prepared to exert their whole strength' to defend this fundamental Australian policy. The officers' plans[24] were 'based on the assumption the enemy (Japan) would attack at a time Australia was isolated from British or American naval aid and would seek a quick decision'.

Returning from the Paris Peace Conference in 1919, Hughes as prime minister declared that 'For us the Pacific problem is for all practical purposes the problem of Japan.'[25]

With the defeat of Germany in 1918, agreement on ship numbers between Japan and the other great naval powers, and British insistence that its navy could protect its empire in the east, Australian governments switched emphasis from self-defence to Empire defence. An Imperial Conference in 1923 endorsed creation of a major base at Singapore to support Empire interests in the region.[26] Australia would rely on the British navy. 'While I am not clear as to how the protection of Singapore is to be assured,' Prime Minister Stanley Bruce remarked, 'I am quite clear on this point, that apparently it can be done.' The 1923 conference established, military historian Gavin Long wrote wryly, 'the principles on which Imperial and incidentally Australian defence were to be built – in framework built so securely, as it turned out, that nothing short of war could shake them.'[27] (Though only shake them – the principles would prove tenacious.)

In Australia, army leaders objected.[28] Australian army Lieutenant-Colonel Henry Wynter argued in September 1926 that if war broke out in the Pacific it would be at a time when Britain was prevented by events in Europe from detaching a sufficient force to the Pacific to defeat a first-class naval power. Singapore, he pointed out, was vulnerable from the landward side. He concluded that Australia needed a stronger army and a fleet base on its own territory. An Australian Defence Committee appreciation two years later concluded that, despite the plan for a Singapore base, a Japanese invasion of Australia was 'not so improbable as to allow it being definitely ruled out'.[29] The army was indignant that the Singapore strategy rationalised spending on the navy rather than the army. The Bruce–Page Government spent twice as much on the navy as the army, and nearly ten times as much on the navy as on the air force. By 1928 the navy had 5000 personnel. The permanent military (not counting an average 40 000 in the part-time Militia) had 1750.

In Australia, the most powerful advocate of the Singapore strategy was a civilian: Frederick Shedden, Secretary of the Defence Committee from 1929, after his return from the Imperial Defence College, London. The army contested Shedden's strategic views. In a 1929 paper for the Chiefs of the General Staff, Colonel John Lavarack wrote far-sightedly that Japan would wait until Britain 'was so involved in Europe that its capacity to respond to a threat in the Far East would be substantially diminished'. In those circumstances 'Japan might then seek to exploit British weakness by landing an invasion force at one of three vital places in Australia – Sydney, Melbourne or Newcastle.'

By 1935 it was becoming harder to take a benign view of Japan's military aspirations. Under the influence of radical nationalists, Japan had resumed skirmishing with China in 1931, and another major war between China and Japan seemed likely. In 1931 Britain decided to go ahead with the Singapore base, a decision widely criticised in the British press as hostile to Japan.[30] There were increasing tensions between the United States and Japan. Offended by the criticism from its members, which included China, Japan had withdrawn from the League of Nations in 1933. The following year it abandoned the Washington Treaty limiting the size of navies. Germany, too, had withdrawn from the League by 1935, and was openly rearming. At the British Admiralty the planners could see that another war in Europe was possible, and it would require the presence of most of the British fleet. This time, Japan might not be a friend.

In November 1935 Piesse would darkly declare he did not know whether or not Japan had plans to annex Australia.[31] But if it did, it would be consistent with 'ideas that have long been prevalent in Japan'.[32] In the same month Curtin was elected Labor leader, the former prime minister, Hughes, published *Australia and War Today*, a polemic stridently warning of Japan's aggressive intentions.

Disliking Australia's involvement in distant wars, remembering the conscription split of 1916, less attached to Britain, the Labor Party had for its own reasons formed defence views akin to those held in the Australian army. Labor liked the new technology of air power. Frank Anstey had been an early advocate of aerial defence as an alternative to dependence on Britain and the British fleet, which implied reciprocal support for Britain. Anstey influenced Curtin in this, as in so much else. Curtin was in favour of aerial defence as early as 1914. He spoke at the 1918 Seventh Commonwealth Conference of the ALP (in Perth) in favour of aircraft, instancing the possibility of sending aircraft freighted with high explosives against enemy ships of an invading fleet.[33] At the same conference, Labor inserted into its platform a requirement for a referendum on any future decision to send troops out of Australia. By 1923 Labor leader Matthew Charlton was advocating that Australia rely on submarines and planes to deter attack.[34] Relying on the British navy risked getting caught up in foreign wars. In July 1923 he announced Labor's total opposition to the Singapore base.[35]

As left-wing Labor member Maurice Blackburn said, the big difference between Labor and the anti-Labor parties was that the anti-Labor parties wanted defence as part of Imperial defence and Labor wanted it to be independent and self-reliant.[36] It was also the difference between Curtin and Menzies. From this, much followed: the different priorities between the surface navy and submarines, between navy and air force, between navy and army, the relative importance of domestic production of munitions, the willingness to despatch expeditionary forces, the support for a British naval base at Singapore. Labor was more concerned with the Pacific than with Europe, with threats to Australia as opposed to threats to Britain. Because the League's collective security arrangements mostly related to European conflicts, Labor was opposed to Australian adherence to collective security arrangements. What Blackburn did not say was that after the split during the Great War, Labor was opposed not only to the Singapore strategy, Imperial defence and collective security with the League but also to conscription, and the sharply higher defence spending that would be necessary for Australia to maintain a useful professional army, air force or navy. In 1935 Curtin's party favoured self-reliance, but not the means to attain it.

Long schooled in Labor's preference for a more independent defence, remembering the Labor split over conscription for the trenches of France, Curtin as Labor leader would soon join the army views of Wynter, Piesse and Lavarack to his own.

(8)

In 1935 there was a unifying legend, a successful democracy, a people much alike. In the little more than three decades of its national existence, however, Australians had been bitterly divided over conscription in the Great War, and again over measures to address the economic breakdown of the Great Depression. The political conflict over conscription was at root a battle over the nature of Australia's relationship with Britain. In one of its most difficult aspects, so too was the battle over economic policies during the Depression, since the most crucial problem was the payment of interest to London holders of Australian debt.

Australians in 1935 had yet to resolve the right relationship between this vast new nation and the mother country, a decision that in turn involved decisions about its security. They had yet to find the right balance between the states, the former colonies, and the Commonwealth created from them. Within its own sphere, the Commonwealth had yet to determine which powers Cabinet should exercise, and which should be exercised independently of Cabinet. Australians had yet to prepare and equip themselves to secure their domain, so distant from their ancestral home, so big and still so puzzling and so little known, from whatever threat the wide world might pose. They had yet to gather their destiny in their own hands. Yet even then, even as Curtin prepared to lead his tiny Federal Parliamentary Labor Party, in cheerless Japanese army compounds in Manchuria, in the military headquarters in Tokyo, officers debated plans that would soon oblige Australians to see their world in a new way. It would be the most shocking, revelatory and consequential event in the new nation's short history, and it would fall to Curtin to contend with it.

CHAPTER 9

LEADER

(1)

A former prime minister, James Scullin was a national figure. Representing an electorate in Australia's remotest capital city, Curtin was publicly known in the eastern states only to those who remembered the conscription debates of 1916 and 1917, or the Labor caucus battles over the Premiers' Plan in 1931. He was only fifty, but he felt old. He told Labor journalist Henry Boote that the party leader should be a 'young snoozer of thirty or thirty-five'. He sometimes gave out that he was a reluctant leader, though thirty-five years of political struggle suggested otherwise. He had three times attempted to win a seat in Parliament before winning on his fourth try, in 1928. Defeated in 1931, he tried again at the first opportunity. Losing in the first ministerial ballot he could run for, he took to drink. He was often quiet, shy and withdrawn but he was not diffident about power.

He now had staff, and an office on the southern side of Parliament House, opposite the doors of the House of Representatives chamber. There were three rooms. His then secretary, Alice Hodges, recalled that Curtin had 'a big room with a couch and easy chairs and a lovely desk'. She and Curtin's male secretary, Eric Tonkin, shared the second room. Later, press secretary Don Rodgers took the third room. At the time, Hodges recalled, Curtin 'always wrote his own speeches and then we typed them out'.[1]

His job was to take the party to government, a daunting task in October 1935. Under Scullin, Labor had picked up four additional House seats at the 1934 election. Even so, Curtin had just eighteen Labor members in the House, including himself. The House chamber was not big but the members of the Federal Parliamentary Labor Party had plenty of room to spread themselves on their benches to the Speaker's left. Only those with very safe seats had remained after 1931. They knew each other well. On the right side Joe Lyons had to cram in forty-seven members, including those from the United Australia Party, the Country Party, and the five members of South Australia's Liberal and Country League. There were nine members of Jack Lang's New South Wales Labor Party on the cross benches, who would generally vote with Labor. Even with those members – and they were sometimes as hostile to their former Labor colleagues as to the government parties opposite – Curtin needed to win eleven seats from the Government to have a majority in the House.

Lyons had been prime minister for nearly four years. He was popular and well regarded. His cleverer colleagues did not mistake Lyons for an exceptionally bright man. They claimed he was too often influenced by the most recent opinion he had encountered, though his most ambitious colleagues would on the whole prefer an amiable and popular leader, open to their influence, to a leader of more certain opinions who might disregard theirs. It was not a troubled government – or did not appear so. After all, Lyons had pulled Australia out of the Great Depression – or so it was said.

In 1935, the UAP was not only successful, but also rich with young talent. At forty-one, already successful as a barrister and a state politician, already on terms of the easiest familiarity with His Majesty's Government in London, already acquainted with President Roosevelt and his principal cabinet members, Bob Menzies now sat opposite Curtin as deputy leader of the UAP and second in seniority in that party. He shone. His assured and good-humoured manner, his sallies of arch wit, rested on an unshakeable conviction of his pre-eminence. If older and less talented party members found his easy condescension grating, they could hardly deny the good humour and cleverness. Married to the daughter of the irreproachably respectable Senator John Leckie, a close friend of Melbourne stockbroker Stan Ricketson, a player on the national stage who had advised Sir Robert Gibson in his battle with the Scullin Government and advised on a legal way to rid New South Wales of Jack Lang, Menzies was as prominent as Curtin was obscure. And he was not alone as a new talent. There were others – Richard Casey and Geoffrey Street among the younger members, Jim Fairbairn and Henry Gullett among the more experienced. This was a party with a future.

Labor, by contrast, was a party at war with itself. It had twice split while in government. Curtin's party did not have a single member of the House from the biggest state, New South Wales.

As a leading anti-conscriptionist, an opponent of the Premiers' Plan, Curtin had been on the left of caucus. A protégé of Frank Anstey, and earlier of Tom Mann, his main supporter in the leadership battle was another left-winger, Jack Holloway. As a former trade union official and editor of a Labor paper, Curtin had many allies in the party organisation outside Parliament. He was close to the powerful Australian Workers' Union, which dominated party affairs in Queensland and was influential elsewhere including Perth. His political career had begun in Melbourne, where he retained contact with the party leaders. He could rely on support from Western Australia. In managing the Federal Parliamentary Labor Party he would often depend on the support of the Federal Executive, the Federal Conference and powerful men in the state party branches.

As leader, Curtin began to abandon his past. Scullin campaigned hard for banking reform in the 1934 election. The Country Party was also critical of banks. Following coalition between the UAP and the Country Party, Lyons in 1935 appointed a royal commission into banking headed by Justice Napier of the Supreme Court of South Australia. Treasurer Richard Casey sought Curtin's views on a Labor appointment to the commission. In one of the most important decisions he would make in the first months of office, he declined Anstey's appeal for the job.

Anstey had tutored Curtin in political economy, supported him through alcoholism and depression, fostered his career in Melbourne and arranged his job in Perth. Curtin had fought side by side with Anstey in caucus during the turbulent days of the Depression; he had been his friend and his drinking partner. Leaving Parliament, Anstey had offered his seat of Bourke to Curtin. But there had always been a side to Anstey that Curtin deprecated. He took money from the corrupt Melbourne businessman John Wren. He had a relationship with a woman not his wife. Now aged seventy and decaying in Sydney, as Ted Theodore said, 'paying obeisance to the Langites', Anstey wrote to Curtin begging off-handedly for the job. Curtin refused. Instead he nominated a former colleague from the Scullin Government, a leader of the official Labor Party in New South Wales, Ben Chifley. He transformed Chifley's career by giving him a two-year immersion in banking and finance. He created the alliance which would underpin Labor in government. For Chifley and Curtin, the 1937 report of the Napier Royal Commission would be the blueprint for banking reform.

Returning to Perth by train in mid-December 1935, Curtin was welcomed at a civic reception. Some of the bleakness of the Depression was lifting, even for Curtin. He told the crowd Australia might develop 'a standard of civilisation greater than the world has yet known'. It would be racially unmixed. Australians, he said, 'desire not only to be one people but that we shall be kindred from a common stock; that we shall, in fact, be a white people predominantly of British origin'.[2] He was a man of his times.

(2)

Curtin had relied on the left for support in the ballot against Frank
Forde. Even so, he had often been strikingly independent in his views.
He would later enhance the financial authority of the Commonwealth
over the states, but unlike many of his Labor colleagues, he did
not believe even in principle that the states should be abolished.
The ALP Conference in Perth in 1918 had committed the party to
a centralisation objective. As a Western Australian, however, he
was well aware of the importance of the state government in Perth
and the immensity of the distance between the western and eastern
coasts of Australia. Speaking in the House in November 1934[3] he had
questioned the Commonwealth's capacity to formulate successful
employment projects, arguing they should be designed by the states.
The following week he again criticised the federal role.[4]

After election as Leader, Curtin distanced himself from the
centralising planks of Labor policy. He declared that no problem could
be tackled effectively unless it was realised that the Federation was a
concern of the states. 'The Commonwealth must be a coordinating
instrument for the States. The States must regard the Commonwealth
as an associate. One must be the complement of the other.'[5] A few
days later the *Sydney Morning Herald* editorial asserted correctly that
Curtin was a moderate rather than extreme protectionist, and that he
was 'no unificationist'.[6]

The bedrock of his economic ideas had not changed much.
He still thought capitalism was unstable, and that it worked in the
interests of owners of capital. The Depression had confirmed his
views. Capitalism enriched owners and impoverished workers, and so
demand would not be able to keep up with supply. But his objective
now was to make it work, not to overthrow it. 'Our main aim,' he said
around this time, 'should be to ensure means of livelihood to every
citizen, and thus make him capable of consuming the production
of the nation.' Writing on 'The Census and Social Services' for a

conference in May 1936 he used an essentially Marxist account of politics and society. He thought of the state as a committee of the ruling class. 'The business of the State,' he wrote, 'is the protection and furtherance of the economic interests of the nation, and in a capitalist nation the State protects and furthers the interests of capitalism.' In capitalist countries there was conflict between those who had property and those who didn't, between the rich and the poor. For capitalism to survive, governments needed to soften the 'disparity between the rich and the poor, by enabling the latter to share in the general progress to a greater extent than their unaided revenues would have made possible. Thereby, internal order was maintained and life and property made more secure.'[7]

Taken in the very depth of the Depression, the 1933 census depicted misery, unemployment and poverty. Curtin said it showed a great many people lived in 'dire penury'. In Australia, 'the great mass of the people have personal resources which are absolutely deficient to enable them to live in a condition of either economic security or comfort. But for the elaboration by the state of a comprehensive and costly system of social services, the poverty of the propertyless in the Commonwealth would be so intolerable as to endanger life and property and jeopardise the existing interests of even those who profit by the current economic order.' Because demand could not keep up with production, unemployment would continue to rise – as the Depression demonstrated. At the time of Curtin's writing, unemployment was still, he believed, around 14 per cent – well below its 1932 peak of over 30 per cent, but still very high. 'It is generally agreed,' he wrote, 'that in future capitalism will have a steadily rising normal volume of unemployment apart from periods of crisis in which the rate will rise to very large and even disastrous dimensions.'

If rising unemployment was endemic to capitalism, it should be regarded as part of the cost of the system. Therefore 'the total income of the people collectively, rather than their individual resources, should constitute the pool from whence the general provision for social service is maintained'.[8] Curtin concluded that taxes must be increased to pay for new social services. 'As early as possible', he wanted to see federal unemployment allowances, child endowment, widows' pensions, and health care. There would be an inquiry first, but the Government probably needed to raise taxes on higher incomes: 'Not only must social services operate as a salvage medium for the victims of the system, but they must also be used in increasing degree as a contributory agency for the remodelling of the industrial and economic life of the nation.' Governments, he was saying, should redistribute money from the rich to the poor and also intervene in the economy to remodel it.

From Marxist premises, Curtin concluded with a program to save capitalism. It was only endangered, he argued, if it failed to provide adequate social services, and it could only do so with more tax on high incomes. Much of the program of social democratic governments after the Second World War was in those few sentences.

In 1936 Australia already possessed a quite extensive social security safety net. With Labor support, and giving effect to a specific constitutional power, Deakin had introduced old age and invalid pensions in 1908. Before the Great War the Fisher Labor Government had introduced maternity allowances and compensation for work-related injury. In 1907 the Harvester judgement of the Arbitration Court had adopted a basic wage, a minimum necessary to sustain a man, wife and two children. State governments provided various forms of unemployment relief, and Queensland had unemployment insurance. But, as Curtin argued, there was 'no system of unemployment insurance or family allowances generally applicable . . . in the Commonwealth'. These 'social services are urgently needed'. By mid-1945, all of the measures proposed by Curtin had been legislated. Menzies introduced child endowment in 1941. Under Curtin, pensions for widows were introduced in 1942, and Commonwealth unemployment and sickness benefits followed in July 1945.

Blatant socialist language soon disappeared from Curtin's public statements. The underlying ideas remained. For capitalism to survive, government would need to redistribute income from rich to poor. He would make it possible for the Commonwealth Government to do just that.

(3)

Before any of these goals could be achieved Curtin needed to win an election, and to win an election he had to reunite and then rebuild a party on the edge of ruin. Lyons had won elections in 1931 and 1934. Curtin could expect the next in 1937, giving him less than two years to rebuild and reunite his party, and craft a platform. Curtin's party was split in South Australia and Victoria, as well as in New South Wales. There were sharp disagreements between the unions and the parliamentary party. Even within the federal parliamentary party there were keen differences over foreign policy and over support for union strikes. He needed a deal with the leader of the New South Wales party, Jack Lang. Scullin had been an implacable and unforgiving opponent of Lang's. Curtin would have to conciliate him. His earlier opposition to the Premiers' Plan counted not only with members of the federal caucus, but also with the nine Lang Labor members sitting in federal Parliament.

Four years before Curtin became party leader, he had been one of the leading figures forcing the expulsion of the New South Wales branch of the party. Scullin remained hostile, but by 1935 many influential Labor leaders were willing to recognise Lang commanded the loyalty of trade unions and Labor voters in New South Wales. Sacked as premier in 1932 by the Governor, Sir Philip Game, Lang would not again win a state election. The federal party had not won a single seat in New South Wales in the 1934 election, however, and the official Labor executive in New South Wales commanded little authority. Lang's allies dominated the Trades and Labour Council and the party branches. With the Depression ending and Labor in opposition in Canberra, the fights over the Lang Plan and the Premiers' Plan no longer mattered. So long as it was on his own terms, which meant that he remained in control in New South Wales and extended his reach into other states, Lang wanted his New South Wales executive recognised once again as the official party in his state.

Curtin accepted that the federal party had tried to replace Lang, but failed. During the Depression, Curtin had shared Lang's opposition to the Premiers' Plan. His objection to Lang was the New South Wales leader's assumption that he could direct the votes of federal caucus members or overrule decisions of the Federal Executive. If this could be settled, the Lang party could be readmitted.

In January 1935, the Victorian State Conference had recognised Lang Labor as the true Labor Party in New South Wales. Queensland and the official party in New South Wales remained opposed. Preparing for a deal with Lang to bring the New South Wales party back into the federal party, Curtin had earlier in 1935 persuaded his Western Australian colleagues to back recognition of Lang. Western Australia's change of position signalled the shift in majority opinion within the party. The deal done behind closed doors, Lang was invited to attend a Federal Conference in February 1936. At that conference the March 1931 expulsion of the New South Wales branch was rescinded.

Five months after his election as leader, Curtin had repaired the split which forced the defeat of the Scullin Government in 1931. It was as much the absence of Scullin as the presence of Curtin which permitted the change, but it was nonetheless an important win for the new leader. It consolidated his leadership and began to bring the federal party back into contention as an alternative government. It was not without risks. It reincorporated into the party populist militants like Jack Beasley, Eddie Ward and Rowley James, who would become critics of Curtin's style as leader. Chifley and his allies, who had stood by the official party in New South Wales, would have to make the best terms they could with Lang. Lang and his allies would now be present at federal conferences. At any point Lang could withdraw, imperilling the federal party. For all the risks, however, Curtin now had twenty-six instead of seventeen colleagues sitting behind him in the House, and he could look across at Lyons, Menzies and the rest of the ministry opposite with more confidence. Labor was once again a threat. On 10 March 1936, Curtin offered a 'sincere and cordial welcome' to the nine members of the Lang faction, now sitting in the caucus room after a five-year absence.

(4)

Even so, Curtin's hold on the party was fragile. Economic issues continued to divide caucus. Meeting in Melbourne on 24 July 1936, caucus debated but defeated a proposal to make banking a 'public monopoly'. Bank nationalisation nevertheless remained a lively issue in the ALP. So too conflicts over the rights of the Commonwealth and of the states spilled over into caucus. With New South Wales only just back in the party and state party branches elsewhere influenced by their state leaders, Curtin chose not to insist on the federal party's right to determine federal issues. That fight would have to wait for another day.

Two cases in point were the Lyons Government's proposed referendums on aviation and marketing. Aviation was not mentioned in the Australian Constitution of 1900. By default, it would be a state responsibility, but there was a good case to make it a federal responsibility. The High Court had found that certain rural marketing arrangements set up by the federal government violated section 92 of the Constitution, which made trade between the states 'absolutely free'. Only a referendum could give clear powers to the Commonwealth. Lang was opposed to both affirmations of federal powers. It was an issue for the federal caucus, but Lang could argue that a decision over the respective powers of the states and Commonwealth was also an issue for the state party.

Unwilling to test his strength, Curtin avoided an early clash with Lang. He would bide his time. In the caucus meeting of 18 November 1936 Curtin moved that Labor should support the Referendum Aviation Bill but that 'members who have received instruction or directions from their State Executives have freedom to vote in accordance with such instruction or direction'. He ruled that the marketing and aviation proposals were 'non party issues', with members having 'absolute freedom' to oppose or support them.[9] Queensland had opposed the marketing bill. In caucus Ward and Brennan also opposed it, arguing it did not go far enough. They wanted the Commonwealth given wider powers – for example, over the length of the working week.

Curtin played no part in the referendum campaign as party leader.[10] The federal executive, however, reaffirmed that no state executive could instruct the Federal Parliamentary Labor Party on the federal platform or legislation. Curtin was developing a political tactic of using the party machine, where he had strong support, to affirm his views and authority in a divided caucus. Both constitutional amendments were lost when put to referendum in March the following year – the marketing amendment overwhelmingly. The aviation amendment gained a national majority, but a majority in only two of the six states.

Foreign policy issues agitated Labor. Curtin trod warily. The USSR had joined the League of Nations in 1934 and through the Comintern pressed for a united front against fascism. The Labor left supported League sanctions against aggressor nations in Europe, while most of the party including Curtin remained resolutely opposed to involvement in Europe.

Two days after Curtin's election as Leader of the Opposition in October 1935, Italy invaded Abyssinia. The United States was not a member of the League of Nations. Germany and Japan were sympathetic to Italy (and leaving the League). This left Britain, France and the Soviet Union as the major powers who were both members of the League and disapproving of Italy's invasion of a weak fellow member of the League, Abyssinia. The USSR was preoccupied with a power struggle, and in any case did not enjoy good relations with France or Britain. If Italy was to be discouraged from seizing Abyssinia it would only be by Britain and France.

In Australia the warm debate over sanctions was more imaginary than real. French Premier Pierre Laval had already made concessions to Italy in North Africa, and had no great interest in offending his southern neighbour. Italy was a potential ally against Germany, as Mussolini's angry response to the Nazi murder of Austrian Chancellor Engelbert Dollfuss earlier in the year had shown. For his part British Foreign Secretary Sir Samuel Hoare was all for conciliation. The British navy kept well out of Italy's way in the Mediterranean, Italy was permitted to use the Suez Canal while invading Abyssinia, and such economic sanctions as were eventually imposed on Italy excluded the only thing that really mattered: oil. Had it not been for its exposure, and had its exposure not forced the resignation of both signatories, the December 1935 Hoare–Laval Pact between Britain and France would have recognised Italy's takeover of Abyssinia.

Though in reality a feeble and obligatory protest by the League, sanctions against Italy were a considerable issue in Australian politics. As a League member Australia adopted and applied the sanctions, though Australia's High Commissioner in London, Stanley Bruce, and Lyons – both well disposed to Mussolini – had privately urged the British Government against them. Curtin spoke against sanctions, his public argument remarkably similar to the private views urged by Bruce and Lyons. Economic sanctions, he argued, would lead to military sanctions, which would in turn lead to war. Australia might find itself in a European conflict not its concern. He did not support Italy, but he did not think it Australia's business to intervene.

Many of his colleagues were Catholic, and sympathetic to Italy. Other colleagues agreed with Curtin's refusal to join European quarrels. There was very little confidence in the League or its capacity to prevent war through collective action. Japan was able to ignore the League in its takeover of Manchuria, and the League had not been able to prevent Germany rearming. Even so, within the Labor Party there were many who supported the ideals of the League, many who were sympathetic to Abyssinia, and many who shared the Soviet Union's hostility to the fascist powers.

As early as 9 October 1935, within a week of the invasion, Curtin spoke in the House against supporting League sanctions on Italy.[11] When his Labor colleague Maurice Blackburn[12] dissented and argued in favour of economic but not military sanctions, Curtin bluntly opposed him.[13] Enforcing economic sanctions could lead to war, he said, and 'If we do not intend to fight for sanctions we ought not undertake to enforce them.' Whatever the private views of Lyons, Menzies and their colleagues, they thought the Empire must have one voice in foreign affairs.

Opposing involvement in European conflicts but recognising increasing threats, Curtin emphasised the defence of Australia. At the 1936 Federal Conference the party platform sought 'adequate home defence against possible aggression'.[14] Responding to the Lyons Government argument that Australia must support the Empire, which would in turn support Australia, Curtin argued for a more independent defence policy. He wanted more weapons made in Australia, and a bigger air force. Logically, self-defence would require a much bigger army, and perhaps conscription to maintain it. Curtin wasn't calling for either.

He was critical of the Government's trade diversion policy, which saw increased preference for Empire trade. Why would Australia injure its trading relationship with Japan and the United States, the two great powers of the Pacific? In November 1936, he spoke in support of maintaining trade relations in the Pacific region.[15]

If his authority was not yet secured in 1936, he at least avoided major mistakes and kept his eye on the coming electoral contest. Remembering the caucus fights while Scullin was overseas, Curtin declined to leave the country. In November 1936, he asked Frank Forde to represent the Opposition at the planned coronation of Edward VIII in London in 1937. Not long after, the British Government forced Edward to choose between marrying his mistress, the divorced Mrs Simpson, or remaining King. Within caucus there was some sympathy for Edward's pose as the workers' friend. Curtin backed the Lyons Government, which supported the British Government. Since the King of the United Kingdom was also the King of Australia, dominion views mattered. British Prime Minister Stanley Baldwin looked for Australian support. On 9 December 1936, caucus unanimously approved the text of Curtin's speech supporting the British Cabinet.

(5)

As Opposition leader, Curtin's personal life remained simple. East coast members left for home on Thursday or Friday during the session but Curtin usually stayed on. Canberra was still a tiny town, with great ambitions. Reporter Harold Cox recalled that when he arrived in the mid-1930s there were clusters of bungalows and small shops – Red Hill, Manuka, Civic – with open fields or scrub between them. Avenues, circuits and streets had been marked out, though there was not much traffic. Dotted along otherwise empty streets through vacant land, he noticed, were bright red fire hydrants. As he had during the Scullin Government, Curtin stayed at the Kurrajong Hotel, a ten-minute walk from Parliament House. Managed by Isabelle Southwell, known to her friends as Belle, the Kurrajong was austere, though companionable. Southwell was close enough to Curtin to give plausibility to the later legend that it was she who had persuaded him to stop drinking when he became Labor leader.[16] Her rules were sensible and unbending. Meals were served at the announced times, and no other. Residents sat in their assigned places, and no other. The accommodations were modest. There was a bright log fire downstairs but no central heating in Canberra's chilly winters, and no central cooling in its hot, dry summers. The showers and toilets were at the ends of the corridors.[17] Chicken was served once a week, though Curtin preferred lamb, of which there was plenty.

He watched a local football match on weekends, and played bowls or tennis on the members' grounds near Parliament House. Always fond of cards, Curtin took up bridge. His companions in his regular foursome at the Kurrajong were Southwell, Miss Betty Jackson, a secretary at Government House, and a public servant, Frank McKenna, later Deputy Secretary in the Prime Minister's Department. The same four would play on when Curtin became prime minister.[18] He had few other friends in Canberra. He later became very close to Ben Chifley, but like Curtin he had lost his seat in 1931 and would not return to the Kurrajong and to Parliament until re-election in 1940.

Not drinking now, Curtin was amiable but distant. In those days, one of his staff recalled, political differences were not noticed out of the chamber. The members, reporters, staff and public servants played bowls and tennis together, drove out on picnics to the streams and valleys of the Brindabellas together, and yarned round the fire at the Kurrajong. Sometimes on weekends Curtin would call Horrie Cleaver, a hire car owner who drove a seven-seat Buick. Curtin would invite two or three women from the Kurrajong, and with a hamper provided by Belle Southwell in the boot, Cleaver would drive them out for an afternoon picnic to Tharwa or Uriarra. In dry times, Cleaver remembered, 'the kangaroos would eat out of our hands'. Then as later, Curtin 'loved walking in the hills'.[19]

There was still time for the family. Early in April 1936, Curtin had travelled from Canberra to Adelaide to meet Elsie, who sailed from

Perth on the *Katoomba*. They spent April touring South Australia, Tasmania and Victoria, with Curtin speaking at meetings and talking to Labor and union officials. He now saw less of his children. Early in October he wrote a father's letter to his son, with its timeless admonishments. He addressed him as Jack, as he himself was accustomed to be addressed, and signed it 'your loving father'. It was a 'solid word' to keep him 'up to the collar' for his own good. 'Do spend time at study,' he advised. 'It is vital you attend practice for cricket, which is necessary. But practice for manhood and its jobs is also imperative. We – Mummie and myself – cannot do for you what you must do for yourself. All we can do is to give you the opportunity. Now do not waste it, my son!'[20] Like his dad, John would leave school as soon as he could. Australian federal politicians see less of their families than other parents, and Western Australian federal politicians less than most of their colleagues. Curtin later regretted seeing so little of his children after his election as Leader.

CHAPTER 10

DEFENDING THE EMPIRE

(1)

War and the threat of war changed Curtin. He found himself speaking less about jobs, economics and social services. He spoke more about war. A year after his election as leader he gave one of his finest speeches. It is among the most prophetic ever delivered in the House of Representatives. It announced as clearly as possible the growing divide between Curtin and the Lyons Government over Australia's defence. An accurate prediction of what would happen, it would resonate through the years. Not the least of its interest is that having so strikingly seen into the way events must evolve, Curtin himself later lost the clarity of vision he then displayed.

The speech on 5 November 1936, drew on Lieutenant-Colonel Henry Wynter's ideas and those of other army leaders, but also on Curtin's own, developed over decades. Among Labor leaders Curtin was unusual in his concern with questions of Australia's defence. Representing what was unaffectedly a trade union party, federal Labor leaders often talked about union preference, industrial disputes, pensions, wages, child endowment, tariffs and government projects such as railways and airports. They usually pushed domestic issues. Curtin might have done the same. In the Depression years he often had. As Leader he put increasing emphasis on defence and foreign policy.

He would persist, meeting the Lyons and then the Menzies Government on its own terms, insisting in the 1937 and the 1940 campaigns (and later in the 1943 campaign) that Labor had strong views on defence policy, that Labor was right, and that there was no greater issue in Australian politics.

And not only insisting during campaigns, but insisting within his own party, so that the party itself had to change, Curtin dragging it along, platform clause by platform clause, with the same persistence he applied to reuniting the party's warring factions. It was a surprise to many in his own party, and it was certainly a surprise to the Government, and to its defence minister, Sir Archdale Parkhill. Defence was an issue for Great War veterans, mostly former officers, most of whom sat on the government side. Curtin had been a notable agitator against conscription, widely though wrongly said to be a pacifist.[1] He had no military training, let alone war experience. He was not of the officer class. He had left Australia only once, and that more than a decade earlier. While not themselves war veterans, Menzies, Lyons, Parkhill and their colleagues were familiar with the leading figures in Empire defence and foreign policy-making. They had had lunches and dinners with them, been invited to their clubs. Curtin had never met them.

Other men of his generation had fought at Gallipoli, in the Middle East and in France. They would become the heroes of Australia's story, related each year in the Anzac Day memorials to the dead. It would be recounted after his death that Curtin had twice volunteered to join the Australian army fighting abroad, and been twice rejected. Perhaps the story arose from a need to rewrite his past to better fit with his later place in Australian history. There is no record of Curtin himself claiming he had volunteered, no family memory of his saying so, and no official record of an application has turned up. As his daughter, Elsie, would write to Lloyd Ross, one of Curtin's biographers, neither of her parents ever mentioned in her hearing Curtin seeking to enlist in the Great War.[2] She thought it highly unlikely, though not impossible. War heroes were uncommon in Australian political leadership. Bruce had served at Gallipoli, but Lyons was a pacifist and neither of Curtin's later political opponents, Fadden and Menzies, had volunteered for the AIF in the Great War.

Curtin's speech on 5 November 1936 was one no other prominent figure on either side would have been able to deliver, except perhaps Billy Hughes. When they had time both Curtin and Menzies wrote their own speeches. Menzies would decades later write that Curtin spoke well and thoughtfully but had a journalist's mind, one that touched on many things but did not, by unspoken contrast, have Menzies' forensic rigour and illuminating power. In its analytic quality, in its insight, this Curtin speech on defence strategy contrasted with Menzies' charming, orotund, wonderfully clever speeches, speeches that reassured his supporters and dismayed his opponents, but rarely saw into necessity, the ineluctable course which events must take. Menzies' speeches were the product of a talented mind trained to make as well as possible whatever case he had been paid to make, but which could not display the harsh logic and occasional brilliance of Curtin, whose journalist's mind sought always to capture reality. Curtin was fine at polemics. Sometimes he was good at the far rarer political gift of insight.

For decades the Australian army and the federal Labor Party had pursued parallel paths on the defence of Australia. Both wanted stronger land and air defence of Australia. Both wanted to shift spending away from the Australian navy, which in time of war would be integrated into the British fleet. The British Government and the Australian 'blue water school' of Empire Defence adherents counter-argued that the British fleet and only the British fleet could protect Australia against Japan. The Singapore base was at the heart of the debate. Curtin had long been a proponent of an independent defence of Australia, a line of thought he shared not only with most of his Labor colleagues but also with former Defence Minister, Sir George Pearce, and an influential group of army strategists.

The most vocal and insistent of these strategists was Wynter. One of Wynter's sympathisers was the Great War veteran, Major-General Charles Brand, since 1933 a UAP senator from Victoria. Brand gave Curtin a copy of a lecture by Wynter. It eviscerated the Singapore strategy.[3]

On 5 November 1936,[4] with the Lyons Government declaring itself to be more loyal to Britain and the Empire than the Labor opposition, Curtin went on the attack. He united in one speech Labor and army views, separately developed over past decades. Drawing on the talk by Wynter, given to a small group sixteen months earlier, he argued that the Singapore strategy, the basis of Australia's defence, was misconceived.

Again challenged by Germany, Britain was realising it could not be powerful in the Atlantic as well as the Indian and Pacific oceans. Curtin spoke the unspeakable. 'There is no escape from the conclusion,' he announced, 'that with the development of air power and the re-emergence of Germany, Great Britain is becoming more and more a European and less and less a world power. Who can deny then that Australia, too, must look to its own security.'

Responding to a statement from Parkhill, Curtin said that 'Singapore cannot be regarded as a measure of Australian's defence, except in conjunction with a fleet based upon it'. But would a fleet be based there when Australia needed it? Would a fleet 'busy in European waters be capable of despatching sufficient ships to the western Pacific to deny it to the enemy?' Surely, 'If an Eastern first-class power sought an abrogation of a basic Australian policy, such as the White Australia Policy, it would most likely do so when Great Britain was involved with or threatened to be involved in a European war.'

In those circumstances, would 'the British government dare to authorise the despatch of any substantial part of the fleet to the East to help Australia?' He instanced the British Admiral Richard Webb saying of this possibility in 1930, 'The British people would not tolerate it.' Curtin believed that 'dependence of Australia upon the competence, let alone the readiness, of British statesmen to send forces is too great a hazard upon which to found Australia's defence policy'. To an interjection from a government member that 'Great Britain has never failed us', Curtin responded, 'History has no experience of the situation I am visualising.' Curtin said the real purpose of Singapore was to defend India from 'hostile cruisers'. He warned that this first-class Eastern power could capture Hong Kong and Singapore, and might then attempt to take Australian ports to prevent them being used by the British navy.

'It is fashionable for the Blue Water school to voice the opinion that Australia need only fear minor raids by a naval visit and the depredations of a commerce raider like the *Emden* and the *Wolf*.' That opinion depended on the belief that 'the British fleet will arrive in Singapore in time, that it will find a properly equipped base not captured or seriously damaged by naval or air bombardment, and that it will win the naval battle when forced into action.' But it is 'unreasonable to think that the British Fleet will leave European waters until the situation there is thoroughly satisfactory'. Delay in arrival of a fleet presents an opportunity for the enemy to 'capture or damage the Singapore base'. The first steps in a Pacific War, he predicted, would be the capture of Hong Kong and Singapore.

The 'great wars in which Australia's security is imperilled will not be European wars' he told the House. 'They will be wars in the South Pacific.'

He did not call for a separate navy. On the contrary, he said, 'An Australian navy would by itself be an absolutely futile force in Australian waters because it would always be the inferior naval force if an attack was made on us.' He had learned 'there was nothing so inferior as an inferior fleet' and that an inferior fleet at Singapore 'would be chased across the Ocean and sunk'. Nor could Australia rely on air forces alone. 'In the last resort the principal factor in our local defence will be our land forces.'

Curtin wanted less emphasis on the Australian navy and more on air, though 'to rely wholly on aircraft for defence would be unwise'. He also favoured friendlier relations with the United States, and disapproved of trade limits on Japan. (He had criticised an iron ore embargo imposed by the Lyons Government.) 'A greater degree of self reliance in Australian defence policy is essential.'

Curtin did not mention Wynter, but listening to the debate Parkhill immediately recognised the argument. When Parkhill was accused by Labor member Brennan of reading a speech prepared for him by a bunch of 'militarist imperialists', Parkhill replied, 'The honourable member might with more justification pass that comment on the speech of his leader.'[5] Four months after Curtin's speech Wynter was transferred to a 'very junior post'.[6] Parkhill thought Wynter's treatment 'lenient'.[7]

It was a pertinent and far-sighted speech. It foreshadowed Japan's strategy in 1941, and its consequences. But it was also true that, obedient to the party platform, Curtin opposed reintroduction of compulsory military training, and complained of additional defence spending. He was unwilling to propose the spending necessary to create the vastly expanded land and air forces on which Australia should rely. Newly elected to the leadership of his party, he had embraced the right theory but was stuck with the wrong practice.

The Singapore strategy was now a point of contention between Curtin and the Lyons Government. Lyons clung to it. Australia could rely on the Singapore strategy. Back from the 1937 Imperial Conference in London and planning the federal election for October, Lyons in late August would offer the House a reassuring account of British naval commitments to Australia. In Spain the Republican loyalists were fighting Franco's rebels, Japan was at war with China, while in Europe Hitler was rebuilding the German navy, air force and army. There was, said Lyons, 'widespread fear' of another major war.[8]

But Britain had renewed its assurances to Australia that 'an adequate fleet would proceed to Singapore in an emergency'. No doubt referring to Curtin's criticisms, Lyons acknowledged that 'It may be suggested that Singapore might be captured or neutralised before the fleet arrived', but on that point Australians should feel no unease. 'This cannot be dealt with in public beyond stating that the base is now a very powerful fortress and its defences are being further strengthened.' Lyons believed the Singapore base was 'the keystone of Empire defences in the Eastern hemisphere' and 'its capacity to fulfil its functions should be undoubted'.

At the Imperial Conference the Admiralty had reassured Australia that a Japanese expedition aimed at Australia, New Zealand or India was 'a highly improbable undertaking so long as our position at Singapore is secure, and the Fleets of the British Commonwealth of Nations are maintained at such a strength as to enable a force capable of containing the Japanese to be dispatched to the Far East, should the occasion arise'.[9] In this assurance the British misled Lyons and Parkhill, and also misled themselves.

For the British planners, the problem was not just defending Australia and New Zealand against a potential Japanese threat, but also of defending Hong Kong, Malaya, Burma and India, all vulnerable to attack by Japan. But if Britain was at war with Germany, and especially if it was at war with Italy as well, the British navy could not send to Singapore a fleet superior to Japan's. It could not defend the larger part of Britain's colonial Empire, or the dominions of Australia and New Zealand.

Curtin had said it in 1936. To the British Admiralty, it was well known. The strategic problem of defending the eastern Empire against Japan while at war with Germany was the Admiralty's biggest problem. If Italy with its Mediterranean fleet joined Germany, the problem was insoluble. Slowly, the awareness of that problem was influencing other British policies, including appeasing Germany, and placating Italy and Japan.[10] Curtin's 1936 speech had grasped one part of the problem. He was perhaps unaware of how big a problem it was, and how much influence it would have on British policy towards Germany, Japan and the United States in the next few years.

(2)

A by-election for the seat of Gwydir in May 1937 was Curtin's first test as a vote winner, and the usefulness of his reconciliation with Lang. Busier now, he saw less of Elsie. Writing a wedding anniversary letter to her from Canberra on 21 April 1937, he reflected that their marriage

> has been a happy time & I still think that you are the nicest lady in the land . . . I bless you for all the years of loveliness you have given me; for the sticking-to-me in all sorts of weather & for the sweet kindness which has marked all your spirit from the day I first saw you. And we will celebrate the 20 years on the day the Gwydir poll is taken – for I'll be home that day. I have not time to say more now – two interruptions to this note already & now I have to go to an appointment . . . We may win Gwydir. And in any case the result is not everything.[11]

His campaigning done, Curtin boarded a train to Perth. 'My goodness I'll be glad – a very tame monkey – when I get home,' he wrote Elsie. 'I am just aching to get to Port Augusta which is, as I see it from here, a Perth suburb.' He felt 'very tired, a bit nervy, but no worse than the others. Cheers & loud cheers! We want Gwydir & if that is won then we are on the threshold of a move upward. Keep your face smiling, old girl, this note will beat me home, but I will be following it hot footed.'[12]

Based in the New England region of New South Wales, the seat of Gwydir stretched north to the Queensland border and west to Bourke. It had been held for the Country Party by C L Abbot, but that party was now split. Curtin campaigned hard for the by-election in May 1937, in company with Lang. Labor's W J Scully won the seat. Curtin's leadership was strengthened. The pact with Lang was proving its value.

By mid-1937 Curtin was gaining confidence and Labor's fortunes had improved. It had comfortably won Gwydir, and W J Riordan had held on to the seat of Kennedy after his uncle David 'Darby' Riordan's death. The Victorian party had readmitted Blackburn after an expulsion. The caucus was 'now larger than it has been for years', Curtin told a party meeting on 17 June. Curtin was sufficiently well-prepared to be able to read his policy speech for the forthcoming general election to caucus early in September.[13] His theme was the defence of Australia. He was taking the offensive against the expected attack on Labor for disloyalty to the Empire. Congratulating their leader during a special caucus meeting on Friday, 10 September, Curtin's colleagues rose to sing 'For He's a Jolly Good Fellow'. Lyons adjourned the House the following Wednesday and called the election for 23 October.[14]

(3)

Curtin's thrust into defence and foreign policy issues was timely. They were soon all that mattered. Heading towards the election, Australian support for Britain was electorally potent. As European tensions increased through 1936 and into 1937, Lyons and his fellow ministers and their newspaper supporters had pledged their loyalty to the Empire. They would support Britain, and through its mighty navy Britain would support Australia. Curtin opposed involvement in Europe, and did not trust the assurances of British naval support in a Pacific war with Japan. It was a debate Lyons hoped would dominate the federal election. It was one Curtin was not reluctant to join.

Speaking in Adelaide in July 1937, Curtin said, 'To be drawn into a war in spite of everything would be bad enough, but deliberately to indicate some willingness to be a participant, for or against certain European groups, would be a piece of national madness . . . The wise policy for Australia in regard to Europe is not to be embroiled in the perennial disputes which mark the old world.'[15]

In Melbourne, Curtin defined Labor defence policy 'as one of resistance to foreign aggression, provided that no forces are sent outside Australia, and that no promises are made of participation by Australian troops outside of Australia, except after a decision by the people'. He believed that 'In view of the growing strength of European nations, Australia could not reasonably expect Britain to assure Australia's safety. Australia had to be self reliant.' If Britain was at war with Germany, Australia would have to rely on its own defences in a Pacific war.

In preparing for the election Curtin was helped by Don Rodgers, a reporter for the *Labor Daily*. Born in Newcastle, Rodgers trained as a reporter on the Newcastle *Herald*, and in 1931 joined the *Labor Daily* as a reporter in the Parliament House press gallery. A party newspaper, the *Labor Daily* generally reflected the views of Jack Lang. It had at first ardently supported League of Nations sanctions against Italy during the invasion of Abyssinia. When Lang announced his opposition to sanctions in September 1935, the *Labor Daily* seamlessly switched, bringing as fervent a conviction to the case against as it had to the case for sanctions. Rodgers was schooled in a world of political pragmatism. (Curtin himself knew the rules. As editor of the *Westralian Worker* he had written favourably of the One Big Union idea until the AWU became the majority owner of the paper. Its officials thought the AWU was all that was required by way of one big union. Curtin promptly changed the paper's line.[16]) Assigned by the *Labor Daily* to help Curtin as press secretary during the 1937 election campaign, Rodgers would be invited to stay on. Then thirty-one, he was twenty years younger than Curtin. He was, he later claimed, the first full-time press secretary for a political leader in Australia.

Rodgers was a journalist, and Curtin enjoyed the company of journalists. Rodgers had been a cricketer and was then the honorary secretary of Canberra's rugby union club, so they had sporting interests in common. They were temperamentally akin. Both had bleak spells. Rodgers and Curtin got to know each other well in that first campaign, travelling together from meeting to meeting on all-night train journeys, staying in country pubs, briefing reporters. Rodgers would discover the usual jostling around the throne. There was no love lost among courtiers. For all that Curtin was, for a press officer, the ideal boss. He knew all the important reporters, he knew what a story was. Other staff might call Curtin 'Leader', a common Labor style or, around the office, 'Mr Curtin' and later simply 'Prime Minister'. Rodgers called him 'boss'. It was deferential but also slightly ironic, good-humoured and collegiate. No well-trained public servant could call Curtin 'boss'.

Rodgers helped Curtin's relationships with reporters, already good. Curtin gave the press time and attention, then and later. Before it was increased in size in 1949 the House had about seventy-five members. Journalist Alan Reid remembered of that time:

> we used to virtually live together, travel together, see we'd stay at the same hotels, drink together. In those days there used to be a veranda at Parliament House (which) was a meeting place for the Press and the Parliamentarians, it was a much easier, closer and more intimate thing. Very few of them had homes here, they lived in the same hotels as us, we'd go on picnics together, we'd go fishing together, we'd drink together. It was a much closer and more intimate association than now.[17]

As Lyons hoped, the campaign was fought on foreign policy issues – which were also issues of Australia's place in the Empire and its loyalty to Britain. Curtin advocated more air power, a defence of Australia that would not rely entirely on the British navy. He seemed to have forgotten his earlier demand for a bigger army. In his policy speech in Fremantle on 20 September he said 'the strength of Australian defence must lie in aviation'. The Lyons Government provided for eight squadrons or ninety-six planes while there is 'not far away from us, a power equipped with a sea-borne plane strength of not less than 300 planes'[18].

Protecting himself from claims he was disloyal to the Empire, Curtin invoked the threat from Japan. 'Australia First is the Labor Party's policy for the elections', he told a crowd in Perth.[19] Some of Curtin's defence material for both the 1937 and then the 1940 campaigns, Rodgers recalled, came via Rodgers from Lieutenant-Colonel Horace (Red Robbie) Robertson, then the second-in-command at Duntroon and an advocate of the army line. Rodgers knew him from the Canberra Rugby Union Club.[20]

Labor went into the election united and with high hopes. Curtin was on the train home on election day, Saturday, 23 October. He wouldn't reach Perth until Monday morning. He had plenty of time to ponder the disappointing results, heard over the train radio. Labor had won two additional seats, but in New South Wales the vote was not much better than the vote for the Lang party at the 1934 election. It did well in the Senate, but not well enough to win control.

Curtin had decided early to fight on the defence and foreign policy issues preferred by the Government. Though he was still a long way from winning government his colleagues and the press thought he had played his cards well in his first two years as leader.

(4)

War was on Curtin's mind when the Parliament first convened on 30 November 1937. All 'countries are resorting to arms', Curtin told the House the following day. He insisted that Australia should be 'increasingly self reliant in its own defence'. Gloomily, and in the event wrongly, he predicted another downturn and rising unemployment.[21]

Britain and France were preparing to make a deal with Italy, he could have read in *The Argus* that morning, but there was a new conflict to report. Japan was preparing to attack Canton. War in Europe was still nearly two years away. War in China, soon to have much greater pertinence for Australian security, was already being fought.

A pacifist by early conviction, Lyons reluctantly augmented Australia's defence spending. His internal party critics pressed for compulsory military training, terminated by the Scullin Government during the Depression. Lyons resisted, but defence spending greatly increased, as did the threat of war in Europe. In March 1938, after Hitler annexed Austria to Germany, Lyons announced plans to more than double defence spending over the following three years. For the first time the air force was allocated more than the army and both were given a higher share of total spending than in past years.

While preparing for the possibility of war in Europe, Lyons was doing all he could to avert it. The Prime Minister, his cabinet, and the Australian High Commissioner in London, Bruce, threw Australia's support behind the British proponents of appeasement, led by the Prime Minister, Neville Chamberlain. For both Britain and Australia, appeasement of Germany was not least a way of minimising the threat from Japan. If preoccupied in a war against Germany, the British navy could not protect British possessions in Asia. At the very least, postponing a war with Germany would allow completion of more British warships – though Japan was also building more ships. Britain's inability to protect its eastern empire against an expansionist Japan, a problem long foreseen but unattended, would be a persistent influence on British policy in Europe, and on Australia.

For both the Australian and British governments, the high tide of appeasement was the 1938 crisis over Czechoslovakia. It was the last

European episode in which Australian Government views mattered in London. It was also the crisis in which the appeasers claimed their greatest success and discovered their final failure. Throughout the crisis Curtin was an interested observer, learning much. The left of his party was opposed to appeasement of Germany. He himself opposed sending Australians troops to fight European wars. It followed that he would regard British policy towards Germany as a matter for the British Government, not the Australian Government. Not so for Bruce, Lyons or Menzies. To them it was Australia's business also.

Hitler had sent troops into the demilitarised but German-controlled Rhineland in March 1936, and into Austria in March 1938. He then claimed for Germany the lands occupied by the German minority in Czechoslovakia, the free Baltic port of Danzig (largely German in population and under League of Nations control as part of the Versailles settlement), and a road and rail line through Polish territory to connect Germany to the port. By the second half of 1938 Germany was using pro-German parties in Sudeten Czechoslovakia and in Danzig to press its claims.

Lyons preferred the sunny side. Discussing the resignation from Chamberlain's government of the Foreign Secretary, Anthony Eden, a signal of increasing disenchantment with appeasement in the Conservative Party leadership, Lyons had told the House in April 1938 that tensions over Germany's takeover of Austria had 'lessened when Great Britain announced that assurances had been received from Germany that the independence of and integrity of Czechoslovakia would be respected.'[22] He assured the House that 'Great Britain is at this moment using its best efforts to ensure appeasement'.

Vansittart's warning gave Lyons pause in 1935, but by 1938 Menzies was as firm a supporter of Chamberlain's appeasement policy as Lyons or Bruce. In London on other matters in July 1938, Menzies arranged to visit Germany to see for himself. A meeting with Hitler proved impossible but the German Foreign Office and the British Embassy in Berlin arranged a useful program. With Pattie, his secretary, Peter Heydon, and the Australian external affairs officer in London, Alfred Stirling, Menzies flew to Berlin on Wednesday, 27 July for a four-day visit.[23] He met German foreign affairs officials, and the President of the Reichsbank. He visited factories and workers' housing, new highways and the Olympic Stadium. Each day he spoke with the British Ambassador, Sir Nevile Henderson, a proponent of appeasement, whom Menzies thought 'an extremely clear headed and sensible fellow'.[24]

From London on 6 August 1938, Menzies reported his conclusions to Lyons, and copied them to British Foreign Secretary, Lord Halifax.[25] He esteemed Chamberlain and Halifax, who 'enjoy high reputations'. He was sympathetic to Germany, and critical of Czechoslovakia. He thought the German Foreign Office was 'optimistic about an amicable settlement of the Polish Corridor affair' but 'depressed about the Czechoslovakian position'. He had sensed 'a gloomy feeling in the German mind' that Czech President Benes 'egged on by France, will refuse to do the fair thing and trouble may ensue'. Menzies thought Germany would be satisfied with 'a loose federal system' in Czechoslovakia, 'for some time at least', rather than actual incorporation of Sudeten Germans. He concluded, 'I am more than ever impressed with the view that this problem requires a very firm hand at Prague, otherwise Benes will continue to bluff at the expense of much more important nations, including our own.' No doubt that was Henderson's view as well.

Hitler evidently wanted to move into Czechoslovakia on 1 October. Well-disposed to Mussolini, Bruce and Lyons urged the British Government to seek his intercession to prevent war over Czechoslovakia. Chamberlain took their advice, telling the House of Commons that as a consequence of a call from Lyons he had asked Mussolini to attend a conference in Berlin. It was a decisive intervention. The German march into Czechoslovakia was averted as

Hitler agreed to four-power talks at Munich at the end of September 1938. Returning to London with an agreement, Chamberlain declared 'peace for our time'.

Curtin did not join a debate about appeasement, and found himself in a sunnier spot than Lyons. Responding to Lyons, he complained of the 'staggering increase' in defence spending foreshadowed by the Prime Minister.[26] After all, 'all the evidence on central Europe suggests that tension is far less grievous than it was'. Was this therefore a time when Australia should be 'embarking on a stupendous burden for national defence?'

Curtin was not an appeaser. In common with most of his colleagues, he wanted no Australian involvement in Europe at all. He most particularly wanted to keep his party united – even at the cost of a gaping contradiction between the defence self-reliance he advocated, and his opposition to the means to attain it.

Curtin remained outside the debate on policy towards Germany. If there was to be war, he told the House at the height of the crisis, then Australia 'should not be involved in it'. It was his 'prayer' that 'if war cannot be averted in some parts of the world then at least the people of Australia will be spared it'.[27]

After the Munich Agreement, Menzies acclaimed Chamberlain. The British Prime Minister's conciliation 'has resulted in a triumph of reason in Europe', he told the House.[28] He objected to Curtin's notion of a separate foreign policy from Britain. Australian leaders 'ought to have minds sufficiently informed and sufficiently strong, positive and constructive, to be able to say useful things at the right time to the government of Britain'. But, he continued, if 'what we are asked to produce is a separate foreign policy of the kind I have been discussing, I say without any hesitation that I would regard such a thing as folly.' Britain was still 'the world's greatest power',[29] certainly in Menzies' mind.

Peace had been declared, but Curtin wasn't convinced. Three days after Chamberlain's statement, Curtin repeated that Labor's attitude remained as he had put it a week earlier: 'Whatever we may do as a Dominion of the British Commonwealth of Nations, no men shall be sent out of Australia to participate in another war overseas.'[30]

(5)

John and Elsie's anniversary had come around again. Curtin, his staff busy around him in the Leader of the Opposition's room on the southern side of the House chamber, wrote to Elsie that 'I bless every hour of all the days that have passed. You have been gracious & loving always; no man has been more fortunate than myself. I love you more & more & my greatest happiness is when I am home with you. All I hope is that you will have happiness & content for ever. That is my prayer.'

His father had died years before. Late in September 1938 his mother, Kate Curtin, died, aged eighty-one. He was in Melbourne for her funeral on 26 September. 'Words are hard things when they fail and they fail me fairly often,' he reflected. 'My mother did live to be a great age as the saying goes, but somehow I have felt but a small boy and she a comparatively young woman. I do not think years matter much in cases like this.'[31]

Sometimes it was all too much. Troubled by disputes within Labor as much as by the contest with the UAP, Curtin spent time lying on his office couch, smoking, looking at the ceiling. Reporter Harold Cox of *The Argus* and then the Melbourne *Sun* recalled that when he spoke to Curtin in the Opposition leader's office he was often prone on his couch, one 'made of some light-coloured wood with not very soft-looking cushions on it', chain-smoking cigarettes and complaining of headaches and neuralgia. He was 'almost a hypochondriac', Cox believed.[32] Curtin developed 'a troublesome smoker's cough', his daughter remembered, despite Craven A's assurances.[33]

(6)

The Munich Agreement avoided war in October 1938, but by January 1939 it was apparent that Chamberlain's satisfaction with the agreement was not shared by Hitler. The 'triumph of reason in Europe' had been very brief. On 25 January 1939, the Dominions Secretary, Malcolm MacDonald, cabled Lyons with a prescient and 'Most Secret' appraisal of recent intelligence reports on the German leader.[34] Lyons shared the cable with Curtin, alerting him to the renewed threat of war in Europe. The cable proved to be remarkably accurate.

The reports, wrote MacDonald, throw 'a most disquieting light on Hitler's mood and intentions.' Hitler was 'bitterly resentful' of the Munich Agreement

> which baulked him of a localised war against Czechoslovakia, and demonstrated the will to peace of the German masses in opposition to the war mongering of the Nazi Party. He feels personally humiliated by this demonstration. He regards Great Britain as primarily responsible for this humiliation and his rage is therefore directed principally against this country which he holds to be the chief obstacle now to the fulfilment of his further ambitions.

Referring to both German and non-German sources, the cable said that Hitler was now contemplating 'an attack on the Western Powers as a preliminary to subsequent action in the East'. He might, MacDonald speculated, attack Holland and take possession of its coasts and give the Netherlands East Indies to Japan. He might encourage Italy to war with France. He might launch a sudden air attack on Britain. All these designs 'may seem fanciful and even fantastic' but 'it is impossible to ignore them particularly in view of the character and proven reliability of the many informants.

Moreover, Hitler's mental condition, his insensate rage against Great Britain and his megalomania which are alarming the moderates around him are entirely consistent with the execution of a desperate coup against the Western Powers.' By January 1939 Lyons and Curtin had every reason to recognise that Hitler could not be appeased by anything Britain could offer.

CHAPTER 11

MENZIES TO POWER

(1)

As the risk of war in Europe increased, Curtin's doubts about Britain's willingness to send a fleet to Singapore to deter Japan were more widely shared. British newspapers covered the issue, as did Australian newspapers. The Melbourne *Herald*, for example, reported on 3 October 1938 an unsourced but evidently authoritative British view that control of the Pacific would require twelve battleships, leaving just one for the defence of Britain. For the British Government, threatened by Germany, that would not be a sensible disposition of its fleet.

Behind the scenes, invisible to Curtin and the press, the Lyons Government was troubled. Though one of the earliest exponents of the Singapore strategy, High Commissioner Stanley Bruce was now sceptical of the British commitment to send a fleet to Singapore if necessary to deter Japan. A few years earlier the Admiralty had put a fleet for Singapore and for Australia's defence second only in priority to the defence of Britain itself. More recently, the Admiralty had had to plan for the possibility that Italy was allied to Germany; to defend the Suez Canal and other Middle East possessions, Britain would now need to provide a stronger fleet in the Mediterranean. The defence of Australia slipped to third priority, after the defence of Britain and the Mediterranean.

Bruce told the Lyons Cabinet of his misgivings on a visit to Australia early in 1939. The Australian naval commander, Admiral Sir Ragnar Colvin, himself on loan from the British navy, was conflicted. He cabled the Admiralty's First Sea Lord, Admiral Sir Roger Backhouse, early in March 1939 to warn that Bruce was telling the Cabinet 'that in his opinion Britain will not be able to send capital ship forces to Singapore in event of war with Japanese while at war in Europe'. Colvin was 'vigorously confuting' Bruce's view. It might encourage Australia to turn to ideas of 'military self dependence which though in my opinion illusory or impossible is attractive to uninstructed public opinion'. He wanted more indications of willingness to support, from Admiralty.[1]

Backhouse replied on 17 March 1939:

> there has never been doubt that a force of capital ships would have to be sent East in the event of war with Japan. What is uncertain is the strength of this force as this would necessarily depend on situation in Europe. In any case I feel sure force sent would be sufficient to safeguard communications in the Bay of Bengal and the Indian Ocean, and act as a strong deterrent to any Japanese expedition against Australia.[2]

This was less than Australia expected – though more than the Admiralty would actually be in a position to provide.

Australians in London were similarly conflicted, as was the British Government. Around the same time as Backhouse was cabling Colvin, the Acting Australian High Commissioner in London, J S Duncan, saw something he was not meant to see. It was the minutes of a meeting of the top-level Committee of Imperial Defence held early in 1939. The meeting record revealed a conflict within British Government over sending ships to Singapore in the event of war with Japan. The minutes showed the Prime Minister, Chamberlain, understood there was a 'categorical and unqualified commitment' given to Australia that 'an adequate fleet would be despatched to the Far East'. Yet on Chamberlain's reading of an Appreciation on Empire Foreign Policy before the committee, 'the undertaking in its entirety may not be able to be carried out'.

This record plainly said that the British Prime Minister now queried the assurances he himself had given Australia. At British request, Duncan agreed not to send the minutes to Canberra but Chamberlain was forced to qualify British assurances. Replying to an earlier message from Lyons, Chamberlain cabled on 20 March. Bruce would later describe this message as a 'bombshell'. Chamberlain assured Lyons that if Britain was at war with Germany and Italy 'it would still be His Majesty's Government's full intention to despatch a fleet to Singapore' in the event of war with Japan also. But such a combination, Chamberlain wrote, 'was never envisaged in our earlier plans'.[3] There was now no assurance about the size of the fleet. It would depend on the circumstances.

War against Germany, Italy and Japan simultaneously had certainly been envisaged in earlier assurances, Bruce insisted. And these assurances had specified a considerable fleet for Singapore.

It was surely quite clear to Lyons' Cabinet by March 1939 that if Britain was at war with Germany and Italy it could not be relied upon to provide a fleet at Singapore superior to the fleet Japan could bring against it. Had the Australian Government been more determinedly probing, it would have been apparent much earlier. Bruce would claim to have been sceptical of British assurances since 1938. It was certainly apparent to the British.

Curtin had predicted this outcome in his 1936 speech. It is unlikely that he was briefed by the Lyons Government on how contingent British assurances had become. It had every reason to be dubious about the value of British assurances which supported its one and only plan for the defence of Australia, yet the Lyons Government made no other. Nor at first would Curtin when he came to power. Instead, they pressed the British for what could not be given.

One result of this official dependence on a fleet and an Empire defence was undisguised defeatism at the heart of Australian plans for its own defence.

(2)

By contrast with the intensity of Australia's involvement in the Munich crisis, the Australian Government was preoccupied by its own internal struggles when the appeasement policy abruptly crashed. Germany occupied Czechoslovakia on 15 March 1939, demonstrating for his remaining sympathisers in Britain and Australia that Hitler's promises were not to be relied upon. Two days later Chamberlain announced in Birmingham that German aggression would now be resisted, a policy approved by the British Cabinet the following day. Lyons spoke to Chamberlain by phone on 19 March before announcing that 'there can be no doubt about Australia supporting Britain in any development that might occur'. Chamberlain's secret cable to Lyons on 20 March qualifying the assurance of naval support in the event of war with Japan, was simultaneous with public news that the appeasement policy had been abandoned. On 21 March the Australian Cabinet endorsed Lyons' position. Australia had committed to join Britain in a possible war with Germany, without a credible assurance its own security could be protected against Japan.

On 31 March 1939, Chamberlain announced in the House of Commons a joint British and French guarantee to Poland. The following month, after Italy invaded Albania, the guarantee was extended to Greece and Romania. Lyons was told of the Poland guarantee by the Acting British High Commissioner. Despite implicitly committing Australia to war with Germany if Germany offended Polish independence, and despite Bruce's long-standing objection that Australia had been taken to war in 1914 without consultation, there is no record of Australian Government involvement in the guarantee to Poland, though some such guarantee would follow from the change in the British position and it was widely discussed.

By then Bruce was in Australia and angling to become prime minister, Menzies had resigned from the ministry, the Lyons Government was in turmoil, Lyons himself was dying, and the governing coalition was about to erupt in a leadership struggle. For Curtin, as for his opponents, the political contest was abruptly changing.

(3)

In the crisis over Czechoslovakia, Lyons, Bruce and Menzies had more influence over the British Cabinet than Australian governments had ever had before or would have again. They had importantly contributed to making the Munich Agreement, the apogee of appeasement. Yet they mostly missed the foreign developments of far greater consequence to Australia. Actively supporting appeasement of Germany, debating the security of Britain and the future of Europe, with Australia's only diplomat making the round of London ministries on European issues, the Lyons Government had shown very little awareness of the struggle in the Pacific – far closer to home, and directly threatening to Australia. What happened in London or Berlin was vivid, interesting and intelligible to Australians. What was happening in Canton or Nanking was unclear, remote – and vital to the unfolding of the Pacific War.

While Australia debated the threat of war with Germany, Japan and China were already fighting. Within a few years Japan's war for control of the immense resources and possibilities of China would draw in the United States, Britain, Australia and Holland. It would become the Pacific War, transforming a European war into a global war.[4]

Though he spoke of the threat from Japan more often, Curtin shared the Government's ignorance of the war in China, and its implications for the United States.

By the time of the Munich Agreement in September 1938, Japan had more than a million troops in China, with many more to come. Yet while it won most battles, Japan could not entirely destroy Chiang Kai-shek's Nationalist forces, or those of the Chinese Communists. First Britain and the Soviet Union and later the United States supported the Chinese resistance, recognising that if Japan could conquer China and control its immense resources it would become a more formidable world power, and one already allied with Germany.

Through Burma, Britain and the United States sent war supplies to Chiang. The United States and Britain had a far more potent weapon at their command if they chose to use it. Until Japan could conquer China and command its resources, it was dependent on the rest of the world for raw materials. It especially needed oil from the United States or the Netherlands East Indies, without which it could not indefinitely make war. If Japan was to conquer China it needed oil. If the United States chose not to provide it, Japan must sooner or later slow its offensive against China, or seize oil wells in the Netherlands East Indies. To seize and hold the oilfields, Japan would probably have to knock out the United States Pacific fleet, and then build a defensive perimeter to protect the sea lanes on which its newly acquired oil would be shipped.

In trying to subdue China, Japan would find itself at war with the United States, Britain, the British dominions including Australia, and Holland. The Pacific War was the unintended though ultimately unavoidable outcome of Japan's war with China.[5] That was the implacable logic, as yet invisible to Australia's leaders. Much would follow from it: the humbling of British power in Asia, Australia's peril, Curtin's chance at greatness, America's Pacific triumph, China's re-emergence as a great power, the remaking of the political map of Asia and the Pacific, Japan's success as a prosperous democracy, China's later rise as a global power, and Australia's discovery of itself in a world neither Curtin nor Menzies imagined.

(4)

Curtin was well aware of the drift to war in Europe. He must also have been well aware that he could not warn of the threat from Japan and, at the same time, continue to oppose more defence spending and oppose conscription for the home defence of Australia. Bound by a party platform written for different circumstances, he felt his way cautiously. A federal Labor Party conference on 4 May 1939 deplored Australia's lack of preparedness, while continuing to reject conscription for Australia's defence. Evidently a compromise, it could not long be sustained.

At the same conference the party adopted a motion moved by Queensland Premier Forgan Smith that 'we will defend all our people in all States against aggression from any force'. It implicitly rejected the longstanding army view that in the event of invasion Australia's forces would need to be concentrated in the south-east, to defend Sydney and Melbourne and their regions. To defend a greater area, however, Australia would need a much bigger army. Curtin remained opposed to the League of Nations' idea of collective security, but denied his policy was isolationist. It was a policy of self-reliance, he explained, one designed to secure Australia with its own defence.[6]

Not isolationist, but self-reliant – that would be the theme. Self-reliance, however, required planes, soldiers and ships.

(5)

Troubled by a bad heart, the 59-year-old Lyons died on Good Friday, 7 April 1939. For the United Australia Party, it was particularly awkward timing. For the first time since his election as Opposition leader nearly four years earlier, Curtin could stand back and watch his opponents destroy their own parties instead of his. He could be an interested bystander – and the only likely winner from the UAP – Country Party coalition's conflicts.

Lyons' most obvious successor, Menzies, had resigned from the ministry on 14 March, purportedly on the refusal of the Government to proceed to set up a national insurance scheme. His probable real purpose was to force a leadership change, which Lyons' death several weeks later both realised and complicated. Resigning also as Deputy Leader of the UAP, Menzies threw in 'issues of defence preparedness' as contributing to his dissatisfaction.[7] National insurance would not win him party support. Defence preparedness might.

Four months earlier Menzies had given a speech to the Constitutional Association in Sydney calling for 'inspiring leadership'.[8] Reporters surmised he did not include his prime minister in that category. His design was perhaps to force a crisis in his relations with Lyons, which would prompt Lyons either to resign in Menzies' favour, or settle on a definite time to fulfil what Menzies believed to be Lyons' promise to give way to Menzies as his successor. There was, reporter Alan Reid remembered, 'no doubt about it, whatever the subsequent denials, that Menzies was intent on making his run then, and whether Joe had lived or died Menzies was determined to replace him with Menzies'.[9]

Offended by Menzies' speech to the Constitutional Club and perhaps judging that Menzies would not be able to hold the party together, Lyons not only declined to pass the leadership to Menzies but begged Bruce to accept it. While Bruce was on a prolonged visit to Australia, Lyons asked to see him in Canberra. 'You've got to come back,' Bruce recalled Lyons saying in late March or early April. 'I am absolutely beat.'[10]

Lyons' sudden death soon after his conversation with Bruce, widespread hostility in the governing coalition toward the talented Menzies, Country Party leader Earle Page's grievances against Menzies and ambitions for himself, and Bruce's evident availability combined to create what even *The Argus*, accustomed to the quirks of politics, would call a 'strange political position'[11] among Curtin's political opponents.

Page loathed Menzies, and blamed him for Lyons' death. Harold Cox had joined the vigil outside Lyons' room at Sydney's St Vincent's Hospital. Page was there, he recalled, with other ministers. Page was 'sitting at one end of the table and in the most objective, unemotional, cold-blooded way possible was tracing the course of Lyons' heart condition as a doctor and linking its development to the attacks which he alleged Menzies had made on Lyons'.[12]

Following Lyons' death Page became Prime Minister pending election of a new leader of the major party in the Coalition, the UAP. Together with Richard Casey, the Treasurer, he sought out Bruce as a candidate who could stop Menzies. To hinder Menzies, Page let it be known that the Country Party would not join a coalition with the UAP if Menzies was leader. In this Page sought to replicate his veto of Hughes, which had brought Bruce to the prime ministership in 1923.

At the party meeting in Canberra on Tuesday, 18 April 1939, Menzies won the leadership against Casey, the veteran Hughes, and a former customs minister, Thomas White. That same day a majority in the Country Party caucus voted in favour of Page's veto on a coalition led by Menzies.

Page resigned as Prime Minister, advising Gowrie to send for Menzies. His last throw was to attack Menzies in what is probably still the most notoriously ill-judged and spiteful speech ever delivered in the House of Representatives. Menzies, he reminded the House, had resigned his Melbourne University Regiment commission soon after the outbreak of the Great War. He had been disloyal to Lyons and contributed by his conduct to Lyons' heart attack and sudden death. He was widely loathed, and rightly so.

Menzies affected to respond to the speech with dignity, and more in sadness for Page's folly than indignation for the offence.

His wonderful control won over the House. It also won over Artie Fadden, a Queensland member of the Country Party and a rival to Page for the leadership. Dissociating himself from Page's speech, Fadden with one other colleague formed his own little independent bloc. He could wait for Page to destroy himself.

Menzies was for a time hampered because his party did not have a majority in the House. If Labor and the Country Party joined together, he would be defeated. It took the declaration of war later that year to sufficiently alter the power configuration of the Country Party to allow it to rejoin a coalition with the UAP. By then Menzies was strong enough to accept Country Party ministers in his government only on the condition that Page was not among them. Only after the 1940 election would Page return to the ministry.

All Curtin had to do as the Government's leaders fought over the succession was stand back. What the episode demonstrated, he told the House after Page's attack on Menzies, was that the UAP had been created for Lyons and depended on Lyons. Without Lyons it would not hang together.

Menzies' ascent and the slow disintegration of the UAP beneath him came at the same time as Europe moved towards another war.

CHAPTER 12

MENZIES VERSUS CURTIN

(1)

Five years after Curtin had won back Fremantle and Menzies had first won Kooyong, they were the principal antagonists in Australian politics. Both led divided parties and both were more unkindly harassed by their own party colleagues than by each other. Both were disfavoured by the major press barons, Sir Keith Murdoch in Melbourne and Warwick Fairfax in Sydney. Each responded to the better qualities of the other, and their personal relations were cordial. Curtin was well aware of the political risks of too savagely attacking or obstructing the Government in a time of global crisis, and was content to wait for the general election due the following year. Following long-established Labor policy and his own strong preference, Curtin was adamantly opposed to entering a national coalition government with the UAP. Menzies found Curtin respected his problems and recognised the country could soon be at war. He reciprocated Curtin's courtesies.

In Menzies, Curtin had an opponent distinctly unlike Lyons. Though an Empire man and a traditionalist, the young Menzies had a keener sense of Australia's coming place in the world than most of his conservative party colleagues. In his first talk to the nation as Prime Minister on 26 April 1939, he marked his departure from Lyons. He redefined Australia's role within the Empire, in a way quite congenial to Curtin's thinking. 'Little given as I am to encouraging the exaggerated ideas of Dominion independence and separatism which exist in some minds,' he said, 'I have become convinced that in the Pacific Australia must regard herself as a principal, providing herself with her own information and maintaining her own diplomatic contacts with foreign powers.'

Menzies reversed the position he had taken only a short while before, when his view on separate diplomatic representation for Australia was sought by Lyons. He had then advised Lyons against it. Perhaps he had since reflected that while Australia was well informed about London, it had no independent diplomatic reporting in Asia. Even by 1939 Australia had no consular offices other than in London. Canada then had seven.[1] Soon Australia would have its own diplomatic contacts, in the United States, China, Japan, Canada and New Zealand. For their part, the British preferred Australia not be represented separately in Washington, and dragged their feet on the formalities.

But while Menzies changed his mind about separate foreign missions, he otherwise emphatically enclosed himself in the Empire view. The 'peace of Great Britain is precious to us, because her peace is ours,' he said. 'If she is at war, we are at war' – though Menzies tellingly qualified his commitment by adding 'even though that war finds us not in European battlefields, but defending our own shores.' It was an interesting qualification, a recognition that if Germany was at war with Britain, Japan might be also. Even so, Menzies added, the defence of Australia 'depends on British sea power as its first element' and Australia could not refuse cooperation to Britain in times of danger. Despite Neville Chamberlain's qualifications, despite the scepticism even of Stanley Bruce, Menzies clung publicly to the British navy for Australia's defence. Privately, Menzies should have been well aware by May 1939 that if Britain was at war with Italy as well as Germany, the British navy was unlikely to be able to send to

Singapore a fleet superior to the sea and air power Japan could bring against it.

Minister for External Affairs Sir Henry Gullett slightly amended the commitment to Britain's wars in a statement to the House on 9 May 1939, just two weeks after Menzies' talk. He said Menzies' words were not meant to suggest that Australia was at war under any and every set of circumstances which led Britain to war, or vice versa, but in today's circumstances 'there is no sort of disagreement' between the two governments. In the ensuing debate Curtin said Gullett's 'qualification' of the Prime Minister's statement 'squares entirely with the conception of Australia's position as held by the Opposition'.

Leading a weary and rancorous government, Menzies focused on the great issues of war and peace. His predecessor had sharply increased defence spending. With the threat of war now more immediate, Menzies warned of still higher spending. As Leader of the Opposition, Curtin was ready to contend with Menzies on the same issues.

Lyons' sudden death and Menzies' succession created three political themes for Curtin to manage. All three were as much about controlling his own party as about contesting the UAP for government. The first theme was the slow but steady self-destruction of the UAP following Lyons' death. That would require of Curtin decisions about how much support to give a divided government, how much courtesy to show Menzies, which in turn would require managing the impatience of his own caucus to push Menzies out. The second theme was the increasing likelihood of war in Europe, the uncertainty about Japan's plans, and the vacancy in Australian defence planning. That would require Curtin to tug his own party away from isolationism towards readiness for war. And the third was the unresolved struggle within his own party over Jack Lang. That alone might prevent Labor coming to power.

(2)

Accepting the probability of war with Germany, Britain and France sought an alliance with the Soviet Union – though without zeal. An alliance would mean that Germany would have to fight a two-front war but it also meant Britain and France would have to fight Germany if Germany attacked the Soviet Union. Many British politicians were as hostile to the Soviet Union as to Germany. If the Soviet Union fought Germany it would have to cross Poland, a possibility rejected by the Polish Government. These obstacles were suddenly irrelevant when, on 22 August 1939, newspapers reported that Germany and the Soviet Union had negotiated a non-aggression pact, to be signed the next day.

In Tokyo, Hiranuma Kiichirō's government was shocked. It fell eight days later. Japan had supposed Germany was an ally against the Soviet Union, not an ally of it. Menzies also was astonished and embarrassed. He sent an impatient note to Bruce asking for more information. Returning from Paris, Bruce found it difficult to discover more than the newspapers had reported. Even without knowing of the secret agreement between Hitler and Stalin to carve up Poland, the implication of the new pact was clear enough. Freed from a threat from the east, Hitler could now if necessary take on Britain and France. The British intelligence appraisal Lyons had shared with Curtin eight months earlier had been prescient.

As war in Europe approached, Curtin reiterated his opposition to committing troops to fight Germany. On 24 August 1939, he said that 'He would be a bold man who would commit the Commonwealth and the lives of Australians as pawns in this matter. For my part, I say that the safety of the Australian people impels us to recognise our inability to send Australians overseas to participate in a European war.'[2] As the Comintern's anti-fascist front was disassembled on Stalin's orders, Australian Communist Party support for a strong stand against Germany evaporated. Within the

Labor Party, Curtin's stand was now supported by many on the left as well as on the right.

Hoping to avert the war the pact between Germany and the Soviet Union portended, Bruce and Menzies pressed the British Government to negotiate with Germany over Poland. On 26 August 1939, Hitler told the British he would offer a comprehensive settlement as soon as he had resolved the 'Polish German problem'.[3] Bruce told the British that Menzies' view would be that 'Hitler's proposals must be treated with the utmost seriousness'.[4] He urged Menzies to cable Chamberlain as his views 'would strengthen the Prime Minister's hand'.[5] Menzies did so immediately, suggesting to Chamberlain that while British obligations to Poland would not be modified, arbitration should be possible. Menzies said he 'regarded the merits of Danzig and the Corridor as quite open to argument' though 'we must not connive at a Polish settlement' that could lead to a takeover, as in Czechoslovakia. He suggested Chamberlain invite Hitler to London. Unlike the earlier Munich Agreement, the Australian Government was well behind events and had no influence on them.

The Australian Cabinet now met in Melbourne each day, reviewing cables from London. Much of the news was contradictory. Bruce told Gullett on 28 August, who then told Cabinet, that the situation was 'much easier than twelve hours earlier', following Britain's reply to Hitler. Bruce told Menzies he was urging Britain 'to induce the Poles to make reasonable concessions'.[6] Bruce was so persistently advocating compromise with Germany that he irritated some of his British contacts. Hankey noted in his diary on 23 August that Chamberlain 'told me very confidentially that Bruce had been to him the previous evening and had expressed doubts about the message being sent out after the cabinet reaffirming our policy of support to Poland, notwithstanding the Russo German pact of non aggression. This had much reduced his confidence in Bruce – never, I gather, very high.'[7] Foreign Office head Alexander Cadogan would a few weeks later note in his diary that the High Commissioners 'are the most undependable busybodies' and in particular 'Bruce is bad'.[8] Bruce was still busy advocating negotiation on 31 August. Responding to him on 1 September, Menzies replied that 'we all agree' the German proposals 'are surprisingly reasonable'. But 'Ministers here' were concerned that undue pressure on Poland would create another Czechoslovakia.[9]

By that evening it was clear that Hitler did not want another Munich to cheat him of a conquest. German troops crossed the border into Poland. Following the expiry of the British ultimatum to Germany the following day, Britain declared war on Germany. At 9.15 p.m. on 3 September 1939, an hour and a quarter after the British declaration was heard in Australia on short-wave radio, Menzies told Australians it was his 'melancholy duty to inform you officially that, in consequence of the persistence of Germany in her invasion of Poland, Great Britain has declared war upon her, and that, as a result, Australia is also at war'.

CHAPTER 13

WAR IN EUROPE

(1)

Britain was at war, and therefore Australia was at war. Had he been prime minister, Curtin might have done it differently. He might have asked for the approval of Parliament and then advised the King to sign a declaration of war by Australia. This is what Prime Minister Mackenzie King was doing in Canada. The Canadian declaration was not formally made until 7 September 1939. Or Curtin might, like acting New Zealand Prime Minister Peter Fraser, have issued a declaration of war separately from, but simultaneous with, that of Britain. That is what Curtin would do in 1941. Either way the point would have been made that Australia acted separately from Britain. But one way or another Curtin would have taken Australia to war. No Australian prime minister in 1939 could have maintained neutrality as Britain, France and Poland went to war with Germany. In a society almost entirely British, that choice did not exist. The substance of Menzies' announcement that Australia was at war was not criticised by any member of the Australian Parliament. The enemy shared Menzies' conception. Germany then and Japan later did not separately declare war on Australia.

Curtin and Menzies met on 3 September. Curtin said he had told Menzies 'the Labor Party could be relied upon to do the right thing for the defence of Australia and the integrity of the British Commonwealth of Nations'. The rest of the conversation, he said, was of a 'confidential nature'.

While there would not be differences over the announcement itself, there would be plenty over the implications. Should Curtin and his party join Menzies in an all-party national government, as Australian newspaper editorials demanded? Would Australia send troops to fight Germany? Would it send troops to support Singapore and its Malayan hinterland against a possible Japanese attack? If so, would Curtin support that? Would Australia conscript young men into the military full-time, and, if so, would it legislate to permit the conscripts to be sent anywhere in the world? What balance would it strike between Australia's own security in the event of war with Germany's ally, Japan, and the security of Britain? Menzies had a number of options, and Curtin would need to be prepared to respond to each.

These considerations partly turned on how long the war with Germany would last, and how it would be resolved. Menzies shared the hope of many British Conservatives that peace could be arranged once Germany had secured its objectives in Poland, and before Britain and France became seriously engaged. The duration of the war in Europe would in turn influence Japan's calculations.

At five minutes to four on the afternoon of 6 September 1939, following a speech by Menzies in the House, Curtin rose to declare Labor's position on the war. He said that the ALP would 'preserve its separate entity', a formula which excluded a coalition but permitted some kind of participation in government. He explicitly opposed a government of all parties. He declared that 'the safety of this Commonwealth must be the paramount consideration influencing every feature of government policy', putting the security of Australia before the security of any other nation, including Britain. He thought there might be differences over conscription and over sending expeditionary forces – both of which he opposed – though he understood the Government had announced the previous night that it did not contemplate sending expeditionary forces.

The question of sending Australian forces to the war against Germany was unsettled within the Menzies Government. Responding to Curtin, Gullett said that he was unaware of any statement that the Government did not propose to send expeditionary forces overseas. 'The Government had not yet seriously discussed the question.' On 10 September, Curtin reiterated Labor's opposition to sending troops overseas. He went further on 22 October, promising to 'strenuously challenge' reintroduction of compulsory military training.[1] In moving his party to recognise the threats to Australia, in reconciling his own warnings about Japan with his refusal to accept conscription even for the defence of Australia, Curtin had a very long way to go.

The war strengthened Menzies' position, though he thought a peace deal with Hitler was quite likely, quite soon. As an older man, a former prime minister who would understand Menzies' circumstances but who could not now be regarded as a rival for his job, an official under an obligation of secrecy, Bruce invited Menzies' confidence. Menzies could and did reveal things to Bruce he could reveal to no other colleague. A week after the declaration of war Menzies wrote 'in a rambling and personal way'[2] to put his thoughts both on the war and on Menzies' political circumstances. Despite German troops now overrunning Poland, and despite the earlier invasion of Czechoslovakia, Menzies still hoped for and expected a negotiated solution that would leave Germany with Danzig and a corridor through Poland. In this his views were shared by Bruce, and by members of the British Government.

Menzies told Bruce that 'I feel quite confident that Hitler has no desire for a first class war' and that when he had occupied Poland Hitler would offer to guarantee the integrity of Poland and just carve off Danzig and the corridor. The United Kingdom and its allies could then say yes or no – if no, 'we must settle down to a war in which Germany's defensive position is incredibly strong'. He thought that 'some very quick thinking will have to be done when the German offer arrives'. He believed 'Germany has always seemed to me to have an almost unanswerable case in relation to the Corridor'. He suggested Roosevelt call a conference to 'extract' the corridor. He asked Bruce what the possibilities might be for having a German proposition 'broadened out to provide for a re-settlement of the whole map of Europe with joint and several guarantees all round?' He also suggested Britain and the United States should offer joint mediation of the China–Japan conflict. He wanted Italy conciliated. He remarked on the 'amazing unity of political opinion' on the 'justice of our action'.[3] Hitler was also hoping that France and Britain would now negotiate a peace. He wanted Poland and Czechoslovakia, but he did not want war with France and Britain, or not in 1939. His ambitions were in the east, not the west. On 6 October he made a peace offer to France and Britain. Chamberlain's Cabinet rejected the offer four days later.

On domestic politics Menzies was no less candid. 'I have now been in office 4 1/2 months,' he related. 'Page gave me an unexpectedly good start by making a martyr of me, though he did not think so at the time, and I certainly thought that his attack upon me would discredit me sufficiently to end me politically.' He thought the Government had a better public than it had had for four years, and 'the cabinet is united and loyal'. Menzies had not had one day off in four and a half months, 'and though I am reputed to be as strong as a horse, I know this cannot go on indefinitely'. He told Bruce that Page was angling for a coalition government but Menzies had made it clear 'I could not have him in the cabinet'. He could possibly do business with John McEwen, but it would be more difficult with Archie Cameron. 'In point of fact,' he claimed, 'Curtin has privately made it clear to me that his people will not put me out to put the Country Party in, and that his own greatest ambition is to remain Leader of the Opposition for the duration of the war.' Keith Murdoch's papers 'have been a little difficult', demanding an expeditionary force. Menzies thought he was 'ace-high with the outside public'. If he was asked to go to London for a meeting of dominion prime ministers, 'I honestly don't know who could run the show, particularly in Parliament, in my absence'. Richard Casey was working hard but 'it is an open secret that he would like to get the Washington appointment'. Street was 'largely a mouthpiece for the Chiefs of Staff'.[4]

Menzies' vanity and his misunderstandings (including of opinion within his own Cabinet) are startling. It is possible Curtin shared Menzies' view that the war in Europe could soon be settled by agreement between Germany, France and Britain, and that consequently he would remain as Opposition leader during what might be a short period. Remaining Opposition leader was after all a consequence of refusing an all-party government. It was also true that Curtin could see no advantage in pushing Menzies out in favour of another UAP or Country Party prime minister. But the notion that Curtin would be content to remain Opposition leader for an indefinite period was fanciful. An election would have to be held the following year, and Curtin would seek to win it. Curtin had already fought one general election and several by-elections. Menzies dangerously underestimated Curtin, as he did his opponents within his own party.

(2)

Japan's response to the war in Europe was still unclear. Menzies was at first extremely cautious in committing troops to support Britain in fighting Germany. He was sensitive to the force of Curtin's argument that Japan might well pose a more immediate threat. It was not yet clear if Japan would soon join Germany. Though the bargain was not put so bluntly, Menzies wanted British assurances of naval support against Japan in return for an Australian army contingent. On 5 September 1939, he told Bruce that 'Until the position of Japan has been cleared up it will be useless even to discuss the sending of expeditionary force and in any event we have great doubts as to just how war is to be carried on and the ultimate use of our troops.' Through the British High Commission, Menzies queried Dominions Secretary Anthony Eden's view that Japan would remain neutral, suggesting that she will 'probably play a purely selfish game and at any time during the war may engage actively without notice on either side and more probably with the enemy'. On Japan's attitude depends the part 'Australia will be able to take in the war, though the question of a possible Australian force for Singapore is not being overlooked'.[5]

Before agreeing to send an Australian volunteer division to fight with the British[6], Menzies sought reassurances about naval and other measures against Japan should Japan enter the war.[7]

In an appreciation sent to Menzies on 17 November, the British assured him that Japan would 'continue to concentrate her efforts' on China and 'will sit on the fence' in respect of the war in Europe.[8] A supporting naval appreciation claimed that a Japanese attack on Singapore would require at least 50 000 troops to undertake siege operations for four to five months, with a long line of communications. This was 'not considered likely'. (The Japanese force in Malaya would be 36 000, and the capture of Singapore would take a little over two months. No siege was necessary.) Invasion of Australia was 'even less likely'. So long as there was a 'superior British fleet in being in any part of the world it is needless to suppose such an enterprise would be attempted'.

The appreciation notably omitted to specify the British fleet that would be sent to Singapore. It argued that the British navy did not need to allocate ships to Singapore specifically because the 'Power of predominant fleet is exercised simultaneously in all quarters of the globe in which it has bases irrespective of the station it occupies at any given moment provided it is not permanently tied to that station.' This was a new rationale for the Australians. Nonetheless, the message said, 'The Admiralty accept full responsibility of defending Australia or Singapore from a Japanese attack on a large scale and have forces at their disposal for these essential purposes.' The Admiralty regarded 'the defence of Australia and of Singapore as a stepping stone to Australia as ranking next to mastering of the principal fleet to which we are opposed, and the duty of defending Australia against serious attack would take precedence over British interests in the Mediterranean'. Thus, there were 'no naval grounds' to 'prevent the despatch of Australian Army to decisive battlefield where the name stands so high'.[9, 10]

These assurances that Singapore would not be attacked, and that the existence of a powerful British fleet in any part of the world would be enough to deter Japan, fell well short of Australia's earlier requests for a powerful force based in Singapore or able to reach it quickly. The declaration that the defence of Australia ranked higher than British interests in the Mediterranean would be repeated, though quite what it meant would prove obscure. It was anyway an easier assurance to give when France was in the war and Italy was not. Those circumstances would soon change.

From London, visiting Minister for Supply and Development Richard Casey pressed Menzies to commit to sending troops. On 23 November he urged that Australia should 'send special division abroad at the earliest'. The worst risk, he argued ingeniously, was that Britain would be defeated in Europe, which would encourage Japan.[11]

Menzies was wary of Curtin. The British High Commissioner, Sir Geoffrey Whiskard, saw Menzies the same day.[12] He reported Menzies' disclosure that one reason for postponing the decision on troops was that Curtin and the ALP were 'definitely opposed' but that opposition would disappear once activity on the Western Front flared up. 'It seemed undesirable to force Labour into strong opposition unless there was real necessity.' In any case, Menzies thought it was 'infinitely more important' for Australia to cooperate in training air crews than to send one or two divisions overseas.

Whatever he had in mind, Menzies' bargaining position was then cut out from under him by New Zealand, which publicly announced despatch of a force to Egypt. Menzies had asked New Zealand to delay its announcement. But by 10 p.m., when Whiskard saw Menzies again and news of the New Zealand announcement had been received, Menzies told him that Australia was now in 'considerable embarrassment'. Whiskard reported Menzies was 'obviously highly incensed at the New Zealand Government', and had told Whiskard that Australia would probably have to follow suit. Cabinet 'will decide on the question Monday' and would almost certainly send a division.[13]

Cabling Casey, Menzies revealed his annoyance. He complained that 'We have been forced into a course of action which we would not otherwise have adopted'. Not consulted before their departure, he resented being told ships were on the way to collect the troops. 'There has been in this matter,' he told Casey, 'a quite perceptible disposition to treat Australia as a Colony and to make insufficient allowance for the fact that it is for the Government of Australia to determine whether and when Australian forces shall go out of Australia'.[14]

The first AIF contingent embarked on 9 January 1940. The British appreciation that Japan was unlikely to go to war was as much as Menzies would get in return.

(3)

By January 1940 Australian volunteer troops were on their way to the Middle East. In Europe the phony war continued, encouraging hopes that a negotiated peace was still possible. Bruce continued to press for peace with Germany, with Menzies' sympathetic support. Neither understood Hitler's ambitions and intentions. To them, war between Britain and Germany over Poland had never made sense. Both continued to believe Hitler would settle for Danzig and the corridor. Italy remained neutral. Both thought Mussolini might be helpful in arranging a negotiation. As Chamberlain acknowledged at the time, Bruce and Lyons had successfully pressed for Italian good offices during the Munich crisis. Perhaps Mussolini could do it again. Bruce mingled with the Conservative Party's appeasement group, led by Chamberlain and Lord Halifax, the Foreign Secretary. Its unremitting opponent was Churchill, whom Chamberlain had reluctantly brought into government at the outbreak of war as First Lord of the Admiralty, the job he had held from 1911 to 1915. Bruce and Menzies loathed Churchill.

Writing to Bruce in early January 1940 Menzies remarked:

> My impression from your various communications is that Chamberlain and Halifax are very largely in accord with your own views, while Winston is opposed to them. I cannot tell you adequately how much I am convinced that Winston is a menace. He is a publicity seeker; he stirs up hatreds in a world already seething with them and he is lacking judgement, as witness his recent speech on the position of the neutrals.[15]

The relationship between Churchill and Menzies was never as good-hearted as they later chose to portray it.

Menzies was as much concerned with the threat of Russian Bolshevism as of German power in Europe. He told Bruce:

> Your remarks about Russia seem to be most appropriate. I cannot doubt that if the war lasts long enough there will be a rapid spread of Bolshevism in Germany and in the Danubian states. Under these circumstances a new alignment of nations in which not only Great Britain and France but Germany and Italy combined to resist Bolshevism is by no means impossible.

His ruminations were sometimes fanciful. He thought an international air force and army and navy could keep the peace when the war was over – nations would be 'immeasurably more disposed' to that.

(4)

In September 1939, Menzies had claimed to Bruce that he was highly regarded by the Australian people, and strongly supported in Cabinet. Perhaps so, in the immediate aftermath of Britain's declaration of war. As the months went by, his support slowly evaporated. As Paul Hasluck later pointed out, by the time Menzies took over in 1939 there were enough backbenchers bitter about being passed over for the ministry, and ministers who wanted the leadership, to make the UAP a difficult party to manage.

And far from acting as if he wished to spend the war in Opposition, Curtin was pressing hard. Since he had become Opposition leader, by-elections for vacancies in the House had gone against the Government. Though the Lyons Government won the general election in October 1937 – the first Curtin had fought as Opposition leader – the Country Party had earlier lost Gwydir to Labor in the May 1937 by-election. Labor then won the South Australian seat of Wakefield from the UAP in December 1938. Not long after Menzies became Prime Minister, Labor won Lyons' old seat of Wilmot from the UAP and retained Griffith. Casey resigned from the ministry in late January 1940 to take the appointment as Australian Minister in Washington. In the subsequent by-election for his seat of Corio Labor again won, and well. In each by-election, Curtin proved to be a relentless campaigner. After Corio and despite the lift that the war had given him, it was apparent that Menzies had not restored the electoral fortunes of the UAP. It was equally apparent to the more confident Labor caucus that as a vote-winner Curtin was doing quite well.

Responding to the deterioration in the Government's support, Menzies took the Country Party into government on 14 March – twelve days after the shock of losing Corio. Page, who had lost the leadership, was obliged to remain on the backbench. Country Party leader Archie Cameron, second in seniority in the Menzies Government, became Minister for Commerce and Minister for

the Navy. A general election would have to be held before the end
of 1940. Given the trend in by-elections, it was for Menzies an
unpleasant consideration. Lifted by the declaration of war in
September, Menzies found his stocks drifting lower in the prolonged
quiet of the phony war months following the rapid conquest of Poland
by Germany and the Soviet Union.

(5)

Party disunity was as troubling to Curtin as to Menzies, and publicly
more vivid. The Lang group had rejoined the federal caucus in
1936 but the struggle within the Labor Party in New South Wales
would not go away. Pressed by Curtin and his allies, a Federal
Conference in May 1939 appointed a provisional executive to
control the New South Wales branch. Curtin wearily explained that
his 'experience in New South Wales was that you could not expect
to believe everything everybody said and damned little anybody
said'.[16] Following a 'unity' conference on 26 August 1939, William
McKell had beaten Lang for leadership of the state parliamentary
party. McKell and his ally, R J Heffron, were supported by an
anti-Lang and left-wing group of union officials based in Trades
Hall. It seemed Lang's control might finally have been broken in
the biggest state, the one most vital to Curtin's chance of electoral
success, but global politics now began to tear the fragile fabric of
the Labor Party in New South Wales. The Soviet Union invaded
Finland at the end of November 1939. Under pressure from outraged
public opinion, Britain and France contemplated sending troops
to help the Finns. Through the Comintern, Communist parties
were instructed to oppose intervention by the allies, and their
propaganda work coloured the attitude of the left more widely. At
the New South Wales state Labor conference in March 1940 the left
carried a 'hands off Russia resolution', which also claimed the war

with Germany was 'being pursued in the interests of big finance and the monopolists'.[17]

The Lang forces appeared to have let the resolution through, either voting for it or abstaining. Lang saw that the resolution was electorally lethal – especially to Curtin and the federal parliamentary party – and must one way or another damage Lang's left-wing opponents.[18] Curtin promptly responded by publicly repudiating the resolution, declaring that 'No State conference can present a new set of principles or declare a new defence policy'. Federal policy must prevail, and federal policy was 'to maintain Australia as an integral part of the British Commonwealth of Nations'. Accordingly, 'we are with Britain and against Germany, because Germany went to war and set the world aflame. If any nation lines up with Germany, we are against that nation.'[19] At that point the Soviet Union was arguably lined up with Germany, though in the early stages of the conflict Germany secretly sent support to Finland.

The squabble seriously embarrassed Curtin. It gave Lang and his allies sufficient excuse to again break away from the main party. Creating the pointedly named New South Wales Labor Party (Non-Communist), Lang was still powerful enough in the party branches to take with him a majority of Labor House of Representatives members from New South Wales.

By the end of April 1940 Curtin was back where he had been before the New South Wales members re-entered caucus in 1936. Outraged, he said, 'Once again Mr Lang, assisted by his tool Mr Beasley has wrecked the solidarity of Labor at a time of great crisis and in circumstances in which the power of Labor to protect the workers should be at its maximum . . . This is their second deliberate offence, carefully planned, incapable of excuse, treacherously designed to stab Labor in the back.'[20]

Curtin pointed out that Beasley, who now claimed to be anti-communist, had once sponsored a resolution at a Labor conference to affiliate with the Communist Party. Beasley responded with a recollection of his own, which was that in a conversation with him in Melbourne earlier in April Curtin had confided that 'I would not ask a dog to accept the nomination of that crowd', meaning the present ALP executive in New South Wales. Beasley claimed Curtin had told him communist 'control' of the ALP would have to go.[21] On 2 May Beasley duly announced in the House that he and his group had withdrawn their membership of the ALP New South Wales and now represented the ALP (Non-Communist) in New South Wales. The group included Beasley, Sol Rosevear, Dan Mulcahy, Joe Gander and Tom Sheehan, but not Rowley James or Eddie Ward. The Lang group had itself split.

(6)

The turmoil in the New South Wales Labor Party coincided with the sudden flaring of war in Western Europe. Germany abruptly ended the phony war in early April by invading Norway and Denmark, pre-empting a British occupation and securing the land route through Norway for the transport of iron ore from Sweden. British and French forces contested the German occupation, holding Narvik before the German attack on France forced their withdrawal. Speaking in the House on 18 April, nine days after the German invasion of Norway began, Menzies was hopeful about the outcome of the first major clash of arms between the Germans and the Allies. He expected German troops and equipment in Norway 'must in the near future fall into allied hands'. Menzies hoped 'we have entered upon a phase of the war which may well prove crucial'. Meanwhile, 'the success of the allied actions must surely have a tremendous effect' upon the neutrals.

Replying, Curtin said there was 'no question of any difference of opinion' in respect of the 'outrageous behaviour of the aggressor powers'. On war aims, his position was close to that of Menzies and Bruce, a position quite unlike that the Allies would evolve over the course of the war. In early 1940 the British Government had not given up on a negotiated peace with Hitler. 'We do not seek necessarily to destroy what is called "Hitlerism",' Curtin said. 'The form of government in Germany is not a matter we seek to influence.' He remained concerned about Japan, remarking, 'There is not even today any certainty that powers which are not now involved in the war may not later become involved in it.' Accordingly, 'we lull ourselves into an absolutely false sense of security if we assume that the struggle in which we are engaged will be restricted to the continent of Europe'.[22]

Government members interjected that Curtin was saying 'our men should not go near Europe', and 'not too much to Great Britain'. Adair Blain, an independent from the Northern Territory, asked if Curtin would 'leave Suez undefended?'. Curtin responded that 'I think so much of the Honourable Member for the Northern Territory that I would not, on any account, leave undefended that part of Australia which is his particular responsibility'.

For all that, Curtin knew the Labor Party's position would have to change – and that he would have to risk his leadership to change it. Labor was still formally opposed to conscription even for home defence, still formally opposed to sending forces abroad, still isolationist in outlook. He could not take that platform to a general election. As Menzies had expected, once Britain and Germany were actually fighting Australians cheered Britain on. It was clearly not possible to withhold support from the AIF in the Middle East.

(7)

Faced with a growing demand for a national government, a proposal unwelcome to Curtin and difficult for Menzies, the party leaders assured the nation that their relationship was cordial. Both had been attacked by critics in their own party for their unwillingness to demean the other. Menzies perhaps had in mind that a national government, which required Curtin's support, would free him from the leadership struggles within the UAP. Accordingly, there was no point in alienating the Leader of the Opposition. Curtin knew that until the next general election he could not have a majority in the House or in the Senate. Forcing Menzies out would not help Labor. Both leaders were aware that with a war on and Australians fighting overseas the electorate would respond unkindly to Canberra catfights.

Accordingly Curtin and Menzies insisted on courteous treatment of the other. Menzies told the House on 10 May that Curtin had displayed 'a sympathetic spirit and a cooperative attitude' and 'we have frequently discussed with each other the progress of affairs in the war and the progress of Australia's national war effort'. He said that 'I have been criticized from time to time . . . for neglecting to fight in a bitter fashion those who sit opposite to me. I have been patient and I have neglected opportunities for such a fight.'

Curtin responded that 'I have refused systematically to manufacture political causes against the government'. The Prime Minister 'has not been provocative; all the time he has been fair minded'. Curtin added that 'except with regard to two or three fundamental points of view I am entirely satisfied with what the government has been doing'. He had supported the Government's financial measures and gave it all the legislation it had sought.

For all the goodwill, the two or three fundamental differences mattered. One was, as Curtin explained, 'we are opposed to con-scription'. Government members interjected, 'So are we', presumably meaning conscription for overseas service. Curtin responded: 'Then that point completely disappears.' He thought a difference remained in his belief that Australia may be 'subject to actual aggression'. If so, Australia would need conscription. His position was inconsistent.

(8)

The war was not going well for Britain or its allies. On 10 May, Germany followed up the invasion of Norway and Denmark by attacking the Netherlands and Belgium, preliminary to the invasion of France. The same day Chamberlain resigned and Churchill was invited to form a government into which he brought the Labour Party. Australian newspapers pressed for a national government in Canberra. In a 3 p.m. statement to a sombre House on 15 May, the Minister for External Affairs, John McEwen, reported that the Dutch commander-in-chief had ordered the Dutch army to cease resistance. He thought the possibility of Italy joining Germany could not be ignored. (It would join on 10 June, when the defeat of France was apparent.)

Within days of their entry to France through the Ardennes, German Panzer divisions wheeled west to get between the main body of the French army and the British and French forces that had moved forward to fight in Belgium. To avoid being trapped between the Panzers behind and the Germans advancing through Belgium, the British were forced to retreat towards the coast around Dunkirk.

Speaking to the House at 3 p.m. on 22 May, four days before the evacuation of the British Expeditionary Force from Dunkirk began, Menzies said, 'As British people, we have reached a stage of emergency without precedent in the history of the Empire.' He could not have been at all confident but he nonetheless told the House, 'We do not doubt' that 'France will rally in the next few days, and ultimately defeat the invader.' Four days later any remaining confidence Menzies might have had in France's capacity to resist the German attack would have vanished, with the British secretly informing him that their troops were withdrawing 'forthwith' to Britain. 'We have to face the possibility,' Menzies was told, 'that the French were not going to carry on.'[23] Responding to the rapid deterioration, Menzies proposed to raise a third army division for service abroad, and increase spending on the navy.

Curtin understood the threat. As the British evacuated from Dunkirk and the Germans prepared to drive on Paris, he told the House the 'British Commonwealth of Nations' was 'engaged in a veritable struggle for its existence'.[24] Refusing to join newspaper attacks on Menzies, Curtin instead defended him. The fact that Menzies was Prime Minister when war broke out, he said, 'is no justification whatever for laying all the blame for what has taken place in Australia on the shoulders of the right honourable gentleman'.

(9)

Hitler would soon be able to concentrate the whole might of the victorious German forces on Britain. There was every chance Italy would now join Germany in war with Britain, threatening British naval control of the Mediterranean and its hold on Egypt and the Suez Canal. To Bruce and the Tory group around Halifax, a negotiated peace with Germany was the only alternative to an invasion of Britain. In London Bruce was agitated. Cabling Menzies on 27 May, before Italy joined with Germany, he warned the 'French collapse may come at any moment'.[25] He thought it 'criminal' that the British Government had not worked out the next steps and consulted the dominions. He wanted a consideration of whether 'we can carry on with a prospect of victory', or that 'we cannot carry on'. He suggested that 'Mussolini has the ambition to be the peace maker of Europe'. If Britain and the Commonwealth could not carry on with a prospect of victory he suggested Mussolini and Roosevelt be stimulated to propose an 'immediate conference'.

While posing it as a question to Menzies, Bruce himself believed that Britain could not carry on without France, and was pressing the British Government to negotiate with Hitler. During a tense British War Cabinet meeting on the morning of 27 May, ministers discussed whether Britain should fight on or negotiate.[26] Chamberlain asked what the dominions should be told.[27] He recounted to Cabinet that Bruce had said the night before that he did not think Britain could continue the war if France fell out, and that Britain had to learn something about possible terms – perhaps through Mussolini. Chamberlain said he would tell Bruce that Britain was determined to fight on.[28] Churchill won the Cabinet debate, and would have taken note of Bruce's meddling and defeatism.

Hostile to and a little contemptuous of Churchill, openly allied with Churchill's enemies in the appeasement wing of the Conservative Party, and now eagerly though vainly pressing for negotiations with Germany, by May 1940 Bruce had ceased to be an asset to Australian interests in Britain. He was instead rapidly becoming a liability. His ineffectiveness in London, his misreading of shifts in power and policy, would contribute to tensions between Australia and Britain during the next five years. Not the least of the problems was that Churchill now disliked him. Neither Menzies nor Curtin appeared to be aware of Bruce's diminished standing, either then or later.

With France facing surrender and Britain in danger of German invasion, Curtin could no longer pretend war in Europe was not Australia's business. The party's position on the war would have to change. In May 1940 Curtin asked caucus to support a call for a special federal conference of the ALP to revisit the defence platform. The left of the party resisted. When on 17 May Curtin agreed with Menzies on changing the Parliament's sitting times he was attacked in caucus by Blackburn and Ward, who said Menzies wanted to cut short the parliamentary session. They protested in the House. When caucus met again on 22 May, Curtin complained that his leadership had been impaired. Caucus backed Curtin.

After months of phony war and fading interest, the military disaster in France rallied Australians behind Menzies. The carping within his government faded. The conquest of France and Holland, however, meant that their colonies in the Pacific were left without plausible defences. The Netherlands East Indies produced oil. Possession of airfields in French Indo-China would bring Japanese air power closer to Malaya and Singapore, as well as southern China. French islands in the Pacific could provide forward bases for the Japanese navy and for Japanese air power, threatening Australia's sea route to the west coast of the United States.

Britain was threatened with invasion and would require all the power of its fleet to deter it. Italy was now in the war and deployed a formidable fleet in the Mediterranean. The strategic problems of the Pacific both Britain and Australia had evaded for so long could no longer be ignored. Nor could Curtin continue to ignore the contradiction in Labor's position – warning of war in the Pacific, while opposing conscription for home defence. Sometime in the second half of the year Menzies would take the country to the polls. By then Curtin would need a plausible defence policy.

CHAPTER 14

AUSTRALIA DEFENCELESS

(1)

Depending on the British fleet and Singapore for protection, Australia was unprepared to defend the country against attack. At the outbreak of war Australia's tiny regular army had no anti-aircraft guns, modern field artillery, mechanical transport, armoured vehicles, or light machine guns. Its paper structure included two cavalry divisions with sabres. Until 1 January 1940, when Menzies introduced conscription for home defence, the Militia was entirely volunteer and without more training would have been incapable of fighting a battle-hardened enemy. The air force had no modern fighters, and few recent planes of any kind.[1] Lyons and then Menzies had increased defence spending, but after decades of neglect and penny-pinching there was not much on which to build. Australia's home defence was all the more threadbare after two volunteer divisions were recruited, officered, equipped and sent to the Middle East for training. The best of the Militia was cannibalised to support the AIF.

Australia could only be invaded, the Imperial Defence story went, if the British navy could not present a credible threat to an invading force. While the army had a few posts in Papua and New Guinea, the basic theory of the army general staff was that an invading enemy would seek an early and decisive battle with Australia's army, and it would force that by launching an attack on the centres of industry and population without which Australia could not continue to fight. The attack would be on Australia's urban centres in the south-east corner of the continent. That is where Australian forces would have to concentrate in the unlikely event of enemy invasion.

Australian forces would later be assigned to defend Malaya and the Singapore base but a powerful forward defence was not part of Australian army planning in September 1939.[2] A serious attack would presumably come to Australia directly by sea, and in any case Australia did not have sufficient forces to meet an enemy elsewhere. If the enemy had sea control, it would cut off both the resupply and the retreat of troops deployed forward in the islands to Australia's north.

With the sudden and catastrophic collapse of France, Italy's declaration of war on 10 June, and the real possibility that Britain might be invaded and the British fleet sunk or captured, Australian attention returned to the possible threat from Japan. Menzies was urged to more rapidly build Australia's capacity for war. Though his focus was on defending Britain rather than preparing for war in the Pacific, publisher Sir Keith Murdoch was a particularly virulent, persistent and damaging critic of Menzies.

Hoping to neutralise Murdoch, Menzies appointed him Director-General of Information on 8 June 1940.[3] Answerable only to Menzies, Murdoch was given sweeping powers. On 12 June 1940, Menzies met him in Melbourne for a war-planning briefing with his top defence officials.[4] The officials included home defence chief, Sir Brudenell White, Secretary of the Department of Defence Co-ordination, Fred Shedden, as well as Major-General Sir Carl Jess, Essington Lewis, and J B Brigden. In the Great War Murdoch had relentlessly pressed for White to replace John Monash as commander of the Australian forces on the Western Front. The exchange between White and Murdoch, recorded in a verbatim note of the 12 June meeting, was revelatory. The discussion turned on the objective of 130 000 troops for home defence.

Murdoch: What would you do with your 130 000 men? How would you face the enemy on a large scale?

White: The 130 000 does not envisage invasion.

Murdoch: No that would be out of the picture. Nor can we contemplate it in our present circumstance. But would you fight an invasion? That is one of the things in the public mind.

White: Really looking at it in hard fact that there are two things that stand against you as brick walls – the lack of ammunition and guns. If the enemy landed they would not last over a month's fighting. There is no use blinking at that.

Murdoch: Well, that is something you cannot tell the public.

White: The second is that in my view I should be allowing for the British Navy to be wiped off and Japan had complete control. Even if we were able to defend ourselves against invasion Japan within six months could probably subdue us by action at sea.

Murdoch: Then you reach this stage – there is no possible need in this country for more than 130 000 trained men?

White: One would need to be careful of using that.

Murdoch: Well, make it 150 000 or 200 000 . . . In other words, there would be no need to train for local defence more than 130 000 men. They would be all you could equip and would be an adequate number for raids which are reasonably contemplated.

White: That is so.

Murdoch: I would suggest that is a very important fundamental fact.

Essentially, White's argument was that no invasion could take place with the British navy in being, since Japan's supply lines would then be vulnerable to interruption and the invading force could be cut off and destroyed. If the British navy had been destroyed, an invasion of Australia would anyway be unnecessary because Japan could force surrender or a favourable outcome by cutting Australia off from the rest of the world. For contingencies less than invasion – a coastal raid, or a more sustained attack by a few divisions – the home defence goal of 130 000 troops would be sufficient to meet the attack. There was no point in having more troops in Australia because there was ammunition and guns for only one month's fighting by the Australian forces. Even if Australia did have the means to 'defend itself', Japan would 'subdue' Australia within six months by naval action alone. To Murdoch's question, whether he planned to fight an invasion, White's roundabout answer was no. It was the logical conclusion of Imperial Defence.

This exchange left many issues unexplored, including the probability that the British navy might remain in being but be unable or unwilling to send considerable forces to the Pacific. If Australia chose to fight on against a strong Japanese force it would need more guns, more ammunition, more tanks and planes, more war supplies of all kinds. It would need to stockpile more oil, chemicals, rubber and metals. Eight days earlier Churchill had declared Britain would fight on the beaches and fields and never surrender. Australian planning against a Japanese landing was instead based on the two alternatives of defeating a small Japanese force, or surrendering to a larger one. Sir Keith, who claimed credit for exposing the military disaster at the Dardanelles in the Great War, had nothing to say about this disclosure. On the contrary, he would later attack Curtin for putting the defence of Australia before the defence of Burma.

The military assessment was confirmed six days later, with no objection from Menzies or his ministers. In the bleak week between the surrender of Paris on 14 June 1940 and the armistice between France and Germany on 22 June, the defence chiefs were called to a War Cabinet meeting in Melbourne.[5] At issue was the risk that following France's surrender Japan might move south to occupy the French colony of New Caledonia and the joint British–French condominium of the New Hebrides. It was in this context that the Australian navy chief, Sir Ragnar Colvin, he who in March 1939 had 'vigorously' refuted Bruce's warning that a fleet might not be sent to Singapore[6], said:

> if Japan should come in and the United States should not, there would be no point in holding Darwin, and the naval oil supplies there should be drained in such a contingency. The whole position in regard to the defence of the northern part of Australia hinged on a battle fleet based at Singapore. If such was not possible, the situation became radically changed.[7]

Chief of General Staff White repeated the view he had offered to Murdoch and Menzies that 'Japan's attack would be against British naval forces and bases, and with their defeat and capture Japan could bring the Commonwealth to terms by the exercise of sea power alone, without the need for invasion'.[8] The Australian army could resist only a 'minor scale of attack'.[9] The two most important armed forces chiefs in Australia were clear-eyed, hard-headed, unabashed defeatists. If there was no British battle fleet at Singapore, if the United States did not come into the war, Australia would have to come to terms with Japan. Against this assessment Menzies' Cabinet made no remonstrance.

Billy Hughes later recalled that in War Cabinet White had said: 'Our strategy is based on the navy being here to help us when it is needed. Our strategy is based on us holding in the Middle East, holding the canal; on us holding Singapore; on Japan not coming into the war.'[10] White was, as Horner remarks, a 'firm supporter' of Imperial Defence.[11] So was Murdoch.

It would later be alleged that the Menzies Government plan in the case of a Japanese invasion was to concentrate its forces along the east coast from Melbourne to Brisbane, the 'Brisbane Line'. Such plans existed, but it is evident that as late as the middle of 1940 the Menzies Government and Australian armed forces had not actively planned to defend Australia against invasion at all. Brudenell White's strategy, openly declared to Menzies and his War Cabinet and meeting no objection from them, was that a Japanese invasion would be unnecessary because Australia would 'come to terms'. Or, more plainly, surrender.

Australia's peril was far greater than Curtin warned of in his most strident speeches. Decades after defining it as the most likely military threat Australia would face, Australia was completely unprepared for war with Japan – a fact accepted with evident placidity by the Government, the army and the navy. Menzies claimed to have kept Curtin informed of major developments in the war. He surely did not tell him of this bleak assessment.

(2)

Menzies knew more than Curtin, but neither of them was aware that with Germany's victory in France and Italy's entry to the war, British military planners were reluctantly facing the truth about Singapore. Now without the allied French navy to watch the Italian navy, the British navy alone would have to guard the Mediterranean, while also preparing to contest an expected German invasion and guard Atlantic convoys on which Britain's survival depended.

On 31 July 1940, a month or so after Colvin and White had told War Cabinet that Australia could not be defended without a British fleet, the British chiefs of staff acknowledged in their planning that there would be no fleet for Singapore. Without a fleet, how could Malaya be defended, let alone Australia? Important in its own right, the loss of Malaya would also open Burma to attack, and then India. 'In the absence of a Fleet,' the British chiefs' memorandum recorded, 'our policy should be to rely primarily on air power. The air forces required to implement that policy, however, cannot be provided for some time to come. Until they can be made available we shall require substantial additional land forces in Malaya, which cannot in present circumstances be found in British or Indian resources.'[12] One obvious place to look for additional land forces would be Australia. The defence of Malaya and Singapore would require at least 336 aircraft. At the time, the appreciation noted, the command had about one-quarter of that requirement.

There would be no fleet. There were insufficient aircraft. British and Indian troops were committed elsewhere. To defend Malaya, to defend Singapore, additional troops would have to come from Australia. The Singapore strategy had acquired an entirely new meaning.

Menzies would soon be formally requested to send the newly recruited 8th Division to Malaya. Later, after Japan came into the war, Churchill would suggest sending one or perhaps two Australian divisions from the Middle East to Singapore and Malaya. But they were not going to defend the fleet base. There would be no fleet. They were going to defend a British colony, its tin and rubber and its United States dollar contributions to the Exchequer. And they would not be supported by adequate air power, because the British chiefs knew that was not possible. In this there was no deceit or betrayal. The British had or would plainly tell Australia there would be no fleet, and Australia would be well aware of the deficiencies of the air force.

(3)

While Germany prepared to invade Britain, Japan found victory in China still infuriatingly out of reach. It now had well over a million troops deployed in China. Though it usually won battles, it would sustain 600 000 military casualties in China before the end of 1941.[13] The United States and Britain were now supplying useful assistance to Chinese forces[14], prolonging Chinese resistance and increasing the cost to Japan. So was the Soviet Union.

Japan had earlier pondered an invasion of the Soviet Union's eastern territories, part of a Northern Advance plan long cherished by the Japanese army. In May 1939, however, a tentative Japanese border advance had been hurled back by Marshal Zhukov's tanks. Japan had been forced to a humiliating ceasefire in September of that year. Stalin now had a non-aggression pact with Hitler. For Japan, the pact made the Soviet Union easier to live with and much more costly to annoy. The navy's Southern Advance plan, which the army opposed but which might cut off China's support through Burma, remained an option.

It also became increasingly apparent to Japan that the United States wished to check its growing power in East Asia, and would sooner or later have the means to do so. In July 1940, Roosevelt signed a two-ocean navy bill that would create a navy with four times the tonnage and air power of Japan's. Though the United States then possessed only a small regular army, an air force far inferior to the Luftwaffe, and the equivalent of a one-ocean navy, its industrial might was many times Japan's. The arithmetic of the rival shipbuilding programs was clear: Japan's naval power would peak in 1941, then rapidly decline compared to that of the United States.[15]

In support of China, the United States had denounced its trade treaty with Japan in 1939. In July 1940 it announced an embargo on high-grade aviation fuel sales to Japan. In Tokyo the southern strategy found greater support. In a 1 August 1940 declaration the Konoe

Government sought a new order for Greater East Asia, under Japanese direction.[16] Press backgrounders confirmed the declared sphere of interest would include the Netherlands East Indies and Indo-China, then held by Vichy France. On 30 August Japan put words into deeds by reaching an agreement with the feeble Vichy regime permitting it to enter northern Indo-China. Seeking to build its alliances and deter the United States, less than a month later Japan signed a tripartite pact with Germany and Italy. Aimed at the United States, the pact declared that if another power not then involved in the war in Europe or China went to war against a pact member, the members would 'assist one another' against that power. Unaware of the direction Hitler's mind was now turning, Japan may have imagined that the Soviet Union would also join the pact.

Washington's firmer stance on Japan paradoxically coincided with Roosevelt's recognition that the gravest military threat to America would likely come from Europe, not Asia. This assessment created a continuing tension in the heart of Washington policy-making that would soon perplex Curtin's political strategy in the Pacific War.

Germany did not possess a powerful surface navy, but if it successfully invaded Britain, seized the British fleet and also took control of the French fleet at Toulon, it would outweigh the US fleet and control the Atlantic. Roosevelt pressed against navy resistance to move some ships from the Pacific to the Atlantic. At around the same time the President accepted State Department advice that Japan would be deterred by a nearer United States naval presence. Overcoming navy objections, in April 1940 he ordered the Pacific fleet to change its main base from San Diego to Pearl Harbor[17]— disregarding a military assessment from 21 April 1939 that the Japanese might well strike Pearl Harbor without warning.[18]

With the fleet committed in the Atlantic and then the Mediterranean after the fall of France, the British sought US naval support against Japan in the Pacific.[19] In naval talks in October 1940 Britain asked the United States navy to station a fleet in Singapore if there was war with Japan.[20] War Secretary Henry Stimson was sympathetic. Then and later President Roosevelt rejected the idea.

Not the least cause of hesitation in the Roosevelt Administration was that even by late 1940 the United States was incapable of fighting a war with a major power. Its vast and now accelerating military build-up was only just beginning. As a 2 October 1940 paper by US army chief General George C Marshall made clear, the United States could not fight a war with anyone for eighteen months.[21] By 30 September 1941, he showed, the United States would be able to put only 130 000 men into the field – the same number as in Australia's home army. Six months later it would be able to deploy more than ten times as many, though munitions, aircraft, artillery and especially shipping would all be limited. Campaigning on war preparedness while insisting that America would stay aloof, Roosevelt was elected for a third term in November 1940. While resisting a military alliance, the United States moved closer to Britain. In a fireside chat broadcast at the end of December Roosevelt warned that if Britain went down, the Axis powers would control 'Europe, Asia, Africa, Australasia and the high seas'. The United States must become 'the great arsenal of democracy'.

Discussion between Britain and the United States about Japan and China, so portentous for Australia, took place almost entirely over the head of the Australian Government, and without its knowledge. Though he closely followed the war in Europe as Hitler prepared to invade Britain and battles flared in the Western Desert, Menzies was less attentive to the war in China. Yet it was this conflict that led directly to the Pacific War, which would shortly threaten Australia. Australia had some intelligence-gathering capability of its own, but only the beginnings – and only in 1940 – of embassy representation abroad. Casey had only recently arrived in Washington, and Australia's new minister to Japan, Sir John Latham, would not reach Tokyo until the end of 1940. Relations with the nationalist government of China did not begin forming until 1941.

Australia depended on the newspapers for its understanding of Japan, and on such British reports as Menzies and his colleagues were shown. Australia did not have independent sources of information on which it could formulate an independent foreign and defence policy. The information gap was most serious in Asia, the region from which any security threat must arise. Bruce and the Dominions Office could keep Australia well informed about Europe; about Asia, less so. Menzies was not well informed about Asia. Nor was Curtin.

(4)

Unable to send a fleet to Singapore, unable to persuade the United States to send one, the British pressed Australia to do more to protect the Empire in the east. Following discussions in May and June 1940, the Menzies Government sent three RAAF squadrons to Singapore and three Australian navy ships to the East Indies. With no likelihood of a fleet using Singapore as a base at this stage of the war, the purpose of Australia's deployment had changed from the defence of Singapore as a naval base to the defence of Malaya. In Australian thinking the two objectives mingled. Menzies did not query the value of holding Malaya. Nor did Curtin, who was himself moving towards endorsing the despatch of Australian troops there. Japan was, after all, over-extended in China, menaced by the Soviet Union in the north, and incapable of matching the fighting qualities and technical superiority of British forces – or so it was widely believed. If it chose to attack Malaya, it might well be defeated.

The AIF, intended to fight in other countries, now had a requirement for 132 527 men – slightly larger than the requirement for home defence. To Parliament later in June, Menzies proposed a force of 250 000 for 'local land defence'. It was nearly twice the size of the force General Brudenell White had that month said was the maximum that could be supported by the arms, ammunition, artillery and transport available – and even then for only four weeks of warfare.

(5)

With a general election expected sometime in 1940, Curtin needed to adjust his position on the war to better accord with Britain's danger, and the possibility that Japan would seize the moment to attack British interests in the east. Led by Curtin, a special federal conference of the ALP in Melbourne on 18 and 19 June 1940 committed the party to winning the war.[22] Dropping the isolationist planks in the platform that would impede it in the next general election, it also approved conscription for home defence. The AIF overseas would be supported, and kept up to strength. The 8th Division, newly raised, should defend Australia. Labor said it would join an advisory council on the war – but it would not join a national government.

It was a great victory for Curtin – his most important win in changing party policy since his election as leader. Though displeased by the refusal to join a national government,[23] newspaper editorials commended what *The Argus* called the biggest decision in the party's history. Curtin won against opposition from both New South Wales and Victoria. Left-wingers in New South Wales still thought it was an imperialist war. In Victoria, anti-conscription sentiment remained strong.

In June 1940, Menzies tightened the national security legislation on the model already enacted in Britain. Curtin won support for the amendments at the June ALP conference. In the House, Menzies said the legislation was necessary for 'the greatest emergency in our history'. Following him, Curtin said the paramount consideration was 'assuring the safety of the country against imminent danger'. Labor supported the amendments. For the Lang group Beasley claimed that 'there is no need for this measure' and his group would not support it. Eddie Ward, who had remained in the Labor caucus, also opposed it, disagreeing with Curtin 'with regret'.[24]

(6)

Following the defeat of France, with Italy now in the war and preparations for a German invasion of Britain apparent in French channel ports, Churchill's great hope was military alliance with the United States. In mid-June Menzies was copied a note sent to Washington to guide the British Ambassador, Lord Lothian, in his contact with the United States Administration. The note accurately forecast that Britain would resist invasion by retaining air superiority over Britain, and also local sea control. Germany could not be defeated, however, without the United States. The key passage for Menzies was item 8:

> The collapse of France would provide Japan with the temptation to take action against the French, British or Dutch interests in the Far East. We see no hope of being able to despatch a fleet to Singapore. It will therefore be vital that the United States of America should publicly declare her intention to regard any alteration of the status quo in the Far East and the Pacific as a casus belli.[25]

Lothian was instructed to seek this outcome. It formalised British policy of seeking American support for its Far Eastern commitments, including Australia. There was 'no hope' of a fleet for Singapore.

If Menzies had cared to read it closely, there was another important implication in the note. Lothian would urge the United States to take responsibility for resisting Japan, and protecting French, British and Dutch interests in Asia and the Pacific. The

British Government was quite prepared to contemplate war between Japan and the United States. After all, the conflict might well also bring the United States into war with Germany. That was the logic of the Tripartite Pact.

Ten days later the British shared with Menzies the chiefs of staff review of Far East strategy following the defeat of France. It was a clear and momentous message. It confirmed there would be no fleet. It asked Australia to undertake responsibility for defending Malaya and Singapore. The chiefs stated:

> Formerly we were prepared to abandon the Western Mediterranean and despatch a fleet to the Far East relying on the French Fleet in the Western Med to contain the Italian Fleet. Now if we move the Med Fleet to the Far East there is nothing to contain the Italian Fleet which will be free to operate in the Atlantic or reinforce the German Fleet in home waters using bases in North Western France. We must therefore retain in European waters sufficient naval forces to watch both the German and Italian Fleets and we cannot do this and send a fleet to the Far East.[26]

For Australia, the Dominions Secretary, Lord Caldecote, added that because Britain could not send a fleet, and because of the threat of a Japanese advance into Indo-China and the increasing range of military aircraft, the chiefs of staff thought Australia should move an army division and two squadrons of aircraft to Malaya 'as an added immediate deterrent'. 'They realise that you could not equip these troops up to full western standards nor would this be necessary in view of the unlikelihood of the Japanese being able to bring mechanized troops with the latest form of equipment to attack them.'[27]

Unable to supply a fleet, unable to defend Australia, the British now asked Australia to defend British possessions in the Far East – and to do so without heavy weapons. The Menzies Government refused the request on 3 July 1940.[28] It was unable to agree to sending an Australian division to Malaya because it could not be equipped with other than small arms. Australia also wanted a more detailed military appreciation. Bruce told Menzies to ask for 'a great deal more information as to United Kingdom appreciation of the situation resulting from the French collapse and of their plans and strategy for the future conduct of the war'.[29] Disfavoured by Churchill, Bruce was seeking ways to force himself back into the inner counsels of British government. He saw the request for Australian help in Malaya as a useful lever. His underlying aim may well have remained a peace agreement with Germany. He could scarcely have been less helpful to Australian interests.

Over a year or so the strategic conception of Australian defence policy had completely changed. The year before the discussions had been about the size of a fleet that would be sent to Singapore to deter Japan. Now there was no fleet, except perhaps in the event of an invasion of Australia. But while there would not be a fleet, Australia was being asked to defend the British colony of Malaya (and thereby contribute also to the defence of Burma and India) against attack by Japan, on the argument that, to defend Singapore, it was necessary to defend Malaya.

(7)

As Japan asserted itself, its relations with Britain deteriorated. Japanese forces pressed in on British concessions in China. External Affairs Minister John McEwen publicly warned of the increasing danger early in August.[30] Responding in the House, Curtin commented, 'the minister says that the situation in the Far East and South Seas gives ground for graver concern than at any time since the war began. Those are not his words; they are my construction on what he said.'

He proposed a secret session at which more could be said about 'an Eastern power'.[31]

In response to Japan's assertion, Britain conciliated. Churchill's bulldog defiance did not extend to Japan. Under continuing Japanese pressure, and unable even to bluff the Japanese that it was capable of defending its position in China, Britain announced on 9 August that it would withdraw all its forces from Peking, Shanghai and Tientsin by the end of the month.

Two days later Churchill sent Menzies a personal message preceding a longer Pacific situation paper prepared by the chiefs of staff.[32] He wrote:

> We are trying our best to avoid war with Japan both by conceding on points where Japanese military clique can perhaps force a rupture and by standing up where ground is less dangerous as in arrests of individuals. I do not think myself that Japan will declare war unless Germany can make a successful invasion of Britain. Once Japan sees that Germany has either failed or dares not try I look for easier times in the Pacific. In adopting against the grain yielding policies towards Japanese threat we have always in mind your interests and safety.[33]

The accompanying situation paper argued that if Japan went to war its objective would be the oil in the Netherlands East Indies. The United States 'would not like this'. Accordingly, the United States main fleet in the Pacific must be 'a grave preoccupation' to the Japanese admiralty. Even if Japan did declare war, the appreciation argued that an invasion of Australia and New Zealand was 'very unlikely', not least because it would leave the United States fleet between the Japanese invasion force and home.

Churchill agreed with his military advisers that a Japanese invasion of Australia was unlikely. He thought Singapore 'ought to stand a long siege'. He told Menzies Britain would also 'base on Ceylon a battle cruiser and a fast aircraft carrier which with Australian and New Zealand ships which we would return to you would exercise a powerful deterrent upon hostile raiding cruisers'. Britain could also send the Mediterranean fleet through the Suez Canal but 'we do not want to do this even if Japan declares war until it is found to be vital to your safety'.

Invasion was unlikely but Churchill assured Menzies that if 'contrary to prudence and self interest Japan sets about invading Australia or New Zealand on a large scale I have explicit authority of cabinet to assure you we would then cut our losses in the Mediterranean and proceed to your aid sacrificing every interest except only defence position on this island on which all depends'. It was a comforting statement. Early the following year Menzies would discern its complications.

Again, Dominions Secretary Caldecote pressed for an Australian division for Malaya. An appreciation three years earlier had assumed that the threat to British interests in the Far East would come by sea. Now, Japan's greater penetration in China, amenable Vichy authorities in French Indo-China, and Thailand's isolation, would 'enable Japan to develop an overland threat to Malaya, against which even the arrival of the fleet would only partially guard'.[34]

It was in any case impossible to send a fleet. The defence problem was accordingly seen in terms of Japanese intentions on Singapore. The appreciation pointed out that Japan would have to reckon the United States might send a fleet to the Philippines. It correctly saw that 'Only if she could rapidly gain complete control of raw materials especially oil, rubber and tin of Malaya and the Netherlands East Indies would she have a chance of withstanding British and American economic pressure.'

The appreciation readily conceded that 'Until . . . we have defeated Germany and Italy or have drastically reduced their naval strength we should be forced in the event of Japanese aggression to attempt to defend our Far Eastern interests without an adequate fleet'.[35] Britain 'should not be justified in going to war' if Japan moved into Indo-China and Thailand. The loss of the Netherlands East Indies would be very serious but under present conditions Britain could not contest it. The appreciation concluded that the most probable line was a Japanese move into Indo-China possibly followed later by a move into Netherlands East Indies, rather than Singapore.

Reviewing the British appreciation the Australian chiefs concluded on 23 August that Singapore must be held to provide a base for a British fleet that would be sent in the extremity of an invasion of Australia.[36] To hold Singapore, it was essential to hold Malaya.

Endorsed by Churchill and Cabinet, and stamped with the authority of the British chiefs, this August 1940 appreciation could hardly have been more candid or clear in its analysis, or more portentous for Australia. Britain would not resist Japan even if it took the Netherlands East Indies. It would not send a fleet to Singapore, which in any case was now vulnerable to attack by land. Australia should reinforce Malaya with troops and planes – though it was apparent that if the Japanese did take the Dutch East Indies, Australian troops in Malaya would be cut off from their home country.

The only deceit in the British position was that it would send a fleet from the Mediterranean to protect Australia if it was about to be invaded by Japan. If Japan had triumphed so far as to be able to contemplate an invasion of Australia, as Australia's civilian defence head, Fred Shedden, would point out, it would have taken Malaya and Singapore already, and the proposed British fleet would have lost its base in the region. And, as Menzies himself would later point out, the British Mediterranean fleet could not be sent through the Canal without abandoning the British army in the Middle East, which now included Australian divisions.[37] It was fanciful. The real British position, or hope, was that Japan could not attack southward without bringing in the United States.

On 13 August 1940, as the nation absorbed the news of the British withdrawal from China, there was another shock. Australia's Army Minister Geoffrey Street, Air Minister Jim Fairbairn, senior minister Sir Henry Gullett and General Brudenell White were all killed when their air force transport plane crashed into a hill near Canberra. His most loyal ministers killed, facing the prospect of humiliating defeats like that in Corio in by-elections for their seats, Menzies gambled that he would be better off with a prompt general election. A week later he announced the federal election would be held on Saturday, 21 September 1940.

CHAPTER 15

KNIFE EDGE

(1)

He gave far more prominence to the threat of Japan and to the poor state of Australia's capacity to meet the threat, but otherwise Curtin went to the election with few differences with Menzies on the war. Covered by the decisions of Labor's federal conference in June, he now supported deployment of the AIF to the Middle East, and conscription for the home defence army. He promised loyal support for Britain. Launching the campaign in a national broadcast on 24 August 1940, he said Australia should ensure its own defence before it 'rushed to do battle across the world'. The results on 21 September were unpleasant for Menzies but not decisive for Curtin. Labor won an additional three seats. Including Lang Labor, it had the same number of seats as the Menzies Coalition Government, which depended on two independents for survival.

Though Labor gained nationally, Curtin had an uncomfortable time in his own electorate of Fremantle. On election night the primary vote went against him so strongly it was reported he might well lose the seat. On 23 Monday the *West Australian* wrote that Curtin 'seems certain' to have been beaten. Curtin himself was so far convinced of his loss he wrote that day to the caucus secretary, Norman Makin, asking that 'whoever is appointed Leader' retain the four staff members who had been working for him.[1] Labor member Rowley James offered to give up his own safe New South Wales coalmining seat to Curtin, should he lose Fremantle. Curtin's daughter, Elsie, later said Menzies offered to appoint Curtin as High Commissioner to New Zealand if he lost his seat. Curtin affected to be prepared to leave politics if he lost, but his daughter also recalled that he refused Menzies' offer because he intended to remain in politics, one way or another.[2] He was publicly quoted as saying, 'I shall not chase my destiny. If Fremantle, which sent me to Federal Parliament, rejects me from the Federal Parliament, that will be the end of politics for me.'[3]

He evidently thought better of that declaration. He told a meeting a little over a week later, 'If I had lost the Fremantle seat I would not have been lost to the Labor Movement, whether or not another seat was found for me.'[4] It was the weekend following the election before it became apparent that second preferences were running towards him much more strongly than expected, and that he would win handily. When they came in, the soldiers' votes from overseas also went Curtin's way, though by that time he was anyway the clear winner.

Curtin had shown so much good sense and restraint in his attacks on Menzies and so well curbed the radicals in his own party, his opponents were as alarmed by his possible loss as his friends. Writing about it three years later, the *Sydney Morning Herald*'s Ross Gollan recalled when Curtin appeared to be losing Fremantle 'there was general consternation in the Parliamentary UAP and the Country Party'. When Curtin's opponent, F R Lee, later visited the eastern states he 'had been made to feel . . . that if he had won the seat for his party the party itself would have regarded him as having committed an unpardonable political sin'.[5]

The 1940 election dramatically changed the political circumstances of Menzies and Curtin. Despite the new split in Labor in New South Wales, the election saw a big swing in that state towards

Curtin's federal Labor Party, and away from the governing Coalition. It was the only significant swing to Labor throughout the country. In Tasmania, Labor lost two seats.

One of the independents on whom the balance of power now rested was Arthur Coles, a successful businessman and former Lord Mayor of Melbourne. Elected as an independent, he supported the UAP and attended its party meetings. Coles had won the Melbourne seat of Henty, left vacant by the death of Sir Henry Gullett – the Canberra air crash still reverberated.

The other independent was Alexander Wilson, from the wheat-growing electorate of Wimmera. He also supported the Coalition, though he had links with Labor in his electorate. After the Coalition had provided a Speaker, it needed the votes of both Coles and Wilson to have a majority in the House. Menzies was soon confident enough of their support to remain in office. Their changing views would be crucial to Australian politics and Curtin's ambitions over the coming year.

(2)

The interregnum between the counting of the close primary vote in Fremantle and the discovery of the strong preference vote for Curtin flushed out the leadership ambitions of Labor's star new candidate, former High Court judge Dr H V Evatt, who won the southern Sydney seat of Barton. Curtin had met him in Fremantle as early as 1926, when Curtin was editor of the *Westralian Worker* and Evatt was already a distinguished Labor lawyer.[6]

Evatt maintained a wide range of correspondents, with whom he shared a belittling estimate of Curtin. He was too cautious, Evatt thought. Frank Brennan had written to him in January 1940, sharing his criticism of Curtin's broadcast for the Corio by-election. Brennan thought it was 'calamitous', he told Evatt. It might have been taken 'from a speech by Pearce or Hughes 1914–18'. It was fatal for Curtin to say he would support Menzies on war issues. The truth was that 'he had always wished to support them and that the main preoccupation of the Executive was to pump sufficient oxygen into him to enable him to stand up and look like a Labor leader'. Brennan was 'sick to death of his pale imitation of Menzies' policy'.[7] Writing to Evatt 'from abroad' in October 1940, reporter Massey Stanley, who had enlisted in the AIF, told Evatt that 'the important thing appears to be that you have stiffened JC sufficiently to keep him from sacrificing Labour'.[8] Corrupt Melbourne powerbroker John Wren was another correspondent with whom Evatt would share his poor opinion of Curtin. Intelligent, ambitious and politically clumsy, Evatt would prove to be a good minister – and a nuisance to Curtin.

Evatt was in a hurry. In 1939 he had hoped Menzies would appoint him minister in Washington, the job that went to Casey.[9] In October that year he also met with UAP politician and fellow barrister Percy Spender, by then a minister in the Menzies Government. Evatt was interested in a national government, he told Spender, asking him if he, Evatt, would be acceptable 'as its leader'. Spender thought or claimed to think Evatt had meant leader of the UAP, but whatever he meant he had raised it with the wrong person.[10] Spender was then and remained a political enemy.

Evatt had very little understanding of what people actually thought about him, or perhaps he didn't care. He made enemies thoughtlessly. Looking around for a federal electorate in 1940 he choose Macquarie.[11] Chifley had lost the seat in the 1931 landslide to Lyons, and won it back in 1940. An outraged Chifley warned Evatt off.

Running for Barton, Evatt had clearly hinted his preference for a national government. In a speech on 9 September 1940, he claimed that 'Labor believes that, in an emergency like the present, the best brains of the nation should be invited to come to the assistance of the nation. It is evident that, unless the UAP – Country coalition shares that belief, all the talk of a national ministry is a sheer waste of time.' He was confident anyway that Labor would win and 'Labor will be the national ministry of Australia'. Labor had already proposed a war council as an alternative to Menzies' national government proposal. On 16 September, Evatt creatively adapted that proposal as a kind of national government. He called it the National War Council. It would not be confined to members of Parliament, and would be 'endowed with great powers'. Hughes should be a member, and it would include the UAP and Country Party. It would have perhaps five members. The chairman, he suggested, would be 'Prime Minister Curtin'. It was pretty clearly an executive authority, not an advisory body.[12] When Curtin appeared to have lost his seat, Evatt reiterated his claim that Labor 'did accept the principle of national government', a statement that was widely and probably correctly interpreted as either a bid for party leadership or for the party to join a national government, or both.

With the House of Representatives evenly divided, the political temperature increased. Curtin led a stronger parliamentary party but it was also more factious. Reading the New South Wales result, Beasley began manoeuvring to bring his group back into caucus. Evatt had a considerable intellect, prestige and force of personality. He also wanted to be in government as soon as possible, and promptly took the lead in pressing for either an all-party government, or a minority Labor government. He made common cause with the left, which pressed for a more belligerent and uncompromising stance towards Menzies.

Curtin remained adamantly opposed to a coalition, and could rely on the support of most of his colleagues. But Curtin was also in favour of a degree of cooperation with Menzies. Australia was, after all, at war. Australians would not welcome another election so soon after the last – especially if brought about by a truculent Labor Party intent on seeking office. Nor would it necessarily help

Labor to force Menzies' resignation, knowing it had no more seats in the House than the Coalition. Curtin's policy was to build towards the 1943 election, or to fight an election sooner if it was brought about by internal troubles of the Coalition, or to accept office only when the Coalition was clearly no longer capable of governing. If he was to form a government in the existing parliament, he would need the support of the independents, as Menzies did. Evatt was Curtin's main opponent on these tactical issues, and to fight them Evatt was prepared to find allies wherever he could.

Recognising how precarious his government was, acknowledging newspaper publishers' advocacy, Menzies responded to the outcome of the September 1940 election by attempting to put together an all-party coalition government on the model Britain had adopted earlier that year.

Evatt was keen but he was easily played. Curtin negotiated, proposing terms too difficult for Menzies. After exhaustive negotiation, caucus backed him on 23 October. Instead, Labor proposed an advisory war council, already agreed at the June 1940 Labor conference. Failing to win an all-party coalition, Menzies accepted the proposal and constituted the Advisory War Council on 28 October 1940. Caucus chose Curtin, Deputy Leader Frank Forde from Queensland and Norman Makin from South Australia as its representatives, overlooking Evatt.[13] Still officially separated from the Labor caucus, Beasley represented the non-communist Labor Party on the Advisory War Council, soon to be widely known simply as the War Council.

Evatt wrote Curtin what one of his biographers called a 'plaintive' letter, complaining he had been sick and unable to defend himself against 'those who refused to endorse' him for the War Council.[14] Earlier, Evatt had signalled his intention to run for Deputy Leader of the party, then withdrew for want of support.[15] His eagerness to claim the deputy leadership probably cost him a spot on the War Council.[16] Though elected to the caucus executive[17], he was finding the Labor caucus tough going. Writing to Curtin he complained that 'your friendly attitude towards myself was not continued after the day of polling'. He said (rightly) that Curtin had ignored his advice as one of the three negotiators appointed by caucus. Evatt thought better of offending his leader and probably didn't send the letter.[18] But he did tell the AWU's Henry Boote that Curtin was 'woefully timid'.[19] Boote was not the first to note that Evatt was 'passionately desirous of office'.[20]

(3)

The War Council would be Curtin's school of government. After five years as Opposition leader Curtin would sit around the same table as the Government's principal ministers, deciding or at least discussing the great issues of war.

The War Council convened for its first meeting on Tuesday, 29 October 1940, at Victoria Barracks, Melbourne – the heart of wartime decision-making. In the photograph recording the meeting Curtin sits on Menzies' right, with Hughes on Menzies' left.[21] Curtin was now at the centre, part of a kind of government, for the first time in his life. He had access to highly classified war intelligence. He could no longer be ignored, or considered lightly. He began falteringly to better understand the drift of events, the considerations that influenced Australia's safety, the way others thought about the war, the personalities and motives of the navy, army and air force chiefs and of civilian defence officials.

To reporters, he was now a more considerable figure, someone who knew many secrets. He was also suddenly elevated in the estimation of caucus, as were his Labor colleagues on the War Council. He now knew so much more than other caucus members. His limitation was Menzies' limitation – neither of them was well informed of British and American talks on the threat from Japan, or knew very much about Washington or Roosevelt. Of Japanese plans, of the circumstances of the war between Japan and China, they knew very little.

Because the defence headquarters was in Melbourne the War Council normally met in that city, though it also often met in Canberra when Parliament was sitting. As Prime Minister and chairman of the Council, Menzies imposed no restriction on the matters which could be brought forward by its members. He also provided members with a good deal of secret information. They would see, he told the first meeting, the Australian chiefs of staff weekly summaries, material relating to decisions of War Cabinet, and copies of cables from the Dominions Office. The Opposition members did not see all that Menzies saw, and there would be instances where major war decisions were made without their knowledge, but they saw many of the major defence communications. A year before he became prime minister, Curtin began to be inducted into the problems of wartime strategy and national political management which would preoccupy him for the rest of his life.

Not much noticed, the War Council also inducted Jack Beasley into the responsibilities of government in time of war, and in a circumstance in which he would work closely with Curtin. They became surprisingly close allies.

The War Council was able to function as it did because, once Australia was at war, the political differences between Menzies and Curtin were muted. Curtin and Beasley had handed Menzies a list of nine guiding principles during earlier discussions of an all-party government which illustrated the issues over which the parties divided. They included soldiers' pay, financial policy, stabilisation of wheat prices and output, social policy, trade union cooperation and post-war reconstruction. It was a big list but the differences were on details, or issues that would only arise when the war was won. The listed principles did not by then include defence strategy, commitment of Australian troops to the Middle East, or conscription for home defence.

Even at this first meeting Curtin was concerned about Japan's southward expansion. It was apparent from his first contribution that he had not been informed of the momentous exchanges between London and Canberra during the previous six months. He had evidently not been told that the British had said they would not send a fleet to Singapore, or that British defence planning for Malaya now recognised the attack would come by land and would be best opposed by air, or that the plan now was that Australia should help defend Malaya and Singapore rather than that Singapore defend Australia. If the naval base at Singapore was the bastion of British power in the region, Curtin asked at this first meeting of the War Council, if it was the barrier to Japan's ambitions to acquire the rubber of Malaya and the oil of the Netherlands East Indies, why was it not supported by a powerful British fleet?[22] Curtin had much to learn.

It rapidly became apparent that the War Council would become a forum for resolving domestic political issues. Hoping to reach agreement before the Budget was presented to Parliament, Treasurer Artie Fadden brought the main proposals before the War Council in early November. They included higher taxes on the wealthy to finance war spending. But the Budget also included a reduction in the tax-free threshold for income from £250 to £150, to which Labor strongly objected. Agreement in the War Council proving difficult, Fadden introduced his Budget to Parliament on 21 November 1940. One week later Curtin moved an amendment which, if passed, would have brought the Government down. With more bravado than confidence Menzies took it as a challenge to test the Government's support. In the course of the debate, however, it became apparent that Wilson was wavering.

Though he preferred a compromise with Menzies, Curtin was evidently quite prepared as early as November 1940 to bring the Government down if Menzies refused to negotiate – and if the two independents supported Labor.

Caucus was again divided. Evatt was opposed to compromise and pressed for a vote in the House. Ward and his allies also opposed negotiation with Menzies. Curtin wanted the Menzies Government to fall apart, not to bring it down. Neither Ward nor Evatt were members of the War Council, which was the forum for a Budget negotiation in Canberra on 4 and 5 December. Curtin and his Opposition colleagues on the War Council reached a compromise with the Government. The tax-free income level was increased to £200 from a proposed £150. When caucus met on 5 December 1940, to consider the compromise plan worked out by Menzies, Fadden, Curtin and Beasley, Evatt attacked.[23] He argued that a compromise should be refused and the question should be put to the vote. Supported by other New South Wales members, Evatt was seeking another general election, or a national government. Ward also rejected the Budget compromise, and some of Curtin's usually loyal supporters sought a higher pension rate. Curtin's compromise was endorsed, but only by twenty-four votes to nineteen. The vote was unexpectedly close.[24] (Beasley's group had supported the compromise with Menzies but would not rejoin caucus until February the following year.)

The Budget dispute illustrated how precarious were the positions of both Menzies and Curtin. It also demonstrated the usefulness of the War Council to both men. At the meeting on 8 November, Beasley had widened the range of topics by saying he wanted to discuss the recent appointment of the secretary of the Department of Labour and National Service, petrol rationing and so forth. Like the Budget, these were issues only loosely connected with war. Menzies offered no objection. Instead, he suggested that members had the right to raise any matters they saw fit – though preferably with some notice beforehand.

Following the Budget negotiations Menzies and Curtin affirmed in the resulting statement that whenever practicable questions would be brought to the War Council before being raised in Parliament. The wider role was apparent through November and December as Menzies and his ministers sought Labor's suggestions on new conciliation procedures to cut strikes, particularly on the coalfields where industrial disputes had cut production. The Labor Party was based on the trade unions, but the political leadership of Labor was as hostile to the coalfields strikes as was Menzies. The Soviet Union and Germany were observing a non-aggression pact. So far as communists among the coalfields leaders were concerned, it was not their war. During 1940, 1.51 million working days were lost in industrial disputes in Australia, of which 1.37 million were in coalmining – mostly in New South Wales.[25] (The strikes would continue long after the Communist Party changed its line. The miners had their own ideas.)

Menzies was discreetly drawing the Opposition leaders into an unacknowledged national government. Government members submitted to the Opposition members a proposed list of names of conciliation commissioners. Menzies said he would like to appoint a 'Labour representative' to a vacancy on the Australian Broadcasting Commission, a suggestion readily agreed. If he could claim proposals had the backing of the War Council, Menzies could be a little less bothered by the discontent in his own party.

With the House of Representatives on a knife edge, a by-election for the UAP-held Perth seat of Swan at the end of 1940 threatened the Menzies Government. In the complicated world of local politics, Curtin did not care for the left-winger running as the Labor candidate. Run down, Curtin let it be known he had been ordered to take a complete rest. He did not return to Perth until Christmas Day, and remained at home resting through early January. His party critics said Curtin was running dead, frightened of winning government. Evatt campaigned hard, contrasting his vigorous presence with Curtin's absence. The Labor candidate, James Dinan, lost badly, and complained of Curtin's conduct. He said he had 'nothing but contempt' for 'those who should have backed me' and that failure of Labor leadership to support him when government hung in the balance showed it did not want to take office.[26] In the federal caucus Curtin managed his critics carefully. In Perth, he commanded loyalty. Dinan was promptly expelled.

(4)

By the end of 1940 both Menzies and Curtin were troubled by the risks of a southward advance by Japan and the shortcomings of British defences at Singapore. With United Kingdom and New Zealand colleagues, Australian military officers took part in a military conference in Singapore on 22–31 October. It was a month since Japanese troops had moved south and established bases in Vietnam, bringing Japanese naval and air power closer to British-held Malaya.

Reports from the conference for the first time gave Menzies and then Curtin a clear picture of Singapore's defences. It was probably the first important secret information given to Curtin on the weakness of the British position in Malaya and Singapore. Curtin's response to the startling conclusions of the conference marked an emphatic shift in his strategic thinking. He now advocated forward defence of Australia in Malaya. Menzies and the military chiefs shared the change in thinking. Menzies' Cabinet had earlier rejected the British request to send the 8th Division to Malaya. The request would be repeated.

Constructed at enormous cost, the 54-square-kilometre Singapore naval base was equipped with what was, in 1940, the world's largest dry dock and sufficient fuel in storage to sustain the entire British fleet for six months. Built on the north side of the island facing Johore, the naval base was defended at either end of the access channel between Johore and Singapore by great guns trained east and south-west. The 15-inch batteries made the base all but impregnable to attack by ships. It had been designed to withstand attack by sea, but not by air or land. Since its construction had first been approved decades earlier, the range and firepower of warplanes had dramatically increased.

By the time the base was officially opened in February 1938 it was already vulnerable to land-based air attack if the Japanese could establish landing fields in southern Indo-China or Thailand. If the enemy occupied Johore, they would command the base and the access channels. The biggest guns defending the base could not be rotated to fire north. Lesser guns in the batteries could, but their shells were designed to pierce armour and then explode. They would prove useless against troops advancing over the soft soil of Johore. The only way Singapore's vulnerability could be addressed, the planners agreed, was by defending the Malayan side in depth.

At the October 1940 Singapore conference the analysis was affirmed. British officers argued that the Singapore naval base was the key to the region's defence. If Singapore was attacked it would probably be from Malaya, so to defend Singapore it was necessary to defend Malaya. The colony produced large supplies of rubber and tin, Malaya-based planes could obstruct the pathway to India through Thailand and Burma, and it was the land route to an attack on the Singapore naval base. As the British civilian authorities in Malaya pointed out, the colony was a 'dollar arsenal'.[27] In the eleven months to July 1941, Malayan rubber and tin contributed 135 million US dollars to the Bank of England. In a Pacific war Japan would want to secure the oil of the Netherlands East Indies, but it would probably first need to eliminate whatever threat the Singapore base presented to its forces heading south. The military conference concluded Japan would therefore strike Malaya as its first key target in a Pacific war.[28]

The conference also concluded that the defence of Malaya could not depend on the British and Commonwealth troops in Malaya, or on the presence of a small fleet. It depended on air power. The British forces should be able to deploy enough bombers and fighters to prevent a Japanese fleet landing an invasion force, and to break up any remnant Japanese army which did manage to get ashore. Part of the air power would be seaborne, because the plans assumed an aircraft carrier would be sent to Singapore if war was imminent. Most would be based on land.

The officers had agreed that the army and air force were 'far below requirements' to secure Malaya against direct attack.[29] Of the 534 modern aircraft the conference deemed required for the defence of Malaya, there were then only eighty-eight in the colony. There were no modern fighters, and only a few modern bombers.[30] In total there were forty-eight modern planes for all of Malaya and Burma.[31] No doubt the planners were conscious that in Britain's current circumstances no substantial fleet could be expected. The Admiralty and Churchill had already made that quite plain. But it was surely at least as improbable that Britain could or would supply planes in the number thought to be required. The British chiefs would later respond that 336 planes would be sufficient, and that was anyway all that could be supplied. In the event, Churchill vetoed even that number.

Presenting the conclusions of the military conference to the War Council in Canberra on 25 November, Menzies discussed the 'alarming position in regard to the defence of Singapore'. He said Britain was likely to request Australian support for the defence of Malaya.[32] Curtin asked again about sending a British capital warship to Singapore and about deploying Australia's navy north of Australia.[33] Menzies said that the circumstances demanded he visit London for a discussion with Churchill. On 17 December Menzies asked Bruce to see if the British Government would agree to his leaving for London in mid-January.

The ostensible aim of Menzies' visit was to persuade Churchill to send more ships, planes and troops to Malaya and Singapore. In the circumstances of late 1940, that was surely a forlorn hope, as Menzies had every reason to know. The British had repeatedly said they would not send a fleet unless Australia was being invaded –

a circumstance which could probably only arise after Singapore (and Malaya) were lost. Still threatened with invasion and fighting the Luftwaffe in the skies over Britain, there was also very little chance Churchill would send more planes to Malaya. Even before he left Australia, Churchill would again reject Menzies' request for ships and planes for Singapore.

Menzies' attention to London would necessarily be at the expense of his attention to home defence. It remained desperately feeble. It was only six months since General White had told Murdoch he could command only 130 000 men for home defence, and even for that number would not have sufficient small arms, ammunition and artillery for more than a month of warfare. By the end of 1940 not much had changed.

If Curtin agreed to the London visit, Menzies could for a while secure his government against a vote in the House, and his leadership against a vote in the UAP party room. But it would be at best a furlough, and perhaps at the expense of greater discontent on his return. Menzies had a mix of motives, including placing himself in the British War Cabinet as representative of the dominions.

Slow to grasp Britain's circumstances, evidently not well informed about the cables to Menzies, Curtin continued to press for a British fleet for Singapore. At a 2 December meeting the War Council agreed, on Curtin's initiative, to request London to base 'three or four capital ships at Singapore, as a deterrent to Japanese action in the region'. The War Council decision would give a plausible character to Menzies' proposal to absent himself from Australia for several months, though Menzies was well aware the British Government had already rejected the request Curtin pressed.

The day before, Menzies had sent a cable to London expressing concern and offering Australian support for strengthening Singapore and Malaya. Apparently without discussion in the War Council he offered to send brigade groups from the 8th Division then being trained in Australia for proposed deployment to the Middle East.[34]

Churchill rejected the request for three or four capital ships at the end of the month. Menzies showed the cable to a Melbourne meeting of the War Council on 8 January 1941. Churchill wrote that the fleet was at the 'fullest naval strain I have seen either in this or former war. The only way in which a naval squadron could be found for Singapore would be by ruining the Mediterranean situation.' Nor was he confident about supplying the requested aircraft for Singapore. He recognised that the Singapore conference recommended 'dispatch of considerable numbers of aircraft' but 'it is difficult to commit ourselves to precise numbers of aircraft which we can make available for Singapore'.[35]

Churchill thanked Menzies for the offer of troops for Malaya.[36] He anyway thought 'if Japan should enter the war, the United States will come in on our side, which will put the naval boot very much on the other leg, and be a deliverance from many perils'. Meanwhile, he wearily advised 'we must try to bear our Eastern anxiety patiently and doggedly until this result is achieved, it always being understood that if Australia is seriously threatened by invasion we should not hesitate to compromise or sacrifice the Mediterranean position for the sake of our kith and kin'.

Churchill's refusal went somewhat further than he told Menzies. On 8 December the British chiefs of staff had proposed to provide 336 aircraft to Malaya and Burma by the end of 1941. On 13 January 1941, Churchill told them 'the political situation in the Far East does not seem to require, and the strength of our Air Force by no mean warrants, the maintenance of such large forces in the Far East at this time'.[37] Churchill, as Chancellor of the Exchequer, had opposed the Singapore base plan in the 1920s.[38] His priorities, as ever, remained Britain, the Mediterranean, and India.

The War Council discussion on a battle fleet for Singapore had been at Curtin's initiative and the request to Churchill had his full support. For Curtin this was a puzzling change of direction. In past years he had argued against depending on a British naval presence in

Singapore for the defence of Australia. He had been an early advocate
of the importance of air power against ships, and of the land defence
of Australia. Now he was pressing for a British navy force in Singapore,
a demand which even before Churchill's reply had been refused – and
refused for the very reasons Curtin had listed in his striking speech
four years earlier.

By the end of February 1941 most of the 8th Division would be
deployed in Malaya. Most of Australia's trained troops were in the
Middle East. General Sir Archibald Wavell had opened the first Allied
offensive in the Western Desert with the Battle of Sidi Barrani on
10 and 11 December 1940. Australia's 6th Division was fighting in
the offensive.

Menzies pressed on with arrangements to visit London. He told
War Council on 8 January he had now been invited to visit the British
leadership in London. He thought it was an opportune time to go,
with the Australian Parliament in recess and the winter minimising
military activity in Europe. Curtin was in Perth and missed the
January 1941 War Council meetings, though he was kept informed.
Menzies needed Opposition agreement to the visit, because, unless it
gave him a pair, the House would be deadlocked. He wanted to feel,
he told the Council, that 'in anything he said in London as Prime
Minister, he was expressing the united opinion of the Australian
people'. He especially proposed to discuss the Far Eastern position in
the light of the Singapore military conference.[39]

After the caucus row on the Budget, Curtin was guarded in
offering support for the visit. Evatt and his allies would rightly
understand that Menzies was making his precarious government
invulnerable while he was abroad. When the War Council met
again the following day, Forde said he had spoken to Curtin and
they thought 'it is the responsibility of Full Cabinet to take any
decision regarding the visit of the Prime Minister to London'. The
critical question remained whether the Menzies Government would
face a confidence vote in his absence. Forde was prepared to say that

'Though non-government members of the Council could not give any undertaking in respect of their parties', he felt that 'the common sense of members should not give rise to any embarrassment to the Government during Prime Minister's absence'. Forde was reluctant to be more definite. He candidly explained that an 'impression was held by some Labour followers that Labour could have taken office during the recent crisis, in order to achieve the objectives of the Labour Party's policy, and as they had not done so the Labour members of the War Council were in the pocket of the government'.[40]

Menzies relied on Curtin, leaving for London on 21 January. Treated unkindly by some of his colleagues and press proprietors, dependent on two independents for his House majority and still troubled by the unpredictability of his Country Party allies, he yearned for a larger sphere and a grander role.

(5)

Menzies would be spending most of his overseas visit in the wrong capital. Locked into the British point of view, a political relationship with the United States still new, Australian leaders did not grasp the increasing risk of war between the United States and Japan. Curtin and Menzies both thought Japan might well attack British and Dutch colonies, threatening Australia. They hoped that if Japan attacked the British Empire, the United States might sooner or later join the war. It was not evident to them that Japan's long and costly war against China had injured its relationship with the United States. For Japan the serious enemy in the Pacific was not Britain and certainly not Australia. It was the United States.

War between Japan and the United States had long been contemplated in the naval plans of both sides. Ever since there had been a United States Naval War College it had used war game scenarios, and in those scenarios 'the enemy was always Japan'.[41] It was after all the only naval power in the world with any likelihood of being both hostile to the United States and effective against it. It was usually assumed that the war would begin with a surprise attack on the Philippines. The United States navy would then advance across the Pacific from the west coast of the United States to the relief of United States forces dug in on the Bataan Peninsula. Somewhere along the way the Japanese and United States navies would fight a fleet action. In the War College scenarios, the outcome of the war commonly turned on that fleet action. This was Plan Orange, adopted after the Great War. As the American naval historian, Thomas Buell, wrote, the Japanese used the same scenario.

When war came to the Pacific it would not be as either Menzies or Curtin imagined. It would be both very much worse and very much better. It would be between Japan and the United States, with Britain promptly knocked out as a significant belligerent after the first nine weeks and Australia remaining as the only important fighting ally of the United States in the Pacific War. It would change the world and Australia's place in the world so completely and abruptly that Curtin himself, who understood and responded to its demands, would not grasp its consequence.

While leaders in Washington, London and Canberra speculated through 1940 on Japan's intentions, opinion in Tokyo had shifted gradually towards widening the war against China. By tradition focused on Russia, the Japanese army high command only reluctantly agreed that to win the war in China it might need to take South-East Asia as well. By September 1940 the Japanese army had begun to give serious consideration to a southward thrust.[42] On 1 January 1941, as Australia began planning to send the 8th Division to Malaya, the 'Taiwan Army Research Section' opened in Formosa. Its job was to collect information on Malaya, the Netherlands East Indies, the

Philippines and Burma. The Imperial Japanese army began more intensive study of amphibious warfare.

At the same time, Roosevelt's position on Japan steadily hardened. Churchill closely followed. As Prime Minister he had obliged Japan by closing the supply route to the Chinese Nationalists through Burma in July 1940. Thereafter he opposed concessions and supported Roosevelt's harder line.[43] He was well aware that Britain did not have the means to counter Japan, but if the United States was drawn into a war with Japan it would probably also find itself at war with Germany. This Churchill ardently sought. Roosevelt was not seeking war, or not at that point. He concluded, however, that Japan could not be permitted to occupy China, Indo-China, and then, in all probability, Malaya and the Netherlands East Indies unopposed. He, too, would have assumed that war with Japan would likely also involve war with Germany.

At the beginning of 1941 neither Menzies nor Curtin seemed to be aware that British and American thinking about Japan was changing. There was a bigger game.

CHAPTER 16

CURTIN WARNS OF WAR IN THE PACIFIC

(1)

With Menzies away, Curtin became the dominating figure on the War Council. When it met in Melbourne on 5 February 1941, with Artie Fadden chairing as Acting Prime Minister and Acting Minister for Defence Co-ordination, Curtin complained that the Council had been dealing with too many matters of 'minor importance'. He wanted regular discussion of the international situation. He may have been startled by the vigour and importance of the discussion that followed. Army Minister Percy Spender, recently returned from a visit to Singapore and Malaya, promptly declared that war with Japan might be imminent. Despite Japan's fear of an alliance against it by the United States and the British Empire, he said, there is 'every possibility of Japan making a move against us in the next three months'. The situation was 'veering towards Japanese intervention in the war', with European politics the determining factor. He evidently meant that Germany was pressuring Japan, with the aim of 'diverting the efforts of the British Empire and interfering with supplies to Great Britain from the United States'.

It was not clear which agency or individual was providing the 'advices' mentioned by Spender, but his prediction would have shocked fellow War Council members. Spender may well have drawn on preliminary Australian military intelligence, which formally advised on 8 February that a Japanese attack could come in the following month.[1] It was less than three weeks since Menzies had left the country in the hands of the Acting Prime Minister, only a month since Churchill had refused a major naval reinforcement for Singapore 'unless or until the Japanese danger becomes far more menacing than at present'. After Menzies' discussion of the Singapore conference report, Council members were well aware that the service chiefs believed Malaya and Singapore had only a fraction of the army, naval and air strength required to meet a threat from Japan. Now the Army Minister was telling Curtin and his colleagues that from advice received and his visit to Singapore he had concluded Japan could well attack within three months. Spender did say that in the view of the military advisers 'it was doubtful whether an invasion of Australia' would take place, but also said that serious harm would be done by continuous and effective raids on Australia.

Curtin followed Spender's alarming assessment and dominated the remainder of the meeting. He thought the threat quite grave. He said that Japan's policy was 'opportunism. If she thought the situation favoured it, she would make war against us tomorrow' and use her navy to immobilise Australia.[2] There would be 'disastrous effects' on commercial and economic life. Curtin said he could not overlook the possibility of a 'temporary occupation' of some part of Australia. The psychological effect would be great, because the Axis would say Britain was losing territory.

To Curtin the threat underlined the need for additional naval forces. Australia relied on Indian Ocean routes for reinforcement of its troops abroad, and also for its overseas trade. He acknowledged, however, that it was 'not practicable' to reinforce the Australian naval squadron because of pressures in the Atlantic and the Mediterranean. It was a reversal of his earlier view that Australia needed planes and also of his view that there was nothing so inferior as an inferior navy.

Curtin thought 'the next six months would be fatal to one side or the other', so it was 'essential that we should dissipate internal friction and that all sections of the Australian community should put their best efforts forward to maintain both Australian and Empire integrity'. Curtin deplored strikes on the waterfront and in coalmining, but there was more to it than his annoyance over lost production. He wanted the state premiers and Parliament to be told of the situation. He wanted naval strength doubled. He claimed the 'danger to Australia would come in the first place from the sea, secondly from the air, while the army would only be brought into full action after both the Navy and Air Force had failed'.

The chiefs of staff were then brought in. They were evidently unconvinced that Japan planned an imminent attack. The Chief of the Naval Staff, Admiral Ragnar Colvin, thought that in the event of war Japan would 'maintain a cruiser and a submarine force and possibly an aircraft carrier' in the Pacific Islands. While Allied forces could not be regarded 'as sufficient to meet this menace', the Australian Squadron would be able to maintain Australian trade. Unless he meant the coastal trade alone, and even in respect of coastal trade the submarines and aircraft would have posed risks, it was not at all clear that the Australian squadron of light cruisers and destroyers had the capability required. When Curtin asked whether cruiser attack could do great harm to Western Australian shipping, Colvin assured him it could not 'in view of the 9.2-inch battery at Rottnest', a judgement which surely overlooked the possibility that Japanese cruisers would decline to operate within its range.

When the War Council reconvened later that evening Spender said more about his visit to Singapore. He said there were 'little or no land defences' on the Malayan Peninsula, though it would be very difficult for an attacking force to penetrate through the jungle. He concluded that 'the general picture regarding Singapore was not good'. He thought 'it would be very difficult to defend against a heavy major attack, which would probably come from the rear' (as the British Far

Eastern Command expected, the Japanese planned, and as, indeed, happened).

Curtin wanted to rebalance Australia's war effort from the Middle East to the Pacific. Evidently unaware that Menzies had offered the 8th Division for Malaya two months earlier, Curtin interjected that Australia should 'reinforce Singapore instead of sending troops to the Middle East'.[3] Spender then 'divulged information' that a brigade group was on its way to Singapore. Curtin thought more troops should be sent to Singapore, and perhaps to New Caledonia as well. Defending the Government's stance, Fadden said the British chiefs of staff thought the Singapore conference conclusions on the defence of Singapore 'were unduly pessimistic' but that 'the present weaknesses of the land and air forces in the Far East were fully recognized and that everything possible was being done to remedy the situation, having regard to the demands of theatres which are the scenes of war'.

Curtin and his colleagues on the War Council had now been advised there was a good chance Japan would come into the war within months. That kind of advice would usually be associated with a developed scenario of how, when and where the Japanese would attack. In this case, it was not. (Fred Shedden was travelling with Menzies, so the War Council discussion was less coherent than usual.) The War Council did not, for example, discuss Japan's problems in operating freely without first incapacitating the United States navy, whether or not the United States was already in the war. Colvin grossly and almost flippantly underestimated the likely form and size of the Japanese naval force. Curtin thought or found it convenient to suggest the unlikely possibility that a Japanese attack on Australia might be a priority as a propaganda weapon – principally for Germany. The War Council considered the real possibility of imminent war with Japan and discussed publicly disclosing the gravity of the situation, without initiating an urgent assessment of what Australia needed to do to meet an attack. The only strong response was to look to Britain. Australian political and strategic thinking about Japan, including Curtin's, was still undeveloped and uninformed in the early months of 1941.

Pressed by Curtin, the War Council agreed to issue a statement to bring the position 'nearer home' to the public. The agreed statement asserted that 'all members of the Council realize Australia, equally with the Empire as a whole, is now entering upon a period on which its very existence is at stake'. A 'maximum effort' was required from 'all sections of the community'.

Though issued under Fadden's name as Acting Prime Minister, the statement was urged at Curtin's suggestion and with the concurrence of the non-government members. As would become more apparent in coming months, Curtin was now assuming a national leadership role – one uncontested and probably encouraged by Fadden.

In his account of these events of February 1941, the official historian, Paul Hasluck, suggested Curtin was deliberately creating a crisis atmosphere in Menzies' absence. Curtin, in Hasluck's view, had thought over the Japan threat during his break in January, and returned to work convinced it was more serious than he had formerly supposed. Hasluck thought the declaration of a crisis was aimed at strikes on the coalfields. Hasluck may be right about Curtin, but the record clearly establishes that the sense of crisis was brought on by the Government rather than the Opposition. It displays Menzies' Army Minister Percy Spender volunteering to the War Council on 5 February 1941 his view that Japan would attack within three months – well within the time Menzies expected to be travelling abroad. Spender's views corresponded to those of Army Intelligence, finalised formally a few days later but presumably already communicated within the military leadership. It is also possible that, in Menzies' absence, Spender was playing his own game. He was a Sydney King's Counsel, a rival of Menzies and ambitious to lead the UAP.

Speaking to an Australian Workers' Union conference on 11 February 1941, Curtin publicly developed his argument that Japan was under German pressure to launch an attack in the Pacific, with Australia an objective. He also expounded his case for a forward defence in Malaya, implicitly at the expense of further commitments to the Middle East. 'If Britain should be most heavily pressed,' he said, 'it would be in the interests of both Germany and Italy to endeavour also to press heavily on the outer parts of the British Commonwealth of Nations.' Australia was as vulnerable as Great Britain, a theme Curtin would develop. His party accepted an obligation to 'resist invasion, raid or attack'. In particular, 'we must see to it that there are land forces available so that there is no back door entrance to Singapore'. He did not demand 'the recall of any of our men already abroad' but he did insist that 'the paramount principle in the reorientation of the Australian military, naval and air forces shall be the defence of this part of the Empire'.[4]

His language was designed to block criticism. Defending Australia was defending the British Empire. Curtin's conception of the defence of Australia now extended to Malaya, a line of thought pressed by London and accepted by Menzies. Singapore's danger was its 'back door'. In the deployment of additional Australian forces Malaya should have priority over the Middle East. His approach paralleled the conclusion affirmed by the chiefs of staff a few days later.

Accused of creating a false scare, Fadden and Curtin had good reasons for alarm. Though Spender did not then publicly reveal it, there was very much more to the sense of crisis in January and February 1941, and to the judgement that Japan might go to war in three months. In London and Washington, too, there had been 'a momentary scare'.[5] On 27 January the UK Ambassador to Japan, Sir Robert Craigie, had reported a widespread feeling that the crisis was at hand. Three days later there was a report from Ottawa that the Japanese Government was commandeering Japanese merchant vessels. On 6 February, British intelligence reported, Japanese officials in London had been told to prepare to leave at short notice. Churchill speculated that recent German mining of the Suez Canal was designed to test the effectiveness of the action in blocking a British navy move into the Red Sea to oppose Japan. The Dominions Office cabled Australia about a heightened alert on 11 February, and the following day British commanders were warned to make unobtrusive precautions against Japanese attack.[6] On 15 February 1941 Churchill shared his concerns in a cable to Roosevelt, suggesting Japan might be planning a move south. Australia was most open and public about the scare, but Fadden's and Curtin's concern was widely shared.

By the time the War Council next met eight days later in Sydney there had been more troubling signs of Japanese war preparations. Australian intelligence reported that the Commonwealth Bank had received a number of applications for withdrawals by Japanese women leaving Australia. It also reported that a Japanese shipping company had asked all except essential employees in Sydney to return to Japan. The Dominions Office cabled that Japan might have already decided to push southward, even if it meant war. Another Dominions Office cablegram reported the landing of Japanese troops north and south of the British colony of Hong Kong. Australia was copied a message from the British chiefs of staff to naval commanders-in-chief that 'there are a number of indications pointing to aggressive action by the Japanese in the near future which may involve us in war with them'.[7] Curtin and Fadden had not invented the alarm.

The 13 February 1941 War Council discussion focused more clearly on Japan's likely strategy. To attack Singapore Japan would probably go through Malaya, and to go through Malaya Japan would find it useful to have a foothold in Thailand. The government of Thailand was appealing to Britain and the United States to resist pressure from Japan. Neither had offered any worthwhile support. Spender said Thailand had 'found herself literally forced into the hands of the Japanese'.

Everything, they now agreed, depended on the United States. Curtin thought that Japan might attack Hong Kong, hoping to avoid war with the United States. In remarks revealing a clear understanding of the priority the United States would give the war against Germany, he said that if Japan attacked British positions in the Far East, 'eventual American intervention was probable' but 'should the war show signs of going against us she might, in the first instance, concentrate on strengthening Britain in the Atlantic and help to get back the outposts of the Empire later'. Curtin may have had Hong Kong in mind, though Australia might also be considered an outpost of the Empire. The transfer of American naval forces from the Pacific to the Atlantic in these circumstances would be 'disastrous to Australia.' (This transfer was under discussion in Washington, prompted by increasing British merchant shipping losses and the possibility Britain could be invaded. In mid-May Roosevelt would order one-quarter of the Pacific fleet to the Atlantic.[8])

It was therefore an immediate priority, Curtin said, that naval forces at Singapore be strengthened, and Australian air defence be brought to the 'utmost efficiency'. It was clear in his mind that 'if we were drawn in we must stand alone for the time being'. Curtin rightly understood that 'Even if America intervened immediate assistance would not be available'. He urged Fadden to conduct a test mobilisation of Australian defences because 'whatever the cost, strain or provocation, a test mobilization would show our determination to withstand the enemy'. He thought 'all sections of the community would stand fully behind the government' if it declared an immediate test mobilisation.

Behind closed doors Curtin was demonstrating an increasing grasp of the broad strategy then being debated in Washington and London. He was evidently aware of at least the outlines of the Germany First doctrine, agreed in secret discussions in Washington between United States and British military staffs around that time. On 8 February 1941, the Australian naval attaché in Washington, Commander Henry Burrell, had cabled that a conference between military staffs of the United States and Britain had agreed Europe would be the decisive theatre, if Japan entered the war.[9] Fadden may have shown the message to Curtin during a War Council meeting.

Fadden and Spender may have hoped Labor would develop a higher sense of anxiety about Japan, and this might reduce strikes. But to declare an immediate mobilisation of Australian defence forces, even if just a test, was something else entirely. Spender demurred, saying he already had plans in hand for a partial test mobilisation. Curtin repeated his suggestion, however, requesting – apparently in written and formal form – that War Cabinet put Australia on a 'war footing'. He also wanted the 'leaders of industry' to be given some of the information seen by the War Council that morning. Fadden was reluctant either to call a test mobilisation or brief industrial leaders but the War Council agreed that in view of the 'menacing attitude of Japan', plans for 'a mobilization of the Armed Forces of Australia should be taken in hand so that Australia could be put on a war footing immediately the necessity should arise'.[10]

Curtin proposed a press statement. After some discussion, however, the War Council agreed his draft 'might create a panic'. Fadden and Curtin worked up another draft which was released to the press that evening. It included Curtin's phrase from his earlier draft: 'the war has moved to a new stage involving the utmost gravity'.

With no further Japanese moves to support it and with a sceptical note entering the press reporting of the War Council, the new mood of 'utmost gravity' was hard to sustain through the Australian summer. By late February 1941, the perceived crisis was over. Elements of Australia's 8th Division had arrived in Singapore on 18 February. Meeting in Sydney on 28 February, the War Council reached the highly improbable conclusion that 'the press statement made by the Council after its meeting of February 13 . . . combined with the despatch of a brigade of Australian troops for service in Malaya, had been effective in staying the hand of Japan in regard to any southward penetration she may have had in mind'.[11]

Writing to Elsie on 3 March 1941, Curtin summarised his thinking over the month of crisis. It is clear from the letter that he understood that Japan would join the war when the opportunity offered, that the United States would give priority to the Atlantic, and that Australia ought to defend itself as far forward as it could.

My Dearest,

The weather map in the paper today shows a big depression in your nor'west . . . Maybe Perth may get a big rain by the time this reaches you & give a good break-up for the summer. It was very sultry here yesterday & on Saturday.

I enclose a cheque for £100. It will keep the home fire glowing for a while.

Our war news is not good. The attacks on shipping are constant and serious. Another convoy of 14 boats has been knocked about with heavy losses. The squeeze economic is on the old country. Bulgaria has joined the Axis and the road from Berlin to Greece & Turkey opened up. Japan is ready & waiting the day of maximum opportunity. This is dependent on how Britain stands up & on the Japanese reading of the USA policy. My own view of America is that Gt Britain & the Atlantic Ocean mean much more to that country than does Australia & what is called Oceana. And that means Australia would be mad not to exert the maximum precautions in and on all the stepping places & approaches to ourselves.

I am well. I send you my love, pride & gratitude for what you have been & are. Keep your heart glowing my beloved.

Your loving husband

John[12]

Curtin's mind had turned to forward defence, to the 'stepping places and approaches to ourselves'. By now, so was the thinking of the Australian chiefs of staff. When the Singapore-based head of the British Far East Command, Sir Robert Brooke-Popham, flew in for discussions with the Australian chiefs of staff in February 1941, they had already concluded that Japan was a substantial threat. They wanted to reinforce Australia's 'outer line of defence'. They wanted air bases, but the air force rightly refused to have air bases without army protection. The army reluctantly agreed to send a battalion group to Rabaul. It also agreed to hold in reserve similar formations for Ambon and Timor should war be imminent. Both were foreign territories, which could only be invested with the permission of the colonial authority. The chiefs agreed the 8th Division not be sent on to the Middle East as earlier planned. It should be held in the 'Malaya – Australia area'.[13]

(2)

The alarm raised by Fadden and Curtin embarrassed Menzies. He had gone to London ostensibly to press for British support for Singapore. He found there growing antagonism towards Japan, particularly in the Foreign Office. Britain supported Roosevelt's hardening line as Japan moved south into Indo-China. If war between Japan and the United States brought the United States into the war against Germany, Churchill's grand strategy would be fulfilled. Australia, on the front line of a Pacific war, saw the situation differently.

Menzies was of two minds. Travelling to London, he cabled Fadden a line should be drawn, beyond which Japan would risk war with the British Empire if it moved further south.[14] Arriving in London he suggested a more accommodating attitude towards Japan, while at the same time urging more war resources for Singapore. The alarming statements from Fadden and Curtin did not quite fit what he now saw as his mission – especially since, if the crisis were genuine, he ought to be in Australia to manage it.

Churchill was reassuring. When Menzies attended the British War Cabinet for the first time on 24 February, Churchill told him Japan had no aggressive intention towards Australia. He said the British Ambassador in Tokyo agreed.[15] Churchill had other things to discuss in that meeting, most importantly a campaign in Greece to be led by Australian and New Zealand troops.

Speaking in London on 3 March, Menzies said 'we aimed and are aiming at getting nearer to Japan. We are not aiming at sitting suspiciously in our corner.'[16] The remark was directed at the British Foreign Office, but was taken also as a rebuke to Fadden and Curtin. Yet in a cable sent from London on 12 March, Menzies told the Australian War Cabinet that they should not rely on Churchill's undertaking to cut losses in the Mediterranean to come to Australia's aid – or, at least, that it was unlikely to be prompt. Troops – including the three Australian divisions in the Middle East – would have to be withdrawn, and shipping arranged for the purpose. It would be 'unwise to delude ourselves regarding the immediate dispatch of a fleet of capital ships to Singapore'.[17]

(3)

Criticised for creating a false scare, Fadden convened a secret session of Parliament on Wednesday, 12 March 1941. It was the same day Beasley announced to the House that his group had once again rejoined the Labor Party. So sour was the mood in Parliament and so divided the views within the three main political parties that some members from all three objected to having a secret session at all. On the Labor side, Arthur Calwell, Eddie Ward and Frank Brennan complained that secret sessions were designed to prevent them publicly debating the issues. Brennan refused to attend the proposed session. On the government side, John Perkins from Eden-Monaro complained that, if the secret session was like the last, 'we shall only be wasting our time'. The Country Party's former leader, Archie Cameron, agreed with Perkins. The following day Ward said in open session that the 'grave warning' issued by Fadden and Curtin was a 'hoax'. Curtin adamantly insisted, 'I stand by it today.'[18] He was used to Ward.

In his speech to the secret session Fadden recounted most of the intelligence warnings presented to the War Council, and added two pieces of information which would have resonated with Curtin and his colleagues.[19] The first referred to an 8 February meeting between Roosevelt and the new British Ambassador to the US, Lord Halifax. While the United States would declare war on Japan if its own possessions were attacked, Roosevelt was reported as suggesting, it would not if the Japanese attacked only the Netherlands East Indies or British possessions.

Fadden's next point demonstrated that the Germany First doctrine was well known to the Australian Government, and presumably now to the Australian Parliament. He said that 'even if the United States were to be involved in war with Japan, it was felt that to fight an active war in the Pacific would mean a dangerous diversion of forces and material from the main theatre of operations which, in American opinion, was the Atlantic and Great Britain'.

When War Council met in February, Fadden recalled, 'we were at the greatest danger point we had reached since the beginning of the war'. It was 'impossible' to tell the Australian people what he had just told honourable members but the War Council had wanted to give warning that:

> a new stage in this terrible war had been reached and that this
> new stage brought with it a distinct possibility of fighting,
> if not on our own soil at least near our shores. Nothing has
> happened since those meetings of the War Cabinet and the
> Advisory War Council to change that outlook.

Fadden acknowledged that despite the alarming news, there was no British fleet on its way to Singapore. Echoing Churchill he told the secret session that 'it would be folly to have too many units idly standing by to meet the possibility of a threat to Singapore'. However, 'in the event of Japan entering the war against us we are assured by the British Government that an immediate redistribution of Naval Forces would be made should the threat to our communications in the Pacific and Indian Oceans be relatively greater than that in the Atlantic' – a formula his audience should not have found at all reassuring. The military plans, Fadden said, did not envisage the active intervention of the United States. Marking a more determined shift to a forward defence of Australia, Fadden said Australia was developing or strengthening defence positions at Rabaul, Port Moresby, the Solomon Islands, Darwin, Thursday Island and Nauru.

For senators and members in the secret sitting, the disclosures were gravely disturbing. Army Minister Percy Spender told them Australia's home defences were so weak a Japanese armoured division could advance from one end of the country to the other without serious opposition. Curtin later recounted that he noticed the member for the Riverina, Joe Langtry, eagerly taking notes of this highly sensitive information. Well known mostly for his dramatic renditions of 'The Man from Snowy River', the description of the Japanese armoured division rolling across Australia's deserts caught Langtry's attention. 'That's good, very good,' he told Curtin. 'It's something new to tell my branches in the Riverina.'[20]

(4)

When Fadden spoke of American concern about a 'dangerous diversion' of forces to the Pacific from the Atlantic in the event of war with Japan, and its disinclination to fight an 'active war' in the Pacific against Japan, he was referring to secret discussions in Washington between British and American defence officials.

The Australian Legation in Washington had already reported on the 8 February discussion between Roosevelt and Halifax.[21] Roosevelt left it doubtful that the United States would come into a war if Japan attacked only Malaya and the Netherlands East Indies. Importantly for the Australians, he also said that even if it were involved in war with Japan, the United States would have to fight a 'holding war' in the Pacific rather than divert resources from the Atlantic. The American position that Germany would have to be beaten first had been worked out some time before Roosevelt's discussion with Halifax.[22] It had been agreed by Roosevelt and the American military leadership in November 1940, and later in staff talks between the American and British military leadership.

From mid-February 1941, when the telegram arrived, the Australian War Cabinet had reason to be despondent about the likelihood of American involvement if Japan attacked south – though this message would change. Whatever Roosevelt said, it was difficult to believe the United States could stand by if Japan threatened to seize Indo-China, Malaya and the oil wells of the Netherlands East Indies, or that Japan would attempt to do so while the United States Pacific fleet was capable of intervening. But the proposed priority for the Atlantic was entirely credible. Curtin was probably not informed of the detail of these cables, but he understood it was the United States (and British) position.

Some of the detail was worked out during Anglo-American staff conversations in Washington from late January through to March 1941.[23] At these staff conversations, designated as ABC-1, there was no disagreement between the British and the Americans over the priority to be accorded to the war against Germany. But there was a good deal of disagreement over other issues of considerable strategic interest to Australia. The British claimed to be tied up in the Mediterranean and wanted one carrier and four cruisers from the United States

Pacific fleet sent to Singapore.[24] The United States refused, arguing that Singapore was not all that important. The Americans said that in the event of war with Germany and Japan, the United States would not be able to prevent the Japanese from taking the Netherlands East Indies, the Philippines and Malaya. They also argued that the conquest of Singapore did not necessarily mean Australia or India would be cut off from Allied support. When the talks concluded in March there was some gesture to the British position, with the United States agreeing to move some ships from the Pacific to the Atlantic.[25] This would in principle allow the British to augment its naval forces in the east. The conclusions were incorporated in the new United States Rainbow 5 war plan in May 1941.

It was an important discussion for Australian Pacific War planning. According to a later account by Shedden, Curtin was not informed of what came to be called the Germany First agreement. He was, however, certainly aware of the general idea that priority would be given to the war against Germany. On 7 February, the Australian naval attaché in Washington, Commander Henry Burrell, advised the Australian Chief of the Naval Staff, Sir Ragnar Colvin, that the British view in the ABC-1 talks was that the policy should be to 'defeat the Germans and Italians first and then deal with Japan'. The material was shown to Fadden on 13 February.[26] An immediately following cable mentioned the weakness of the US Pacific fleet. As Paul Burns points out, Fadden may well have shown the cable to Curtin at the 13 February War Council meeting, which would explain some of Curtin's remarks.[27] Shedden later claimed that Curtin was unaware of the ABC-1 agreements. But Shedden was with Menzies, and may not have been aware of what Fadden had shown to Curtin or revealed to Parliament. Curtin showed understanding of the 'Germany First' doctrine in his letter to Elsie on 3 March 1941. He had listened to Fadden's secret speech. So long as Fadden had followed the written text, Curtin would have understood the key point.[28]

(5)

While Fadden and Curtin anxiously pondered Japan's intentions, Menzies was drawn into Churchill's most hapless wartime scheme. In late February 1941, Menzies, then in London and attending the British War Cabinet, told Fadden that the British Government wanted two Australian divisions then deployed in the Middle East to help Greece fight Italian forces and an expected attack by German forces.[29] The British War Cabinet, he told Fadden, 'is unanimously in favour of the enterprise'. Menzies thought political arguments for supporting Greece were strong, and he said he was impressed with the military argument that enemy bases in Greece would threaten the British position in the Middle East.

Despite his earlier personal reservations, Menzies was evidently finding Churchill difficult to resist. 'It may help you in your discussion,' Menzies confided to Fadden, 'if I tell you most secretly that I spent the entire weekend with Churchill, that he has been in closest communication with Roosevelt via Hopkins.' Churchill had told Menzies that 'if Japan goes to war against us America will unquestionably come in'. If Australia was attacked and America was not in, adequate naval reinforcements would be despatched to Australian waters. With these private assurances, Menzies thought 'we should concur' in the proposal to use the Australian divisions in the Greece expedition.

The clear implication of Menzies' communication to Fadden was that Australian agreement to the Greece campaign was in return for an assurance of 'adequate naval reinforcements' if Japan entered the war and America did not. Yet this cable to Fadden was only a couple of weeks after an earlier Menzies cable telling Fadden not to rely on British assurances of naval support. Churchill's private assurances about American intervention were at odds with Halifax's report of Roosevelt's views, of which Churchill would have been well aware, and which Fadden had earlier disclosed in the secret session of the Australian Parliament. Menzies would certainly have been aware of it. Why Menzies credited these new assurances, if Churchill indeed gave them, was not clear. Australian and British reports from Washington around the same time made it plain the United States would not go to war with Japan if only British colonies were attacked.

Menzies was then unaware that on Saturday, 22 February 1941, three days before his cable to Fadden, British Foreign Secretary Anthony Eden in a meeting in Athens with the Greek Government had committed Australian and New Zealand troops to the defence of Greece. The meeting presumably occurred on the same weekend Menzies was staying at Chequers. When he discovered in early March that Eden had already committed the Australians, Menzies was not pleased. He would have been less pleased if he had known that Churchill's military advisers strongly opposed the Greece campaign, and supported the view of the Middle East command that it should instead finish the destruction of Italian forces in North Africa.[30] Nonetheless, Menzies agreed to deployment of the Australians, and secured the agreement of War Cabinet in Australia.

In late March and early April Australia's 6th Division was deployed to Greece, along with the New Zealand 2nd Division and a brigade of a British armoured division. The Germans then invaded Greece in overwhelming force. Like the Gallipoli campaign, another Churchill project in which Australian troops based in the Middle East were landed on the Aegean shore, the Greece campaign proved to be a very bad idea. Without air cover, facing armoured German divisions, the Allied landing in Greece was defeated in two weeks. It so weakened the British position in North Africa that General Erwin Rommel was able to drive the British out of Libya and into Egypt. It was a political calamity for Churchill, and for Menzies.

(6)

Despite the private assurance from Churchill he sent to Fadden, Menzies had no success in London in winning a guarantee of British navy support. In late February the Dominions Secretary, Viscount Cranborne, reiterated a promise of one battle cruiser and aircraft carrier for Singapore, if necessary.[31] That was as good as it got. Menzies would have been disappointed in a meeting with the Vice-Chief of the Naval Staff, Admiral Sir Tom Phillips, in early March. Perhaps posing as a devil's advocate – or perhaps prompted by Bruce – Menzies asked Phillips what were the plans for the Commonwealth forces in the Middle East if, as Churchill had promised, circumstances arose in which the British fleet abandoned the Mediterranean to sail to the Far East. Surely the troops – including three Australian divisions – 'could not just be left to their fate'.

Phillips said bluntly Britain would not go to war if Japan occupied the Netherlands East Indies. Evidently weary of it all, Menzies said 'in the general reference to reinforcing our position in the Far East with capital ships we have only been deluding ourselves', which had, indeed, been so for decades. Ominously, Phillips told Menzies that he 'would have no hesitation in engaging the Japanese fleet with 60 per cent of their number of British ships'.[32] Later that year Phillips commanded HMS *Prince of Wales*, a modern battleship sent with the battle cruiser HMS *Repulse* to Singapore. In the event, Phillips had no chance to engage a Japanese fleet. In a reckless sortie without adequate air cover *Prince of Wales* and *Repulse* were sunk off the coast of Malaya by land-based Japanese aircraft. Phillips went down with his ship.

Brooke-Popham underestimated the quality of the Japanese air force. Phillips underestimated the quality of the Japanese navy. Both would pay a heavy price for underestimating Japan's war-fighting capabilities. The British higher command shared their illusions. Evidently responding to questions about Singapore's defences posed by Menzies, the British chiefs of staff concluded in April that the 'majority of the 450 shore-based aircraft which the Japanese can marshal against us are of obsolete types, and, as we have said, we have no reason to believe that Japanese standards are even comparable with those of the Italians'. The British were seeking Buffalo aircraft from the United States which would 'probably prove more than a match for any Japanese aircraft'.[33] Menzies claimed to have stood up to Churchill in the British War Cabinet, and been the only person around the table to do so. Perhaps so, but he did not get what he came for, and agreed to the use of Australian troops in a foolish military campaign which ranked among Churchill's greatest errors of judgement.[34]

(7)

Curtin was becoming convinced that Japan would move south and Singapore's naval strength had to be reinforced. He had moved to support a forward deployment to Malaya. By late March 1941 he had reached the conclusion that the threat from Japan was sufficiently serious to warrant return of Australian troops from the Middle East. It was an important change, if not in his thinking then in what he was prepared to say in front of his political opponents on the War Council. He could be – no doubt would be – portrayed as abandoning Britain in its Middle East fight against Germany and Italy, to guard against an attack in the Pacific which might well not occur.

Curtin approached the issue cautiously. Discussing the findings of another Allied conference in Singapore in the previous month, Curtin told his colleagues at a 26 March meeting of the War Council that the 'defence of Australia and New Zealand must, in the present international position, be regarded as of paramount importance'. It followed that 'serious consideration should therefore be given to the return of some, if not all, of our troops from the Middle East'.

He reminded Fadden non-government members had recommended earlier in the year that Australia should not undertake any additional commitments in the Middle East.

Four days later Rommel began a counteroffensive in the Western Desert, sweeping the Allied troops back and leaving Australian troops besieged at Tobruk. At the same time the 6th Division was being hurled from Greece. Discussion of withdrawing the Australians from the Middle East for a time ceased.

(8)

Curtin and Beasley had been working towards readmission of the Beasley Six to caucus.[35] In March 1941 they returned, their reappearance in caucus coinciding with four days of caucus uproar in seven successive meetings.[36] The challenges came from the existing radicals of the party rather than the newly readmitted Beasley group. They included Ward, Reg Pollard, Bert Lazzarini and Rowley James.

On Tuesday, 11 March Ward moved in caucus that Labor withdraw from the War Council, and that it move no confidence in the Menzies Government the following day in the House. During a five-hour debate in the caucus room Curtin was stridently attacked by Ward and his allies. Curtin had collaborated with Menzies. Curtin had joined with the Government in condemning strikes. It was noisy and rancorous, but Curtin had the numbers. When contested, Curtin's procedural ruling in the debate was upheld by thirty-four votes against twelve.[37] Compared to the Budget negotiations vote the previous year, Curtin had more supporters and fewer opponents, suggesting that Beasley and his group were now in the Curtin column. Ward persisted, and Curtin pounced on him with equal truculence. Ward leaked stories to the newspapers, Curtin alleged. Ward had been observed talking to reporters. Ward was disloyal to the party. Curtin's long run of by-election successes, his trenchant arguments in the House, commanded caucus respect. Even so, it was apparent to Curtin that caucus was impatient for government.

After a difficult session, Curtin left for Perth on 9 April. He would remain until 25 April. While he was in Perth Menzies sent a cable from London offering an all-party government. Returning by train from Perth, Curtin met the Governor-General, Lord Gowrie, at Port Augusta on Saturday, 26 April. Gowrie thought Australia ought to have an all-party government in time of war, as Britain did. If it was pressed on him by Gowrie, Curtin was unmoved. With caucus support Curtin rejected Menzies' latest offer.[38]

The murmuring did not stop. On 10 May Curtin was forced to publicly deny a breach with Evatt and Beasley, and a challenge to his leadership. By the end of the month he was seriously unwell. He spent over two weeks, from late May to 12 June, in bed in Melbourne, recovering from pneumonia. Later in June he had to issue a public declaration that he was not planning to resign the leadership on health grounds. He and Menzies were both struggling with opponents in their own parties.

CHAPTER 17

PREPARING FOR GOVERNMENT

(1)

Menzies returned to Australia on 24 May 1941. He had travelled 42 000 miles, 36 000 of them by air. He had been in the Middle East for twelve days, and in Britain for ten weeks. He had also visited Ireland, Canada, the United States and New Zealand. It was, he said, 'the most valuable experience of my life'. Despite repeated refusals, he had hoped to win a firm British commitment to send a fleet to Singapore in the event of war with Japan.

After nearly four months of talks, however, the 'only definite commitment remained the dispatch of a battle cruiser and an aircraft carrier to the Indian Ocean'.[1] (The British had already agreed this with the Americans, part of the bargain in which the United States would deploy more ships to the Atlantic.) Menzies had committed Australian troops to Greece. By the time he arrived in Australia the battle for Greece was long over, with Allied troops defeated with heavy losses. With their British and New Zealand allies, the remaining troops of the 6th Division were making a fighting retreat from Crete under heavy German attack. Though Allied troops fought well against vastly superior German forces, the campaign had been a military calamity. Nearly four thousand Australians had been captured, wounded or killed during the campaign.

Menzies had also hoped the British would agree to a dominion representative in an Imperial war cabinet – preferably himself. Churchill did not agree. Nor did the Canadian Prime Minister, Mackenzie King, or the South African Prime Minister, Jan Smuts.

Construe it as he might, Menzies' mission had not only failed in its ostensible objective of securing a British naval commitment, but also associated Menzies with the military disaster of the campaign in Greece and Crete. His remarkable self-confidence was intact. He loftily complained of how disheartening it was to return to Australian politics. He was decidedly cool to Fadden, whom he left alone at the airport after a ceremonial welcome home. Fadden would remember it.

Menzies had spent three weekends with Churchill and delighted in his company, but after the Greece disaster he did not care to remark on his intimacy with the British leader. He could not easily relinquish his ambition to be the dominion representative in the British War Cabinet, though he had found support for it nowhere except among Churchill's Conservative Party enemies, and his resentful advisers. Maurice Hankey, the former Cabinet Secretary, supported Menzies' ambition, and persuaded Halifax in Washington to support Menzies as the dominion representative in the War Cabinet.[2] When Menzies left London, Churchill's principal military assistant, General Ismay, wrote to Brooke-Popham that Menzies 'went down very well over here, and there was a large body of opinion which hoped that he might stay as a permanent member of the War Cabinet'.[3] On Menzies' behalf, Fred Shedden was more ambitious. 'Radical as it may sound, why should not a Dominion statesman lead the Empire in war?' he asked his diary.[4]

Travelling home through Canada in May, Menzies formally wrote to Mackenzie King, Jan Smuts of South Africa and Prime Minister Peter Fraser of New Zealand proposing the leaders of the four self-governing dominions press for an Imperial war cabinet in London, which these leaders would attend. None agreed. Churchill told him the other dominion prime ministers would not agree to one of them representing the others in an Imperial war cabinet.[5] In Canada, Menzies found Mackenzie King unhelpful. King divined that Menzies had himself in mind as the representative. It may or may not have been in Menzies' mind, but if he had been the dominion representative in the War Cabinet, if something happened to Churchill, would he not have to be considered among the candidates to succeed him? After all, as he told Mackenzie King, Churchill might go anytime.[6] Menzies would again press the proposal, cabling Smuts and King on 3 July.[7] Again they would refuse.

Back home, Menzies found his own party fractious, and Curtin increasingly confident. Among the Labor leaders only Evatt was still pushing for a national government, drafting a two-page letter to Menzies. Evatt appeared to be offering to serve under Menzies. This letter was probably not sent; even so, Curtin may have heard about it.[8] The letters Evatt did not send are far more interesting than those he did.

Speaking to the War Council on 28 May 1941, Menzies said that in attending the War Cabinet in London he had been 'somewhat disturbed at the manner in which this body worked'. He did not consider there was 'an effective cabinet as ordinarily understood'. This was 'owing to the personal domination' of the Prime Minister, who directed war strategy. 'The only discussions on strategy that were originated by anyone' other than Churchill, Menzies claimed, were raised by Menzies himself. Mentioning Lloyd George's support for his proposal, Menzies said the War Cabinet needed dominion representation, not least because 'Mr Churchill has no conception of the British Dominions as separate entities . . . the more distant a problem from the heart of the Empire, the less he thinks of it.' Churchill was not interested in war finances, and had told Menzies that he 'never did understand sums'. Menzies had 'the lowest opinion of the efficiency of the Foreign Office', particularly its 'utterly negative' attitude to Japan and 'resignation to the inevitability of a conflict'.

Curtin disliked flying, preferring the train. His journey from Perth to Canberra could take five nights and four days, half of it travelling across his home state of Western Australia. Curtin was attached to his travelling rug, which was acquired for his visit to Geneva in 1924.

John Curtin with his parents outside their home in Creswick, Victoria. He was born there in the previous year, 1885.

John Curtin in his twenties, leading the 'life that thrills' in the Victorian Socialist Party.

Curtin found some contentment by moving to Perth and marrying Elsie Needham. In this 1922 photo he poses with Elsie and the two children, also named Elsie and John.

Curtin in his 'planter suit' with Elsie and children in the garden of their Cottesloe home, 1927. The following year he would be elected to federal parliament on his fourth attempt.

Source: National Archives of Australia

The 'temporary' Parliament House, Hotel Kurrajong, the public service East Block and much bare ground, in 1926, two years before Curtin's arrival in Canberra.

Source: National Archives of Australia

Curtin in the front row of the Federal Parliamentary Labor caucus in 1929. Though he had performed well in Opposition, he was passed over for the Labor ministry, which came to office in 1929.

James Scullin, Labor leader and Prime Minister from late 1929 to early 1932, voted against Curtin as his successor but later became a warm supporter.

Curtin and Frank Anstey, his early political mentor, fought against the policies of both the Scullin government and the Opposition in the troubled Labor caucus of the Depression.

While the Scullin government tore itself apart during the Depression, Japan invaded Manchuria. Within a decade Japan's war on China led to the Pacific War.

Curtin as the unexpected Leader of the Opposition, 1935.

The Curtin family's California bungalow in Cottesloe, 1939.

United Australia Party
Prime Minister Joe Lyons.
His ministerial colleagues
derided his intellect but
he successfully controlled
a factious government
and won elections.

Prime Minister Robert Menzies took Australia to war in September 1939, a decision supported by Curtin and the Opposition. When France and Holland fell, in May 1940, the Dutch and French colonial empires in the Pacific were left unprotected against Japan. After Dunkirk, Britain was preoccupied by the threat of German invasion.

Following the knife-edge 1940 election Curtin and his senior colleagues joined the Australian Advisory War Council. To Curtin's right is Francis Forde, to his left Robert Menzies and Billy Hughes. The War Council would be Curtin's school of government.

Country Party Leader Arthur Fadden (middle row, centre) became Prime Minister when Menzies was ousted in August 1941. A little over a month later Curtin won a confidence vote in the House of Representatives and Labor took office with Curtin as Prime Minister.

The Curtin government was sworn in on 7 October 1941. To Curtin's right sits his Treasurer Ben Chifley and Jack Beasley, his Minister for Supply and Development. To his left are Governor-General Lord Gowrie, Minister for Army Frank Forde, and the Attorney-General Herbert Evatt. Expected to be short-lived, the cabinet faced the Japanese onslaught in the Pacific eight weeks later.

Curtin convened his first Cabinet meeting soon after the government was sworn. Challenging then, Curtin's job would soon become much harder.

Source: JCPML 00376/115

In November, the month following his appointment as Prime Minister, reporters discovered, to their surprise, that Curtin made decisions quickly and acted without hesitation.

Source: JCPML 00004/24

Source: JCPML 00139/30

Within months of taking office Curtin and Treasurer Ben Chifley had asserted Commonwealth authority over the central bank and prepared plans to monopolise income tax for the federal government. These changes would profoundly alter Australia.

Source: Chronicle, Alamy

In the surprise attack on Pearl Harbour, Japanese planes damaged or sank seven battleships of the US Pacific Fleet. Hours earlier, Royal Australian Air Force planes had attacked Japanese transports landing troops near Kota Bharu in north-east Malaya.

Governor-General Lord Gowrie signs the declaration of war on Japan, watched by members of the Australian War Cabinet. The declaration followed those from Britain and America.

During an ill-timed visit home in January 1942, Curtin found himself isolated in Perth as Japan invaded Rabaul, the first Australian territory to be attacked.

The fall of Singapore confirmed Curtin's warnings of Britain's unpreparedness for war against Japan.

After taking Malaya and Singapore, Japan invaded Java.

As Japanese troups moved south, Curtin warned Australians that 'every human being here is henceforth at the Government's service, and every material thing in the country can be diverted to war purposes at the government's direction'.

By March 1942 Curtin feared that Japan would follow its conquest of Singapore, Java, Rabaul and north-east New Guinea with an attack on Port Moresby and an invasion of Australia.

His explained that his speech in London was to counter that view and urge serious discussion with Japan, not to argue for appeasement of Japan.[9]

At a War Council meeting in Melbourne on 5 June, Curtin was clearly influenced by Menzies' account of Churchill's style. He said that too many decisions were taken in Whitehall that should be taken in the field. He also wondered if it would be better to close the Suez Canal, scrap the African Empire, and try to hold Palestine. Menzies replied that if the fleet left the Mediterranean the Germans could go to the Persian Gulf and ultimately to India. Menzies did not emphasise that this was the same fleet Australia was asking to come to its assistance in the event of war with Japan.

Meeting his War Cabinet colleagues on 10 June, Menzies told them 'it is now evident that, for too long, we readily accepted the general assurances about the defence of this area'. On the question of a fleet, the British chiefs had replied, 'All we can say is that we should send a battle cruiser and a carrier to the Indian Ocean. Our ability to do more must be judged entirely on the situation at the time.' If they did abandon their Mediterranean interests, the British chiefs pointed out, the fleet would have to remain 'until the end in order to cover the withdrawal of the armies'.[10]

Curtin's concern over Churchill remained. With Australian and other Allied troops forced out of Greece and Crete, rolled back in the Western Desert, besieged in Tobruk, and with the occupation of Syria mainly by Australian troops only beginning on 8 June, the British position in the Mediterranean was dire. Meeting in Melbourne on 12 June to discuss the Middle East, Curtin told the War Council he was concerned about the priority Churchill gave to the Mediterranean. Curtin was probably unaware, as the whole Australian Government and its High Commissioner in London were unaware, that the British chiefs were also bothered by Churchill's emphasis on the Middle East.

As the War Council met, British newspapers were running front-page stories about the German troop build-up on the borders of the Soviet Union and Soviet-occupied Poland. Hitler was either planning to invade, the papers suggested, or perhaps demand control of Soviet oilfields. British intelligence had known for some time of the impending German invasion of the Soviet Union. Operation Barbarossa would begin ten days later, on 22 June.

Preoccupied with a German attack, the Soviet Union would no longer pose a threat to Japan. Curtin told the War Council the 'impending German-Soviet crisis' might help Japan decide its course of action. He was also concerned that in a battle Britain might lose its Mediterranean fleet. Japan might take a decision 'regarding the Netherlands East Indies'. He asked again whether it would not be better to evacuate the position in the Mediterranean 'before a severe defeat was inflicted on us'. He thought Churchill was prepared to fight in the Mediterranean 'regardless of cost' and to the prejudice of the capacity to defend communications – including in the Indian and Pacific oceans.

The threat from Japan was uppermost in his mind. He thought it ought to be met as far forward as possible. Curtin said the War Council could not leave out of account 'the possibility of having to put Australian forces into the Netherlands East Indies'. He said 'a losing fight in the Middle East was an open invitation to Japan to attack the Netherlands East Indies'. After the lessons of Greece, Curtin said he wanted Churchill's assurance that adequate air power would be provided in the Middle East. Curtin referred again to a March War Council decision that Australia could not provide more troops for the Middle East, given the Malayan situation.[11]

Earlier, on 4 June, Menzies had submitted to War Cabinet a review of Pacific defence informed by his visits abroad. The tone was decidedly glum, the purpose exculpatory. Britain had written down the aircraft requirement for Burma, Malaya and Borneo from 582 to 336, saying this 'would give a fair degree of security'. The actual number in the command was 118, including three Australian squadrons. Menzies claimed astonishment at the weakness of the British and Commonwealth position in the Far East, about which he had known all year.

The review lacked what was then most needed: a rethink of strategy, based on reality. Menzies claimed it was only at the Singapore conference towards the end of 1940 that the 'Australian representatives discovered the weakness of the local defence position in Malaya. It is only recently that the real situation in regard to a fleet for the Far East has become apparent.'[12] The latter assertion was certainly untrue.

At a War Council meeting the following day Curtin explored the possibility of reaching agreement between Japan and Australia.[13] It was a weirdly errant trajectory. Australia could hardly reach an agreement with Japan independently of the United States and Britain, and then hope to sit out a war between the major players. Nor could it assist in reaching agreement between Japan and the United States or Britain, since it was insufficiently informed, had no mandate from its allies, and was anyway too tiny a player. Avoiding the issue of whether Australia could or should attempt to reach agreement with Japan independently of the United States and Britain, Menzies replied that such arrangements depended entirely on the Japanese. At the time Curtin was having discussions about the prospects for peace with the Japanese minister in Australia, Tatsuo Kawai. The War Council affirmed it had no objection to him continuing his discussions. Menzies perhaps hoped to set Curtin up for a tumble.

Much was behind closed doors, but much was also public. Speaking in the House in June, Curtin said that instead of being a bastion for Australia, the Singapore base 'would become merely a service station for the enemy'.[14]

Following the German invasion of the Soviet Union, Churchill was quite clear about his priorities. They were the defence of the United Kingdom, the struggle in the Middle East, and supplies to the Soviet Union. 'Last of all,' Churchill wrote after the war, was 'resistance to a Japanese assault'. He thought that if the Japanese came in, so would America. If America did not, Churchill saw he had no means of defending the Dutch East Indies 'or indeed our own Empire in the East' in any case. He remained prepared to sacrifice the Middle East 'if Japan invaded Australia'.[15] Quite how that could be done in time and with sufficiently overwhelming naval force (and without abandoning British and Australian troops in the Middle East) remained unspecified. Even if it was clear to Churchill, it was not at all clear to Curtin or Menzies.

(2)

It was becoming harder for Curtin to keep Menzies in office. He had refused Menzies' offer of a national government in April. As Menzies stumbled and his internal party opponents became more openly hostile, the Labor caucus grew impatient. On 27 June Curtin defeated another caucus motion supported by Ward to oppose Menzies in the House on the Budget, or before it was brought down.[16] Parliament then rose for the winter recess, the stability of Menzies' government unresolved.

Leaving Canberra on Tuesday, 1 July, Curtin travelled home to Cottesloe. He would remain in Perth until early August, gratefully living in his own home, sleeping in his own bed, eating at his own table with Elsie, and Grandmother Needham. He attended some local Labor meetings, gave a few speeches, strolled with Kip along the Cottesloe waterfront. Free of caucus and its troubles, free of urgent War Council business, free of the demands of the House, he had time to think. Though not entirely free. On 28 July he had to deny he planned to resign the leadership because of poor health. 'My health is very much better than that of many of the defenders of Tobruk,' he told reporters. 'They are not talking of giving up, neither am I.'

While Curtin was in Perth, German troops sliced through the Soviet armies. Japan and the United States moved towards war.

(3)

Annoyed by British and American help for China, by the middle of 1941 the Japanese army and navy had resolved their dispute over a southward thrust. A Tokyo Liaison Conference of the army and navy on 12 June 1941 decided to occupy southern Indo-China as a tentative first move. This would provide airfields closer to Malaya. After Germany attacked the Soviet Union ten days later, the decision was confirmed. An Imperial Conference in Tokyo on 2 July approved the southward advance and resolved that the Japanese Empire would not flinch from war with the United States and Britain, if necessary.[17]

By this time, United States signals intelligence had broken a Japanese diplomatic code. Three days after the Imperial Conference, United States Secretary for War, Henry Stimson, informed Roosevelt of its decisions. When on 12 July the Japanese presented an ultimatum to Vichy France requiring bases in southern Indo-China, the Americans again intercepted it. Even so, Roosevelt hoped to avoid or at least postpone war in the Pacific. As he wrote on 3 July, 'it is terribly important for the control of the Atlantic for us to help keep the peace in the Pacific. I simply have not enough Navy to go around – and every little episode in the Pacific means fewer ships in the Atlantic.'[18]

Japan's move into southern Indo-China demanded a response from Washington. A year earlier the United States had imposed mild sanctions on Japan. Pressed for harsher action by members of his cabinet, Roosevelt had for some time been warning that cutting off oil supplies to Japan would cause it to seize the Netherlands East Indies. At an 18 July cabinet meeting Roosevelt began by repeating this view, and then agreed to two new sanctions. Exports of oil to Japan would be cut off, and Japanese assets in the United States would be frozen. It was a momentous decision, and one that was soon joined by Britain, Australia and the other dominions.

The following day United States intelligence decoded a 14 July Japanese cable indicating that the move into southern Indo-China prepared the way for conquest of Singapore and the Netherlands East Indies.[19] On 20 July, the United States and Britain announced the new sanctions. They cut off three-quarters of general trade and nine-tenths of Japan's oil imports. Japanese assets in Britain, the United States and the dominions were frozen. By August all oil exports to Japan were banned. As Roosevelt had earlier warned, the sanctions had the effect of speeding up rather than slowing down Japanese preparations to seize the Netherlands East Indies oilfields. Undeterred, Japanese forces landed in southern Indo-China on 28 July. The following day a Vichy–Japan pact gave Japan eight airfields in Indo-China.

Once tighter sanctions were imposed in July 1941, the clock was ticking. The key was oil. As Japan's wartime Prime Minister General Hideki Tōjō later observed, oil was needed in war and 'in the end, came down to 'the matter of the Netherlands East Indies'.[20] Both Japan and the United States saw this. Roosevelt told the Japanese Ambassador in Washington that if Japan attacked the Netherlands East Indies it would 'immediately mean war with Britain' as well as the Dutch authorities, and, with respect to the United States, 'an exceedingly serious situation'.[21] Australia would have been alert to Japan's predicament, since Australia's petrol supply was drawn from the oil of the Netherlands East Indies.[22]

(4)

In Perth, Curtin followed the dramatic developments as best he might through the newspapers. In Canberra and Melbourne, Menzies and his ministers were better informed. The Australian Government had access to important secrets. Some of the American intelligence from its Magic code-breaking device was shared with British and Australian intelligence. By early July the Australian Government knew that the Japanese had decided to occupy southern Indo-China.[23] Richard Casey followed up on 9 July, reporting to

Menzies a conversation with Sumner Welles, Acting Secretary of State during Cordell Hull's absence.[24] Welles 'believes that secret information available and the known concentration of Japanese naval forces make it evident that the Japanese have decided on a southward expedition probably in the next fortnight'.[25]

Menzies shared some of the information with the Opposition, but not all. He guardedly told a meeting of the War Council on 16 July that 'various indications had been received pointing to an early move by Japan'. Opinions differed 'as to whether it would be north against the Soviet Union or south against Indo-China'. A Japanese move into Indo-China 'might not cause war' but it 'would have very sharp repercussions short of war, and it would be probable that economic and financial sanctions would be imposed by the United States'.[26]

CHAPTER 18

CURTIN TO POWER

(1)

Japan had moved into Tonkin in 1940 and into southern Indo-China in July 1941. It was threatening to move into Thailand.[1] Each move south brought its airfields closer to Malaya. By mid-1941 Churchill wanted Roosevelt to join him in drawing a line against further Japanese advance. With the United States Senate reluctant to go to war, Roosevelt had no intention of joining Churchill in such a public statement. Britain and Australia then had to ponder whether they were prepared to draw a line against Japan without United States support. That would mean war with Japan if it continued the southward advance. But since the British could not send a fleet, or provide sufficient planes to meet even the minimum requirement for the defence of Malaya, or deploy armies of size sufficient to intimidate Japan, it was quite clear that the British Empire could not go to war with Japan without America.[2] That was the reality, even if the British Government might pretend otherwise. At this point and long beforehand the United States was deciding strategy towards Japan, and Britain had no choice but to support Washington. Step by step, Roosevelt was preparing for war in the Pacific.

For some years the United States had planned to abandon its position in the Philippines at the outbreak of a war with Japan.

In July 1941, US Army Chief of Staff General George Marshall reversed policy, deciding instead to defend the islands. Roosevelt appointed General Douglas MacArthur, then in the Philippines, commander of United States Army Forces in the Far East. He also commanded the Philippines army. Heavy bombers capable of reaching Japan from the Philippines were sent to MacArthur's new command. Roosevelt's appointment of MacArthur signalled an intention to meet Japan. So, too, the deployment of the B-17 long-range bombers. To support the new command Australia agreed to construct airfields at Darwin, Townsville, Rabaul and Port Moresby for American planes flying between the Philippines and Hawaii.[3]

By the time Curtin returned to the eastern states in early August 1941, the threat of war in the Pacific had much increased. Through August and into September Curtin hoped war with Japan would be averted. Attending a War Council meeting in Melbourne on 6 August, Curtin listened as Menzies briefed on Australia's response to the sanctions imposed by the United States and Britain. Churchill was seeking a joint statement with the United States warning Japan against going into Thailand, Menzies reported, but 'no clear statement had evolved so far'. Menzies was not pleased with the United States. He 'could not describe the position as satisfactory'. The United States would not make any statement before the Japanese entered Indo-China but had 'taken drastic action' after it. Of course, he added bleakly, it was 'important to keep in line' with the United States.[4]

Menzies supported Churchill's proposal that the United States should warn Japan. There was a difference in objectives between Britain and Australia which Menzies was slow to see. Churchill would welcome war between Japan and the United States. If the United States went to war with Japan, Churchill rightly surmised, it would probably find itself at war with Germany as well.

Australia did not want a war with Japan at all. Its finest troops fighting in the Middle East, its home army poorly equipped, without a formidable air force or tanks or adequate artillery, and in all probability without the protection of a British fleet, Australia was forced to a different view from that of the British Government. Japan could not attack Britain and probably not the continental United States. It could certainly attack Australia, and dominate its region. A year earlier Australia had no better defence plan than surrender, if Japan was unobstructed by a hostile fleet and able to threaten an invasion. After a year of grave warnings, by mid-1941 the forces Australia could immediately deploy against a Japanese attack were not much more formidable than they had been in the middle of 1940, and a British fleet for Singapore had been clearly and repeatedly denied. Britain had an interest in encouraging the United States to take a stronger stand against Japan. Australia did not.

Perhaps influenced by his discussions with Tatsuo Kawai, the Japanese minister in Canberra, Curtin had a more sympathetic understanding of the Japanese point of view. He was also determined to avoid Australia being drawn into a war with Japan without United States support, and with Britain unable to help. This led him by early August to place a charitable interpretation on Japan's motives, and miscalculate the chances for preventing war. Like Menzies, he urged negotiations with Japan. He was reluctant to decide in advance the line beyond which Japan's advance would mean war with Britain and Australia. He thought there was a division of opinion in Japan, and that the Japanese believed their action in Indo-China was legitimate because it had been agreed by the Vichy government.

Curtin's analysis was elaborate, hopeful, and not well informed. He told the War Council that Japan's move into Indo-China was 'based on pressure by Hitler to give some token of her adherence to the Axis', with the implication that without German pressure Japan would not be extending its military reach. He said that Japan was 'still susceptible to a face saving arrangement'. There should be frank talks to ascertain if a solution was possible. He thought that 'Hitler was aiming to involve Japan, the British Empire and the United States in a naval war in the Pacific, and if this happened he would turn south, towards Suez. The effect of such a war on the battle of the Atlantic was not hard to see.'

Curtin argued the Australian Government should suggest to Britain 'the wisdom of British ministerial consultations, with or without the United States, with the Japanese government, in an attempt to delimit by agreement the expansionist policy of Japan'. Crucially, Curtin was sceptical of the military strength of the United States. 'Support by the United States,' he said, would not be 'as great as the Japanese opposition', presumably meaning that Japan would be more formidable in the western Pacific than the United States. He later added that if Japan came into the war American naval forces 'might not be sufficient to preserve the lines of communication between Australia and the Middle East and to safeguard our shores'. He said he was 'not confident of fighting power in the U.S.A.'. He thought that American strategy was 'founded on the protection of jumping-off places which were an advantage to them in their own defence and which it was essential to deny to an enemy'. If necessary, therefore, 'Britain and Australia should take up the matter alone with Japan'.[5]

Influenced by his discussion with the Japanese minister, Curtin was now right out of his depth. Germany's encouragement or discouragement did not have much influence on Tokyo's decisions. Sensibly enough, British policy was now to work closely with the United States, which deployed a battle fleet in the Pacific far more powerful than anything the British navy might be able to spare. Now that oil sanctions were biting, Japan's military leaders thought they must either seize the Netherlands East Indies or withdraw from the war in China. There was no possibility of reaching agreement with Britain alone to stop the push south. With Britain or Australia, Japan had very little to discuss – though it would no doubt seize any opportunity to split its probable opponents. Like Menzies, Curtin was slow to grasp that Japan and America would decide whether there would be war in the Pacific. Britain was an onlooker, as was Australia.

Curtin sensibly wanted to avoid any situation in which Britain declared war on Japan without United States backing, leaving Australia to bear the brunt of the Japanese response. If war with Japan was considered to be inevitable, he said, 'we should bring pressure on the United States to knock Japan out now'. But if not, 'we should not be pushed into war when it is to our great prejudice in other theatres'. He wanted a 'frank discussion' with a view to drawing a 'chalk line to mark the limits of Japan's southern advance'. But to draw the line before talks 'would be to prejudice the possibility of a satisfactory discussion'. To Hughes' objection that no arrangements with Japan could be taken seriously, Curtin responded that the Anglo-Japanese Treaty indicated the trustworthiness of the Japanese word, as did the treaty with the Axis. But if Hughes was right, 'The AIF should return to Australia from the Middle East.'

Now a member,[6] Evatt brought to the War Council a pertinacity it had lacked. Was 'the occupation of Thailand by Japan', he asked, to be considered 'grounds for war'? Government members thought it would be dangerous to act without the United States, a view with which Evatt agreed.

Curtin concluded a discussion he had dominated by instancing the AIF position in the Middle East and the 'large supplies' Australia was sending overseas while 'faced with the prospective entry into the war of Japan, which will be active in areas in which we are vitally interested'.

Curtin said the United States would not move until the Netherlands East Indies was attacked by Japan. He thought the Japanese blow would fall on Siberia and that Japan's threat to the south was an attempt to immobilise Australia's cooperation with the other parts of the British Empire in the war against Germany and Italy. The United States might ultimately come in, but in the meantime enormous damage would have been done by Japanese raids. The AIF would be away from the country and a state of affairs would arise which would be politically unmanageable. It was a puzzling and strangely round-about argument, but the end point was that even if Japan did now attack the Soviet Union, as many suggested, it could still raid south to Australia. The AIF in the Middle East should be brought home.

(2)

Preparing for war with Japan, Roosevelt agreed to meet Churchill in early August 1941. Conferring on battleships in Placentia Bay, Newfoundland, on 9 and 10 August, Roosevelt was charming, easy, hospitable and elusive. Churchill wanted an alliance against Germany. Judging the power of isolationists in the Senate too great to defy, Roosevelt refused even to discuss one. If not an alliance against Germany, Churchill at least wanted a joint ultimatum to Japan.[7] Roosevelt refused that too. He did say, however, that while the United States would not go to war with Japan if it went into Thailand, it would be a different matter if it attacked the Netherlands East Indies.[8] Since Roosevelt had told his cabinet that Japan might well invade the Netherlands East Indies if the United States banned oil exports to Japan, it was a significant shift.

The American–British staff talks in February 1941, had reached useful understandings and the Placentia Bay meeting now reached others. An alliance between Britain and the United States was developing. Even by the first half of 1941, however, the United States had no substantial army or air force. Its navy was formidable but barely adequate for the jobs assigned to it in the Pacific and the Atlantic. United States army offensive strength was 'still close to zero'[9] as the official history later recounted. It would not be until early September 1941 that Roosevelt's 'Victory Plan' for an enormous expansion in the United States armed forces and weapons production would be finalised.

To Churchill's surprise, Roosevelt at Placentia Bay produced for agreement a statement of principles very distant from those for which

Churchill stood. The British were asked to agree to 'respect the right of all people to choose the form of government under which they shall live', or at least agree to issue a declaration to that effect. They also agreed to trade 'on equal terms'. The Atlantic Charter was issued on 14 August 1941, and widely reported in Australia. The world was shifting. The price of American goodwill was agreement to principles quite at odds with the old Empire rules. An actual alliance might require Churchill to be still more accommodating of Roosevelt's views.

(3)

Informed of the forthcoming summit, which coincided with the threatened Japanese move into Thailand, Menzies had cabled congratulations to Churchill on 8 August.[10] The meeting should discuss American and British strategy in the Pacific. At Bruce's urging, Menzies suggested Churchill and Roosevelt 'clarify the Far Eastern position'. On Sunday, 10 August, Menzies cancelled plans for a speaking tour and called a Cabinet meeting for Melbourne the following day. Formally, the main agenda item was policy to be adopted if, as Menzies later told the War Council, 'Japan should invade Thailand'. The real agenda was Cabinet agreement that Menzies again go to London. His government troubled by division, his leadership attacked, his slender parliamentary majority threatened, it was Menzies' last card.

Following the meeting Menzies floated to reporters the idea of returning to London.[11] He and Fadden met Curtin on the night of Monday, 11 August, also in Melbourne. The Menzies Government now depended on Curtin and the Opposition. Menzies wanted agreement that he could again visit London to plead for help against Japan, remaining Prime Minister while abroad. Following the caucus battles of early March and again in June, Curtin should have been wary of agreeing with Menzies. Evatt, Makin and perhaps Forde had signalled to reporters covering the 6 August War Council meeting that they were impatient to take office.[12] Curtin had returned from Perth the previous day and remained publicly silent. Beasley was said to back Curtin. As so often, Beasley's authority as the leader of the New South Wales group in caucus was considerable. Too cautious, too impressed by Menzies' insistence that in London he could make a difference, convinced that Japan and Australia could soon be at war and that Australia's security depended on holding Malaya, Curtin let himself be persuaded. Puzzlingly, Curtin does not seem to have consulted his colleagues on Menzies' request, and was unprepared for the unanimity of their response. It was one of the few times he lost touch with his senior colleagues' views. He would not make the same mistake again.

The War Council met on Thursday, 14 August in Melbourne, the same day Roosevelt and Churchill issued the Atlantic Charter. Menzies opened by briefing on Japan. London and the dominion governments had been discussing a declaration by the British Empire 'or preferably, by the British Empire and the United States'. He emphasised that the 'highest degree of secrecy' must be maintained on these discussions between Empire governments. Cabinet, he said, had earlier concluded that Britain should send capital ships to Singapore to deter Japan, but the commitment of the British navy to the Battle of the Atlantic 'appeared to preclude this'. Japan should be told that an attack on Thailand 'could not be disregarded'. It was 'essential', said Menzies, that this view should be accepted by the British Empire 'and the United States'.[13] If Singapore was Japan's next objective, Menzies thought it would be 'better to oppose her in Thailand rather than wait until she had been allowed to consolidate her position'.

So far the discussion had not moved far beyond that of the previous War Council meeting. Japan should be told that further southward advance meant war, but the Menzies Cabinet and the Labor Opposition agreed that the United States would have to join an ultimatum before it could be issued. Menzies now announced a

startling view. Agreement with the United States was 'important',
he acknowledged, 'but if the concurrence of that country could not
be obtained, the British Empire should make this statement alone'.
Evatt asked the obvious question, the same question he had asked
eight days before: did this mean that if Japan attacked Thailand,
Australia would go to war? Menzies replied that 'such was the case'.
Evatt then asked whether the Empire would go to war without the
United States. Menzies said the answer was yes, 'provided the United
States did not object'.

This was a weird irruption in Menzies' thinking. He was acknowledging that the British fleet was committed to the Atlantic and the
Mediterranean, and at the same time saying the British Empire should
issue a declaration guaranteeing Thailand's independence. If Japan
attacked Thailand, the Empire would go to war – if necessary, without
the United States. Preoccupied elsewhere, Britain would be of no help.
Menzies was proposing to commit Australia, unaided, to war against
Japan. This proposal was surely either a subterfuge, or reflected what
may well have been a complete misunderstanding of Japan's capacity
for war. If a subterfuge, it was to justify Menzies' proposed visit to
London rather than to Washington.

Having responded to Evatt, Menzies seemed to change tack. He
said New Zealand had advised that the Empire should survey its
capacity before acting. He then added that Churchill and Roosevelt
had been conferring about a joint statement, a reference to the
Placentia Bay meeting. Menzies had emphasised to Churchill that
the Far East was important and 'should not be regarded as something
subsidiary' – a wild misreading of Churchill's actual position. It also
nearly exactly foretold a phrase Curtin would use not many months
later. He said the statements were to be made on war aims and on a
proposed neutralisation of Thailand and withdrawal of Japan from
Indo-China. (In the event, they were not made because Roosevelt
would not be drawn into what was effectively an ultimatum to Japan.
The Atlantic Charter did indeed cover the first point, but Roosevelt

did not agree to Churchill's request for a strong joint position on Japan.)

According to the War Council record, Curtin had been 'in consultation' with Menzies during the Cabinet deliberations earlier in the week. Whatever goodwill Curtin had found in earlier discussions with Japanese diplomats had vanished. He now found they had an 'intimidatory attitude' regarding the necessity for Japan to break up the American, British, Chinese and Dutch powers in the Pacific. He said it was important to have a capital fleet in Singapore or a United States fleet in the Philippines. It would be unwise, he said, 'to make any threat to Japan without the power to carry it out'.

Menzies then read out the telegram he had sent to Churchill on Monday, 11 August.[14] During his London visit Menzies had told the British Government that Australia would join a British guarantee to the Netherlands East Indies against attack from Japan, if necessary without American support.[15] Menzies had now told Churchill the Australian Government believed the 'British countries' should tell Japan 'any attack on Thailand by Japan' would be regarded as a cause of war with the British Empire – with or without American participation. He mentioned Australia assumed that, in the event of war with Japan, Britain would send a fleet to the Far East with 'a nucleus of five capital ships'.

It was an extraordinarily reckless cable. It invited Britain to threaten war with Japan at a time it was already at war with Germany and Italy. It did not have the ships and planes in the theatre to counter Japan or any prospect of sending them. Evatt immediately pointed out that Cabinet had threatened war, without consulting the War Council. Beasley, Forde and Makin supported Evatt. Contradicting Evatt, Curtin said that the cablegram 'stated the views that had been put forward by non-Government members of the Council over a period'. It was then agreed that the War Council should be consulted before any decision or communication was made by the Government which might involve Australia in war.

Menzies then revealed his plan. He told the War Council his Cabinet had requested him to go to London as prime minister 'to represent the Commonwealth to the United Kingdom War Cabinet'.

The case for visiting London only four months after returning from his last visit was not in the least compelling. In agreeing, Curtin had made an astonishing misjudgement. Menzies' demand for a fleet at Singapore had been rejected last time, and nothing had changed to make it more likely now. So, too, Churchill had refused to send to Malaya the planes the command required. In his visit Menzies had, as he freely said, obtained nothing. He had instead been gulled into agreeing to deployment of Australian troops in Greece. If war with Japan was imminent, there was much to be done in Australia to meet the threat. Menzies' place was to remain home and direct it. If he was visiting abroad, by mid-1941 it was surely more useful to visit Washington than London.

For Menzies the visit would serve two purposes. The first was to return him to London and the high sphere of wartime decision-making. The second was to avoid a vote on his leadership by either his own party or the House of Representatives. He had presumably discussed with Curtin reports of the meeting between Churchill and Roosevelt, and stressed the growing danger from Japan. It may have been part of Menzies' calculations that if he could hang on as prime minister until a Pacific war began, it would be very hard for either his party opponents or Curtin to then dislodge him.

Menzies' rationale was unconvincing. He had lost support as party leader, and everyone knew it. As soon as he proposed the visit to London, Forde objected. He said the Prime Minister's duty should be discharged in Australia. Curtin immediately contradicted his deputy. He said the Council had long been dissatisfied with Australian representation in London, where there was 'a lack of recognition in some quarters of the vulnerability of Australia'. In what would prove to be a recurrent theme he said that there 'appeared to be an inability on the part of United Kingdom ministers, which might be quite reasonable from their angle, to see the War through Australian eyes'. He was agreeable to the Prime Minister going abroad. In an implied rebuke of Forde he said that 'the paramount consideration' was 'the safety of Australia'. This consideration 'separated the conduct of the war from every other consideration in the political sphere'.

Forde's most striking characteristic, in the memory of Hazel Craig, was that he wanted everyone to like him. That Curtin was in conflict with the amenable Forde showed how seriously Curtin had lost touch with caucus sentiment. That Forde was contradicting his Leader also showed how unconvincing Menzies' arguments were. In losing authority within his own party, Menzies was also undermining Curtin within his.

Evatt also disagreed with Curtin. It was left to Makin to bring the discussion back to earth by saying he doubted Menzies had the confidence of Parliament, and this would be determined at its forthcoming meeting. Among his Labor colleagues, Curtin was now on his own. It was a serious lapse of judgement of his colleagues' views, and of the case for Menzies to visit London.

Menzies gave some examples of issues on which his presence in London had been useful, including the appointment of Blamey as Deputy Commander-in-Chief, Middle East. As to the 'possibility of proceeding to London in any other capacity than that of Prime Minister', Menzies said that 'the representation of Australia could not be satisfactorily carried out by a deposed Prime Minister'. Evatt voiced the point that Menzies would therefore wish to go on the condition that he not be deposed – which was, indeed, Menzies' intention.

Curtin said that 'the façade of a united country' was necessary, as it would have a 'great influence' on Japan and the United States. He thought granting supply would enable unity to be maintained for the 'next few vital weeks'. Somebody should be in London to speak for Australia.

Evatt and Curtin clashed again, and this time openly, on the tactical questions that divided caucus. Evatt said that he was 'not prepared to act on the assumption that the present government would continue for the duration of the war'. Curtin said he was not in favour of an early election since 'public opinion was fully reflected in Parliament'. To Fadden's ambivalent comment that the 'present position is an intolerable one for the government', Evatt promptly replied that it was 'equally so for the Opposition'.

The 14 August War Council was the apogee of Curtin's willingness to permit Menzies to remain prime minister through to the 1943 election. It was obvious that Curtin's position was untenable, as was Menzies'. In supporting Menzies' second request Curtin was fighting not only his own party, but Menzies' party as well. It was the last time he would differ with his senior caucus colleagues on such a fundamental issue of political strategy.

(4)

Events moved swiftly.[16] On Wednesday, 20 August Menzies told the House that his Cabinet had asked him to 'to pay another visit to London', but he would not go without 'the approval of all parties'. Even at this point Curtin was offside with his own colleagues, supporting an unrecorded, private session of Parliament to discuss the proposed visit, in the face of opposition from Ward, Evatt and Rosevear. When caucus met the following day, 21 August, the issue was no longer in doubt. It resolved to oppose the visit. Menzies' place was in Australia. When, later that day in the House, Menzies moved he be sent abroad, Labor voted in opposition. Curtin's belated refusal to support Menzies' plan initiated the crisis that would make Curtin prime minister six weeks later.

Menzies' tactics were perhaps too transparently artful. Recognising that his support was draining away he tried shock tactics. When the

Labor caucus refused on 21 August to support his visit to London, Menzies called a Cabinet meeting.[17] He told his colleagues he had come round to the view that he should resign – and advise the Governor-General to send for Curtin. His colleagues were aghast. He implicitly posed their alternatives as sticking with Menzies, or accepting Curtin as prime minister or – much worse – a general election in which a good many would lose not only their ministerial jobs but also their seats. By way of explanation, Menzies told them, 'it was better to have Labour in without an election and under circumstances which enabled us to control them from the Opposition benches than after an election at which they would probably have a sweeping majority and go back for a three year term'.

Compared to the equally dismal alternatives of an immediate election or a Curtin government, the idea of again offering a national government was attractive – not least because, if indeed an election was unavoidable, it would give the Government an issue on which to fight it. It was unanimously approved by Cabinet. Most if not all members would have known Curtin and his colleagues would not join an all-party government, and for many of them that was perhaps the point. Menzies then proposed it in a letter to Curtin the following day, Friday, 22 August, and released it publicly.

It was a sign of Menzies' desperation that he offered Curtin half the seats in Cabinet as well as the prime ministership. The Labor caucus executive discussed it on Friday, and held a decision over to caucus on the following Tuesday. Most newspapers – Menzies sadly recorded – saw it merely as a tactical exercise.[18] 'Labor unlikely to accept offer of national government', *The Argus* headlined on Saturday, 23 August, noting unkindly that, in making an offer certain to be rejected, Menzies had at least given himself something on which he could fight an election.

No doubt Curtin was aware Menzies might contemplate this option. In the 1940 election Menzies had made an issue of Curtin's refusal to join a national government. Curtin thus had to tread cautiously between the radicals of his party seeking to destroy the coalition government as soon as possible, and the very lively possibility that Menzies would go to an election as prime minister, warning of imminent war with Japan and portraying Labor as the wrecker of national unity.

Curtin scheduled a meeting of the parliamentary party executive and caucus for Tuesday, 26 August. The executive met in the morning, with caucus scheduled to meet at 3 p.m. There could not be much doubt about the outcome. Curtin had frequently reiterated his refusal to join a national government. Even those like Evatt, hungry for office, would prefer to be a powerful minister in a Labor government than to jostle with Menzies and others in a coalition. Caucus unanimously endorsed Curtin's reply, refusing to join an all-party government, and advising Menzies to resign as prime minister.

Two days later Curtin made one of the big gambles of his political career. The House would reconvene at 2.30 p.m. on Thursday, 28 August. Rightly suspecting Evatt would press in caucus for an immediate no-confidence vote in the House, Curtin called a meeting of the parliamentary party executive. Convincing his colleagues that the only thing that could now prevent Labor coming to power was a premature and unpredictable challenge in the House, he persuaded the executive that no attempt should be made by Labor to defeat the Government in the current session.

When caucus met later that morning Evatt was locked in. Curtin had made it clear he would resign his party's leadership if it forced a confidence vote in the House before the end of the session. Disregarding the threat, Calwell moved for immediate action. As with similar resolutions in March and June, Curtin won thirty-five votes, the radicals fifteen.[19] The rest were prepared to wait until the Budget session.[20] Ward recorded that he was for the challenge.[21] His list of those against includes Curtin and Evatt, and many of the former Lang group including Beasley and James.

Decades later Calwell was still indignant. Recalling the 28 August caucus meeting, he wrote he had moved the resolution to challenge the Menzies Government and try to bring it down 'at the solicitation of Dr Evatt'. But Curtin heard of it and opposed it at the party executive, so when it came up in caucus Evatt voted against it. 'Curtin,' Calwell wrote, 'took a long time to forgive me.'[22] Sticking with the strategy of letting the Government collapse rather than be seen to force it out, Curtin kept his grip on caucus. In his private record of his fall, Menzies noted that in the Labor caucus 'Shrewd counsels prevailed'.[23]

At 9.30 p.m. on Thursday Menzies announced his resignation as prime minister to a meeting of the UAP. The Country Party was called in and Fadden was unanimously elected as leader of the joint parties. The following morning Menzies visited the Governor-General and advised Gowrie to send for Fadden.

Weakened by the strain of the last month and suffering in the Canberra winter, Curtin left for hospital after the 28 August caucus meeting 'to seek treatment for a chill'. He was well enough to announce to the House on Tuesday, 2 September that 'we are ready to govern'. It was a momentous announcement. It meant that when it was presented Labor would move to amend Fadden's Budget, and if possible bring down his government. Curtin was ready – but the time was not yet ripe. The left had pressed for the early destruction of Fadden. At a meeting on 21 September the Federal Executive backed Curtin.[24] He would choose the moment.

Throughout his time as prime minister, Menzies and Curtin had been cordial. After his resignation Menzies wrote to Curtin as 'My dear John', thanking him for his 'magnanimous and understanding attitude'. Curtin's personal friendship, he wrote, was 'a pearl of great price'. Replying to 'Dear Bob' the same day, Curtin thanked him for 'the consideration & courtesy which never once failed in your dealings with me'. Menzies' personal friendship 'is something I value, as I hope and know you do, as a very precious thing'.[25]

Despondent about Australia, Menzies hoped to find a seat in the British House of Commons. Lord Gowrie tried for him in October. Churchill refused, courteously but firmly replying that Menzies was too valuable where he was. British High Commissioner, Sir Ronald Cross, himself a Conservative member of the House of Commons, tried for him early the following year, also without success.[26]

(5)

With Menzies, Curtin had a courteous relationship. With Fadden, Curtin had a warm and easy relationship. An accountant from central Queensland, Fadden was astute, amiable, honourable and without Menzies' offending assumption of superiority. Decades later Fadden would write that Curtin was the greatest Australian leader of Fadden's time, a judgement that notably reflected on the prime minister he would serve as Treasurer and Deputy Prime Minister during the long years of Menzies' post-war political success.

Earlier in the year Curtin and Fadden had collaborated in dramatising the threat of war with Japan. By the beginning of September, war was much closer than either Fadden or Curtin supposed. In London, Churchill took a cheerful view of Pacific affairs. Cabling Fadden on 31 August, Churchill told him the risks of war with Japan had diminished. 'Events about Japan seem to have taken a favourable turn in the last month,' Churchill wrote, linking it to the 'hard line' he claimed he had persuaded Roosevelt to adopt. America was now negotiating with Japan. The Soviet Union was also taking a hard line, and Japan had problems in China. In a war the Japanese 'would thus have about three quarters of the human race against them, and I do not wonder they are placed in deep anxiety and hesitation. I cannot believe the Japanese will face the encounter now developing around them. We may therefore regard situation not only as more favourable but as less tense.' The more tangible news was that 'the growth of our battleship strength' will 'make it possible in the near future for us to place heavy ships in the Indian Ocean'. Churchill again assured the Australian Government that 'we shall never let you down if real danger comes'.[27]

As prime minister Fadden chaired the next War Council meeting on 2 September, with Menzies now attending as his Minister for Defence Co-ordination. Reviewing the Far East, the War Council welcomed the American negotiations with Japan. They agreed with Churchill that it was useful to gain time 'so long as there were no further encroachments by Japan'.[28] Council members agreed time was running more in favour of the Allies than Japan. The Battle of the Atlantic, for example, was improving.

They also agreed on one central point: if there was war with Japan, the United States and not Britain would be the principal antagonist. As the minute recorded, 'The results of the discussion between Mr Churchill and President Roosevelt have now established the United States as the spearhead of opposition to Japan, with United Kingdom support.' This was a big change in Australian understanding. It had taken a while, but both Curtin and Fadden now recognised that the key decisions would be made in Washington.

Even now, however, they still pressed for a fleet for Singapore, and sent a Cabinet representative to London to plead for support. The United States was the spearhead, and in a war it would be Japan's main enemy. But as the Australian leaders now knew, the United States doubted the importance of Singapore and regarded Malaya as entirely a British responsibility. If Curtin and Fadden thought that Singapore was important for Australia's defence, and if Singapore had to be defended in Malaya, then Australia's safety could still be influenced by decisions made in London.

That, anyway, was how things must have seemed in early September of 1941. Curtin himself had over the last year or so become an advocate of 'forward defence' in Malaya. His idea presumably was that even the chance that a British fleet could use the base would be enough to convince the Japanese they must take it before moving further south and that, fighting in Malaya, Australians would be fighting with British and Indian allies. There did not seem to be a discussion at that point of how the troops could be brought out if there was no British fleet, and Japan controlled the seas. The brilliance of Japan's war-making was not then imagined.

Meeting ten days later in Canberra, the War Council members remained optimistic that war would be averted. Menzies had declined Fadden's request he go to London. Sir Earle Page, the Minister for Commerce, would go instead. Discussing his planned visit Page said he thought Japan could be deterred if Singapore had sufficient naval and air strength. His objective was to persuade Britain to provide it. Curtin shared Page's view. He linked the presence of Australian troops in the Middle East to London's willingness to send additional ships to Singapore. The degree to which Australia could 'participate in the overseas war effort' depended on the resources needed for local defence. Therefore, Curtin concluded, 'the strategy of the war insofar as it affected Australian cooperation depended on the presence of capital ships at Singapore'.

Curtin added that a recent discussion he had had with the Commonwealth Bank 'indicated the need for a reconsideration of the war effort'. In the bank's view, evidently, Australia's resources were strained. Choices needed to be made. In Curtin's opinion the war effort should now be limited to the existing AIF divisions, the present commitment to the Empire Air Training Scheme, and existing naval forces. The fact that Curtin and the bank had such a discussion at all underlined a growing expectation that Labor might shortly become the government. It is unclear, but the comment may also suggest Curtin was not at this point seriously expecting war in the Pacific or could not imagine its scale. When it happened, it would call for a vastly greater war effort and the views of the Commonwealth Bank would be immaterial.

When the Council met again a week later, on 19 September, the mood was even brighter. Fadden presented cables exchanged with Churchill who had raised the possibility of sending capital ships by the end of the year. Churchill's message that 'we shall never let you down if real danger comes' was 'noted with satisfaction'.

The Fadden Government's parliamentary support, however, was about to be tested.

Curtin had declared that Labor was ready to govern. It was now only a matter of waiting for Fadden to produce the Budget, which would test his strength in the House. It made for a difficult month for Curtin, wearied by the ceaseless and repetitive speculation that accompanies political crisis. He spent some time lying on his bed in the Kurrajong troubled by 'nerves'. Writing to Elsie on Tuesday, 30 September to wish her a happy birthday on the following Saturday, Curtin penned his finest surviving personal letter.[29] A birthday was, he wrote:

> a timetable & records what we do not like to feel. I find I am growing old, as the song says. We cannot avoid what life brings. To me the finest occurrences have been you & the two children. I dreamed about Jack last night. I'm afraid my nerves need a rest. And here crisis follows crisis & there is no spell at all. More than ever my nature is crying out for a holiday from strife. What with Royal Commissions, debates in the House, the conflict & conferences in the caucus, and the too-neglected work of the war Council I find myself dragged into the commonplace and not able to attend to what would be worth doing.
>
> But enough of complaint. Let me look at the credit side. And you alone have supplied that. I have had a kindly life. You have given me a deep well of content & met the urges of my nature completely. I have had supreme happiness in your love and loveliness. And no man has ever had more than

that. Not a moment's anxiety have you given me regarding your housewifery. My affairs have been managed far better than I could ever have done. If I heap blessings on your head as I do, it is because not a day have I been in doubt of your prudence, good sense, generosity and cheerfulness. And all you have been & what you are in essence is all that I have relied on. Know that firmly on your birthday, my dearest dear. I cannot do more now as the Executive is waiting. We have the Budget to consider & I am sick of millions for that and for this & everybody assuming no one should pay & that the thin air gives money and not oxygen.

All of my love & all my heart & all my gratitude for all you have been & are, the wife – the stouthearted sweet natured wife – of my manhood & the beloved of my soul.

He enclosed a cheque for £200. He was left, he calculated, with £560 in his account. That and what Elsie had in her bank balance was all the cash they had by then amassed, though 'there is that £100 war loan svgs in addition'. In 2014 dollars their financial wealth was then around $50 000. By then they also owned the house they lived in and another nearby.

(6)

Fadden introduced the Budget on Thursday, 25 September. Caucus met the following Tuesday, 30 September, and, on Evatt's motion, readily agreed to reject the Budget on the ground it 'should be recast to ensure a more equitable distribution of the national burden'. Curtin spoke against the Budget in the House the following day, 1 October. Fadden sat across from Curtin, holding his chin, a finger across his lips. On Fadden's extreme left Menzies watched Curtin intently. It was a moment on which their lives would turn.

Caucus spirits were rising. On Thursday morning caucus met again, congratulating Curtin on the sixth anniversary of his leadership and singing 'For He's a Jolly Good Fellow'.[30] Debate on the Budget continued through Thursday and into Friday. The protracted debate permitted both the Government and the Opposition to work hard on Coles and Wilson, on whom the outcome of the debate depended.

Arthur Coles had been attending UAP meetings. Claiming to be offended by the party's treatment of Menzies, however, he had withdrawn and become increasingly sceptical of the Fadden Government's performance. His fellow independent, Alexander Wilson, was already somewhat inclined to Labor since he depended on Labor support in his electorate. Wheat-farming groups to which he was affiliated supported Labor in state politics. Working on this advantage, Evatt cultivated Wilson. When Coles took Wilson aside to suggest they vote against the forthcoming Fadden Budget, Wilson was already there. (Though others had a different story. Harold Cox and some other reporters had assumed Wilson would vote with Fadden, right up to the moment when he didn't. Alan Reid claimed he was told by Wilson a few days beforehand that he would vote against Fadden. Neither Cox nor Reid suggests Wilson was influenced by Coles – or Evatt.)

There was, in the final moments of this long-lived ruling UAP – Country Party coalition, not much of substance to say, although that did not shorten the debate. Fadden had not been a bad prime minister, the Budget was not particularly objectionable. On war policy, the Government and the Opposition had few disagreements.

It was now just under a decade since the December 1931 election in which the Scullin Government had lost thirty-two seats, including Curtin's. It had left Labor with fourteen seats in the House against forty for the new UAP Government lead by Joe Lyons. Since Lyons' death the UAP had steadily deteriorated, in large part because, as Curtin had said of Page's attack on Menzies (and Hasluck later wrote), the leadership of the UAP had been arrayed around Lyons. On his death, it lost its equilibrium. Labor had improved its standing under Curtin and strengthened its numbers in the House, but there was no overwhelming groundswell for Labor in the 1940 election.

The UAP was destroying itself. The generational change to Menzies was too much. He was too young, too clever, too scathing, too commanding, too ambitious, too superior for some of his older colleagues. Unconnected with the landed families that produced Street and Fairbairn, the son of a shopkeeper, not then or ever a member of the Melbourne Club, Menzies lacked a comfortable legitimacy. Page was brutal, vindictive and foolish, but he said publicly of Menzies many things his colleagues, veterans of the Great War, said privately. Whatever Fadden's qualities, he was the leader of the minor party in the coalition. He was prime minister only because a decade after its creation the UAP was now leaderless. Since he had arrived in federal Parliament in 1934, Menzies had been the force to which his non-Labor colleagues had had to respond. After Lyons' death Menzies had been Curtin's principal opponent, and to Curtin's views it was Menzies who presented the principal alternative. The force of his character, abilities and ambitions had dominated his side of politics for seven years – and would for another quarter-century.

The Budget debate climaxed on Friday, 3 October, when Coles rose to say that he had very little objection to the Budget but he wanted stability in government. In resigning, Coles reminded the House, Menzies had said his government was unworkable. Coles thought the Government was still unworkable. 'I stand up today,' he declared, 'to say I have come to the same conclusion as the former Prime Minister did a month ago. I have decided to vote against the Government.' Labor cheered him on. Fadden was as direct as usual. When Coles claimed he had told Fadden he could not be regarded as a supporter of the Government, Fadden interjected: 'Unless I put you in the Government.'

The result of the vote was announced at 4.15 p.m. The House rejected the Budget thirty-six to thirty-three. Fadden spoke to his

Cabinet and the Coalition parties, and early Friday evening advised Gowrie to commission Curtin to form a government. Accepting Fadden's advice and after confirming with them that Coles and Wilson were prepared to support Labor, Gowrie saw Curtin later on Friday evening and invited him to form a government. Curtin telegraphed Elsie with the news. 'This is your birthday gift,' he wrote, 'and Coles and Wilson are providing it.'

After the political tumult of the last three months, the biggest question was not what the Curtin Government would do, but how long it would last. On Friday night Curtin could not say who his ministers would be, or what his government would do – but he did tell reporters that 'I am confident the Labor Government will be a stable government'.[31] He could not have firmly believed it. The press was sceptical. Depending as it did on a factious caucus, on the same two independents in the House who had just brought down the Fadden Government, led by a man widely thought to be hesitant and diffident about power, reporters had no reason to suppose the Curtin Government would last long.

(7)

As the Australian political crisis moved towards its climax in the early southern spring, German armies had prepared to hurl themselves against the Soviet armies in a final, decisive offensive in the northern autumn. By early September the Germans had occupied Kiev, besieged Leningrad and begun the final assault on Moscow. In a miscalculation that would cost the Germans, on 25 September Hitler ordered an attack south towards Kharkov, the Crimea, and the oilfields beyond. The new attack on Moscow was delayed.

Japan meanwhile finalised plans to go to war in the Pacific. On 6 September 1941, a Cabinet Conference in the presence of Emperor Hirohito agreed to continue negotiations with the United States while preparing for war.[32] It set a deadline of 10 October for the talks, later extended. In the same month Admiral Yamamoto submitted to the Navy General Staff plans for a Japanese offensive, including an attack on Pearl Harbor. His plan called for five separate and simultaneous operations. The American-held islands of Wake and Guam would be captured, marking a new eastern defence perimeter. There would be landings in the Philippines, Malaya and the Moluccas. To attack the United States fleet at Pearl Harbor Yamamoto planned to send four large carriers, and later added two smaller carriers. The Japanese consul in Hawaii had been instructed in late September to map Pearl Harbor into five zones and to report back the precise number of warships in each zone. There were then eight battleships and three carriers in the Pearl Harbor base of the United States Pacific fleet.[33]

British intelligence misread the picture. A 26 September 'Review of the Situation in the Far East' by the General Headquarters, Singapore, argued that since May the position in the region had changed against Japan. The signs included the 'more positive attitude' of the United States. It believed that Japan had been confused by the German attack on the Soviet Union soon after Hitler had encouraged Japan to sign a non-aggression pact with Stalin. The report noted that Foreign Minister Matsuoka, thought to be pro-German, had been forced to leave the Japanese Cabinet. British and American hostility to Japan's move into Indo-China had checked Japan. The British believed it would be 'madness' for Japan to attack south while the Soviet Union had substantial forces. Finally, the weather in the South China Sea from November to February is bad. As a result, 'it is improbable that Japan can be contemplating war in the south for some months'.[34] On 29 September a conference in Singapore chaired by the British resident minister, Duff Cooper, concluded Japan would attack the Soviet Union rather than move south.[35]

Even so, the Singapore command recognised that Japan held good cards. Two days before the vote which brought down the Fadden

Government, Page reported to Fadden from Singapore. Meeting with Cooper and the military leadership, they agreed the 'only real deterrent to further Japanese aggression would be a British fleet based at Singapore and in the absence of this fleet there is little doubt that Japan will be able to strike at her selected moment'.[36]

The British Admiralty did not see it quite the same way. Its strategy to counter Japan was now to base a task force at Ceylon, to guard the routes across the Indian Ocean. The force would be able to move to Singapore as and when the situation demanded, but it would not be based there. The Admiralty planned to send the task force by March 1942.[37]

CHAPTER 19

CURTIN FORMS HIS GOVERNMENT

(1)

When the House of Representatives next met at 3 p.m. on Wednesday, 8 October 1941, Curtin sat on the Speaker's right, at the table where Fadden had been sitting the week before. Behind him, the front bench was crowded with the new ministers. In speaking to the House, Curtin read from notes. As prime minister it was no longer possible to speak off the cuff, or not as often.

Curtin's health had never been robust, but at fifty-six he had worn well. He looked to be in his early forties, the *Courier-Mail* remarked encouragingly.[1] In the new job he would age quickly. From his meeting with Gowrie on the evening of Friday, 3 October, Curtin's life had abruptly changed. He had been busy enough as Opposition leader. As prime minister in wartime he would have to demand more of himself than he had ever been called on to give. The first business was his own office, and taking advice from the Prime Minister's Department on the procedures for forming government. The second order of business was the composition of the ministry. On the details of the transition he would have been closely engaged with the secretary of the Prime Minister's Department, Frank Strahan.

His personal office was the easiest part. Don Rodgers would stay as press secretary, Eric Tonkin as private secretary. In Opposition he had a stenographer, Gladys Joyce, who moved to the Prime Minister's office with him. Other staff, including stenographer Hazel Craig who was assigned to work with Rodgers, had been working for Menzies and then Fadden. Shedden sent up Department of Defence Co-ordination public servant Fred McLaughlin as the private secretary responsible for Curtin's war business. There would be others, but that was a start. Curtin moved from the Opposition leader's office off the corridor on the southern side of the House chamber to the Prime Minister's office in the north-eastern corner of Parliament House, looking out towards the War Memorial. He was close to the House chamber and the Cabinet Room. He worked at a large desk inlaid with green leather in a grand wood-panelled room.[2]

Though based in Melbourne, the secretary of the Department of Defence Co-ordination, Fred Shedden, would highly likely have taken himself to Canberra to brief the new leader. He would certainly have advised Curtin to take the Defence portfolio himself. With his usual diligence, Stanley Bruce got in early. He cabled Curtin on Saturday, 4 October, not very long after the vote in the House and well before the Prime Minister-designate was formally invested. The presumed urgency of the cable was belied by its content, which concerned negotiations between the United States and Britain over post-war rules on international trade. No immediate decision was required of Curtin on Imperial Preference versus American insistence on free trade, and none was recommended. It was useful, though, as a reminder that while there was a war to fight, there was also a peace to plan.

Composing Cabinet was complicated, as usual. The Menzies and Fadden ministries had each had nineteen members, some of them with more than one portfolio. Curtin decided he, too, would have nineteen ministers, including himself. Norman Makin, Bert Evatt and others lobbied him over the weekend, arguing for their preferred portfolios. Convening caucus on Monday, 6 October, Curtin was re-elected Leader by acclamation. He immediately asked that Deputy Leader Frank Forde should likewise be re-elected by acclamation, and caucus did so. Of the nineteen ministers, he proposed that five should be senators and the rest in the House, with the House taking nine of twelve senior ministries.

Arthur Calwell later claimed that Curtin ran a 'ticket' or list of preferred candidates for the ministry, which notably did not include Calwell. Others said there was no Curtin ticket, but he did make his preferences known.[3] Of the ministry of nineteen, thirteen were elected on the first of seven ballots. The rest fought over the remaining jobs in six more ballots in a three-and-a-half-hour meeting. Among the top vote winners were Jack Beasley and Evatt, who sometimes but not always worked together so closely that Makin would describe them as 'twins'.[4] Ben Chifley and John Dedman also did well in the ministerial poll. If he had tried, Curtin did not succeed in keeping Eddie Ward out of the ministry. According to journalist Alan Reid, who was close to Beasley, Curtin strongly supported Beasley in the poll, despite some remaining antagonism in caucus to his earlier defections. Curtin reckoned Beasley would be more tractable within the ministry than without. It would prove to be a good decision.[5] At seventy-six, Senator Collings from Queensland was the oldest minister; at forty-two, Ward was the youngest.

Under Labor Party rules, caucus elected the ministers and the prime minister allocated the portfolios. Scullin initiated an amendment, one influenced by the memory of his own chaotic ministry and the presence in Curtin's ministry of factious personalities. He proposed that the prime minister be given the power to sack a minister, a resolution that caucus promptly carried. Scullin's timing was deft. After a decade out of power, caucus was sufficiently jubilant to cede a little of its authority to the leader. It was not a power Curtin would ever use, though he would have to stand down one minister and threaten to sack another. It was a handy power to have.

After earlier saying he would give three senior portfolios to ministers in the Senate, Curtin changed his mind. Defending the omission, he announced that because of the war all senior portfolios would be in the House. 'Had it been a time of peace,' he said in a statement, 'my allocation would have been different.'[6] Australia had been at war for a while, so that did not explain his abrupt change of view. On reflection Curtin had probably decided the senators elected to the ministry would not be up to the senior jobs.

Allocating the ministries, Curtin gave big jobs to his closest ally, Chifley, and to talented though potentially troublesome colleagues. As Treasurer he chose Chifley over Forde, who not only keenly wanted it but perhaps also thought that as deputy leader of the party he had a right to select his own portfolio. After his experience on the Royal Commission on Banking, Chifley was much the better choice. Like Menzies, Curtin himself became Minister for Defence Co-ordination (later the Minister for Defence), a job that brought with it the tireless Shedden. Curtin made Evatt both Attorney-General and Minister for External Affairs. Beasley got the ministry of Supply and Development, making him responsible for much war-related production. Curtin would come to rely on his steady support in caucus. Taking a chance, Curtin gave Ward the ministry of Labour and National Service. His job was to sort out the labour disputes. Until his passion for controversy got the better of him, he was a more than competent minister. Curtin put the armed services portfolios in the House.

In a seniority ranking of the ministry, Forde was second to Curtin, then Chifley third, Evatt fourth and Beasley fifth. To War Cabinet, Curtin appointed himself, Chifley, Evatt, Beasley, Navy Minister Makin and Air Minister Arthur Drakeford. In December Dedman, Minister for the War Organisation of Industry, would be added. It would be the heart of government. 'Nine-tenths of the business was done in the Barracks in Melbourne,' recalled Hazel Craig, though Curtin convened War Cabinet in Canberra far more frequently than Menzies had. Craig remembered that War Cabinet 'took precedence' and the 'general cabinet just fell away really'.[7]

Probably because he already had too much to do in Canberra, Chifley was spared membership of the Advisory War Council. The government members of the Council would be Curtin, Forde, Evatt, Beasley and Makin. Chifley's high standing was the standout detail in the ministerial appointments.

Curtin had come to office during wartime, without an election, and without his own party having a majority in the House. The immediate need was to reassure Australians that the country was in safe hands. That imperative determined his first public comments. He committed to fighting the war with vigour. In a cable to Churchill he declared his government's loyalty to the British Empire, informing the House of the message soon after it met on Wednesday, 8 October. He publicly denied reports he would bring the Second AIF home from the Middle East, though in War Council in past months he had raised that possibility.

Curtin confirmed the jobs of a number of prominent former political opponents who served the previous government. The ambassadorial and diplomatic appointments of the previous government 'would not be interfered with', he announced on 4 October.[8] Reporters thought he might replace Casey in Washington. Curtin publicly supported him as the head of the Australian legation, despite Evatt's dislike of Casey. He confirmed Bruce as High Commissioner in London, and would come to value him more the more he dealt with him. In this he was mistaken: Bruce was no longer close to British ministers. Even Page was permitted to continue his mission through the United States and on to London, where Churchill would allow him to attend the War Cabinet if Australian matters were under discussion. (Bruce concealed for a while his displeasure at the arrival of a more senior Australian representative, one who had been his junior partner in government, while maintaining a careful diary record of Page's shortcomings. With Page it was only a matter of waiting for him to trip himself up, as he would in February 1942.) So, too, some of Menzies and Fadden's advisers were retained. Douglas Copland remained as economic adviser. The Financial and Economic Committee, a very loose group of academic and government economists, also remained. Essington Lewis, who as BHP chief executive might have evoked antagonism from Labor, remained as Director-General of Munitions. Chifley had once been his director for manpower, and admired Lewis. Later there would be bigger jobs for him.

(2)

The country reassured, ministers elected by caucus and allocated portfolios by Curtin, the next priority was the Budget. Fadden had lost office when the House refused to accept his Budget. Curtin and his ministry had now to produce another that would win a majority in the House and the Senate. After granting supply for a short period, the House was adjourned. The Budget was not only about financing government. Its financing raised two fundamental questions of how Australia worked. One was whether the states of the Commonwealth should have priority over the biggest source of revenue, income tax. The other was the extent of government authority over the Commonwealth Bank, and the publicly owned Commonwealth Bank's authority over the privately owned banks. Those two questions would be the basis for two far-reaching reforms in the Curtin Government, changes which would shape government influence over the economy for decades to come.

(3)

There was the Budget, and there was the war. Three divisions of Australian troops were now fighting in the Middle East. Troops from the 9th and 7th divisions were holding Tobruk against the

Germans. They had been besieged since April. Some had been relieved in August, but the British commander in the Middle East and Churchill had asked Fadden to allow them to delay the relief of the others. After seven months most of the Australians were still there, living in trenches and tunnels, bombarded from the air and by land artillery, with little air support, the sea at their back.

Most of the 8th Division was now in Malaya. Australia's AIF commander in the Middle East, General Sir Thomas Blamey, still pressed for it to be deployed to the Middle East as soon as replacement units from the Indian Army had arrived in Malaya. Australian air crews were part of the Royal Air Force in Britain, and Australian ships part of the British navy. There was now a substantial conscript army in Australia, organised as the Australian Military Forces. It was already too big, in Blamey's opinion. He thought Japan very unlikely to go to war. The real need, Blamey thought, was production, and more recruits for the Second AIF in the Middle East. Neither the Menzies nor Fadden governments, newspapers and top officials complained, had done enough about mobilising manpower for war production. Strikes continued to disrupt coalmining and the waterfront.

The military forces deployed to defend Australia were still pitifully weak. With Australian air crews mostly in Britain or the Middle East, its naval ships under Admiralty control and often in distant waters and with three of its five volunteer divisions in the Middle East and a fourth in Malaya, Australia's home defence relied on a conscript army which was quite large but mostly only partly trained, inexperienced, and poorly equipped. When Curtin came to office there were 113 887 people on full-time duty in the military in Australia, including 61 396 in the Citizen Forces, 11 050 in garrison battalions and 36 357 in the AIF (including the Ist Armoured Division, scheduled to be sent to the Middle East in December).[9] Many more Militia soldiers had been trained and released, so there was a capacity for rapid expansion of that force. Even so, the home army in being was smaller than the

130 000 Brudenell White had described to Murdoch and Menzies the previous year.

Australian military intelligence in Melbourne did not share Blamey's conviction that Japan would stay out of the war. Nor did the Americans. Curtin's assessment changed by the week. Earlier in the year he had thought a Japanese attack imminent. He still thought it quite a high risk, and since Australia could be imperilled by a Pacific war this risk was an important one. But he had also thought for a while that the negotiations in Washington might be successful. He would have to take account of Churchill's view that Japan would not go to war in the Pacific, an assessment shared by the British command in Singapore as well as by Blamey.

Though he had warned of war with Japan earlier in the year, Curtin had not come to office convinced that war in the Pacific was imminent, or that the Australia-based army should be rapidly expanded, or that Australia must rapidly expand its air force or bring its ships back into Australian waters and under Australian command. As prime minister, he had specifically said he would not recall the AIF divisions from the Middle East.

The threat of war with Japan or the adequacy of Australia's defence were not the reasons Curtin was prime minister or that Fadden had lost office, though it was true that from the beginning of the war in Europe Curtin had warned of the danger of war in the Pacific. Between the Government and the Opposition there was at this point no important disagreement about the conduct of the war.

A zealous campaigner in 1916 against conscription for overseas wars, Curtin was now prime minister. The leader of the largest Opposition party would shortly be Billy Hughes, the prime minister who had gaoled him in 1916. But the Opposition was not then calling for conscription for overseas service. There was not now a disagreement about conscription for service within Australia or its territories, or assignment of the all-volunteer Second AIF to the Middle East and Malaya. Curtin had long been a sceptic of the British Government's ability to send a fleet of sufficient size to trouble Japan, if war came. But for the last year or so he had joined with the Menzies and Fadden governments in demanding assurances of British navy protection, which he should have known were unlikely to be given – or if given, plausible.

Curtin may well have reasoned to himself that even if Britain could not send a fleet, there was a good argument for Australia to fight in Malaya. The Japanese could not safely seize the Netherlands East Indies and its oil if Singapore remained under British control. Japan would want to take Singapore if only to protect its conquests further east. Since Singapore's big guns made it hard to attack by sea, a Japanese army would have to come through Malaya. Curtin had been assured that British and American warplanes were much superior to Japanese warplanes. It was widely said that while Japanese troops might overcome poorly trained Chinese troops, they would be no match for the better trained and better equipped British, Indian and Australian troops. A Japanese southward thrust might well be blocked in Malaya.

Curtin may also have been aware of America's refusal to support the defence of Singapore. If Australia was to fight in Malaya, only the British could help. That anyway was the logic of fighting in Malaya, even without the British navy. Its fault was that if the British defence of Malaya was as poorly resourced as the Australian Government had been repeatedly told, if Japanese warplanes were better than expected (and as good as American advisers in China were reporting), if the Japanese proved able to defeat the British Imperial forces, those forces would be hard to rescue.

In the mind of the man who now became his principal war adviser, not much had changed in Australian defence policy in the last decade or two. In an early conversation Shedden recorded that he gave Curtin a paper he had given Scullin when he became prime minister twelve years earlier. Australia was an island continent, the paper argued, so its first line of defence was sea power. Even if Britain was at war with both Japan and a European power, 'multiple enemies made multiple

allies certain, the most sure one being the United States'.[10] Perhaps.
If indeed the paper had been handed to Scullin twelve years earlier,
and if it had said what Shedden said it said, then the truth about
Empire Defence and the Singapore strategy Shedden had so strongly
pressed for over a decade was that it depended not on Singapore, not
on a British fleet, not on the Empire at all, but on the chance that if
there was war with Japan, the United States would join it. No such
rationale had been offered hitherto.

(4)

The new Cabinet met first on Tuesday, 7 October at 12.15 p.m. The
first priority was a new Budget. Curtin said he wanted preparation
of the Budget 'without any delay'. He proposed that after securing
supply Parliament adjourn for three weeks 'to enable ministers
to make themselves acquainted with the work of their respective
departments'. He proposed that the full Cabinet meet in Canberra,
and War Cabinet in Melbourne. Defining the style of his government
he recognised a wide autonomy of ministers to make decisions
without reference to Cabinet, telling them 'Each minister would be
responsible for his own administration'. It was an important note,
though he also said 'in coming to any decision naturally a minister
would conform to the Government's general policy'. Some matters
'require Cabinet consideration and it was assumed that Ministers
would take action in accordance with recognised procedures'. Curtin
did not plan to scrutinise routine decisions of ministers but he did
think ministers should be frugal. Curtin troubled himself to detail
the amount and method of paying travel allowances and outlined
'suggestions for economies' in the use of cars by ministers and staff.
Meeting again on Thursday, Cabinet noted that 'no titles of any kind
were to be recommended' – a policy later breached for Shedden.[11]

Appointed rather than elected to office, depending for his working majority on two independents in the House of Representatives and facing a Senate controlled by his political opponents, leading a party that only a year ago had very nearly rejected his Budget compromise with the Government, his own physical health unreliable and subject still to occasional and unaccountable spells of gloom, Curtin could hardly be confident of the Labor Government's durability or his own as its leader. The year or so on the War Council had familiarised him with the military leaders and officials on whom he would now depend, and showed him the ropes of government decision-making. But he had never been a minister, and never run anything bigger than the Victorian Branch of the Timber Workers Union or the editorial office of the *Westralian Worker*.

Curtin's government was widely expected to be short-lived. For the next few months, Calwell later recalled, there would be 'plenty of speculation about an early election'.[12] Speaking from the Labor backbench on 8 October, Frank Brennan advised the government to go to an election as soon as it sensibly could. It may well have been in Curtin's mind. Writing in his column on Monday, 6 October, the *Sydney Morning Herald*'s Ross Gollan warned that the Curtin Government could be fragile. The Senate could reject its Budget if it introduced 'radical finance'. Labor's opponents had a majority of two in the Senate. Even if one voted with Labor, the chamber would be deadlocked. A deadlock would be enough to refuse to pass the Budget, and perhaps the House would be forced to an election. Gollan and his employer, Warwick Fairfax, loathed Menzies, but admired Fadden and regretted his loss of office. Curtin as prime minister was an unknown.

One strength, difficult to calculate, was the moral authority Curtin had gained by his earlier reluctance to force the Coalition Government from office. The *Sydney Morning Herald* acknowledged this in its leader of Thursday, 9 October, praising the new prime minister and his party for 'cooperating with the party's opponents in office without compromising its independence' and 'restraining the impatience of his followers until the appropriate moment arrived'. Curtin did not have a majority but he did have 'the present trust of his whole party, the liking and respect of the Opposition, and the hopeful good will of the nation'. The paper thought he had made 'an excellent beginning'.

Another strength, far more reliable, was the weakness of the Opposition. Menzies had lost not only the leadership of the country but was about to also lose the leadership of his party, the UAP. While still nominally leader of his party, Menzies fought a gallant but hopeless battle to displace Fadden as Leader of the Opposition. In a UAP party meeting called for Wednesday, 8 October, the last day before the adjournment, he resigned the leadership ('to secure for himself', as he wished it to be known, 'full rights of expression') and sought a resolution that as the major coalition party the UAP should determine the leadership of the Opposition. This was quite opposite to his view six weeks earlier that the joint party meeting should elect its leader, who would be prime minister. The party instead voted nineteen to twelve in favour of a 'combination' with the Country Party,[13] meaning the two parties jointly would determine the coalition and therefore Opposition leadership. Facing certain defeat Menzies did not then stand for the UAP leadership, which was won by Hughes. At a subsequent joint meeting of the parties Fadden was proposed for the leadership by two UAP allies, and elected Leader of the Opposition unopposed.

Menzies thenceforward posed as an isolated, grand figure, free at last to pursue a private legal practice, patiently waiting for the conservative parties and the country to turn to him. His successor as UAP leader, the 79-year-old Hughes, enjoyed the support of his New South Wales colleagues but was widely and correctly seen as an astute survivor of five decades of political wars whose best times were long past. He had split the Labor Party in 1916, adroitly destroyed Bruce in 1929, and contributed to Menzies' destruction. He was better at wrecking than building. For the UAP in 1941, there was no one else. Menzies was widely disliked. Casey was in Washington. Fairbairn, Street and Gullett were dead. None of the younger members had the strength to claim the leadership.

Hughes' simple and for a time successful strategy to retain leadership was not to call a party meeting at which it might be contested. With the shock of the UAP's political collapse still recent, party meetings seemed not to be missed. Hughes, anyway, was only leader of the UAP. The chief figure in the Opposition was Fadden. As leader of the minor party in the Coalition, Fadden's leadership had to be thought temporary. But if the UAP could do no better than Hughes to lead them, they could hardly claim to lead the Opposition.

Certainly, the Opposition controlled the Senate. But the utmost it could do there was make governing so difficult for Curtin he would be forced to ask the Governor-General for a general election. And what then? An election, and one imposed on the Government in wartime by an obstructionist Senate, was the last thing the Opposition wanted. The weakness of the conservative parties, which would continue until Menzies captured both the leadership of his party and of the Opposition after the 1943 election, remained one of Curtin's strengths. Another source of durability for Curtin's government, an event that would in eight weeks instantly sweep away all thought of an early election, was even then being planned, checked and rechecked in painstaking detail by Admiral Yamamoto and his staff.

(5)

While relying on goodwill, Curtin did not neglect the usual wiles of political patronage. Under the Constitution, the Speaker of the House cannot vote except in the case of a tie, when the Speaker's vote becomes the casting vote. It was therefore helpful to Labor when the Coalition Government's speaker, W M Nairn, agreed to remain, together with the Chairman of Committees in the House, the Country Party's J H Prowse. If it came to an important vote, that would reduce the Opposition vote by one, and possibly two. Coles and Wilson had been looked after by the preceding governments. Curtin would find things for them to do. Coles would soon find himself appointed to the board of the Commonwealth agency organising housing for war workers. It was something. As Don Rodgers remarked, Curtin knew his politics and how to play them.[14]

As prime minister Curtin would prove to be an able chairman, as he had in leading the Labor Party in Opposition. It would be one of his strengths, on display in caucus, Cabinet and War Council meetings, difficult conferences with miners and mine owners, and with state premiers. Chairing meetings was an important part of the prime minister's job. He made decisions promptly. Interviewed later or recalling Curtin's style in their memoirs, Curtin's ministers would remark on his collegial style of government. By and large Curtin let ministers make their own decisions. Where necessary he would support them against Cabinet opponents. The latitude he encouraged may have been partly the exigencies of a wartime government, where all ministers and especially the prime minister had so much to do they had little time left to see what other ministers were doing. But it was also an aspect of his character. He was not vain and overbearing. He did not think his own qualities so superior to his ministers that they required his supervision and correction. He was mostly liberal in his views and character.

There was another aspect of his character, however, which his colleagues also noted. He was or had become a loner. Other than with a very few of his close colleagues he did not exchange confidences or encourage banter or share problems – or not with his ministers.

He appeared to have a more congenial relationship with Canberra political reporters than with his ministers, perhaps because reporters were easier to please and were satisfied with less of what he had to give, perhaps because they were in a different game, and perhaps also

because – after years of editing and writing and running the Australian
Journalists Union in Perth – he was in his own mind as much a
journalist as a politician. Curtin still wore his AJA badge on the watch
chain across his waistcoat. Working with Don Rodgers, he was closer
to Canberra press gallery reporters than any prime minister before
him, and perhaps any since. Rodgers privately doubted Curtin could
have earned a living as a journalist – an unreasonable judgement,
since Curtin *had* earned his living as a journalist, and all up for over
a decade. He had learned to type – not a usual accomplishment
for men at the time. He could and still did type some speech drafts,
some letters.

Rodgers, too, recognised Curtin was shy of both intimacy and easy
camaraderie. Perhaps that was what his drinking had been about, and
he had foresworn geniality with the beer. Rodgers said that Curtin's
favourite word was 'mateship'. He used that term with his political
colleagues. But what Rodgers and Curtin meant by mateship was
loyalty. Curtin valued loyalty. Political leaders usually do. He did not
value back-slapping geniality. Rodgers had been close to him now for
four years. Along with the shyness were spells of sadness. Thirty years
later Rodgers would recall the 'black melancholia' that sometimes
afflicted Curtin, a condition he would well recognise since he was
similarly afflicted himself.[15]

The Prime Minister's suite of offices was in the north-eastern corner
of the main floor of Parliament House, not far from the chamber
of the House of Representatives and the Cabinet Room. Ray Tracey
usually drove Curtin in at 9 a.m. and took him back to the Lodge at
midnight.[16] Sometimes Curtin walked. He could get to the Lodge in
twenty or thirty minutes, walking across the Capital Hill fields behind
Parliament House, watched by kangaroos and wallabies feeding on
the grass. The corridor entrance to the offices was attended by Oliver
Chidgey. 'One of the best known characters in Parliament House for

many years,' according to Cox, Chidgey had long been orderly and Cabinet messenger for Australia's prime ministers. Inside the office were Curtin's private secretaries Eric Tonkin and Fred McLaughlin, the typists Hazel Craig and Gladys Joyce and office assistants. Don Rodgers had an office nearby and of all the staff members was the one most constantly with and closest to Curtin. Ray Tracey was on call. Curtin's manner with his staff was courteous, thoughtful, friendly, and correct. He asked after their families, their health, their weekend plans. His most frequent request was for a cup of tea.

Close to his own offices Curtin located one for Chifley, and another for Scullin. The former leader had not run for the ministry and had no official responsibility, but Curtin liked having him close by. The three offices linked three of the threads of the Curtin Government. Curtin himself had command over the Government as a whole and in particular military matters and relations with the Allied leaders. Chifley took care of the Budget, including monetary policy and taxation. 'Has Chif seen this?' Curtin would often ask his staff of finance papers.[17] Later Chifley would, with Curtin, take major responsibility for post-war planning.

Scullin was a forceful advocate for a Commonwealth takeover of income tax, and a veteran anxious to see that the caucus troubles that destroyed his government did not destroy Curtin's. Widely respected and experienced, Scullin's close association strengthened Curtin in the Government Members Room. Shedden would later say that the big four of Cabinet were Curtin, Chifley, Beasley and Evatt, but the big three of the Government were Curtin, Chifley and Scullin. (Shedden left himself off the list. Don Rodgers recalled that Shedden was 'closest to Curtin'. Others remarked that the man closest to Curtin was Rodgers.)

Little remarked, the head of the Prime Minister's Department kept the paper moving. Frank Strahan had been in the job since 1935 and would remain until 1949. He often said he was 'just a clerk' and though he had won both an arts and a law degree through night classes he adhered to a narrow conception of the departmental secretary's role. He remained nearly invisible. He attended full Cabinet and took notes and arranged agenda but he did not provide extensive policy advice. He said with good humour that the department was a letter-writing machine. When Curtin went away on his one visit overseas, Strahan stayed behind. In wartime the pre-eminence of the secretary of War Cabinet and of the Department of Defence was unchallengeable.[18]

CHAPTER 20

EARLY DECISIONS, AND CAUCUS CRISIS

(1)

As Curtin told its first meeting, the first order of business for Cabinet was a new Budget. Parliament had adjourned on 8 October, 1941, and the next sitting was scheduled to begin three weeks later. Consideration of the Budget would be the Parliament's major business.

Even before the Budget, Curtin at Shedden's urging initiated what the defence head thought of as a 'general mobilization for a total war effort'. Signed off on 16 October, nine days after the defeat of the previous government, the new government created a Production Executive bringing together ministers responsible for Munitions, Supply and Development, Labour and National Service, and War Organisation of Industry. Its formation was announced on 5 November. Coordinated by the Minister for War Organisation of Industry, John Dedman, it initiated a transformation of the civilian economy that would accelerate after Pearl Harbor. Intended to remove impediments to war production, Shedden called it 'a feat without parallel in Australian history',[1] perhaps because it was his idea. Confident in Dedman, Curtin did not put himself on the Production Executive.

The burden of Budget preparation fell to Chifley. Pondering Labor's task in writing a new Budget in his *Sydney Morning Herald* column on Monday, 13 October, Ross Gollan depicted Chifley as 'an able high priest of orthodox Labour financial unorthodoxy', quoting his minority views in the 1937 report of the Royal Commission on Banking opposing the private ownership of trading banks. Chifley now wanted the banking system 'entirely under national control', Gollan wrote, with the Commonwealth Bank having clear regulatory authority. The Budget would test how far Labor was prepared to go in carrying out its program for banking.

A minister in the second year of the Scullin Government, Chifley was defeated in his Bathurst-based seat of Macquarie in 1931 and had not returned to federal Parliament until the September 1940 election. He had prepared well. Asked by Casey in 1935 to nominate a member of the Royal Commission on Banking, Curtin had chosen Chifley, then fighting a lonely battle in New South Wales against Jack Lang. For Chifley, who was taken out of school as soon as it was legally possible to do so and who learned most of what he knew in night schools and adult education courses, the Royal Commission was a fine education in economics and finance.

Curtin was drawn to Chifley. Both came from Irish Catholic families, both left school early, both were union officials and both keenly pursued economic knowledge at night courses. Both had been strong opponents of conscription in the Great War. They had first been sworn in as members of the House in the same hour. Both resisted the orthodox economic policies the Scullin Government was forced to adopt, and both fought Lang. Both were firm supporters of White Australia, and equally ready to deploy racist rhetoric. During the Great War Curtin had warned that Australian soldiers killed in France would be replaced at home by Asians. In the 1928 federal election campaign, one of Labor's themes was that the Bruce Government's immigration policies weakened White Australia, with Chifley criticising Bruce for permitting the migration of 'so many Dagoes and Aliens into Australia'.[2] They did not agree on centralisation. Chifley favoured abolition of states. Curtin sometimes spoke up for states' rights.

In war the distinction did not matter. The Commonwealth required greater powers in war, and it would assume them. They also disagreed about nationalisation of banking. Curtin had not supported the nationalisation of banking that Chifley favoured in a dissenting note in the Report of the Royal Commission on Banking. That, too, was a question that could be put aside in wartime. They wholeheartedly agreed on how to handle the Commonwealth Bank, an issue on which Curtin was as forceful as Chifley.

As the war claimed more resources, the problem of financing it became more acute. Even in October 1941, fighting a distant enemy in distant theatres, around one-fifth of males fourteen years and older – a total of 554 000 – were either in the services or in war production. Another 74 000 women were either in the services or in war production. Two years earlier only one occupied man in a hundred had been involved in war work. A little over 430 000 men were in the defence services, compared to 14 000 when the war with Germany began.

Australian war spending would soon rise so dramatically that the level of spending when Curtin formed his Cabinet would seem quite modest. Even so it was very considerable. When Curtin took office war spending was a little more than one-seventh of total national output or GDP, double the share a year earlier.[3] Australians were not as hard pressed as the British. In that year war spending in Britain was around half of total national expenditure or more than three times the Australian share – though Australia's share was above the United States, Canada and Japan.

Australia had not settled on a reliable way of financing the war. Commonwealth Revenue, mostly tax, was around a seventh of GDP in 1941. Commonwealth Government spending was a quarter of GDP. The gap between spending and revenue was around one-ninth of GDP. It had to be covered by bond issues, short-term borrowing from banks, and loans from the Commonwealth Bank. The states competed with the Commonwealth in income tax. The assent of the Commonwealth Bank board was required for war financing by the bank, and the private banks thought of their cooperation in buying government debt as voluntary, as it was. That would soon have to change, and quickly.

In his earliest instruction in economics, Curtin had learned not to confuse money with resources. Things were produced by workers, machines, land and mines, not by money. The financing transaction was necessary only to facilitate production, which was limited not by money but by the availability of workers and machines and land and mines. The war could be financed either by borrowing or by taxes. The borrowing could be from the public, through war loans, or directly from the Commonwealth Bank, which could create money. But if the Commonwealth Bank just created additional money there would be no reduction in demand for non-essential goods such as occurred when people paid additional taxes or saved to buy war bonds.

In financing part of war spending, Fadden had agreed to a scheme in which the Commonwealth Bank essentially borrowed from the trading banks, and paid them interest. Curtin objected. He discerned the greedy hands of the banks. As Opposition leader he had told the House at the beginning of October 1941 that all the government needed could be done through the Commonwealth Bank. He said the 'Commonwealth Bank Board itself is too responsive to the interests I am now criticising'. He did not care for its chairman, Sir Claude Reading. He thought Sir Claude's 'conception of how this country can best be served is not in the best interests of Australia as a nation'.[4] Those arrangements, too, would have to change.

Taxation could help shift resources into war production and restrain the growth of non-war spending. But income tax, the biggest source of revenue, was also imposed by the states for their own purposes. They claimed the major share of income tax revenue. The Commonwealth had to add tax on top of the state takings. In wartime, with a sudden large addition to Commonwealth spending and with a requirement to constrain private demand, these old arrangements did not work. Fadden could not resolve the issue without offending the states and running against the grain of the Coalition's views. Scullin, by contrast, was an unequivocal supporter of Commonwealth authority. He had told the House in May 1940 that 'I have yet to learn that it is the obligation of this parliament and this taxing authority to adjust to the taxation of the States'. Instead, the Commonwealth should impose 'whatever tax we think is equitable'.⁵ Sooner or later the banking and tax issues would have to be addressed. When they were, Curtin would change Australia in ways both important and enduring.

With only a few weeks to write the new Budget and a fragile majority in the House, Curtin and Chifley did not have time or inclination for major changes to the Fadden Budget they had rejected. They wanted higher pay for the armed forces, higher taxes on the wealthy and lower taxes on the poor.

More fundamentally, they wanted clear and direct federal control over the banking system, exercised through the Commonwealth Bank. Fadden had accepted voluntary cooperation from the trading banks. Curtin and Chifley insisted the framework be compulsory, and at the discretion of the Commonwealth Bank rather than the private trading banks. Both knew that the Budget could not be so radical as to tempt the Senate to reject it.

By Friday, 17 October, ten days after the Government had taken office, the proposed Budget was far enough along to bring to what turned out to be a two-day meeting of Cabinet. It began at 2 p.m. Friday. After a dinner break the discussions went though to 10.15 p.m., resuming at 10.35 a.m. on Saturday and continuing through the evening. On the agenda were two big issues. They discussed the Commonwealth Bank, including the makeup of its board, its policies, and financing the war. They also discussed tax, including the respective income tax powers of the Commonwealth and the states. Scullin attended as a tax expert.

If all his revenue proposals were accepted, Chifley explained, there would still be a gap of one hundred million pounds. On Monday he and Curtin would discuss the gap with the Commonwealth Bank. In his policy speech for the 1940 election, Curtin had promised to lift the old age pension to twenty-five shillings per week. The Budget now proposed twenty-two shillings and sixpence. Curtin expected the caucus debate on the draft Budget to be difficult. He wanted all ministers to support the Budget proposals that had now been agreed by Cabinet, emphasising the 'necessity for cabinet solidarity'. It would be the first test of Cabinet solidarity and of Curtin's authority in caucus as prime minister.

Cabinet met again on Monday, 27 October at 2.10 p.m. in Canberra. As he often did, Gollan offered some public political advice to the new government. He warned Curtin in his usual Monday column that, of the two perils to a Budget, the Senate would be more of a problem than caucus. There would have to be a general election if the Budget was 'completely unacceptable' to the Opposition. As to caucus, the left was 'disintegrating'. Gollan thought it was 'safe betting' the Senate would pass the Budget unless the Government proposed 'permanent and unacceptable changes to the financial structure'.

To Cabinet, Chifley recounted his discussions with the governor of the Commonwealth Bank and the chairman of its board. He had told them he wanted closer control of private banks and of interest rates, an expansion of the activities of the bank, and the bridging of the 100 million pound gap. He read out to Cabinet the Budget speech text on the issue.[6] To exert greater influence over the Commonwealth Bank, Cabinet also discussed and apparently agreed to the appointment of the ACTU secretary to its board. (In the event, the ACTU secretary, Percy Clarey, did not wish to retire from the Victorian Legislative Council, and for that reason could not be appointed to the Commonwealth Bank board. Cabinet instead appointed a Sydney lawyer and senior vice-president of the New South Wales Labor Party, W Taylor.)

Gollan was wrong on the greater peril. The new Budget drawn up by Chifley proposed marginal rather than fundamental changes to Fadden's spending and financing proposals. Soldiers' pay and old age pensions were increased. Taxes on profits were increased. The changes were not enough for Curtin and Chifley's caucus colleagues, who revolted. On 29 October, on a motion moved by Rosevear and seconded by James, caucus carried a motion to withdraw Chifley's Budget, instructing him to provide twenty-five shillings a week for pensioners rather than the twenty-two shillings and sixpence proposed. Ward voted with the majority against his Cabinet colleagues.[7] It was a humiliating defeat for Curtin and Chifley.

For Curtin it was a startling reminder of the authority and assertiveness of caucus, despite attaining office after a decade of Opposition, despite their fragile hold on government – and despite the war. Rosevear, James, Calwell and Ward were implacable when aroused. Faced with the first big setback since coming to office three weeks earlier, Curtin and Chifley quickly crafted a compromise. After the dinner adjournment caucus accepted Chifley's suggestion that twenty-five shillings would be introduced 'early in the new year'.

A caucus rebel himself in the days of the Scullin Government, Curtin did not dispute the authority of caucus. But disunity would be fatal. Meeting in Canberra on Tuesday, 4 November at 8.35 p.m., with the caucus upset still fresh in mind, Curtin sternly lectured Cabinet on Cabinet responsibility, and speaking to the press. His target was no doubt Ward, who was unrepentant. As he had in the early days of his Opposition leadership, Curtin readily compromised with his caucus opponents. He would be less accommodating as his strength increased.

Delivered in what Gollan described as his 'hacksaw' style to an attentive House, Chifley's Budget speech when Parliament reconvened on 29 October confirmed his authority on financial issues. Of the Opposition speakers, only Menzies raised serious objections, and he was crushingly rebutted by Curtin. Chifley announced what he had already told the Commonwealth Bank, which had then told the private banks: Fadden's plea for voluntary cooperation from the private banks would be replaced by black letter regulation. Banks would now be licensed. They would be told what to do by the Commonwealth Bank, and the Commonwealth Bank would be told what to do by the Treasurer.

In a broadcast the same day Curtin explained that the new Budget proposed to draw on central bank credit to finance expansion of production. The Budget 'establishes proper control of the trading banks through the Commonwealth Bank acting under a policy laid down by the Treasurer on behalf of the Government'.[8] The regulations would be issued 'at an early date'. As economic historian S J Butlin wrote, the assertion of authority over the banking system, including licensing of private banks and increasing the authority of the Commonwealth Bank over the financial system marked 'a revolutionary change in the position of the Commonwealth Bank as a central bank'.[9]

Responding for the Opposition, Menzies defended the private banks and the financial orthodoxy of the Gibson era. Curtin replied, reminding the House on 6 November that the Menzies Government had used central bank credit 'in a perfectly proper manner' on the outbreak of war in 1939, yet in the Great Depression Scullin 'had the door bolted against him, while the country was forced through the misery of a depression which need not have been so serious but for the action of those who had no responsibility, and who used their power for their own ends and to defeat the Government'. The Great Depression conflicts were still warm.

By the Cabinet meeting of 17 November the Budget was out of the way, and ordinary business returned – apples and pears, eggs, butter and milk, and wheat. Curtin asked ministers not to send Christmas cards, as an economy measure and as an example.

(2)

The war between Germany and the Soviet Union remained in the balance. Otherwise, the war in Europe had lost its urgency for

Australians. Germany securely controlled its Western European conquests, but while it was locked in battle with the Soviet Union Britain was safe from invasion. The British fleet still controlled the North Atlantic, the Royal Air Force controlled the skies over Britain and was developing its capacity to bomb Germany. A well-trained and well-equipped army garrisoned Britain. In the Middle East, the battle for control of the Suez Canal and for a southern route to the oilfields of Persia swung between the British and Commonwealth forces, and those of Germany and its allies. At home, petrol rationing had been introduced towards the end of 1940, but otherwise civilian life in Australia had not been much changed by war. Food was not rationed, beer production was not restricted, and race meetings, movie screenings and theatre performances continued. Household consumption was higher when Curtin took office than it had been a year earlier.

As Minister for Defence Co-ordination, soon to be renamed the Minister of Defence, Curtin's principal adviser and departmental head was Australia's most powerful public servant, Fred Shedden. Secretary of the Department of Defence, secretary of War Cabinet and Secretary of the Advisory War Council, Shedden held all the strings. Nothing came on to the agenda of War Cabinet or the War Council without his say-so. When these bodies made decisions, Shedden recorded them, interpreted their intent, and then supervised their implementation. Fluent in the ways of bureaucratic power, a protégé of the creator of the Cabinet Secretariat in Whitehall, Sir Maurice Hankey, Shedden had long been an advocate of Imperial Defence and the Singapore strategy. When that defence foundation collapsed, as it shortly would, he would adroitly manoeuvre not only to retain but to increase his authority.

Shedden was a stayer. His influence was so trenchant, his intentions so persistent, he would still be in his job and still advocating a close military alliance with Britain years after Curtin's death. Long after the Second World War ended, he would still seek Cabinet agreement to an Australian commitment to the defence of the Middle East – now, presumably, to protect it against the Soviet Union – as if the Pacific War, the independence of India, Egypt's demand for control of its own affairs, the first Palestine War and the creation of Israel, nuclear weaponry, the exhaustion and collapse of the whole Imperial ideal, national rebellions against European colonialism, had not happened. In December 1951 he would get Menzies and his Cabinet to agree to an Australian military role in the Middle East though even Menzies, himself locked in the Imperial past, would complain of the 'dead hand of Fred Shedden'.[10]

In October 1941 Shedden was the indispensable man, the one Curtin would later call his 'right and left hand and head too'.[11] Some of Curtin's ministers didn't care for his reliance on Shedden and the service chiefs bridled, but Don Rodgers had no doubt. The press secretary and Shedden grated on each other. Each had to reckon with the other.

The central issue for Curtin, Shedden and for the War Cabinet and War Council meetings Curtin would chair in the first two months of his prime ministership was the threat of war with Japan. A week after Curtin became prime minister, Prince Fumimaro Konoe's Cabinet in Tokyo resigned. It had toyed with accepting Roosevelt's terms, which would probably mean sooner or later withdrawing from China. General Tōjō was now Prime Minister and Minister for War. On Sunday, 19 October, Curtin responded to the news of the fall of the Konoe government with a public warning of 'ominous portents on the Pacific horizon'.

To some faction leaders in Tokyo, Tōjō hinted at a willingness to meet the American terms; to others he was uncompromising.[12] Whatever his private views, he was unable to stop the slide towards war.

Through intercepts, the United States followed some important Japanese decisions and shared much of the information with

Britain and Australia. In Washington, Casey was closely following the negotiations between the Secretary of State, Cordell Hull, and the Japanese Ambassador, Admiral Kichisaburō Nomura – the last serious hope of avoiding war. Four days after Curtin had been sworn in, Casey cabled a report of a conversation with Roosevelt. The President thought the 'prospect of anything (save gain in time)' from the Washington talks between Hull and Nomura was not good.[13]

Nor were Singapore and Malaya much better prepared for a Japanese attack than they had been when the conference there at the end of 1940 had demonstrated the wide gap between the forces available and those that might be required. More fighter planes had been promised, but they hadn't arrived. The British claimed there were 200 planes in Singapore, Earle Page reported to Curtin from London on 16 November.[14] The target was now 300 – considerably fewer than the 586 earlier thought necessary for Malaya and Burma. (On 14 November, two days earlier, Page had cabled Curtin his understanding that there were actually only 110 warplanes in the Singapore-based command.[15]) The Australian 8th Division – most of it – was now there. Blamey was demanding it be sent through to the Middle East. The Indians, it was said, were more suitable than Australians for guard duties in tropical conditions.

The secret American–British conversations of early 1941 agreed that the British navy would strengthen its presence in the Indian Ocean, in return for which the United States would strengthen its naval presence in the Atlantic. This was not an outcome which suited Australia's interest, since it would gain very much less from more British naval forces around Ceylon than it would lose from fewer American naval ships in the Pacific. Australia was not involved in these talks, but it was told of their broad conclusions. They were a consideration in Churchill's earlier cable to Fadden, informing him of the decision to deploy a force of capital ships into the Indian Ocean.

(3)

By the second week of his prime ministership Curtin was deep into the details of war planning. Much of the agenda already concerned defence cooperation with the United States rather than Britain. Though it had originated in talks between the United States and Britain, and the United States would continue for some time to deal with Australia as part of its arrangements with Britain, some of the defence cooperation between Australia and the United States was now discussed directly with Washington rather than through London. As part of a supply route to the Philippines, for example, the United States wanted to use the port and airfield of Rabaul on the island of New Britain, part of Australian-mandated New Guinea.

Curtin called a meeting of War Cabinet in Melbourne on Wednesday, 15 October. It discussed improvement of the Rabaul defences, and agreed to military talks with the Manila-based United States commander in the Far East, General Douglas MacArthur. It decided to approach Portugal to permit an Australian deployment in Timor. War Cabinet discussed reinforcement of Ambon and Koepang, and agreed to invite Blamey back for consultations after the Tobruk withdrawal was completed. It agreed to ask London for 'a modern capital ship' in the proposed Indian Ocean squadron.[16]

On Thursday, 16 October, nine days after the new government was sworn in, the Singapore-based British commander in the Far East, Air Chief Marshal Sir Robert Brooke-Popham, briefed Curtin and his colleagues at a War Council meeting in Melbourne.[17]

'Malaya', the ever-hopeful Brooke-Popham assured the War Council, 'is going from strength to strength.'[18] He was also reinforcing Hong Kong. The Philippines to the east and Hong Kong would 'form a pincers' to crush Japanese forces if they came south. (Churchill rightly thought Hong Kong indefensible in a war with Japan. The United States thought the same of the Philippines, though it had recently decided to defend it.) But Japan was anyway unlikely to move south. Brooke-Popham said Japan was now looking north. He said the north-east monsoon made naval operations off the east coast of Malaya almost impossible from November to March. When the Japanese did move, they were more likely to attack the Soviet Union than Malaya. As an air force officer, he was confident that, if and when Japan did attack Malaya, they would find British air power formidable. The Buffalo Brewster fighters, he said, 'are superior to the Japanese and well suited to the work in Malaya'. The British air forces could cope with the planes the Japanese could base on aerodromes within range of Malayan targets.

Curtin was not entirely convinced. He pointed out that 'vital deficiencies' reported earlier in 1941 appeared to be still outstanding. Short of threatening resignation, Brooke-Popham replied, he was doing all he could to wrest more resources. But while the War Council may have had doubts about British and Australian superiority in aviation, one of Brooke-Popham's messages was comforting: the strong force of British navy capital ships would be deployed in the Indian Ocean by the beginning of 1942.

Brooke-Popham calmed the country. He gave a press conference at Victoria Barracks in Melbourne, reporter Harold Cox recalled. Brooke-Popham

> exuded confidence. He told us that anybody who thought the Japanese would enter the war was stupid. They would not come into the war. If they did come into the war, which was immeasurably improbable, it would not be against Australia they would move but against Russia, so that the western allies had nothing at all to fear from Japan. In any case, even if the Japanese did wish to attack the western allies through the Pacific, they realised that Singapore was impregnable and they would be wasting their time.

While it was hard to argue with Brooke-Popham, Cox had second thoughts not long after when he spoke to a delegation from the Netherlands East Indies. They were 'quite convinced that it was a matter of weeks only before the Japs would be in the war. They were completely philosophical about it. They told me and they told anybody who liked to ask them that there was nothing in the East Indies to hold the Japanese and that the Japanese would overrun the Indies whenever they wanted to.'[19]

Brooke-Popham hadn't studied his predecessors' reports. After careful assessment the then General Officer Commanding Malaya, Major-General W G Dobbie, had reported four years earlier that if the Japanese attacked it was not only possible for them to land on the east coast of Malaya during the monsoon period from October to March, but highly 'probable'. The bad visibility would be no great hindrance to an amphibious attack, but it would make British air reconnaissance difficult. Kota Bharu, he concluded, was a likely landing point. Contrary to the common military assumption, he reported the following year, Johore was not impassable for infantry, and an attack on Singapore would likely come from that direction.[20]

British planning in Malaya relied on air power to oppose an attack by sea. Instead of being concentrated to meet the main enemy force, British land forces were accordingly divided and assigned to defend the air bases in northern Malaya. It was a strategy that might have made sense if Brooke-Popham had possessed the required number of modern fighters and bombers. As he readily conceded to Curtin, he didn't. He had less than a third of the number of planes specified in earlier assessments, all of them obsolete.

(4)

At Blamey's request, Fadden had insisted on relief of the remainder of the Australian troops holding Tobruk. On 13 October Churchill had cabled Curtin seeking a reversal of the Australian decision. Curtin refused and, with the support of War Cabinet and the War Council, reaffirmed the Australian request on 16 October.[21] He also asked Churchill for a 'first class capital ship' to be included in the Indian Ocean squadron.[22]

Ten days later Churchill testily cabled that the relief was being carried out 'in accordance with your decision which I greatly regret'. He still thought Japan would not 'run into war' with British or American forces 'unless or until Russia is decisively broken'. But he confirmed the British navy's newest battleship, the *Prince of Wales*, would be sent to the Indian Ocean, joining *Repulse*. Later, other, older battleships would be sent.[23] Curtin thanked Churchill, who responded on 2 November, 'I am very glad you are pleased about the big ship. There is nothing like having something that can catch and kill anything.'[24]

Churchill had met some opposition to sending the big ship. On 20 October he had had to overcome Admiralty objections to persuade the Defence Committee of Cabinet to send the *Prince of Wales* to Cape Town.[25] Churchill thought of it as a demonstration. He told the same meeting that he 'did not foresee an attack in force on Malaya'.[26] Intended to be accompanied by the aircraft carrier *Indomitable*, British plans were upset when the carrier ran aground during training in the Caribbean. The *Prince of Wales*, together with *Repulse*, was sent on anyway, berthing in Singapore on 2 December. Japanese torpedo bombers would shortly demonstrate that the battleship, the heart of the both the British navy and the United States Pacific fleet, the central weapon in the fleet action naval doctrine of the United States and Britain – and, for that matter, Japan – was made instantly obsolescent at the outbreak of the Pacific War by the striking power of aircraft.

(5)

Driven by Evatt and with Curtin's endorsement, there were stirrings of a stronger assertion of Australian independence in foreign policy. Direct defence cooperation with the United States had begun under the previous government, and both widened and deepened under the Curtin Government. The War Cabinet submission[27] for the 13 October meeting made it clear that while the Dominions Office had transmitted the American request for facilities to support an air route to the Philippines, the next stage would involve direct contact between Australian and United States authorities. Australia would also enter direct discussions with MacArthur.

Meeting on 30 October, War Cabinet considered a British proposal that the British commanders at Singapore and Hong Kong should have authority to seize Japanese fishing boats when they thought war with Japan was imminent. Evatt argued that the proposal was 'highly dangerous' because it meant military commanders could initiate hostilities without civilian political authority. War Cabinet agreed; Evatt's point was well taken. Churchill was also alert to the possibility local commanders would initiate hostilities, at enormous political cost to Britain and more importantly its prospective ally, the United States.

To Churchill's annoyance Australia also pressed for a prompt declaration of war against Finland, then fighting the Soviet Union, in addition to declarations against Hungary and Romania. Responding to a British cable canvassing the pros and cons of a Soviet request for a declaration of war against Finland, on 30 October War Cabinet agreed to tell London it would be 'disastrous' to Russian morale to refuse the request. The War Council subsequently agreed, and the Dominions Office was informed of Australia's views the same day. Churchill hoped that Finland and the Soviet Union would begin peace talks before Britain was obliged to declare war. If Britain did declare war, he thought, Scandinavian opinion would be offended, and Britain would lose the little influence it had over Finland.

In late November Churchill cabled Curtin[28] complaining of a press report that Evatt had criticised Britain for not declaring war on Finland. Replying on 29 November Curtin suggested that Evatt had been misquoted, adding that Churchill should welcome Australia's 'independence of thought' on issues. As Australia accepted more of a burden on foreign policy 'sometimes it is inevitable that the Commonwealth Government will formulate a policy at variance with yours'.[29] In the event, Churchill found Stalin's pressure too strong and Finland's claims too weak. Britain and the Commonwealth declared war on Finland in early December.

At the same War Cabinet meeting Evatt won agreement to an exchange of diplomatic representatives with the Netherlands East Indies, and a proposed Australian delegation to the Soviet Union. Both moves had been initiated under the previous government. Between the Government and the Opposition, there were at this point few differences on foreign policy.

In September 1939 Menzies had declared that Britain was at war, so Australia was at war. Australia did not separately declare war on Germany. In discussion of war declarations against Finland, Hungary and Romania, Evatt argued that Australia's declarations of war should not follow from a British declaration but be made independently. Canada and New Zealand had already adopted this procedure. The declarations would still have to be assented to by the King, who was constitutionally Australia's head of state. But the form would make it clear that the King acted as the head of state of Australia and not Britain. Curtin instructed Bruce[30] that Australia's war declaration would be made only if Britain had made one. In the event, all three declarations were conveniently bundled with a fourth when Japan attacked.

(6)

Despite cryptographic intelligence otherwise, Churchill and Brooke-Popham were not alone in thinking Japan was more interested in attacking the Soviet Union than the British in the Far East. Casey reported on 17 October that the United States navy also expected this. Page reported it from Singapore, and from a conversation with MacArthur. The possibility prompted Curtin and Evatt to press for an agreement between the Soviet Union and Britain which would see each aiding the other if one was attacked by Japan. On 30 October War Cabinet approved a War Council recommendation that Japan should be told that if it attacked the Soviet Union, the British Commonwealth would then declare war on Japan – 'irrespective of the attitude of the United States'. The British Commonwealth should seek a reciprocal assurance from the Soviet Union that it would declare war on Japan if it instead attacked southward, but the commitment to support the Soviet Union 'should not be conditional upon such an assurance'. Committing to war with Japan without the United States was surely not a sensible idea, though it evidently had the support of the Opposition as well as the Curtin Government.

Such a pact, Curtin argued in a message to London on 4 November, would commit the Soviet Union to a war in the Pacific if Japan attacked. Certainly, there would be a price to pay in recognition of post-war Soviet territorial claims, but it was well worth paying. Churchill primly refused. The Atlantic Charter would not permit him to accept claims without the consent of the people involved. Curtin denied that he had intended otherwise. With the Soviet Union fighting for its life against the German war machine, there was very little likelihood Stalin would invite a war with Japan. His Siberian troops were needed to build the armies that a year later would appear out of the snowstorms either side of Stalingrad, joining up to encircle and destroy General Friedrich von Paulus's 6th Army. Stalin shared Churchill's view: Germany first.

Curtin was trying out various possibilities, not all wise and some plainly silly. Then and through early November he pressed for the early arrival of the promised capital ships, the reciprocal pact with the Soviet Union on Japan, support for China (including his agreement to Churchill's plan to send Australian 'volunteer' pilots to Chiang Kai-shek's air force[31]), and an immediate declaration of war by Britain if Japan attacked the Netherlands East Indies.

But among the options raised, one was missing. Curtin did not mention his past preference, pressed at the War Council earlier in the year, that Australia should bring its troops back from the Middle East to meet a new danger from Japan. An announcement that Blamey would return from the Middle East for consultations sparked speculation that the AIF divisions would be withdrawn. 'The government had no intention' of recalling the AIF, Curtin told the House on 5 November.[32]

(7)

In the cable traffic between Curtin and Churchill, small annoyances accumulated. Speaking to the War Council on 11 and 18 November, Blamey criticised the gap between the forces promised for the campaign in Greece, and those actually provided. If Australian troops were to be used in a campaign in Turkey, then being considered, Australia should insist on better preparations. Curtin cabled Churchill to this effect on 22 November, citing details of the problems in the Greek campaign. A cable based on such detailed information, clearly provided by a general who possessed the facts, was not one that could be easily contradicted. Churchill deftly replied that there was much that might be said, but he thought Curtin would not wish him to reply in full at that moment.[33]

In public remarks Blamey reprimanded Australians on their complacency and lack of understanding of the reality of war. It was

Blamey who misunderstood. In mid-November he was still pressing for the 8th Division to be transferred from Malaya to the Middle East, still demanding strong air and naval support if and when the AIF joined the operations in Turkey, still arguing that the conscript home army was too big, and still insisting that Japan would not enter the war – or, if it did, it would attack the Soviet Union. Flying back to his command, he was astonished to be told over drinks in Karachi that Japan had attacked at Pearl Harbor.[34]

For his part Curtin had decided he wanted the 8th Division to stay in Malaya. He told a Canberra meeting of War Cabinet on 18 November 1941 that Australia 'can't expect the United States to help' unless 'we are doing something for ourselves'.[35] Well before Pearl Harbor, Curtin's thinking had turned to America.

Still, he thought the AIF in the Middle East should be reinforced. As Dedman later recounted, 'So long as it thought that there was a possibility that Japan would not go to war', the Curtin Government 'was unwilling to weaken the British position in the Middle East, where the second western desert offensive was about to be launched'.[36] Much of the reinforcement for the AIF came from the Militia, which was depleted of its best commanders and best-trained troops. Even if there was war with Japan, it was assumed there would be plenty of time to train new armies.[37]

(8)

It was quite evident to Curtin that Japan was preparing for war, but he still hoped it might be averted. The day before his government had been sworn in, Australia's Combined Operational Intelligence Centre in Melbourne had reported that Japan's preparations for war were 'considered to be almost complete'.[38] Three weeks later it reported that the Japanese navy was now 'fully mobilised on a war footing'. Around the beginning of November, in an operational planning directive, the home commander, Major-General Sydney Rowell, advised that 'The general situation is such that war between the British Empire and Japan must be regarded as a probability.'[39] In order of likelihood, the Japanese might be expected to attack Malaya to seize Singapore, to attack the Netherlands East Indies and British North Borneo, and to invade Australia or New Zealand. The probability of war was increasing. In late November Tatsuo Kawai, the Japanese minister in Canberra, told Curtin the momentum towards war was too great to be stopped, a conversation Curtin later recounted to *Sydney Morning Herald* war reporter Gavin Long. Curtin learned soon after that Kawai's staff were burning their papers. Despite Evatt's objection, Australian intelligence had bugged the Melbourne offices of the Japanese diplomatic mission.[40]

From Washington, Casey cabled Curtin that talks with Japan had entered a new, final phase. Reporting a 14 November meeting, Casey wrote that Under Secretary of State Sumner Welles thought Japan would refuse to evacuate China, and the United States would insist on nothing less.[41]

At the end of November 1941, the uncertainty abruptly ended. From Washington on Saturday, 29 November[42] Casey reported a sudden change in the United States assessment.[43] He told Curtin he had that day spoken to Henry L Stimson, the 74-year-old Secretary for War, a Republican whom Roosevelt had brought into his cabinet to counterbalance the isolationist sentiment of the Senate. In conversation with Casey, Stimson had been joined by General Sherman Miles, the head of United States Army Intelligence. As Secretary of State for President Hoover in 1932, Stimson had refused to recognise Japan's 1931 conquest of Manchuria, a policy affirming American interest in unobstructed access to China. At around the time he met Casey, Stimson had confided to his diary a discussion with the President, who had said the Japanese might attack as early as Monday, 'for the Japanese are notorious for making an attack without warning, and the question was what we should do. The question was how we should manoeuvre them into the position of firing the first shot without allowing too much danger to ourselves.'[44]

Stimson and his intelligence chief told Casey that the United States assessment was now that Japan would not attack the Soviet Union, even though it had superior forces in the region after the westward movement of Soviet troops. Instead, Japan was clearly preparing to attack south. A naval task force was being assembled in Hainan and Taiwan. According to Army Intelligence, 'A task force of about 5 divisions, supported by appropriate air and naval units has been assembled for the execution of these plans. This force is now en route southward to an, as yet, undetermined rendezvous.' The United States navy had sent out precautionary warnings to all its commanders.

Plans for an attack would be put into effect, Army Intelligence concluded, as soon as the talks in Washington, now led for Japan by special envoy Saburō Kurusu, definitely failed. On 30 November, Dominions Secretary Cranborne cabled Curtin that 'there are important indications that Japan is about to attack Thailand'.[45] From Kota Bharu on the north-east coast of Malaya, Royal Australian Air Force planes were now patrolling the arc of sea through which a Japanese task force would move south. A day earlier, United States navy chief of operations Admiral Harold F Stark signalled fleet commanders that 'if hostilities cannot be repeat cannot be avoided', the policy of the United States was that 'Japan shall commit the first act'.

What would prove to be an even more momentous intercept decoded by the Americans was a report of a 29 November meeting between the Japanese Ambassador in Berlin and the German Foreign Minister, Joachim von Ribbentrop. Encouraging Japan to attack British and American forces, Ribbentrop said the Führer was determined to go to war with the United States if Japan did.[46]

At the beginning of December the Combined Operational Intelligence Centre in Melbourne reported that Japan 'is now ready to strike in any direction from Indo-China at any moment'.[47]

Aware of the concentration of forces to attack south, United States intelligence was unaware of the far bigger naval force now heading east in the North Pacific towards Honolulu.

As war tension increased, the Australian navy suffered ill fortune. The light cruiser HMAS *Sydney* was sunk off the coast of Western Australia by the German raider, *Kormoran*, on 19 November. All 645 of *Sydney*'s crew died. For Curtin it was the worst news of the war, thus far. He shared his sorrow with a sympathetic Gowrie. They couldn't print it, but he told reporters anyway. 'You can write this and have it ready, and you can tell Sir Keith [Murdoch],' Curtin told Cox. 'You can't publish it, of course, until censorship releases it and that can't be until next-of-kin are informed.'[48] Eleven days after it sank, Curtin announced the loss of the ship. A few days later the Government announced the loss of HMAS *Parramatta* in the Mediterranean.

Unprepared for war in the Pacific, Curtin wanted to avert it. If under a peace plan China had to accept continuing occupation by Japan, so be it. With Curtin's support, Evatt pressed to the last moment for a new start to the Washington talks. Chiang Kai-shek's Nationalist Government had strongly exerted itself to prevent the United States compromising on Japan's China claims. China should compromise its demand for a Japanese withdrawal, Evatt argued, if that was the obstacle to an agreement. Evatt told the House on 27 November that an 'honourable arrangement with Japan' was possible if it withdrew from Indo-China – a very much less demanding condition than withdrawing from China. Two days later Evatt cabled Sir Frederic Eggleston, the Australian Minister to China, instructing him that China's 'intervention in preventing agreement' may have the objective of forcing war between Japan and the United States, taking the pressure off China. He quoted a conversation earlier that morning in which Curtin had said to Evatt, 'China does not want to be treated as a pawn in this game. But neither does Australia.' Evatt asked Eggleston to spin to the Chinese an implausible line that their opposition to an agreement between Japan and the United States on this point might result in fiercer attacks on China by Japan, without necessarily bringing the United States into a conflict with Japan. He also encouraged Casey's suggestion that Casey seek a meeting with the Japanese special envoy in Washington, Kurusu.[49] Casey did, but without useful result.

Meeting in Canberra on 1 December, War Cabinet considered a Dominions Office cablegram in which the Commander-in-Chief Far East, Brooke-Popham, asked London for permission to move into Thailand if Japanese ships approached. War Cabinet agreed, while also asking Britain to press the United States to reach a 'modus vivendi' with Japan. Curtin said Japan intended to occupy Thailand.[50] Troop leave from Darwin was deferred.

The same day Bruce reported to Curtin a meeting with Churchill.[51] Always aware of Roosevelt's political circumstances, Churchill said he was reluctant to authorise a strike into Thailand before an actual attack by Japan. It would allow isolationists in the United States, still powerful in the Senate, to say Britain had provoked a war. The British plan to move pre-emptively into Thailand was cancelled. Regretted by the army, Churchill's decision was certainly correct. Nothing mattered more than America coming into the war.

On 1 December, around the same time as War Cabinet was meeting in Canberra, an Imperial Conference was assembling in Tokyo. During it Emperor Hirohito accepted that the deadline for diplomacy had passed. He approved a decision to go to war with the United States, Britain and the Netherlands. Australia was not separately mentioned.[52]

The ordinary business of government continued. Meeting in Canberra on Tuesday, 2 December, Cabinet agreed that female workers were needed in wartime, so long as priority for men was restored after the war. The following day Cabinet discussed wheat, apples and pears. Curtin said he planned to be in Western Australia from 14 December. Forde would be Acting Prime Minister. Curtin had not been home since August.

In Washington, the Roosevelt Administration was expecting war. Still hopeful, on 3 December Evatt cabled Bruce, Casey and Eggleston to thank them for their help in preventing the breakdown of talks in Washington. 'It is now obvious,' he wrote, 'that our efforts have not been without some measure of success.'[53]

By then Japanese troop transports were at sea, and in radio silence the carrier task force was steaming towards Hawaii.

(9)

There was plenty of discussion of the threat from Japan, but in Curtin's first two months in office there had been only a few steps to increase Australia's capacity to meet an attack. Curtin had begun to remove obstructions to war production. He pressed for bigger British navy battleships for the Indian Ocean, there were negotiations over Australian naval vessels expected to be returned to Australian waters if Japan entered the war, and there was the cooperation with the United States in building up Rabaul as a naval base and Australian airstrips as part of the Philippines supply route.

The defence of Australia against a possible invasion was not a top priority. Australia continued to supply aircrew for training in Canada and posting to Britain, and its ships continued to be under Admiralty command and part of the British navy. The AIF in the Middle East was reinforced as necessary. War Cabinet pressed for more and faster aircraft production, but many of the planes were intended for Britain.

There was discussion of the size of the Militia. Not, as might be expced, that it was too small or that it was not sufficiently trained, but that it was too big and had too many men in full-time training who might otherwise have been making munitions or other war products. During the War Cabinet meeting of 30 October, for example, the minutes recorded that 'it was observed the number of Militia called up for full-time duty represented a heavy demand on manpower and financial resources', and a reorganisation might permit 'release of men from the Army for munitions production and essential industry'. During his November visit Blamey reinforced the message: the Militia was too big.

Whatever he said publicly at this time, whatever he had said when in Opposition, the actions of Curtin and his government in the first two months of office suggest that he relied on the promised British navy Indian Ocean task force, on a quite false British assessment of the capabilities of the Japanese navy, army and air forces, and on the hope that war in the Pacific against Japan either wouldn't happen or would bring in the United States if it did. It had been much the same for Menzies and Fadden. Though he had for years warned of a Pacific war, Curtin did not prepare for one with much greater urgency than Fadden or Menzies.

That said, the entry of Japan into the war would be less surprising to Curtin and his ministers than the shock of Japan's rapid, bold and extraordinary success. It was that – Japan's success – which would overturn Australia's understanding of the world.

As late as 4 December, Curtin asked at a War Cabinet meeting in Melbourne for a review of the strength and organisation of the three services 'to meet the probable forms of attack on Australia', bearing in mind that the 'primary requirement is to prevent an enemy landing on these shores'. The review should particularly consider 'the possibility of reducing the establishment of the Military Forces by, say, 20 000 to 30 000 men to enable additional manpower to be made available for the Navy and Air Force and for munitions production.'[54] The War Cabinet decision reflected the views of Shedden, but it is difficult to reconstruct the reasoning behind a preference, with war imminent, to reduce the size of the Australian army. Australia lacked ships and planes, but not crews. In War Council Curtin had earlier discussed reducing the size of the Militia. In due course, Fadden would put that discussion to good political use.

Meeting in Melbourne on Friday, 5 December, War Cabinet's agenda included discussion of rifles, oil, the role of women in production, munitions and aluminium. War Cabinet would meet next in Victoria Barracks at 4.10 in the afternoon of Monday, 8 December. By then, Australia would be at war with Japan.

(10)

In two months as prime minister, Curtin and his ministers had brought new energy and direction to government. They had impressed their critics. Above all, the Government had survived. Curtin's standing had been transformed, not so much because of what he suddenly became but because the earlier portrayal of him had been off the mark. In 1940 and 1941 Curtin's strategy had been to avoid the appearance of obstructing the Government, though he continued to express differences. After the 1940 election he recognised that, while Menzies' support was weakening within Cabinet and his majority in the House was precarious, Curtin could at the time no more command a majority in the House than could Menzies. Curtin might be able to force an election, but an election so soon after the 1940 ballot would not be welcomed. Labor might lose rather than gain seats. He remained resolutely opposed to an all-party government, reasoning that Labor would have to accept responsibility without being able to implement its program.

While Curtin's strategy was sensible and ultimately successful, it involved a considerable cost. The newspaper owners seeking a national government portrayed Curtin as a weak leader avoiding the responsibility of office. Menzies encouraged this interpretation, not least because his political survival depended upon a national government. In his eagerness for office and hostility to Menzies, Evatt portrayed Curtin in the same way. Evatt did so in private letters, including to Melbourne powerbroker John Wren.[55] The result was a widespread view that Curtin was a reluctant leader, an impression which made his conduct in office all the more surprising.

In those first eight weeks, press opinion of Curtin sharply changed. His ways were unaltered. Even as prime minister he had no police guard and he could still be seen catching a tram from the Victoria Palace Hotel to War Cabinet meetings at Victoria Barracks.[56] As prime minister Curtin used the 'blue-and-gold suite' at the Victoria Palace. He sometimes took his meals in the dining room area the staff knew as 'the manager's alcove', where it was quieter. Often, the staff recalled, if he saw a serviceman dining alone he would ask him to join him. He still liked the plainest of food. His favourite dish at the Victoria Palace was Irish stew, according to the dining-room manager Mollie Morgan. Assistant head porter Mac McKernan recalled that as prime minister 'Mr Curtin never made any fuss'.[57] His 'personal elusiveness' and 'deliberative nature' were still remarked upon by reporters.[58] His personality hadn't changed, but reporters now discerned in him a new authority and decisiveness. Reporting in the *Sunday Sun* on 9 November, for example, Alan Reid wrote that '"Plain John" Curtin', who, his opponents had said, was afraid of taking office, 'is amazing his former critics'. Curtin had 'ripped Menzies to pieces' during the Budget debate.

Sun News-Pictorial reporter Harold Cox spoke of the same transformation. When Curtin was Opposition leader, Cox said he used to lie on his office couch complaining of headaches and neuralgia.

> But when he became Prime Minister, the position changed fantastically. In the matter of two days, he seemed to be completely on top of the position. He was never aggressive, never flamboyant. He didn't seek to make spectacular changes.

He just carried on and there was a new direction seemed to develop in the Parliament which had been obviously floundering.[59]

By the time of his *Sydney Morning Herald* column of 17 November, Ross Gollan was still missing his hero, Fadden, but reconciling himself to the new government. Factional disputes in caucus seem to have disappeared, he reported. Even 'non Labour quarters' – perhaps Fadden – agreed that Curtin has 'so far come through every test with credit to himself and Australia'. With his Budget speech Chifley had established himself as 'one of the major political forces in this parliament', after saying very little in Opposition since his return to Parliament. Beasley and Evatt were also deemed successes.

Curtin continued to cultivate the Opposition, and the press. By the time of Gollan's column on Monday, 1 December, Curtin ranked up there with Fadden among Gollan's admired politicians; at all events, he extended to Curtin the same unwillingness to disbelieve he had extended to Fadden. Gollan reported that Curtin wanted a 'recess long enough to enable Parliamentary committees to present reports which could serve as a basis for legislation', reflecting Curtin's 'faith in the committee system' and his 'desire for inter party cooperation'. Curtin was thus praised for an intended recess of three or four months, on the grounds he wanted to elevate Parliament. At the same time Gollan decided Curtin was 'steadily elevating the status of the Advisory War Council'.

Writing on Sunday for his Monday, 8 December column, Gollan recognised that the 'showdown' with Japan 'may come any day now'. Curtin had been in office two months, prompting Gollan to sum up the Government's performance: 'Mr Curtin, as Prime Minister, seems to all his closest observers a miraculously changed person from Mr Curtin, as Leader of the Opposition.' There had been a theory that 'Mr Curtin would not be able to stand up to strains of Prime Ministership for more than a couple of months because of illnesses 'thought to be of nervous origin, which had a way of attacking him whenever heavy political weather arrived'. Curtin also had shown a 'knack of indecisiveness in some small political matters'. But 'the plain fact about Mr Curtin since he took the Prime Ministership is that the bigger the matter that has come to him, the more decisive has been his handling of it – the more the load of work and worry upon him, the better his apparent physical trim'. Curtin displayed 'hard unemotional thinking'.

A literary man (he had been annoyed by the previous government's ban on James Joyce's *Ulysses*), Gollan wrote that:

> Mr Curtin's ultimate biographer may trace the transformation in him since assuming the Prime Ministership to a release of inhibitions first caused by his omission from the Labour Cabinets of 1929–31. They were possibly accentuated by his defeat in the 1931 general election and by his later uphill though eventually successful fight as leader of a party which, when he returned to Canberra after his one Parliament's absence, had almost ceased to be a living political force.

By the time Gollan's column was published, Japanese forces had attacked Pearl Harbor, landed in Thailand and Malaya, and begun fighting their way down the Malay Peninsula towards Singapore.

CHAPTER 21

IT HAS COME

(1)

Recruited from the foothills of the Himalayas, in December 1941 the men of the third battalion of the 17th Dogra regiment of the India Army found themselves on the flat shores of the South China Sea, 4000 kilometres from their mountain homes. Their job was to watch the beaches, rivers and swamps and protect the nearby airfield at Kota Bharu on Malaya's north-eastern coast, just south of the border with Thailand. Not long after midnight on the morning of Monday, 8 December, soldiers of A and B companies guarding the Bandang and Sabak beaches saw small boats near the mouth of the Kemassin River. They alerted the Royal Air Force base nearby. The duty officer was Wing Commander Reginald Davis, the thirty-year-old commander of the Number One Squadron of the Royal Australian Air Force. Soon after the telephone call Davis heard the crash of naval guns as Japanese warships shelled the Dogras and their shore defences. In the shallow waters off Kota Bharu, 5600 troops from Major-General Hiroshi Takumi's 56th Infantry Division scrambled from their transport ships into landing barges. Two and half kilometres inland, RAAF crews dashed to their Hudson bombers to attack the Japanese. Nearly two hours before Japanese planes reached Pearl Harbor, the Pacific War had begun.

At 6 p.m. on Friday, 5 December, Curtin had been leaving a War Cabinet meeting at Victoria Barracks, Melbourne, to catch the Spirit of Progress train to Canberra. Shedden caught up with him and drew him aside. 'I am sorry to have misled you gentlemen,' Curtin then told the waiting reporters, 'I am not returning to Canberra tonight.'[1] Army Minister Frank Forde and Air Minister Arthur Drakeford were called back, War Cabinet reconvened for half an hour, and the ministers then adjourned to await news over the weekend.

Curtin called some reporters to his room in the Victoria Palace Hotel at nine o'clock that night. It was 'an austere and inexpensive hotel with oilcloth on the floors, polished oilcloth – it smelt of soap – narrow corridors, funny little pot plant stands with aspidistra plants on them, funny little brassbound tables', Cox recorded. Curtin told them of a warning that a Japanese fleet was at sea and heading to Malaya. Cox recalled that Curtin said, 'There's probably nothing in this and if it clears early next week I'll take my holiday. But I think you'd be wise to remain in touch.'[2]

'Ominous Moves in the Pacific', *The Argus* reported on Saturday morning. Negotiations in Washington had failed. A Japanese amphibious expedition was moving southward, possibly to attack Malaya, or the Netherlands East Indies, or perhaps the Philippines. It was now highly likely, the newspaper reported, that if Japan attacked in the Pacific the United States would be involved. War Cabinet had cancelled Christmas leave for forces in Darwin, and placed a large order for gas masks. It was a big page-one story – though not as big as the main story reporting the fighting in Russia.

Elsie was returning to Perth, and Curtin had been planning to return to Canberra and then follow her for a Christmas break. He spent the weekend at the Victoria Palace instead, and visited old friends in Melbourne on Saturday. They found him anxious and preoccupied. On Sunday evening he turned in at the Victoria Palace, not knowing what the week might bring. Cox remembered it was 'a very dreary week-end. Nothing happened on the Saturday;

nothing happened on the Sunday.' The first report of the landing at Kota Bharu reached the Navy Office in Melbourne at 4.30 a.m. on Monday, an hour and a half after the attack began[3] and a few minutes after Japanese planes began their attack on Pearl Harbor. The Department of Information picked up broadcast news of the Hawaii attack at 5.45 a.m. Curtin had gone to bed in his small suite at the hotel at 1 a.m., around the time the Japanese task force had arrived off Kota Bharu. Don Rodgers woke him with the news the war with Japan had begun. 'Well, it has come,' Curtin said. Rodgers called Cox to say there were reports Japanese attacks had begun 'and the boss thinks it's on. He's getting dressed and he's going down to the Barracks. Will you tell the others. You'd better try and get them down there early, too.'[4]

By the time Curtin and his colleagues met as War Cabinet in Melbourne's Victoria Barracks later that day, Australian airmen of the First Squadron at Kota Bharu had sunk the first Japanese naval vessel lost to Allied action in the Pacific War, and suffered their first casualties from Japanese fire. The British Admiralty, Curtin was told, had ordered all its commanders to 'Commence hostilities against Japan' at once. War Cabinet agreed immediately that 'the situation should be accepted as involving a state of war against Japan'.[5] The formal declaration would come a little later.

On the morning of Monday, 8 December Melbourne was expecting cloudy, unsettled weather with more rain. The morning papers were well behind events. *The Argus* ran a story with a Singapore by-line reporting that Japanese naval ships were in the Gulf of Siam, crossing from Saigon to Bangkok, probably intending to attack Thailand rather than Malaya. They were being closely observed by RAAF Hudsons from Malaya. The British Eastern Fleet was reported to be 'ready for immediate action'. There was still a hope for peace, with Roosevelt sending a message to Emperor Hirohito. The *Sydney Morning Herald* reported that full Cabinet was expected to meet later that day in Melbourne to declare war on Finland, Hungary and

Romania. Getting in first, New Zealand Prime Minister Peter Fraser had done so the previous day.

At 7 a.m. in Tokyo, 9 a.m. Melbourne time, Japanese preparing for the week's work were astonished and then delighted to learn Japan had entered war with the United States and Britain in the Pacific before dawn, successfully raiding Pearl Harbor and the Philippines and attacking Malaya. Shortages of rice and luxury goods were annoying, but if Japan could through war secure the raw materials it needed the sacrifice would perhaps be worthwhile.[6] In any case, they were told, the United States had given Japan no alternative.

The Pearl Harbor raid astonished them, but American leaders were expecting a Japanese surprise attack somewhere. Earlier that year the United States Ambassador in Tokyo, Joseph Grew, had alerted Secretary of State Hull to Tokyo rumours of a 'surprise mass attack on Pearl Harbor'.[7] At the urging of the State Department, Roosevelt had wanted to deter or at least postpone war with Japan with a show of American naval might. Deployed to Pearl Harbor from its San Diego base on Roosevelt's insistence and over Navy objections, the United States Pacific fleet presented to Japan's planners an attractive target.

Cox remembered that:

Curtin was at the Barracks well before a normal breakfast time, stayed there throughout the day and he held three press conferences in that first day of the Japanese war. The notable feature always was his complete calmness, lack of flap, and his obvious knowledge of precisely where he was going, what he was doing. He announced one after another a whole series of most important decisions and he did it without any fuss and without any sign of anxiety or anything else.[8]

Keeping an earlier commitment to speak at a public meeting to raise money for a replacement for HMAS *Sydney*, Curtin warned that the Japanese might attack Australia. 'This is the first time in the history of this land,' he said, that an enemy could 'enter here and break down the defences that have kept our houses from attack.'[9]

Fortunately, the British Empire was well prepared, or so Australians were assured. As the *Sydney Morning Herald* confidently reported on Tuesday, 9 December, 'the ability of Singapore to defend itself against any form of attack – either by sea, land or air, or by all three methods together – has never been questioned by military and naval experts'. 'The great fortress and its approaches have been so strengthened since the outbreak of war in 1939 that there is little reason to doubt that they are impregnable.'

(2)

It had come. The Pacific War would both simplify and intensify Curtin's life. It enlarged him. For a while there would be no caucus revolts, no cross-purposes within government, no day-to-day threat of a vote in the House of Representatives that would bring the Government down. The risk of being forced to an election, hanging over the Government for the last two months, vanished. So, too, did Curtin's option of calling an election. The long debate over Japan's intentions, over the likelihood of America being drawn into a war against Japan, was at once resolved.

The nation was shocked, astonished. Australians looked to the prime minister as never before in their short history. People cooperated. An obscure politician from Perth unexpectedly elected Leader of the Opposition and six years later appointed prime minister without a vote of the people, a prime minister without a party majority in either House and whose first Budget had been promptly amended by his own party, Curtin was now asked to be the national leader in what might be the first threat to the nation's survival it had ever had to face.

It would not become apparent for a while, but it was not only Australia's security that was at issue. It was also the way Australians thought about themselves, their country and its place in the world. Those ideas would be changed not so much by Japan's entry into the war or by its final defeat as by its extraordinary early victories. They would be changed also by Curtin's decisions during war, though he and the colleagues who supported him were themselves schooled in the thought patterns they were rearranging, and did not always foresee or welcome the changes they brought about.

Very often what they would say they were doing and sometimes even what they thought they were doing would not be what they actually did, or had consequences quite other than those intended. War in the Pacific changed too many things, too abruptly, for Curtin to see where it would take Australia and Asia. Things that might have happened sometime, war speeded up. The best Curtin and his government could do was to find a way through each successive problem. Only later would they begin to understand what they had done – to begin to understand what was enduring, what was temporary, what mattered and what did not.

For all its vast scale, ferocity and savagery, the war in Europe was familiar. The combatant nations in Europe had fought a war a quarter-century earlier in which they had taken much the same parts and fought on much the same ground. Germany fought Britain, France and Russia. The naval war in the Atlantic, the battles in the Middle East, the battles on the Eastern front and Western front had been fought before.

There had never been a Pacific war. Japan had never fought Britain and America. It was entirely new. The military strategies were new; some of the weapons such as aircraft carriers were, if not new, then used in a new way. Amphibious landings were usual in the Pacific War before the landings in North Africa, Italy and France. The theatre of war – the mix of big and little islands, the coastal jungles, the expanses of the sea, the peninsula of south-east Asia – was also new. In Russia, hundreds of German and Soviet divisions, thousands of tanks, were clashing against each other on great open plains. In the Pacific War a single division would be a big force; very often battles would be fought by battalions or even platoons, with the tactics of battle decided not by generals directing the movement of great armies but by captains or lieutenants fighting over jungle tracks on which at their widest only a few men could actually engage the few enemy, similarly constrained.

Hitler injected into the invasion of the Soviet Union a racial distinction, of Teutons against Slavs, that was not there in the campaigns against France and Britain. But from the beginning, from before the beginning, the Pacific War was also a race war. The war in Europe remade boundaries and spheres of influence. The war in the Pacific destroyed empires and created nations. It would change Australia's world.

(3)

As the shock of the surprise attack on Pearl Harbor wore off, morale in Australia rose.

While Japan had successfully landed troops in Thailand and on the east coast of Malaya and was now attacking British and Indian troops on both sides of the country, this southern thrust might well be parried. American Hudson bombers and Brewster Buffalo fighters were said to be better than their Japanese counterparts, the Japanese navy was said by the British to be no better than the Italian. Japanese army units were not necessarily better than the Indian army units they were fighting in Malaya – and certainly not equal to the Australian and British units they would soon encounter. The larger part of the Japanese army was still fighting in China. It had to watch the Soviet Union, which had routed a Japanese incursion not long before. The whole southern army first deployed by Japan in the attacks on Malaya, the Philippines, Hong Kong and scattered islands in the Pacific was by the standards of European engagements quite small.

Japan had sunk or damaged the eight great battleships of the United States Pacific fleet. But even after the losses at Pearl Harbor, the allied navies remained a formidable threat to Japan's plans. The British navy deployed a strong task force in Singapore and other ships at Ceylon. United States navy aircraft carriers had fortunately been away from Pearl Harbor on the day of the attack. Japan was now fighting the world's strongest nation, the United States, which for all the losses so far inflicted was already building a far superior navy

Curtin's mood was grave. Elsewhere, Japan's attack on the United States and the British Empire was good news. In China, Chiang was so delighted with what he thought of as his deliverance he played 'Ave Maria' on his gramophone. In the Soviet Union Stalin would see that at one stroke Japan had ceased for some time to be a threat to the eastern borders, and America would quite likely join the war against Germany. While the Roosevelt Administration was incensed and embarrassed by the success of Japan's attack on Pearl Harbor, it had long thought war likely and hoped Japan would make the first move.

For Churchill, it was the best news of the entire war. It had solved Roosevelt's political problems and brought a mighty ally to Britain's side.[10] 'Greater good fortune has rarely happened to the British Empire,' Churchill would minute the following year, recalling 'the blessing that Japan attacked the United States and thus brought America wholeheartedly into the war'.[11] Even in Curtin's government in those first few days there was solemnity and fortitude, not dismay. War with Japan had, after all, long been expected. As Evatt told War Cabinet with his usual pertinacity on the morning of Monday, 8 December, 'United States entry on our side' assured eventual victory.[12] Half a world away, Churchill said much the same. His delight at Japan's attack was all the greater because he had not expected it. Only four days earlier he had described the idea of a Japanese attack as a 'remote contingency'.[13]

Churchill's joy was complete when a few days later Germany declared war on the United States, as promised. Hitler wanted Japan to attack the Soviet Union also. Even the possibility might oblige Stalin to keep a powerful force in Siberia. If he won the war in the east, Hitler would be more than ready when Britain and America came at him from the west. The increasingly active and hostile stance of the US navy in the Atlantic suggested that America would sooner or later join the war against Germany. How much better for Germany if America was tied down by Japan in the Pacific? It was a reasonable gamble – so long as Japan attacked the Soviet Union, or the Soviet Union behaved as if it might, and so long as American resources were diverted to the Pacific War. A reasonable gamble, though unsuccessful. Recognising their mutual interests in fighting wars on other fronts, Japan and the Soviet Union would leave each other alone until the final days of the Pacific War. Roosevelt was already committed to defeating Germany first. The Soviet Union would in any case prove a far more formidable adversary than Hitler had reason to believe in December 1941.

Nothing had or could have adequately prepared Curtin for leading Australia in its time of peril. Unlike Churchill and Roosevelt he had never been in the armed forces, or even visited a war zone. War Council had familiarised him with the issues, but until he became prime minister and Minister for Defence Co-ordination two months before Japan went to war in the Pacific he had no experience of making war decisions. Yet Curtin accepted the vast new responsibilities without bother or complaint. He seemed, as the *Sydney Morning Herald*'s Gollan observed, to be rather more comfortable, easy and clear-headed in making big decisions than in making small ones. There were times he worried and worry was not good for his heart. His unreliable health intermittently interfered. The spirit was willing.

(4)

The day, the hour and the places were unknown, but by early December war with Japan was not unexpected in Washington. Roosevelt knew from the imposition of deeper American-led Allied sanctions against Japan in July 1941 that war was all but inevitable. Japan had only two choices. It could either seize oil in the Netherlands East Indies, which would mean war with the United States, or accede to the United States demand and withdraw from China. It went to war in December 1941 not to defeat the United States, which was impossible, but to secure oil, rubber and other resources and thus to secure its empire in Korea, Taiwan, Manchuria and China. Already at war with China and with good reason to be wary of the Soviet Union, Japan's southward thrust was a gamble undertaken only because the military leadership was convinced it had no alternative. The oil wells of the Netherlands East Indies produced 65 million barrels of oil a year, more than Japan consumed in any year of the war. Every military move of the opening phase of the war was designed to attain and then secure that objective. Japan was to find the prize worth very much less than it had supposed.

American intercepts of Japanese messages showed war was coming. Even the surprise attack was no surprise – it was a typical Japanese move, demonstrated with great success in the Russo-Japanese War of 1905. What was unexpected was that the surprise attack would be on Pearl Harbor and on Thailand, Malaya, Wake Island, the Philippines, more or less simultaneously – and be so rapidly successful. All the comforting assurances about the quality of Japanese planes and pilots, its navy and its army were refuted in the first few hours of battle. Japanese Zeroes were better planes than American or British fighters; the Japanese pilots were as well trained and used better tactics. Japanese naval command and tactics, the British and Americans rapidly discovered, were better than their own, and their ships better built and more numerous. The Japanese soldier was superbly trained and experienced, courageous, disciplined and well equipped. In the early months of war Japanese army tactics were far superior to British, Australian or American combat tactics.

With the benefit of the records we can now see clearly what to Curtin and his military advisers was entirely conjectural.[14] Japanese pre-war planning was thorough and detailed. Unlike most military plans, the Japanese plan for the opening attacks in the war was followed quite closely. The only major deviation from the plan was that most of its objectives were achieved in three months instead of the planned six.

Japan's planners saw that it would be necessary to take Malaya and then Singapore to prevent British interference from the west, and necessary to take the Philippines to remove a threat from American air bases. They correctly saw that success in achieving the plan's objectives and then securing them would depend on air power, based either on land or carriers. Much of the planning turned on either acquiring strategically useful places for airfields, or denying them to the United States and its allies. Japan moved into Indo-China to bring air bases closer to Malaya. Rabaul and then Timor were early objectives because Allied possession of Rabaul threatened the southern naval base at Truk, the right flank of Japan's naval disposition against the expected US counterattack from the east. Japanese possession of Rabaul strengthened Truk's defence. The timing, the required forces, and the command structure of the forces for the attack on Rabaul, the first Australian controlled territory to be invaded, were planned in detail well before the war began.

There was a forward impetus built into this strategy. Each conquest further south, each new airfield seized to assist in the defence of an airfield or base further north, was itself vulnerable to Allied attack. This threat became more and more pertinent as the range of bombers increased. It was part of the original plan to take Rabaul to defend Truk. Once established in Rabaul, it would become apparent to Japanese planners that Rabaul was threatened by Port Moresby – although an attack on Moresby was not part of the original plan. Had the Japanese succeeded in taking Port Moresby, they may well have then wished to take Darwin, which would have been the base for attacking a Japanese-held Port Moresby. Darwin was not part of the plan on 8 December, but was seriously discussed in the Japanese high command a few months later. Following the logic of the war, British and Australian assessments anyway assumed that sequence highly likely.

Possession of the oil of the Netherlands East Indies was the central objective. There was no other point or purpose in Japan's southward thrust at a time it was still fighting to conquer China. The only way to secure oil in the long term, however, was to reach a peace settlement with the United States in which Japan was left in possession of the oilfields. And the only hope Japan had of forcing the United States to negotiate such a settlement, the planners had long thought, was if Japan could destroy the United States navy in the Pacific. It would replicate the successful outcome of the Russo-Japanese War, where the Russian Baltic fleet, sent around Africa and across the Indian Ocean, was annihilated by the Japanese navy as it steamed north to Vladivostok. Negotiation with Russia soon followed. Between great powers, war could be a contest of forces, followed by a negotiated settlement.[15]

(5)

Curtin would not be a war leader like Churchill or Stalin, demanding of his generals a new front here or a more vigorous push there. He could not be commander-in-chief, as Roosevelt was. He would never dismiss a general (though he made one general's resignation inevitable), nor order an offensive. He was reluctant to break the chain of command. He relied on Shedden. He would give command to MacArthur, and he would respect the undertaking. Australia would have the right to refuse the use of its forces, but not to determine the strategy directing their use.

For all that, Curtin's job in the Pacific War would be hard. He would always struggle against the limits. As the leader of a small, imperilled nation at war with a much larger power, as the smaller partner in alliance with a great power, as the leader of a dominion in the British Empire, he must exert the utmost political skill, the most cleverly shaped arguments, deploy the most delicate and the most brutal of pressures, to exercise what little influence he could to protect his country and create for it the most congenial place in the post-war world. His was a deadly serious game, and if he sometimes seemed too shrill, sometimes too plaintive, sometimes simply implausible, those aspects too were part of the game.

He had both to conciliate and frighten the Opposition, rally the people, awe his enemies in the press and in his own party. If he had to, he would grovel. He had to find the funds to continue the war, and he had to decide how money and resources would be shared between the many urgent claims. But above all, in 1942, 1943 and 1944 he had to manage personal relationships with five men who were important to the conduct of the war and to Australia's survival: Churchill, Roosevelt, MacArthur, Blamey and Shedden. Curtin had to deal with them as only the prime minister of his country could. Those five occupied his thoughts and filled his working days. While Australia and its concerns were a very small part of the considerations of Churchill and Roosevelt, those two leaders were a very large part of Curtin's considerations. On their decisions, much depended.

(6)

Always seen in a suit and tie and sometimes with a homburg, of medium height and medium build, his expression entirely neutral,

Fred Shedden was a self-effacing presence in the background when prime ministers and defence ministers held press conferences or greeted important visitors. For Menzies, he had felt admiring devotion. Roosevelt had charm and command, Shedden thought after accompanying Menzies on his 1941 visit to London and Washington, and Churchill might have wonderful language and some brilliant ideas, but Menzies had all these qualities and more besides – including good sense. As Secretary of the Defence Department, Shedden's services to Menzies went well beyond his official duties. He advised Menzies on whom to appoint to his ministry, and on how a coalition government with Labor might work. Whether his views on these matters had been solicited is not entirely clear.[16]

For all that, he adjusted easily to Curtin as prime minister and he to him. They knew each other well from War Council, of which Shedden was secretary – one of the ways he had implanted himself as the central figure in defence planning. For Curtin he would become his eyes and ears and brains, too, or so he recorded Curtin saying.

Seven years younger than Curtin and born, like him, when Victoria was Queen, Shedden had joined the Defence Department as a sixteen-year-old in 1910. His first job was to master the filing system. It remained a useful accomplishment and a source of power in a four-decade career that made him one of the most influential public servants in Australia's history. It was said of Shedden that he had never thrown away a document – everything was filed, everything was in its proper place, everything could be retrieved when necessary. 'Documentation, thy name is Shedden,' said Menzies.[17] Defence ministers, prime ministers, uniformed officers came and went, but Shedden was always there, always with his files. Churchill and Roosevelt would soon enough see the product of the files. Even after he was pushed out of his job as secretary of the department in 1956, Shedden returned every day to work for a decade and a half, looking through his files and compiling a history of Australian defence policy so long, so dreary and so tendentious it could not be published.

Shedden was bright and focused. He had no interests other than defence, worked long hours and was untiring in advancing his career. From his beginnings as a file clerk and then a pay accountant, by the late 1920s he had sufficiently won the confidence of his civilian superiors to be sent to the Imperial Defence College, London – an experience that gave him the confidence to discuss defence policy issues with the service chiefs who had hitherto monopolised advice to the minister. Soon he found ways to intervene between them and the minister, engendering a nearly universal dislike and suspicion among service chiefs who found themselves powerless, despite their high rank, ribbons and medals, knighthoods and braid, despite their battle scars and war experience and the public awe their splendid uniforms inspired, to discompose the Secretary of the Department of Defence Co-ordination in any way whatsoever.

The Imperial Defence College commandant was a naval strategist, and Shedden had absorbed from him a view of Australia's proper place in Imperial defence. Australia must for its own defence rely on sea power, which meant relying on the British fleet, which in turn meant the Singapore base. By doctrine the fleet must be under one command, so in time of war Australia's navy would become part of the British fleet. Australia needed ships to contribute to the fleet; it needed a skeletal army organisation that could in time of war recruit and train an expeditionary force to support the mother country. It needed coastal defences, mostly fixed guns, against raids. It specifically did not need a home army to defend the country, because the British fleet would prevent invasion. Shedden's colleague in the 1928 Imperial Defence College intake, Colonel John Lavarack, disputed this view then and would continue to dispute it through the following decade.

As Secretary of the Defence Committee from 1929, Shedden deliberated with the uniformed chiefs of staff of the services, and began to influence policy. The army continued to argue that Japan would only strike if Britain was fighting in Europe and unable to send a fleet of sufficient size to deter an invasion of Australia.

When the army pressed for development of a mobile striking force to guard against this possibility, Shedden in alliance with the navy opposed it. With the Depression forcing cuts to defence spending, and the army seeking a large expansion, Shedden had little difficulty in holding the Scullin Government to the Singapore strategy.

When Australia joined the war on Germany, Shedden persuaded Menzies to adopt an administrative scheme that gave priority to defence policy, to Menzies, and to Shedden. Defence Minister Geoffrey Street was made Army Minister, with Menzies appointing himself Minister for Defence Co-ordination. Shedden proposed that Menzies establish a War Cabinet, with himself as secretary. It was the first time a public servant had regularly attended Cabinet meetings, formally recorded the decisions, and overseen their implementation.

Menzies had found Lavarack's criticism of the Singapore strategy uncongenial, as had Shedden. As Chief of the General Staff, Lavarack was replaced by a British general, Ernest Squires. The British Ragnar Colvin was the naval chief, and another British officer, Air Chief Marshall Sir Charles Burnett, was recruited as air force head. Until Squires' sudden death, the three service chiefs under Menzies were British officers. Brudenell White was brought out of retirement to succeed Squires. All the early decisions of the Cabinet were ones Shedden pushed, sometimes against Menzies' hesitation. An expeditionary force was recruited to support Britain, RAN ships were placed under Admiralty control, and Australia undertook to supply aircrew for Britain under an Empire Air Training Scheme.

Shedden's defence views were quite opposite to those of Curtin, who had queried the Singapore strategy, spoken up for both the army and the air force against the navy, and warned of the threat from Japan. Yet Shedden and Curtin found no discord. For all his deep immersion in the Singapore doctrine and Imperial Defence over decades, Shedden could adapt quickly when necessary.

He portrayed himself to Curtin as disappointed with the British and critical of Churchill, as indeed he had become. Shedden claimed to have queried the AIF commitment to the campaign in Greece, and to have found the British military authorities unhelpful when, with Menzies in London, he had sought more assurance of British naval support for Singapore. Within a day of Pearl Harbor he would claim to have devised a new story about the Pacific War, one Curtin readily adopted. His analysis had the happy effect of blaming Britain for failing to support a Singapore strategy, an outcome Australian critics (including Curtin) had long said was likely if Britain was at war in Europe.

The criticisms of the Singapore strategy were those Shedden had done all he could to rebut, ignore and suppress through several decades of strict loyalty to the doctrine now demolished. Excusing himself for his failure to correctly interpret the plain meaning of London's discouraging cables on the likelihood of a fleet for Singapore, Shedden instead blamed Britain for failing to redeem promises which had been withdrawn at least three years earlier. Britain's betrayal of Australia over the Singapore base was a fiction Shedden found convenient to sustain. It excused his long adherence to the Singapore base doctrine. Astonishingly, he would rebound to it in a few years, bringing Curtin with him.

(7)

Once at war in the Pacific, Curtin and his War Cabinet and key officials spent much of their time in the offices and War Cabinet rooms of Victoria Barracks in Melbourne. The press gallery followed. 'I actually left Canberra for a period of six months and I boarded in Melbourne, and all our work was done in Melbourne for about the first six months,' Cox remembered.[18] There, just off St Kilda Road, in the bluestone 'New Wing' constructed during the Great War to house the Commonwealth Department of Defence, Curtin and Shedden had offices. Curtin and his War Cabinet colleagues met in a spacious, high-ceilinged room on the first floor behind double doors lined with green baize, seated in brown leather chairs around a vast table. On the walls, pull-down maps marked the Japanese advances in green felted pins. An extractor sucked up the cigarette and pipe smoke, expelling it into the typing pool room nearby.

Meeting in Cabinet on Monday, 8 December, the news of the Japanese attack only a few hours old and its full extent not yet clear, Curtin and his ministers recognised that they were already at war. 'Accept situation as being at war with Japan,' Shedden's assistant Vincent Quealy wrote at the top of his handwritten Cabinet notes. The declaration was a formality. With declarations against Romania, Finland and Hungary already pending and a process for getting the Crown's signature already agreed, Evatt could use the same procedure to issue the declaration against Japan. The declaration itself would be Australia's, with the instrument signed on Tuesday by the Governor-General, Lord Gowrie, in Curtin's presence. The timing depended on the British declaration, which in turn depended on the American declaration.

Unlike Menzies' announcement of the war against Germany, Australia was not at war because Britain was at war. Formally at least, it was at war of its own decision. Japan declined to reciprocate. In its declaration of war on 8 December, Japan did not recognise the separate status Australia and the other dominions claimed. It declared war on the United States and 'the British Empire'. In the declaration, republished every week in Japanese newspapers throughout the war to remind the Japanese of their duty, Australia was not mentioned.

Cabinet was advised that the undersea cable to Singapore had already been cut. Colvin briefed on the navy's dispositions. Even at that first meeting of Cabinet following the Japanese attack, some important decisions were made or confirmed. Mobilisation of some of the part-time Militia had already begun.[19] The army confirmed it was proposing to send a battalion to Port Moresby. It would send another to Rabaul, if requested by the Americans, to secure the American air supply route through Australia to the Philippines. Curtin gave authority to move troops to Koepang in Dutch Timor. It was already clear that Australia expected to fight alongside the Americans. It was also clear that Australia was prepared to defend airfields in the islands north of Australia, though not in considerable force.

Three-quarters of Australia's volunteer army was fighting in the Middle East. Its return to fight the new enemy was discussed, but still not sought. Curtin told the meeting he did not intend to recall the AIF from the Middle East.[20] He said Malaya would need more air support, a theme of Australian requests to London and Washington that would be frequently and stridently repeated over the next few months. Curtin's decision to leave the AIF in the Middle East suggested he thought Australia's circumstances were serious but not perilous. He would have thought the main battle against Japan would be fought in Malaya, and Australia would fight there as part of the Empire. He probably calculated that if necessary the British would reinforce Singapore, including more ships to add to the squadron led by HMS *Prince of Wales*. For this, the exchanges of the last two years gave no grounds for hope. There was some consideration of recalling Royal Australian Air Force units from Britain and the Middle East. Air Chief Marshal Burnett thought it would be difficult to withdraw an Australian flying boat squadron then in Britain, and a fighter squadron in the Middle East.

After the service chiefs had departed, Shedden briefed War Cabinet on the cold reality of Australia's ability to defend itself. He told the ministers that the chiefs doubted that even one division could now be put into the field in Australia 'as a good fighting force'. Australia's home defence was much weaker than appeared on paper. Shedden also suggested Curtin ask Churchill for an up-to-date appreciation of the Far East war situation, and also formally ask the Australian chiefs for their views.

Shedden astutely portrayed himself as extremely dissatisfied with the military heads. After the meeting he wrote a note to Curtin saying he had been 'very disappointed with the showing of the Chiefs of Staff' at the meeting, with only 'scrappy and meagre' information presented, and a general sense that 'this new and nearby threat to Australia was merely another incident in the present war in which we had added to our enemies by one' and 'gained another ally'. Shedden suggested, in words Curtin would then adopt, 'the Government must press it right home that this is a new war'.[21]

It was indeed a new war in the Pacific, one that had arisen out of an old war between China and Japan and was influenced by the concurrent war in Europe. A new war, but it was also true that on 11 December Germany declared war on the United States. What had been a European war became a world war. For all that, the Australian perception of the Pacific War as a new and separate conflict would colour all Curtin's dealings with the two great Allied leaders, Roosevelt and Churchill.

(8)

That evening, Monday, 8 December 1941, Curtin broadcast to the nation. His talk was preceded by a stirring brass band rendition of 'Advance Australia Fair'. Introduced by an ABC announcer with the typically clipped English accent of the time, Curtin spoke in a full, confident voice, without hesitation. His accent was characteristically Australian, but not broad except in the short 'a'. He pronounced Japan as J-pan, with a short harsh 'a'. Australia, he said, had struggled to avoid a breakdown of discussions between Japan and the United States. The guilt of war was upon Japan. It had 'chosen the Hitler method', going to war 'like an assassin in the night' while its negotiators were still talking in Washington.

Australia would formally declare war the following day. Curtin called for 'your courage, your physical and mental ability, your inflexible determination that we as a nation of free people shall survive'.

It was, he said, the nation's 'darkest hour', but Australians would 'hold this country, and keep it as a citadel for the British-speaking race and as a place where civilisation will persist'. The Australian Government, he said, with more confidence than truth, was 'fully prepared'. Petrol consumption 'for pleasure' was to be rationed. Military leave was cancelled. Ward was to leave for Darwin immediately to organise labour. Other preparations were 'secret', but added up to 'complete provisions for the safety of the nation'. That, as he well knew, was very far from being the case. He finished with a quote from Algernon Swinburne's 'Eve of Revolution', a celebration of Mazzini's unification of Italy and a popular poem in the socialist groups of Curtin's youth: *Hasten thine hour and halt not, till thy work be done.*

He did not explicitly warn of a Japanese invasion of Australia, but in promising Australians would 'hold this country and keep it as a citadel for the British-speaking race' his listeners would assume an attempted invasion was a possibility. It was already widely discussed. The Secretary of the Department of the Army, F R Sinclair, wrote to his minister the following day to warn of a 'distinct probability of Japanese land raids in strength' resulting in Japanese troops 'establishing themselves' along the Australian coast. Army chief of staff Lieutenant-General Vernon Sturdee was indignant. He told Forde it was 'complete defeatism'.[22]

But that same Tuesday morning, when War Cabinet met, Curtin was using similar language. He had learned of the Japanese attacks across the Pacific only the morning before, but he was already prepared to tell his colleagues that Australia must be prepared to resist invasion.[23] In a marked change of tone clearly influenced by Shedden, Curtin told War Cabinet that it was now a 'new war'. The most urgent requirement, he said, was air support. Curtin cited an April 1941 British assurance that air resources would be redisposed in the event of war with Japan. Cabinet discussed the lack of command machinery uniting American, British and Dutch forces fighting Japan. It would have to be created.

With the Japanese only beginning their attacks on the Philippines and Malaya, invasion of Australia was not an immediate threat or perhaps even a distant one. Remote as it might be, Curtin had no motive to minimise the threat to Australia which Japan presented. Defence of the homeland was the most potent rallying cry Curtin could choose.

Australia had very few bombers or fighters. It did have the nucleus of what could become a formidable army. The army chief, Sturdee, told War Cabinet that there were 134 000 Australian Military Forces troops in training or full-time duty.[24] He said another 112 000 should be called up. After discussion of the needs of industry, War Cabinet agreed that 25 000 should be called up – a modest number, given Curtin's view that the country must be prepared for invasion.

The United States, Britain, Holland, Australia, New Zealand and Canada all had forces in the Pacific and were at war with Japan. How should these forces fighting Japan be coordinated? Chairing a War Council meeting later that day, Curtin led a discussion of the need for a 'supreme authority' to guide the Allies in the war in the Pacific.

(9)

By Thursday, 11 December, when Curtin again convened War Cabinet, the war looked a lot worse. The Japanese were now securely established on both sides of the Malay Peninsula. Recklessly sortieing without air cover to intercept Japanese troop transports, both *Repulse* and *Prince of Wales* – the ship that could catch and kill anything – had been sunk off the Malayan coast. Japan commanded the skies over Malaya. Singapore was now a fleet base without a fleet, and with no immediate possibility of getting one. While some transports continued to get through, the remaining British navy fighting ships in the Indian Ocean sailed further west to avoid Japanese planes.

Bad as it looked, Curtin and his advisers were probably unaware of quite how appalling the Allied position in Malaya had become. The *Sydney Morning Herald* told its readers on Tuesday, 9 December that while the Japanese navy might be formidable, the Japanese air force was weak. It was wrong. Japan deployed an air force in Malaya four times bigger than that of the defenders.[25] Within twenty-four hours of the Japanese attack the Allied air force in Malaya had been all but destroyed. The British commanded an army of three divisions. Numerically vastly superior to the Japanese force, much of it was scattered in defence of widely separated northern Malaya air bases – now useless. The British command had argued that a battle in Malaya would depend on air power. The Japanese had come to the same conclusion.

Responding to Curtin's request for an evaluation, the Australian chiefs of staff presented on Thursday a sombre and very different view from their position on Monday. Their appreciation argued that the attack on Malaya 'might well be a first step in the Japanese plan for a major attack on Australia', a dramatic shift unwarranted by any new information. The possibility of a 'direct move on Australia', beginning with Japanese occupation of New Caledonia, Port Moresby and Rabaul, must now be considered. It was necessary to 'train now the forces that would be necessary to prevent and to meet an invasion'.[26] This time, War Cabinet readily agreed to call up an additional 112 000 men – more than four times the number agreed four days earlier.

For their 11 December appreciation the chiefs had been asked to assess the requirements for the defence of the core industrial region of Sydney, Newcastle, Lithgow and Wollongong, without which Australia could not continue resistance to Japan. They were also asked to assess the defence of strategic points in the islands to Australia's north, including Port Moresby.[27] They recommended that Rabaul's defence be strengthened. It would, they rightly predicted, be an early Japanese target. Invasion of Australia was possible, but only after the island bases had been taken.

This first appreciation reaffirmed two concepts central to defence planning. One was the idea of forward defence of Australia to deny island air and sea bases to Japan, and to sustain communication with American forces. Curtin had long argued that a Japanese attack should be met as far forward as possible, which was also the chiefs' view, and the view of the Menzies Government. In Malaya the British Empire had substantial forces, not yet tested. To defend the airfields on the islands to Australia's north, however, Australia had been able to deploy only a few planes and ships, and small army units. These forces could not hope to do more than impede the southern thrust of Japanese forces. They were more accurately described as an 'outer screen' than a forward defence.

The other concept affirmed in this early appreciation was that in the event of invasion, Australia would concentrate its forces to defend the key industrial region. This was narrowly the area from Wollongong to Newcastle, and broadly from Melbourne to Brisbane. It would likely be the initial objective of a Japanese invasion, and Australia would have no choice but to concentrate to defend it. Both forward defence or an 'outer screen', and concentration of forces in the south-eastern corner of the continent to meet the invasion, were standard ideas in Australian defence. Later controversies would obscure the coexistence of these two elements.

When Japan attacked in the Pacific, on paper the Australian army was structured into thirteen divisions, including four overseas.[28] (Divisions were usually around 20 000 men.) Only the AIF was battle-trained. Australia's sea power and air power were at that point negligible. Including the AIF divisions, the total strength of the Australian defence forces in December 1941 was 369 800.[29] The total included 20 000 in the RAN and 61 000 in the RAAF.

While he had publicly denied an intention to bring the three AIF divisions in the Middle East back to join the Pacific War, Curtin was exploring other possibilities. At War Cabinet and a later meeting of the War Council that day the option of recalling Blamey to command

Australia's armed forces was discussed. Since he commanded the AIF in the Middle East and there were few battle-trained troops in Australia, the return of Blamey would inevitably suggest a discussion of the return of the AIF as well. It was a significant shift. In the course of five days Curtin had moved from an explicit denial of interest in bringing back Australian troops from the Middle East, to an explicit consideration of the threat of invasion and of appointing Blamey to overall command of Australian forces.

The British were reassuring. In a cable Dominions Secretary Viscount Cranborne told Curtin there was 'no immediate large scale threat to Australia'. He also confirmed the British view that 'We must not forget that Germany . . . is still the main enemy'[30] and Germany was in trouble in the Soviet Union and Libya.

Curtin was not reassured. On 13 December he cabled Roosevelt directly, seeking whatever help the President could give to deny Rabaul and New Caledonia to the enemy.[31] It was an early sign of his readiness to deal directly with Washington.

A few weeks earlier Curtin had wanted to reduce the size of the home army. He told his colleagues in a War Cabinet meeting in Canberra on 18 December that 'immediate defence is the urgent need'.[32]

With the war much closer to home and decisions needed quickly, it made no sense for War Cabinet and the War Council to meet successively with the same agenda and, for the Government, most of the same people. At the War Cabinet meeting on December 11 Curtin proposed to simplify the process by proposing that something decided in the War Council with the concurrence of ministers would be taken to be a decision of War Cabinet.[33] This rule might suggest that the War Council had pre-eminence over Cabinet. When it came to the most important decisions, however, the Government's views would prevail over those of the non-government members of the War Council. Decided earlier, the change was announced on 17 December. It was as close as Curtin would come to a national government, and it was on his own terms.

While War Cabinet and its military advisers pondered Japan's astonishing success in the first week of war, Elsie continued her slow train journey back to Perth for Christmas. In Adelaide reporters sought her comment on the war. Don Rodgers was said to be anxious whenever she encountered reporters – there was no knowing what she might say. As usual, she acquitted herself well, and with her usual directness. She was deeply upset by the loss of *Prince of Wales*, she told reporters. It vindicated her husband's long preference for 'bombers before battleships. For years he has been urging a bigger and bigger Air Force.' She had hoped her husband 'would be able to fly to Perth in time to join the family at Christmas, but that arrangement probably would have to be cancelled now'.[34] A train perhaps, but she well knew Curtin was unlikely to fly – war or no war.

CHAPTER 22

TURNING TO AMERICA
CURTIN APPEALS TO
ROOSEVELT AND CHURCHILL

(1)

By the second week of the Pacific War it was apparent that the British
command arrangements in the Far East no longer suited Curtin.
He was excluded from direct contact with the commander. On
20 December[1], Curtin cabled Churchill complaining that Sir Robert
Brooke-Popham, still Commander-in-Chief Far East, had not
replied to Curtin's request for a briefing on the situation in Malaya,
or to his request for a briefing note three times a week. British
Minister Duff Cooper's report on a Singapore services conference
of 18 December reached Curtin via Cranborne. At a Canberra War
Cabinet meeting on 22 December, Curtin and his colleagues agreed
to send additional troops to Malaya.[2] With the 8th Division already
there, Australia was committed. It was also at the end of its trained
army units. The machine gun unit sent to Malaya was the last trained
AIF battalion in Australia. Two thousand additional men sent a little
later were 'largely untrained'.[3] It was a telling measure of Australia's
unpreparedness.

Without direct and prompt reports from Brooke-Popham,
Curtin depended on news reports to follow the war. Early reports of

the successes of British and Indian troops in resisting the Japanese invasion of northern Malaya were soon superseded by less confident accounts. Assigned to positions in the south of the Malay Peninsula, it was a while before the 8th Division was engaged in the fighting. Reporters covering the fighting further north cabled back news of Japanese advances down the peninsula, of unimpeded Japanese naval movements, and evident air superiority.

It was a new war for reporters also. Unlike the battles in the Middle East, most of the engagements in Malaya involved small formations – platoons or battalions. The Japanese were sometimes able to use small tanks. When they did they were usually effective. More often the Japanese advance relied on moving down roads or tracks, often on bicycles, until they encountered the Indian, British or Australian troops. They then outflanked them by moving into the jungle on either side of the position. To outflank the defending troops the Japanese used small boats where the fighting was near the coast, and sometimes trucks. Mostly, they walked. Harassed by Japanese bombers, unused to the flanking tactic, reluctant to use the jungle as the Japanese did, the British and Indian troops were forced from the airfields and railroad hubs they defended, back down roads towards Singapore.

The Australian commander of the 8th Division, Major-General Gordon Bennett, reported the military reverses. So did the Australian civilian representative in Singapore, Vivian Bowden, who observed that Japanese planes attacked the city with little loss. As early as 13 December Bennett told Forde he was worried by the want of air support. He told Army Headquarters, 'I fear another Crete.'[4] On Christmas Eve, Bowden reported deterioration of the position in Malaya was 'assuming landslide proportions'. Without air reinforcement, he believed, Singapore would fall.[5] It was just sixteen days since the Japanese landing at Kota Bharu.

(2)

In Singapore itself the extremity of the crisis had yet to dawn on the British authorities. British Minister Duff Cooper convened a conference in Singapore on 18 December. While pleading for reinforcements and acknowledging a 'serious' situation it warned against 'undue pessimism'.[6]

So rapid was the Japanese advance that reinforcement in Malaya was already urgently needed. The previous week Curtin had put aside the option of withdrawing the AIF from the Middle East. By the second week of the Pacific War it was already under discussion in the British Government and the Australian army. Using Commonwealth troops to reinforce Malaya in the event of war with Japan had long been part of British planning. Sailing across the Atlantic to his first meeting with Roosevelt since the United States entered the war, Churchill cabled Britain's chiefs of staff around 18 December suggesting one or two of the three Australian divisions in the Middle East be withdrawn, either to India to replace an Indian army division being sent to Singapore, or directly to Singapore. Around the same time Bennett had requested an Australian division from the Middle East for Malaya.

Curtin cabled Churchill on 20 December requesting advice on the measures the British Government proposed to take to reinforce Malaya. On the same day Earle Page, now in London, cabled Curtin – most immediate, most secret, for the prime minister himself alone – reporting a discussion in the British Defence Committee. The issue of moving Australian troops from the Middle East to Malaya had also come up, in Churchill's absence but on his prompting. Page steered that discussion back to the immediate needs in Malaya, arguing that on past occasions – Greece was the most vivid example – Australian troops had had to fight without adequate air support. He thus linked the return of Australian troops to his demand for more fighters and bombers for Malaya.

Page told Curtin the British chiefs' understanding did not meet the urgent need to 'prevent Singapore capitulating and to save the Netherlands East Indies'. It would be months before troops now in the Middle East could be brought into the Malaya battle, and meanwhile the Japanese were rapidly advancing down the peninsula. If Singapore was to be saved, he rightly supposed, it had to be 'by air forces immediately'. Demanding planes, Page recognised that 'we might have only three or four weeks to save the position'.[7] Burma and its air bases that might have refuelled British warplanes flying east were now under attack. The British chiefs pointed out that fighters, like troops, could now only be brought in by sea. That would take some time.

In the urgency of the moment there was no time to reflect on the ignominious outcome of the twenty-year Australian debate about the vital importance of the Singapore naval base. The two modern ships based there had been lost almost as soon as the war began. Without air cover, the transports bringing troops to Singapore were in constant peril. The discussion was no longer about the size of the British fleet that would be deployed there to protect Australia, but about the number of fighter planes necessary to protect both British control of Malaya and the base itself from destruction.

The logical conclusion might have been that without both sea and air control it would be difficult to defend the base and there was, in any case, no point in having it. The logical conclusion was not drawn, or not by Curtin or his advisers. Churchill was quicker to see it. Australia continued to believe in the base, and demand British action to secure it. Shedden, devoted for a decade to an Imperial Defence idea based on Singapore, was no doubt the principal drafter of Curtin's messages on the issue. But Curtin probably amended them, took responsibility for their content, and signed off on them.

(3)

The suddenness and sweep of the Japanese victories extinguished the rancour of Australian politics, at least for a while. Curtin called for Australians to do their duty calmly and without question, and for many months they did. There was little panic[8], though both the American Minister, Nelson Johnson, and the British High Commissioner, Sir Ronald Cross, would report to their governments that Australians were shocked and fearful. Curtin had announced that Australians could no longer use petrol for pleasure drives, and it was accepted without too much complaint. Controls that had been thought hard to impose or politically controversial proved possible to implement.

Within days of Pearl Harbor, Curtin proposed a new Manpower Directorate reporting to the Minister for Labour and National Service, Eddie Ward. Cabinet approved the Directorate on 19 January 1942. It would have complete control over distribution of people between the armed services and civilian employment, and allocation of labour between industries. Curtin promptly resolved a long-running dispute between the Commonwealth Aircraft Corporation and the Aircraft Production Commission, with the Corporation made subordinate to a new Director-General of Aircraft Production. A Civil Constructional Corps was set up, and an Allied Works Council to coordinate Australian and American requirements for new defence construction.

In the following months Australia would be mobilised for war. Curtin displayed a new zealotry in curbing beer consumption and horse racing. Unions dragged their feet but women were encouraged to take jobs in industry and to join the armed services. So pressing was the need for air bases and support buildings in northern Australia that Cabinet agreed to an American request to bring in Javanese workers, an abrogation of the White Australia policy inconceivable before Pearl Harbor. As it happened the Japanese moved too quickly, and Java was in their hands before labourers were recruited. Reluctantly, Cabinet would also decide not to refuse units of black troops among those coming from America.

Justifying all the new controls and regulations was the suddenness and enormity of the change Australia had to make. The armed forces were rapidly enlarged. Before Pearl Harbor there were 382 100 Australians in the armed services, including the four divisions abroad. By March 1942 there would be 554 700 – an increase of nearly 200 000 in four months, most of whom were withdrawn from civilian jobs.[9] At the same time war production increased, and construction began on new airfields, docks, training camps, defence works and roads in remote country. Where it could, Australia developed alternatives to imports threatened by the war with Japan, and rationed their use. No Australian prime minister had ever overseen the doing of so much, so quickly.

(4)

Focusing on the Japanese push down the Malay Peninsula towards Singapore, there was less attention to what was happening with American plans to fight the Pacific War. Pearl Harbor changed everything, including command of the United States navy. With most of its Pacific fleet battleships on the bottom of Pearl Harbor, its aircraft carriers fewer in number than those Japan could bring against them, its small Far Eastern flotilla already fleeing from the Philippines, it might have been an option for the United States navy to guard the approaches to Hawaii and the United States west coast until it could be reinforced. Appointed Commander-in-Chief of the United States fleet on 30 December 1941, Admiral Ernest King thought otherwise. His first order was to instruct Admiral Chester Nimitz, the new Pacific fleet commander, that his fleet's 'primary objective' was 'the protection of the lines of communication from Hawaii to Australia and to Midway'.[10] Unbidden, unnoticed, the United States navy in the Pacific had been ordered to secure the sea passages south-west to Australia.

Washington decisions assumed greater importance for Curtin in other ways. At the first War Cabinet after Pearl Harbor, he had spoken of the need for a unified command in the war against Japan. Meeting in Washington in late December to concert war plans, Churchill and Roosevelt discussed Allied command of the Pacific War. Dick Casey had told Bert Evatt on 22 December that Roosevelt wanted an American commander for the Pacific and Far East, and had MacArthur in mind. It would be a good idea, Casey proposed, for Australia to itself ask for an American supreme commander. The command might, he suggested, be based in Australia.[11] Casey was probably the 'informed source' for a 23 December *Sydney Morning Herald* report from Washington that MacArthur would be made the Allied commander-in-chief for the Pacific.

It would be another three months and more calamitous defeats before Roosevelt had his way. In the Washington discussions, from which Australia was excluded, Churchill resisted the appointment of a theatre commander with control of naval forces as well as air and land forces. One and indivisible in naval doctrine, the British Admiralty resisted any authority over its fleet other than its own. Marshall got round Churchill's objection by proposing that the theatre commander be the British general, Sir Archibald Wavell.[12]

British participation in the higher command of the Pacific War was secured by creation of a United States and British combined chiefs of staff. Churchill agreed only reluctantly to the combined chiefs being based in Washington. In practice, decisions in the Pacific War and often in other theatres of joint operations would be made by the American chiefs. Roosevelt had already said to Stimson that henceforth Washington and not London would be the head-quarters of the Allied war command.[13] In Australia Shedden said the same.

(5)

Informed of the Washington meeting between Churchill and Roosevelt, Curtin cabled both leaders warning that Singapore might fall. In a well-informed report from Canberra, the *Sydney Morning Herald* pointed out on Wednesday, 24 December that Curtin's cable to Roosevelt had been 'direct' and not via Britain, an unusual approach for Australia. Curtin told Churchill and Roosevelt that promised reinforcements were 'utterly inadequate' – especially fighters. He warned Roosevelt that 'the fall of Singapore would mean the isolation of the Philippines, the fall of the Netherlands East Indies, and an attempt to smother all other bases'. This setback 'would be as serious to United States interests as to our own'.[14] With Casey's cable in mind, he also told the leaders that Australia would gladly accept an American commander in the Pacific area – a suggestion Churchill would not have welcomed. Evatt sent Bowden's recent report from Singapore warning of a 'collapse', with the fall of Singapore 'a matter of weeks'.[15]

It was clear enough that by late December, a couple of weeks after the Pacific War had begun, Curtin had placed his hopes for his country in America. So, too, had Churchill, for his. There, already, was the conflict between Australia and Britain. For American resources and attention, Curtin and Churchill, Australia and Britain, were now competitors.

The cable drafted and sent to Churchill and Roosevelt, Australian reporters were then briefed. Like the *Sydney Morning Herald*, the Sydney *Daily Telegraph* reported on 24 December that Curtin had 'yesterday cabled Mr Churchill and President Roosevelt Australia's views on what should be done urgently to meet war developments in the Far East'. Curtin was not waiting to be told. For a dominion prime minister to be warning the American president of the possible 'fall' of the major British base east of India two weeks after Japan launched the Pacific War would have disturbed Churchill, then pressing the priority of the war against Germany. As much as the content of the cable, the prompt reporting of it would also have annoyed Churchill. Menzies would later claim that he himself had suggested cabling Roosevelt directly, and Curtin would say privately that Hughes, Fadden and Spender had urged him to press Australian views.[16] Publicising the cable, however, annoyed the Opposition as well as Churchill. The suggestion in the stories was that Curtin understood the gravity of the Pacific War, while Churchill and Roosevelt did not. That is the way British High Commissioner Cross indignantly reported the stories to London.

Differences over the Pacific command went to the heart of the rapidly emerging distinction between Australian and British interests, and between American and British interests. Japanese objectives against the United States were primarily strategic. Japan had for a time disabled the United States Pacific fleet, and was well on its way to occupying the Philippines and other United States outposts in the Western Pacific. It wanted to build a defensive screen against the United States, but it did not want to occupy substantial United States territory. (Now vigorously defending the Philippines, the United States had earlier been prepared to let it go and take it back later.)

In the French, British and Dutch colonies of south-east Asia, however, Japan had quite different objectives. It had already assumed military control in Indo-China. It wanted to seize the tin and rubber resources of Malaya and the oil and other resources of the Netherlands East Indies. It planned to take Burma. It had some oil but, more importantly, control of Burma would close the main supply line to China and also threaten the British position in India. In this region the United States had no substantial naval forces, no troops and little interest. Roosevelt disapproved of British and Dutch imperialism. The United States had no intention of supporting British possession of Malaya. It had repeatedly said the strategic importance of Singapore was overstated. Its interest in Burma, which was keen, was only to protect supply routes to its ally, China.

The United States had long believed that sea power supplemented by carrier-borne air power were better counters to Japan than land forces, because Japan was after all an island nation and its economic might and leadership was located in its islands. If the Allies commanded the seas and skies of the northern Pacific, the homeland could be threatened even if Japanese forces continued to control south-east Asia and coastal China. If a south-west Pacific regional base was needed for this strategy, it could be Australia.

(6)

Dominions Secretary Viscount Cranborne ('Bobbety' Cecil, among his peers) had urged Curtin not to forget that Germany was the main enemy, an unhelpful piece of advice for an Australian prime minister whose military advisers thought a Japanese invasion quite possible, quite soon. Germany was certainly not Australia's main enemy, or not in December 1941. Curtin had long been aware that this was the British point of view. From Washington, reporters wrote that Churchill and Roosevelt had agreed the war on Germany was the first priority. For Churchill, reaffirmation of that priority was the main objective of his Washington talks with Roosevelt.

Curtin was probably unaware that a formal policy of defeating Germany first while only holding a line against Japan in Asia and the Pacific had already been agreed by the Australian Government – and well before the war with Japan began. Certainly, his main military adviser insisted that Curtin was unaware of the decision by the previous government. Shedden recorded that War Cabinet had approved the American and British war plans on 15 May 1941. Menzies was still abroad, so the meeting would have been chaired by Fadden. The Advisory War Council on which Curtin and his Labor colleagues sat was not informed of the material or the decision.[17] Fadden had, however, referred to the Germany First doctrine in his secret speech in 1941, and Curtin had anyway worked out for himself that the United States would see Germany as the main enemy – as, indeed, for the United States it was. As he had written to Elsie, 'My own view of America is that Gt Britain & the Atlantic Ocean mean much more to that country than does Australia & what is called Oceana.'

As we have seen, the Germany First strategy was formally agreed during the secret American–British staff talks in Washington from January to March 1941. Churchill's talks with Roosevelt and the accompanying staff talks at the end of 1941 (the Arcadia conference) confirmed the Germany First policy, agreeing that 'our view remains that Germany is still the prime enemy'. Once Germany was defeated, the defeat of Japan 'must follow'. Therefore, 'only the minimum of force necessary for the safeguarding of vital interests in other theatres should be diverted from operations against Germany'. Australia was not forgotten in this agreement. The 'vital interests' in the Asia–Pacific region included the security of Australia and New Zealand, and holding Singapore, East Indies, Rangoon, and the Philippines. Much was included that would shortly be lost. The military planners had committed to holding 'vital interests' without the means to do so.

Though Page may not have reported it to Canberra, Churchill referred directly to Germany First and the Arcadia agreement at a January 1942 meeting of the Cabinet Defence Committee of the British Cabinet at which Page was present.[18]

The reaffirmation was one of Churchill's great strategic victories, but he had met no real opposition. Roosevelt and Marshall had long held the same conviction. Germany was unquestionably the stronger power. If it succeeded in defeating the Soviet Union, as it very well might, its supremacy in Europe would be incontestable. A German victory against the Soviet Union would free Japan from a threat from Siberia and release forces to reduce China and defend its new perimeter. It would permit Germany and its allies to support Japan through Siberia. It was also true that to a much greater extent than Germany, Japan would always be vulnerable to superior sea power and air power. Sooner or later the United States would attain dominance in the seas and skies of the Pacific and either force Japan to surrender or to negotiate. That was the impeccable logic of beating Germany first.

Curtin could understand the logic of giving priority to the war against Germany. He would later say he did not disagree with it. But Britain was garrisoned by a strong army, the British navy was in secure command of the home waters and the RAF was now in command of the daytime skies over the Channel and Britain. Britain was not in danger. In the east, the Soviet Union was now holding the German attack. It would be quite a while before the Allies were in a position to land in Europe. Meanwhile, as General MacArthur would soon urge, there was an opportunity to strike against Germany's axis partner, Japan. It was also true that the defensive line against Japan agreed at the Arcadia talks looked likely to be broken. The Philippines, Malaya, Singapore and Burma were all threatened. Australia might be next. Responsible for Australia's defence, Curtin could not accept Churchill's or Roosevelt's perspective. As he would tell Australians on 27 December, Australia could go and Britain remain. He was determined it should not go.

(7)

As the end of 1941 approached and Japanese troops won more battles in Malaya, British understanding ran well behind reality. On 23 December, Cranborne cabled Curtin with the details of a Defence Committee evaluation of strategy in the Far East. Britain was not able to provide a fleet for Singapore 'at present', but intended to assemble a fleet of nine capital ships and four aircraft carriers in the Indian Ocean at some future time.[19] This would be an enormous fleet, equivalent to the Home Fleet, so Curtin should have assumed that the future time would be very distant indeed. Meanwhile, the United States and Britain would not combine their fleets to battle the Japanese fleet, as the Australian chiefs had urged.

It was clear enough that British military planners thought Australia should now look to Washington, not London. They advised American assistance would be essential to resist the Japanese attack. With considerable aplomb the British chiefs advised that it would not be sufficient for the United States 'to maintain a defensive attitude'. That, as it happened, was exactly the content of the earlier American–British agreement, ABC-1, reaffirmed between Churchill and Roosevelt that very day in Washington. It was also the policy position of Britain's chiefs, who would relentlessly protest against what they regarded as diversion of American war resources to the Pacific. For their part, Cranborne's cable informed Curtin, the British were sending part of their 18th Division and more Indian army troops to Malaya. (The timing of this commitment would later be pertinent.) Air reinforcements were planned for Malaya and Burma, but would not be available for some weeks. Although Churchill had suggested it, there was no mention of sending Australian divisions from the Middle East to Malaya or India. The candour of this appreciation and its meagre offerings must have been startling – even to Curtin and Shedden, to whom the refusal of a fleet for Singapore should have been no surprise.

There would be no fleet, British or American or combined. Nor would there be substantial reinforcement of the remnants of the Royal Air Force and RAAF squadrons fighting a far superior Japanese air force in Malaya. Curtin had demanded prompt air support for Malaya, but as Casey cabled on 27 December, prompt air support was impossible. After consultation with Churchill in Washington and British and American officials, Casey reported that there were 'no modern aircraft in India' and no British aircraft 'of any consequence closer than the Middle East'. Fighter aircraft could no longer be flown

from the Middle East because the Japanese now controlled the skies
of northern Malaya and southern Burma. The Americans 'cannot be
induced to risk sending one of their few aircraft carriers' to Singapore
or even Australia.[20] In Washington it was already accepted that the
Philippines would be lost.

Preparing for his meeting with Churchill, Roosevelt had been
told the Australians were 'panicking'.[21] Curtin had warned Singapore
might be lost. On Christmas Day, Churchill cabled Curtin from
Washington that he did not agree. The 'Singapore fortress' would
be defended with the 'utmost tenacity'. Churchill suggested that the
rapid retreat of Allied forces southward was part of a plan to avoid
losing troops and instead concentrate on the defence of Singapore
and its immediate north. With Rommel hurling back the British
8th Army in North Africa, and Germany still pressing hard on the
Soviet front, Churchill had other problems.

(8)

As the news from Malaya worsened, Curtin's exhortations to greater
efforts became more frequent, and his warnings about the possibility
of invasion more dire. In a national broadcast on 26 December,
Boxing Day, he said, 'I would be misleading you were I to tell you
that the end of our reverses has come. There will be more.' He left
no doubt Australia might be attacked. 'I am telling you bluntly that
war has come to Australia and Australians must conduct themselves
accordingly.' But 'we can, one and all, as a nation by greater efforts
hold this country.' He called for 'unstinted service; undaunted
courage; unswerving determination'.

The following day the Melbourne *Herald* carried the most
memorable statement of Curtin's life, and the most celebrated
document in Australian foreign policy. Written ostensibly to stir
greater Australian efforts in the demanding year ahead, the piece was

also directed to an audience of two in Washington: Churchill and Roosevelt, then still conferring on strategy for the war against Japan.

Invited by the *Herald* to contribute to its Saturday, 27 December magazine, Curtin offered a piece on The Task Ahead.[22]

In the 1500-word piece, Curtin said that his policy was grounded on two 'facts'. One fact was that the war against Japan was a 'new war' and not just a phase of the struggle against the Axis. He refused 'to accept the dictum that the Pacific struggle must be treated as a subordinate segment of the general conflict' – the dictum, as it happened, that Roosevelt and Churchill had reaffirmed in Washington four days earlier, and which Curtin would later say he accepted.

Curtin regarded the 'Pacific struggle as primarily one in which the United States and Australia must have the fullest say in the direction of the democracies' fighting plan', an arrangement that would elevate Australia's role and one Churchill was determined to prevent. It was in that context he then made his famous declaration that 'Without any inhibitions of any kind, I make it quite clear that Australia looks to America, free of any pangs as to our traditional links or kinship with Britain.' There was a sting in the next paragraph:

> We know the problems that Britain faces. We know the dangers of dispersal of strength, but we know too, that Australia can go and Britain can still hold on. We are, therefore, determined that Australia shall not go, and we shall exert all our energies towards the shaping of a plan, with the United States as its keystone, which will give to our country some confidence of being able to hold out until the tide of battle swings against the enemy.

The second 'fact' that Curtin developed was quite different and largely for an Australian audience. It was also in a characteristic tone, one that went back to the struggle to enlighten the workers of Melbourne to the need for a socialist revolution. Political leadership for Curtin was often about persuading people to see the error of their ways, and accept the light of truth. Older, eminent, working long hours, Curtin was becoming a scold. 'Australia must go on a war footing,' he declared, and that meant 'the reshaping, in fact the revolutionising, of the Australian way of life until a war footing is attained quickly, efficiently and without question'. With unusual candour he confessed that the Government had 'found it exceedingly difficult to bring Australian people to a realisation of what, after two years of war, our position has become. Even the entry of Japan, bringing a direct threat in our own waters, was met with a subconscious view that the Americans would deal with the short sighted, underfed and fanatical Japanese.'

Curtin's reproof of the 'lackadaisical' ways of Australians had a good deal to do with strikes, stoppages and work bans, particularly on the wharves and coalfields. Speaking to an industrial relations conference the day after his article was published, Curtin said that peacetime industrial practices 'must be overridden by the stern duty of defending Australia from attack'.[23]

Don Rodgers would later claim to have drafted the Melbourne *Herald* piece. In some accounts, Rodgers claimed Curtin hadn't read it before it was published. This is very unlikely to be true. The ideas, the force of statement and logic, the play of the mind are Curtin's and the jagged, rhetorical style of the prose are recognisably his. Even the opening quote from the poet Bernard O'Dowd is characteristic of Curtin. An old colleague from the Victorian Socialist League, O'Dowd was an assistant editor of *The Socialist* around the time Curtin wrote for it. Asked directly by the Melbourne *Age* reporter Herbert Mishael about the rumours that Rodgers had written the piece, Curtin indignantly denied it.[24] Mishael recounted that Curtin had 'laughed derisively' and said, 'Do you think any Prime Minister worthy of the name would leave an announcement like that to his press officer? Of course I drew up the statement myself.' He also told Mishael 'our attitude was already well known to both the British and American governments. It was not all that new. Those two governments knew exactly what we proposed.' With his long working experience in journalism, Curtin was accustomed to typing out speeches, articles and letters directly on his typewriter, using a 'two finger peck'.[25] It was an unusual accomplishment. It is certainly possible Rodgers wrote parts of the piece on Curtin's instruction; Curtin's claim that he 'drew up' the piece does not preclude Rodgers' contribution. They may have been shared by Rodgers, but the ideas in the piece were certainly Curtin's.

The chief offence of this piece to Churchill, which was considerable, was not the celebrated tilt towards the United States and away from Britain. This was after all the inevitable result of the Pacific War. Churchill, Cranborne and the British chiefs of staff were insisting Australia find its chief military support with America – as Britain itself was now doing. The real difficulty was Curtin's demand to accord the war against Japan equal weight with the war against Germany, and to admit Australia into direct discussion with the United States in planning the Pacific War.

Shut out of the Washington talks, Curtin was demanding to be let in. Both propositions were at odds with Churchill's chief objective at the Arcadia talks, which was to reaffirm the priority of the war against Germany. To sustain that priority Churchill was determined to discourage direct, high-level discussion between Australia and the United States over allocation of war resources to the Pacific. To support his standing with the Americans he also had to claim he was not only the leader of embattled Britain. He spoke for an Empire, which included Australia. Yet Britain and Australia now competed for America's attention, and for troops, weapons, ships and planes. Coming on top of the dispute over Tobruk, the annoyances over the declaration of war on Finland and then pressure to seek Soviet intervention against Japan, Curtin's public declaration was altogether too much for Churchill.

The annoyance to Churchill was all the greater because it coincided with the British leader's most crowded and difficult times in Washington. He had strenuously fought Roosevelt and Marshall's insistence that much war planning be based in Washington rather than London. Losing that debate, he then found he had to fight back the objections of his own military chiefs. To great acclaim, he had addressed a joint sitting of the United States Senate and the House of Representatives on 26 December. That night he experienced symptoms of a heart attack while opening a window at the White House, an episode kept secret by his personal doctor, Sir Charles Wilson. Early in January 1942, Churchill told Wilson he had sent a 'stiff telegram' to Curtin, who was 'jumpy about invasion' because of the setbacks in Malaya. 'London had not made a fuss when it was bombed,' he told Wilson. 'Why should Australia?' Curtin's government did not represent the Australian people, Churchill said. Curtin's attitude reminded him that 'Australians came of bad stock'.[26] Churchill's indignation, nursed at length in his book, *The Second World War*, helped to give permanence to what *The Age* at the time correctly described as a gross misinterpretation.

While Curtin's piece was deeply disturbing to Churchill, the reaction within Australia was more muted. An Anglican bishop was furious, but his response was not widely shared. Even the *Sydney Morning Herald*, which described the sentiments about Britain as 'deplorable', conceded that the United States 'must lead' in the Pacific War, and was so far innocent of the strategic debate as to query whether anyone had declared the Pacific struggle subordinate. The Melbourne *Herald*, the Sydney *Telegraph* and the Melbourne *Age* all supported Curtin. Surprisingly, so did newspaper baron Sir Keith Murdoch, then in London, who sympathetically drew attention to Curtin's article in pieces he contributed to the British press. Murdoch, it is true, had his own agenda to which Curtin's piece made a nice fit. *The Argus* was unusual in perceiving the obvious and important point that the

United States and Australia now had a new relationship, a 'military alliance'[27] – as, indeed, they did.

As leader of the UAP, Billy Hughes declared that 'we should be undone without Britain', but readily accepted Curtin's explanation that no slight was intended against the mother country. There was just enough of a controversy in Australia for Curtin to respond in a press conference. His article, he was reported as saying, 'was not to be construed as in any way suggesting a weakening of the ties between Britain and Australia'.[28] Even so, he went on, Australia now looked to America. Not even Churchill could query that.

Murdoch's game was more complicated. He was agitating for both an all-party national government in Australia, and for a dominion representative in an Imperial War Cabinet, objectives Menzies had pursued. Menzies had had himself in mind as the dominion representative. Murdoch perhaps thought he would fit the part. The notion of a dominion representative in an Imperial War Cabinet, someone independent of British political parties and of the sentiment of the House of Commons, was supported by Churchill's enemies in the Conservative Party.

Publicising Curtin's Melbourne *Herald* message in London, Murdoch used it as an argument for an Empire War Cabinet.[29] The (Sydney) *Daily Telegraph*'s London editor reported on 31 December that 'the idea of an Empire War Cabinet has again been brought right to the forefront by the "we look to America" statement'. Sir Keith had written to *The Times*, the Melbourne *Herald* reported dutifully on 29 December, claiming that Churchill 'dominates much too greatly those around him'. The problem might be addressed by appointing a dominion representative. Menzies had said much the same. The following day the *Sun* demanded for Australia a place in the British War Cabinet. (The *Sydney Morning Herald* that same day ran a leader rejecting the idea that the Pacific conflict was ' a new war'.) Neither of the big proprietors saw that Washington was now the key to what was for Australia certainly a new war. It was an ingenious interpretation by

Sir Keith, but, while he formally supported the idea, Curtin's intent was quite opposite to having a dominion representative in the British War Cabinet. He wanted, as he said, Australia and America to jointly direct the Pacific War.

Shedden thought Curtin made two supreme declarations in the *Herald* piece. They were that 'We are determined that Australia shall not go' and that this was to be achieved by 'the revolutionising of the Australian way of life until a war footing is attained'.[30] The language about the United States and Britain did not strike Shedden as marking any significant policy change. Speaking to Curtin on the following Monday morning, Shedden suggested he might have saved himself trouble if he had written 'without any lessening of the bonds with Britain' instead of 'free of any pangs'. Curtin smiled, Shedden recounted, and said that 'he was as staunch a supporter of the British Commonwealth as anyone else'.[31]

In his account of it, Shedden missed the point: in calling for America and Australia to jointly make policy for the Allies in the Pacific War, Curtin was either excluding London or proposing to act on the Empire's behalf.

Even years later, when he came to write his history of the war, Churchill was still grumbling. The embarrassment to him in the White House must have been considerable. He wrote that Curtin's article 'produced the worst impression in high American circles and Canada'.[32] It is surely unlikely that Canadian leaders were appalled by the content of Curtin's article, though the tone might have been considered too blunt. Canada had long established direct relations with its great neighbour. Its prime minister, Mackenzie King, was far more insistent on Canada's independence of British decisions than was Curtin. He was no doubt still furious at the capture of Canadian battalions in Hong Kong, sent to garrison the British outpost on Churchill's assurance that Japan would not go to war. As the long-time leader of America's northern neighbour, Mackenzie King had a personal relationship with Roosevelt. Canada valued the British Empire connexion as a balance to its relationship with the United States, not as a channel for it.

Primed perhaps by Churchill, Roosevelt told Casey that if Curtin was attempting to drive a wedge between Britain and the United States, he would be disappointed. Roosevelt was nearly as reluctant as Churchill to recognise Australia's independent status. A 'ridiculous statement', Shedden puffed, noting also that 'Nevertheless, Roosevelt did not discourage the trend towards Washington' as 'the centre of gravity in the Pacific', which inevitably meant 'the decline of the Pacific War Council in London'.[33]

The article caused Churchill irritation not only in his relationship with Roosevelt, but also with King George. Addressing his anxieties, Churchill wrote to the King that 'in spite of all the arguments we have used, the Commonwealth government, which has a majority of two, is determined to have recourse to the United States. They have the idea that they can get better service and more support from the United States than they can from us. It would be foolish and vain to obstruct their wishes.' He told the King the Australians would get a 'very awkward reception in Washington . . . I do not think they will succeed in displacing the effective centre of gravity from London.'[34]

It was a fib, as Churchill knew. The British chiefs and Churchill himself were not only well aware that Australia must now depend on the United States, but had urged Australia to recognise it and were now urging Roosevelt to take responsibility for the region. He might be reluctant to recognise that Washington had indeed replaced London as the centre of gravity, but his military leaders and Cabinet ministers saw it plainly. Churchill later wrote that he contemplated 'making a direct broadcast to the Australian people'. As Shedden remarked, it would have been 'a gross constitutional intrusion'. Churchill, Shedden wrote after the war, 'sought to minimise the dangers that Australia was under, and to make rhetorical assurances of aid, which he could not fulfil. He was thus imperilling the frail fabric of British

Commonwealth relations by projecting Australia increasingly into the orbit of the United States.'[35]

What may have prompted the tone of his letter to the King and the misleading information it offered was not any actual outrage at Curtin's comments, but Churchill's need to conciliate the King. George VI was now close to Churchill, who lunched with him once a week. But Churchill had been the leading opponent of his brother's abdication. The King had found friends in Chamberlain's wing of the Conservative Party, which still nursed its grudges against Churchill. This was not a relationship to be taken for granted. Any public conflict between Britain and one of his dominions, especially any dispute which saw Australia looking beyond the Empire for support, was awkward for the King.

If Curtin's article was at all shocking – and it was certainly front-page news in Britain – it was partly because Australian and British opinion was still behind the flow of events in the Pacific War. Churchill was well behind, and would remain so until the surrender of Singapore. At the end of December, American and Philippine troops were still fighting the Japanese in the Philippines; the Japanese had taken the northern half of Malaya but had not yet reached Kuala Lumpur. It would be another two weeks before they first engaged Australian troops in southern Malaya. Churchill had only just proposed redeployment of Australian troops in the Middle East to the support of Malaya, and other British and Indian reinforcements were on the way. The United States was sending fighter planes and other supplies to MacArthur in the Philippines. The Netherlands East Indies had not yet been attacked. Singapore would not fall for another six weeks. The defeat of the local Allied naval forces in the battle of the Java Sea was still two months away. What was shocking to British opinion was not so much Curtin's turn to the United States, as it was the judgement of Japanese success and British peril in Malaya which underlay it.

Even at the end of December 1941, the scale, speed and completeness of the Japanese victory in the south-west Pacific was not yet imagined. To those expecting the Japanese to be stopped in the encounter with Australian and British troops in Malaya and American troops in the Philippines, Curtin's appeal suggested faintheartedness or panic. His recognition of the Japanese as a 'powerful, ably led and unbelievably courageous foe' was not one Churchill was willing to accord. Curtin's message was that an invasion of Australia was a serious possibility, and Britain would be unable to help. This in turn implied that the Empire forces would be beaten in Malaya and Singapore. This was not an outcome Churchill was at that point prepared to contemplate. The Japanese in Malaya, as he wrote to Curtin, had not yet encountered white troops (though they had elsewhere, pushing aside the Canadian battalions in Hong Kong and forcing American units in the Philippines to retreat to Bataan).

It was that: the revelation of the danger. To the British press the thought that Australia was in peril was new, and controversial. So, too, was the implication that impregnable Singapore might be lost. Churchill, Roosevelt and their advisers had long seen that the United States would lead the Allies in a war against Japan, but the implication for Australia had not perhaps been so clearly seen, or not as widely. There was also a political element to the story in Britain, which to Churchill made Curtin's declaration all the more inconvenient. Churchill was in trouble. Britain and its allies had lost the campaign in Greece, Rommel had beaten the British in Libya and threatened Egypt, shipping losses in the Atlantic remained high, Hong Kong had been lost and its Canadian defenders captured or killed, and now Japanese troops were rapidly advancing down the Malay Peninsula.

His enemies within the Conservative Party pressed for limits on Churchill's authority, or for an alternative leader. In the penumbra of the Conservative Party, Stanley Bruce was busy promoting Stafford Cripps as an alternative to Churchill. Staying in London, Keith Murdoch criticised Churchill and seized on Curtin's comments to press for dominion representatives in the British War Cabinet. His ostensible purpose was not only to enhance Empire solidarity, but also to bring into War Cabinet people who would stand up to Churchill – the role Churchill's enemies, Menzies' flatterers, assured Menzies he had performed. Part of Churchill's annoyance was the political threat to him.

Curtin was surprised by the controversy his statement had created, or claimed to be. Meeting with him six weeks later, British High Commissioner Sir Ronald Cross discussed what Cross referred to as the 'without inhibitions' message. He reported to London that Curtin had told him he 'regretted making this statement and would never have done so if he had appreciated how it would be interpreted'. What Curtin had in mind, Cross reported, 'was that the Australian government had ceased to think of the United States as a mutineer against Britain'. The Australian Government was now 'willing to be friends' with the United States 'without any thought of past differences'.[36] In this ingenious reinterpretation, the 'inhibitions' Curtin referred to were not those arising from its traditional ties to Britain, but those arising from Australia's supposed objections to the American Revolution. The interpretation was plainly at odds with the text. Curtin did not care for Cross, then or later. It was a measure of Curtin's craft that he could offer this unlikely interpretation with a straight face, and of Cross's innocence that he would report it to London without pointing out that it was daft. It was later copied to Churchill, who was not so innocent.

CHAPTER 23

AIF FOR THE PACIFIC WAR

(1)

He turned to the United States, but what did Curtin expect the United States to provide? Perhaps before and certainly after Pearl Harbor, its Pacific navy was inferior to the Japanese navy. As Curtin had said in 1936, there was nothing so inferior as an inferior navy. Its shipyards would soon produce the world's greatest navy, but in late 1941 and early 1942 the United States kept its big ships out of fights. Roughly the same size as Australia's, its army was still relatively small. Much of it was still being trained. The United States had only recently dropped restrictions on where conscripts could be sent. With the immense needs of Britain and the Soviet Union, even cargo ships and troop transports were scarce. The United States Army Air Force was being rapidly expanded, but much of American aircraft production was committed to the Soviet Union, and the British bombing campaign over Germany – as well as to the United States build-up.

In early 1942 the United States did not have the means to substantially assist Australia with ships or planes or troops – and didn't. Even when it did, the distance from San Diego to Sydney was twice the distance from New York to London, so at best the same shipping capacity within the same time could transport only half the amount from the United States to Australia as from the United States to Britain. A troop transport would take a month from Monterey to Brisbane, compared to ten days or so from Brooklyn to Belfast. It would be well into the second half of 1942 before American troops or planes made a difference to Australia, and into 1943 before American ground troops bore more of the burden of fighting in the south-west Pacific than Australian ground troops.

Not so the United States navy. The superiority of its intelligence making up for the inferiority of its fleet, the United States navy in the Pacific would make its own luck.

(2)

Curtin warned Australia that Japan could invade. The military chiefs agreed. For all that, Curtin and his military chiefs did not act as if invasion was imminent. There were air raid trenches dug around Parliament House and in Melbourne parks. Some civilians stocked up on canned food. Road signs would be removed and blackouts imposed. Australians were not otherwise acting as a people about to be invaded.

The British had mined their beaches, uncoiled barbed wire around possible landing sites, dug posts into possible landing fields, protected cities and factories with anti-aircraft batteries and barrage balloons, deployed squadrons of advanced fighters to meet incoming bombers, kept most of the British fleet in home waters to meet an invading force, and deployed a powerful army to garrison the island.

By contrast, Australia was and remained poorly prepared to meet invasion. Its coastline was too long, its war resources too tiny, to replicate the British defences, even if Curtin and his military advisers really did think an invasion imminent. When Japanese bombers attacked Darwin a few months later, they were opposed by only a few land-based anti-aircraft weapons. Australia had no tanks, few planes and few ships. If they were able to sail transports to the Australian coast, Japanese forces would not find it hard to make and secure a landing in Australia, probably not hard to create ports and airfields, and probably not hard to bring in tanks, especially if the Allies could not contest the seas or skies.

(3)

Mostly themselves British officers, the Australian chiefs of staff were as unhappy with the British chiefs' Pacific assessment sent by Dominions Secretary Cranborne on 23 December 1941 as were Curtin and Shedden. In the Australian chiefs' response there was now an unexpected element of fantasy, of a refusal to make do with what they had or were likely to have. They wanted a joint British and American armada to come together to fight a fleet action against the Imperial Japanese Navy, and bring the whole nightmare to an end. Cabling Churchill on 29 December, Curtin gave him the Australian chiefs' comments on the earlier British appreciation.[1] The chiefs expressed surprise that the United States Pacific fleet was 'unable or unwilling to assist', and sharply criticised the British conclusions that it would not be possible to combine a British and American fleet to attack the Japanese navy. They claimed that the British fleet of nine capital ships and four aircraft carriers mentioned in the vaguest terms in the British chiefs' appreciation would be inferior to a fleet Japan could bring against it, a criticism premised on this British Indian Ocean fleet actually existing. It didn't, or not then. If it did, it would certainly be formidable – and somewhat bigger than American task forces that would later turn back the Japanese advance. The chiefs referred to the ABC-1 conversations of March 1941, at which fleet coordination had been discussed. (The chiefs were evidently well aware of the detail of ABC-1 conversations, even if Curtin was not.) The Australian chiefs wanted the Allies to destroy Japan's sea power. They suggested that Britain replace United States naval losses, permitting the United States Pacific fleet to seek a fleet action and regain sea mastery. The alternative idea of building up a British Indian Ocean fleet was 'obviously unsound, and must have been forced on us by the American attitude'.

The Australian chiefs of staff were out of touch with American and British thinking. The request to combine British and American fleets to overcome the Japanese navy was a bold idea and in a certain imaginary world had much to commend it. But the British had no such fleet in the Indian Ocean and no plans to send one soon. The United States navy battle fleet in the Pacific was only then being hauled up from the bottom of Pearl Harbor. The Australian chiefs' proposal begged the question of how long it would take to move a large British force into the Pacific, given that a big Indian Ocean fleet did not yet exist and there was no schedule for its creation. Nor did it recognise the new reality of the Pacific naval war, which is that what mattered was not so much ships as planes carried by ships, or land-based planes that could attack ships. That was already evident in the Pearl Harbor losses, and the sinking of *Prince of Wales* and *Repulse*. The Australian military leaders shared a view that a decisive Allied naval victory 'would render any enemy successes in the meantime worthless to him', since Japan's connexion with its conquests was by sea. One day that would be true, but not in December 1941.

Far from seeking a fleet action, the Commander-in-Chief United States Fleet and Chief of Naval Operations, Admiral Ernest King, had determined to protect his most powerful pieces for later in the game. He had issued a strategy explicitly ruling out attacks in the Marshall Islands designed to draw Japanese strength from Malaya and the nearby islands, or support for British forces south of the equator and west of longitude 155 degrees east, a meridian that excluded Australia and the Netherlands East Indies as well as Malaya and Singapore. The Australian chiefs may not have been aware of his instruction to protect the line from Hawaii to Australia.

Responding to the Australian suggestions on 3 January, 1942, First Sea Lord, Admiral of the Fleet Sir Dudley Pound, deprecated the idea of a fleet battle with Japan. The Japanese navy would not provide such a battle, he cabled Curtin, unless in circumstances where it had air superiority. The British and American navies could not chance their arm on a single engagement.[2] Churchill endorsed Pound's comments. It was a sensible view. The Americans would chance their arm – but not until they had a clear advantage of superior intelligence, and the capacity to deploy air power at least comparable to their opponent. Battleships unsupported by air cover were more hindrance than help. The naval strategy that underpinned Australia's defence planning had vanished. There was no fleet – and if there was, it would likely be the wrong kind. The theory carried on regardless.

(4)

At the end of December, 1941, Churchill told Curtin about the new command arrangements in the south-western Pacific agreed with Roosevelt in Washington. Curtin and his government had wanted a United States commander and representation on a decision-making body in Washington. In the Washington agreement, United States Joint Chiefs had been allocated direction of the Pacific theatre. The Indian Ocean and Middle East were under British command. The European–Atlantic theatre would be joint. But while Washington had overall command of the war against Japan, the operational command in Australia's region went to General Archibald Wavell – to be based in the Netherlands East Indies. Wavell had formal command over MacArthur in the Philippines, but no power to remove him or his forces. Some United States naval units came under joint command. The main United States Pacific fleet was not under Wavell's control. An American air force officer, General Howard Brett, became Wavell's deputy.

In this first cut at the command arrangements, Australia was left out. The American navy was quite uninterested in risking its remaining ships in the Pacific in support of the British in Malaya and Singapore, or for that matter in support of American troops in the Philippines. It was also reluctant to assume any responsibility for Australia itself. Under the agreed arrangements, the defence of Australia and of its territories other than Darwin was not Wavell's responsibility, nor was it the responsibility of the United States Pacific fleet. It was an Australian responsibility. This was not the kind of independence Curtin or his government had in mind.

For Curtin, looking for United States support, direct access to Washington, and naval and air reinforcement in the area, the agreement was very disappointing. Now to be based in the Netherlands East Indies, Wavell had a major responsibility for the defence of the misnamed 'Malay Barrier'. He looked to the Indian Ocean, to Malaya, Burma and the Netherlands East Indies. In principle he commanded all the Allied forces in the region from the Philippines in the north, Burma in the west and the Netherlands East Indies and Darwin in the south.

Reporting the same day, Casey said the US Army Chief-of-Staff General George Marshall was the moving spirit in these arrangements, which mostly consolidated control of sectors already under British command, with the additions of the Netherlands East Indies and the Philippines. Since the Philippines was already well on the way to being lost, the addition of this command meant little. The restrictions on Wavell in any case prevented him removing MacArthur from the Philippines command, or moving MacArthur's forces elsewhere. The Dutch, with small forces of their own, readily assented. Curtin's concern, he rapidly made clear, was that neither Wavell nor the United States Pacific navy had responsibility for the defence of Australia. A follow-up from Casey on 30 December made it clear that in subsequent revisions all of Australia and all of Australian New Guinea, together with the Solomons, Fiji and the New Hebrides, would be excluded from the command arrangements and thus be an Australian responsibility.[3]

Without substantial air and naval forces, it was a responsibility Australia was reluctant to assume. Curtin replied to Churchill on 1 January 1942 that the Australian chiefs of staff believed adoption of the command proposals would result in Australia and New Zealand 'being isolated and left to defend the Australian area' without Allied assistance, and with entirely inadequate forces.[4]

Notwithstanding Curtin's objections, the joint command was announced in Washington.

(5)

By the end of 1941 Curtin was pondering Churchill's proposal to move an AIF division from the Middle East to fight the Japanese. During a War Council meeting on 31 December Curtin referred to a cablegram dated 27 December from Churchill recounting that 'A week ago I wirelessed from the ship to London to suggest that you recall one Australian Division from Palestine, either to India to replace other troops sent forward or to go direct if it can be arranged to Singapore.'[5] When queried about this, Bruce had replied on 31 December that the transport and escort of the troops had not been worked out. During the War Council meeting on the last day of 1941, Curtin said flatly that he was not in favour of sending the troops to India[6], an early and prompt decision foreshadowing the crisis in Australia's relations with its two great allies, the United States and Britain, six weeks later. War Council including the Opposition members then agreed on refusing India. It also resolved that if a request was received to transfer an AIF division from the Middle East to the Far East, Australia would agree. At that point, the Australian Government was not demanding return of the troops. It was saying that it would agree to a request to move a division to the 'Far East', if such a request was made.

On 3 January 1942, the British Government formally asked Curtin to agree to the despatch of two Australian divisions from the Middle East to the Netherlands East Indies, a request they recognised would split the Australian corps. Two days later both War Cabinet and the War Council agreed to the request, adding the possibility that Blamey should accompany the troops. Curtin then told the British that Australia would agree to the despatch of the 6th and 7th divisions of the AIF to Singapore, and other troops to the Netherlands East Indies.[7]

With only one Australian division to be left in the Middle East and the 6th and 7th joining the 8th in the Pacific theatre, Blamey suggested these three divisions be commanded in the same way as was the case in the Middle East – as a corps and, as he no doubt intended, under Blamey. He added that the 9th Division could also be transferred if the further Soviet advance was successful. He wanted Lavarack to go with the troops moving east, after which Blamey would go with the AIF headquarters.

In a submission drafted by Shedden[8], Curtin told a War Council meeting on 19 January that a concentration of the AIF in the Pacific would not only strengthen the area's defences and shorten the communication line for reinforcement and supplies, it would also 'have a stimulating effect on the spirit of the Australian people' and strengthen 'our claim to a voice in the higher direction of operations in this region and makes undeniable our claim for a Joint Allied Council for the Pacific theatre'. It would allow the Australian Government to 'get inside the President's mind more readily through his Commanders here. Every opportunity is thus presented for the Commonwealth to develop, by weight of hard facts, a position which will render the Government largely independent of the ineffectual pleadings hitherto necessary with Mr Churchill.'[9]

The submission claimed that it was 'never contemplated, with war in the Far East, that our Expeditionary Forces would proceed further afield than Singapore or Malaya, as the whole of the Forces that we could raise would be required for the local defence of Australia and for reinforcing the outer screen extending from Singapore at one end to New Zealand at the other. An Expeditionary Force was sent to the Middle East because Japan was not an enemy.'

No doubt drafted by Shedden, it was a retrospective rationale of that official's advice to the Menzies Government. It was quite clear in this submission that Curtin did not want Australian troops deployed west of Singapore – in India, for example, or Burma.

Though Curtin had discussed that possibility with Shedden, he was not at this point asking that the AIF be returned to Australia. In this 19 January submission he wanted the whole of the AIF to be concentrated in the Pacific theatre, a far more specific term than the 'Far East' and one that would exclude both India and Burma. 'In the last resort,' he argued, 'should fortune still further favour the Japanese, it gives a line of withdrawal to Australia for our Forces, which we do not possess at present with the AIF in the Middle East.'

Even in early January, Curtin must have been keeping an open mind on where the returning troops would land. By then Curtin and his colleagues were aware that the Allied position in Malaya was crumbling. Both Bennett and Bowden had said so in their reports to Canberra. Australian war correspondents sent back gloomy accounts of retreats down the peninsula and of Japanese control of the air and sea. By early January the Japanese controlled most of northern Malaya and were ready to take the capital, Kuala Lumpur. It could not be long before they engaged the Australian 8th Division in Johore, the most southerly state and the last defence point before Singapore itself.

Curtin himself had told Churchill that Singapore might well be lost, unless promptly reinforced. Early in January, however, there was little likelihood of prompt reinforcement. It would be at least another month before the Australian divisions from the Middle East could join the battle in Malaya. There were no better guarantees of adequate fighter support for the troops in Malaya than there had been earlier.

On the contrary, Casey had pointed out that prompt and substantial air reinforcement was impossible.

Why then would Curtin agree to commit two of Australia's three divisions in the Middle East to Malaya and Singapore's defence? Once landed, they would be difficult to retrieve. The answer presumably is that Curtin could not press the British Government for support for Malaya unless Australia was also willing to commit troops. That, and the likelihood that long before the troops actually reached Singapore it would be clear whether or not it could be held.

Churchill himself publicly announced that Australian divisions would leave the Middle East. Speaking in the House of Commons on 27 January 1942, Churchill said there would be no impediment to the return of 'the splendid Australian troops' from the Middle East to wherever the Australian Government wished to deploy them. The transport movement would be classified; the fact that Australian troops were being redeployed from the Middle East would not be. Three days after Churchill's speech the leading elements of the 7th Division embarked from an Egyptian port of Tewfik at the Red Sea end of the Suez Canal, in the first of five convoys taking the division east through the Indian Ocean. The 6th would soon follow.

The likely destination was the Netherlands East Indies. Singapore remained a possibility, but by the end of January it would have been clear that army reinforcements which would not arrive for a month could not save it.

(6)

Through those early weeks of January 1942 Curtin and Churchill exchanged cables. In the decoding rooms Curtin was JOHCU, Churchill WINCH. The privilege of making direct contact with Churchill and Roosevelt was one of Curtin's few means of influence over Allied planning. He used it fully. Churchill had earlier encouraged

Menzies to cable directly rather than through high commissioners, not least to cut Bruce out as an intermediary. From 17 December 1941 to 27 January 1942, Curtin sent thirteen personal cablegrams to Churchill on the position in the Pacific. Civility and courtesy was sometimes strained in these exchanges. Annoyances accumulated. Offended by the demand for direct access to Washington decisions, annoyed by Curtin's unceasing requests for British planes and ships to resist the Japanese advance, Churchill by the end of January thought of suspending 'special premier-to-premier telegrams to Canberra'. He explained that it was 'in view of Mr Curtin's tone'.[10] If it was ever more than a late night and intemperate thought, or merely a polite evasion of Cross's demand to see the telegrams, Churchill found it inconvenient to implement. The direct cables continued. Curtin's tone would not improve – nor would Churchill's.

Curtin pressed Churchill to bring the Soviet Union into the war with Japan. He pressed him to persuade Portugal to permit Australia to land troops in Timor. He was anxious, insistent, repetitive. Above all in the early days of January he complained of the command arrangements in the region. He wanted the United States navy to be explicitly responsible for defending Australia from Japanese naval attack. He wanted Australian officers given bigger jobs in Wavell's command. He wanted the Australian Government to be represented on a council that would direct the Pacific War, and he wanted the council to be in Washington rather than London.

Churchill sparred, but gave no ground. He wanted the British dominions and the Dutch on a council in London, chaired by him. Churchill would ascertain the views of the council, and convey them to Washington. He fought against separate representation for Australia in a Washington war council, resisting Curtin and Evatt. His argument to Curtin was that China, the Netherlands and New Zealand would also have to be represented, and decisions would be difficult. Unspoken to Curtin was his determination to keep the American focus on Germany – on ships to protect the Atlantic

convoys, planes for British bombing of Germany, war supplies to the
Soviet Union, the battle against German submarines in the Atlantic,
the battle against Rommel in North Africa. Churchill did not want
Australia competing for resources for the war against Japan. They were
needed for the war against Germany.

Churchill's relationship with Roosevelt was his chief asset, his
long-fostered, gently developed, and now jealously guarded prize.
Curtin got no help from Australia's London representatives. Through
early January Page and Bruce supported the British view. They, too,
thought London should be the centre of decision-making on the
Pacific War, and they should represent Australia on a Pacific War
Council there. As Churchill told King George, London would remain
the centre of Allied war planning. Roosevelt left him his illusions.
Facts would in the end prevail.

Responding to Curtin, Churchill was also blunt. He may well
have been enjoying himself. Composing cables, after all, was
something he did well. He wrote for the record, for history – and
not only in the sense that historians would use the record of his
cables. Churchill's own six-volume war history would essentially be
a sequence of his telegrams. He was writing his next book as he went
along. The intent of his cables was often (and brilliantly) exculpatory.
All he did was justified, either by result, or by the information
available at the time, or in terms of the choices he faced at the time –
or in terms of rationales he thought up later. Composing cables
brought forth his talent for delicate sarcasm, trenchant argument and
calibrated insult. It called forth from Curtin insistence, truculence,
aggression, powerful argument – but not wit. Later in 1942 Curtin's
cables would fade into redundancy and irrelevance – but by that
time Churchill's views on the Pacific War no longer mattered. It had
become an American show.

Churchill's cables were usually characteristic of his style, and
could not have been drafted by anyone else. Curtin's varied.
Shedden's bureaucratic logic, grey prose, and devotion to the record

and precedent are evident in many of Curtin's cables. One or two have Evatt's distinctive force, pertinacity and recklessness. Some have Curtin's own reasonable, direct and sensible style.

Later that year Evatt would tell Bruce (who promptly recorded it in his diary) that the 'great majority' of cables were drafted by Shedden and that Curtin 'had probably not given them any consideration'.[11] That may have been so for routine cables to Bruce and other officers, as it should have been. For the exchanges between Churchill and Curtin there is little doubt that with one or two possible exceptions the JOHCU designation and Curtin's name at the bottom meant he was thoroughly familiar with the content. Which words he had actually drafted in any particular cable is now unknown. What is known is that in those three months after Pearl Harbor and before the loss of Singapore knocked Britain out of serious engagement in the Pacific War, Curtin was in frequent cable exchanges with Churchill and Roosevelt. These exchanges were personal conversations on high matters, of a level, drama, urgency and weight an Australian leader had never engaged in with two great leaders of the democracies before, or might ever again.

The exchanges were often long and frosty. On Monday, 5 January 1942, Curtin wrote to Elsie:

> The war goes very badly and I have a cable fight with Churchill almost daily. He has been in Africa and India and they count before Australia and New Zealand. The truth is that Britain never thought Japan would fight and made no preparations to meet that eventuality.
>
> In addition they never believed air power could outfight sea power and now they will not risk ships uncovered by air support and there is no early probability of air support. In Australia we have to produce our own aircraft. Notwithstanding two years of Menzies we have to start production.
>
> But enough, I love you, and that is all there is to say.[12]

In his private letters to Elsie, unquestionably his own, Curtin displays a sure understanding of Australia's strategic circumstances, one sometimes obscured in his public communications.

Despite the gloomy war news and the conflicts with Churchill, Curtin appeared unperturbed. As reporters said, he thrived in the job. On 28 December the *Sun* ran a photo of him, gazing downward, fist on his cheek, hair glossy, face unlined. On 8 January he celebrated his fifty-seventh birthday.

Bad enough already, Curtin's fights with Churchill would shortly become very much worse.

CHAPTER 24

RESISTANCE COLLAPSES IN MALAYA, RABAUL IS INVADED, AND CURTIN MAKES AN ILL-TIMED VISIT TO PERTH

(1)

Associating himself with a key decision taken in Washington some weeks earlier, Churchill cabled Curtin on 8 January 1942, with momentous news. Under the Pacific command arrangements Churchill had negotiated in Washington, Australia would be primarily responsible for the 'defence of Australian soil' – but the United States would provide 40 000 to 50 000 troops to reinforce Australian home defences.[1]

It marked a major development in Allied strategy in the Pacific War, a change of great significance for Curtin and Australia. The United States Joint Chiefs now recognised that Australia would be a useful base for future American operations against Japanese forces in the south-west Pacific. Soon after Pearl Harbor, Marshall's deputy, Dwight Eisenhower, had proposed to Marshall that Australia be used as a south-west Pacific base – initially for the United States Army Air Forces.[2] The idea built on the existing agreement to use Australian airfields as part of an air route to the Philippines. Eisenhower thought the Philippines would probably be lost, but in the meantime could be supported from Australia. If the Philippines was lost, Australia would then be a good base – perhaps the only one left – for American operations in the western Pacific. Marshall agreed on 17 December, a few days before the Arcadia talks between Churchill and Roosevelt began in Washington.

General Brett from the Army Air Force was appointed to the command of United States forces in Australia, and Wavell's deputy in the American British Dutch Australian (ABDA) command. In their meetings and in the parallel staff talks, Churchill and Roosevelt agreed to defend a chain of small bases across the Pacific, and to send around 30 000 troops – mainly aircrew and support people – to Australia. This decision approved Marshall's earlier decision.

Churchill would not agree to Curtin's demand that Australia be directly represented on a war council in Washington. Instead, he cast himself as the intermediary between Washington and Canberra, one who had in mind Australia's best interests. With American troops based in Australia, Curtin's contact with the Americans would become more direct.

(2)

As late as 12 January, when he cabled Curtin from Washington in response to Curtin's earlier message, Churchill was still optimistic about Malaya, or at least Singapore. He still doubted the quality of the Japanese soldier. The Japanese, he told Curtin, 'have only had two white battalions and a few gunners against them the rest being Indian soldiers'. Singapore was being reinforced. Wavell hoped to launch a counteroffensive in late February, when more troops would have arrived. Curtin had referred to the lack of air support of Australian troops in Crete and Greece. Churchill refused 'to accept any censure'. Britain, he pointedly wrote, had imposed universal conscription. It had lost two fine ships in defending Singapore.[3]

Curtin now had a different view of the Japanese soldier. They were not the short-sighted, underfed Orientals of the cartoons. They were, as he had written in the Melbourne *Herald*, 'a powerful, ably led and unbelievably courageous foe'. Curtin was also closer to Malaya and Singapore, and knew of the rout. On 13 January, War Cabinet discussed evacuation of European women and children from Malaya, and the awkward subject of the admission of Chinese and Eurasian refugees into Australia.[4] There was no recorded discussion of evacuating troops from Singapore, if necessary.

On 17 January, Curtin responded to Churchill with a lengthy reiteration of the Singapore strategy, and the assurances given under it since Bruce had placed it in the centre of defence policy in 1923. The cable had Shedden's touch, the master of the files, recalling the history and the various assurances given. For Shedden it was exculpatory. For Australia, for Curtin, these reminiscences now served no useful purpose. 'I repeat these earlier facts,' Curtin asserted, 'to make quite clear the conception of Empire and Local Defence in which we have been brought to believe.'[5]

Influenced by Wynter, Curtin had not in fact believed it. Shedden did, or had. Curtin had no hesitation in picking up Churchill's reference to universal conscription. 'We make no apologies,' he wrote, 'for our effort or even for what you hint we are not doing.' (Churchill appeared to be unaware that Australia imposed conscription, though conscripts could not be sent to fight beyond the limits of Australia or its territories.)

The 8th Division had gone into action against the Japanese on 14 January. Bennett had tersely reported that day, Curtin told Churchill, 'Our air support absent.' Curtin had made the position public because, he told Churchill, 'I believe it is better they should know the facts than assume all is well and later be disillusioned by the truth.'[6]

Quite a lot was becoming public. Curtin had plainly and publicly
warned of a possible Japanese invasion. The broad content of his cables
to Roosevelt and Churchill had been given to Australian reporters.
There was the Melbourne *Herald* piece. There was discussion over
command arrangements. Now there was the absence of air support
for the 8th Division. Soon the issue of London versus Washington for
a Pacific War council would be made public. Part of this was to avoid
blame for the developing catastrophe in Malaya and Singapore, and to
sustain Curtin's fragile hold in the House of Representatives. Part was
to sustain the argument for assigning higher priority to the war against
Japan, the 'new war'. There was little in these public discussions to
help the enemy. Of its air and naval supremacy Japan was well aware.
Reading the disclosures in Canberra, Sir Ronald Cross raged.

Much of the news of the Allied retreat down the Malay Peninsula
was suppressed. The *Sydney Morning Herald* complained of the
'official silence'. But there was enough in the official communiqués,
and no doubt more in war correspondents' reports that could
not be printed, to stir criticism and alarm in the Australian press.
By Friday, 16 January the *Sydney Morning Herald* was belatedly
wondering if Singapore was indeed the fabled fortress the paper
had long supposed, or if it was a 'delusion and a snare', a 'Maginot
Line' that would, like the French fortifications, prove no fortress
at all. It was not only Australians who were 'astonished' at 'British
weakness', who thought it 'incredible' that it had not been promptly
and effectively reinforced, but the Dutch and Chinese governments
as well. And as Churchill was well aware, the critical ferocity of the
Australian newspapers was quite mild compared with those he read
every morning over a late breakfast. As the *Sydney Morning Herald*
remarked, 'nothing said or written elsewhere compares in asperity'
with what was being published in London as the British position
collapsed. While Curtin's cables annoyed Churchill, the clamour of
the British press and of his critics in the House of Commons was
something else entirely, and much more threatening.

Responding two days later to Curtin's cable of 17 January, Churchill thanked Curtin for his 'frank expression of views', a sure sign of some unpleasantness to follow. When it came to exculpation, no one could do it better than Churchill. If there was now a problem in Malaya, it was not his doing. He pointed out that 'I have not been responsible for the neglect of our defences and the policy of appeasement which preceded the outbreak of war'. With provocative candour he wrote that 'I deem the Middle East a more urgent theatre than the now christened A.B.D.A. area'. He added that recent victories against Rommel and the Soviet Union's successes in holding the Germans from driving through to the Caspian permitted him to release the 7th and 8th Australian divisions, the British 18th and several more Indian divisions for the Far East. (Churchill misnamed the 8th for the 6th – an indication that he himself had written the text, though the language is anyway unmistakable.) It would have been wrong to send forces earlier, when the campaign against Rommel hung in the balance and the Germans might have swept into the Middle East from the north and east through Persia. No one could have foreseen the naval disaster of Pearl Harbor, nor the loss of *Prince of Wales* and *Repulse*, and thus the temporary command of the sea Japan had won.

By May, Churchill wrote, the United States would have a superior fleet at Hawaii, and the British navy would send two and perhaps three modern carriers to the Indian Ocean. Churchill's language was private to Curtin, and wonderfully stirring. 'We must not be dismayed or get into recrimination,' he wrote, 'but remain united in true comradeship. Do not doubt my loyalty to Australia and New Zealand. I cannot offer any guarantees for the future and I am sure that great ordeals lie before us, but I feel hopeful as never before that we shall emerge safely and also gloriously from the dark valley.'[7]

To someone of Curtin's sensitivity to words, Churchill's language may have been softening. But to someone with his long background in politics and policy, the grand public language may also have been disappointing. He wanted planes, not wonderful words. On 20 January, when Curtin received the cable, the 8th Division was pressed hard in Johore and falling back to Singapore. To Curtin, May would have seemed a very long way away – even if Curtin could still credit Churchill's assurances of eventual naval support.

Churchill had arrived back in London from his Washington talks with Roosevelt on Saturday, 17 January. He would only then be registering the distressed mood in Fleet Street and in the House of Commons.

(3)

Curtin was feeling the strain. It was not only the relentless Japanese successes, the disagreeable exchanges with Churchill, the obscurity of decision-making in Washington. He was also troubled by local problems. A former trade union official and radical socialist, Curtin now found strikes infuriating. On the coalfields of New South Wales strikes were unpredictable, and frequent. In mid-January Curtin threatened that striking coalminers would be called up. Strikes by stevedores were also frequent, and hurt war production. Curtin told the Waterside Workers' Federation the navy would be ordered to work the ships if the stevedores refused.[8]

Exhausted after nearly four months as prime minister, Curtin left Melbourne by train on Wednesday, 21 January for Adelaide, on his way to Perth. The *Sun Pictorial* mentioned the following day that Curtin had left by train for a 'brief rest'.

Tired, unwell, Curtin would have found it hard to relax. He hadn't been home since returning from Perth to Melbourne the previous August, to find the Menzies Government collapsing. Churchill spent his weekends at Chequers. Roosevelt frequently visited his estate at Hyde Park, New York. Hitler had the Berghof at Berchtesgaden, and Stalin had his dacha. In Melbourne, Curtin stayed in a two-room suite at the Victoria Palace Hotel in Little Collins Street and in Sydney at the Commercial Travellers Association. It was not a comfortable or splendid life. In Canberra Curtin had the Lodge, hot in summer, cold in winter, and often lonely. He had spent Christmas alone at the Lodge, inviting a local RAAF crew to Christmas dinner. His colleagues mostly returned to their homes on weekends or when Parliament was not sitting. Taking care of her mother, Elsie stayed at home in Cottesloe, thousands of kilometres and a long train journey from Canberra.

To work as he did Curtin needed rest, and the only way he knew how to rest was to ride the train west, back to his home in Cottesloe. Reporters were told he would stay in close touch. Some travelled with him, including the *Sunday Telegraph*'s Richard Hughes. Curtin travelled with a teleprinter and phone scrambler.[9] In principle he could stay in close communication. In practice his staff found the facilities in Perth less adequate than those in Melbourne or Canberra. With a Japanese army advancing down the Malay Peninsula, and Japanese task forces scouring the Java Sea for Allied ships, there was no good time to take a break. As it happened, Curtin chose a very bad time to be away from the military headquarters in Melbourne. It was the first time since he had become prime minister that Curtin's health, his physical fragility, his distant home, affected his work.

As Curtin travelled west, the war news became dramatically worse. Through to late January, as Japanese troops moved down the Malay Peninsula, Australian newspapers had kept a grim but hopeful tone. The Japanese were losing surface ships and submarines in battles with Allied navies, they reported. Japanese progress in Malaya was obstructed by Allied air raids. The Japanese bombed Singapore, but the casualties were light. When the Japanese reached Johore, Australian correspondents in Malaya reported that the advance had been checked by the cleverness of the tactics of the Australian 8th Division under Major-General Gordon Bennett, who issued frequent and encouraging press statements. Each day brought reports of new Allied successes in the Australian newspapers, yet each day the Japanese advanced further south down the peninsula.

Curtin and his colleagues had been hearing a different story, and would have been less surprised when, on 23 January, Bowden cabled a report of a conversation with Ian Fitchett. A war correspondent attached to the 8th Division, Fitchett told Bowden the situation in Johore was 'desperate and perhaps irretrievable'.[10] Around the same time Bennett reported that part of his force had been cut off, without possibility of relief.[11]

Two days after Curtin left the command headquarters at Melbourne's Victoria Barracks on his long train journey to Perth, the tone of Australian newspaper reporting abruptly changed. The catalyst for the newspapers on the morning of 23 January was not the approach of the Japanese towards the Singapore causeway. It was the sudden Japanese attack on Rabaul, 5400 kilometres east of Singapore. Northern Queensland was much closer to Rabul than it was to Melbourne. Overnight, what had still seemed a distant war in the jungles of Asia became a war on nearby Australian territory. In Malaya the Australians fought under the higher command of the British as part of the Empire forces. Rabaul was defended by an AIF unit and some Militia troops – and only by them.

For Japanese war planners, Rabaul, the major port of the island of New Britain, had been a key objective. A Japanese base there would help defend the major naval base at Truk, and allow ships and aircraft to annoy communications between Australia, New Guinea and the United States. In American hands, Rabaul could become a B-17 bomber base against Truk. The Japanese command also hoped for a major battle between the Japanese and American navies, the fleet action on which Japan depended to force a peace settlement. The engagement, the Japanese thought, would take place east of the Marianas and north of the Marshall Islands. Rabaul, 2800 kilometres south of Truk, was the extreme right flank of a line of naval and air bases watching against the American fleet.[12] But while the Japanese might think of it as the right flank of a line facing east, Curtin and his fellow Australians would think of it as the left flank of a line facing south – towards them.

Escorted by ships of the Japanese navy, the nine ships transporting the Japanese South Seas Force ordered to seize Rabaul had sailed from Apra on Guam on the afternoon of 14 January. The following evening the escorts detected what was thought to be a small hostile ship on the horizon. Suspecting it could be a US naval ship taking MacArthur from the Philippines, the *Tsugaru* chased it down. It turned out to be a Japanese tuna fishing boat, the fishermen relieved to find they were not being hunted by an American destroyer.[13] On 20 January, the convoy crossed the equator – the first Japanese army unit ever to do so. By 11.40 on the night of 22 January, as Curtin's train travelled further west, the South Seas Force was landing at Rabaul.

After a sharp fight with defending Australian troops, the Japanese occupied the town. All Australian communications with Rabaul had ceased, *The Argus* reported on Friday, 23 January. A RAAF plane flew over the Rabaul port in the evening, observing a strong Japanese escort, troop transports, and every sign confirming the Japanese had taken the town. The nearby island of Bougainville at the northern end of the Solomons was also under attack.

Both New Britain and Bougainville were Australian mandates, the first Australian territories to be invaded by the Japanese in the Pacific War. Tokyo radio announced the successful invasion of Rabaul at 5.15 (Tokyo time) on the evening of Saturday, 24 January. Backgrounding the announcement, Imperial Headquarters explained the capture of Rabaul was 'extremely significant in terms of our ability to attack and menace Australia'. It also 'increases the possibility of blockading the line of communications between the United States and Australia'.[14] Curtin's assessment, that of his military advisers, was exactly the same.

The Japanese counted 300 Australians killed, and 833 taken prisoner, including the force commander. The Japanese lost sixteen killed. Earlier war reporting had been filtered by military censorship in Singapore, London or Washington. Much of the news about New Guinea now being read by Australians came directly to Melbourne from Australian military sources. The Australian Government had no interest in minimising the threat.

(4)

Chaired by Frank Forde in Curtin's absence, War Cabinet discussed the Japanese attack on Rabaul and the rapid deterioration in Johore at a Melbourne meeting on Friday, 23 January. The chiefs of staff attended. Four days earlier, Bennett had told Sturdee that Indian troops were unreliable and British troops inexperienced. Bennett had since reported the advancing Japanese had cut off two Australian battalions in Johore. The meeting was also told the Japanese navy had attacked Rabaul that morning. The possibility of an attack on Australia was discussed, with Chief of the Naval Staff, Vice-Admiral Sir Guy Royle, saying he thought Japan had 'so much on her hands' that Australia 'did not offer a very attractive target'. Even so, he could not discount the possibility of an attack on Port Moresby.[15]

War Cabinet chose to disclaim responsibility and blame the British Government. It concluded, the note-taker Quealy bluntly recorded, the 'Australian people' were 'to be told that United Kingdom government has not been able to supply forces necessary for the defence of Malaya'.[16] A stiff cable demanding reinforcement of Singapore was to be prepared and sent to Churchill over Curtin's name.

In London, the Defence Committee of Cabinet had also been meeting. The occupation of Rabaul coincided with Churchill's return from Washington and his sudden recognition that the British position in Malaya might well be irretrievable, threatening Britain's hold on Burma. On 19 January, Wavell warned Churchill that he doubted Singapore could be held for long once Johore was lost. General Sir Alan Brooke, the Chief of the Imperial General Staff, noted in his diary on 20 January that 'News from Far East is bad and I am beginning to be very doubtful whether Singapore will hold out much longer'.[17]

Warned by Wavell that Singapore might not be able to hold out for more than a few weeks, Churchill asked the British chiefs of staff committee on 21 January whether it would not be better to 'at once blow the docks and batteries and workshops to pieces and concentrate everything on the defence of Burma and keeping the Burma Road open'.[18] Reinforcements intended for Singapore would instead go to Burma. The chiefs discussed the paper on the morning of 21 January, without decision.

The British Defence Committee meeting that evening had before it the cable from Wavell reporting that an Indian infantry brigade and two Australian battalions had been cut off in southern Malaya. It might be necessary to withdraw to Singapore. In light of this impending withdrawal across the causeway, the Defence Committee discussed whether evacuation of Singapore should be considered. If it was evacuated, the reinforcements intended for Singapore could instead be sent to Burma.

The intended reinforcements at this stage were the remaining elements of the British 18th Division, but the two Australian divisions were either already at sea or shortly to embark from Egypt for Malaya. The first eight ships transporting the Australians would not reach Colombo until the end of January, so the British discussion may not have specifically referred to them. If not explicit, it would have been implicit that, if Singapore was to be abandoned in favour of a stronger stand in Burma, and if reinforcements intended for Singapore were to be redirected to Burma, those reinforcements should logically include the Australians. If so, it was the first time the option of sending the AIF troops to Burma had been raised implicitly or explicitly in the presence of an Australian representative. Unhelpfully, the British chiefs said the decision on evacuating Singapore should be left to Wavell, as the regional commander.

According to Churchill, Page did not attend the chiefs of staff meeting or the Defence Committee but 'somehow' had access to Churchill's minute. Page claimed in his diary that he told a meeting of War Cabinet, which immediately followed, that 'Australia would never stand our men being deserted' and that the proposed evacuation 'would be more fatal and injurious to the lives and fortunes of the army and the war than standing and fighting at Johore on the line that was there'.[19] If Page did indeed say so to the War Cabinet, and not only to his diary, it was not recorded in the meeting minutes. He also claimed to have said that Churchill's paper was a 'defeatist note'. Had he said it out loud, Churchill's eruption would have been something to behold.

While Curtin's train was travelling to Perth, Page cabled him with the dramatic news of these meetings of the British Defence Committee of Cabinet and the War Cabinet. His cable reporting these conversations arrived in Australia on 23 January, but evidently not in time for consideration at the War Cabinet meeting chaired by Forde that day. Page reported that the question had been raised as to whether 'evacuation should not now be considered' and reinforcements for Malaya diverted to Burma. The diversion of troops en route to Malaya which could instead be sent to Burma included the British 18th Division and 'any other reinforcements which could have reached Singapore in time'.[20] Page thought evacuation would cause 'irreparable loss of prestige and I think irreparable damage to the allied cause'. It had been decided, he reported, to wait for a couple of days to see if the Australians and Indians could fight their way back to the main army. What difference that would make to an evacuation plan was unclear, as was much else in this discussion.

A cable to Churchill on the conclusions of the Australian War Cabinet earlier that day was drafted under Curtin's name. Evatt amended it to take account of Page's cable. The cable to Churchill bears the stamp of Shedden's long association with the Singapore strategy, and Evatt's intemperate language. 'After all the assurances we have been given,' the cable told Churchill, 'the evacuation of Singapore would be regarded here and elsewhere as an inexcusable betrayal.' The cable also rejected the Defence Committee suggestion that reinforcements intended for Malaya might be sent to Burma. If it was no longer possible to send them to Singapore, they should be sent to the Netherlands East Indies, not Burma.

The cable told Churchill that the Japanese appeared likely to seize Rabaul and attack Port Moresby. It warned of 'public uneasiness' in Australia over the Japanese advances, and clearly implied that Curtin would blame Britain and Churchill. The Australian Government would have 'a duty and an obligation to explain why it may not have been possible to prevent the enemy reaching our shores'.[21] The explanation would presumably dwell heavily on Britain's failure to prepare against Japanese attack. In a separate cable to Page, Evatt asked where the suggestion for the evacuation had come from. Evatt was evidently unaware that it had come from Churchill. Had he been, the tone might have been a little less offensive.

Churchill could easily interpret the implications. In disclaiming responsibility, the Australian Government would throw it upon Churchill – and at a time he was already under political attack. The cable was copied to Casey, with instructions to show it to Roosevelt and enlist American help in preventing evacuation of Singapore.[22] Given the American view of Singapore, Roosevelt was surely the wrong person to ask.

(5)

Sent under his name, and covering matters of great weight, Curtin must have been informed of and agreed to the cable's content. He may have amended it. If the language was not his, the thoughts were those with which he would agree. Travelling west on Friday, 23 January, he had stopped at Kalgoorlie, where he spoke to reporters and sent a telegram east. He made a speech in the town which included his line that 'the man not fighting has no excuse for not working'.[23]

He had access in Kalgoorlie to telegrams from Melbourne. The Western Australian time zone was behind that of the east coast, extending the opportunity to consult Curtin. He would have been able to speak to Shedden, Forde and Evatt by phone, and probably securely. He would have opposed at least for now what amounted to the surrender of Singapore – all the more so if, as British Defence Committee discussions suggested, Singapore would be surrendered to permit a stronger stand in Burma. Curtin had already said he did not want the returning AIF troops to go to India. Had he thought it implied in the British discussion, he would have had an even stronger objection to Burma. As much as any of these documents, it was one for which he was responsible.

The reversals in Johore were troubling but the more immediate concern of War Cabinet on that Friday was the occupation of Rabaul. It was Australian territory, and its occupation raised the possibility of an invasion of Australia itself.

Cabinet was anything but calm and resolute in the face of the news. Forde was particularly excited, to no clear purpose. 'We shall never give in,' Forde martially declared in a radio broadcast that Friday night. It was, he said, the first time in history Australian territory had been attacked, the first time foreign invaders were trying to gain a footing on Australian soil, and the first time the Australian Militia had been in action. He was sure the Japanese would attack mainland Australia. 'I am certain the enemy will make an attack, perhaps not at once, but make it he will.'

Australia, The Argus told its readers the following morning, was 'facing the greatest danger in its history'. It reported there had been no word from Rabaul in two days, and Japanese were said to be landing elsewhere in New Guinea and the Solomons. War Cabinet, it reported, would that day consider a scorched earth policy in Australia to deny food to the invading enemy. Ministers and service chiefs, the paper added, had little doubt that the Japanese were seeking bases in New Guinea 'to press direct attacks against the Commonwealth'. The Australia Day holiday on Monday had been cancelled. Curtin was expected in Perth Saturday morning, when he would speak with Forde. (*The Argus* was well informed. War Cabinet did indeed discuss a 'scorched earth policy' to be implemented in an invasion.[24])

When War Cabinet met the following day, Saturday, 24 January, Evatt discussed Page's cable and said the Australian Government had told London Singapore should not be evacuated. The chiefs of staff concurred, according to the meeting minutes. Importantly for the later row over the episode, a subsequent War Council also endorsed the 'inexcusable betrayal' cable, apparently without discussion. (Spender later claimed that both Menzies and McEwen had dissented from the Government's reply. Shedden responded that neither he nor the minute secretary, Quealy, had any record of this dissent.[25]) The question of 'diversion' of reinforcements to Burma, soon to become one of the most celebrated in Australian history, does not seem to have been discussed.

If he had been there, Curtin might have managed it better. Forde was too amenable and weak, Evatt too pertinacious and heedless, Beasley too blunt and combative. Without Curtin (and sometimes with him) War Cabinet could be irascible. After several months of reassurances that the Japanese advance would be slowed and stopped, that troops and supplies were being hurried to Singapore, War Cabinet was suddenly told that Singapore might be abandoned, and reinforcements at sea – perhaps including the returning AIF – might be rerouted to Burma. War Cabinet had been sceptical of British assurances, but this reversal was too abrupt to permit careful thought or anything other than indignation. Aware of the critical tone of Australian newspapers, ministers could easily imagine the shock and anger that would follow abandonment of the Singapore Fortress. They would not want to appear complaisant in its abandonment.

War Cabinet should have seriously considered the possibility of withdrawal. It should have asked Shedden to seek the views of its military advisers on whether it would be possible, and over what time. It did not.

While War Cabinet discussed plans to burn the country as Australian defenders fell back before a Japanese invasion, several thousand more Australian troops were landed into the melee of Singapore.[26] They were untrained, unready, unfit. Some had not had a week of training in Australia. Many had never fired a rifle. Around them both civilian and military control were beginning to collapse. The last of the Allied troops retreated into Singapore a week later, blowing up the causeway behind them.

Everywhere the Japanese were triumphant. In Washington, Admiral Ernest King wisely refused so far as possible to risk his ships against the Japanese fleet. But after the Japanese capture of Rabaul he did order the Commander-in-Chief, US Pacific Fleet, Admiral Chester Nimitz, to despatch a carrier task force commanded by Vice-Admiral Herbert F Leary and based on the carrier USS *Lexington* to the south-west Pacific. The task force was reinforced by another carrier, USS *Yorktown*.[27] King's decision would prove fateful for Australia.

(6)

Reporters speculated that the emergency in Rabaul and Singapore was so great that Curtin would promptly return to the east coast. Quealy noted in the War Cabinet minutes of Saturday, 24 January: 'PM to return next week'. Astonishingly, Curtin did not return. He did contribute to the alarm and confusion by publicly disclosing the content of recent cables to Churchill. Travelling with him, reporter Richard Hughes reported in the *Sunday Telegraph* of 25 January that Curtin 'had demanded of Mr Churchill immediate establishment of a Pacific War Council and an Imperial War Cabinet'. Like his colleagues in Melbourne, Curtin wanted to pin the blame for the Malaya reverses on London, though how an Imperial war cabinet might improve matters was not at all evident. The subtext of the intermittently raised Imperial war cabinet proposal was often that Churchill's decisions should be queried. Perhaps that was what Curtin was suggesting to Hughes.

For Curtin it was not proving a relaxing break. He had left on Wednesday. He met the South Australian Premier Tom Playford in Adelaide on Thursday, 22 January. According to Syd Gray, son of an old friend and also travelling on the Trans towards Perth, their train was then held up one day out of Kalgoorlie by floods. Probably conflating two separate encounters, Gray recalled that Curtin hailed him, invited him into his carriage for a beer and a sandwich, and told him that if necessary a plane would take them to Perth.[28] But if it happened at all on the way to Perth the train delay could not have been a long one, because Curtin spoke to reporters at Kalgoorlie on Friday (and in all likelihood also spoke to Forde and Evatt on the Secraphone, which his staff carried in its box), and attended Gray's wedding on Saturday in Perth.

Saturday was his first night at home in Cottesloe since leaving the previous August. It could not have been entirely tranquil. Annoyed by more industrial disputes, Curtin repeated that 'the man not fighting has no valid excuse for not working', a statement that unhappily came out at much the same time as a BBC report that Curtin was on holiday.[29]

Furious, Curtin responded angrily but unconvincingly that it was an 'absolute lie' to say that he was on holiday. On the contrary, 'what I am doing in Perth is imperative work associated with my office'.[30] This work, it was disclosed, was to discuss with the West

Australian Premier construction required at Fremantle if it was to become a port for a British fleet. Curtin said navy chief Sir Guy Royle had 'asked me to forward a highly confidential message to the Premier of Western Australia. I am here for this purpose.'[31] It was a lame story. If it was so important to talk face to face the Premier could have come to Melbourne, as the *Sun Pictorial* pointed out.[32] The works would take months if not longer, and would be of no value in the immediate crisis. There was in any case no British fleet to berth in Fremantle.

Curtin spent Sunday with his two children, now young adults. He did not appear in the least relaxed. In a press photo taken at home in Cottesloe that day, Elsie and young Elsie are both in flowered dresses, both smiling as pleasantly as they could manage, while young John in RAAF uniform stands behind his mother, his hands on her shoulders. Curtin stands a little aside, buttoned up in a three-piece suit and bow tie, looking displeased. On that Sunday, with Churchill talking about evacuating Singapore, with Rabaul taken by the Japanese two days earlier and Bougainville and Lae now threatened, with many promises but no actual ships or planes or men delivered by the great allies, with Frank Forde assuming national leadership, declaring an invasion certain and vowing in a national broadcast that Australia would never surrender, with Cabinet announcing the country would be burnt in front of the advancing Japanese, and with Curtin now finding himself haplessly posing with his wife and children in the garden of their California bungalow in Jarrad Street, Cottesloe, thousands of kilometres away from his War Cabinet and his military advisers, a perilous time during which the BBC was telling the world he was on holiday, how could he be other than displeased?

In the east the crisis continued. On Monday, 26 January *The Argus* headlined the evacuation of Lae, and Japanese landings in the Bismarcks. Rabaul had been occupied on Friday, the authorities now disclosed. Curtin was fully informed, the paper reported, but had not yet decided to return east. He was attending to 'a number of defence matters of urgent importance'.

Broadcasting on the night of Australia Day, Curtin warned striking workers and uncooperative employers that the subjugated nations of Europe had paid the price of having done 'too little too late'. He demanded a say in the Allied war strategy and directly attacked Churchill in an unmistakable reference. 'No single nation,' he said, 'can afford to risk its future on the infallibility of one man, and no nation can afford to submerge its right of speaking for itself because of the assumed omniscience of another.'

Curtin's hints were followed up in *The Argus* on Wednesday, 28 January, with a well-sourced but unattributed report that Australia was seeking a Washington council to direct the Pacific War. A London organisation 'would not be acceptable to Australia'. Page and Bruce had both sent cables in the past few days stoutly maintaining London was the best place for a Pacific war council, not Washington. Curtin and Evatt insisted on Washington. This point of contention with Churchill had not hitherto been publicised.

The War Cabinet evidently expected Curtin's early return, according to Quealy's note. Curtin chose to stay a few more days. Perhaps he thought cancelling his Perth program would look like panic. Keeping to his original and announced schedule, he spoke on Monday at a Civic reception and met Premier J C Willcock. On Tuesday he spoke at a lunch put on by the Perth City Council, and on Wednesday he spoke at Fremantle Town Hall. It was then time to go, Curtin leaving by train on Thursday 29 January. That wasn't the end of his troubles. In Melbourne, War Cabinet was pondering with astonishment reports the Japanese had fought their way through southern Johore to the shores opposite Singapore, and successfully seized Rabaul as their base in the south-west Pacific. The Militia army was bigger now, they knew, but Australia still had no tanks or fighters to resist the invasion that Frank Forde had declared likely. In the press, Ward and Cameron blamed Menzies and Spender for Australia's unpreparedness. They replied in kind. Curtin gave a short press conference[33] when he reached Kalgoorlie on the morning of 30 January and travelled on towards Port Augusta. Around Murray Bridge his train was held up for twelve hours by floods, in places several centimetres over the rail line. He was served breakfast, but then the food ran out. Someone had a hamper, which Curtin 'ordered' be shared among the women and children – or so it was reported. He himself had a frugal 'hunk of bread and cheese' for lunch.[34] He arrived in Melbourne on Sunday evening, ten hours late.[35] He missed a War Cabinet meeting he had planned to attend on Sunday, and took the chair for the meeting on Monday. It was, reported *The Argus*,[36] the fifteenth War Cabinet meeting in eleven days. Curtin had missed fourteen of them. At a press conference on Monday he expressed amazement at reports of Empire disunity. Happily, only the BBC made a point of his absence. As Curtin darkly pointed out, Western Australia was after all part of the nation. That Monday, as he prepared to chair War Cabinet, the papers reported the Imperial troops had withdrawn from Malaya across the causeway to Singapore. Curtin travelled on. By Tuesday morning he needed to be in Canberra for a Premiers' Conference.[37]

(7)

Churchill was very annoyed by Australia's cable, over Curtin's signature. The British 18th Division was on the way, he told Curtin. He continued:

> I really cannot pass without comment such language to me as 'inexcusable betrayal'. I make all allowances for your anxiety and will not allow such discourtesy to cloud my judgement or lessen my efforts on your behalf. It would however make it

very difficult for your representative to be present at our most
intimate and secret councils if ex parte accounts of tentative
discussions are to be reported to you and made the basis for
the kind of telegrams you have sent me . . .

When the British War Cabinet met on 26 January, Churchill said he
regretted that Page had not informed the Australian Government
of the Defence Committee's decision to give highest priority to the
defence of Johore and Singapore. According to one witness, Churchill
'then went off the deep end about the Australians generally . . . and
said if they were going to squeal he would send them all home again
out of the various fighting zones'. Page retorted that rather than
looking after themselves the Australians had been looking after the
Empire, 'and if anybody had been looking after themselves it was
the chaps this end'.[38] It was unpleasant.

    Casey, who had extraordinary access, did show the 'inexcusable
betrayal' cable to Roosevelt on 24 January, as instructed. He cannot
have been entirely comfortable with the assignment. Roosevelt
sensibly responded that plans would be made to evacuate 'in ordinary
prudence', even if no evacuation was planned. More importantly, and
here arose the most difficult issue for Curtin, Roosevelt did not agree
that intended reinforcements should be diverted to the Netherlands
East Indies if Singapore was lost. He thought 'it is essential to hold
Burma as the only link to China', telling Casey that the Chinese
would soon be in a position to attack Japanese bases in Indo-China
(a confidence which proved unfounded). Roosevelt raised with Casey
the possibility of United States troops, then being convoyed to New
Caledonia, being deployed to Port Moresby. The beginning of an
offer of more United States troops for Australia's defence in return
for Australian troops for Burma's defence was already becoming
apparent – and as strongly from the American side as the British.
Roosevelt told Casey that he had 'very little anxiety for the security of
Australia itself'.[39]

The United States had long believed Singapore was not all that important – and it was right. Churchill by now also saw it could not be saved. In any case, Japanese air superiority, its new bases in southern Malaya and its demonstrably lethal air tactics against ships had already made Singapore useless as a fleet base. (Useless for the British navy. The Japanese navy would find it quite useful.) But both Britain and the United States had strong interests in defending Burma from the Japanese. Britain thought of Burma as a pathway to India, as indeed it was. The United States saw it as part of the only feasible supply route to China. United States support for China was, after all, the core of the conflict between Japan and the United States. At issue here was a switch of British priorities, from defending Singapore to defending that part of Burma not already lost, and which lay between the Japanese and India.

There was certainly a good argument to evacuate Singapore, which Curtin and his advisers did not canvass. There was an even better argument to withhold army reinforcement from Singapore. Empire ground forces were already more numerous than the Japanese ground forces. The shortcoming was in the air, not on the ground.

Curtin might well have pondered whether it was feasible to evacuate Singapore, even if it was desirable. It was a question he would soon pose in respect of putting the troops into Burma, after Singapore had been lost and its defending troops marched into prison camps. The British navy had been able to land reinforcements at Singapore, but as the Japanese advanced down the peninsula and won control of more airfields the risks to Allied shipping into Singapore increased. The British 18th Division landed only with great difficulty, under constant bombing attack, and only after Wavell had told Commodore John Collins, the Australian commander of the British navy escort, that unless he went through with the landing (despite Collins' reluctance and his assessment Japanese bombing made it too risky), Wavell would let it be known that the British navy had lost Singapore.[40]

British ships were withdrawing to Ceylon or further west to avoid attack. The Japanese navy deployed carriers and other ships in the region, and would have concentrated on Singapore if a large-scale evacuation became apparent to the many flights over the island. The Java Sea battle the following month would demonstrate Japan's easy ascendancy over the combined Allied navies. It was one thing to evacuate an army from Dunkirk, when Britain controlled the seas and at critical times the skies over Dunkirk and safety was as close as the other side of the Channel. It would be quite another when Japan controlled the seas as well as the skies, when the nearest land was Sumatra, and no preparations had been made to evacuate large numbers of troops. If they were able to leave at all it would be without their artillery and other heavy weapons, without road transport and without the immense quantities of food and water needed to sustain thousands of fighting troops. By late January 1942, when the issue was raised, Japanese troops had already occupied Sulawesi and Kalimantan. They would occupy Sumatra within a few weeks. Evacuating the AIF's 8th Division and the remaining British and Indian units, around one hundred thousand troops in all, would have been extraordinarily difficult.

It was, in any case, late in the day. The following day (January 24) Bowden reported that all the fixed defences on Singapore pointed seawards: 'None are directed to mainland.'[41] It would later be pointed out that the lesser guns in the fixed defences could be rotated northwards, but none were supplied with anti-personnel shells. Their armour-piercing ammunition was designed to penetrate the hull of a ship and then explode. Fired north, they buried themselves in the soft soil of Johore. Whatever the capabilities, Bowden would be reporting what he knew.

Had Curtin chaired the meeting, the cable to Churchill might have been a little less inflammatory, the statements from War Cabinet a little less excited, but no decisions were taken which Curtin opposed, or which he would have made differently.

It was an inglorious episode. Curtin was in the wrong place, Evatt was foolish, and the Australian chiefs and Shedden should certainly have informed a sensible discussion of evacuation options. In London, Page should not have rejected Churchill's view without consultation and reflection, and the British chiefs should have given it a great deal more thought rather than idly suggesting such an immense decision, with great consequence for civilian government and higher strategy, should be handed back to Wavell. No participant came out of the episode well, except perhaps Churchill, who had the force of mind to suggest withdrawal.

Subsequently Churchill wrote that Curtin's message did not decide the issue: 'If we had all been agreed upon the policy we should . . . certainly have put the case "bluntly" to Wavell'. Churchill thought a British 'scuttle' would have offended American opinion. He had 'no doubt what a purely military decision should have been', though neither at the time nor later did he plausibly specify how an evacuation would have been arranged. His attention was less on evacuation than on withholding reinforcements from Singapore and redirecting them to Burma. General Brooke, Chief of the Imperial General Staff, later wrote of the decision to send the British 18th Division to Singapore, 'in the light of after events I think we were wrong to send it to Singapore, and that it would have served more useful purposes had it been sent to Rangoon'.[42]

Just so. In the light of after events, much might have been different. As the British official history later recounted, the Singapore naval base 'was doomed before the war started'. Its air force was meagre. Japan's air command was so superior, its ground tactics so clever, its troops so well trained, that five days after the landing at Kota Bharu, 'Malaya already faced defeat'.[43]

(8)

With slender forces, with Wavell establishing his Java headquarters only the previous week, with no additional ships or planes on their way, Curtin and his War Cabinet could do no more than assess the speed of the Japanese advance. Preventing it, still less throwing it back, was not within Australian power. They could not slow the Japanese advance but Curtin and War Cabinet had almost in passing made one very big decision: troops on their way to Singapore and Malaya should not be sent to Burma. That might also include the returning 6th and 7th divisions. Making that decision, and still more affirming it in the face of relentless opposition from Churchill, Roosevelt, Page, Bruce, Fadden, Menzies and Spender, would be the most memorable military choice Curtin made in the Pacific War.

(9)

The Imperial bonds were showing strain. Curtin's unhappiness with Churchill, his public reluctance to risk his country on the 'infallibility' of 'one man', had much to do with Churchill's obstruction of Curtin's insistence on direct and high-level communication with Washington. Even late in January, as the Japanese overran Malaya and attacked Rabaul, Churchill successfully if only temporarily prevented creation of a Washington Pacific War Council. It should be in London. On 24 January 1942, Curtin cabled Churchill, pressing for a Washington-based council – on which Australia would be represented. It had already been agreed, he pointed out, that instructions to the supreme commander in the south-west Pacific area would be issued by the President of the United States.[44] On this issue, Curtin found Australia's London representatives continued to be a hindrance. Bruce told Curtin he supported the idea of a London-based Pacific War Council to coordinate views.[45]

Curtin conceded, for the moment. In a 6 February cable to Churchill, Curtin reluctantly agreed to a Pacific War Council in London.[46] It was better than nothing. The information flow to the Australian Government was sporadic. That same day he had to ask Wavell for regular reports to his cable address (Kindlier, Canberra). But Curtin still wanted the Council in Washington and it would not be long before the arguments for it were irresistible.

Curtin's unhappy relations with Churchill were not helped by the British High Commissioner in Canberra, Sir Ronald Cross. A former Conservative junior minister whom Churchill had found dispensable, Cross admired Menzies and spoke to him frequently. Not so Curtin. A month after Pearl Harbor, Cross had reported to London that the 'crude realities' Australia had suddenly faced had produced a 'stupor', with 'grave anxieties and even jitter'. He told Cranborne that 'strong national leadership' was lacking, though once or twice Curtin did have 'the voice of leadership'. Cross was indignant that Australians were being led to believe that the reverses in Malaya 'are simply the consequences of British stupidity and incompetence' and that Australia had been 'misled by oversanguine British assurances'.[47]

Cross's reading of the Australian newspapers was that the impression was being created that in cables to Roosevelt and Churchill Curtin alone had revealed 'the true nature of the Pacific situation'. In reality, Cross confided, 'Mr Menzies tells me that it was he who, at the Advisory War Council, suggested telegraphing Mr Roosevelt and that he outlined the message to be sent.' Cross doubted that Australians have 'at any time . . . fully realised that the survival of Australia is bound up with the survival of the UK. This limited outlook finds a place . . . even in the mind of Mr Curtin. Indeed, that is the only explanation I can offer of his astonishing statement that the Japanese attack must be recognised as a new war, and not thought of merely as a new outburst of the previously existing war.' Cross thought it was 'this same outlook of narrow horizons (and perhaps shaken nerve) that I believe, influenced Mr Curtin in appealing to the United States of America'. For all that, Cross thought Curtin 'likeable and capable' and that 'contrary to all prognostications' he 'appears to be standing the strain well'.

Cross could have caused much more trouble if he had been more widely respected. Annoyed by what he thought of as an 'anti-British press campaign', Cross felt ill-used. In a cable to Cranborne, received in London on 21 January, he asked he be given authority to threaten trade and other economic sanctions on Australia if the bad behaviour continued. Australia, Cross told Cranborne, was 'ignoring the obligations' of the 'spirit of Imperial partnership'. While he 'did not suspect Curtin of taking an active part' in what he thought was an anti-British campaign, it was 'increasingly clear that Curtin fails to resist his left wing leader Evatt and probably cannot do so.' Cross wanted a 'stiffer attitude' to maintain 'British prestige in Australia'.

Much of what he wanted was specifically about Cross's prestige. He thought it necessary to 'strengthen the position' of the British High Commissioner. He suggested that if Page was to be on the Pacific War Council and attend War Cabinet when Australian matters arose in London, Cross should be able to attend the Australian Advisory War Council, or War Cabinet. He told Cranborne that one reason he was so little regarded in Canberra was that he did not see the cables between Curtin and Churchill. He did not know what was being discussed. He asked to be copied. He thought the Australian Government overlooked his importance. It would perhaps be reminded of the power of Britain if he was given authority to threaten trade or other economic sanctions, of a nature unspecified.

Cranborne wasn't interested. In a 29 January note Cranborne told Churchill that Cross thought 'we should use economic or financial pressure to coerce the Australian government to cooperate with us'. Cross's proposals were printed up in a War Cabinet minute and tentatively put on the War Cabinet agenda.[48] Churchill promptly had the minute deleted from the agenda and made sure copies were not distributed. A secretary reassured him that Page had not been sent a copy. Churchill might not have cared whether or not Cross saw the WINCH–JOHCU exchanges, but he certainly did not want Page or Bruce to see them. His solution was to tell Cranborne on 30 January that 'the Winch-Johcus are ended for the present in view of Mr Curtin's tone'. The proposed sanctions, and Cross's thought of attending the 'Australian Council', were disregarded.

Cross saw Curtin on 5 February, when he returned to Canberra. This is when Curtin told him he regretted his Melbourne *Herald* piece. Curtin mentioned that he had also been publicly critical of the British government during his trip to Perth, when he had spoken to reporters during the journey. This was because, he said, he had been cabling London for five weeks about representation in the British War Cabinet without a satisfactory reply. (Most of his pressure was actually for a Washington-based rather than a London-based Pacific War Council – Cross does not seem to have been aware of this.) While Menzies, Hughes and Spender were now criticising him for this statement 'they themselves had at various times urged [him] to demand representation'. Indeed, Curtin said, he was 'the one who was always endeavouring to use moderate language'. He told Cross there was an anti-Britain 'press campaign' which he would tell editors to stop. Cross told London he had suggested the words Curtin would use to editors. Curtin's duplicity in conversation with the credulous Cross was almost unseemly.

As a diplomat Cross was much less competent than Bruce, though neither was respected by the government to which he was accredited. Cross's shortcomings were widely known, especially to his compatriots. A British businessman with intelligence links, Lieutenant-Colonel Gerald Wilkinson, would later be assigned by Churchill as an informal liaison to General MacArthur in Australia. Wilkinson would find that MacArthur loathed Cross, and Gowrie was also well aware of his shortcomings – as were other senior British in Australia. Meeting him in Canberra, Wilkinson thought Cross wasn't ill-intentioned but might have done better if he had modified his 'Eton manner'. He would tell MacArthur that Cross's problem was simply that he was 'second rate and not very bright'.[49]

CHAPTER 25

FALL OF SINGAPORE
BRINGING THE AIF HOME

(1)

They had fought over evacuation of the Australians at Tobruk, troops, planes and ships for Singapore, command arrangements in the Pacific, and Australian access to the Washington leadership. But until late January 1942 there had been no persistent disagreement between Churchill and Curtin on withdrawal of AIF troops from the Middle East and their reassignment to the war against Japan. Churchill himself initiated their withdrawal from the Middle East in late December 1941 while sailing towards the Arcadia conference with Roosevelt in Washington. Curtin agreed to the request in early January. Curtin and the War Council had made it clear they did not wish the troops sent to India. By inference, it was clear War Cabinet would likely object to sending them to Burma. Curtin had told War Council on 19 January that if they were deployed in the Pacific he wanted the troops to have a clear line of withdrawal to Australia, which would exclude Burma and by late January quite probably Singapore. While it was now clear enough that Churchill and Roosevelt might well want the troops sent to Burma, they had not directly proposed it to Curtin.

Now steaming across the Indian Ocean, led by the fast passenger liner SS *Orcades* and followed by USS *Mount Vernon* and other troop transports, the destination of the 7th Division and later the 6th would become for a few weeks of February 1942 the most important issue in the war with Japan.

With the British, Indian and Australian forces overwhelmed in Malaya and retreating down the peninsula, the Japanese invasion of Burma progressing rapidly towards Rangoon, Rabaul occupied and a Japanese invasion of Sumatra and Java imminently expected, the Allied defence against Japan was crumbling. British forces in Malaya and Singapore were trapped and must soon surrender. Manila had fallen early in January. The United States and Filipino forces on the Bataan Peninsula were also trapped. Well-trained, battle-hardened and freshly rested, the AIF troops sailing through the Indian Ocean were the only uncommitted Allied ground forces capable of encountering the advancing Japanese and inflicting damage. For Churchill, examining the great maps in his war rooms, the markers following the transports' passage east in the Indian Ocean represented interesting possibilities. He was concerned about India, threatened by the Japanese advance west across Burma. Firmly focused on China and with two senior American advisers assigned to Chiang, Roosevelt wanted the Burma Road for supplies to the Nationalists kept open.

By early February the Japanese had forced their way through Johore and had crossed over to Singapore. 'Japanese Forces Land On Singapore', *The Argus* told Australians on Tuesday, 10 February. The paper reported hopefully that 'offensive action is being taken to mop up the enemy' after a 'terrific British artillery barrage'. Gordon Bennett told reporters the situation was 'well in hand'. But by Friday, 13 February *The Argus* reported the Japanese claim to have occupied the whole city. Even on Saturday, 14 February *The Argus* was still reporting that there was 'no talk of surrender' at Singapore. Unable to resist, the island's water supply from Johore cut off, the British commander surrendered his forces on Sunday, 15 February 1942. The *Canberra Times* announced it on Monday morning, along with a Japanese attack on Sumatra and 'heavy fighting' in Burma.

As the Japanese advanced into Singapore, Curtin had declared a new plan for a 'total war effort'. Following agreement at a Tuesday, 10 February War Cabinet meeting, profits, prices and wages would be controlled. Workers would if necessary be directed to jobs. Investment would be controlled by government decision, prices would be pegged, profits pegged to return of 4 per cent on capital and no more, wages would be pegged at their level on 10 February, workers would be directed towards 'fulfilment of a maximum war effort', absenteeism would be illegal, any area could be proclaimed to be under military control. On Tuesday, 17 February a full Cabinet meeting in Sydney agreed to a 'total mobilisation' of Australian human and material resources. Curtin said that 'every human being here is henceforth at the Government's service, and every material thing in the country can be diverted to war purposes at the government's direction'.[1] Asked by Curtin, Ted Theodore agreed to head an Allied Works Council to build the airfields, camps and roads required to turn Australia into the south-west Pacific base for the war against Japan.

Australia itself was becoming the front line. At war with the Soviet Union, Germany had indefinitely postponed an invasion of Britain. Continental America and Canada were invulnerable, as was South Africa. Of the British Empire nations, of white English-speaking nations, of all the unconquered members of the Allied nations except the Soviet Union and China, only Australia faced a serious threat of enemy invasion in the first half of 1942. To Churchill and Roosevelt, it was a world war fought on many fronts, each accorded a priority for war resources. To Australians, to Curtin, there was by February 1942 only one front, one conflict, one war, and it was for their homeland.

The returning Australian troops could no longer be landed at Singapore. The next battle in the south-west Pacific would be Java, but Japan was rapidly closing in on the Netherlands East Indies. Japanese troops had landed in Borneo on 11 January, Rabaul on 23 January. On 4 February they captured Ambon and on 9 February Makassar. By early February it was apparent to the Australian intelligence officer in Java,

Lieutenant-Colonel K A Wills, that Japan would soon take Timor and Sumatra, leaving Java in between and indefensible. The leading elements of the 7th could not arrive before 1 March, and the whole of the 6th and 7th divisions could not reach Indonesia until well into April. By then it would be in Japanese hands. Wills rightly concluded that the forces would be lost if they attempted to land in Java. He also thought their loss would jeopardise 'the defence and safety of Australia'.[2] Briefed by Wills, Lieutenant-General John Lavarack, who had joined Wavell's command, put the argument strongly to army chief of staff Lieutenant-General Sturdee in Australia, who agreed.

So did Wavell, at least about the Netherlands East Indies. As Singapore surrendered, Curtin was copied a cable from Wavell informing London and Washington that if southern Sumatra was lost – which seemed likely – Java could not be held. As for the Australian divisions assigned to defend the Netherlands East Indies, Wavell advised 'there are advantages in diverting one or both divisions to Burma or Australia.'[3] Burma was part of his command, and he wanted the Australians there.

Out of office and feeling its loss more keenly as the decisions facing Australia's leaders became more immense, Menzies wrote to Curtin from his Melbourne chambers on 14 February. Addressed to My Dear Prime Minister rather than the more familiar John, it posed a series of questions, by then commonplace. It looked to the Japanese taking Singapore, then the Philippines, and then Sumatra and Java. With the Japanese holding overwhelming air and naval supremacy, the letter suggested in its sequence of questions, there would be no point in losing forces by trying to resist in the Netherlands East Indies. Instead, Menzies asked, 'would we be in fact ultimately better off in this war by concentrating all available forces in the north of Australia to carry out a Continental defence and not an Island one?' Or would Australia be better off by supporting a concentration of Allied forces in Burma to keep the China road open? He suggested Curtin ask his officials to review these alternatives.

In the letter Menzies revealed a lack of thought about continental defence. Australia did not have the means to move troops quickly over Australia's vast distances, especially under air attack. His proposal that all Australia's 'available forces' be concentrated in the 'north of Australia' if a continental defence was selected was exactly the strategy the Australian army advised against, including earlier to Menzies. If Japan possessed the sea command to invade, it would be free to take Sydney or Melbourne, isolating the Australian army in the north from its support.

Curtin replied briefly two days later, addressing him as Mr Menzies. He told Menzies that the 'questions you have raised have already been considered by the Government, discussed with its advisers and taken up with Britain Government'. He added a sting: 'The evolution of opinion towards a policy which has long since been advocated by me not without some opposition is not without interest.'⁴ Curtin's reply suggests he thought Menzies wanted the troops concentrated in Australia. When it came to the choice, Menzies would opt for Burma.

Their use of formal titles in this exchange was unusual. It tells us much about the mood as Singapore fell. Both recognised they were writing for the historical record in a crisis of national survival. A formal tone was appropriate.

Just before Singapore's collapse, British Minister of State Duff Cooper had offered Menzies what was essentially Cooper's job.⁵ It was the best the British would offer Menzies in Opposition, and it was not very good.

Lieutenant-General Sturdee would only rarely initiate contact with his political superiors but he did so on Sunday, 15 February, the day of Singapore's surrender. It was, as he would have known, a call of momentous importance. He telephoned Curtin in Canberra to advise that the returning Australian troops should be brought to Australia. Speaking to Lavarack's paper, he informed Curtin that 'considerable risks are at present being taken with the security of this country', which was the only base from which a counteroffensive on Japan could ultimately be launched. The return to Australia of the Australian divisions, 'some 100 000 trained and war experienced troops' would in his view 'more than double the present security of this country'.[6] Sturdee wanted the 9th Division back as well.

Curtin and Sturdee would have assumed Singapore was lost. Vivian Bowden had left Singapore by boat the previous day. Curtin would soon know that the 8th Division, one of only four battle-trained divisions Australia possessed, had been surrendered to the Japanese on Sunday evening. For Curtin the capture of Singapore meant invasion of Australia was now possible, and perhaps imminent. It also meant that by default Australia had now become what Eisenhower had proposed in December and Curtin had long urged: the main south-west Pacific base for resisting and throwing back the Japanese push south. For Churchill and for Wavell the loss of Malaya meant the strengthening of Japanese forces in Burma and a greater risk to India.

That day Curtin cabled Page with a detailed review of Australia's defence position.[7] Based on his War Council submission of 19 January it went further by telling Page 'it is a matter for urgent consideration whether the AIF should not proceed to the Netherlands East Indies but return to Australia'. For the defence of Australia, United States and Canadian forces would be helpful but 'nothing can be of assistance as quickly as the AIF'.[8]

Curtin told Page these matters had not yet been considered by the Government. There was no new War Cabinet or War Council decision but Curtin had no hesitation in assuming full responsibility for proposing that the entire AIF be withdrawn from the Middle East and sent to Australia if, as 'appears probable', the Netherlands East Indies could not be held.

He had not yet instructed Page that the troops must be returned to Australia, but he had plainly indicated that was his inclination.

He had instructed him that all the Australian troops in the Middle East – and this would include the 9th Division – should be returned to the Pacific theatre. The Pacific theatre did not include India or Burma.

When the defeat in Singapore was confirmed on Monday, 16 February 1942, Curtin was prepared with a statement. He solemnly announced the fall of Singapore 'can only be described as Australia's Dunkirk. It will be recalled that the fall of Dunkirk initiated the Battle for Britain. The fall of Singapore opens the Battle for Australia.' His statement then lapsed into colourful implausibility. On the outcome of this battle for Australia depended, he said, 'the frontier of the United States of America and, indeed, all the Americas and, therefore, in a large measure the fate of the British-speaking world'.[9] In Washington, the loss of Singapore was not thought quite so important – though the United States now accepted that Australia should be the base for Allied operations in the south-west Pacific. In the circumstances, a little exaggeration could be overlooked. In Tokyo the following day Prime Minister Tōjō called on Australia to end its 'futile resistance' to Japan's plans for the Pacific.[10] In those plans Australia would ultimately find its place in the Greater East Asia Co-Prosperity Sphere. In the meantime it should remove itself from the war.[11]

Singapore lost, the Netherlands East Indies under attack, the returning AIF could go either to Burma or Australia. Asked for their views, the Australian chiefs of staff agreed on Tuesday, 17 February that the 6th and 7th divisions should now be diverted to Australia, and the 9th also recalled. Perhaps papering over some difference of views, the chiefs hedged their response, suggesting that the situation in Burma 'may necessitate some reinforcement there until other troops are available from elsewhere'.[12] This hint of indecision would cause trouble.

Curtin forwarded these views directly to Churchill on 17 February, as well as to Page and Wavell. Casey was asked to communicate them to Roosevelt. In his cable to Churchill, Curtin said directly that the 'government' requested the diversion of the returning troops to Australia. He asked as well for the recall of the 9th Division to Australia, and for a 3000-man British armoured brigade en route to the Far East to also be sent to Australia.[13] There had not been a War Cabinet meeting between Curtin's cable to Page and his cable to Churchill. He was continuing to take personal responsibility, but with no doubt in his mind his colleagues would back him. There was no longer any suggestion that the Australian troops could be sent to the Netherlands East Indies, which had still been a lively possibility when Curtin had cabled Page two days earlier.

Churchill wanted to protect India. Roosevelt wanted to keep a supply route open to China. For different reasons they both thought Burma could and should be held. Churchill and Wavell made much of the need to keep the China land supply route through Burma open, the argument that would appeal in Washington. The need to protect India's eastern approaches, a more direct British interest, was not prominently argued.

Decisions were swiftly taken in London. Responding to Wavell's cable on the difficulty of defending Java after the loss of Singapore, the Defence Committee of the British Cabinet decided on 16 February to withhold further reinforcement of Java and instead concentrate on the defence of India, Ceylon and Australia.[14] This meant abandoning the Netherlands East Indies. Churchill convened a meeting of the Pacific War Council on 17 February to hear the views of the Dutch, whose colony would be lost. It had before it a cable from Wavell suggesting the returning 6th and 7th divisions of the AIF should be sent to Burma. That night the Pacific War Council agreed that the Netherlands East Indies be abandoned and that all Australian forces should be committed to the war against Japan – a decision that would have meant the return of the 9th Division as well. It also decided, with Page's concurrence, that the 7th Division should be sent to Rangoon.[15]

Roosevelt's White House agreed with the British view on Burma, and linked the sending of United States troops to Australia with the diversion of the 6th and 7th divisions to Burma. On the same day the Pacific War Council met in London, Casey[16] saw Harry Hopkins in Washington. The President's aide asked him whether, if the United States sent troops to Australia, the Australian Government would be prepared to send its two divisions to Burma or India.

Casey's message to Curtin reporting his conversation with Hopkins was closely followed by one from Page on 18 February, reporting that the Pacific War Council in London had recommended that the Australian Government permit diversion of the 7th Division, already on the water, to Burma. The 6th Division would go straight to Australia. The Council was chaired by Churchill. Page was a member of the Council and had agreed with this recommendation, though Page would have been well aware that Curtin had told Churchill the troops were to be diverted to Australia.

In this and a following cable Page wrote that Curtin's earlier cables had been fully considered by the Council and by the British. Ignoring Curtin's actual instruction, Page picked up on the chiefs' view that Burma could be considered 'until other troops are available from elsewhere'. Those of the 7th Division were the only troops that could reach Rangoon in time, and keep the Burma Road open and China in the fight. 'The position of this convoy', Page told Curtin, made it 'imperative that permission should be given to this course within 24 hours'. Page himself 'strongly' recommended that Curtin acquiesce in the Pacific War Council decision. Churchill, he said, had assured him that air support for Burma was 'already in train'.[17] (It was not provided.)

The United States and Britain – and Page – were now lined up to send the 7th Division (and perhaps the 6th Division) to Burma, where Japanese troops, reinforced by troops released from the Malaya campaign and supported by overwhelming air superiority, were rapidly advancing towards Rangoon. Though Curtin was unaware of it and it did not determine his decision, the British defence of Burma had been a calamity.

To Page, Curtin immediately and tersely replied on 18 February that there was a very strong probability that the Government would decide the 7th Division should come on to Australia, and the convoy should not be diverted to Burma.[18]

The pressure increased. Following Page's cables Bruce told Curtin that in his view 'it is essential we agree' to send the 7th Division to Burma. Wavell chipped in with a cable to Curtin on 18 February saying Curtin 'might like to know' that Lavarack agreed Australian troops should be diverted to Burma. (It was a foolish misstep by Lavarack. He would later regret it.)

Curtin had travelled to Sydney on Tuesday, 17 February to speak at a War Loan rally. He planned to chair a War Cabinet and War Council he had called for the following day. Falling ill with what was described as a gastric attack, he was admitted on Tuesday night to St Vincent's Hospital, where he would remain until Thursday. From his hospital bed he stayed in close touch with the cable traffic and War Cabinet discussions. His own views had already been made quite clear.

In Curtin's absence War Cabinet on Wednesday, 18 February discussed the 'future employment of the AIF'. It was the first War Cabinet meeting since 10 February. The surrender at Singapore had concentrated his colleagues' minds. Much of the discussion was over the troops on *Orcades*, then landing in Java. Beasley said forcefully (and correctly) that deploying the leading elements of returning AIF to Java was 'sending men to the same fate as those in Singapore'.[19] (The 3400 Australian troops on *Orcades* had been landed at Batavia the day before. The ships transporting the Japanese invasion force to Java were that day leaving Cam Ranh Bay. In the Japanese attack the Australians were captured or killed.) War Cabinet agreed Blamey should return as quickly as possible to command Australia's military forces. Within the government as within the army command there was unanimity. The troops should not be sent to Burma. They should come back to

Australia. When the issue was brought up in War Council following the War Cabinet meeting, however, there was a deep disagreement.

Confined to bed at St Vincent's, where young Elsie visited to find him surrounded by flowers and good wishes, Curtin missed the War Council discussion. The War Council had before it Curtin's 17 February cable asking for return of the AIF to Australia. The members also saw the cables from Wavell and Page supporting the Burma diversion, and from Casey reporting Washington's preference for Burma and its willingness to send United States troops to Australia.

Under Forde's chairmanship, and with Evatt and Beasley leading the discussion from the government side, the War Council meetings were perhaps more acrimonious than they might have been under Curtin. Over the two meetings on 18 and 19 February the Opposition argued that the Pacific War Council was right, Page was right, and troops should go to Burma. Only they could stop the Japanese in Burma. If the land supply route to China through Burma was closed, Japanese divisions could be moved from China to the Pacific, threatening Australia. The Government, they argued, had to understand the war from a larger perspective. Evatt and Beasley fought back, the pertinacity of one and the truculence of the other enraging Fadden, Hughes, Menzies and Spender. On this issue the Government members would concede nothing. Shedden recorded the non-government members agreed with Page's recommendation that the 7th Division should go to Burma.

So far as Beasley was concerned, arriving news of a big Japanese bombing raid on Darwin on 19 February, the first attack on Australian soil, sealed the argument.

The attack on Darwin by carrier-based planes was intended to knock it out as a port supporting Allied naval ships in the region, before the Japanese took Timor. As the first major attack on Australia, it also underlined the nation's unpreparedness to resist invasion. The Japanese task force of four carriers, two battleships and three cruisers, the same task force under Admiral Nagumo that had attacked Pearl Harbor, entered the Banda Sea undetected and launched 150 strike aircraft at the Darwin port. All but undefended, with almost no land-based anti-aircraft defences and no fighters, the port was full of naval shipping. Twelve ships were sunk.

The Darwin base, the reinforcement link to Java and the nearest Australian base to Port Moresby, was for a time disabled.[20] The attack itself was shocking, but the most serious concern for the Government was the demonstration that the Japanese could attack Australia where and when they wished, with impunity. Against sea or air attack, it was all but undefended. Churchill thought the Australians were panicking. When Nagumo steamed his task force towards Ceylon and India, as he shortly would, Churchill himself would respond with far more theatrical alarm than Curtin's.

(2)

Following the War Council meeting on Thursday, 19 February, War Cabinet reviewed the discussion and affirmed the decision to return the AIF to Australia. That day Curtin cabled Page instructing him that the Australian Government 'cannot agree' to the diversion of the troops to Burma. Australia, Curtin said, was in 'imminent danger of attack'.[21] He left St Vincent's on Friday to be driven to Canberra to speak in a secret session of Parliament on the Darwin attack. On Saturday he chaired a War Cabinet meeting.

Replying from London on 19 February, Page astonishingly told Curtin he was 'holding your telegram secret' until Curtin had an opportunity to review War Cabinet's decision.[22] For a government representative, it was a brazen defiance of clear instructions, and at a perilous time. In an abrupt reply dated 20 February, Curtin tersely instructed him that if he had not already done so he should 'act at once' on Curtin's earlier cable.[23] Page replied on 20 February, telling Curtin that the destination of the convoy had not been changed to Burma and the necessary instructions had been issued for it to sail to Australia. Page, it would soon emerge, was not well informed.

Churchill himself weighed in on 20 February, asking Curtin to reverse the Government's decision in what Shedden considered a 'patronizing tone'. Churchill said Curtin had to share the blame for sending the British 18th Division to Singapore, where it had been lost, rather than to Burma, where it would have stopped the Japanese.[24] On his renewed request to divert troops to Burma, he told Curtin he needed an answer 'immediately'. Roosevelt supported Churchill in a message conveyed through Casey to Curtin.

The following day, Saturday, 21 February, War Cabinet met in Canberra. Chaired by Curtin, it discussed the messages and affirmed its earlier decision. Replying to Churchill in a frosty but not insulting tone on 22 February, Curtin said that 'I have received your rather strongly worded request at this late stage, though our wishes in regard to the disposition of the A.I.F. in the Pacific theatre have long been known to you and carried even further by your statement in the House of Commons' on 27 January. (Churchill had told the House he would put no obstacles to the return of the AIF 'to defend their own homeland or whatever part of the Pacific theatre may be thought most expedient'.)

Curtin expanded the argument. He noted that Wavell wanted the whole corps for Burma and, in Washington, Field Marshal Sir John Dill wanted it left open. 'Once one division became engaged,' he pointed out, 'it could not be left unsupported.' He queried whether it could be landed and, once landed, whether it could later be brought out. He again refused Churchill's request to send the troops to Burma.[25]

To Roosevelt, Curtin cabled that Australia, with its small population, 'the only white man's territory south of the equator', was now directly threatened.[26]

In his recollections, reporter Harold Cox perhaps conflates several different conversations from around this time, but it is clear enough that Curtin was sharing his troubles with the press – or at least with Cox. Meeting him in the King's Hall of Parliament House during the crisis, Cox recalled:

Curtin came mooching out of the bar lobby where he'd been to buy cigarettes, and we stopped and talked for a few minutes. Curtin looked the picture of a complete physical wreck, and I said to him 'You're overdoing it. You look dreadful. I've never seen you look worse, and I think you ought to go home and get a good sleep.' We were completely alone and the Hall was deserted. He said to me 'I'm not going to get any sleep tonight. You know what's doing, don't you?' I said 'Yes, I know. You've kept us pretty well informed.' He said 'Well, the position is this: I've talked to the War Cabinet and I've talked to the War Council. I've talked to the soldiers (the Chiefs of Staff). I can't get any unanimity of opinion on what we should do, but by 6 o'clock in the morning they will have reached the point of no return. I've got to go home and between now and 6 o'clock I've got to decide the message I'm going to send.' And Curtin, with his thin, slender gold cigarette case[27], tapping against a cigarette butt, wandered across towards the Government lobby. Then just before he got there, he stopped and called me. He said 'Harold! What would you do if you knew their equipment was on another convoy two days behind them?'

Then he disappeared into the lobby. By the most extra-ordinary coincidence, I met him in pretty much the same circumstances the next evening. He was a changed man. I said 'You look a lot better tonight.' He said 'Yes, I feel a lot better, too. They're coming home.'[28]

Curtin would have assumed his government's refusal of a Burma diversion would be acted upon. It was not. Disregarding Curtin's strong view and without informing Page or Bruce, Churchill had ordered the convoy north towards Burma. He had done so ten minutes before sending his cable to Curtin on 20 February in which he had not revealed the diversion.[29]

He revealed this to Curtin only on 22 February, asking again for Curtin to reconsider. Shedden thought 'It was arrogant in tone and revealed a grossly misleading statement.' After a long walk in the Majura hills in Canberra[30] Curtin replied sharply and briefly on 23 February, insisting on his earlier decision. It was 'quite impossible' to change Australia's decision.[31] This time Churchill submitted, and ordered the convoy back.

Churchill would never surrender, or not completely. On Thursday, 26 February he copied Curtin a plea from the Governor of Burma claiming that Australians troops could 'effect a radical change for the better'.[32] Churchill telephoned Page at 2 a.m. that morning to seek his support. Page refused to raise the issue again.[33]

The destination of the 7th Division was now settled. The use of the 9th and the 6th divisions was not. When Churchill pressed there, however, he would find the Australian Government more accommodating. Curtin had moved on, and so probably had Evatt. By the beginning of March they had shifted most of their attention to Washington. Securing Roosevelt's goodwill became their main aim.

(3)

For Curtin, it had been an exhausting couple of weeks. He had rejected the demands not only of Churchill but also of Roosevelt, and done so against the strongly expressed wishes of his emissaries Page and Bruce in London, and against the advice of the Opposition members of the Advisory War Council, some of whom – Menzies,

Hughes, Spender and Fadden – claimed as much or more experience of wartime decision-making. If Curtin had got it wrong, his political opponents would pursue it vigorously.

For all that, the decision had not been hard to make. The army chief of staff Sturdee strongly supported bringing the troops back to Australia. He may have threatened to resign if they were committed to Burma, an entirely unnecessary threat given the unanimity of opinion on the government side. Shedden pressed for return of the troops, and claimed to have been doing so since early January. War Cabinet was likewise adamant the troops return to Australia. Australia's national interests prevailed over those of Britain. It was not quite clear-cut – the 9th Division remained in the Middle East for another year, and the 6th Division would be left in Colombo for some months. But Burma was out.

For now the debate was over, though it would resonate down the years. The following year Keith Murdoch, campaigning against the Curtin Government before the 1943 election, would insist in a front-page column the troops should have been sent to Burma. So did Menzies. In his memoirs decades later, Page insisted he had been right and Curtin wrong.

An obvious decision, but Curtin had assumed a great responsibility. The Australian Government was not accountable for the loss of Singapore, and the loss of the 8th Division. It was now accountable for the safe return of the AIF. It was the first time an Australian government had assumed so heavy a responsibility. At the Lodge, in Curtin's office, the burden was evident. Curtin's secretary for defence matters, Fred McLaughlin, a Shedden protégé and just as meticulous, was an evangelical adherent of the Moral Rearmament Movement. The light of faith was not shed quite as brightly on his office colleagues; Hazel Craig remembered McLaughlin as someone who expected you 'to do good deeds and live a better life than you were living and so he used to leave notes for all of us round saying how we could make our lives better'. During the dispute with Churchill, McLaughlin was frequently on his knees in his office, praying to Jesus. The worst of the dispute, he later told his family, 'was the most difficult night' he had ever gone through. (Mrs McLaughlin said Curtin was on his knees too, joining her husband in prayer. She did not herself observe it, and it is surely unlikely.[34]) Not sharing McLaughlin's faith, Gladys Joyce recalled that Curtin lay for an hour daily on a couch in his room, looking 'up at the ceiling with his cigarette holder jutting between his teeth . . . thinking through his problems'.[35]

Might the 7th Division have made a difference in Burma? On 20 February the Headquarters of the 7th Division and the 25th Brigade were near Colombo and the 18th Brigade was at Bombay. Only the 21st Brigade was in convoy to the east of Colombo and able to reach Rangoon within a reasonable time.[36] Heavy equipment had been loaded separately so the troops had only their small arms. The evacuation of civilians from Rangoon had begun on 19 February, and on 27 February the Governor and the military commanders decided to withdraw troops from Rangoon and destroy whatever would be useful to the enemy. This was the day after Curtin's final refusal. Wavell countermanded the withdrawal the same day, adding to the confusion. Wavell wasn't actually there to make a judgement, however, while the Governor was. The Japanese onslaught continued and by 8 March the last of the British demolition parties were leaving and the city was in chaos.

As the official British history records, 'Looting, treachery, arson and desertion were then rife through this great port and city.'[37] Had the Australians landed, it would have been without their artillery or transport. Without heavy weapons, without air or naval support, the Australian soldiers would have gone ashore under air attack to a city the British were abandoning. They would have faced a well-equipped enemy, skilled in jungle fighting, supported by a powerful air force, which had already sent British and Indian troops reeling back towards India.

The final British judgement was unambiguous. 'Even if the Australian Government had agreed to the diversion of the 7th Australian Division,' the official British history recorded, 'only one brigade could have reached Rangoon before the port had to be abandoned.' Told that the 7th Division might be diverted to his support, the British Burma commander, General T J Hutton, responded that he 'was certain that Rangoon could not be held'. The British history concluded that Hutton was right and 'the late-minute arrival of an Australian division could have affected the situation no more than the arrival of the Eighteenth did in Singapore'.[38]

Burma was not lost because Curtin refused the 7th Division. It was lost, the official history concluded, because Britain was unprepared 'in practically every respect to meet an invasion of the country'.[39] In December 1941, 'few imagined that that Japanese advance into Malaya would not be halted'. In seven weeks a Japanese army equivalent to somewhat less than two British divisions had taken Rangoon because 'no adequate steps' had been taken by the British command to defend it 'against the relatively small forces the Japanese could maintain across the Siamese frontier'.[40] Wavell's biographer concluded of Curtin's refusal that it was 'a hard but surely a just decision'.[41] Five months later the 7th Division was to help defeat the Japanese land offensive in New Guinea.

The Japanese army did indeed close the land road to Burma, but it was soon replaced by 'the Hump' – an air route from India into China. On 3 May 1944, Churchill would tell Curtin and others at the Prime Ministers' Conference in London that the air supply route was going so well that six times as many stores and war materials were flying the Hump 'as could have been taken over the Burma Road had it been kept open'.[42]

Even a decade later, the war won, Curtin long dead and he himself witnessing the extraordinary changes which had followed, Churchill was still fuming over Curtin's refusal to allow the AIF to be sent to Rangoon. But somehow his chapter on the matter in the fourth volume of his account of *The Second World War* did not address any of the key issues involved.

Burma was not lost because of Curtin's refusal of the 7th, though Menzies would make this claim. Nor was Australia saved from invasion by Japan by Curtin's decision, another persistent myth. Only one brigade could have been landed before the British retreat from Rangoon began in earnest. Had it been committed, the brigade might well have been lost, though the main British and Indian forces successfully retreated west to India. The rest of the 7th Division and all of the 6th probably could not have been landed even if Curtin had agreed. He would soon agree to the elements of the 6th Division remaining for some months in Ceylon, and the 9th Division was not returned until 1943. The returning AIF did not save Australia from Japanese invasion, not least because at the most perilous time most of the AIF was not there. Though the 6th and 7th divisions later performed well against the Japanese, the enemy did not invade Australia and at that point did not plan to.

But Curtin did not know this in February and March 1942. All he knew then was that the Japanese had overwhelming air superiority in Malaya and Burma, that they were pushing back the British and Indian forces in Burma as they had in Malaya, that Wavell had wanted the 6th Division as well as all of the 7th Division for Burma, and that the Japanese were advancing in New Guinea and bombing Australia. He made the right decision.

CHAPTER 26

THE THREAT OF JAPANESE INVASION

(1)

The relentless Japanese advance south continued. The Japanese landed on Timor on 19 February, 1942, four days after the surrender of Singapore and a month after taking Rabaul. They bombed Darwin the same day, to discourage Allied intervention against their Timor landing. Eight days later an Allied naval force under Dutch command sailed to intercept the Japanese fleet invading the Netherlands East Indies. Outgunned and outmanoeuvred, most of the Allied fleet was sunk in what is remembered as the Battle of the Java Sea. The Japanese invaded Java on 28 February. In a five-day operation beginning on 8 March, the Japanese protected their new base at Rabaul by occupying Lae on the New Guinea mainland and Salamaua on New Guinea's north-eastern coast. The small Australian forces posted to protect what had been thought as the outer defence screen withdrew, or were captured or killed.

The Dutch authorities surrendered in Java on 9 March. Dutch radio transmissions from Java ceased with the announcer's final message: 'Goodbye. We are now shutting down. God save the Queen.' It was another low point for Curtin and for all Australians. European authority in the south-west Pacific and in Malaya and Burma had all but vanished. Wavell's command had been dissolved. There was as yet no new Allied commander in the south-west Pacific. The *Sydney Morning Herald* of Monday, 9 March announced the Japanese landing in northern New Guinea, and the probable collapse of resistance in Java. It reported a speech by Major-General Gordon Bennett, who had escaped from Singapore, warning that Australia was in danger not only of Japanese raids but of being 'attacked in force'. Curtin had said on the weekend that 'the British way of life and British institutions' were 'the very core on which to found a free world'.[1] In the Philippines the American and Filipino army garrison at Bataan would resist until 6 May, but was so little threat to the Japanese they were able to send troops elsewhere.

In the first five months of 1942, Japan would take more territory over a greater area than any invader in history. It would capture a quarter of a million prisoners of war, and sink over a hundred Allied ships. In the whole period Japan would not lose a major ship. The deeper shock to Britain, America and Australia was not that Japan had attacked in the Pacific. This had long been possible and, from the tightening of sanctions in July 1941, probable. The deeper shock was Japan's astounding success.

The assumption that the Japanese armed forces were inferior in equipment and training was shown to be false. In Singapore, more than 100 000 Empire troops surrendered to a Japanese army of 30 000.[2] In the Netherlands East Indies 96 000 Allied troops surrendered.[3] In the Philippines the Japanese were cleverer and quicker than the American and Filipino forces, but not more numerous. As Australia's minister to China Frederic Eggleston wrote to Evatt on 4 May 1942, British prestige had been 'completely shattered' by the loss of Malaya and Singapore.[4]

(2)

Where would Japan strike next? Their national interests diverging, Curtin and Churchill thought quite differently about the Japanese threat. In London, the chiefs of staff expected that after taking Singapore the Japanese would take Java, then press the invasion of Burma and capture Ceylon.[5] The Japanese would aim to threaten India, and perhaps try to link with German forces through Afghanistan and Iran. Churchill would tell the House of Commons that an attack on India was more likely than an attack on Australia.

Curtin did not agree. He would prove willing to meet Churchill's request for AIF units to defend Ceylon until relieved by British reinforcements, but was otherwise far more concerned by Japan's advance to the south than its threat to India. By the end of February, an invasion of Australia, the threat Curtin had warned of since the beginning of the Pacific War, a warning earlier intended more to underline the magnitude of the task Australia faced than to describe an impending likelihood, began to look like a serious possibility.

In late February the Australian chiefs of staff would tell Curtin and his War Cabinet colleagues Japan was 'now at liberty' to attack Australia.[6] The nation was in peril. Slit trenches were dug in Canberra gardens; tinned food was stored. Town signs and street signs disappeared to fool the invader. If the Japanese invaded, crops and towns would be burned, railways torn up, airfields cluttered with obstructions as the Australians retreated. The new economic plan stressed austerity, work, vigilance. The military high command pondered how much of the country could actually be defended and how much let go.

(3)

The Americans were coming. In an 18 February cable to Churchill, Roosevelt affirmed a new strategy for the Pacific War. It recognised the new reality. The United States would take responsibility for the 'right flank' of the Pacific, 'using Australia as the base'.[7] Roosevelt wanted Burma held – that was a British responsibility. Wavell's command would dissolve, and the United States would take responsibility for Australia and New Zealand.[8] From Casey and Churchill, Curtin understood the broad outlines. The United States was now Australia's Pacific partner, and its only partner. Britain had lost Hong Kong, Malaya and Singapore. In Burma, British forces were retreating towards the border with India. In mid-February 1942, six weeks after Curtin's declaration of a turn to the United States, Britain was exiting the Pacific War.

On 22 February, in the greatest secrecy, Roosevelt ordered MacArthur to leave the Philippines island stronghold of Corregidor for Australia, where he would take command of all Allied forces in the region. Marshall had already warned MacArthur on 4 February that he would be needed for a higher command.[9] Curtin was not informed. It was a perilous journey by torpedo boat and by air. MacArthur might well be captured or killed during his escape. There would be time enough to tell Curtin if MacArthur got through.

Two days earlier Curtin had cabled Blamey asking him to 'urgently return' to Australia. The AIF would be coming to Australia, and so should its commander.

With Malaya and Singapore gone and the Netherlands East Indies and the Philippines about to go, Australia was – as Sturdee had argued – the only possible base for a future counteroffensive. The Allied policy was still Germany first, but in the meantime Australia must be held. The United States' 41st Division was ordered to Australia in mid-February, reversing previous Washington policy. In early March Churchill asked Roosevelt for more United States troops for Australia to support his argument for the 9th Division and New Zealand troops to remain in the Middle East. Roosevelt replied that the 41st would arrive in April and another division (the 32nd) would sail in April or May.

At the same time as the American chiefs directed two divisions to Australia, they also ordered naval and marine forces to secure island bases linking Australia and Hawaii across the Pacific. These included Palmyra, Christmas Island, Canton Island, Bora Bora, Samoa and the Fiji Islands. Not long after, the Americans secured bases in New Caledonia, the Tonga islands and the New Hebrides. The Japanese had responded to the likelihood the Americans would use Australia as a base by occupying Lae and Salamaua on the north coast of New Guinea in early March, and Buka in the northern Solomons shortly after.[10]

There was now little that could be expected of Churchill. He cabled Curtin on 30 March to inform him that 'During the latter part of April and the beginning of May, one of our armoured divisions will be rounding the Cape. If, by that time, Australia is being heavily invaded, I should certainly divert them to your aid.'[11] By 'invaded' he meant not mere raids, but 'say, eight or ten Japanese divisions'. As Shedden commented, if 'the Japanese had command of the sea to land eight or ten divisions, Australia was beyond any aid that Britain could offer'.[12] Curtin sent cordial thanks.

They would soon be on the way, but until substantial American forces arrived Australia stood alone. There were no major American fighting units in Australia, and there would not be for some time. There were a few planes and a few ships. Otherwise the only forces Curtin could rely on were a small number of well-trained AIF units, and a larger number of Militia. It would be well into 1942 before Australia could deploy formidable forces.

(4)

With British and Dutch forces in the region overwhelmed and the timing and extent of American support still uncertain, Curtin and his government pondered how Australia should dispose its own meagre forces to meet the threat of an invasion.[13] The decisions taken then would still be argued about long after the threat had passed.

Two days after Singapore fell the Australian chiefs of staff and the home defence commander, Lieutenant-General Sir Iven Mackay[14], warned Curtin and War Cabinet that dispersion of forces to defend the whole country against invasion would lead to small detachments being defeated piecemeal. It was necessary to concentrate, on the principle that 'the area most vital to the continuance of the war effort of Australia was the Port Kembla-Sydney-Newcastle-Lithgow area'. More broadly, the 'Melbourne–Brisbane region' was thought 'vital'. Concentration meant that outlying areas such as Tasmania and Townsville would not be defended, except lightly. 'It might be necessary,' the submission continued, 'to submit to the occupation of certain areas of Australia by the enemy should local resistance be overcome.' This was not very different to the advice provided by the army to earlier governments, and reflected such plans as it had to meet an attack on the mainland. With his electorate including Townsville, Army Minister Frank Forde was not entirely happy with this plan. Coming as he did from Fremantle, Curtin could not have been happy either.

As chairman of the chiefs of staff, Sturdee advised that the defence of Newcastle to Kembla required denial of coastline from Melbourne to Brisbane, since possession of either would allow the enemy to attack the vital area with land-based aircraft. To meet the threat, Sturdee reported, Australia had available five divisions in various stages of readiness.

Ten days later, 27 February, the chiefs warned that 'Japan is now at liberty to attempt the invasion of Australia, should she so desire'. Japan might indeed desire to do so, if only to deny the use of Australia as a base for a future counteroffensive. Given its sea supremacy and the forces available at that point to resist Japan, the chiefs evidently decided Australia had no choice but to fight in Australia rather than in the islands to the north. 'The forces are everywhere inadequate to meet the scale of attack that may be brought against them,' they advised, recommending against further reinforcement of Port Moresby.

Given time, Australia would be stronger. The chiefs expected to have two AIF divisions in Australia plus one United States division by the end of April. With the home conscript army in training, Australia would have sufficient troops to meet an invader, on the scale of the attack on Malaya. But Australia did not have sea or air power to support its troops and 'until such time as adequate Naval and Air Forces are available, it is estimated that it would require a minimum of 25 divisions to defend Australia against the scale of attack that is possible'.

Australia could with time raise fifteen divisions, but '10 fully equipped divisions would have to be supplied by our allies'. Allies would also have to provide the chiefs' wish list of a fleet of capital ships based in Sydney, plus 'a capital ship force including carriers' based at Fremantle, plus an air force of seventy-three squadrons. Even as a wish list intended to support requests to Washington and London, the chiefs' requirements were ludicrously out of scale with America's capacity to provide, let alone Britain's.

At Mackay's plan for concentrating forces in the south-east, Curtin and his colleagues cavilled. Forde did not want Townsville abandoned, nor Curtin Fremantle. The Opposition members of the War Council would not accept it either. Meeting on 18 March, War Council affirmed Darwin and Port Moresby 'should be defended to the fullest possible extent'. The civilian leadership presumably understood that if Port Moresby was in Japanese hands, Darwin could not be used as a port and could be seized. The political leadership was reluctant to take decisions explicitly abandoning Australian home territory. The Brisbane Line controversy later that year and into 1943 underlined the political perils.

MacArthur would later write that when he arrived in Australia in early March the Australian army leadership was defeatist, and that it planned to defend only the eastern seaboard of Australia, from Brisbane to Melbourne. By implication Curtin had either approved the strategy, or was so far remiss as national leader that he did not know what the army planned.

The facts were otherwise. Curtin had earlier hoped Australia would be defended by the 'Malay Barrier'. He had urged deployment of Australian troops in Malaya to support that strategy. When Malaya, Singapore, the Netherlands East Indies and then Rabaul all fell by mid-March 1942, New Guinea was the last major land mass between Australia and the southward advance of Japan. New Guinea then became the northern defence line. But since the Japanese navy controlled the seas and skies between New Guinea and Australia, Curtin could not safely send major forces to New Guinea, or evacuate them if overwhelmed.

Cabling the military chiefs' assessment of March in a cable to Evatt in Washington on 4 April, Curtin emphasised three points. The first was that in the opinion of the Australian chiefs of staff (agreed by General Howard Brett, representing MacArthur) 'attacks in force against Australia and Australian lines of communication are likely at an early date'.

The second point neatly twinned the ideas of forward defence and the defence of Australia itself. The chiefs had pointed out that Australia's ability to remain in the war depended on holding the line from Brisbane to Melbourne. This was where the population centres and industrial strength necessary for the 'continuance of the war effort' were located. But in the opinion of the chiefs and of Curtin the 'key' to holding that line was Port Moresby – and a Japanese 'attack on Port Moresby could develop at any time'. Early attacks on Darwin and Fremantle were also likely.

The final point Curtin emphasised was that Allied forces in Australia were insufficient to repel a determined Japanese advance. He needed ships and planes – particularly planes. Curtin's message and the underlying assessment were drafted before MacArthur took up his command. The Brisbane Line could be defended as far forward as Port Moresby, though ships and planes were needed to support the strategy. Even in early April Curtin and his commanders could see the most pressing need was for ships and planes, not troops. Evatt promptly sent the assessment to Roosevelt.[15]

(5)

Curtin's rupture with Churchill was soon repaired. Both were professional politicians. Each needed the other. There would be no permanent difficulty between Curtin and Churchill. Nor did the dispute over return of the troops initiate a parting of the ways between Britain and Australia. Reassured by the promise to send the United States 41st Division to Australia, the progress of the 7th Division AIF home and no doubt recognising that Roosevelt if not Churchill should be conciliated, Curtin had compromised on the timing of the return of the 6th and 9th divisions. He would also have judged that while all or part of the 7th Division would highly likely have been lost in Burma, the roles proposed for the 6th and 9th divisions were unlikely to lead to their destruction. He would bargain.

Even as Churchill reluctantly cancelled the diversion of the 7th Division to Burma, he pondered another destination for it – one quite close by. With the Japanese moving west through Burma and extending their naval power into the Indian Ocean, Churchill was worried about the security of Ceylon. The same day Curtin had told Churchill it was 'quite impossible' to change the Australian Government's refusal of the 7th for Burma, Bruce cabled Curtin the British War Cabinet was discussing the defence of Ceylon.[16] On the following day, 24 February, Page asked Curtin to permit the 7th to reinforce Ceylon for a month or six weeks until relieved by a British division.

Annoyed by Page's conduct in the Burma controversy, Curtin cabled him on 25 February recalling seven earlier cablegrams instructing him to put Australia's case for immediate support against

Japan. Curtin complained that he had no impression that Australia's point of view was being strongly advocated by Page.

Curtin was cranky with Page and no doubt also with Churchill, but he understood Australia's strategic circumstances. Even more than troops, Australia needed fighters, bombers and naval support. Only the United States could supply those resources in the quantities needed, and to obtain them a measure of British goodwill was also necessary. The 7th Division would return as agreed, but on 2 March Curtin and War Cabinet decided to offer the British two brigade groups of the 6th Division, then embarking in Suez. Curtin promptly cabled news of the decision to Churchill and Roosevelt. Both the 6th and 9th were wanted back 'as soon as possible', but the 6th would help garrison Ceylon until relieved.

The relevance of the JOHCU–WINCH exchanges, meanwhile, was fading. London had cabled Curtin the British chiefs' assessment of Japan's probable moves following the Singapore surrender. It predicted Japanese forces would land in New Guinea and attempt to capture Port Moresby. An invasion of Australia was unlikely. The Australians had suggested Britain and the US combine fleets to challenge the Japanese navy. The UK chiefs reiterated there was no base on which the United States navy and the British navy could combine to meet the Japanese fleet. In any case, it would be highly risky. Australia would have to rely on the United States. Over time, Britain would build up its fleet in the Indian Ocean.[17]

The Australian chiefs of staff responded that the British assessment gave too much emphasis to stabilising the present position 'rather than taking the initiative from Japan'. They wanted the enemy attacked. They insisted a fleet of US and British ships should take on the Japanese navy. Churchill refused. The British Government, he replied on 20 March, would not undertake offensive naval operations in the manner suggested by the Australian chiefs.[18]

Curtin and his military advisers took some time to realise it, but by the time Churchill replied, British views were no longer important.

With Wavell back in India, British ships on the western side of the Indian Ocean, and British forces rapidly retreating westward in Burma, it was habit alone that sustained a military conversation between Australia and Britain. Except in supporting Australia's claims in Washington, Britain could now do nothing for Australia and its views about what might happen were no longer informed by any sources of its own.

For all that, the Imperial ties held. Curtin's decision to lend Churchill brigades of the 6th Division to defend Ceylon worked well. The two brigades helped garrison Ceylon during carrier-based raids Nagumo would shortly launch in the Indian Ocean. Churchill adhered to his undertaking that the commitment would be short. In mid-June the Australians would be told the 16th and 17th brigades were to be sent on as soon as possible after 25 June. Their arrival in Australia would be announced on 27 August – several months after any serious threat of invasion had passed, but in good time to help drive the Japanese from New Guinea.

Curtin would find getting the 9th Division back from the Middle East much more difficult. Planning a Middle East offensive, Churchill wanted to hold on to the remaining AIF division. In early March he told Curtin that the United States was prepared to offer another two divisions to the south-west Pacific – one to Australia and one to New Zealand – in addition to the 41st Division already on its way. Claiming these divisions were in exchange for the Australian and New Zealand divisions in the Middle East, Churchill asked Curtin to leave the 9th Division where it was. Consulted, the Australian chiefs recommended acceptance. Curtin did a little bargaining himself, telling Churchill on 20 March he still awaited British responses to his pleas for ships and planes.

In a cable from Washington nine days later Evatt would undermine Churchill's bargaining position by reporting that Roosevelt had said that the American divisions were despatched to Australia unconditionally 'and without any question of Australia's

right to decide the destination of the A.I.F.'. Even so, he reported on
2 April, Marshall wanted the 9th to remain in the Middle East. After
seeking advice from Blamey and MacArthur, by then commanding
allied forces in the south-west Pacific, Curtin would tell Churchill
on 14 April that the 9th could remain – if naval and air strength was
provided to Australia. Churchill blithely replied the following day,
thanking Curtin for 'the present'. He assured Curtin that 'you have
always been and will be perfectly free to decide the movement of all
your troops'. Curtin was almost certainly unaware Roosevelt and
Churchill had already agreed at the Arcadia conference at the end of
1941 to plan a joint invasion of north-west Africa, Operation Torch,
to crush Rommel's army between the jaws of an Allied advance from
the east and the west. In the plans, the 9th Division had already been
assigned its role.

(6)

Curtin and Churchill were not yet done. A spat over Richard Casey,
Australia's minister in Washington, revived discord. Rather than
minimise the dispute Curtin amplified it and made it public. Curtin
was becoming more confident in his handling of Churchill.

Menzies had found Casey's relentless self-promotion daunting,
affecting astonishment that during his visit to Washington in 1941
Casey could ask him for a new decoration, a Companion of Honour,
in the presence of Casey's wife, Mae. He also asked for a 'roving
commission' to cover the Middle East and Britain, as well as the
United States. Menzies thought Casey 'the bitterest disappointment
of my life'.[19] Casey's charm and energy had helped him form
sufficiently good contacts with the Roosevelt Administration to
keep Curtin informed during a time of momentous decisions in
Washington. Complaining of Evatt, Casey took the opportunity of
a December 1941 train journey with Churchill to ask him for a job.

Churchill obliged. Early in March, he offered Casey the post of British minister in Cairo.

Churchill asked Curtin's leave, but not until after offering Casey the job. Curtin was rightly annoyed. Though Casey was a political opponent, Curtin had kept him on. Casey was valuable to Australia in Washington at a time when Washington decisions were life and death for Australians, while a great many competent civilians with political experience could do the Cairo job Churchill offered Casey. Curtin mentioned Churchill's request to his colleagues at a Canberra meeting of War Cabinet on 16 March. They shared his annoyance. Casey concealed his initiation of the job change, affecting to be pressed by Churchill. If Casey wanted to go, Curtin decided, he could not be prevented – but it was against the wishes of the Australian Government. Churchill announced the new appointment in the House of Commons on 19 March. Curtin first heard the public announcement on the BBC news at 10 p.m. in Canberra.[20]

The disagreement over Casey becoming public, Curtin in late March published as a white paper the testy cables between himself and Churchill over the appointment. Curtin no doubt suspected that Churchill got Casey out of Washington exactly because he was so good at his job. Churchill would not have approved of Casey's ready access to Roosevelt and his senior Cabinet members.

By the end of March Curtin had had a lot of rows with Churchill, some of them public. Neither had given much ground. They had by then argued over relief of Tobruk, British support for the battle in Malaya and Singapore, the Melbourne *Herald* declaration, the destination of the returning 6th and 7th divisions, and now the job offer to Casey. Curtin had discovered that, if he insisted, Churchill would have to give way. Churchill had discovered that while Curtin appreciated Churchill's prestige, he would also take the risk of making a dispute with Churchill public. In all these disagreements, Curtin had the support of his Cabinet and of his official advisers.

Curtin was unusual in the directness of his disagreements with Churchill, but not in their frequency. Churchill thrived on opposition, and modified his decisions only reluctantly. Roosevelt often disagreed with Churchill. At the time Curtin was disputing the appointment of Casey, Roosevelt was annoyed with Churchill for sabotaging Stafford Cripps' mission to negotiate self-government in India. Mackenzie King, Canada's long-serving prime minister, also often disagreed with Churchill. He was not reluctant to refuse Churchill what he wanted, and his disagreements were often similar to those Curtin had with the British leader. Churchill treated Mackenzie King with greater respect than he gave Curtin. Mackenzie King was closer to Churchill in his political beliefs, and he had been Canada's leader for much longer than either Churchill or Curtin had led their nations. Mackenzie King also had a personal relationship with Roosevelt. It was not wise to slight Mackenzie King.

Though they had little contact, Mackenzie King was often close to Curtin's point of view. Canada was the richest of the self-governing dominions. From the fall of France to Hitler's invasion of the Soviet Union, it had been Britain's biggest fighting ally. Mackenzie King still resented the loss of Canadian battalions in Hong Kong, deployed there on the British assurance that Japan was unlikely to go to war against Britain. He now put more time into cultivating Roosevelt, less to cultivating Churchill. He closely followed the spat over Casey.

He discussed the Casey affair and Churchill's relations with the dominions in a 21 March conversation with British High Commissioner to Canada, Malcolm MacDonald, the son of former Labour leader and later coalition prime minister Ramsay MacDonald. Churchill had 'not been sympathetic' on India, MacDonald told Mackenzie King, and there was a risk that 'Britain may even lose India'. In the Far East, the situation was 'very dangerous'. Both were concerned about Churchill's treatment of the dominions. 'Since the Churchill-Roosevelt conversations,' Mackenzie King said, 'Canada has sort of been ignored by Britain.' MacDonald said that the British

Government did 'not recognise the importance of the Dominions' and that Churchill was 'apt to forget their significance altogether'. Mackenzie King thought the controversy between Curtin and Churchill over Casey was 'most unfortunate' and that Casey had injured his own position. He told MacDonald he thought 'Churchill really wanted to be free of Australian representation in Britain altogether. He did not like Bruce, nor Earle Page, and was rather disgusted [by] and a bit suspicious of Menzies. By getting Casey he would have him nominally in the Cabinet but not on his back – far enough from London to be out of the way.' They also agreed that Canada had done the right thing in opposing an Imperial war cabinet. New Zealand Prime Minister Peter Fraser had 'lost ground in New Zealand for having been in London so long. Menzies had certainly lost out altogether.' They agreed that 'the Australians were drawing nearer to America and away from Britain'.[21]

Mackenzie King was well ahead of Curtin in understanding that Britain's ejection from Hong Kong, Malaya, Singapore and Burma and its deteriorating position in India would change the Pacific after the war was over. If Britain lost India, Mackenzie King recorded of the conversation, then after the war 'the Pacific Ocean might become, as regards the English speaking people, what the Atlantic had been in the past, namely that America, Canada, Australia and New Zealand would all seek a complete control of the Pacific and feel their common interest' while Britain will 'be left more and more to do the best she could with her relations with Europe, but that America instead of Britain would become the controlling power in world affairs'. Two years later Mackenzie King and Curtin would clash on their understanding of Britain's place in the post-war world, and its relationship to their own nations.

Churchill was not anxious to prolong the dispute over Casey, not because Curtin was indignant but because Roosevelt thought it had got out of hand. 'I am greatly disturbed at the publicity coming out of the Casey business,' Roosevelt cabled Churchill on 22 March 1942.

The story, he thought, 'plays right into the hands of our enemies'. Instead of the 'rather strained relations between Australia and Britain at this time', Roosevelt wanted to see 'good will'. Churchill replied the following day, laying the blame on Australia. 'The matter is complicated by Australian Party politics which proceed with much bitterness and jealousy regardless of the national danger.' Evatt and Beasley, he said, 'have made their way in local politics by showing hostility to Great Britain'.[22] Nevertheless, he let the dispute die. Even a few months earlier Roosevelt would have hesitated to admonish Churchill over his relations with a dominion. Things were changing, as Mackenzie King could see.

Perhaps mordantly, Churchill advised Curtin to appoint Menzies to the now-vacant post of Australian minister in Washington. Eager to be where the big decisions were made, Menzies pressed hard for it, as he had earlier pressed for a seat in the House of Commons. He was 'avid to secure the appointment and made no pretences to the contrary', the US Minister in Canberra, Nelson Johnson, reported to the Secretary of State. 'In his conversations with us he stated he would very much like to go.'[23] If willing to obey instructions from Canberra, Menzies might well have been an outstandingly successful appointment. Curtin probably thought seriously of offering it to him, but after his experience with Page he would have queried Menzies' willingness to take orders. Evatt anyway would have been strongly opposed. He had told the Americans that Casey was a 'swine'[24], and he loathed Menzies even more than he did Casey. Jack Beasley was also said to be interested in the job, complicating Curtin's choices. He took a safer option, appointing High Court judge Owen Dixon.

Menzies was not at all pleased to be refused the Washington job. Lunching around that time with the American Consul in Melbourne, Erle R Dickover, Menzies told him he would be much happier about the war if Australia was not being run by the present government. 'They are scum – positive scum.' Curtin 'is a reasonably safe, solid man, but he cannot control the other members of his cabinet, some of whom like Ward and Evatt are positively menaces to Australia'. Menzies thought Curtin was 'at heart an isolationist and wants to defend Australia only, letting the rest of the Empire go'. He darkly predicted that if the Japanese invaded part of Australia, the Labor Government would 'revolt against Britain, declare their independence, and try to make Australia a second United States'. In his report to Washington, Dickover concluded that Menzies' aversion to the government 'made it difficult to see how he could attempt to represent the Australian government in Washington, as suggested by Mr Churchill'.[25]

CHAPTER 27

AUSTRALIA IMPERILLED

(1)

In the south-west Pacific, only Australian forces remained to oppose the Japanese. Unescorted, across seas patrolled by Japanese planes, ships and submarines, the 7th Division was coming home. With 4600 troops on board the USS *Mount Vernon*, a fast cargo ship converted into a troop transport, was sailing south through the Indian Ocean to Fremantle. All he could see from the deck, recalled Private Bob Hope, was the white wake of the ship and empty sea from horizon to horizon.[1] Curtin's friend Frank Green, Clerk of the House of Representatives, encountered Curtin one night in the grounds of the Lodge, pacing, smoking, sleepless. 'How can I sleep, with our men in the Indian Ocean among enemy submarines?' he asked Green. Curtin was 'haggard with worry', recalled one of the Lodge housemaids. 'He told me he would never forgive himself if anything happened to the troopships carrying the boys home. He did not relax until a telegram arrived informing him that the ships had arrived safely in Australian waters.'[2] Alan Reid recalled travelling on a train with Curtin around this time, and finding him 'staring out of the window' with 'beads of sweat' trickling down his forehead. 'He'd had a nightmare of the ships bringing the troops back from the Middle East being torpedoed and lives being lost, and when he was talking to me his hands were trembling and the sweat was pouring out of him.'[3] Curtin was a worrier. He did not have Churchill's or Roosevelt's temperament, their exuberance and bounce.

In this vast region of the south-west Pacific there was no longer a supreme Allied commander, and little to command. Curtin had earlier asked Roosevelt for an American commander for the theatre. In Washington General Marshall pressed Roosevelt for withdrawal of MacArthur from Corregidor and his appointment as supreme commander of Allied forces in the south-west Pacific. On 22 February, Roosevelt had directed MacArthur to proceed to Australia. Leaving Corregidor by torpedo boat on 11 March, MacArthur arrived by plane at Batchelor Field south of Darwin six days later. MacArthur's arrival confirmed, General Brett telephoned Curtin, apologising for his inability to speak to him earlier. In an astute and gracious letter from Roosevelt which Brett read to Curtin, the President asked Curtin to nominate MacArthur 'as the Supreme Commander of all Allied Forces in the SWP', and submit that nomination to London and Washington. Whatever qualms Curtin may have had about placing Australian forces under American command – and there were very few – were dispelled by conferring on Curtin MacArthur's nomination. War Cabinet considered the request that day, and Curtin's nomination was duly sent to London and Washington. It was announced publicly on 18 March. It would be, Curtin told War Cabinet on 17 March, 'a great inspiration'.[4] Though no doubt as surprised as everyone else, Don Rodgers evidently worked hard on the MacArthur story. The *Daily Mirror* of Wednesday, 18 March revealed to its readers that MacArthur's appointment was the result of a request by Curtin. It was a 'diplomatic triumph'.

After three months of defeats that had brought Japanese forces well within striking distance of Australia, morale soared with the announcement of the sudden arrival of the fabled American general.

(2)

In the hundred days from Pearl Harbor to his Wednesday, 18 March statement announcing the arrival of MacArthur in Australia, Australia's circumstances and Curtin's had changed so completely it would take the country and Curtin another few years to fully see it. Australia was still feeling its way. The war with Japan was the main change, but it had released other changes, long immanent. By taking Malaya and Singapore and then the Netherlands East Indies, Japan had separated British interests in Burma and India from Australia's interests in the south-west Pacific. Japanese forces now stood between the two. Wavell's command in Java was the last flicker of British Empire power in Australia's region until 1945.

Australia's turn to the United States, long endorsed by Churchill and affirmed by Curtin at the end of 1941, was now more completely realised than Curtin, Roosevelt and Churchill might have expected. There was no British fleet in the region able to protect Australia, nor was there likely to be. The nearest British forces were now in Burma, fighting rearguard actions against the advancing Japanese army, harassed by Japanese bombers, and retreating as quickly as they could to India. There was then no time or purpose to reflect on it, but sooner or later it would become apparent that if Australia could not expect Britain to come to its defence, then the unique relationship between Australia and Britain would vanish. It would more closely resemble the relationship between Canada and Britain, or South Africa and Britain – a cultural and ethnic relationship, one that remembered the past. The dependency, the insistent anxiety to influence the British Government to Australian purposes, would wither away. Curtin initiated the change. He would later try to reverse it. He himself could not fully comprehend it, his rival Menzies still less so.

Its Pacific fleet battleships damaged at Pearl Harbor, its aircraft carriers now carefully husbanded by Admiral King, its remaining troops in the Philippines now under siege at Bataan, the US was at bay. Japan had thrown up a defence perimeter in the south-west Pacific from west of Singapore to east of Rabaul. In three months it had thrown up an interlocking sequence of air and naval bases and troop concentrations in the area far more formidable and in shorter order than expected in pre-war United States planning, or in Japanese planning. It was now the major power in Australia's region. But while Britain was fully stretched, the United States had barely begun to mobilise for war. Its vast manpower, its great economic weight, were yet to be deployed against Germany, Italy and Japan. Still scattered in the western Pacific, still cautious, American power was slowly building.

Curtin had proposed a United States commander for the region. Now he eagerly accepted MacArthur, with none of the resentment and injured national pride that had been evident in his dealings with Churchill. The Americans had the weight and purpose to win. With a commander on Australian soil, Curtin would have the opportunity to deal directly with him. He might not, as with Wavell, have to beg for information. From the middle of March 1942, the decades of controversy over the Empire Defence Strategy, the readiness of a British Fleet to defend Australia, the readiness of Churchill to if necessary abandon the Mediterranean to come to Australia's assistance, ceased to matter. Australia's security was now an American responsibility. 'Australia must be held', Roosevelt cabled Churchill on 18 March 1942, the same day MacArthur's proposed appointment as Supreme Commander was publicly announced, and 'we are willing to undertake that'.[5]

Though he would continue to do so, Churchill could no longer authentically claim to broker Australia's interests with America in the Pacific War. The only source of real authority in the war was in Washington, to which MacArthur reported. Evatt was pressing hard for agreement on Australian representation on a Pacific war council.

For Curtin, those hundred days since Pearl Harbor had been a searching test of his intellect, character and stamina, and above all of his political skills in feeling his way to an outcome suiting Australia. Mostly, the events and forces were beyond his control or even influence. Japan's military successes dictated the Allied responses. Australia had had no serious part in command decisions. It had pleaded for reinforcements, but of the Australian commanders only Bennett had so far had an important job in the Pacific War, and only in command of the 8th Division. Blamey was only just returning to Australia, to be offered command over all Australian forces.

But if the events were not of his own making, Curtin had readily seized what he could use to fashion a new story, an interpretation, plausibly connecting Australian interests to the implacable trend of regional circumstances. By the second day of the Pacific War he had adopted Shedden's description of the conflict with Japan as a 'new war', implicitly challenging the subordination of the Pacific War to the war in Europe and building a case for reinforcement from Britain and the United States. Less than three weeks later he had formulated a crude but effective declaration that Australia looked to the United States rather than Britain for its military security.

After Singapore fell he had paced Washington in declaring Australia the only possible base to resist Japan in the south-west Pacific. He did not initiate but readily agreed to return of the Australian troops from the Middle East. Faced with the most urgent request from the two leaders of the western alliance, Churchill and Roosevelt, advised by Page, Bruce and Casey to accede to their wishes, pressed by Menzies and Fadden at home, Curtin steadfastly refused to permit the diversion of troops to Burma. As military historian David Horner rightly argues, it was the most important military decision ever made by an Australian cabinet – though it is also true that Curtin made the decision and communicated it to London before War Cabinet convened to consider it. Curtin then offered to lend two brigades of the 6th Division to defend Ceylon, and agreed to the 9th Division remaining longer in the Middle East. These agreements could be and were seen as helpful in sealing the United States commitment to send two army divisions to Australia.

Curtin did not have Menzies' stamina. He missed two important sequences in the period because of exhaustion or illness. Visiting Perth, he missed a series of War Cabinet meetings as Japan for the first time occupied Australian territories. Had he been present for discussion of Page's cable on Singapore evacuation, or more closely edited the unhappy mix of Shedden's remembered adhesion to Empire Defence and the Singapore strategy with Evatt's ungoverned pertinacity in Australia's reply, had he been on the east coast when the Japanese took Rabaul and himself made the national broadcast, Australia's response might well have been more purposive. Had he been present a month later for the War Council meeting on the requested deployment of the 7th Division to Burma, the discussion might have been less hot-tempered. In neither case would the decision have been different.

In those hundred days the world had changed irreversibly, though in ways Churchill and also Curtin were slow to recognise. The Pacific War shattered not only British prestige, but all Pacific political arrangements. At the White House, Roosevelt was already pondering political arrangements in the Pacific after Japan's defeat. There was no place for Britain. He would tell Mackenzie King on 15 April that the Chinese were confident China and the United States could 'settle the affairs' of the Far East and that Britain 'could not be expected to do much in that area'. He thought there was 'no possession in the East to which self-government could not be given immediately' except New Guinea and Borneo.[6] The way Roosevelt was thinking, Hong Kong would be returned to China, while Indo-China, Malaya, Singapore, Burma and India would all be self-governing (and soon independent) and so would the Netherlands East Indies. China would be a great power. The Philippines was on the way to complete independence, Roosevelt reasoned, why not the rest of colonial Asia? This would be a world Curtin, even Evatt, had yet to imagine and which Curtin would probably not find congenial. The Cairo conference the following year would confirm Roosevelt's insistence on a new order in the Pacific.

It was already evident that in thinking about the post-war Pacific, Roosevelt did not think of Australia as an important player, still less as a 'principal'. China and the United States would settle things in the 'Far East'. He did not mention Australia – or Canada either. Curtin had turned to America. At the White House, the change was recognised but not fully reciprocated. Like Churchill, Roosevelt thought of Australia as a subordinate member of the British Empire.

(3)

The Americans were coming. So were the Japanese. Curtin's invasion alarm was not fanciful, or not entirely. In secret sections of the September 1940 Tripartite Pact, Japan had included the South Seas and specifically Australia and New Zealand in its Co-Prosperity Sphere. Historian Chris Thorne claimed this meant they were 'marked out for eventual conquest'.[7] If not conquest, Australia was already within Japan's sphere of influence, if it could hold on to its victories thus far.

At much the same time Curtin warned of a possible invasion of Australia, Japan's military leaders in Tokyo were arguing about its costs, risks and advantages. An invasion of Australia had certainly not been part of Japan's immediate pre-war planning. Harassment perhaps, but 'invasion, never, no', Prime Minister Tōjō told his interrogators before his execution for war crimes. In its December 1941 planning the Japanese army expected to reduce its southern armies strength from 400 000 men to 200 000 when its tasks had been achieved. Those tasks were the invasion of the Philippines, Malaya and Singapore, the Netherlands East Indies and Rabaul. All had been won by mid-March.[8]

The Japanese navy disagreed with the army. Until the United States was forced to a peace agreement, the offensive must continue.

By late February, their southern thrust completely successful and in far less time than planned, Japanese Imperial General Headquarters in Tokyo pondered new moves. The navy planning staff correctly judged the Americans were building a base in Australia to attack Japan's new defence perimeter. Australia should be promptly invaded, the naval planning staff argued, before the forces there were sufficiently strong to obstruct it. The planning staff calculated it would take three divisions to capture and hold strong points in north-east and north-west Australia.

The army agreed with the navy's judgement of American intentions, but assessed it would need ten divisions for a successful invasion.[9] Australia already had 300 000 troops for home defence, the army calculated, and would soon have more. Invasion would require two million tons of shipping to launch and support the attack, a requirement impossible to meet. The army was still fighting in China, and it had troops watching the Soviet Union. It had yet to complete the conquest of the Philippines and Burma. Japan did not have the reinforcements, the supplies, or the ships to invade Australia, or at least not soon. Commanding the combined fleet, Admiral Yamamoto was also reluctant to use his warships to support an invasion.[10]

In a compromise, the navy and army agreed to threaten the supply line between the United States and Australia by occupying Port Moresby and the southern Solomons. They would then take Fiji, New Caledonia and Samoa, forming a screen of bases across the Allied supply line and isolating Australia. If necessary, Australia could be invaded later.[11] A Tokyo army–navy liaison conference as early as 10 January 1942 had agreed on a blockade to 'force Australia to be freed from the shackles of Britain and the United States'.[12] After a three-hour debate between the army and the navy at a 4 March conference in Tokyo, an invasion of Australia was postponed indefinitely, a decision shortly ratified by the Emperor. The invasion of New Caledonia, Fiji and Samoa was scheduled for July.

Australian and American planners readily understood the Japanese intention. The United States had sought bases across the Pacific precisely to forestall the Japanese. Australian planners expected an early attack on Port Moresby, particularly after Japanese forces moved into Rabaul, Lae and Salamaua. It was the key to the defence of north Australia, and was now within fighter distance of Japanese air bases. On 5 March, Australian Major-General Sydney Rowell predicted the new Japanese moves.[13] In the middle of the following month Imperial Headquarters in Tokyo agreed on the schedule. Port Moresby would be captured on 7 May, Midway on 7 June, New Caledonia on 8 July, Fiji on 18 July and Samoa on 21 July.[14] Imperial Headquarters was now accustomed to the achievement of its objectives, on time or earlier, and with the forces allocated. Australia need not be invaded, but within four months it would be under Japan's control.

ENDNOTES

1 Robert Menzies, *Afternoon Light* (Melbourne: Cassell, 1967), p. 126.
2 Labor spelling adopted 1912.
3 Wilkinson report of Gowrie meeting, 4 October 1942, the papers of
   Gerald Wilkinson, GBR/0014/WILK. Churchill College Archives Centre.
4 John Edwards, 'Australians at War: An American Perspective', *The National
   Times*, 30 January – 4 February 1978, John Curtin Prime Ministerial Library
   (hereafter JCPML): JCPML00709/1.
5 A W Martin & Patsy Hardy (eds), *Dark and Hurrying Days: Menzies' 1941
   Diary* (National Library of Australia, 1993), p. 81.
6 *Sydney Morning Herald*, 8 October 1941.
7 David Horner, *Defence Supremo: Sir Frederick Shedden and the making of
   Australian defence policy* (Sydney: Allen and Unwin, 2000), p. 123.
8 Paul Hasluck, *The Government and the People 1939–1941* (Australian War
   Memorial, 1952), p. 543.
9 John Keegan, *The Second World War* (London: Penguin, 1989), pp. 207–8.

Chapter 1

1 Parliament resumed 13 March 1935.
2 Elsie Curtin, 'The Curtin Story', part 5 of series in *Woman* magazine, 1951,
   JCPML00577/5.
3 William Manchester, *American Caesar: Douglas MacArthur 1880–1964*
   (New York: Dell, 1979), p. 304.
4 Harold Cox, interviewed by Mel Pratt, 1973, sound recording held by National
   Library of Australia (hereafter NLA).
5 Lloyd Ross, 'The Story of John Curtin', *Sun-Herald* 1958 JCPML 00788/1
6 COMCAR, *Going the Extra Mile: A History of the Commonwealth Car Service
   1910–2010* (Australian Department of Finance, 2010), p. 39.

7　*Courier Mail* interview with Ray Tracey, 13 January 1950, p. 2.

8　Geoffrey Higham, *Marble Bar to Mandurah: a history of passenger rail services in Western Australia* (Bassendean, WA: Rail Heritage WA, 2007), p. 101. The Adelaide *News*, 22 January 1942, reports Curtin meeting him at Adelaide railway station, and ran a photograph. This contradicts Gray's account (see Gray interview, JCPML00346/2) that Gray met Curtin on 22 January when, he says, the Trans was stopped by a flood one day out of Kalgoorlie. The *Daily Mirror* and *Newcastle Sun* (23 January) also report it as a meeting at Adelaide station, though these are probably copies of the *News* story.

9　*Australian Women's Weekly*, 1 April 1944.

10　*Sydney Morning Herald*, 9 July 1945.

11　Richard Buckeridge, letter in *Post*, 18 February 1981.

12　Heather Campbell, *Diary of a Labour Man 1917–1945* (hereafter *DOLM*, available at <john.curtin.edu.au/diary>) notes Curtin was in Perth giving the WA case to the Commonwealth Grants Commission from 26 February to 4 March 1935.

13　Lloyd Ross, *John Curtin* (Melbourne University Press, 1996), p. 68.

14　House of Representatives Hansard, 17 July 1930, p. 4242.

15　Higham, op. cit., p. 137.

16　This section relies on the timetable and brochure of the Trans-Australian Railway held in the Mitchell Library, State Library of NSW. It is undated, but shows a steam train. It does not mention air conditioning, so presumably preceded its introduction in 1936.

17　Letter from John Curtin to Elsie Curtin, April 1937, JCPML00402/33.

Chapter 2

1　By 1935 the number had fallen a little, but the Great Depression was still very evident in the 1933 census. In that survey nearly half a million men, one-fifth of the workforce, were wholly unemployed. Two-thirds had been unemployed for over a year.

2　John Connor, *Anzac and Empire: George Foster Pearce and the Foundations of Australian Defence* (Cambridge University Press, 2011).

3　This section draws on Ian McLean, *Why Australia Prospered* (Princeton University Press, 2012).

4　Letter from Victorian Police Commissioner to Lloyd Ross, 11 September 1945, Lloyd Ross papers, NLA MS3939, box 41 11/1.

5　Wray Vamplew (ed.), *Australians: Historical Statistics* (Broadway, NSW: Fairfax, Syme and Weldon Associates, 1987), chapter 8.

6 Chay Fisher & Christopher Kent, *Two Depressions, One Banking Collapse*, discussion paper, Reserve Bank of Australia, June 1999.

7 Ross, op. cit., p. 7.

8 Ross, op. cit., p. 10.

9 Ross, op. cit., p. 11.

10 Curtin would see Tillett again in Geneva in 1924 – see letter to Elsie from Geneva, when an ILO delegate (Black, 2001, pp. 130/131.).

11 Bertha Walker, *Solidarity Forever!* (Melbourne: National Press, 1972). See also Ian Turner, *Industrial Labour and Politics* (Canberra: Australian National University, 1965).

12 David Black, *Friendship is a sheltering tree: John Curtin's letters, 1907–1945* (Perth: JCPML, 2001), p. 2.

13 Edwards (2005), op. cit., p. 85.

14 House of Representatives Hansard, 6 December 1929.

15 Black (2001), op. cit., p. 33.

16 ibid.

17 ibid., pp. 2–5.

18 ibid., p. 109 – letter to Elsie, 6 February 1917.

19 John Curtin, *The late Frank Hyett*, Railways Union Gazette, 7 June 1919, JCPML 00653/28/5.

20 Black (2001), op. cit., p. 170.

21 ibid., p. 57.

22 ibid., p. 79.

23 V J Stout, letter to Elsie Macleod, 14 July 1959, Lloyd Ross papers, NLA box 41 11/2.

24 P Love, 'Stout, James Victor (1885–1964)', *Australian Dictionary of Biography*, vol. 16, (Melbourne University Press, 2002).

25 Black (2001), op. cit., p. 93.

26 Black, ibid., p. 94.

27 The first referendum was defeated 28 October 1916.

28 *The Argus*, 15 November 1916.

29 ibid., p. 8, gives the time as 4.30 p.m.; John Connor (op. cit.) gives it as 2 p.m. *The Argus* has Hughes and 24 supporters meeting; the *Sydney Morning Herald* on the same date has Hughes and 23 others walking out of caucus.

30 *The Argus* states 24, the *Sydney Morning Herald* 23. Ross (op. cit., p. 59) states 24 plus Hughes.

31 Black (2001), op. cit., p. 105, letter to Elsie, 27 December 1916.

32 *DOLM*, 31 January 1917.

33   Ross, op. cit., p. 58.
34   Black (2001), op. cit., p. 110, referencing David Day, *John Curtin: a life* (Sydney: Harper Collins, 1999).
35   ibid., p. 110, referencing *The Socialist* 9 and 16 February 1917.
36   ibid., p. 111, letter to Elsie, 8 February 1917.
37   *DOLM*, c. 16 February 1917.
38   JCPML00480/1.

Chapter 3

1   David Black, 'Biography of Elsie Curtin', JCPML.
2   ibid.
3   Alan Chester, *John Curtin* (Sydney: Angus and Robertson, 1943).
4   Arthur Calwell, *Be Just and Fear Not* (Hawthorn, Vic: Rigby, 1972).
5   *DOLM*, 8 February 1917.
6   Chester, op. cit.
7   Calwell (1972), p. 49.
8   *Westralian Worker*, 30 March and 27 April 1917, quoted in David Day, *John Curtin: a life* (Sydney: Harper Collins, 1999), p. 243.
9   Richard Hall and Clem Lloyd (eds), *Backroom Briefings: John Curtin's War* (National Library of Australia, 1997), p. 168.
10   JCPML 00577.
11   *DOLM*, 12 January 1929.
12   Boris Schedvin, *Australia and the great depression: a study of economic development and policy in the 1920s and 1930s* (Sydney University Press, 1970), p. 108.

Chapter 4

1   House of Representatives Hansard, 6 December 1929
2   Geoffrey Bolton, *A Fine Country to Starve In* (University of Western Australia Press, 1972), p. 188.
3   Patrick Weller (ed.), *Caucus Minutes 1901–1949*, vol. 2 (Melbourne University Press, 1975), p. 349.
4   Calwell, op. cit., p. 47.
5   Schedvin, op. cit.
6   It was all crisply explained by the Commonwealth Statistician E T McPhee and his colleagues in contemporary editions of *The Official Year Book of the Commonwealth of Australia*. In 1928/29, Australians enjoyed a national income of £100 per head. They owed annual interest on overseas debt of £5 per head.

In 1928/29 exports were worth £22 per head, and imports £23 per head. Private business investment inflows helped, but to meet the remaining gap between export income and payments for imports plus net interest payments Australians needed to borrow an additional £5 per head, on average, each year. Without borrowing at least that £5 per head, Australians governments could not pay the interest required on their existing debt, let alone repay debt as it became due.

7 Hasluck (1952), op. cit., p. 38.

8 Schedvin, op. cit., p. 6.

9 House of Representatives Hansard, 10 June 1930, p. 2591.

10 ibid., p. 2599.

11 Theodore resigned 5 July 1930. Niemeyer arrived later that month.

12 Black (2001), op. cit., p. 145.

13 Black (2001), op. cit., letter to Elsie, 2 August 1930, p. 148.

14 ibid.

15 Weller, op. cit., vol. 2, p. 389.

16 ibid., p. 390.

17 ibid., pp. 396–97.

18 Black (2001), op. cit., p. 152.

19 House of Representatives Hansard, debate on the Financial Statement, 12 November 1930, p. 207.

20 ibid., p. 214.

21 ibid., p. 208.

22 Weller, op. cit., vol. 2, p. 431.

23 On 24 June 1931 the ALP Federal Executive permitted a free vote on the Premiers' Plan.

24 John Edwards, *Curtin's Gift* (Sydney: Allen & Unwin, 2005), p. 113.

25 Elsie Macleod, letter to Tom Fitzgerald, JCPML00653/280.

26 Don Rodgers, interviewed by Mel Pratt, 1971, sound recording held by NLA, TRC 121/14. Also held as JCPML00497/1.

27 *DOLM*, 4 December 1931.

28 B Beddie, 'Pearce, Sir George Foster (1870–1952)', *Australian Dictionary of Biography*, vol. 11 (Melbourne University Press, 1988).

29 G C Bolton, 'Green, Albert Ernest (1869–1940)', *Australian Dictionary of Biography*, vol. 9 (Melbourne University Press, 1983).

Chapter 5

1 Black (2001), op. cit., p. 155.

2 ibid., p. 157.

3   ibid., p. 159.

4   ibid., p. 162.

5   Bolton, op. cit., p. 250.

6   *DOLM*, c. 25 April 1932.

7   *West Australian*, 10 August 1934, p. 24.

8   Elsie Macleod, letter to Tom Fitzgerald, JCPML00705/1/84.

9   ibid., JCPML00705/1/62.

10 ibid., JCPML00399/018.

11 *Sunday Times*, 1943 Curtin family scrapbook of press clippings, JCPML00297/3

12 Elsie Curtin, 'The Curtin Story', *Woman* magazine, 1951, JCPML00577.

13 Elsie Macleod, letter, JCPML00399/018.

14 Dianne Sholl, 'John Curtin at the "Westralian Worker" 1917–1928: an examination of the development of Curtin's political philosophy as reflected in his editorials', BA (Hons) thesis, University of Western Australia, 1975.

15 Elsie Macleod, letter, JCPML00399/018.

16 Don Rodgers, JCPML00497/1.

17 'Perhaps losing the Fremantle seat in 1931 was one of the most important factors in John Curtin's life because one of the first things he did was to forgo alcohol, and from that time onwards until his death he remained a teetotaller.' Elsie Macleod, JCPML00399/018.

18 Elsie Curtin, op. cit.

19 Conversation with Barbara Davidson, daughter of John Curtin and Elsie's son John, and Beverley Lane, daughter of John Curtin and Elsie's daughter Elsie, 2014.

20 Elsie Curtin, op. cit.

21 Conversation with granddaughters, 2014, op. cit.

22 Bolton, op. cit., p. 5.

23 *DOLM*, 4 June 1933.

24 Black (2001), op. cit., p. 162.

25 Bolton, op. cit., p. 256.

26 *Sunday Times*, 18 February 1934.

27 Bolton, op. cit., p. 52.

28 ibid., p. 258.

Chapter 6

1   Weller, op. cit., vol. 3, p. 84.

2   John Robertson, *J. H. Scullin* (University of Western Australia Press, 1974), p. 448.

3 Ross, op. cit., p. 148. In his account of the vote, Curtin biographer Lloyd Ross says the difference between victory and defeat for Curtin was provided by Drakeford, who not only voted for Curtin himself but also cast the proxy vote of Maurice Blackburn, which Blackburn had given to him, for Curtin. Since Blackburn and Curtin had long been at odds, Ross's suggestion is that Curtin's victory was entirely accidental. But Blackburn was on the left, and would not have approved of Forde.

4 *Sydney Morning Herald*, 5 October 1935.

Chapter 7

1 Menzies papers, box 579, folio 8, Draft of Diary 1935.

2 A W Martin, 'Menzies, Sir Robert Gordon (Bob) (1894–1978)', *Australian Dictionary of Biography*, vol. 15 (Melbourne University Press, 2000).

3 Anne Henderson, *Joseph Lyons: the people's prime minister* (Sydney: NewSouth, 2011), p. 366. Joe and Enid Lyons joined the ship in Fremantle.

4 Born in 1895, a year after Menzies, George VI shared with the Australian Prime Minister support for Chamberlain, and hostility to Churchill.

5 The draft is handwritten.

6 Hansard Legislative Assembly Parliament at Victoria, 9 October 1930, p. 3049.

7 *The Argus*, 4 May 1931, p. 6.

8 ibid.

9 Address-in-Reply, House of Representatives, 2 November 1934.

Chapter 8

1 Ian McLean, Working Paper 2002–10, University of Adelaide, School of Economics, p. 29 (international comparisons from Angus Maddison).

2 Australian Bureau of Statistics, cat. no. 3412.0 (Canberra: ABS).

3 Net immigration was surprisingly small in the years between the end of the gold rushes and the mid-1930s. In the seventy or so years from 1861 to 1934 the net number of new immigrants was only a little over 1 300 000. They accounted for less than a quarter of the total increase in population.

4 Census, 1933. In 2008 it would be one in four. The proportion of Australian-born in the mid-1930s was higher than it would be after World War II.

5 From 1871 to 1933 the proportion of the population under age fifteen had continuously declined, from 42 per cent in 1871 to 28 per cent in 1933.

6 In the 1933 census there were 6 629 839 Australian residents, exclusive of full-blood Aboriginal Australians. Between 1921 and 1931 the population had

increased by an average annual rate of 1.83 per cent, a rate of growth similar to the previous three decades. In 1934 the population was estimated to be 6 705 677, again excluding full-blood Aboriginal Australians. Including the 58 848 full-blood Aboriginal Australians the number of people on 31 December 1934 was estimated to be 6 760 525.

7   Australia's land area was 2 974 581 square miles, giving it a population density of 2.27 people to the square mile. By contrast, the density in North America was 20 people to the square mile, and 118 in Europe.

8   That is, they did not live in a capital city, or an adjacent urban area, or an incorporated town or city outside of the capital cities.

9   Nearly four out of ten Australians lived in New South Wales and a little over a quarter in Victoria. Together those two states accounted for two-thirds of the population. Queensland accounted for one-seventh of the population, Western Australia for a bit more than one-twentieth and Tasmania for one-thirtieth.

10 *Official Year Book of the Commonwealth of Australia, 1935*, Australian Bureau of Statistics.

11 ibid., p. 547.

12 John Marshall, *The Life of George Washington* (Philadelphia, 1804), vol. 3, pp. 537–43.

13 However, the states were still bound by the repugnancy doctrine laid down in the Colonial Laws Validity Act 1865.

14 The *Australian Women's Weekly*, 1 April 1944.

15 J H Rose et al. (eds), *The Cambridge History of the British Empire*, Volume VII Part I, *Australia* (Cambridge University Press, 1933), p. 622.

16 Henry P Frei, *Japan's Southward Advance and Australia* (University of Hawaii Press, 1991), p. 65.

17 This section relies on Frei, ibid.

18 Neville Meaney, *Fears & phobias: E.L. Piesse and the problem of Japan, 1909–39* (NLA, 1996), p. 4.

19 ibid., p. 5.

20 Frei, op. cit., p. 67.

21 Beddie, op. cit.

22 Lionel Wigmore, *The Japanese Thrust* (Australian War Memorial, 1996), chapter 1.

23 Neville Meaney, 'Piesse, Edmund Leolin (1880–1947)', *Australian Dictionary of Biography*, vol. 11 (Melbourne University Press, 1988).

24 Gavin Long, *To Benghazi* (Australian War Memorial, 1952), p. 25.

25 Wigmore, op. cit., chapter 1.

26 Peter Dennis, *Heading For Disaster? Australia and the Singapore Strategy*, paper presented at the Fall of Singapore 60th Anniversary Conference, National University of Singapore, 16–17 February 2002.

27 Long, op. cit., p. 8.

28 ibid., pp. 8–9.

29 Dennis, op. cit.

30 Wigmore, op. cit., chapter 1.

31 Piesse used the nom de plume of 'Albatross' in his *Japan and the Defence of Australia* (Melbourne: Robertson & Mullens, 1935).

32 Frei, op. cit., pp. 1–2.

33 Hasluck, op. cit., p. 24.

34 Ian Hamill, *The strategic illusion: the Singapore strategy and the defence of Australia and New Zealand, 1919–1942* (Singapore University Press, 1981), pp. 151–152.

35 Long, op. cit. Labor made it clear before the 1923 Imperial Conference that it was opposed to participation in construction of Singapore naval base. Charlton's view then (1923) was consistent with Labor's view as late as 1939.

36 Long, op. cit., p. 16.

Chapter 9

1 Adele Hodges nee Mildenhall, interview by Isla Macphail, JCPML00211/1.

2 *DOLM*, 13 December 1935.

3 House of Representatives Hansard, 14 November 1934, p. 282.

4 House of Representatives Hansard, 21 November 1934, pp. 464–465.

5 *The Argus*, 3 October 1935.

6 *Sydney Morning Herald*, 5 October 1935.

7 John Curtin, 'The Census and the Social Service State' in G V Portus (ed.), *What the Census Reveals* (Adelaide: F W Preece & Sons, 1937). Proceedings of a conference of the Australian Institute of Political Science, Adelaide, 26–28 June 1936.

8 Menzies was pressing for the introduction of an insurance scheme to cover unemployment and sickness. Employees would pay an insurance premium to cover specified payments if they lost their job or fell ill. Curtin may have been in part responding to this model of social welfare.

9 Weller, op. cit., vol. 3, p. 155.

10 ibid., footnote 22, p. 155.

11 House of Representatives Hansard, 9 October 1935, pp. 565–69.

12 Blackburn voted with the government on sanctions. The Victorian Executive expelled him from the party in December 1935. At issue was his association with the Victorian Council against War and Fascism, a group widely believed to be a Communist front. He was not readmitted to the Party until Easter 1937, after he left the Council.

13 House of Representatives Hansard, 18 October 1935, pp. 864–65.

14 Paul Burns, *The Brisbane Line Controversy* (Sydney: Allen and Unwin, 1998), p. 15.

15 *DOLM*, 24 November 1936.

16 Kim E Beazley, *Father of the House* (North Fremantle, WA: Fremantle Press, 2009), p. 59.

17 ibid.

18 Elsie Macleod, JCPML00399/018.

19 Horace Cleaver, interview, JCPML00207/1.

20 *DOLM*, 2 October 1936.

Chapter 10

1 *DOLM*, 1918. In a 17 April 1918 speech in Melbourne, Curtin reminded the audience that the primary struggle of the labour movement was not against the war but against capitalism, and that his opposition to conscription and the war, 'was not due to pacifism'.

2 Elsie Macleod, letter to Lloyd Ross, 15 December 1976, Lloyd Ross papers, NLA Box 41 11/2.

3 Shedden papers, National Archives of Australia (hereafter NAA), A5954, 886/3. Brand's role is mentioned in the correspondence over Wynter's demotion.

4 House of Representatives Hansard, 5 November 1936, p. 1547.

5 Long, op. cit., p. 19. Long suggests Curtin read out Wynter's lecture. It certainly drew heavily on Wynter but as Long acknowledges Labor had held similar views for many years.

6 ibid.

7 Correspondence and minutes in Shedden papers, NAA: A5954, 886/3.

8 House of Representatives Hansard, 24 August 1937, p. 22.

9 Long, op. cit., p. 22.

10 In preparing for the 1937 conference, little attention was given to the most obvious fact about the Pacific and Japan: the might of the United States. The Australian papers prepared for the conference portrayed the United States as 'isolationist' and therefore not a reliable ally in the Pacific. Curtin had no better grasp of America's importance.

11 Black (2001), op. cit., p. 187.

12 ibid., p. 189.

13 8 September 1937, Weller, op. cit., vol. 3, p. 165.

14 House adjourned 15 September 1937, election announced 14 September 1937, House dissolved 21 September 1937.

15 *Sydney Morning Herald*, 28 July 1937.

16 *DOLM*, January–February 1919.

17 Alan Reid, Oral History, NLA. interviewed by Mel Pratt, 1972–73, sound recording held by NLA, TRC 121/40.

18 *Sydney Morning Herald*, 21 September 1937, reporting Curtin policy speech in Fremantle on 20 September 1937.

19 *Sydney Morning Herald*, 24 September 1937.

20 Rodgers, op. cit.

21 House of Representatives Hansard, 1 December 1937, p. 52.

22 House of Representatives Hansard, 27 April 1938.

23 Stirling to Hodgson in Australian Government Department of Foreign Affairs and Trade (hereafter DFAT), *Documents in Australian Foreign Policy 1937–1949*, vol. I, 1937–38 (Canberra: APGS), DFAT document 236, p. 398.

24 Menzies to Lyons, 6 August 1938, in ibid., document 237, p. 400.

25 Menzies sent the same letter to Halifax dated 6 August 1938; Menzies papers NLA folder 4963, box 579, folder 4.

26 ibid.

27 House of Representatives Hansard, 28 September 1938, p. 326.

28 House of Representatives Hansard, 5 October 1938, p. 428.

29 ibid., p. 430.

30 *DOLM*, 3 October 1938.

31 *DOLM*, 24 September 1938.

32 Cox, op. cit.

33 Elsie Macleod, JCPML00399/018.

34 DFAT, op. cit., vol II, 1939, document 10, p. 20.

Chapter 11

1 DFAT, op. cit., vol. II, document 37, p. 60.

2 ibid., vol. II, document 41, p. 68.

3 DFAT, op. cit., vol. II, document 46, p. 75.

4 Some of this argument is influenced by S C M Paine, *The Wars for Asia 1911–1949* (Cambridge University Press, 2012). I am grateful to Mark Johnson for sending me this important and interesting book.

5   ibid.

6   *Sydney Morning Herald*, 5 May 1939.

7   *The Argus*, 15 May 1939.

8   On 24 October of the previous year.

9   Reid, op. cit.

10 Cecil Edwards, *Bruce of Melbourne: man of two worlds* (London: Heinemann, 1965).

11 *The Argus*, 19 April 1939.

12 Cox, op. cit.

Chapter 12

1   Francine McKenzie & Margaret MacMillan (eds), *Parties Long Estranged: Canada and Australia in the Twentieth Century* (University of British Columbia Press, 2003).

2   *The Argus*, 25 August 1939; quoted in DFAT, op. cit., vol. II, p. 187 fn 6.

3   DFAT, op. cit., vol. II, document 153, p. 188.

4   The London cable from Inskip was sent 3.49 a.m., 26 August; Bruce's at 10.15 p.m. was received in Australia at 8.45 a.m., 27 August.

5   At 12.30 a.m., London, 27 August.

6   DFAT, op. cit., vol. II, p. 208.

7   I M Cumpston, *Lord Bruce of Melbourne* (Melbourne: Longman Cheshire, 1989), p. 170.

8   ibid. p. 171.

9   DFAT, op. cit., vol. II, document 176, p. 214.

Chapter 13

1   Eric Tonkin papers, box C40, NLA.

2   Menzies to Bruce, 11 September 1939, papers of Prime Minister Bruce, NAA M103 1938/39. An extract from the letter is in DFAT, op. cit., vol. II, 1939, p. 256.

3   ibid.

4   ibid.

5   DFAT, op. cit., vol. II, p. 258.

6   Menzies to Casey, DFAT, op. cit., document 361, 14 November 1939.

7   Menzies was bargaining. In the War Cabinet agenda of 14 November 1939, vol. II, document 362, p. 406, Street records that the Defence Committee (13 November) had approved despatch of 6th Division to Palestine in response to cables of 5 and 6 November from Casey (DFAT, op. cit., vol. II, documents 327

and 332, pp. 372–375). It also approved raising a second division to be despatched overseas. This was discussed by War Cabinet on 15 and 16 November (DFAT, ibid. note 4, p. 407), which decided to defer it to full Cabinet.

8   DFAT, vol. II, op. cit., document 371, p. 415.

9   DFAT, ibid. Casey to Menzies, ibid., 17 November 1939, document 372, p. 417.

10   DFAT, ibid. Casey to Menzies, ibid.

11   Casey to Menzies, ibid., 23 November 1939, document 384, p. 428.

12   Whiskard to Dominions office reporting conversation with Menzies 'yesterday afternoon', DFAT, op. cit., 24 November 1939, document 386, p. 431.

13   DFAT, op. cit., document 391.

14   ibid., vol. II, document 398, p. 441.

15   Menzies correspondence with Bruce, 22 February 1940; Menzies papers, NLA box 582, Folio 29. Document sent from Melbourne.

16   *The Argus*, 5 May 1939.

17   'State Labor conference carries hands off Russia resolution', *Sydney Morning Herald*, 25 March 1940.

18   *Sydney Morning Herald*, 27 March 1940, suggests the Lang forces permitted the outcome to embarrass their opponents. In the *Sydney Morning Herald* on 30 March 1940, federal secretary McNamara, who was present, said the Langites either voted for it or abstained.

19   *Sydney Morning Herald* on 27 March 1940 reports Curtin repudiated the motion.

20   *Sydney Morning Herald*, 20 April 1940, presumably reporting the event the day before when Curtin 'made a bitter attack on Mr Lang MLA and Mr Beasley MHR for their part in forming a new Labor Party' – a day or two after German attack on Norway as a preliminary to attacking the West.

21   *Sydney Morning Herald*, 20 April 1940, reports Beasley's reply to Curtin.

22   Address-in-reply at 3.57 p.m. on 18 April 1940, Hansard CPD.

23   Caldecote to Whiskard, sent 11 p.m. 26 May 1940 (most secret and personal decode yourself), DFAT, vol III, document 282, p. 334.

24   Hansard HR 28 May 1940, 3.30 p.m.

25   Bruce follows up at 2.15 a.m. 27 May. DFAT, op. cit., document 283, p. 334.

26   These paragraphs based on John Lukacs, *Five Days in London May 1940* (Yale University Press, 1999). He recounts that this Monday, 27 May 1940 was 'a very bad day' because Churchill knew of Belgian King Leopold's decision to surrender and to stay in Belgium, making a separate peace with Germany.

27   ibid., p. 142.

28   According to Lukacs, Caldecote also knew that Bruce was a defeatist but said that Menzies was not inclined to agree with Bruce.

Chapter 14

1   Eustace Keogh, *South West Pacific 1941–45* (Melbourne: Grayflower, 1965), p. 50.

2   ibid., p. 43.

3   Murdoch immediately blundered in the new job, tactlessly issuing without adequate consultation a regulation requiring correction of newspaper reports in extreme cases.

4   Verbatim record from Menzies papers, NLA 574, McNicholl deposit, 4936/40/12: War Cabinet, Melbourne, 12 June 1940.

5   War Cabinet minutes, Melbourne, 18 June 1940. DFAT, op. cit., vol. III, document 399, p. 451.

6   See earlier

7   War Cabinet minutes, Melbourne, 18 June 1940, op. cit.

8   ibid.

9   David Horner, *High Command* (Sydney: Allen and Unwin, 1982), p. 36, and War Cabinet minutes ibid.

10 Horner (1982), op. cit., p. 36.

11 David Horner, 'Australia and Allied Strategy in the Pacific 1941–1946', doctoral dissertation, vol. 1, Australian National University, 1980, p. 37.

12 Peter Lowe, 'Retreat from Power: British Attitudes towards Japan 1923–41' in Barry Hunt (ed.), *War and Diplomacy across the Pacific 1919–1952* (Waterloo, Ontario: Wilfred Laurier University Press, 1988).

13 S C M Paine, *The Wars for Asia 1911–1949* (Cambridge University Press, 2012), p. 185.

14 ibid., p. 145.

15 ibid., p. 176.

16 David Kaiser, *No End Save Victory* (New York: Basic Books, 2014), pp. 109–10.

17 ibid., p. 62.

18 ibid., p. 45.

19 ibid., p. 117.

20 ibid. Kaiser makes but does not reference a plausible claim that Churchill's decision to reopen the Burma Road to China in October 1940 was 'in the hope that confrontation in the Far East might bring the United States into the war'.

21 ibid., p. 120.

22 Burns, op. cit., p. 28.

23 *The Argus*, 20 June 1940.

24 Hansard House of Representatives, 3 p.m. 20 June 1940, vol. 164, p. 15.

25 Caldecote to Whiskard, sent 6.47 p.m. 19 June, received 9 a.m. 20 June 1940. DFAT, vol. III, document 406, p. 458.

26 Commonwealth government re 29 June, sent 8 p.m. 28 June 1940. DFAT, vol. III, document 459, p. 517.

27 ibid.

28 Australian Government to Caldecote, 3 July 1940. DFAT, vol. III, document 5, p. 8.

29 Caldecote to Australian Government. His cable (document 7, p. 10) was sent from London 8 p.m. 3 July 1940, i.e. after Australian cable sent. DFAT, vol. III, document 5, p. 8.

30 McEwen's statement, 6 August 1940.

31   8 August 1940.

32 Caldecote to Whiskard, for Menzies, sent 6.48 p.m. 11 August 1940 – a 'foreword' to a forthcoming appreciation. DFAT, vol. IV, document 64, p. 84.

33 ibid.

34 Caldecote to Whiskard, strategic appreciation, sent from London 7.45 p.m. 11 August 1940. DFAT, vol. IV, document 66, p. 89.

35 ibid., p. 92 is a good summary of those interests, in which defence of Australia and New Zealand was first.

36 Douglas Gillison, *Royal Australian Air Force 1939–1942* (AWM, 1962), p. 141.

37 ibid., 22 March 1941, p. 141.

Chapter 15

1   Black (2001), op. cit., p. 195.

2   Edwards (2005), op. cit., p. 15.

3   *Smith's Weekly*, 11 October 1941.

4   *DOLM*, 30 September 1940.

5   *Sydney Morning Herald*, 26 April 1943.

6   John Murphy, *Evatt: a life* (Sydney: NewSouth, 2016), p. 79.

7   Brennan to Evatt (letter signed F but clearly Brennan, with attached clips) Evatt Collection, F4 460, Flinders University.

8   Sgt Massey Stanley to Evatt, 24 October 1940, Evatt Collection, F4 463, Flinders University.

9   Murphy, op. cit., p. 158.

10 ibid., p. 161.

11 ibid., p. 163.

12 Speeches and Statements 1940–1947, Evatt Collection, op. cit.

13 Evatt had been ill.

14 Murphy, op. cit., p. 31.

15 ibid., p. 174. Murphy says Evatt nominated. Weller, op. cit., vol. 3, p. 237 records that Forde was elected deputy leader unopposed.

16 ibid., p. 75 quotes Crisp to this effect.

17 Weller, op. cit., vol. 3, p. 237.

18 Murphy, op. cit., p. 176.

19 ibid., p. 177.

20 ibid., p. 178.

21 Photo in Chester, op. cit.

22 Hasluck, op. cit., p. 296, and Advisory War Council (hereafter AWC) minutes.

23 Weller, op. cit., vol. 3, p. 255.

24 Hasluck, op. cit., p. 277.

25 ibid., p. 280.

26 Perth *Mirror* and *DOLM*, 4 January 1941.

27 Wigmore, op. cit., footnote 2, p. 5.

28 These paras based on Wigmore, op. cit.

29 Hasluck, op. cit., p. 297.

30 Australia planned to produce 180 Beauforts in 1941, of which 90 were committed to Britain. Wigmore, op. cit., p. 19.

31 ibid., p. 18.

32 Hasluck, op. cit., p. 296.

33 According to Hasluck, the non-government members of War Council were 'more emphatic' about naval reinforcement but do not seem to have raised issue of AIF.

34 Australian Government to Cranborne, 1 December 1940. The Government was 'gravely concerned at the most serious position revealed in regard to the defence of Malaya and Singapore' by the Singapore defence conference. This cable offered the brigade group plus the three squadrons already made available. The Australian Government wanted the brigade group there to be temporary before going to the Middle East and preferred Britain use Indian troops. DFAT, op. cit., document 212, p. 285 (see also document 84).

35 Churchill to Menzies, sent 2.50 a.m. 23 December 1940. DFAT, op. cit., document 236, p. 314.

36 Hasluck (op. cit.) says that Churchill thanked Australia for the offer of troops and said they would be replaced by May 1941 by a division from India – which did not happen. p. 299.

37 Wigmore, op. cit., p. 51.

38 Hamill, op. cit.

39 AWC minutes for 8 January 1941, NAA A2683.

40 AWC minutes for 9 January 1941, op. cit.

41 Thomas Buell, 'American Strategy in the Pacific: its Philosophy and Practice', in Hunt, op. cit., p. 145.

42 Keogh, op. cit., p. 71.

43 Lowe, op. cit., p. 287.

Chapter 16

1 Wigmore, op. cit., p. 57.

2 AWC minutes, op. cit., for 5 February 1941. Text says 'demobilize', presumably meaning 'immobilise' since it is in the context of using naval power to stop trade.

3 Curtin would raise the issue of returning troops from the Middle East to Australia at the 8 May 1941 War Council, and again on 5 and 12 June. See also Hasluck, op. cit., p. 356 et seq. and Curtin speech to the House, Hasluck, ibid., p. 360.

4 *Sydney Morning Herald*, 12 February 1941, p. 11.

5 Paul Haggie, *Britannia at bay: the defence of the British Empire against Japan, 1931–1941* (Oxford University Press, 1981), p. 190.

6 G Hermon Gill, *Royal Australian Navy 1939–1942* (Australian War Memorial, 1957), p. 425.

7 AWC minutes, 13 February 1941.

8 Robert Dallek, *Franklin D. Roosevelt and American Foreign Policy, 1932–1945* (Oxford University Press, 1979), p. 264.

9 Burns, op. cit., p. 34.

10 AWC minutes, 13 February 1941.

11 AWC minutes, 28 February 1941.

12 Black (2001), op. cit., p. 201.

13 Keogh, op. cit., p. 67.

14 Hamill, op. cit.

15 Anne Henderson, *Menzies at War* (Sydney: NewSouth, 2014), p. 109, date given p. 115.

16 *Sydney Morning Herald*, 5 March 1941.

17 Wigmore, op. cit., p. 76.

18 Hansard HR 13 March 1941.

19 Filed with Menzies' resignation diary held in the NLA Menzies papers (series 31, World War II, box 496a), there is also the text of a speech given to a secret meeting of the Parliament – the date is not clear, though 'June 1941' is pencilled on the first page. This may be the time it was received by Menzies' staff. I take it on internal evidence to be a copy of Fadden's speech.

20 Reid, op. cit.

21 This was reported by the Australian legation in a telegram dated 12 February received on 13 February, and in a Dominions Office telegram dated 14 February received 15 February.

22 Hasluck, op. cit., p. 353.

23 Horner (2000), op. cit., p. 124.

24 Kaiser, op. cit., p. 175 and footnote.

25 ibid., pp. 179–81.

26 DFAT, op. cit., vol. IV, pp. 373–74.

27 Burns, op. cit., p. 35.

28 According to Horner there is no evidence that Shedden told Curtin when he became prime minister, though he 'probably' did. Evatt later declared the existence of a Beat Hitler First agreement a surprise to him. Horner (2000), op. cit.

29 Sent from London 9.20 p.m. 25 February 1941. DFAT, op. cit., document 321, p. 452.

30 Noel Annan, 'How Wrong Was Churchill?', *New York Review of Books*, 8 April 1993.

31 Burrell to Colvin, sent by Casey 24 February 1941. DFAT, op. cit., document 318, p. 440. See also document 317, p. 438.

32 London, 8 March 1941, ibid., document 343, p. 482.

33 London, 11 April 1941, ibid., document 400, p. 568.

34 Annan, op. cit.

35 The six were House members J A Beasley, J S Rosevear, D Mulcahy, T Sheehan, and Senators S K Armour and J Armstrong.

36 Graham Freudenberg, 'Victory to defeat: Caucus 1941–49', in Stuart Macintyre & John Faulkner (eds), *True Believers* (Sydney: Allen and Unwin, 2001), chapter 6, note 2, p. 301.

37 *The Argus*, 11 March 1941.

38 Allan Dalziel, *Evatt the Enigma* (Melbourne: Lansdowne Press, 1967), p. 19. Dalziel writes that on the day of Menzies' return Evatt called Dalziel into the Sydney office to type up a letter to Menzies in which Evatt said he 'was ready to serve in any capacity'. It was delivered to the Prime Minister's suite in the Commonwealth Bank building. Other writers are less sure it was actually delivered.

Chapter 17

1 DFAT, op. cit., vol. IV, p. xi.

2 Henderson (2014), op. cit., p. 145.

3 David Horner, 1980, op. cit., vol. 1, p. 53 referencing Brooke-Popham papers V/l, Liddell Hart Centre for Military Archives, King's College, London.

4 ibid., p. 54.

5   Winston Churchill, *The Second World War, Vol. III: The Grand Alliance* (Sydney: Cassell, 1950a), p. 363.

6   Diaries of William Lyon Mackenzie King, held by Library and Archives Canada, available at http://www.bac-lac.gc.ca/eng/discover/politics-government/prime-ministers/william-lyon-mackenzie-king/Pages/diaries-william-lyon-mackenzie-king.aspx.

7   DFAT, vol. V, p. 3.

8   Murphy, op. cit., p. 180.

9   Menzies reviews his visit abroad; War Council minute, 28 May 1941. DFAT, op. cit., document 472, p. 681.

10 Wigmore, op. cit., p. 82.

11 AWC minutes, op. cit., 12 June 1941. The minutes refer to a 26 March War Cabinet meeting at which Curtin emphasised no new commitments.

12 4 June 1941. DFAT, op. cit., document 484, p. 699.

13 War Council minute, Melbourne 5 June 1941. DFAT, op. cit., document 488, pp. 704–5.

14 Hasluck, op. cit., p. 360.

15 Churchill, op. cit., pp. 522–23.

16 Weller, op. cit., vol. 3, pp. 80–81.

17 Kaiser, op. cit., p. 250.

18 ibid.

19 ibid., p. 253.

20 Christopher Thorne, *Allies of a Kind* (Oxford University Press, 1978), p. 52.

21 Kaiser, op. cit., p. 255. Quite how Roosevelt was able to commit Britain to war without committing the United States was not apparent. The British were saying otherwise.

22 Hamill, op. cit.

23 Horner (1982), op. cit., p. 130.

24 DFAT, op. cit., vol. V, document 2, p. 5.

25 Though DFAT 12 July 1941 (op. cit., document 6, p. 11), Cranborne to Menzies, offering intelligence that Japan plans to attack Vladivostok.

26 AWC minute, op. cit., 16 July 1941.

Chapter 18

1   In the event, the move into Thailand was postponed until the major attack in December.

2   Keogh, op. cit., p. 28 is quite clear that the United States took the lead and Britain announced it would follow; for example, in reopening the Burma Road.

3 ibid., p. 69.

4 AWC minute, op. cit., 6 August 1941.

5 See War Council minutes 6 August 1941. Hasluck (op. cit., p. 529) argues that Menzies was the hard one and Curtin thought Japan issues were negotiable. But he also writes that in the preceding twelve months Curtin had argued that war with Japan was inevitable.

6 Following the readmission of the Beasley Six to the Labor caucus in March 1941 the membership of the Council had been rearranged. Evatt was added to the Labor delegates to the War Council. Fadden agreed that Beasley could retain his place, and another government member was added.

7 Hamilton, op. cit., p. 29.

8 ibid., p. 15.

9 ibid., p. 17.

10 Menzies to Churchill, 8 August 1941. DFAT, op. cit., vol. V, document 35, p. 63.

11 *The Age*, 12 August 1941. Reporters were told of Menzies' dissatisfaction with the representation of the dominions in London, and his view that only he could impress on the British the dangers of Japan's advance.

12 *Sydney Morning Herald*, 7 August 1941.

13 DFAT, op. cit., vol. V, document 39 is the text dispatched to London after Full Cabinet

14 ibid.

15 ibid., and footnote 4.

16 *The Age*, 15 August 1941.

17 This section based on Menzies' resignation notes, Menzies papers, NLA, op. cit.

18 ibid.

19 Weller, op. cit., vol. 3, p. 289.

20 *Sydney Morning Herald*, 29 August 1941.

21 Edward J Ward papers, NLA MS 2396.

22 Calwell, op. cit., p. 50.

23 Menzies' resignation notes dated 1 September 1941; Menzies papers, NLA.

24 *Sydney Morning Herald*, 22 September 1941.

25 29 August 1941. Brenda Niall & John Thompson (eds), *The Oxford Book of Australian Letters* (Melbourne: Oxford University Press, 1998).

26 Gowrie's letter was sent to Cranborne on 10 October 1941. Anne Henderson (2014), op. cit., pp. xxi, 5, 8.

27 Cranborne to Fadden, 31 August 1941, giving a personal and secret message from Churchill. DFAT, op. cit., vol. V, document 54, p. 92.

28 This is a quote from cable 608.

29 Black (2001), op. cit., p. 205.

30 Weller, op. cit., vol. 3, p. 292.

31 *Daily Telegraph*, 4 October 1941.

32 Wigmore, op. cit., p. 92.

33 Keegan, op. cit., pp. 207–8

34 Hasluck, op. cit., p. 541.

35 Wigmore, op. cit., p. 92.

36 Page to Fadden from Singapore, 1 October 1941. DFAT, op. cit., vol. V, document 75, p. 125.

37 S W Roskill, *The War at Sea 1939–1945 Vol. II: The Period of Balance*, History of the Second World War, United Kingdom Military series (London: HMSO, 1956), p. 21.

Chapter 19

1 *Courier Mail*, 4 October 1941.

2 Hazel Craig, transcript of interview for the Curtin Library, JCPML00209/1.

3 Norman Makin, 1974 original interview by NLA. Accessible as JCPML00518/1.

4 ibid.

5 Reid, op. cit.

6 *Digest of Decisions and Announcements*, 6 October 1941.

7 Interview of Hazel Craig, JCPML00209/1.

8 *Digest of Decisions and Announcements*, 4 October 1941.

9 War Council minutes, 30 October 1941, Weekly Report.

10 F G Shedden manuscript, 'Victory under the Curtin and Chifley Governments', chapter 16, p. 6. NAA, Shedden Collection A5954, Boxes 1320-1327.

11 Minutes of the Full Cabinet, Volume 1B (Curtin Ministry), 7 October – 15 December 1941, NAA A2703.

12 Calwell, op. cit., p. 53.

13 *The Argus*, 9 October 1941.

14 Rodgers interview, op. cit., p. 18.

15 ibid.

16 ibid.

17 Craig, op. cit.

18 Graeme Powell, 'Strahan, Frank (1886–1976)', *Australian Dictionary of Biography*, vol. 16 (Melbourne University Press, 2002).

Chapter 20

1   Shedden, op. cit., chapter 17, p. 2.
2   NAA, primeministers.naa.gov.au/primeministers/chifley/before-office.aspx
3   S J Butlin & C B Schedvin, *Volume IV: War Economy 1939–42* (Australian War Memorial, 1977), chapter 15. I assume 1940/41 figures are broadly true of October 1941. The big changes occurred after Pearl Harbor. Vamplew op. cit. p. 257, 258 provides numbers for the Commonwealth.
4   ibid., p. 390.
5   ibid., p. 384.
6   NAA Cabinet minutes for the Curtin government, A2700
7   *Sydney Morning Herald*, 3 November 1941, p. 6.
8   *Digest of Decisions and Announcements*, 29 October 1941.
9   Butlin & Schedvin, op. cit., pp. 394–95.
10 David Horner, 'Shedden, Sir Frederick Geoffrey (1893–1971)', *Australian Dictionary of Biography*, vol. 16 (Melbourne University Press, 2002).
11 ibid.
12 Eri Hotta, *Japan 1941: countdown to infamy* (New York: Knopf, 2013), p. 210.
13 DFAT, op. cit., vol V, p. 131.
14 DFAT, ibid., p. 201.
15 DFAT, ibid., p. 192.
16 War Cabinet Notebooks, 15 October 1941, op. cit., NAA A5954.
17 Only Spender and McEwen were present from the Opposition.
18 DFAT, op. cit., vol. V, p. 140.
19 Cox, op. cit.
20 W S Kirby et al., *The War Against Japan Vol. I: The Loss of Singapore*, (London: HMSO, 1957), p. 15.
21 DFAT, op. cit., footnote 4, p. 128.
22 ibid., p. 149, 16 October 1941.
23 ibid., p. 154.
24 ibid., p. 159.
25 Haggie, op. cit., p. 192.
26 Thorne, op. cit., p. 4.
27 DFAT, op. cit., p. 133.
28 ibid., p. 232, 28 November 1941, p. 131.
29 ibid., p. 237.
30 ibid., p. 266.
31 ibid., p. 184.
32 HR Hansard, 5 November 1941.

33 Shedden papers, NAA A5954 Box 1320.

34 David Horner, *Blamey: the Commander-in-Chief* (Sydney: Allen & Unwin, 1998), p. 256.

35 NAA War Cabinet notebooks, A5954 vol. 4.

36 Horner (1980), op. cit., vol. 1, p. 44.

37 ibid., p. 48.

38 Horner (1982), op. cit., p. 134.

39 ibid., p. 135.

40 Horner (1980), op. cit., p. 47.

41 DFAT, op. cit., p. 197.

42 Received in Canberra on Sunday, 30 November 1941.

43 DFAT, op. cit., p. 242.

44 R J C Butow, 'How Roosevelt Attacked Japan at Pearl Harbor: Myth Masquerading as History.' *Prologue Magazine.* 28, 3 (Fall 1996).

45 DFAT volume V, op. cit. p. 243.

46 Kaiser, op. cit. p. 324.

47 Horner (1982), op. cit. p. 134.

48 Cox, op. cit.

49 DFAT, op. cit., p. 241.

50 1 December 1941, War Cabinet Notebooks, op. cit.

51 DFAT, op. cit., p. 256.

52 Hotta, op. cit., p. 278.

53 DFAT, op. cit., p. 265.

54 War Cabinet Notebooks, op. cit.

55 James Griffin, *John Wren: A Life Reconsidered* (Melbourne: Scribe, 2007), p. 287.

56 *Daily Telegraph*, 29 December 1941.

57 Katherine Sheedy, *Home Away from Home: Celebrating 125 years of the Victoria Hotel* (Lane Cove, NSW: CL Creations, 2007), p. 95.

58 Hobart *Mercury*, 6 October 1941.

59 Cox interview NLA aso accessible as JCPML01060/1.

Chapter 21

1 *The Argus*, 6 December 1941.

2 Cox, op. cit.

3 Gill, op. cit., p. 484. This reflects Melbourne time. Others are Malaya.

4 Cox, op. cit.

5 War Cabinet minutes NAA A2673, 8 December 1941.

6 Hotta, op. cit, p. 3.

7   https://history.state.gov/historicaldocuments/frus1941v04, Grew to Hull January 27 1941.

8   Cox, op. cit.

9   *Sydney Morning Herald*, 9 December 1941, from Curtin office scrapbooks of press clippings JCPML00297/2. I did not find these words in the article accessed through Trove: presumably a different edition.

10 Nigel Hamilton, *The Mantle of Command* (New York: Houghton Mifflin Harcourt, 2014), p. 60.

11 Thorne, op. cit., p. 70.

12 David Horner, *Inside the War Cabinet* (Sydney: Allen and Unwin, 1996), p. 77.

13 Thorne, op. cit., p. 4.

14 This based on Bullard, Steven (translator), *Japanese Army Operations in the South Pacific Area: New Britain and Papua campaigns, 1942–43* (Australian War Memorial, 2007).

15 The idea of a war fought to the unconditional surrender of one side or the other came later.

16 Horner (1996), op. cit., p. 78.

17 Patrick Weller, *Cabinet Government in Australia, 1901-2006: Practice, Principles, Performance* (Sydney: UNSW Press, 2007).

18 Cox, op. cit.

19 ibid.

20 ibid., p. 78.

21 ibid., p. 80.

22 ibid., p. 83.

23 War Cabinet minutes, op. cit., 9 December 1941.

24 The Cabinet notebooks for the Monday meeting record the AMF strength was put at 210 000, the AIF 35 000. Presumably the AIF strength referred only to troops in Australia.

25 Kirby et al. (1957), op. cit., p. 460.

26 Horner (1996), op. cit., p. 84.

27 Shedden, op. cit., chapter 8.

28 ibid., chapter 17, p. 7.

29 ibid.

30 Horner (1996), op. cit., p. 85.

31 Shedden, op. cit., chapter 10, p. 4.

32 Cabinet notebooks.

33 Horner (1996), op. cit., pp. 84 and 86.

34 *Daily Mirror*, 11 December 1941.

Chapter 22

1   DFAT, op. cit., p. 330.

2   Cabinet Notebooks.

3   Horner (1980), op. cit., vol. 1, p. 66.

4   Horner (1982), op. cit., p. 144.

5   Horner (1980), op. cit., p. 64.

6   DFAT, op. cit., p. 337.

7   DFAT, p. 333.

8   Butlin & Schedvin, op. cit., p. 5.

9   ibid., p. 6.

10 Buell, op. cit., p. 148.

11 DFAT, op. cit., p. 339.

12 Hamilton, op. cit., p. 140.

13 ibid., p. 113.

14 DFAT, op. cit., p. 341.

15 Winston Churchill, *The Second World War*, Vol. IV: *The Hinge of Fate* (Sydney: Cassell, 1950), p. 6 et seq.

16 Sir Ronald Cross, report of meeting with Curtin, 5 February 1942, UK National Archives, PREM 4/50/7A.

17 Shedden, op. cit., chapter 10, p. 2.

18 Thorne, op. cit., p. 256.

19 DFAT, op. cit., p. 342.

20 ibid., p. 369.

21 Hamilton, op. cit., p. 113.

22 Graham Freudenberg, *Churchill and Australia* (Sydney: Pan Macmillan, 2008), chapter 19.

23 Associated Press, carried in the *New York Times*, 28 December 1941.

24 Mishael's letter is in *West Australian*, 18 May 1978, and elsewhere.

25 Elsie McLeod, letter to Lloyd Ross in Ross collection, box 41, NLA.

26 Lord Moran, *Churchill, taken from the diaries of Lord Moran: The Struggle for Survival 1940–1965* (Boston: Houghton Mifflin, 1960). Sir Charles Wilson became Lord Moran in 1943.

27 *The Argus*, 29 December 1941.

28 *New York Times*, 30 December 1941, carrying a report from Australia dated 29 December.

29 Tonkin papers, NLA folder A16: Foreign Policy.

30 Shedden, op. cit., chapter 12.

31 ibid., p. 9.

32 ibid., p. 11.
33 ibid.
34 ibid., p. 13.
35 ibid., p. 14.
36 Cross, op. cit.

Chapter 23
1 DFAT, op. cit., p. 383.
2 DFAT, ibid., p. 411.
3 ibid., p. 390.
4 ibid., p. 396.
5 Shedden, op. cit., chapter 19, p. 1.
6 ibid., p. 2.
7 Replying to Curtin on 7 January, the British Government thanked him for the 'reinforcement for Malaya'. It warned that it would be unable to provide escorts to the 'degree of security in relation to the possible scale of attack which has been feasible hitherto'. Shedden, op. cit., chapter 19, p. 3A.
8 Horner (1980), op. cit., vol. 1, p. 74.
9 Shedden, op. cit., chapter 19, pp. 3A, 5.
10 Thorne, op. cit., p. 257 and footnote 34.
11 DFAT, op. cit., p. 816.
12 Black (2001), op. cit., p. 210.

Chapter 24
1 DFAT, op. cit., p. 423.
2 Gavin Long, *MacArthur as Military Commander* (London: Batsford, 1969), p. 89 et seq.
3 DFAT, op. cit., vol. V, p. 432.
4 Cabinet Notebooks, p. 629.
5 DFAT, op. cit., p. 441.
6 ibid.
7 DFAT, op. cit., p. 445.
8 Both reported in the *Sydney Morning Herald*, 19 January 1942.
9 *The Argus*, 22 January 1942 (I assume his staff carried the Secraphone scrambler apparatus).
10 DFAT, op. cit., p. 462.
11 ibid, p. 463.
12 Bullard, op. cit., p. 4.

13 ibid., p. 22.

14 ibid., p. 22 et seq.

15 That Page's cable was not discussed at the 23 January War Cabinet meeting is based on a careful reconstruction by David Horner using British and Australian files. Horner (1980), op. cit., vol. 1, pp. 73–85.

16 Cabinet Notebooks, p. 650.

17 Horner (1980), op. cit.

18 Churchill (1950b), op. cit., p. 50.

19 Horner (1980), op. cit., vol 1.

20 Churchill (1950b), op. cit., pp. 51–2, quoted in Kirby et al. (1957), op. cit., p. 467.

21 DFAT, op. cit., p. 463.

22 DFAT, ibid., p. 466 note 10.

23 Melbourne *Herald*, 24 January 1942.

24 Cabinet Notebooks, p. 1754.

25 Horner (1980), op. cit, vol. 1.

26 ibid., p. 125.

27 Bullard, op. cit., p. 51.

28 Syd Gray interview JCPML. Gray says the delay was on 22 January, a Thursday. Curtin was in Adelaide that day, though he may have gone on. Gray's account suggests hold-up was between Kalgoorlie and Perth, which would rule out 22 January. A contemporary newspaper story said Gray met Curtin at the Adelaide railway station on 22 January. The stories made no mention of a train delay outside Kalgoorlie on Curtin's journey to Perth. The reported hold-up was on his way back.

29 In DFAT, op. cit., the editors simply note that Curtin went to Perth 'for a holiday'; vol. V, p. 463.

30 *The Argus*, 27 January 1942.

31 *West Australian*, 26 January 1942.

32 *Sun News Pictorial*, 27 January 1942.

33 *West Australian*, 31 January 1942.

34 *West Australian*, 2 February 1942, with a 1 February dateline on the story.

35 *Canberra Times*, 2 February 1942.

36 *The Argus*, 2 February 1942.

37 *West Australian*, 3 February 1942.

38 Horner (1980), op. cit.

39 DFAT, op. cit., p. 471.

40 Horner (1980), op. cit., vol. 1.

41 DFAT, op. cit., p. 468.

42   Horner (1980), op. cit., vol 1.

43   Bullard, op. cit., pp. 460, 464.

44   DFAT, op. cit., p. 469.

45   ibid., p. 473.

46   ibid., p. 497.

47   Cross, Report to Rt. Hon. Viscount Cranborne, Secretary of State for Dominion Affairs, January 1942, UK National Archives, PREM.

48   War Cabinet, 'Relations with Australia', 22 January 1942, UK National Archives CAB 66/21/13.

49   Wilkinson, op. cit.

Chapter 25

1   *The Argus*, 18 February 1942, p. 1.

2   Keogh, op. cit., p. 83.

3   Horner (1996), p. 99. Paul Hasluck, *The Government and the People 1942–1945* (Australian War Memorial, 1970), p. 74. DFAT, op. cit., p. 528 footnote 5 references the document.

4   NLA: MS 4936, Series 31, Box 497, Folder 8A. Also accessible as JCPML00533/4 (Menzies to Curtin) and JCPML00533/5 (Curtin to Menzies).

5   Henderson (2014), op. cit., p. 10.

6   Keogh, op. cit., p. 87.

7   DFAT, op. cit., p. 521.

8   ibid.

9   *Digest of Decisions and Announcements*, 16 February 1942.

10   Bullard, op. cit., p. 92.

11   ibid., p. 93.

12   DFAT, op. cit., p. 527.

13   ibid.

14   S W Kirby et al., *The War Against Japan, Vol. II: India's Most Dangerous Hour*, History of the Second World War, United Kingdom Military series (London: HMSO, 1958), p. 55.

15   ibid., p. 56.

16   DFAT, op. cit., p. 533.

17   Page's two cables sent 18 February 1942 are in DFAT, ibid., pp. 535–538.

18   ibid., p. 539.

19   Cabinet Notebooks in relation to 1896 and 1914.

20   Roskill, op. cit., p. 11.

21   DFAT, op. cit., p. 540.

22   ibid., p. 542.

23   ibid., p. 543.

24   ibid., p. 546.

25   ibid., p. 551.

26   ibid., p. 553.

27   Elsie recalled the cigarette box was silver.

28   Cox, op. cit.

29   Horner (1996), op. cit., p. 105.

30   Though it has often been written, I am unconvinced of the accuracy of the
     story that Curtin was lost in the hills, and Shedden had advertisements for
     him placed in Canberra cinemas. It has the ring of a good yarn, especially the
     cinema ads, but is unlikely.

31   DFAT, op. cit., p. 564.

32   ibid., p. 576.

33   ibid., 586.

34   From McLaughlin family interviews, JCPML0185/1.

35   This section based on 'Doing the best for the country: Behind the scenes of
     Australia's wartime decision-making 1939–45', 2004, compilation by JCPML.

36   Kirby et al. (1958), op. cit., p. 56.

37   Roskill, op. cit., p. 19.

38   Kirby et al. (1958), op. cit., p. 102.

39   ibid., p. 104.

40   ibid., p. 101.

41   Horner (1980), op. cit., vol. 1, quoting John Connell & Michael Roberts,
     Wavell, Supreme Commander 1941–1943 (London: Collins, 1969), p. 196.

42   Records of the Commonwealth Prime Minister's Conference UK National
     Archives, PREM 4/42/5.

Chapter 26

1   *Digest*, op. cit., 7 March 1942.

2   Lowe, op. cit., p. 280.

3   Hamilton, op. cit., p. 237.

4   Thorne, op. cit., p. 206, and note 19 p. 229.

5   Kirby et al. (1958), op. cit., p. 55.

6   Horner (2000), op. cit., p. 139.

7   Warren F Kimball, *Roosevelt and Churchill, Volume 1: The Complete
    Correspondence* (Princeton University Press, 2015), p. 363.

8   Hamilton, op. cit., p. 211. See also Kimball, op. cit.

9 Hamilton, op. cit., p. 212. See also Long (1969), op. cit.

10 Keogh, op. cit., p. 134.

11 DFAT, op. cit., p. 688. Two days later Churchill amended the cable to read that an infantry division was rounding the Cape, and an armoured division would be sent a month later. See ibid., p. 688 footnote 1.

12 Shedden, op. cit.

13 Shedden, ibid., chapter 21 is the source for this section.

14 War Cabinet Agendum 96/1942 Defence of Australia. See also Burns, op. cit., p. 75.

15 Evatt to Roosevelt, 5 April 1942, appended to Pacific War Council meeting minutes of 1 April 1942, Roosevelt Library.

16 Shedden, op. cit., chapter 20.

17 ibid., chapter 22.

18 DFAT, vol. V, document 432, p. 667.

19 Martin & Hardy, op. cit., pp. 130–31.

20 DFAT, vol. V, note to document 426, p. 658.

21 Mackenzie King diary, 21 March 1942.

22 Kimball, op. cit., p. 428.

23 On April 23. Peter Edwards, *Australia Through American Eyes* (University of Queensland Press, 1979), p. 68.

24 ibid.

25 Edwards (1978), op. cit.

Chapter 27

1 Edwards (2005), op. cit., p. 8.

2 Mrs Harry Seuling, quoted in the *Sunday Telegraph*, 8 July 1945.

3 Reid, op. cit.

4 Cabinet Notebooks, volume 5.

5 Kimball, op. cit., p. 421.

6 Mackenzie King diary, 15 April 1942.

7 Thorne, op. cit., p. 52, attributed to *Documents on German Foreign Policy*.

8 Bullard, op. cit., pp. 75–7.

9 Henry P Frei, *Japan's Southward Advance and Australia* (Melbourne University Press, 1991), pp. 161–62.

10 ibid., p. 168.

11 Keogh, op. cit., pp. 134–35.

12 Bullard, op. cit., p. 79.

13 Keogh, op. cit., p. 135.

14 The order was issued 18 April 1942. Bullard, op. cit., p. 86.

BIBLIOGRAPHY

Books

Albatross (Piesse, Edmund Leolin). *Japan and the Defence of Australia*. Melbourne: Robertson & Mullens, 1935.

Atkinson, Rick. *The Guns at Last Light: The War in Western Europe, 1944–1945*. New York: Henry Holt and Co., 2013.

Australian Bureau of Statistics. *Official Year Book of the Commonwealth of Australia 1935*. Canberra: Australian Bureau of Statistics, 1935.

Beazley, Kim Edward. *Father of the House*. North Fremantle: Fremantle Press, 2009.

Curtin, John. *In His Own Words: John Curtin's Speeches and Writings*. Edited by David Black. Bentley: Paradigm Books, Curtin University, 1995.

Black, David. *Friendship is a sheltering tree: John Curtin's Letters, 1907–1945* (Perth: John Curtin Prime Ministerial Library, 2001.

Bolton, Geoffrey. *A Fine Country to Starve In*. Nedlands: University of Western Australia Press, 1972.

Bridge, Carl, editor. *A Delicate Mission: The Washington diaries of R. G. Casey 1940–42*. Canberra: National Library of Australia, 2008.

Bullard, Steven, translator. *Japanese Army Operations in the South Pacific Area: New Britain and Papua Campaigns, 1942–43*. Canberra: Australian War Memorial, 2007.

Burns, Paul. *The Brisbane Line Controversy: Political Opportunism versus National Security 1942 1945*. Sydney: Allen and Unwin, 1998.

Butlin, Sydney James. *War Economy 1939–42*. Canberra: Australian War Memorial, 1955.

Butlin, Sydney James and Schedvin, Carl Boris. *War Economy 1942–45*. Canberra: Australian War Memorial, 1977.

Calwell, Arthur. *Be Just and Fear Not*. Hawthorn: Lloyd O'Neil in association with Rigby, 1972.

Chester, Alan. *John Curtin*. Sydney: Angus and Robertson, 1943.

Chester, Wilmot. *The Struggle for Europe*. Connecticut: Konecky and Konecky, 1952.

Churchill, Winston. *The Second World War Vol. III: The Grand Alliance*. London: Cassell, 1950.

Churchill, Winston. *The Second World War Vol. IV: The Hinge of Fate*. London: Cassell, 1950.

Commonwealth of Australia. *Digest of Decisions and Announcements and Important Speeches by the Prime Minister*. Canberra: Records of the Commonwealth of Australia, 1941-1945.

Connor, John. *Anzac and Empire: George Foster Pearce and the Foundations of Australian Defence*. Cambridge: Cambridge University Press, 2011.

Crisp, Leslie Finlay. *Ben Chifley: A Biography*. London: Longmans, 1960.

Cumpston, Ina Mary. *Lord Bruce of Melbourne*. Melbourne: Longman Cheshire, 1989.

Curran, James. *Curtin's Empire*. Port Melbourne: Cambridge University Press, 2011.

Dallek, Robert. *Franklin D. Roosevelt and American Foreign Policy, 1932–1945*. New York: Oxford University Press, 1979.

Dalziel, Allan. *Evatt the Enigma*. Melbourne: Lansdowne Press, 1967.

Day, David. *John Curtin: A Life*. Sydney: Harper Collins, 1999.

Denning, Warren. *Caucus Crisis: The Rise & Fall of the Scullin Government*. Sydney: Hale and Iremonger, 1982.

Department of Foreign Affairs. *Documents on Australian Foreign Policy 1937–1949, Vol. I-VIII*. Canberra: Australian Government Publishing Service, 1975.

Donovan, Peter. *Going the Extra Mile: A History of the Commonwealth Car Service 1910–2010*. Canberra: Commonwealth of Australia, 2010.

Drea, Edward J. *Japan's Imperial Army: Its Rise and Fall, 1953–1945*. Lawrence: University Press of Kansas, 2009.

Edwards, Cecil. *Bruce of Melbourne: Man of Two Worlds*. London: Heinemann, 1965.

Edwards, John. *Curtin's Gift: Reinterpreting Australia's Greatest Prime Minister*. Sydney: Allen & Unwin, 2005.

Edwards, Peter (editor). *Australia Through American Eyes, 1935–1945: Observations by American Diplomats*. St Lucia: University of Queensland Press, 1979.

Ehrman, John. *Grand Strategy Vol. V August 1943 – September 1944*. London: Her Majesty's Stationery Office, 1956.

Frei, Henry P. *Japan's Southward Advance and Australia: From the Sixteenth Century to World War II*. Melbourne: Melbourne University Press, 1991.

Freudenberg, Graham. *Churchill and Australia*. Sydney: Pan Macmillan, 2008.

Gill, George Hermon. *Royal Australian Navy 1939–1942*. Canberra: Australian War Memorial, 1957.

Gillison, Douglas. *Royal Australian Air Force 1939–1942*. Canberra: Australian War Memorial, 1962.

Green, Frank. *Servant of the House*. Melbourne: Heinemann, 1969.

Griffin, James. *John Wren: A Life Reconsidered*. Melbourne: Scribe, 2004.

Haggie, Paul. *Britannia at bay: The Defence of the British Empire Against Japan, 1931–1941*. New York: Oxford University Press, 1981.

Hall, Richard and Lloyd, Clem, editors. *Backroom Briefings: John Curtin's War*. Canberra: National Library of Australia, 1997.

Hamill, Ian. *The strategic illusion: The Singapore Strategy and the Defence of Australia and New Zealand, 1919–1942*. Singapore: Singapore University Press, 1981.

Hamilton, Nigel. *The Mantle of Command: FDR at War, 1941/1942*. (Boston: Houghton Mifflin Harcourt, 2014.

Hasluck, Paul. *The Government and the People 1939–1941*. Canberra: Australian War Memorial, 1952.

Hasluck, Paul. *The Government and the People 1942–1945*. Canberra: Australian War Memorial, 1970.

Hastings, Max. *Winston's War: Churchill, 1940–1945*. New York: Knopf, 2009.

Hazlehurst, Cameron. *Menzies Observed*. Sydney: Allen & Unwin, 1979.

Henderson, Anne. *Joseph Lyons: The People's Prime Minister*. Sydney: NewSouth, 2011.

Henderson, Anne. *Menzies at War*. Sydney: NewSouth, 2014.

Higham, Geoffrey. *Marble Bar to Mandurah: A History of Passenger Rail Services in Western Australia*. Bassendean: Rail Heritage WA, 2007.

Horner, David. *High Command*. Sydney: Allen and Unwin, 1982.

Horner, David. *Inside the War Cabinet: Directing Australia's War Effort, 1939–1945*. Sydney: Allen & Unwin, 1996.

Horner, David. *Blamey: The Commander-in-Chief*. Sydney: Allen & Unwin, 1998.

Horner, David. *Defence Supremo: Sir Frederick Shedden and the Making of Australian Defence Policy*. Sydney: Allen & Unwin, 2000.

Hotta, Eri. *Japan 1941: Countdown to Infamy*. New York: Knopf, 2013.

Ike, Nobutaka (Editor) *Japan's Decision for War: Records of the 1941 Policy Conferences*. Stanford: Stanford University Press, 1967.

Kaiser, David. *No End Save Victory: How FDR Led the Nation Into War*. New York: Basic Books, 2014.

Keegan, John. *The Second World War*. London: Hutchinson, 1989.

Keogh, Eustace. *South West Pacific, 1941–45*. Melbourne: Grayflower Productions, 1965.

Kimball, Warren F, editor. *Roosevelt & Churchill, Volume 1: The Complete Correspondence*. Princeton: Princeton University Press, 1984.

Kirby, S W, Meiklejohn, J F, Addis, C T, Wards, G T and Desoer, N L. *The War Against Japan Volume I: The Loss of Singapore*. London: Her Majesty's Stationery Office, 1957.

Kirby, S W, Meiklejohn, J F, Addis, C T, Wards, G T and Desoer, N L. *The War Against Japan Volume II: India's Most Dangerous Hour*. London: Her Majesty's Stationery Office, 1958.

Leahy, William D. *I Was There*. New York: Whittlesey House, 1950.

Long, Gavin. *To Benghazi*. Canberra: Australian War Memorial, 1952.

Long, Gavin. *MacArthur as Military Commander*. Sydney: Angus and Robertson, 1969.

Lukacs, John. *Five Days in London, May 1940*. London: Yale University Press, 1999.

MacArthur, Douglas. *Reminiscences*. London: Heinemann, 1964.

Manchester, William. *American Caesar: Douglas MacArthur, 1880-1964* London, Hutchinson, 1979.

Marshall, John. *The Life of George Washington*. Philadelphia: C. P. Wayne, 1804.

Martin, Allan W. *Robert Menzies: A Life, Vol. 1 and 2*. Melbourne: Melbourne University Press, 1999.

Matloff, Maurice and Snell, Edwin. *Strategic Planning for Coalition Warfare 1941–1942*. Washington: Office of the Chief of Military History, Department of the Army, 1953.

McKenzie, Francine and MacMillan, Margaret, editors. *Parties Long Estranged: Canada and Australia in the Twentieth Century* Vancouver: University of British Columbia Press, 2003.

McLean, Ian W. *Why Australia Prospered: The Shifting Sources of Economic Growth*. Princeton: Princeton University Press, 2013.

Meaney, Neville. *Fears & Phobias: E.L. Piesse and the Problem of Japan, 1909–39*. Canberra: National Library of Australia, 1996.

Menzies, Robert. *Afternoon Light: Some Memories of Men and Events*. Melbourne: Cassell Australia, 1967.

Menzies, Robert, Martin, A W and Hardy, Patsy, editors. *Dark and Hurrying Days: Menzies' 1941 Diary*. Canberra: National Library of Australia, 1993.

Miller, John. *Cartwheel: The Reduction of Rabaul*. Washington: Office of the Chief of Military History, Department of the Army, 1959.

Lord Moran, *Churchill, taken from the diaries of Lord Moran: The Struggle for Survival 1940–1965* (Boston: Houghton Mifflin, 1960)

Murphy, John. *Evatt: A Life*. Sydney: NewSouth, 2016.

Niall, Brenda and Thompson, John (editors). *The Oxford Book of Australian Letters*. Melbourne: Oxford University Press, 1998.

Paine, Sarah C M. *The Wars for Asia 1911–1949*. New York: Cambridge University Press, 2012.

Perry, Mark. *The Most Dangerous Man in America: The Making of Douglas MacArthur*. New York: Basic Books, 2014.

Reynolds, Wayne. *Australia's Bid for the Atomic Bomb*. Melbourne: Melbourne University Press, 2000.

Robertson, John. *J.H. Scullin: A Political Biography*. Nedlands: University of Western Australia Press, 1974.

Rose, J Holland, Newton, A P, Benians, E A, editors. *The Cambridge History of the British Empire Vol. VII Part 1, Australia*. Cambridge: Cambridge University Press, 1933.

Roskill, S W. *The War at Sea 1939–1945, Vol. II: The Period of Balance*. London: Her Majesty's Stationery Office, 1976.

Ross, Lloyd. *John Curtin: A Biography*. Melbourne: Melbourne University Press, 1977.

Santamaria, B A. *Santamaria: A Memoir*. Melbourne: Oxford University Press, 1997.

Sarantakes, Nicholas Evan. *Allies Against the Rising Sun: The United States, the British Nations, and the Defeat of Imperial Japan*. Lawrence: University Press of Kansas, 2009.

Schedvin, Boris. *Australia and the Great Depression: A Study of Economic Development and Policy in the 1920s and 1930s*. Sydney: Sydney University Press, 1970.

Serle, Geoffrey. *For Australia and Labor: Prime Minister John Curtin*. Perth: John Curtin Prime Ministerial Library, 1998.

Sheedy, Katherine. *Home Away from Home: Celebrating 125 years of the Victoria Hotel*. Lane Cove: CL Creations, 2007.

Slim, William. *Defeat into Victory*. London: Cassell, 1956.

Spector, Ronald H. *Eagle Against the Sun: The American War with Japan*. New York: Free Press, 1985.

Spratt, Elwyn. *Eddie Ward, Firebrand of East Sydney*. Adelaide: Rigby, 1965.

Thorne, Christopher. *Allies of a Kind: The United States, Britain and the War Against Japan, 1941–1945*. London: Hamilton, 1978.

Toland, John. *Rising Sun: The Decline and Fall of the Japanese Empire 1936–1945*.
   Barnsley: Pen & Sword Books, 2005.

Turner, Ian. *Industrial Labour and Politics: The Dynamics of the Labour Movement in
   Eastern Australia*. Canberra: Australian National University, 1965.

Vamplew, Wray, editor. *Australians: Historical Statistics*. Broadway: Fairfax, Syme
   and Weldon Associates, 1987.

Walker, Bertha. *Solidarity Forever: A Part Story of the Life and Times of Percy Laidler
   – The First Quarter of a Century*. Melbourne: National Press, 1972.

Weller, Patrick, editor. *Caucus Minutes, 1901–1949: Minutes of Meetings of the Federal
   Parliament Labor Party, Vol. 1–3*. Melbourne: Melbourne University Press,
   1975.

Weller, Patrick. *Cabinet Government in Australia, 1901-2006: Practice, Principles,
   Performance*. Sydney: University of New South Wales Press, 2007.

Wigmore, Lionel. *The Japanese Thrust*. Canberra: Australian War Memorial, 1957.

Chapters

Buell, Thomas. 'American Strategy in the Pacific: Its Philosophy and Practice.' In
   War and Diplomacy Across the Pacific, 1919–1952, edited by A Ion Hamish and
   Barry Hunt, 143–154. Waterloo: Wilfred Laurier University Press, 1988.

Curtin, John. 'The Census and the Social Service State.' In *What the Census Reveals*,
   edited by G V Portus, p154 et seq Adelaide: F W Preece & Sons, 1936.

Falk, Stanley L. 'Douglas MacArthur and the War against Japan.' In *We Shall
   Return!: MacArthur›s Commanders and the Defeat of Japan, 1942-1945*, edited
   by William Leary, 1–22. Lexington: University Press of Kentucky, 1988.

Freudenberg, Graham. 'Victory to Defeat: 1941–49.' In *True Believers: The Story
   of the Federal Parliament Labor Party*, edited by John Faulkner & Stuart
   Macintyre, 76–89. Sydney: Allen & Unwin, 2001.

Horner, David. 'Blamey and MacArthur: The Problems of Coalition Warfare.'
   In *We Shall Return!: MacArthur›s Commanders and the Defeat of Japan,
   1942-1945*, edited by William Leary, 23–59. Lexington: University Press of
   Kentucky, 1988.

Leutze, James. 'Continuity and Change in America's Second Oldest Foreign Policy
   Commitment.' In *War and Diplomacy Across the Pacific, 1919–1952*, edited by
   A Ion Hamish and Barry Hunt, 21–44. Waterloo: Wilfred Laurier University
   Press, 1988.

Lowe, Peter. 'Retreat from Power: British Attitudes Towards Japan 1923–41.' In *War
   and Diplomacy Across the Pacific, 1919–1952*, edited by A Ion Hamish and Barry
   Hunt, 45–62. Waterloo: Wilfred Laurier University Press, 1988.

Menzies, A R. 'Canadian Views of United States Policy Towards Japan, 19451952.' In *War and Diplomacy Across the Pacific, 1919–1952*, edited by edited by A Ion Hamish and Barry Hunt, 155–172. Waterloo: Wilfred Laurier University Press, 1988.

Stanley, Peter. *Australia Under Threat of Invasion in Remembering 1942*. Australian War Memorial History Conference, 2002. Canberra: Australian War Memorial.

Archives, manuscripts, oral histories

Advisory War Council. Minutes. October 29, 1940–August 30, 1945. National Archives of Australia.

Bruce, Prime Minister Stanley. Miscellaneous Official and Private Papers. 1918–1967. AA1970/555, National Archives of Australia.

Cleaver, Horace. Interview. June 30, 1997. JCPML00207/1, John Curtin Prime Ministerial Library.

The Commonwealth Prime Minister's Conference. 1944. PREM 4/42/5, UK National Archives.

Cox, Harold. Interview with Mel Pratt. April 6, 1973. Mel Pratt collection, National Library of Australia.

Craig, Hazel. Interview. June 30, 1997. JCPML00209/1, John Curtin Prime Ministerial Library.

Cross, Sir Ronald. Report of Meeting with Curtin. February 5, 1942. PREM 4/50/7A, UK National Archives.

Cross, Sir Ronald. Report to Rt. Hon. Viscount Cranborne, Secretary of State for Dominion Affairs. January 1942. PREM, UK National Archives.

Department of Defence. Prime Minister's War Conferences. 1937–1956. A5954, Shedden collection, National Archives of Australia.

Gray, Sydney. Anecdotes. 1999. SER0263, John Curtin Prime Ministerial Library.

Harrison, Hector. Interview. 1973. JCPML00016/1, John Curtin Prime Ministerial Library.

Hodges, Adele. Interview with Isla Macphail. July 2, 1997. JCPML00211/1, John Curtin Prime Ministerial Library.

King, Mackenzie. Diaries of William Lyon Mackenzie King. MG26-J13, Library and Archives Canada.

McLaughlin–Ross family. Interview. October 26, 1996. JCPML00185/1, John Curtin Prime Ministerial Library.

Makin, Norman. Monologue by Norman Makin and Interview by Suzanne Walker. Oral TRCs 271/1 and 271/2, National Library of Australia.

Menzies, Sir Robert. Draft of Diary. 1935. Box 579, folio 8, National Library of Australia.

Pacific War Council Meeting, Minutes, Franklin D Roosevelt Presidential Library.

Reid, Alan. Interview with Mel Pratt. October 4, 1972–February 28, 1973. Mel Pratt collection, National Library of Australia.

Rodgers, Donald Kilgour. Interview with Mel Pratt. April 29, 1971. Mel Pratt collection, National Library of Australia. Also held as JCPML00497/1.

Lloyd Ross papers, MS3939, National Library of Australia.

The Shedden collection. A5954, National Archives of Australia.

Shedden, Sir Frederick Geoffery. 'Victory under the Curtin and Chifley Governments.' Shedden Collection, A5954 Box 1325, National Archives of Australia.

Tonkin, Eric W. Papers of Eric Tonkin. MS3668, National Library of Australia.

War Cabinet. Relations with Australia. January 22, 1942. CAB99/26, UK National Archives.

War Cabinet minutes. Menzies and Curtin governments, 1939-1945. A5954, National Archives of Australia.

War Cabinet notebooks, A9240, National Archives of Australia.

Ward, Edward J. Papers. MS 2396, National Library of Australia.

Wilkinson, Gerald Hugh. The Papers of Gerald Wilkinson. 1942–1975. GBR/0014/WILK, Churchill Archives Centre.

Journals, papers, compilations, biographical entries

Black, David. 'Biography of Elsie Curtin.' John Curtin Prime Ministerial Library, last modified June 10, 2017, http://john.curtin.edu.au/resources/biography/ecurtin.html.

Campbell, Heather. 'Doing the best for the country: Behind the scenes of Australia's wartime decision-making 1939–45.' John Curtin Prime Ministerial Library, 2004. http://john.curtin.edu.au/behindthescenes/

Campbell, Heather. 'Diary of a Labour Man 1917–1945.' John Curtin Prime Ministerial Library, 2008. http://john.curtin.edu.au/diary/

Dedman, John. 'The Labor Government in the Second World War: A Memoir, Part II.' *Labour History* 22 (1972): 42–56.

Dennis, Peter. 'Heading For Disaster? Australia and the Singapore Strategy.' Fall of Singapore 60th Anniversary Conference. National University of Singapore, February 16–17, 2002.

Fisher, Chay and Kent, Christopher. 'Two Depressions, One Banking Collapse.' Discussion paper. Reserve Bank of Australia, June 1999.

Horner, David. 'Australia and Allied Strategy in the Pacific 1941-1946.' Doctoral dissertation, Australian National University, 1980.

Robertson, H C H. 'Defence of Australia.' *Army Quarterly* 27 (1934).

Sholl, Dianne. 'John Curtin at the 'Westralian Worker' 1917–1928: An Examination of the Development of Curtin's Political Philosophy as Reflected in his Editorials'. Bachelor of Arts (Honours) thesis, University of Western Australia, 1975.

Australian Dictionary of Biography entries

Anderson, Grant and Dawson, Daryl. 'Dixon, Sir Owen (1886–1972).' In *Australian Dictionary of Biography, Vol. 14*, edited by John Ritchie and Christopher Cunneen. Melbourne: Melbourne University Press, 1996.

Beddie, B. 'Pearce, Sir George Foster (1870–1952).' In *Australian Dictionary of Biography, Vol. 11*, edited by Geoffrey Serle and Christorpher Cunneen. Melbourne: Melbourne University Press, 1988.

Bolton, G C. 'Green, Albert Ernest (1869–1940).' In *Australian Dictionary of Biography, Vol. 9*, edited by Bede Nairn, Geoffrey Serle and Christopher Cunneen. Melbourne: Melbourne University Press, 1983.

Horner, David. 'Shedden, Sir Frederick Geoffrey (1893–1971).' In *Australian Dictionary of Biography, Vol. 16*, edited by John Ritchie and Diane Langmore. Melbourne: Melbourne University Press, 2002.

Love, Peter. 'Stout, James Victor (1885–1964).' In *Australian Dictionary of Biography, Vol. 16*, edited by John Ritchie and Diane Langmore. Melbourne: Melbourne University Press, 2002.

Martin, A W. 'Menzies, Sir Robert Gordon (Bob) (1894–1978).' In *Australian Dictionary of Biography, Vol. 15*, edited by John Ritchie. Melbourne: Melbourne University Press, 2000.

Meaney, Neville. 'Piesse, Edmund Leolin (1880–1947).' In *Australian Dictionary of Biography, Vol. 11*, edited by Geoffrey Serle and Christorpher Cunneen. Melbourne: Melbourne University Press, 1988.

Powell, Graeme. 'Strahan, Frank (1886–1976).' In *Australian Dictionary of Biography, Vol. 16*, edited by John Ritchie and Diane Langmore. Melbourne: Melbourne University Press, 2002.

Newspapers and magazines

Annan, Noel. 'How Wrong Was Churchill?' *New York Review of Books*, 8 April 1993.

Butow, R J C. 'How Roosevelt Attacked Japan at Pearl Harbor: Myth Masquerading as History.' *Prologue Magazine*. 28, 3 (Fall 1996).

Curtin, Elsie. 'The Curtin Story.' *Woman*, 12 March, 1951.

Curtin, John. 'The late Frank Hyett.' *Railways Union Gazette,* 7 June, 1919.

Edwards, John. 'Australians at War: An American Perspective.' *The National Times*, 30 January–4 February 1978.

Ross, Lloyd. 'The Story of John Curtin.' *The Sun-Herald*, 4–5 February, 1958.

Scrapbooks compiled by the Prime Minister's Office. *Scrapbook 2*. JCPML00297/2, John Curtin Prime Ministerial Library.

Scrapbooks compiled by the Prime Minister's Office. *Scrapbook 3*. JCPML00297/3, John Curtin Prime Ministerial Library.

ACKNOWLEDGEMENTS

I am indebted to Penguin Australia's Publishing Director Ben Ball for encouragement and comment on parts of earlier drafts and for guiding the book to completion. Working with Penguin's splendid publishing team is a pleasure. I thank Hilary Reynolds who edited the draft, Mark Evans who painstakingly proofed the text, and Fay Helfenbaum, who kept it all together. Louisa Maggio designed the cover.

Before the final draft reached Penguin it was most carefully read and reread by friend and editor John Nethercote, who brought to the task both his vast knowledge of Australian politics and his attention to grammatical detail. Barry Howarth indexed the book with his customary care and thoroughness.

The book was first commissioned by the then Managing Editor at Penguin Bob Sessions, who responded helpfully to an early version of the beginning of the book. Before she left that interesting but unremunerative business, literary agent Mary Cunnane provided excellent advice, both commercial and literary.

As for my earlier book *Curtin's Gift* I am indebted to Kandy-Jane Henderson, former head of the John Curtin Prime Ministerial Library (JCPML) at Curtin University of Technology for her early guidance and her continuing encouragement and interest. I thank her for reading and commenting on an earlier version of the book draft. Curtin University Adjunct Professor David Black, who has contributed vastly to Curtin materials through his carefully annotated editions of Curtin's speeches and letters, was kind enough to read and comment on large sections of earlier drafts. So too David Wylie, formerly a researcher on the staff of the JCPML, generously gave time to read a draft. Harry Edwards and Alex Edwards helpfully commented on sections of the book. Deborah Hope gave this first volume a careful scrutiny, and made many valuable suggestions. With the late Ian Marsh, a close friend and a distinguished political scientist, I enjoyed many illuminating discussions on Australian political history.

I thank Gail Pearson, Mark Johnson, David Jenkins, David Bell and Brian Toohey for sending me important books and documents.

Thanks to the staffs of the National Archives of Australia, the National Library of Australia, the Bodleian Libraries, the Churchill Archives Centre, the Flinders University Library, the Library of Congress, the Franklin D. Roosevelt Presidential Library and Museum (and especially William Baehr), the Mosman Library, the UK National Archives, and the State Library of NSW. Through this long project the JCPML has been unstintingly helpful in assembling materials and providing a space to work with them, in responding to queries and guiding me though its immense inventory of online resources. I especially thank the Library Archivist Sally Laming. Thanks also to the Department of Defence for facilitating access to the War Cabinet rooms at Victoria Barracks, Melbourne.

Any contemporary account of Curtin, his colleagues, his opponents and his times depends on the earlier work of others. Previous biographies by Lloyd Ross and David Day broke much new ground and are acknowledged in the text. Even now Australia's World War II official histories are indispensable, as is the magnificent series of the *Documents on Australian Foreign Policy*, Volumes I-VIII, published by the then Department of Foreign Affairs. In the course of research and writing I often consulted the work of David Horner, from his two volume dissertation written under Professor Robert O'Neill at the Australian National University (later published as

High Command), through his books on Blamey, Shedden, and the decisions of War Cabinet and War Council. David Black's book on Curtin's speeches and writings, his book on Curtin's letters and his book with Lesley Wallace on Curtin archival sources are now essential materials in writing about Curtin. For the JCPML, Heather Campbell produced an excellent chronology of Curtin's life, 'Diary of a Labour Man', on which I have relied. Finally, thanks to the National Library of Australia for creating the Trove archive of digitised Australian newspapers, a tool that has transformed that aspect of research.

INDEX

Abbot, C L, 126
ABC-1
  Australian chiefs of staff on, 369
  and defensive attitude to Japan, 355
  and Germany First doctrine, 226, 227
Aboriginal Australians, 87–8
Abyssinia
  Italian invasion of, 113–14
Advisory War Council *see* War Council
air power, xvii, xviii, 3, 100, 122, 129–30, 131, 337
  and defence of Malaya, 204–5
  for defence of Malaya, 204–5, 207, 300
  and naval power, 371
  and Singapore strategy, 346
air support
  Greece, 345, 382
  Malaya, 276, 344, 345, 346, 355, 383
  in Pacific War, 337
  Tobruk, 276
air travel
  crash near Canberra (Aug. 1940), 3
  Curtin's aversion to, xi, 1–3
aircraft
  and battleships, 301
  for Burma, Malaya and Borneo, 207, 238
  and defence of Malaya and Singapore, 179, 186, 205, 207, 297
    Buffalo Brewster, 231, 299
  production of, 311
aircrew
  posted to Britain, 311, 332
  training in Canada, 311
Albania
  invasion of by Italy, 141
Allied war command
  head-quarters of in Washington, 349
Allied Works Council, 347, 412
Ambon, 222, 297
  Japanese occupation of, 412

American British Dutch Australian (ABDA)
  command, 382
Anglo-Japanese Treaty, 97, 248
Anstey, Frank, 16–17, 39
  and air power, 100
  Curtin and, 16–17, 19, 21, 22, 28, 30, 34, 40, 44, 90, 105, 106
    encouragement of Curtin to stand for his seat of Bourke, 57–8, 106
  Curtin on, 60
  and economic statement prepared by Fenton, Lyons, Anstey, Theodore and Curtin, 41
  and expulsion of Lang's NSW branch from ALP, 42
  and Lang group, 106
  left Parliament, 60
  and royal commission on banking, 106
  and Wren, 106
Anzac Day, 120
appeasement of Germany, 75, 132, 133, 137, 142
  Churchill and, 162
  collapse of, 141
  and defence of Australia, 131
Arcadia conference and agreement, 382, 410
  and Germany first doctrine, 353, 359
  and Japan, 354
  and Operation Torch, 440
Argentine Government
  and British banking system, 15
Atlantic Charter, 249–50, 251, 252–3, 304
Atlee, Clem, xiii
Australia
  1890s–1935, 78–84
    per capita income, 78
  in 1935, 84–5, 101–2
    age of population, 79, 80
    birth rate, 79–80
    defence policy, 94–5
    economic policy, 102

Australia *continued*
  economy, 81
    wool, 81
  foreign affairs, 93
  foreign representation, 93
  immigrants, 79, 80
  population, 81
  population density, 81–2
  trade union membership, 81
  in 1939
    defences against invasion, 173, 174–6,
      174–8
    foreign representation, 182
  in 1941
    at beginning of war, 321, 323
    war preparedness, 246, 276–7, 311, 312
  to 1935
    defence policy, 98, 100–1
  and Aboriginal Australians, 87–8
  as base for US operations against Japanese
    forces, 381–2, 416, 431, 432, 450, 453
  Japan and, 434
  as British, xx, 84–5, 86–7, 93
    differences from the British, 85–7
    and the Empire, 91, 92, 93–4
    relations with Britain, 90, 101–2, 448
  census 1933
    agriculture, manufacturing and other/service
      occupations, 81–2
    population city/country, 82
    poverty and unemployment, 108
    religion, 80–1
    sheep numbers, 81
  changes after arrival of MacArthur, 448
  competition with Britain for US resources and
    attention, 350, 351, 359
  consequences for of Japanese invasion of
    China, 142
  Constitution, 86
  construction of airfields for USA, 245
  declaration of war on Germany, 153
  defence of
    and assistance from USA, 367–8
    Australian government's responsibility, 372,
      372–3, 381
    Britain and, 417, 448
    forces needed, 436–7
    US Pacific fleet and, 372
    US troops for, 381, 382, 439–40, 451
    Wavell and, 372
  defence of core industrial region, 339, 340,
    434, 435, 436
  defensive capability at beginning of war,
    335
  and Depression of 1890s, 15, 16, 79

diplomatic representation, 149, 303
as European, 91–2, 93
European beginnings
  and the Enlightenment, 85
  nature of conflicts, 86
  nature of first settlers–contrast with
    America, 85
  and European colonial possessions in
    Asia-Pacific region, 91
Federation *see* Federation
government and politics, 86, 88–9
Governors-General, 87
and Great Depression, 34, 47–8
and immigration, 79, 80
  British, 80
  Chinese, 80
  Irish, 78, 80
  see also White Australia Policy
and Italian invasion of Abyssinia, 114
Japanese threat to, xviii, 95–100, 431
MacArthur based in, 432
military traditions, 88
and Netherlands East Indies oil, 242
and Papua and New Guinea, 91
part played in command decisions, 450
possible invasion of by Japan, 337, 338, 339,
  356, 368, 399, 412, 415, 422, 431, 433,
  434, 452, 453
  preparations for, 368–9, 431, 433, 434
racism and xenophobia, 94; *see also* White
  Australia Policy
  and Japan, 96
and religion, 80–1, 85
in Roosevelt's post-war Pacific, 452
sea voyage to Britain, 93–4
sense of vulnerability as British outpost in the
  South Seas, 93
separation of interests of and British interests
  by Japanese conquests in east Asia and
  Pacific, 448
and Singapore military conference
  (Oct. 1940), 203, 208
situation while Germany at war with Soviet
  Union, 295
social services, 109
and Statute of Westminster, 89
trade relations with Japan, 115
trade relations with USA, 115
turn to USA, 448; *see also under* Curtin,
  John (Jack)
US navy securing sea passages south-west to,
  348–9, 370, 432
and USA, 92–3
  USA to take responsibility for, 432
Australia Day holiday (1942) cancelled, 395

Australia–USA sea route
compared with sea route USA–Britain, 367–8
protection of, 348–9, 370, 432
vulnerability of, 172
Australian air force see Royal Australian Air Force
(RAAF)
Australian armed services
numbers, 348
Australian army (AIF)
Australian troops to go to Burma in exchange
for US troops for Australia's defence, 401,
408
Australian troops to remain in Middle East
in exchange for US troops for Australia's
defence, 439
battalion group sent to Rabaul, 222
and compulsory military service, 96
in Crete, xiii
and defence of Malaya and Singapore, 174,
186, 189
and defence policy, 99, 100, 101, 119, 121,
122, 130
divisions to reinforce Singapore
at sea or not yet embarked, 391
embarkation to fight Germany, 161
and Empire military forces, 94, 97
establishment, 312
forces of, 338
in Greece campaign, xiii, 223, 229, 234
last trained troops sent to Malaya, 343
in Middle East/north Africa, xv, 335
numbers for home defence, 175, 183–4, 206
return of troops from Middle East, 231–2,
248, 249, 274, 277, 305, 335, 340–1,
450
to Australia, 415–16
British Government and, 374
Churchill and, 345, 364, 373, 410
question of to where, 375–6, 410–11,
412–13, 415, 416
structure of in December 1941, 335
at Tobruk, xiv
troop movements at beginning of war, 334–5
troops to meet invasion, 435
in World War I
on Western Front, 22–3
Australian army (AIF) 6th Division
in Ceylon, 428
at Colombo, 425
to Greece, 229, 232
in New Guinea, 439
possibility of being diverted to Burma, 428
retreat from Crete, 234
return of from Middle East, 374, 376, 437
to Australia, 418

to Burma, 417
to Ceylon, 438, 439, 450
to where?, 410–11, 412–13, 424
in Western Desert, 208
Australian army (AIF) 7th Division
capture of on Java, 419
on Java, 419
in New Guinea, 427
possibility of being diverted to Burma, 426,
427, 428
possibility of being diverted to Ceylon, 437
return of from Middle East, 374, 376
to Australia, 416, 424, 437, 438
to Burma, 417, 418, 451
to where?, 410–11, 412–13
21st Brigade in convoy east of Colombo, 426
18th Brigade at Bombay, 426
25th Brigade near Colombo, 426
at Tobruk, 275–6
Australian army (AIF) 8th Division, 450
and defence of Malaya and Singapore, xv, 179,
203, 208, 210, 215, 220, 222, 276, 297,
306, 343, 344, 374
in action against Japanese, 383, 387
difficulties of evacuating from Singapore, 403
difficulties of evacuation of, 403
at Johore, 375, 386
loss of, 415, 425
Australian army (AIF) 9th division
in Middle East, 425
and Operation Torch, 440
to remain in Middle East, 432, 439, 440, 450
return of from Middle East, 416, 417, 437
to Australia, 428, 438, 439
possibility of, 374, 415
to where?, 424
at Tobruk, 275–6
Australian chiefs of staff
all British, 94, 369
and command arrangements in south-western
Pacific, 373
on defence of core industrial regions, 434,
435, 436
on defence of Port Moresby, 436
on dispersal of forces to meet invasion, 434
expectations of British and American assistance
in response to threat of Japanese invasion,
369–70
on forces needed to defend Australia, 436–7
and forward defence against Japanese threat, 222
on imminence of invasion, 434, 436
and possible invasion of Australia, 431
and situation in Burma, 416
6th and 7th Divisions to be diverted to
Australia, 416

Australian chiefs of staff *continued*
  9th Divisions to be recalled, 416
  and threat of Japanese invasion, 339
  on troops to meet invasion, 435
Australian Journalists Association
  Curtin and, 6, 27, 284
Australian Labor Party (ALP), 86
  and abdication of Edward VIII, 116
  and advisory council, 184, 196, 197
  after 1916 split, 25
  and bank nationalisation, 112
  centralisation objective, 107
  defence policy, 100, 101, 115, 119, 121, 128
    and air power, 100
    and conscription in World War II, 155, 156,
      167, 184
    and conscription in World War II for home
      defence, 144
    and defence of Britain and defence of
      Australia if Japan entered war, 155
    isolationist, 167, 184
    and sending troops out of Australia, 100,
      155, 156, 160, 167
  election 1931, 47, 49
  election 1934, 25, 60, 104, 105
  election 1940, 193–4
  electoral successes after 1937 election, 163
  expulsion of Lang's NSW branch, 42
  first government of, xix
  foreign policy issues after 1934 election,
    113–15
  fragmentation and unification of after 1934
    election, 110–12
  fragmentation of after 1934 election, 111
  in Great Depression, 48
  leaders of, 63
  and Menzies' return to London, 257
  and national government, 155, 184, 196, 258
  NSW Branch
    divisions in, 164; *see also* Lang
      faction/group: Lang Labor
    'hands off Russia resolution', 164–5
    readmission of Lang group to, 110–12
  special federal conference (June 1940)
    commitment to win war, 184
  splits
    Lyons group (1931), 12–13, 76
    in NSW, 60
    over conscription, xix, 12–13, 24–5, 46,
      63, 101
  and UAP national security legislation, 184–5
  Western Australia
    Curtin and, 27
  see also Curtin Government; Fisher
    Governments; Scullin Government

Australian Labor Party (Non-Communist), 166,
  197
Australian Military Forces, 276
Australian military intelligence
  and likelihood of Japan going to war, 277
Australian navy, 205
  under British Admiralty control, 94, 276, 311,
    332
  and British navy, 121
  and compulsory military service, 96
  Curtin on, 123–4, 213, 214
  and protection of shipping, 214
  return to Australia if Japan entered war, 311
  strength of, 340
Australian Workers' Union (AWU)
  and *Australian Worker*, 49
  and Curtin, 34, 105, 128
  and *Westralian Worker*, 128
Austria
  and Germany, 131, 132
aviation
  proposed referendum on, 112, 113

Backhouse, Admiral Sir Roger
  and sending of British fleet in defence of
    Australia, 139
  and Singapore strategy, 139
Bainbrigge, Cec, 4
Baldwin, Stanley, 69
  and abdication of Edward VIII, 116
  and Germany, 71
Balfour Report (1926), 89
banking system
  bank nationalisation
    ALP and, 112
    Chifley and, 289
    Curtin and, 289
  central banking, 36
  and exchange rate, 41
  federal control of through Commonwealth
    Bank
  Curtin Government, 291, 293–4
  in Great Depression, 35, 48
  regulation of, 293–4
  royal commission on (Napier, 1937), 106,
    273, 288
  in 1890s, 15–16, 35
  see also Commonwealth Bank
Barton, Edmund, 83
Bataan *see under* the Philippines
Beasley, Jack, 32, 111, 395, 420
  and bombing of Darwin, 420
  Churchill on, 444
  and Churchill's suggestion of making Menzies
    Australian minister in Washington, 444

and Curtin, 165–6, 232, 233, 251
and Curtin ministry, 272
  ministry of Supply and Development, 273
  ranking in ministry, 273
and Curtin War Cabinet, 273
and Curtin War Council, 274
and Lang faction/group, xiii, 42, 165, 166,
  184–5, 196, 201
  rejoining ALP, 223, 232
and Menzies threatening war without
  consulting War Council, 253
and Niemeyer proposals, 39
and not forcing no-confidence motion to
  topple Menzies Government, 258
in photo of 7 October 1941, xiii
the press on, 315
and Scullin government, xiii, 44
and Singapore and protection of Australia,
  xvi–xvii
and War Council, 197, 199, 201
Belgium
  German invasion of, 169
Benes, Edvard, 133
Bennett, Major-General Gordon, 387, 450
  and need for air support in Malaya, 344, 383
  and possible invasion of Australia, 430
  on quality of British and Indian troops in
    Malaya, 390
  request to move Australian troops from Middle
    East to Malaya, 345
  on situation in Malaya, 375, 388, 390
  on situation in Singapore, 411
Bismarcks
  Japanese landings on, 398
Blackburn, Maurice, 171
  on ALP defence policy, 100
  and Curtin's election as leader of federal
    parliamentary Labor Party, 461
    (Chapter 6 note 3)
  and Italian invasion of Abyssinia, 115
  readmission to ALP, 127
Blain, Adair, 267
Blamey, General Sir Thomas, xiv, xx, 255
  to be offered command over all Australian
    forces, 450
  consideration of recall of to command home
    forces, 340–1
  and Curtin, 329
  and Greece campaign, 305
  on Japan in October 1941, xvi
  and Japanese attack on Pearl Harbor, 306
  on Militia, 312
  on need for more production and more
    recruits, 276
  and possible campaign in Turkey, 305, 306

recalled for consultations, 297, 305
and relief of Australian troops at Tobruk, 300
on return of 9th Division, 374
to return to Australia, 419, 432
suggestion that 6th, 7th and 8th Divisions
  become a corps, 374
thought Japan unlikely to go to war, 276, 277
  or would attack Soviet Union, 306
wanted 8th Division in Malaya to be sent to
  Middle East, 276, 297, 306
Boote, Henry, 103, 198
  and AWU's *Australian Worker*, 49
Bora Bora, 433
Borneo
  Japanese invasion of, 412
Bougainville
  Australian mandated territory, 389
  Japanese attack on, 389
Bowden, Vivian, 415
  on fixed defences of Singapore, 403
  and imminent fall of Singapore, 350
  and need for air support in Malaya, 344
  on situation in Malaya, 375, 388
Brand, Senator Major-General Charles, 122
Brennan, Francis (Frank), 113, 124, 194
  on early election for Curtin Government, 280
  and secret session of Parliament, 223
Brett, General Howard, 371, 436, 447
  in command of US forces in Australia, 382
  and Wavell, 382
Brigden, J B, 174
'Brisbane Line', 178, 435, 436
Britain (British government)
  and ABC-1 talks
    and Germany First doctrine, 226, 227
  advice to Australia to look to USA in resisting
    Japan, 355
  and air reinforcements for Malaya and Burma,
    355
  Australia pressing for agreement between
    Britain and Soviet Union re mutual
    assistance if either attacked by Japan, 304
  and Australian request British and US navies
    challenge Japanese navy, 438
  and Australia's diplomatic representation, 149
  and Canada, 442, 442–3
  and China in war with Japan, 143, 180
    consequences for of Japanese invasion of
      China, 142
  competition with Australia for US resources
    and attention, 350, 351, 359
  declaration of war on Germany, 153
  and defence of Burma, 402
  and diversion of American war resources to
    Pacific, 355

Britain (British government) *continued*
and European affairs, 122, 131–4
exiting Pacific War, 432
and German invasion of Czechoslovakia, 141
and German peace offer, 157
and Germany First doctrine, 219–20, 226,
      341
and Italian invasion of Abyssinia, 114
and Japan
   drawing a line on southern advance, without
      USA, 244
   on Japan's probable moves after fall of
      Singapore, 438
and likelihood of Japan entering war, 159,
      161
and negotiated peace with Germany, 167
preparations to meet German invasion, 185
pressed by Australia to negotiate with
      Germany over Poland, 152
and promise of battle cruiser and aircraft
      carrier for Indian Ocean, 234
proposal that military commanders at
      Singapore and Hong Kong could
      effectively initiate hostilities without
      civilian political authority, 302
and reinforcing forces in Malaya with
      Australian troops, 345
relations with Australian government after fall
      of Singapore, 438–9
request from for transfer of two AIF divisions
      from Middle East to Netherlands East
      Indies, 374
secret talks with USA (1941), 297
seeking alliance with Soviet Union, 151
and sending British and Indian troops to
      Malaya, 355
and Singapore strategy, 95
situation while Germany at war with
      Soviet Union, 295
war with without USA, 244
Britain and the British Empire
alliance with Japan, 96–7, 97, 98
and Asia, 91
Australia and in 1935, 84–5, 91, 92, 93–4;
      British subjects, 84–5, 87
      everyday goods from, 84
      government and politics: contrast with 1778
         America, 88–9
and Australian foreign policy, 93
and China, 93
colonies protecting sea route to Australia, 91
Curtin and, 90
east of Suez, 95
and India, 91
Lyons and, 115

Menzies and, 75, 90, 115, 149
and USA, 92
see also Balfour Report (1926); Statute of
      Westminster (1931)
British Admiralty
and Australian navy, 94
British Defence Committee
abandonment of Netherlands East Indies. in
      favour of defence of India, Ceylon and
      Australia, 417
abandonment of Singapore in favour of
      stronger stand in Burma, 391, 394
evacuation of Singapore should be considered,
      391
if Singapore evacuated, the reinforcements
      intended for Singapore could be sent to
      Burma, 391
and intention to assemble fleet in Indian
      Ocean, 354–5
and issue of moving Australian troops from
      Middle East to Malaya, 345
British intelligence
and misreading plans for Japanese offensive,
      268–9
British navy, 92
and Australia navy, 121
capital ships to be sent to Indian Ocean, xvii,
      234, 237, 261, 269, 297, 299, 301, 311;
      see also HMS *Prince of Wales*; HMS *Repulse*
at Ceylon as deterrent to Japan, 189, 269, 297
and defence of Australia, 90, 94–5, 97, 98,
      122–3, 124–5, 131, 138, 149, 159–60
existence of sufficient for, 159, 176
fleet required for, 138
no fleet for, 179, 185, 186, 190, 205, 206,
      207, 208, 223, 225
and requirements for war in Europe, 138, 179
substituting US fleet for British at
      Singapore, 181–2, 185
defending the eastern Empire against Japan
      while at war with Germany, 125, 149–50
in Indian Ocean, 438, 439
non-British command of unacceptable, 349
at Singapore as deterrent to Japan, 205, 207–8,
      223, 230, 251, 253, 261, 262, 263, 269,
      277–8; *see also* Singapore strategy
Singapore base, 95, 98, 123
British 18th Division
loss of, 422
reinforcements for Singapore, 391, 392, 400,
      402, 404
Brooke, General Sir Alan
on sending British 18th Division to Singapore,
      404
warning of imminent fall of Singapore, 391

Brooke-Popham, Air Chief Marshal Sir Robert, 222, 235
  and briefing of Curtin, 343
  briefing of Curtin War Council, 298–9
  on Japan in October 1941, xvi, 298–9
  and Japanese air force, 230, 299
  and likelihood of Japanese attack on Soviet Union, 304
  and move into Thailand if Japanese approached, 310
Bruce, Stanley, xiv, 13, 33, 377
  and appeasement, 131, 162
  Australian High Commissioner in London, 69, 71, 274
  and British Cabinet re Czechoslovakia crisis, 142
  and Churchill, xiv, 162, 171, 187, 424
  and Cripps, 365
  and Curtin, 405, 424, 450
    on defence of Ceylon, 437
    first cables to as Prime Minister re post-war rules on international trade, 271
    on London as centre of decision-making in Pacific War, 378
  and defeatism, 171
  and Evatt
    on authorship of Curtin's cables, 379
  on German claim for Polish Corridor, 161
  on German claim to Danzig, 161
  and German non-aggression pact with Soviet Union, 151
  and London-based Pacific War Council, 405
  and Lyons, 33
  and Menzies, 156, 157
  and Munich Agreement, 142, 162
  and Mussolini, 114, 133, 161, 162, 170, 171
  and negotiated peace with Germany, 156, 161, 170–1
  and Page, 146, 274
  pressing British Government to negotiate with Germany over Poland, 152, 153
  Prime Minister, 27
  and reinforcements for Singapore being diverted to Burma, 405
  responses of to looming world slump, 32
  and return of troops from Middle East, 373
  return to Parliament, 69
  and Roosevelt, 170
  and sending of British fleet in defence of Australia, 149
  on Singapore, 98
  and Singapore strategy, 138, 139, 383
    in event of war in Europe, 140
  and US–Japan negotiations, 311
  visit to Australia, 142
  and Winch–Johcu cables, 408

Bruce–Page Government, 13, 27
  and expenditure on navy, 99
  and immigration
    and small farms, 82
    and White Australia, 288
Brunswick (Vic), 16
Buka
  Japanese occupation of, 433
Burma
  air bases under Japanese attack, 346
  British forces fighting in, 448
  British forces retreating, 432
  defence of
    Britain and, 402
    USA and, 402
  evacuation of civilians, 426
  the Hump, 427
  Japanese invasion of, 411, 415, 418, 426, 427, 453
  pathway to India through, 204, 351, 411
  return of Australian troops from Middle East to, 392, 393, 395, 404, 405, 410, 413, 417, 418, 420, 450
  situation March 1942, 426
  as supply line to China (Burma Road), 143, 180, 211, 351, 391, 411, 417, 418, 420, 427
  withdrawal of troops, 426
Burnett, Air Chief Marshall Sir Charles, 332
Burrell, Commander Henry, 219, 227

Caldecote, Lord, 186, 189
Calwell, Arthur
  and Chifley Budget, 293
  and Curtin, 259
  on Curtin, 28–9, 29
    and election of ministry, 272
  on early election for Curtin Government, 280
  and no-confidence motion to topple Menzies Government, 258
  and secret session of Parliament, 223
Cameron, Archie, 157
  leader of Country Party in coalition with Menzies Government, 163–4
  and Menzies, 399–400
  and secret session of Parliament, 224
  and Spender, 399–400
Canada, 442
  and Britain, 442, 442–3
  and British Empire, 362–3
  British in, 90
  declarations of war made independently, 303
  defeat of troops at Hong Kong, 362, 365, 442
  foreign representation, 93
  and Lord Durham's 1839 report, 88

Canada *continued*
  Menzies on, 74
  opposition to an Imperial war cabinet, 443
  and USA, 362
  see also King, Mackenzie
Canberra
  in mid-1930s, 116
Canton Island, 433
capitalism
  Curtin on collapse of, 20, 44
  Curtin on nature of and reform of, 53–4, 107–10
  and Great Depression, 47–8
Carroll, Senator William, 46
Casey, Mae, 440
Casey, Richard (Dick), 84, 105, 106, 158, 182, 242, 282, 363, 393, 422
  on air reinforcements for Malaya, 376
  and air support for Malaya, 355–6
  and American supreme commander in Pacific, 349, 350
  Australian Minister in Washington, 163, 195, 274
  and Bruce, 146
  and Chifley, 146
  and Churchill
    offer of British job, 440–4
  on command arrangements in south-western Pacific, 372, 372–3
  and committing troops to support Britain in fighting Germany, 160
  and Curtin, 450
  and Evatt, 274, 440
  Evatt on, 444
  and Hopkins, 418
  and 'inexcusable betrayal' cable, 401
  and Kurusu, 310
  and Menzies, 146, 440
  and negotiations between USA and Japan, 297
  and Roosevelt Administration, 440
  on Stimson and imminence of Japanese attack southward, 307–8
  and US offer of Australian troops to Burma in exchange for US troops for Australia's defence, 420
  and US view of likelihood of Japanese attack on Soviet Union, 304
  and US–Japan negotiations, 311
  on US–Japan negotiations, 307
Catholicism
  Curtin and, 16
central bank, 36, 84
  see also Commonwealth Bank

Ceylon
  Australian 6th Division and, 428, 438, 439, 450
  British ships at as deterrent to Japan, 189, 269, 297
  defence of, 417, 439
  Japanese threat to, 421, 437
  see also Indian Ocean
Chamberlain, Neville, 171
  and appeasement, 131, 162
  Churchill and policies of, 72
  and German invasion of Czechoslovakia, 141
  and Menzies
    on Hitler, 71, 72
    on Japan, 71–2
  and Munich Agreement, 136
  resignation of, 169
  and sending of British fleet in defence of Australia, 139–40, 149
Charlton, Matthew
  leader of ALP, 63
  and Singapore strategy, 100
Chiang Kai-shek, 143, 305, 309
  and news of Japanese attack on USA, 324
  see also Chinese government
Chidgey, Oliver, 284–5
Chifley, Ben, 32, 111–12, 195
  and bank nationalisation, 289
  and Budget, 287–8, 291, 292–4
  and centralisation, 288
  and Commonwealth Bank, 292
  and conscription in World War I, 288
  and Curtin, 117
    similarities and differences, 288
  and Curtin ministry, 272, 274
    ranking in ministry, 273
    Treasurer, 273, 285
  and Curtin War Cabinet, 273
  and Curtin War Council, 274
  and economic statement prepared by Fenton, Lyons, Anstey, Theodore and Curtin, 41
  education, 288
  and Evatt, 195
  and Lang, 288
  and Lewis, 275
  office near Curtin's, 285
  parliamentary history, 288
  in photo of 7 October 1941, xii
  and post-war planning, 285
  and Royal Commission on Banking, 106, 273, 288
  and Scullin Government, 288
  and White Australia, 288
child endowment *see* Royal Commission on Child Endowment or Family Allowances

China
  Britain and, 180
  and Japan, 93, 96, 99, 131, 143, 180, 210,
    307, 309, 453
    and beginnings of Pacific War, 142, 143
    and resources of, especially oil, 143
    USA and, 209
  Japan and British concessions in, 187
  in 1920s, 28
  in 1930s, 93
  Soviet Union and, 180
  supply line to through Burma, 143, 180, 211,
    351, 391, 402, 411, 417, 418, 420
  USA and, 93, 180, 402
Chinese Communists, 143
Chinese government
  and Singapore situation, 384
  see also Chiang Kai-shek
Christmas Island (Pacific Ocean), 433
Churchill, Winston, xx
  and the Hump, 427
  and ABC-1, 355
  and appeasement, 162
  and Arcadia conference and agreement, 353,
    359, 382, 410
  and Australia, xiv, 452
  and Australian request for fleet at Singapore to
    deter Japanese attack, 207, 263
  and Australian requests for ships to defend
    Singapore and Australia, 206, 207, 208
  and Australian 9th Division and New Zealand
    troops to remain in Middle East, 432
  and Australia's turn to USA, 448
  on Beasley, 444
  and Blamey, xiv
  and bombing of Darwin, 421
  and Bruce, xiv, 162, 171, 187, 443
  and Burma and defence of India, 411
  cable from Curtin pledging government's
    loyalty to British Empire, 274
  cable from Roosevelt to
    'Australia must be held', 449
  cable to from Curtin
    Curtin insisted; Churchill submitted, 424, 437
    ignored, 424
    3000-man British armoured brigade en
      route to the Far East to be sent to
      Australia, 417
    6th and 7th Divisions to be diverted to
      Australia, 416–17
    9th Division to be recalled to Australia,
      416–17
  and Casey
    offer of British job, 440–3
  and Chamberlain's policies, 72
  and Chinese Nationalists, 211
  and Cross, 408
  and Curtin, xiv, 329, 380, 406, 437, 438, 450
    acceptance of Australian Government decision
      on AIF returning to Australia, 424
    appointment of Menzies as Australian
      minister in Washington, 444–5
    Australian Government decision on AIF
      returning to Australia, 422
    British aid if Australia invaded, 433
    British job for Casey, 441–4
    and Casey, 440–1
    competition for US resources, 377–8
    criticisms by re Greece and Crete and lack of
      air support, 382
    direct contact with, 376
    ignores Australian Government decision on
      AIF returning to Australia, 424
    responsibility for sending British 18th
      Division to Singapore, 422
    thoughts of on Japanese threat, 430–1
    tone of cables, 377, 378
    topics of cables, 377–8
  on Curtin Government, 360
  Curtin on, 399
  and Curtin's demand for direct representation
    on war council in Washington, 382, 405
  and Curtin's refusal to allow AIF to be sent to
    Rangoon
    in The Second World War, 427–8
  and Curtin's 'The Task Ahead' article in
    Melbourne Herald, 359–60, 362
  and King George VI, 363–4, 378
    in The Second World War, 360, 362
  and declaration of war on Finland, 302–3
  and defence of Australia, 240
  on defence of Burma and Burma Road, 391
  on defence of Hong Kong, 298
  and defence of India, 415, 417
  and defence of Singapore, 401
  and defence of Singapore and Malaya, 207
  and deployment of capital ships to Indian
    Ocean, 297, 301
  and dominion representative in an Imperial
    war cabinet, 235, 236
  and Evatt, xii
  on Evatt, 444
  and Fadden on diminished risk of war with
    Japan, 260–1
  on fighting ability of Japanese, 365
  and Gallipoli, 229
  and Germany First doctrine, 352, 378
  and Greece campaign, 228, 229, 231, 305
    Australian and New Zealand troops for, 223
  health, 360

Churchill, Winston *continued*
  on holding Singapore, 356
  and imminence of war with Japan, 218
  and 'inexcusable betrayal' cable, 393, 400–1,
    403, 404
  and Japan, 211, 223
    not likely to go to war, 277
  and Japanese occupation of Rabaul, 390
  and Japanese threat to Ceylon, 421, 437
  and King George VI, 363–4
  and likelihood of Japanese attack on Soviet
    Union, 304
  and London as centre of decision-making in
    Pacific War, 378
  and London-based Pacific War Council, 405,
    406
  and Mackenzie King, 442
  and Menzies, xi, xiv, 162, 235, 366, 443
    and assurance of naval support in event of
      war with Japan in exchange for troops
      to Greece, 228–9
    direct contact with, 376–7
  Menzies on, 72–3, 73
  and Menzies' search for seat in House of
    Commons, 260
  and Middle East if Japan invaded Australia,
    240
  and military alliance with USA, 185
  on new command arrangements in
    south-western Pacific, 371–3, 381
  and news of German declaration of war on
    USA, 325
  and news of Japanese attack on USA, 324
  and Operation Torch, 440
  and Page, 274, 424, 443
  and Placentia Bay meeting (with Roosevelt),
    249
    Roosevelt's statement of principles: Atlantic
      Charter, 249–50, 252–3
  political threat to leadership of after military
    reverses, 365–6
  Prime Minister, 169
  priorities after German attack on Soviet
    Union, 239–40
  and promise of battle cruiser and aircraft
    carrier for Ceylon, 189
  and proposal of sending Australian troops from
    Middle East to Malaya, 364
  and proposal that Australian troops remain in
    Middle East in exchange for US troops for
    Australia's defence, 439
  and proposal that military commanders
    at Singapore and Hong Kong could
    effectively initiate hostilities without
    civilian political authority, 302

  on quality of Japanese soldiers, 382
  and reinforcements for Malaya, 364
  and reinforcements for Singapore being
    diverted to Burma, 404, 405
  on release of British, Australian and Indian
    units for deployment to Far East, 385
  and reliance on USA, 350
  and relief of Australian troops at Tobruk,
    300–1
  and return of Australian troops from Middle
    East
    to Burma, 410, 424
    decision, 376
    disposition of, 422
    suggestion of sending Australian troops to
      India or Singapore, 345, 364, 373
  and Roosevelt, 378
    and Churchill's offer of job to Casey, 443–4
    disagreements, 442
    request for more US troops for Australia,
      432
  and Roosevelt's new strategy for Pacific War,
    431–2
  and Singapore strategy, 207, 346
  and situation in Malaya, 390
  and strategy for winning war, 185–6
  and suggestion of evacuation of Singapore, 393
  and supreme commander in Pacific, 349
  and Thailand, 310
  on US troops for Australia, 381
  and USA in event of Japan entering war, 207,
    211
  and war between USA and Japan, 186
  and war situation (October 1941), xiv
  on war situation (January 1942) and his
    responsibility for it, 385
  warning from Curtin of imminent fall of
    Singapore, 350–1
  and Winch–Johcu cables, 376, 379, 408,
    438
    not to be seen by Page or Bruce, 408
  and withdrawal from Singapore, 404
  and writing cables, 378
Churchill Government
  appreciation of Japanese objectives in
    South-east Asia, 189–90
  and avoidance of war with Japan, 188
  and Japan in October 1941, xvii
  on unlikelihood of Japanese invasion of
    Australia or New Zealand, 188–9
  and withdrawal of British forces from China,
    188
Civil Constructional Corps, 347
Clarey, Percy, 292
Cleaver, Horrie, 117

Coles, Arthur, 194
and Curtin Government, 283
and fall of Fadden Government, 265, 266, 267
Collier, Philip, 57
and Curtin, 58
Collings, Senator Joseph
and Curtin ministry, 272
Collins, Commodore John, 402
Colvin, Admiral Sir Ragnar, 332, 334
on defence of Australia by battle fleet at
Singapore, 177
and Germany First doctrine, 227
and imminence of war with Japan, 214, 215
and Singapore strategy, 139
Combined Operational Intelligence Centre,
Victoria Barracks
and Japan, xvi
on Japan's preparations for war, 306, 308
Comintern
instructions to Communist Parties re Soviet
Union's invasion of Finland, 164
and united front against fascism, 113
and German non-aggression pact with
Soviet Union, 151
command arrangements in south-western Pacific,
371–3, 381
Australia excluded from, 372
Australia, New Guinea, Solomons, Fiji and the
New Hebrides excluded from, 372–3
command machinery uniting American,
British and Dutch forces fighting Japan,
337, 338
Committee of Imperial Defence see Imperial
Defence
Commonwealth Aircraft Corporation
and Aircraft Production Commission, 347
Commonwealth Bank, 288, 289
authority of over banking system, 293–4
and central banking, 36
Chifley and, 292
and Curtin Government, 275, 291
federal control of banking system through,
291
Curtin on, 47
and Curtin re preparedness for war, 262
deflationary program of, 36–7
and exchange rate, 83
and privately owned banks, 275
and Scullin Government, 46
and Theodore's economic plan, 39
and war financing, 289–90
see also Gibson, Sir Robert
Commonwealth Court of Conciliation and
Arbitration
and basic wage, 31

Commonwealth Grants Commission
Curtin and Western Australia's submission
to, 57
Commonwealth prime ministers' conference,
67
Commonwealth vis-à-vis states, 50, 57, 107
and proposed referendums on aviation and
marketing, 112–13
Commonwealth/states financial agreement, 83
Communist Party of Australia
and German non-aggression pact with Soviet
Union, 151, 202
conscription in World War I, 23, 101–2
ALP and, 101
Curtin and, 23–4
gaoling of over, 13, 25
referenda on, 23, 24, 27
splits in ALP over, xix, 12–13, 24–5, 46, 63,
101
Constitution, 86
Cooper, Duff, 268, 269, 343, 345
and Menzies, 414
Copland, Douglas, 275
Co-Prosperity Sphere see Greater East Asia
Co-Prosperity Sphere
Corio
by-election, 163
Cottesloe (WA), xi, 5, 27, 48, 50, 53, 240,
387
Curtin home in, 51–2
wife Elsie and, 55
Country Party, xii, 11
and banking, 105–6
and coalition with Menzies Government, 147,
163
election 1934, 59, 104
refusal of coalition with Menzies as UAP
leader, 146
Cox, Harold, 3, 146
on Brooke-Popham, 299, 300
on Canberra, 116
on Curtin, x, 135, 314–15, 318
and AIF returning to Australia, 423
on first day of war, 320
on Menzies, 3
on Page, 146
and sinking of Sydney, 309
on War Cabinet in Melbourne, 333
on Wilson, 265
Craig, Hazel, 2, 271, 285
on Curtin, x
on Curtin War Cabinet, 273
on Forde, 255
on McLaughlin, 425
Craigie, Sir Robert, 217

Cranborne, Viscount, xi, 343, 406, 407
on Cross, 407
on imminent Japanese attack on Thailand, 308
on possible invasion of Australia, 341
and promise of battle cruiser and aircraft
carrier for Singapore, 230
on strategy in Far East
Australian chiefs of staff response to, 369
possibly sending fleet to Singapore, 354–5
sending British and Indian troops to Malaya,
355
Creswick (Vic), 15
Crete
Australian troops in, xiii
Churchill and, 382
retreat of Australian troops from, 234
Cripps, Stafford
Bruce and, 365
Cross, Sir Ronald, 347, 351, 377
on Australian reaction to Pearl Harbor, 406–7
and Curtin, 366, 384, 406, 407, 408
'The Task Ahead' article in Melbourne
Herald, 366, 408
as diplomat, 408–9
Gowrie and, 408–9
on imposing trade and economic sanctions on
Australian, 407
MacArthur and, 408, 409
on maintenance of British prestige in Australia,
407
and Menzies, 406
and Menzies' search for seat in House of
Commons, 260
and position of British High Commissioner in
Australia, 407
Wilkinson and, 408, 409
Curtin, Elsie (née Needham)—Curtin's wife, xi,
3, 28, 398
birthday, 263
gift: Curtin Prime Minister, 267
and caring for her mother, 387
character of, 55
at Cottesloe home, 55
and Curtin, 4, 7, 21–2, 23, 24, 25, 29, 51,
117–18, 126, 135, 240, 387
his drinking, 45, 54
on Curtin, 31–2
as housekeeper, 55
returning to Perth (December 1941), 318,
342
Curtin, Elsie—Curtin's daughter, 14, 28, 32, 51,
52, 55, 398
birth of, 27
and Curtin, 51
his drinking, 45, 54

on Curtin's purported volunteering for military
service, 120–1
Curtin, John—Curtin's father, 15, 78
death of, 135
Curtin, John (Jack)
defence and foreign policy:
and ABC-1 talks, 227, 369
and acceptance of American commander in
Pacific, 350
on advantage to Germany of Japan entering
war, 217
and air power, 3, 100, 122, 129–30
and air support for Malaya, 355
and appeasement, 134
and assertion of independence in foreign
policy, 302
Australia as south-west Pacific base against
Japan, 415, 450
and 'Australia looks to America' statement, 357
and 'Australia shall not go' statement, 357, 362
and Blamey
to return to Australia, 432
and 'bombing of Darwin, 421
and British assessment of Japanese forces, 312
British officers and officials not briefing him
on war situation, 343
and British position in Malaya and Singapore,
203
and British position in Middle east, 237
broadcast to the nation after fall of Rabaul
Australia would never surrender, 398, 451
broadcast to the nation at beginning of war,
336–7
and Bruce, 378, 405, 424, 450
cable from on defence of Ceylon, 437
cable to Churchill, Wavell and Page
all troops to be returned to Australia, 418, 419
3000-man British armoured brigade en
route to the Far East to be sent to
Australia, 417
6th and 7th Divisions to be diverted to
Australia, 416–17, 419
9th Division to be recalled to Australia,
416–17
and capital ships in Indian Ocean, 312
and Casey, 450
and China, 309–10
and Churchill, 237, 329, 380, 405, 406, 424,
437, 438, 450
agreement to 9th Division remaining in
Middle East, 440, 450
appointment of Menzies as Australian
minister in Washington, 444
and Australian Government decision on AIF
returning to Australia, 422

cable to re government's loyalty to British Empire, 274
cables to: authorship and style, 377–9
cables to and from: topics, 377–8
and Casey, 440–3
competition for US resources, 377–8
demand for direct representation on war council in Washington, 382, 405, 408
disagreements, 441–2
and job for Casey, 441
and Middle East, 238
offer of British aid if Australia invaded, 433
re reinforcement of Malaya, 345
and responsibility for sending British 18th Division to Singapore, 422
thoughts on Japanese threat, 430–1
Winch–Johcu cables, 376, 379, 408, 438
on Churchill, 399
and command arrangements in south-western Pacific and defence of Australia, 372–3
and Commonwealth Bank, 262
and consultations with Japan, 247
and control of profits, prices and wages, 412
critical of British government, 408
and Cross, 406
and dealing directly with USA, 341, 350
and decision to leave troops in Middle east, 335
and declaration of war against Finland, 303
and declaration of war on Germany, 154–5
and declaration of war on Japan, 154
and defence planning, 150
and defence policy, 101, 115, 119, 127–8, 132, 144
 5 November 1936 speech, 119–20, 121, 122–4, 140
 experience in, 120
 forward defence, 203, 217, 221, 222, 238, 261–2, 340
 and self-reliance, 144
 and views of Wynter, Piesse and Lavarack on, 101
and defence spending, 134, 144, 150
direct contact with Churchill and Roosevelt, 376, 379
and dominion representative in Imperial War Cabinet, 362, 408
and establishment of a Pacific War Council and an Imperial War Cabinet, 397
and evacuation of Singapore, 402
and Evatt
 cable outlining military chiefs' strategy for defence of Australia, 436–7
on fall of Konoe Government, 296

on fall of Singapore, 416
on fighting ability of Japanese, 365
on first day of war, 320
and 'general mobilization for a total war effort', 287
and Germany, 134
and Germany first doctrine, 353, 354
going public with truth about war situation, 384
 reasons for, 384
and Hitler and Japan's move into Indo-China, 246–7
and idea of agreement with Japan, 239
on imminent loss of Singapore, 356, 375
and independent defence of Australia, 121
and 'inexcusable betrayal' cable to Churchill, 403–4
and Japan
 and German invasion of Soviet Union, 238
 imminence of war with, 212, 213, 217, 218, 220, 277
 likely strategy of attack, 218–19
 naval defence against, 253
 southern advance, 200
and joint direction of Pacific War with USA, 362, 374
and Kawai, 239, 246, 307
and Mackenzie King, 442
 and Britain's place in post-war world, 443
knowledge of imminence of war with Japan, 306, 307, 308
lack of information
 about Britain and USA re Japan, 200
 about British situation, 206
and London-based Pacific War Council, 406
and MacArthur, 328–9
 supreme Allied commander, 447, 449
and 'Malay Barrier', 436
and Menzies' 'if Britain is at war, Australia is at war' policy, 150
military experience of, 120
and mobilisation of the people for war effort, 358
 total mobilisation, 412
and naval forces, 123–4, 213, 214, 219
and need for a 'supreme authority to coordinate Allies', 349
and 'new war', 336, 337, 357, 450
and Operation Torch, 440
Pacific War and enlargement of, 321–2
and a Pacific war council in Washington, 399, 406
and pacifism, 120

Curtin, John (Jack) *continued*
  and Page, 378, 415–16, 424, 437–8, 450
    cable from on moving 7th Division to
      reinforce Ceylon, temporarily, 437
    Page's refusal to pass on to British Government
      Australian Government decision on AIF
      returning to Australia, 421–2
  and possible invasion of Australia, 337, 338,
    354, 356, 368, 384, 415, 422, 431, 452
  and possible Japanese attack on Netherlands
    East Indies, 238
  and possible Japanese attack on Soviet Union,
    248–9
  pressing for agreement between Britain and
    Soviet Union re mutual assistance if either
    attacked by Japan, 304
  and proposal to defend only core industrial
    regions, 435, 435–6
  and quality of Japanese soldiers, 383
  reactions of on news of Japanese fleet nearing
    Malaya, 318–19
  reactions of on news of Pearl Harbor, 319
  and rebalance of Australian forces between
    Middle East and Pacific, 215, 217
  and recognition that key decisions would be
    made in Washington, not London, 261
  rejection of suggestion that reinforcements
    intended for Malaya be sent to Burma, 405
  rejection of suggestion that troops withdrawn
    from Middle East be sent to Burma, 410,
    427, 428, 450
  and reliance on USA, 350
  and relief of Australian troops at Tobruk, 301
  reply to Menzies' question of Australian forces
    to be concentrated in northern Australia
    or Burma, 414
  request for Britain to send capital ships to
    Singapore, 205, 206, 207–8, 261, 262
  response to Dunkirk, 170
  response to German invasion of Norway, 167
  and retention of 8th Division in Malaya, 306
  and return of troops from Middle East, 231–2,
    248, 249, 274, 277, 305, 341, 373, 374,
    450
    to Australia, 415–16, 420, 422, 423, 425
    benefits of, 374
    not to India, 410
    reasons for sending troops to Middle East,
      374–5
    whole of AIF to be concentrated in Pacific
      theatre, 375
  and Roosevelt, 329, 424, 437
    appointment of supreme Allied commander,
      447
    possible invasion of Australia, 422

  and sending of British fleet in defence of
    Australia, 138, 277–8
  and sending of troops overseas/to Europe, 113,
    127, 135, 151
  and Shedden, 271, 285, 329, 330, 333
  and Singapore and protection of Australia,
    xvi–xvii
  and Singapore strategy, 122, 124–5, 332, 346
    reiteration of, 383
  and sinking of *Sydney*, 309
  and strikes, 214, 232, 386, 394, 397, 399
    threat of using navy to break strike on
      wharves, 386
  and subordination of Pacific war to war in
    Europe, 357, 359
  'The Task Ahead' article in Melbourne *Herald*
    (27 December 1941), 356–8, 364–5,
    366, 408
    Australian reaction to, 360–2, 364
    authorship of, 358–9
    British reaction to, 364, 365
    Churchill and, 359–60, 362
    Cross and, 366
  and test mobilisation of Australian defences,
    219, 220
  and turn to USA, 364, 432, 448, 450
  and US Germany First doctrine, 219–20, 221,
    227
  and US military strength, 247
  and War Cabinet meetings missed, 400
  and War Council, 197, 212
    experience on, 280
  as war leader, 328–9
    men he depended on, 329
    preparation for, 325
  and war planning
    consultations with USA, 298
  and war production, 311
  and war with Japan without USA, 246, 248
  warning to Roosevelt and Churchill of
    imminent fall of Singapore, 350–1
  on Washington as centre of decision-making in
    Pacific War, 377
  and Wavell, 449
economics:
  alternative economic plan, 41
    and Keynes, 41
  and banking system, 36, 38, 47, 105–6
    bank nationalisation, 289
    Commonwealth Bank, 47, 289, 290
  on Budget, 294
  and budgetary equilibrium, 40, 47, 75
  and Central Reserve Bank Bill, 36
  and economic direction of Fenton and Lyons,
    41

and economic statement prepared by Fenton, Lyons, Anstey, Theodore and Curtin, 41
and exchange rate, 41, 47
and function of the state, 108
and Gibson, 76
and Great Depression, 47–8
and loan repayment, 40
and Lyons Government trade diversion policy, 115
and monetary policy, 40, 43, 76
and money and resources, 290
and Niemeyer plan, 40
and old age pension, 292
and Premiers' Plan, 42–3, 61, 62, 76, 110, 111
and Reading, 290
and Shann, 27, 31, 41, 56
and social services, 107–9
and state governments v. federal government, 47
and tariffs, 50
and war financing, 290
employment:
and Australian Journalists Association, 27, 284
and Boote re employment, 49
and preparation of Western Australia's submission to Commonwealth Grants Commission, 57
sports writer for *Westralian Worker*, 51
as journalist, 56, 359
editor of the *Westralian Worker*, 4, 6, 24, 25, 26, 27, 28, 44, 53, 58, 128, 280
on Metropolitan Milk Board, 57
publicity officer for the Perth Trades Hall Council, 51
secretary of Timber Workers' Union, 6, 20, 21
at Titan Manufacturing Company, 20, 30
unemployed, 50
personal:
ability as speaker and writer, 21, 28, 29, 104, 121
accommodation away from Perth, 387
accommodation in Canberra, 32, 116–17
activities in Cottesloe and Perth, 53, 56
and air travel, xi, 1–3, 342
and alcohol, x, 21, 22, 27, 35, 45, 54, 117
and clinic at Lara, 22, 26
and congeniality, 284
assets in 1941, 264
behaviour of after becoming Prime Minister, 314
birth of, 15
break back in Perth (January 1942), 386–8, 396, 397–9
return, 394, 396, 399, 400
and Britain and the British, 90
and cast in left eye, 54
and Catholicism, 16, 90

congenial relationship with Canberra political reporters, 283–4
and daughter Elsie, 51
death of, 5
and depression, 4, 14, 31, 40, 280, 284
dress and clothing, 6–7, 53, 54
and driving, 4
education, 18
economics, 27, 31
family life in Cottesloe after loss of seat, 51, 56
feelings while troops crossing Indian Ocean, 446–7
fifty-seventh birthday, 380
and Gowrie, xi
health, x, 14, 31, 54, 135, 233, 240, 259, 263, 270, 386, 387, 419, 420
and his children after election to Parliament, 118
and his mother, 135
home in Cottesloe, 51–2
humility of, 56
immediate post-school life, 16
and Irish nationalism, 90
journalist's mind, 121
and kelpie Kip, 51, 52, 53, 240
lonely, 387
loner, 283, 284
and McLaughlin, 426
manner with his staff, 285
mannerisms, 29
marriage, 14, 24, 26, 27
anniversary, 126, 135
move to Western Australia, 26, 27
and music, 53
personal life as Leader of the Opposition, 116–18
personality of, 7, 14
press opinion of
changes in after becoming Prime Minister, 314–15
reading, 8, 18, 21, 56, 90
and Reid, 53
and religion, 54
and Salvation Army, 16
and sea travel, 3–4
and smoking, 6, 14, 35, 54, 135
sociability of in Perth, 55–6
and Southwell, 116–17
and Tracey, 5
and train travel, xi, 5–6, 8
and White Australia, 30, 106
and wife Elsie, 4, 7, 21–2, 24, 29, 51, 117–18, 240, 387
letters, telegrammes to, 21–2, 23, 25, 26, 40, 126, 135, 221, 263–4, 353, 379–80

Curtin, John (Jack) *continued*
politics—labour movement:
and Australian Workers' Union, 34
and AWU, 34, 105, 128
and capitalism, 20, 44, 56
  reform of, 30, 53–4, 107–10
and conscription in World War I, 23–4, 27,
  47, 277
  gaoling of over, 13, 25, 277
and education, 18, 20
and International Labour Organization,
  Geneva, 4
and Mann, 17–18, 19, 29, 44, 56, 90, 105
and Adela Pankhurst, 26
and red revolution, 16–17, 20, 21
and socialist politics and economics, 19, 20,
  29–30, 30, 31, 90
  language of, 110
  move from revolution to reform, 53–4
and Stout, 22, 45
and Tillet, 17, 29, 63, 90
and Timber Workers' Union, 6, 20, 21, 280
and VSP, 17, 19, 20, 22, 26, 31
politics—parliamentary:
and accusation he did not want to win
  government, 200, 202
and ALP centralisation objective, 107
and ALP in Great Depression, 48
and ALP in WA, 27
and ALP machine, 105, 113
and Anstey, 19, 21, 22, 28, 30, 40, 44, 90,
  105, 106
  encouragement of Curtin to stand for his
  seat of Bourke, 57–8, 106
and expulsion of Lang's NSW branch from
  ALP, 42, 110
and readmission of Lang's NSW branch to
  ALP, 111
and appointment of Duke of Gloucester as
  Governor-General, 57
and authority of caucus, 293
as backbencher, 34, 47
and Beasley, xii, 165–6, 232, 233
and Cabinet responsibility, and speaking to the
  press, 293
and Calwell, 259
and campaign for WA secession from
  Federation, 51, 57
as a chairman, 283
and Chifley, 117, 285
  similarities and differences, 288
and Collier, 58
  election to caucus executive, 60
  electoral history, 103
and Evatt, xii, 197–8, 233
and Fadden, 260, 424, 450

and Fairfax, 148
and fall of Scullin Government, 44–5
and federal seat of Balaclava, 30
and federal seat of Bourke, 57–8, 106
and federal seat of Fremantle, 32, 33, 34, 45,
  58, 59
  in 1940 election, 192–3
  loss of seat (1931), xiii, 13, 19, 47, 49
and federal seat of Perth, 31
and Forde, 63, 255
and fragmentation and unification of ALP
  after 1934 election, 110–12
and Green, 12, 45, 61
and Gwydir by-election, 126, 127
and Holloway, 61, 62, 105
and Hughes, 424
and Italian invasion of Abyssinia, 114–15
and journalists, 129, 284
and Lang, 126, 127, 150, 165
and Lang group, 34, 62, 232
leader of federal parliamentary Labor Party, xii,
  62–4, 75, 77, 78, 461 (Chapter 6 note 3)
  arguments against becoming, 61
  possibility of becoming, 49, 58, 60–2
  press coverage of, 63
  qualities and background for, 103, 105
and McCullum, 58
and Menzies, 75, 77, 148–9, 167–8, 259, 266,
  424, 450
  contrast, 105
  election 1940, 193, 195
  foreign policy, 134
  negotiation with in 1940 parliament, 200–1
  and relationship to Britain, 84
  return to London, 250–1, 254–5, 255, 256
  willingness to let him remain Prime Minister
  till 1943 election, 256
Menzies on, 444–5
and Murdoch, 148
and national government/all-party
  government, 148, 196, 233, 257, 258,
  313–14
and not forcing no-confidence motion to
  topple Menzies Government, 258, 280–1
and NSW Branch 'hands off Russia resolution',
  165
and parliamentary road to socialism, 20, 30
in photo of 7 October 1941, ix–x, xx
policy of after 1940 election re government, 197
policy of in 1940 election, 192, 195
Prime Minister, ix, x
  and Defence portfolio, 271, 273
and rejection of Fadden Budget, 264
respect for, 14
and Rodgers, 129, 285

and role of Commonwealth vis-à-vis states, 50, 57, 107, 112–13
and Royal Commission on Child Endowment or Family Allowances, 30–1, 54
and Scullin, 285
and Scullin Government, xii, 12, 38
and Spender, 424
staff and accommodation in Parliament House
   as Leader of the Opposition, 103–4
   as Prime Minister, 270–1, 284–5
and states rights, 288
strategy in government, 313
and Swan by-election, 202–3
and Theodore, 34–5, 37–8, 42, 43, 49–50
and Ward, xiii, 201, 224, 232, 240
winning back of seat (Fremantle, 1935), 14
Curtin, John—Curtin's son, 14, 28, 32, 51, 52, 53, 118, 398
   birth of, 27
Curtin, Kate—Curtin's mother, 78
   death of, 135
Curtin Government, x
   and Australian forces in Greece and Crete, xiii–xiv
   and Australian forces in Middle East, xv
      reinforcement of, 306
   beginning of, 267
   and British and US navies challenging Japanese navy, 438
   as British and white, xix–xx
   Budget, 275, 279, 288; see also under Chifley, Ben
      Cabinet and, 291–2
      caucus and, 293
      and Fadden Budget, 291
      Senate and, 280, 291
   Churchill on, 360
   and command arrangements in south-western Pacific, 371, 372
   commitment to war with Japan without USA, 304
   and committing Soviet Union to war with Japan, 304
   and Commonwealth Bank, 275
      and trading banks, 293–4
   and declaration of war against Finland, 302
   diplomatic appointments of previous government to stand, 274
   and extermination of Jews by Hitler regime, xv
   and Financial and Economic Committee, 275
   and income tax, 275
   and Japan, xvi, xvii, xviii
   Menzies on, 444–5
   ministry, x–xi
      autonomy of ministers, 279, 283
      election of, 271–3

and news of Japanese attack on USA, 324
not in agreement with diversion of Australian troops from Middle East to Burma, 421
and prosecution of the war, xiv
reactions of on news of Japanese fleet nearing Malaya, 318
relations with British government after fall of Singapore, 438–9
and responsibility for fall of Singapore, 425
and responsibility for loss of Burma, 427
and responsibility for loss of 8th Division, 425
revenue gap, 291–2
and Roosevelt, 424
and Senate, 280, 282
7 October 1941 photo, ix, xviii–xix
and Singapore and protection of Australia, xvi–xvii
situation of in House of Representatives, 282–3
survival of after first two months, 313–16
War Cabinet, 273
War Council, 274
Curtin War Cabinet
   and appointment of MacArthur as supreme Allied commander, 447
   and attack on Rabaul, 390
      blamed British Government, 390
      demand for reinforcement of Singapore, 390
   cable to Churchill
      Britain's failure to prepare against Japanese attack, 393
      evacuation of Singapore 'an inexcusable betrayal', 393, 395
      evacuation of Singapore and reinforcements for Singapore being diverted to Burma, 393
      Japanese on point of capturing Rabaul and attacking Port Moresby, 393
      rejection of suggestion that reinforcements intended for Malaya be sent to Burma, 393, 395
   and Churchill's offer of job to Casey, 441
   and commencement of hostilities against Japan, 319
   and declaration of war on Japan, 334
   discussion of Chinese and Eurasian refugees, 383
   endorsement of 'inexcusable betrayal' cable, 395
   on evacuation of women and children from Malaya, 383
   and landing of troops on Java, 419
   meetings missed by Curtin, 400
   Melbourne offices, 333–4
   and refusal to send of AIF to Burma, 422

Curtin War Cabinet *continued*
  rejection of suggestion that reinforcements
      intended for Malaya be sent to Burma, 405
  rejection of suggestion that troops withdrawn
      from Middle East be sent to Burma, 410
  and return of AIF to Australia, 422, 425
  and return of Blamey, 419
  and total mobilisation, 412
  and troops not to go to Burma but return to
      Australia, 419–20
  and War Council, 341
  weaknesses of in Curtin's absence, 395–6
Curtin War Council
  Beasley and, 274
  briefing of by Brooke-Popham, 298–9
  Chifley and, 274
  Darwin and Port Moresby to be defended, 435
  Evatt and, 274
  meeting at outbreak of Pacific War, 334–5
  Opposition members on
      and proposal to defend only core industrial
          regions, 435
      supporting sending Australian troops from
          Middle East to Burma, 420
  return of troops from Middle East
      acceptance of British request of sending
          Australian troops from Middle East to
          Netherlands East Indies, 374
      affirmation of decision to return AIF to
          Australia, 421
      Blamey to accompany troops, 374
      on possible transfer an AIF division from
          Middle East to the Far East, 373, 375
      rejection of Churchill's suggestion of sending
          Australian troops from Middle East to
          India, 373, 394, 410
      submission of 19 January 1942, 374–5
  and War Cabinet, 341
Czechoslovakia
  crisis over (1938), 131–2, 133
  Lyons, Bruce and Menzies and, 142
  Germany and, 136
  invasion of, 141

Danzig, 132
  Bruce on German claim to, 161
  Menzies on German claim to, 152, 161
Darwin
  bombing of, 420–1, 429
  defence of, 435
Davis, Wing Commander Reginald, 317
Dawson, Peter, xv
Deakin, Alfred
  and Defence Bill, 96
  on Japan, 96

Deakin Government
  and Japan, 97
  and old age and invalid pensions, 109
debt *see* government debt owed to British lenders
declaration of war
  Evatt: to be made independently, 303
  on Japan, 334
  by Japan on USA and 'British Empire', 334
  made independently, 334
  Menzies: Britain at war, so Australia at war,
      153, 154, 303
  role of King in declarations of war by
      Australia, 303
Dedman, John
  and Curtin ministry, 272
      Minister for the War Organisation of
          Industry, 273
  and Curtin War Cabinet, 273
  and Production Executive, 287
  and reinforcement of forces in Middle East, 306
defence policy, 94–5, 98, 100–1
  changes in by 1940, 187
  Curtin *see under* Curtin, John (Jack)
  forward defence, 225, 340, 436; *see also under*
      Curtin, John (Jack)
  or 'outer screen', 340
  Labor *see under* Australian Labor Party (ALP)
  Labor and anti-Labor, 101, 115, 119, 121, 132
  Labor and Army, 100, 101, 121, 122, 130
  Lyons, 115, 127
  see also Singapore strategy
Denmark
  German invasion of, 166
Depression of 1890s, 15, 16, 79
Dickover, Erle R
  and Menzies on Curtin and his government,
      444–5
Dinan, James, 202, 203
Director-General of Aircraft Production, 347
Dixon, Owen, 66, 444
Dobbie, Major-General W G
  on difficulties of Japanese attack on Malaya, 300
Dollfuss, Engelbert, 114
Dominions, 89–90
  status of in British Empire, 89
  see also Balfour Report (1926); Statute of
      Westminster (1931)
Dover Castle, 68
Drakeford, Arthur, 318
  and Curtin ministry
      Air Minister, 273
  and Curtin War Cabinet, 273
  and Curtin's election as leader of federal
      parliamentary Labor Party, 461
      (Chapter 6 note 3)

Duke and Duchess of York, 70
see also George VI, King
Duke of Gloucester
appointed Governor-General, 57
Duncan, J S, 139, 140
Dunkirk, 169, 403, 416
Dutch government
and Singapore situation, 384
Dutch Timor *see* Koepang, Dutch Timor

Eden, Anthony, 132
and commitment of Australian troops to
Greece, 229
and Japanese neutrality, 159
Edward VIII, King, 116
Eggleston, Sir Frederic, 309–10, 430
and US–Japan negotiations, 311
Eisenhower, Dwight
on Australia as south-west Pacific base, 381–2,
415
election 1917, 30
election 1928, 32, 47
election 1929, 32, 36
election 1931, xiii, 44, 45, 46, 47, 49, 265
election 1934, 59, 60, 104, 105, 110, 130
election 1937, 4, 6, 120, 127, 130, 163
election 1940, 120, 147, 191, 192, 193–4,
257–8, 266
election 1943, 1, 120, 282
election (NSW) 1930, 39
Elizabeth II, Queen, 70
Empire Air Training Scheme, 262, 332
Empire Defence Strategy, 449
Engineers' Case (High Court)
and federal–state relations, 66
European affairs
pre-war, 114, 122, 131–4
European–Atlantic theatre
under joint US–British command, 371
Evatt, Dr H V (Bert), xx, 194, 195, 196, 197,
285, 393, 395, 404, 407, 420, 430
and air travel, 3
and American supreme commander in Pacific,
349
and assertion of independence in foreign
policy, 302
and Bruce
on authorship of Curtin's cables, 379
cable from Curtin outlining military chiefs'
strategy for defence of Australia, 436–7
passed on to Roosevelt by, 437
and Casey, 274, 440
on Casey, 444
and China, 309, 310
Churchill on, 444

and Churchill's suggestion of making
Menzies Australian minister in
Washington, 444
and Curtin, xii, 197–8, 233
on compromise with Menzies, 201
on Curtin, 194–5, 198, 314
and Curtin ministry, 272
Attorney-General and Minister for External
Affairs, 273
ranking in ministry, 273
and Curtin War Cabinet, 273
and Curtin War Council, 274
and declaration of war on Finland, 303
and declaration of war on Japan, 334
and declarations of war to be made
independently, 303
and diplomatic representation in Netherlands
East Indies and Soviet Union, 303
on evacuation of Singapore, 393
and grounds for war with Japan, 248
and imminent fall of Singapore, 350
and Indo-China, 309
on Japanese invasion of Thailand and war with
Japan, 248, 252
and London told Singapore not to be
evacuated, 395
on Menzies, 444
and Menzies Government continuing for
duration of war, 255–6
Menzies on, 445
and Menzies' return to London, 255, 256
and Menzies threatening war without
consulting War Council, 253
and motion to reject Fadden Budget, 264
and national government, 195–6, 197, 236,
258
and news of Japanese attack on USA, 324
and no-confidence motion to topple Menzies
Government, 258
and a Pacific war council in Washington, 399
in photo of 7 October 1941, xii
the press on, 315
pressing for agreement between Britain and
Soviet Union re mutual assistance if either
attacked by Japan, 304
and proposal that military commanders
at Singapore and Hong Kong could
effectively initiate hostilities without
civilian political authority, 302
reporting on Roosevelt
US troops being sent to Australia without
conditions, 439–40
and Singapore and protection of Australia,
xvi–xvii
and style of Curtin's cables, 379

Evatt, Dr H V (Bert) *continued*
  and US–Japan negotiations, 311
  and War Council, 197, 248
  and Wren, 314
  exchange rate, 41, 47, 83

Fadden, Artie
  and 1940 Budget, 200, 275
  and Australian forces in Tobruk, xiv
  and Churchill's decision on deployment of
    capital ships to Indian Ocean, 297
  and Curtin, 260, 450
  on Curtin, x, 425
  and Curtin War Council, 420
  and defence of Singapore, 215
  and Fairfax, 280
  and forward defence, 225
  and Germany First doctrine, 224, 352–3
  and Greece campaign, 228
  and grounds on which USA would declare war
    on Japan, 224
  and imminence of war with Japan, 217, 218
  and income tax, 290–1
  Leader of the Opposition, 281, 282
  and Menzies, 147, 235
  and Page, 147
  Prime Minister, x, 259, 265, 266
  and recognition that key decisions would be
    made in Washington, not London, 261
  and reinforcements for Singapore being
    diverted to Burma, 405
  and relief of Australian troops at Tobruk,
    300
  and request for Britain to send ships to
    Singapore, 261, 263
  and request that Menzies go to London,
    262
  and secret session of Parliament, 223, 224,
    228–9
  and test mobilisation of Australian defences,
    219, 220
  and voluntary cooperation from the trading
    banks, 291, 293
  and War Council, 212, 216, 224–5
  and war financing, 290
Fadden Government, x
  1941 Budget, 263, 264–5, 266–7
  end of, 267
Fairbairn, Jim, 105
  death of in air crash near Canberra, 191
Fairfax, Warwick
  and Curtin, 148
  and Fadden, 280
  and Menzies, 148, 280
Federation, 86

Commonwealth powers after, 16, 82–4
  evolution of, 83
  see also under Western Australia
female workers
  in wartime, 310, 347
Fenton, James
  Curtin and economic direction of, 41
  deficit reduction plan, 39
  and economic statement prepared by Fenton,
    Lyons, Anstey, Theodore and Curtin, 41
  and loan repayment, 40
  and Melbourne Agreement, 38
  and reinstatement of Theodore as Treasurer, 42
Fiji, 433
  Australia responsible for, 372
  Japanese invasion of scheduled, 453
Financial and Economic Committee, 275
financing of war, 289–90, 291
  Commonwealth Bank and, 289–90
  war spending, 289, 290
Finland
  declaration of war on, 302–3, 319, 334
  war with Soviet Union, 164, 302
Fisher, Andrew, 13
  as ALP leader and Prime Minister, 63
Fisher Governments, 13
  and compulsory military service for army and
    navy, 96, 97
  and maternity allowances and workers'
    compensation, 109
Fitchett, Ian
  on situation in Malaya, 388
Forde, Frank, 116, 318, 390, 398
  attack on Rabaul first attack on Australian
    territory, 394
  Craig on, 255
  and Curtin, 63, 255
  and Curtin War Council, 274, 420
  and defence of Townsville, 434, 435
  deputy leader, 272
  on Menzies' London visit, 208–9
  and Menzies' return to London, 254
  and Menzies threatening war without
    consulting War Council, 253
  and party leadership, 61, 62, 107
  in photo of 7 October 1941, xi–xii
  and possible invasion of Australia, 399
  and Premiers' Plan, 61, 62
  ranking in ministry, 273
  and Scullin, 62
  and War Council, 197
France
  German conquest of, 171, 177
    and Indo-China and Pacific possessions,
      172, 177

German invasion of, 166
and German peace offer, 157
and Italian invasion of Abyssinia, 114
possessions in South Pacific and Asia, 91, 92
seeking alliance with Soviet Union, 151
see also Vichy France
Fraser, Peter, 443
and declaration of war on Germany, 154
and dominion representatives in an Imperial
war cabinet, 235–6
'free trade' and 'protection'
meaning of in Britain and Australia, 86
French Indo-China
airfields, 172, 241, 242, 244
Japan and, 181
see also Vietnam
Friedman, Milton, 41

Gallipoli, 88
Churchill and, 229
Game, Sir Philip, 110
Gander, Joe, 166
George V, King
Silver Jubilee of, 65–70
George VI, King, 70
and Chamberlain's wing of Conservative Party,
364
and Churchill, 363–4, 378
German New Guinea, 97
Germany
advantage to of Japan entering war, 217
and Austria, 131, 132
conquest of France, 171, 177
and Czechoslovakia, 131–2, 133, 136
invasion of, 141
declaration of war on USA, 325
and division of Poland with Soviet Union,
153, 164
and economic and political consequences of
Great Depression, 64
Hitler in power in, 71
invasion of Belgium, 169
invasion of Denmark, 166
invasion of Greece, 229
invasion of Holland, 169
invasion of Norway, 166
invasion of Poland, 153
invasion of Soviet Union, xv, 238, 267, 268,
412
racial element of, 323
and Japan's southern advance, 247
and League of Nations, 100
non-aggression pact with Soviet Union, 151,
202
and Poland, 141

politics in 1920s, 28
preparations for invasion of Britain, 185
rearmament of, 71
re-emergence of, 122
rise of fascism in, 28
threat of in 1935, 92
and Treaty of Versailles, 71
tripartite pact with Japan and Italy, 181, 186,
452
war with Soviet Union, 294–5
and war with USA if Japan attacked USA,
308
Germany First doctrine, 219–20, 221, 224, 226,
227, 341, 352–3, 353, 377–8, 432
logic of, 353–4
Gibson, Sir Robert, 105
and Curtin, 76
economic policy of, 36, 37, 38
and Menzies, 76
and Pearce, 46
and Scullin Government, 46
Gollan, Ross
on Chifley, 288, 293
on Curtin, 193, 315, 315–16, 325
on Curtin Government, 280, 315
and Budget, 292
on Fadden, 280, 315
on imminence of war with Japan, 315
on Menzies, 280
government debt owed to British lenders, 35,
102
repayment of, 36
governors-general
first Australian-born, 87; *see also* Isaacs,
Sir Isaac
role of, 89
Gowrie, Lord, xi, 146
and all-party government, 233
and Cross, 408–9
and Curtin, xi, 270
invitation to form government, 267
and declaration of war on Japan, 334
and Fadden, 259
and Menzies
and search for seat in House of Commons,
260
in photo of 7 October 1941, ix
and sinking of *Sydney*, 309
Grants Commission, 57
Gray, Syd, 396
Great Depression, xii, xix, 11, 28, 32, 33–4,
35–6, 47–8, 83
economic and political consequences of, 64
Great War *see* World War I
Great Western Express, 1, 7, 8

Greater East Asia Co-Prosperity Sphere
  Australia and, 416
  Australia and New Zealand and, 452
Greece
  British and French guarantee to, 141
Greece campaign
  Australian troops and, xiii, 223, 228, 234,
    305, 345
  Churchill and, 228, 382
  military advisers and, 229
Green, Albert (Texas), 12, 14, 446
  and Curtin, 12, 45, 61
  and Lyons, 46
  and Scullin Government, 12
Grew, Joseph, 320
Griffith
  by-election, 163
Gullett, Sir Henry, 105, 156
  death of in air crash near Canberra, 191, 195
  and defence policy
    Menzies' 'if Britain is at war, Australia is at
      war' policy, 150
    trip to Britain for Silver Jubilee of King
      George V, 67
Gwydir, 126–7
  by-election, 126, 127, 163

Halifax, Lord, 133, 162, 170, 226, 228
  and grounds on which USA would declare war
    on Japan, 224
Hankey, Sir Maurice, 73, 295
  on Bruce, 152–3
Harvester judgement
  and minimum wage, 109
Hasluck, Paul
  on Curtin, in Menzies' absence in London,
    216
  on internal conflicts in Menzies Government,
    163
Hawaii, 91
  see also Pearl Harbor
Heffron, R J, 164
Henderson, Sir Nevile, 133
Hilton, John
  and Westralian Worker, 24
Hindenburg, Paul von, 71
Hiranuma Kiichirō, 151
Hirohito, Emperor, 267, 310
  and approval for war with United States,
    Britain and the Netherlands, 310
Hitler, Adolf
  Chamberlain on, 71, 72
  and extermination of Jews, xv
  on German offensive against Soviet Union, xv
  Malcolm MacDonald on, 136–7

Menzies on, 72
  and Munich Agreement, 136
  and Munich talks, 134
  and news of Japanese attack on USA, 325
  in power in Germany, 71
  and treaty of Versailles, 71
  Vansittart on, 73
HMAS Parramatta, 309
HMAS Sydney, 309, 320
  sinking of, xi
HMS Indomitable, 301
HMS Prince of Wales, xviii, 230, 301, 335, 338,
    342, 346, 370, 385
HMS Repulse, 230, 338, 346, 370, 385
Ho Chi Minh, 92
Hoare, Sir Samuel, 114
Hoare–Laval Pact between Britain and France,
    114
Hodges, Alice, 103, 104
Holland
  capitulation of, 169
  and command arrangements in south-western
    Pacific, 372
  consequences for of Japanese invasion of
    China, 142
  German conquest of
    and Netherlands East Indies, 171
  German invasion of, 169
  and Netherlands East Indies, 91
    views on British abandonment of, 417
  see also Dutch government
Holloway, Edward (Jack), 60
  and Curtin, 61, 62, 105
home defence, 183–4
  Australian army numbers for, 175, 183–4, 206
  Murdoch and White on, 174–6, 183, 206
  Murdoch on, 176–7
  Spender on, 225
Hong Kong, 91, 362
  Churchill on defence of, 298
  defeat of Canadian troops at, 362, 365, 442
  loss of, 432
Hope, Private Bob, 446
Hopkins, Harry, 228, 418
Horner, David
  on Curtin's refusal to permit the diversion of
    troops to Burma, 450
  on White, 178
Hotel Kurrajong (Canberra), x, xi, 116–17
  'cupboard' bar, 35, 45
Hughes, Billy
  as ALP leader and Prime Minister, 63
  and conscription in World War I, 23
    split in ALP over, 12–13, 24
  and Curtin, 425

and Curtin War Council, 420
and Curtin's 'The Task Ahead' article in
    Melbourne *Herald*, 361, 408
and dominion representative in British War
    Cabinet, 408
on Japan, 96, 98, 100, 248
leader of UAP, 277, 281, 282
and Page, 146
at Paris Peace Conference, 93
Prime Minister, 12, 23, 27
and White Australia Policy, 30
Hughes, Richard
on establishment of a Pacific War Council and
    an Imperial War Cabinet, 397
Hughes Governments, 13, 25, 27
Hull, Cordell, 243, 297, 320
Menzies on, 74
Hungary
declaration of war on, 302, 319, 334
Hutton, General T J, 427
Hyett, Frank, 19

Imperial Conference (London, 1937)
and defence of Australia, 124, 125
Imperial Defence
and conflict in British Government over ships
    to Singapore, 139
view on Japanese invasion of Australia, 173–8
income tax
Fadden and, 290–1
powers of federal and state governments, 291
Scullin and, 291
states and, 290
on wealthy and on poor, 291
India
defence of, 415, 417
Burma and, 204, 351, 411
return of Australian troops from Middle East
    to, 345, 364, 373, 410
Indian Ocean
Britain to send capital ships to, xvii, 234,
    237, 261, 269, 297, 299, 301, 311, 312,
    354–5
Japanese raids in, 439
see also Ceylon
Indian Ocean and Middle East theatre
under British command, 371
Indian troops, 179, 262, 276, 278, 297, 390
and Japanese landing at Kota Bharu, 317
to reinforce Malaya, 345, 364
Indo-China *see* French Indo-China; southern
    Indo-China; Tonkin; Vietnam
Ireland
and Britain, 90
Irish in Australia, xiii, 87, 90

Irish nationalism
Curtin and, 90
Isaacs, Sir Isaac, 38, 87
Isaacson, Peter, 2
Ismay, General Hastings
on Menzies, 235
Italy
entry into war on German side, 169, 170, 172
and invasion of Abyssinia, 113–15
and invasion of Albania, 141
Menzies on, 73
rise of fascism in, 28
tripartite pact with Germany and Japan, 181,
    186, 452

Jackson, Betty, 117
James, Captain L V, 65
James, Rowley, 111, 166, 193, 232
and Chifley Budget, 293
and not forcing no-confidence motion to
    topple Menzies Government, 258
Japan
achievements in first five months of 1942, 430
advantage to Germany of its entering war, 217
alliance with Britain, 96–7, 97, 98
approval for war with United States, Britain
    and the Netherlands, 310
armed forces of, 326–7
attack on Pearl Harbor, xvii–xviii, 306, 319,
    326
    plans for, 268
and Australia, 102
    forces needed for invasion of, 453
    invasion of, 428, 452
    invasion of postponed, 453
and Australian racism—White Australia Policy,
    30, 96, 97
bases in Pacific, 449
bases in Vietnam, 203
at beginning of war, 220
and beginnings of Pacific War in China, 142,
    143
and Bismarcks
    attack on, 398
and Borneo
    invasion of, 412
and Bougainville
    attack on, 389
British and Australian views of likelihood of
    attack on Soviet Union by, xvi, 248–9,
    249, 268, 299, 304, 306
and British concessions in China, 180
British views of fighting capability of, 230–1
and Buka
    occupation of, 433

Japan *continued*
  and Burma, 351
    control of skies, 356
    invasion of, 411, 415, 418, 426, 427, 448,
      453
  and China, 93, 96, 99, 131, 143, 180, 210,
    307, 309, 453
    consequences of re USA, 209
  and Chinese resources, especially oil, 143
  Curtin and idea of agreement with Japan, 239
  and Darwin
    bombing of, 420–1, 429
  declaration of war on USA and 'British
    Empire', 334
  diplomatic code broken, 241, 242
  and economic and political consequences of
    Great Depression, 64
  expansion of empire in 1920s, 28
  expansion of in east Asia in 1930s, 98, 99
  finalisation of war plans, 267–8
  and French Indo-China and French Pacific
    islands, 171
  and German invasion of Soviet Union, 180,
    238, 268
  and German non-aggression pact with Soviet
    Union, 151
  and Germany
    at war with USA if Japan attacked USA, 308
  and Greater East Asia Co-Prosperity Sphere,
    180–1, 416, 452
  grounds on which USA would declare war on,
    224, 226
  and Hong Kong
    capture of, 362, 365
  initial phases of war, xviii
  judgement of Japanese success by end of
    December 1941, 364–5
  and League of Nations, 100
  and Malaya, 200, 204, 218
    control of skies, 356
    invasion of, 317, 319, 323, 344, 345, 364,
      375, 411, 452
    landings and action at Kota Bharu, 317,
      319, 344, 404
    occupation of, 338–9
    raw materials in, 189
    rubber, 204, 351
    southward movement, 278, 384, 387, 388,
      390
  and Manchuria/Manchukuo, 72, 115
  Menzies on, 73
  and Micronesian islands, 72
  navy, 92
  and Netherlands East Indies
    capture of Australian troops on Java, 419

    invasion and occupation of occupation of
      Sumatra, 403, 411
    invasion of, 452
    invasion of Borneo, 412
    invasion of Java, 411, 412, 413, 419, 429
    occupation of Ambon, 412
    occupation of Kalimantan, 403
    occupation of Makassar, 412
    occupation of Sulawesi, 403
    occupation of Sumatra, 411, 413
    occupation of Timor, 413, 420
    oil, 171, 200, 204, 242, 247, 326, 327,
      351
    raw materials in, 189
    surrender of Java, 429, 430
  and New Guinea
    occupation of Lae, 429, 433, 454
    occupation of northern coast, 429, 430
    occupation of Salamaua, 429, 433, 454
    plan to occupy Port Moresby, 453
  Northern Advance plan and attack on Soviet
    Union, 180, 243
  objectives of against French, British and Dutch
    colonies of south-east Asia, 351
  objectives of against USA, 351
  and oil, 241, 242
  and the Philippines
    fall of Manila, 411
    fighting US troops, 364, 365, 411
    invasion of, 351, 452, 453
    US and Filipino forces trapped at Bataan,
      411, 430, 448
  plan for screen of bases across Allied supply
    line and isolating Australia, 453
  power of in Asia-Pacific region, 92
  pre-war planning, 327–8
  quality of armed forces, 430
  and Rabaul
    attack on and occupation of, 388–90,
      394–5, 398, 399, 411, 454
    base at, 429
    invasion of, 452
  raids in Indian Ocean, 439
  and Russia, 96, 97
  Russo-Japanese War of 1905, 326, 327
  sanctions against, 241, 242, 243, 245, 247,
    249, 326
  and separation of Australia from British
    interests by conquests in east Asia and
    Pacific, 448
  and Singapore, 242, 278, 402
    forces at, 399
    invasion of, 452
    surrender of, xviii, 411, 413, 415, 416,
      429

situations in which USA would not declare
war on, 227, 229
and Solomons
plan to occupy, 453
southern advance, 241, 243, 308, 453
Germany and, 247
Southern Advance plan, 180
and southern Indo-China, 241, 241–2, 244
and Soviet Union, 180, 268
Japanese–Soviet Non-aggression Pact,
268
and Thailand, 218, 244, 245, 249, 250, 310
invasion of, 323
and Timor
attack on and occupation of, 429
and Tonkin, 244
tripartite pact with Germany and Italy, 181,
186, 452
and USA, 99, 180
after Pearl Harbor, 448–9
as main enemy of in Pacific, 209
negotiations with, 260, 261, 267–8, 277,
296–7, 307, 308, 311, 318
and Vichy France, 181
and Indo-China, 241
views of imminence of war with, 212, 213,
214, 215, 217, 218, 220, 277, 300
in early 1941, 212–16, 217–18
war situation in March 1942, 428
war with USA, 210
Java
Australian troops landing on, 419
difficulty of defending after loss of Singapore,
413, 417
imminent Japanese attack on, 411, 412
Japanese invasion of, 429
surrender of to Japanese, 429, 430
Java Sea
Battle of, 364, 429
Javanese workers, 347–8
Jeparit (Vic), 65
Jess, Major-General Sir Carl, 174
Jews
extermination of by Hitler regime, xv
Johnson, Nelson, 347, 444
Johnston, Senator Bertie, 46
journalists at Parliament House
Alan Reid on, 129
Curtin and, 283–4
Joyce, Gladys, 2, 271, 285
on Curtin, 426

Kalgoorlie (WA), xi, 2, 7, 8, 12
Kalimantan
Japanese occupation of, 403

Karrakatta (WA)
Curtin's burial there, x
Kawai Tatsuo
and Curtin, 239, 246, 307
Kennedy by-election, 127
Keynes, Maynard, 31
and Curtin, 41
The General Theory, 40
King, Admiral Ernest
order for US Pacific fleet to protect sea
passages south-west to Australia, 348–9,
370
order for US Pacific fleet to south-west Pacific,
396
King, Mackenzie
on changes in Pacific after war, 443
and Churchill, 442
on Churchill, 443
and Churchill's offer of job to Casey,
442–3
and Curtin, 442
on Britain's place in post-war world, 443
on Curtin, 29
and declaration of war on Germany, 154
and dominion representative in an Imperial
war cabinet, 235
and dominion representatives in an Imperial
war cabinet, 235–6
and independence of British decisions,
362
and Malcolm MacDonald, 442
and Roosevelt, 442
on China in post-war period, 451
and troops sent to Hong Kong, assured of no
war with Japan, 362
King, the
role of in declarations of war by Australia,
303
see also George VI, King
Koepang, Dutch Timor, 297
troops to be sent to, 335
Konoe Fumimaro, Prince, 296
Konoe Government
and Greater East Asia, 180–1
resignation, 296
Kormoran, 309
Kota Bharu, Malaya, 300, 308
landing and action at, 317, 319, 344, 404
Kurrajong *see* Hotel Kurrajong (Canberra)
Kurusu Saburō, 308
and Casey, 308

Labor Conference, Perth 1919, 3
Labor Daily, 128
Labour Daily, 6

labour movement
and banking system, 15–16
see also Australian Labor Party (ALP);
    Australian Workers' Union (AWU);
    Timber Workers' Union (Federated
    Saw Mill, Timber Yard and General
    Wood Workers Employees' Association
    of Australasia, Victorian Branch); trade
    unions; Victorian Socialist Party (VSP)
Lae
    Japanese occupation of, 429, 433, 454
Landon, Alf, 74
Lang, Jack, xii, 14
    and Chifley, 288
    and Commonwealth vis-à-vis states,
        112–13
    and Curtin, 126, 127, 150, 288
    dismissal of, 105, 110
    and Gwydir by-election, 127
    and *Labor Daily*, 128
    and McKell, 164
    and Melbourne Agreement, 39
    and Menzies, 75–6
    and Premiers' Plan, 111
    and proposed referendums on aviation and
        marketing, 112–13
    and Scullin Government, 42
Lang faction/group: Lang Labor, xiii, 42, 104
    and ALP NSW Branch 'hands off Russia
        resolution', 165
    and Curtin, 34, 62, 110–12, 127, 165
    election 1934, 34, 130
    and fall of Scullin Government, 44
    formation of New South Wales Labor Party
        (Non-Communist), 165
    and Premiers' Plan, 110
    readmission of into ALP, 110–12
    rejoining ALP, 223
    and Scullin, 60, 64
    and UAP national security legislation, 184–5
    see also Australian Labor Party
        (Non-Communist); Beasley, Jack;
        New South Wales Labor Party (Lang);
        New South Wales Labor Party
        (Non-Communist)
Langtry, Joe, 225
Latham, Sir John, 46, 59, 77, 182
Laval, Pierre, 114
Lavarack, Colonel John, 332, 374, 413, 414
    Australian troops to be diverted to Burma, 419
    and Curtin's defence policy, 101
    on Japan, 99
    and Menzies, 332
    and Singapore strategy, 331
Lazzarini, Bert, 232

League of Nations
    ALP and, 113
    Australia and, 93
    and German rearmament, 115
    Germany and, 100, 114
    and Italian invasion of Abyssinia, 114
    Japan and, 100, 114
    and Japanese invasion of Manchuria, 115
    Soviet Union and, 113
    USA and, 93, 113–14
Leary, Vice-Admiral Herbert F, 396
Leckie, Senator John, 105
Lewis, Essington, 174, 275
    and Chifley, 275
Liberal and Country League (SA)
    election 1934, 104
Lloyd George, David, 236
Loan Council, 83
    and spending of states, 83
London dockers' strike of 1889 strikes
    Broken Hill (1909)
    Mann and, 18
Long, Gavin
    on Curtin, 307
    on Imperial Conference 1923, 98
Lothian, Lord, 185
Lyons, Enid
    and campaign for WA secession from
        Federation, 50
Lyons, Joe, 11
    as Acting Treasurer, 38
    and appeasement, 131
    and bond conversion, 41–2
    and British Cabinet re Czechoslovakia crisis,
        142
    and Bruce, 145
    and campaign for WA secession from
        Federation, 50–1
    Curtin and economic direction of, 41
    and Czechoslovakia, 132
    death of, 144, 146
    and defence policy, 127
    experience in, 120
    deficit reduction plan, 39
    and economic statement prepared by Fenton,
        Lyons, Anstey, Theodore and Curtin, 41
    and Green, 46
    leaves ALP to lead Opposition, 46
    and loan repayment, 40
    and Melbourne Agreement, 38
    and Menzies, 66, 69, 76–7, 145, 148–9
    and Munich Agreement, 142, 162
    and Mussolini, 114, 133, 162
    pacifist, 121, 131
    and Page, 146

as Prime Minister, 60, 104
and reinstatement of Theodore as Treasurer, 42
split from Scullin Government and ALP,
    12–13, 76
and succession as UAP leader, 145
trip to Britain for Silver Jubilee of King
    George V, 67, 69
UAP after death of, 265–6
Lyons Government, 11, 13, 66
and abdication of Edward VIII, 116
after 1934 election, 104
and air power, 130, 131
and appeasement, 142
and British Government position on German
    invasion of Czechoslovakia, 141
defence policy, 115
defence spending, 131, 134
and Italian invasion of Abyssinia, 114
proposed referendums on aviation and
    marketing, 112–13
and sending of British fleet in defence of
    Australia in event of war in Europe, 140
and Singapore strategy, 124–5
and Statute of Westminster, 84
and struggle in Pacific, 142
trade diversion policy, 115

MacArthur, General Douglas, xx, 349, 436
and air travel, 3
arrival in Australia, 447
on Australian army leadership and their
    defence strategy, 435
based in Australia, 432
and Cross, 408, 409
and Curtin, 328–9, 329
formally subordinate to Wavell, 371
    restrictions on Wavell, 372
on Japan in October 1941, xvi
and likelihood of Japanese attack on Soviet
    Union, 304
ordered to leave Philippines, 432, 447
ordered to take command of Allied forces, 432
and the Philippines, 245
reinforcements for in the Philippines, 364
supreme Allied commander, 447, 449
McCullum, Alex, 28, 58
MacDonald, Malcolm
on Hitler, 136–7
and MacKenzie King, 442, 443
MacDonald, Ramsay, 69, 442
McEwen, John, 157, 169, 187
and 'inexcusable betrayal' cable, 395
Mackay, Lieutenant-General Sir Iven, 434
McKell, William
and Lang, 164

McKenna, Frank, 117
McKernan, Mac, 314
McLaughlin, Fred, 271, 285
and Curtin, 426
and Moral Rearmament Movement, 425
Mahon, Hugh, 26
Makassar
Japanese occupation of, 412
Makin, Norman, 192, 255
and Curtin ministry
    Navy Minister, 273
and Curtin War Cabinet, 273
and Curtin War Council, 274
and Menzies threatening war without
    consulting War Council, 253
and War Council, 197
'Malay Barrier', 372, 436
Malaya
air support for, 355–6
Curtin War Cabinet on evacuation of women
    and children from, 383
defence of, 179, 214, 239, 244
    air power and, 204–5, 207, 300, 335, 338
    by Australia, 174, 179, 183, 186, 189, 221
    by Australia—8th Division, 179, 203, 208,
        210, 215, 220, 222, 276, 297, 306
    and defence of Singapore, 187, 190, 204
difficulties of Japanese attack on, 300
Japan and, 200, 204, 218
Japanese invasion of, 317, 319, 323, 344, 345,
    364, 375, 411, 452
    movement southward, 278, 384, 387, 388,
        390
Japanese occupation of, 338–9
loss of, 432
nature of warfare in, 344
RAAF preparations for Japanese attack in, 308
reinforcements for, 345, 364
retreat of Allied forces southward
    Australian and British press and, 384
    Australian press and, 384
rubber and tin, 179, 189, 204, 351
US action in event of Japanese attack on, 227
Manchuria
Japanese conquest of, 72, 115
Manila
fall of Manila to Japanese, 411
Mann, Tom
and Broken Hill strike (1909), 18
career after leaving Australia, 18–19
and Curtin, 17–18, 19, 44, 56, 63, 90, 105
and education, 18
and London dockers' strike of 1889, 17
and VSP, 17
Manpower Directorate, 347

Marshall, General George C, 245
  and Australia as south-west Pacific base, 381,
    382
  and Australian 9th Division to remain in
    Middle East, 440
  and command arrangements in south-western
    Pacific, 372
  and Germany first doctrine, 353
  and MacArthur, 432, 447
  on war preparedness of USA, 182
Matsuoka Yōsuke, 268
Melbourne, 15
  population mid-1930s, 82
Melbourne Agreement, 38, 42
Melbourne offices of Japanese diplomatic mission
  bugging of, 307
Menzies, Pat/Pattie, 65, 67, 69, 70, 105, 133
Menzies, Robert Gordon (Bob), ix, 399, 443
  and air travel, 3
  and all-party government after 1940 election,
    197, 233, 313–14, 361
  ambitions in Britain, 235, 236
  and appeasement, 75, 132, 133
  and Australian troops in Greece and Crete,
    xiii–xiv
  Australian troops should have been sent to
    Burma, 425
  background, 266
  and balanced budgets, 75
  and Britain and the Empire, 149
  on Britain and the Empire, 90
    preparedness for war, 75
  and British assurances of naval support against
    Japan, 158–9
  and British Cabinet re Czechoslovakia crisis,
    142
  and British navy and defence of Australia, 149
  and Bruce, 156, 157
  on Canada, 74
  and Casey, 146, 440
  and Chamberlain, 71, 134
    on Hitler, 71, 72
    on Japan, 71–2
  and Chifley Budget, 293
    defending private banks and financial
      orthodoxy, 294
  and Churchill, xi, xiv, 162, 235, 366
    and assurance of naval support in event of
      war with Japan in exchange for troops
      to Greece, 228–9, 230
    direct contact with, 376–7
  on Churchill, 72–3, 73, 162, 236, 237
  and Churchill's suggestion to Curtin to make
    him Australian minister in Washington,
    444–5

and committing troops to support Britain in
    fighting Germany, 158, 160, 160–1
  and conciliation of Italy, 157
  as Constable of Dover Castle and Lord Warden
    of the Cinque Ports, 68
  and Cooper, 414
  and Crete campaign, 235
  and Curtin, 75, 77, 148–9, 167–8, 259, 266,
    424, 450
    in 1940 Parliament, 201
    contrast, 105
    election 1940, 193
    foreign policy, 134
    and relationship to Britain, 84
    responsibility for loss of Burma, 428
  on Curtin, x, 158
    and his government, xii, 444–5
    journalist's mind, 121
  and Curtin War Council, 420
  and Curtin's 'The Task Ahead' article in
    Melbourne Herald, 408
  and Czechoslovakia, 133
  declaration of war: Britain at war, so Australia
    at war, 153, 154, 303
  declaration of war on Germany, 153, 154, 303
  and defence policy, 100
    experience in, 120
    if Britain is at war, Australia is at war, 149,
      153
  and defence spending, 150
  and diplomatic representation for Australia,
    149
  and Dixon, 66
  and dominion representative in an Imperial
    war cabinet, 235, 236, 361
  and dominion representative in British War
    Cabinet, 235, 408
  and dominion representatives in an Imperial
    war cabinet, 235–6
  and Duke and Duchess of York, 70
  early life, 65–6
  elected deputy leader of UAP, 76–7, 104–5
  elected leader of UAP, 146
  election to federal Parliament, 59, 66
  and English history, 68, 69
  on Evatt, 445
  Evatt on, 444
  and Fadden, 147, 235
  and Fairfax, 148, 280
  focus of on defending Britain, not defending
    Australia, 174
  on Foreign Office
    on Japan, 236–7
  on German claim for Polish Corridor, 133,
    152, 156–7, 161

on German claim to Danzig, 152, 161
on German invasion of Norway, 166
and German non-aggression pact with Soviet
    Union, 151
and Germany, 133
and Gibson, 76
Gowrie and, xi
and Greece campaign, 228, 229, 234, 235,
    254
and guarantee to Thailand in event of Japanese
    attack, 253
on Hitler, 72
on Hull, 74
and 'implied immunities' and 'reserved State
    powers', 83
and 'inexcusable betrayal' cable, 395
and Japan, 222–3
    briefing and possible ultimatum, 251–2
on Japan, 73
    conciliation, 75
and King George V and Queen Mary, 69–70
and Lang, 75–6
and Lavarack, 332
lawyer's mind, 121
loss of UAP leadership, 281
and Lyons, 66, 69, 76–7, 145, 148–9
in Lyons Government, 66
marriage, 105
and mediation of the China–Japan conflict,
    157
Minister for Defence Co-ordination, 261
and Munich Agreement, 142
and Murdoch, 148, 157, 174
on Mussolini and Italy, 73
and national government, 197, 236, 257
and national insurance scheme, 145
and negotiated peace with Germany, 155,
    156–7, 158
offer of resignation in favour of Curtin, 257
on Opposition, 281–2
on Pacific defence, 238–9
and Page, 145, 146, 147
on Page, 157
and Premiers' Plan, 76
pressing British Government to negotiate with
    Germany over Poland, 152, 153
Prime Minister, 146
proposal to return to London, 250–1, 254–7
    declines Fadden's request to, 262
    purpose of, 254
reading, 67
and reinforcements for Singapore being
    diverted to Burma, 405
resignation as Prime Minister, x, 259
resignation from Lyons ministry, 142, 145

response of to Dunkirk, 169
on Roosevelt, 74
and search for seat in House of Commons,
    260
and Shedden, 330, 332
and Singapore strategy, 332
speech to Constitutional Association
    and UAP leadership, 145
and suggestion of cabling Roosevelt directly,
    351
and threat of Russian Bolshevism, 162
trip to Britain for Silver Jubilee of King
    George V, 65, 67–8
    in Britain, 68–71
    'Jubilee Pilgrim', 67, 68, 69, 70
and UAP internal conflicts, 150
UAP under, 266
and US sanctions on Japan, 245
and USA, 92, 245
on USA, 74–5
and Vansittart
    on Hitler, 73
and Victorian Parliament, 66
visit to Canada and USA, 73–4
visit to Germany, 132–3
visit to London (1941), 205, 206, 208–9,
    234, 235
    aims of, 234
    results of, 254, 255
and War Council, 197, 201
on Ward, 445
and Young Nationalist/Melbourne Nationalists
    group, 46, 76
Menzies Government
    and Australian forces in Greece and Crete,
        xiii–xiv
    and Australian forces in Tobruk, xiv
    and British request for Australia to defend
        Malaya, 187, 189
    changes in defence policy by 1940, 187
    coalition with Country Party, 163
    and committing troops to support Britain in
        fighting Germany, 161
    and contradictory news from London, 152
    and defence of Singapore, 183
    and forward defence, 340
    and home defence, 183–4
    and independents after 1940 election, 194
    and industrial relations, 202
    and information on Japan, 182–3
    on internal conflicts in, 163
    and Japan
        drawing a line on southern advance, without
            USA, 244
    and national security legislation, 184

Menzies Government *continued*
   request to Britain for capital fleet at Singapore
      to deter Japanese attack, 206, 223, 230,
      251, 253
   and war between USA and Japan
      consequences for Australia of, 245–6
   and war in China, 182
Metropolitan Milk Board (Perth)
   Curtin on, 57
Micronesian islands
   Japan and, 72
Middle East/north Africa
   Australian troops in, xv; *see also* Tobruk
Midway, 349
   scheduled capture of by Japanese, 454
Miles, General Sherman, 307
Militia, 99, 173, 276, 306, 311–12, 313, 334,
      399, 433
   in action at Rabaul, 394
Mishael, Herbert, 358
Mitchell, Sir James, 57
Monash, John, 174
Moncrief, Gladys, xiv–xv
Morgan, Mollie, 314
Mulcahy, Dan, 166
Mulford, Clarence E.
   Hopalong Cassidy westerns, 8
Munich Agreement, 134, 136, 142
Murdoch, Sir Keith
   and all-party national government, 361
   Australian troops should have been sent to
      Burma, 425
   and Churchill, 361, 365–6
   and Curtin, 148
   and Curtin's 'The Task Ahead' article in
      Melbourne *Herald*, 360–1, 361
   Director-General of Information, 174
   and dominion representative in an Imperial
      War Cabinet, 361–2
   on home defence, 176–7
   and Menzies, 148, 157, 174
   and White
      on home defence, 174–6, 183, 206, 277
Muscio, Mildred
   and Royal Commission on Child Endowment
      or Family Allowances, 31
Mussolini, Benito, 73, 114, 133, 161, 170, 171

Nagumo Chūichi, Vice Admiral, xviii, 421
   raids in Indian Ocean, 439
Nairn, W M, 282
Napier, J M, 106
National Labor Party, 25
Needham, Abraham—Curtin's father-in-law, 20,
      21, 52, 54

Needham, Annie—Curtin's mother-in-law, 29,
      52, 240
Needham, Elsie *see* Curtin, Elsie (née
      Needham)—Curtin's wife
the Netherlands *see* Holland
Netherlands East Indies, 91, 92
   British proposal to abandon, 417
   imminence of Japanese attack on, 300
   Japan and, 181, 188, 241, 242, 247, 326,
      327
   oil, 143, 171, 188, 241, 242, 326, 327
      Australia and, 242
   Singapore in British hands and, 278
   US action in event of Japanese attack on, 227
New Caledonia, 433
   Japanese invasion of scheduled, 453
New Guinea
   Australia and, 91
   Australian 7th Division in, 427
   as Australian northern defence line, 436
   Japanese landing in, 394
   Japanese occupation of northern coast, 429,
      430
   see also German New Guinea; Lae; Port
      Moresby; Salamaua
New Hebrides, 433
   Australia responsible for, 372
New South Wales Labor Party (Lang)
   election 1934, 104
   see also Lang faction/group: Lang Labor
New South Wales Labor Party
      (Non-Communist), 165
New Zealand
   Britain and defence of, 125
   British in, 90
   Churchill's proposal that troops remain in
      Middle East in exchange for US troops to
      defend New Zealand, 439
   and committing troops to support Britain in
      fighting Germany, 160–1
   and declaration of war on Germany, 154
   declaration of war on Japan, 320
   declarations of war made independently,
      303
   Maori minority, 90
   and Singapore military conference (Oct.
      1940), 203
   and Statute of Westminster, 89
   troops for Greece campaign, 223, 229
   and USA
      USA to take responsibility for, 432
   in World War I
      on Western Front, 22
   see also Fraser, Peter
Niemeyer, Sir Otto, 37, 38, 40

Nimitz, Admiral Chester, 396
   order for US Pacific fleet to protect sea
      passages south-west to Australia, 348–9
Nomura Kichisaburō, Admiral, 297
Norway
   German invasion of, 166
Nullarbor Plain, xi, 2, 9, 10, 11

O'Dowd, Bernard, 358
oil
   in China
      Japanese need for, 143
   in Netherlands East Indies, 143, 171, 188,
      242, 326, 327
   Japan and, 143, 188, 241, 242, 326, 327
old age pension
   in Chifley Budget, 293
   Curtin and increase in, 292
One Big Union, 128
Operation Torch, 440

Pacific fleet see under United States navy
Pacific theatre
   under direction of US Joint Chiefs, 371
Pacific War
   beginning at Kota Bharu, 317, 319
   beginnings in China, 142, 143
   Britain exiting, 432
   consequences of, 143
   early assessment, 323–4
   a 'new war', 336, 337, 450
   racial element of, 323
   Roosevelt's new strategy for, 431–2
   United States and British combined chiefs of
      staff based in Washington, 349
   and wars in Europe, 322–3
Pacific War Council
   Churchill and, 399, 405
   Curtin and, 397, 405, 406
   in London, 363
      and abandonment of Netherlands East
         Indies, 417
      all Australian forces to be committed to war
         against Japan, 417
      Australian representative on, 378
      7th Division to be sent to Burma, 417, 418
   London versus Washington, 384, 408
Page, Sir Earle, xvi, 401, 404, 407, 424
   on abandonment of Australian troops in
      Malaya and Singapore and evacuation of
      Singapore, 392
   and air support in Malaya, 346
   on aircraft in Singapore, 297
   and Australian troops fighting without air
      support, 345

Australian troops should have been sent to
   Burma, 425
and British fleet at Singapore as deterrent to
   Japan, 269
and British suggestion of sending Australian
   troops from Middle East to Malaya, 345
and Bruce, 146, 274
and cable to Churchill from Curtin re return
   of Australian troops to Australia, 416, 417
and Churchill, 424
and Curtin, 415–16, 437–8, 450
   on London as centre of decision-making in
      Pacific War, 378
   on moving 7th Division to reinforce Ceylon,
      temporarily, 437
   Page's refusal to pass on To British
      Government Australian Government
      decision on AIF returning to Australia,
      421–2
and diversion of Australian troops from
   Middle East to Burma, 420
   Curtin Government not in agreement, 421
and Fadden, 147
and Hughes, 146
and likelihood of Japanese attack on Soviet
   Union, 304
loss of Country Party leadership, 163
and Lyons, 146
and Menzies, 145, 146, 147
mission to London
   aims, 262, 274
Prime Minister, 146
and reinforcements for Singapore being
   diverted to Burma, 405
reporting on Pacific War Council decision, 418
response to British Defence Committee and
   the War Cabinet deliberations, 392
opposition to evacuation of Singapore and
   to reinforcements for Malaya being
   diverted to Burma, 392
and source of suggestion of evacuating of
   Singapore, 393
and Winch–Johcu cables, 408
Palmyra, 433
Pankhurst, Adela
   and Curtin, 26
Papen, Franz von, 71
Papua
   Australia and, 91
Parkhill, Sir Archdale
   and Curtin's defence policy, 122, 124
   and defence policy, 120, 125
Parliament
   secret session of (March 1941), 223–4, 228–9
Paulus, General Friedrich von, 394

pay for armed forces, 291, 293
Pearce, Sir George, 12–14
  and ALP splits, 12–13, 24, 46–7
  and Bruce–Page Government, 13
  and campaign for WA secession from
      Federation, 50
  and defence, 13–14, 96, 97, 121
  and Fisher Government, 13, 97
  and gaoling of Curtin over conscription, 25
  and gaoling of Curtin over conscription In
      World War I, 13
  and Gibson, 46
  and Hughes Governments, 13, 25
  and Japan, 14, 96, 98
  Leader of the Opposition in the Senate, 34, 36
  and Lyons Government, 13
  in Lyons Government, 66
  and Scullin Government, 46
  and United Australia Party, 46
Pearl Harbor
  Japanese attack on, xvii–xviii, 319, 326
    Japanese reaction to, 320
    plans for, 268
Perkins, John
  and secret session of Parliament, 224
Perth Trades Hall Council
  Curtin publicity officer for, 51
petrol rationing, 295, 337, 347, 412
the Philippines, 91
  Bataan, 365
    US and Filipino forces trapped, 411, 430,
        448
  Corregidor
    MacArthur ordered to leave, 432, 447
    fighting in, 364, 365
    imminent loss of, 356
    Japanese attack on, 326, 351
    Japanese invasion of, 453
    reinforcements, including fighter planes, for,
        364
    US action in event of Japanese attack on, 227,
        244–5
    USA on defence of, 298–9
    Wavell and, 371, 372
Phillips, Admiral Sir Tom
  death of, 230
  and Japanese navy, 230
Piesse, E L
  and Curtin's defence policy, 101
  on Japan, 98, 100
Placentia Bay meeting (Roosevelt and Churchill),
    249, 252
  and Roosevelt's statement of principles:
      Atlantic Charter, 249–50
Playford, Tom, 396

Poland
  Britain pressed by Australia to negotiate with
      Germany over, 152, 153
  British and French guarantee to, 141, 142
  division of between Germany and Soviet
      Union, 153, 164
  German invasion of, 153
Polish Corridor
  Bruce on German claim for, 161
  Menzies on German claim for, 133, 152,
      156–7, 161
Pollard, Reg, 232
Port Augusta (SA), 10
Port Moresby
  defence of, 435, 436
  Japanese attack expected, 454
  Japanese plan to occupy, 453
  possibility of Japanese attack on, 390
  reinforcement of, 434
  troops to be sent to, 334, 401
Portugal
  talks re deployment of Australian troops to
      Timor, 297
Pound, Admiral of the Fleet Sir Dudley
  on idea of a fleet battle with Japan, 371
Premiers' Plan, 14, 42–3, 61, 62, 76, 110, 111
Production Executive, 287
Prowse, J H, 283

Quealy, Vincent, 334, 390, 396, 399
  no record of Menzies and McEwen dissenting
      re 'inexcusable betrayal' cable, 395

Rabaul, New Britain
  Australian casualties and prisoners taken,
      389
  Australian mandated territory, 389, 394
  Australian troops sent to, 222
  defences of, 297, 388
  Japanese attack on and occupation of, 388–90,
      394–5, 398, 399, 411, 451, 454
  Japanese base at, 429
  troops to be sent to, 334
  and Truk, 327, 328, 388
  use of by USA, 297, 311
racism and xenophobia, 94
  and Japan, 96
  see also White Australia Policy
railway lines, 8–9, 12, 46
  gauge changes, 9, 10
  see also train travel
Reading, Sir Claude, 290
Reid, Alan
  and Beasley, 272
  on Curtin, 272, 314

on Curtin's feelings while troops crossing
    Indian Ocean, 446–7
on journalists in Parliament House, 129
on Menzies, 145
on Wilson, 265
Reid, Alec
    and Curtin, 53
Ribbentrop, Joachim von, 308
Ricketson, Stan, 46, 105
Riordan, David (Darby), 60, 62, 127
Riordan, W J, 127
RMS *Otranto*, 65
Robertson, Lieutenant-Colonel Horace (Red
    Robbie), 130
Rodgers, Don, 1, 6, 55, 103, 128–9, 270, 271,
    447
    and authorship of Curtin's Melbourne *Herald*
        article, 358–9
    and Curtin, 129, 285
        and news of Pearl Harbor, 319
    on Curtin, 284
        his drinking, 45, 284
    and Curtin's defence policy, 130
    on Elsie Curtin, 342
    and Shedden, 296
    on Shedden, 285
Romania
    British and French guarantee to, 141
    declaration of war on, 302, 320, 334
Rommel, General Erwin
    in North Africa, 229, 232, 440
Roosevelt, Franklin D, xx, 74, 228
    and ABC-1, 355
    and Arcadia conference and agreement, 353,
        382, 410
    and Australia, 452
    and Australian 6th and 7th Divisions to be
        sent to Burma, 418
    and Australian troops to Burma in exchange
        for US troops for Australia's defence, 401,
        418
    and Australia's independent status, 363
    and British and Dutch imperialism, 351
    and Burma, 431
    and Burma as supply line to China, 351, 401,
        411, 417
    and cable from Curtin to Evatt outlining
        military chiefs' strategy for defence of
        Australia, 437
    and cast in Curtin's left eye, 54
    and Churchill, 378
        'Australia must be held', 449
        and Churchill's offer of job to Casey,
            443–4
        disagreements, 442

and Curtin, 437, 450
    appointment of MacArthur as supreme
        Allied commander, 447
    appointment of supreme Allied commander,
        447
    direct contact with, 376, 379
    deployment of Pacific fleet from San Diego to
        Pearl Harbor, 320
    and Evatt, xii
    and Germany First doctrine, 181, 352, 353,
        377–8
    and grounds on which USA would declare war
        on Japan, 224, 226
    and 'inexcusable betrayal' cable, 401
    and Japan
        more certain of war with, 211, 222, 241,
            245
        and Netherlands East Indies, 241, 242
        preparing for war in Pacific, 244, 245, 249
    and Mackenzie King, 442
    on China in post-war period, 451
    MacArthur ordered to leave Philippines, 432
    and maintaining peace in Pacific, 241
    and Malaya, 351
    Menzies on, 74
    and movement of Pacific fleet from San Diego
        to Pearl Harbor, 181
    and negotiations with Japan, 297
    and new strategy for Pacific War, 431–2
    and news of Japanese attack on USA, 324
    and Operation Torch, 440
    and the Philippines
        in event of war with Japan, 244–5
    and Placentia Bay meeting (with Churchill),
        249
        Roosevelt's statement of principles: Atlantic
            Charter, 249–50, 252–3
    and possibility of US troops on way to New
        Caledonia being diverted to Port Moresby,
        401
    and post-war Pacific, 451–2
        Australia's place, 452
    and reinforcements for Singapore being
        diverted to Burma, 405
    return of Australian troops from Middle East
        to Burma, 410
    and sanctions against Japan, 241, 242
    and Singapore, 351
    substituting US fleet for British at Singapore,
        182
    and suggestion of evacuating Singapore, 393
    and support for Churchill in trying to reverse
        Australian Government decision on AIF
        returning to Australia, 422
    and supreme commander in Pacific, 349

Roosevelt, Franklin D *continued*
two-ocean navy bill, 180
US troops being sent to Australia without conditions, 439–40
'Victory Plan', 249
on war preparedness of USA, 182
warning from Curtin of imminent fall of Singapore, 350–1
Rosevear, Sol, 166
and Chifley Budget, 293
and Menzies' return to London, 256
Rowell, Major-General Sydney
on expected Japanese moves, 454
on expected Japanese southern advance, 307
Royal Australian Air Force (RAAF)
forces of, 338, 340
and forward bases, 222
and landings at Kota Bharu, 317, 319
and preparations for Japanese attack in Malaya, 308
question of recalling elements from Britain and Middle East, 335
Royal Commission on Banking, 106
Chifley and, 106, 273, 288
Royal Commission on Child Endowment or Family Allowances, 30–1, 54
Royle, Sir Guy, 390, 398
rural marketing arrangements
proposed referendum on, 112, 113
Russia
and Japan, 96, 97
Russo-Japanese War of 1905, 326, 327
see also Union of Soviet Socialist Republics (Soviet Union)

Salamaua
Japanese occupation of, 429, 433, 454
Salvation Army
Curtin and, 16
Samoa, 433
Japanese invasion of scheduled, 453
Scullin, James (Jim), xii, 103
and appointment of Australian-born Governor-General, 87
and Curtin, 38, 285
and election 1934, 59
electoral win in 1929, 32
and Forde, 62
and Great Depression, 34
health of, 60
and Imperial Conference, London, 37, 38–9
and Lang, 14, 64
and Lang Labor, 60
leader of ALP after 1934 election, 60, 63–4
leader of ALP and Prime Minister, 63

and loan repayment, 40
office near Curtin, 285
and power of prime minister to sack a minister, 103
and Premiers' Plan, 42, 61
and reinstatement of Theodore as Treasurer, 42
resignation as leader, 61
and tax, 291
Scullin Government, xii, xiii, xix, 33, 34, 54
Chifley and, 288
Curtin and, 12, 288
defeat of, 19
disintegration of, 39, 42, 43–4
Gibson and Commonwealth Bank and, 46
and Great Depression, 36, 37
Green and, 12
and Lang, 42
and Melbourne Agreement, 38, 42
Pearce and, 46
and Singapore strategy, 332
split (1931), 13
Scully, W J, 127
Shann, Edward, 27, 31, 41, 56
Shedden, Sir Frederick, 174, 215, 271, 273, 318, 329–32, 374, 396, 404
briefing on Australian defensive capability, 335
on British appreciation of Japanese objectives in South-east Asia, 190
and Churchill, 330, 332–3
and British aid if Australia invaded, 433
on Churchill, 363–4, 424
and Curtin, 271, 285, 329, 330, 333
on Curtin, 4
on Curtin Government
big four of Cabinet, 285
big three of the Government, 285
and Curtin's 'The Task Ahead' article in Melbourne *Herald*, 362
and dependence on USA for defence, 278–9
and 'general mobilization for a total war effort', 287
and Germany First doctrine, 352
and Imperial Defence College, London, 99, 331, 346
and McLaughlin, 425
and Menzies, 330, 332
on Menzies' ambitions in Britain, 235
and Menzies War Cabinet, 332
and military forces establishment, 312
and military heads, 335–6
no record of Menzies and McEwen dissenting re 'inexcusable betrayal' cable, 395
and Pacific War, 333
as 'new war', 336
in post-war period, 295–6

retrospective rationale for sending troops to Middle East, 375
and return of troops to Australia, 425
and Rodgers, 296
roles under Curtin Government, 295, 296
and Roosevelt, 330
and Singapore strategy, 99, 279, 331, 332, 333, 346, 393
and reiteration of, 383
and style of Curtin's cables, 378–9
and Washington as head-quarters of Allied war command, 349
Sheehan, Tom, 166
Silver Jubilee of King George V, 65–70
Simpson, Wallis, 116
Sinclair, F R, 337
Singapore
Admiralty estimates re protection of, 159–60
Allied troops fall back on, 396, 400
Allied troops trapped in, 411
army reinforcements for, 376, 391, 402
Australian forces to defend, xviii, 183, 186, 200
8th Division, 179, 203, 208, 210, 215, 220, 222, 276, 297, 306, 343, 344, 374
Australian reinforcements sent to, 396
base at, 203–4
in British hands and Netherlands East Indies oil, 278
defence of, 179, 203–4, 205, 214–15, 404
by defending Malaya, 187, 190, 204
defences, 278, 297, 321, 338
difficulties of evacuation of, 403
economic value of, 204
fall of, xviii, 411, 413, 415, 416, 429, 432
fixed defences of, 403
Japan and, 242, 278
Japanese at, 399
no British fleet to defend, 179
no reinforcements, naval or air, for, 355, 375
question of evacuation of, 391, 392, 393, 395
question of withdrawal of troops to, 391
reinforcements for to be diverted to Burma, 391, 392, 393
US action in event of Japanese attack on, 227, 278
USA and, 401
Singapore military conference (Oct. 1940), 208
and southward advance of Japan and defence of Singapore, 203
Singapore strategy, xvi–xvii, 95, 98–9, 100, 121, 122, 123, 125, 138, 173
and air power, 346
Bruce and, 138, 139
Chamberlain and, 140

Curtin and, 332, 346
Curtin and Lyons Government, 124–5
and defeatism, 141
in event of war in Europe, 140, 149–50
Lyons Government and, 140
new meaning of, 179
Shedden and, 99, 279, 331, 332, 333, 346, 393
Smith, Adam
Wealth of Nations, 85
Smith, Forgan, 144
Smuts, Jan
and dominion representative in an Imperial war cabinet, 235
and dominion representatives in an Imperial war cabinet, 235–6
social services
Curtin on, 107–9
Solomons
Australia responsible for, 372
Buka
Japanese occupation of, 433
Japanese landing in, 394
Japanese plan to occupy, 453
South Africa
British in, 89
southern Indo-China
Japan and, 241, 241–2, 244
see also French Indo-China
Southwell, Isabelle (Belle)
and Curtin, 116–17
Soviet Union *see* Union of Soviet Socialist Republics (Soviet Union)
Speaker of House of Representatives
power of, 282
Spender, Percy, 195, 399
and Curtin, 425
and Curtin War Council, 420
and Curtin's 'The Task Ahead' article in Melbourne *Herald*, 408
and defence of Malaya and Singapore, 214
and dominion representative in British War Cabinet, 408
on home defences, 225
and imminence of war with Japan, 212–13, 216, 217, 220
and Menzies, 216
on Menzies and McEwen and 'inexcusable betrayal' cable, 395
and reinforcements for Singapore being diverted to Burma, 405
and test mobilisation of Australian defences, 220
on Thailand, 218
Squires, General Ernest, 332

SS *Katoomba*, 26, 32, 118
SS *Orcades*, 410, 419
SS *Wollongbar*, 4
Stalin
    and news of Japanese attack on USA, 324
Stalingrad, 304
Stark, Admiral Harold F, 308
Statute of Westminster (1931), 39, 84, 89
    adoption of by Australia in 1942, 89
Stimson, Henry L, 182, 241, 307–8, 349
Stirling, Alfred, 133
Stout, Vic
    and Curtin, 22, 45
Strahan, Frank, 270, 285–6
Street, Geoffrey, 105, 332
    death of in air crash near Canberra, 191
strikes
    1941, 276
    Broken Hill
        Mann and, 18
    coalfields, 202, 386
    Curtin and, 214, 232, 386, 394, 397, 399
    Liverpool dock strike
        Mann and, 18
    London dockers, 17
    of 1890s, 16, 78
    stevedores, 386
Sturdee, Lieutenant-General Vernon, 337, 338,
        390, 413
    Australia as base for US operations against
        Japanese, 432
    and Curtin
        advising that returning Australian troops be
            brought to Australia, 414–15, 425
    on defence of industrial core regions, 434
Sudeten Czechoslovakia, 132, 133
Sulawesi
    Japanese occupation of, 403
Sumatra
    Japanese attack on and occupation of, 403,
        411, 413
Swan by-election, 202–3
Sydney
    population mid-1930s, 82

'Taiwan Army Research Section' (Japanese),
        210–11
Takumi, Major-General Hiroshi, 317
Tasmania
    defence of, 434
taxation, 291
    on profits, 293
    and war production, 290, 294
    see also income tax
Taylor, W, 292

Thailand, 91
    British move into if Japan attacked, 310
    and Japan, 218, 244, 245, 249, 250
    Japanese invasion of, 323
        as cause of war with British Empire, 248,
            252, 253
    pathway to India through, 204
    report of imminent Japanese attack on
        Thailand, 308
Theodore, Ted
    and Allied Works Council, 412
    and Anstey, 34
    and Curtin, 34–5, 37–8, 42, 43, 49–50
    on Curtin as possible Labor leader, 49, 58
    Curtin on, 60
    economic plan, 39, 42
    and economic statement prepared by Fenton,
        Lyons, Anstey, Theodore and Curtin,
        41
    and exchange rate, 41
    and Great Depression, 34, 36
    and Lang group, 34
    left Parliament, 60
    and Premiers' Plan, 42
    reinstatement of as Treasurer, 42
    resignation of as Treasurer, 37
    on Scullin Government, 54
Thorne, Chris
    on Australia and New Zealand in Japan's
        Co-Prosperity Sphere, 452
Tillett, Ben, 90
    and Curtin, 17, 29, 63, 90
    and London dockers' strike of 1889, 17
Timber Workers' Union (Federated Saw Mill,
        Timber Yard and General Wood Workers
        Employees' Association of Australasia,
        Victorian Branch)
    Curtin and, 6, 20, 21
Timor, 222
    Japanese attack on and occupation of, 413,
        420, 429
    talks with Portugal re deployment of Australian
        troops to, 297
    see also Koepang, Dutch Timor
Titan Manufacturing Company
    Curtin's employment at, 20
Tōjō Hideki, General, xvii–xviii, 242
    call for Australia to surrender, 416
    on invasion of Australia, 452
    Prime Minister and Minister for War, 296
Tobruk
    Australian troops at, xiv, 232, 275–6
    relief of, 300–1
    withdrawal of, 297
Tonga Islands, 433

Tonkin
    Japan and, 244
Tonkin, Eric, 103, 270, 285
Townsville
    defence of, 434, 435
Tracey, Ray, 4–5, 285
    and Curtin, 5, 284
trade unions
    membership, 81
    and war mobilisation, 347, 358
    see also Australian Workers' Union (AWU);
        Timber Workers' Union (Federated Saw
        Mill, Timber Yard and General Wood
        Workers Employees' Association of
        Australasia, Victorian Branch)
train travel, xi, 5–6
    Perth to Canberra, 7–10, 11–12
    see also Great Western Express; railway lines;
        Trans-Australian Railway
Trans-Australian Railway, 8, 9–10, 46
Treasury (federal)
    powers of in 1935, 84
Treaty of Versailles, 71, 72
Tripartite Pact, 181, 186, 452
Truk (Micronesia)
    Japanese naval base, 72, 327, 328, 388
Tsugaru, 389
Tudor, Frank
    leader of ALP, 63
Turkey
    Australian troops and possible campaign in,
        305, 306

unemployment relief, 109
Union of Soviet Socialist Republics (Soviet
        Union)
    alliance with sought by Britain and France,
        151
    Australia pressing for agreement between
        Britain and Soviet Union re mutual
        assistance if either attacked by Japan, 304
    and China in war with Japan, 143, 180
    and division of Poland with Germany, 153, 164
    German invasion of, xv, 238, 267, 268, 412
    Japan and, 180, 238, 268
        racial element of, 323
    invasion of Finland, 164
    and Italian invasion of Abyssinia, 114
    and Japan, 180, 238, 268
    Japanese–Soviet Non-aggression Pact, 268
    Japanese Northern Advance plan of attack on,
        180, 243
    and League of Nations, 113
    likelihood of Japanese attack on, xvi, 248–9,
        249, 268, 299, 304, 306

non-aggression pact with Germany, 151, 202
    war with Finland, 302–3
    war with Germany, 294–5
United Australia Party (UAP), x, xii, 11
    after death of Lyons, 265–6
    election 1931, 46, 265
    election 1934, 59, 104
    internal conflicts after beginning of war, 163
    internal conflicts after death of Lyons, 144–6,
        150
    leadership of in opposition, 277, 281–2
    under Menzies, 266
    Pearce and, 46
United States army
    black troops allowed in Australia, 348
    fighting in the Philippines, 364, 365
    32nd Division ordered to Australia, 432
    41st Division ordered to Australia, 432, 437,
        439
United States Army Air Force, 367
United States Joint Chiefs
    and direction of the Pacific theatre, 371
    recognition by that Australia convenient base
        for US operations against Japanese forces,
        381
United States Naval War College
    and war with Japan, 209–10
United States navy, 92, 367
    after Pearl Harbor, 348
    and likelihood of Japanese attack on Soviet
        Union, 304
    Pacific fleet
        and defence of Australia, 372
        deployed from San Diego to Pearl Harbor,
            320
        and Japanese access to Netherlands East
            Indies oil, 143
        transfer of part to Atlantic, 219, 227, 297
        and Wavell, 371
    and preparations for Japanese attack, 308
    and securing sea passages south-west to
        Australia, 348–9, 370, 432
    and support for Malaya, Singapore, the
        Philippines, 370, 372
United States of America (USA)
    in 1935, 92–3
    and Australia as south-west Pacific base for
        operations against Japanese forces in,
        381–2, 416, 431, 453
    Australia dealing directly with, 341, 350
    and breaking of Japanese diplomatic code,
        241, 242
    and Britain, 92
    and China, 93, 180, 402
    and China in war with Japan, 143, 180, 211

United States of America (USA) *continued*
　Churchill seeking military alliance with,
　　185
　consequences for of Japanese invasion of
　　China, 142
　and defence of Burma, 402
　and defence of Singapore, 227, 278
　dependence on for Australia's defence
　　Shedden on, 278–9
　and direct consultations with Australia, 298,
　　302
　and economic and political consequences of
　　Great Depression, 64
　and fall of Singapore, 416
　fighting Japanese in the Philippines, 364
　German declaration of war on, 325
　Germany First doctrine in event of war with
　　Japan, 219, 221, 226
　Great Depression in, 33–4, 48
　and grounds on which USA would declare war
　　on Japan, 224, 226
　and Japan, 99, 180
　　declaration of war, 334
　　and negotiations with, 260, 261, 267–8,
　　　277, 296–7, 307, 308, 311, 318
　　in October 1941, xvii
　　and war in China, 209
　and knowledge of Japanese plan for southern
　　advance, 241
　as main enemy of in Pacific, 209
　Menzies and, 92
　Menzies on, 74–5
　mobilisation, 449
　and no war in event of Japanese attack on
　　British colonies, 229
　and no war in event of Japanese attack on
　　Netherlands East Indies, the
　　Philippines, and Malaya and Singapore,
　　227
　and Pacific possessions (including Hawaii),
　　91
　and the Philippines, 91
　politics on 1920s, 28
　and responsibility for Australia and New
　　Zealand, 432
　and sanctions against Japan, 241, 242, 243,
　　326
　and sea power supplemented by carrier-borne
　　air power, 352
　secret talks with Britain (1941), 297
　and Singapore, 402
　and south-west Pacific regional base
　　(Australia), 352
　troops for defence of, 381, 382, 439–40,
　　451

　war preparedness of, 182, 249
　war with Japan
　　attack on Pearl Harbor, xvii–xviii
USS *Lexington*, 396
USS *Mount Vernon*, 410, 446
USS *Yorktown*, 396

Vansittart, Sir Robert
　on Hitler, 132
　and Menzies
　　on Hitler, 73
Vichy France
　and Japan, 181, 241, 242
Victorian Artillery Corps
　Curtin's father and, 15
Victorian police
　Curtin's father and, 15
Victorian Socialist Party (VSP), 17
　Curtin and, 17, 19, 20, 22, 26, 31
　Young Comrades Contingent of the Socialist
　　Army, 19
Victorian Timber Workers Union *see* Timber
　　Workers' Union (Federated Saw Mill,
　　Timber Yard and General Wood Workers
　　Employees' Association of Australasia,
　　Victorian Branch)
Vietnam, 92
　Japanese bases in, 203
　see also French Indo-China

Wake Island, 326
Wakefield
　by-election, 163
War Council, 197, 198–9, 201, 201–2, 215,
　　216, 218, 220, 224–5, 238
　agenda, 200, 201
　Curtin and, 197, 212
　discussion of imminence of war with Japan,
　　212–16
　and domestic political issues, 200
　　and Budget (1940), 200, 201
　and Japan's likely strategy of attack,
　　218–19
　and Menzies' London visit, 208–9
　press statement re situation of 'utmost gravity',
　　220
　in war with Japan USA would be main
　　protagonist, not Britain, 261
　see also Curtin War Council
War Loan rally, Sydney, xiv–xv
war production, 311, 347, 348
　taxation and, 290, 294
war resources
　manpower, 289

Ward, Eddie, xx, 111, 113, 166, 171, 185,
    232
    and Chifley Budget, 293
    and Curtin, xiii, 224, 232, 240
        on compromise with Menzies, 201
    and Curtin ministry, 272
        ministry of Labour and National Service,
            273
    and Manpower Directorate, 347
    and Menzies, 399–400
    and Menzies Government, 232
    Menzies on, 445
    and Menzies' return to London, 256
    and no-confidence motion to topple Menzies
        Government, 258
    to organise labour in Darwin, 337
    and secret session of Parliament, 223,
        224
    and Spender, 399–400
    and War Council, 232
Washington agreement on command
    arrangements in south-western Pacific
    see command arrangements in south-western
    Pacific
Washington Naval Arms Limitations Treaty,
    95
Washington Naval Treaty, 92
Waterside Workers' Federation
    threat by Curtin of breaking strike with
        navy, 386
Watson, Chris
    as ALP leader and Prime Minister, 63
Wavell, General Sir Archibald, 208, 404,
    405, 413, 419, 439, 448
    and Brett, 382
    and Burma as supply line to China,
        417
    cable to Churchill from Curtin re return
        of Australian troops to Australia,
        416
    countermanded withdrawal of troops from
        Rangoon, 426
    and Curtin, 449
    on decision to evacuate Singapore, 392
    and defence of Australia, 372
    and defence of India, 415
    on difficulty of defending Java after loss of
        Singapore, 413, 417
    and diversion of Australian troops from
        Middle East to Burma, 413, 420
    and landing reinforcements for Singapore,
        402
    and MacArthur, 371, 372
    and 'Malay Barrier', 372

    and operational command in Australia's region,
        371, 372, 377
    to be dissolved, 431–2
    dissolved, 429
    on situation in Malaya
        Indian and Australian troops cut off,
            391
    on 6th and 7th Divisions of AIF to be sent to
        Burma, 417, 428
    warning Churchill of imminent fall of
        Singapore, 390–1
    on whole AIF to be sent to Burma, 422
Webb, Admiral Richard (British), 122–3
Welles, Sumner, 243, 307
Wellington Hotel (Canberra), 32
West Leederville (WA), 27
Western Australia
    campaign for secession from Federation, 50–1,
        57
    price for joining Federation, 12
    price for joining federation, 8–9
Western Australia's submission to
    Commonwealth Grants Commission
    Curtin and, 57
Westralian Worker, 28
    Curtin as sports writer for, 51
    Curtin editor of, 4, 6, 24, 25, 26, 27, 28, 44,
        53, 58
    Hilton and, 24
Whiskard, Sir Geoffrey, 160, 161
White, Sir Brudenell, 332
    death of in air crash near Canberra, 191
    on defence of Australia by battle fleet at
        Singapore, 177, 178
    and Murdoch
        on home defence, 174–6, 183, 206,
            277
White, Thomas, 146
White Australia Policy, 80, 86
    Chifley and, 288
    Curtin and, 30, 288
    Japan and, 30, 97
    partial relaxation of during war, 347–8
Wilkinson, Lieutenant-Colonel Gerald
    and Cross, 408, 409
Willcock, J C, 399
Wills, Lieutenant-Colonel K A, 413
Wilmot
    by-election, 163
Wilson, Alexander, 194, 200
    and Curtin Government, 283
    and fall of Fadden Government, 265,
        267
Wilson, Sir Charles, 360

Wilson, Woodrow
   and League of Nations, 93
World War I
   and Australian government debt, 35
   Australians on Western Front, 22–3
   Britain after, 92
Wren, John
   and Anstey, 106
   and Evatt, 314

Wynter, Lieutenant-Colonel Henry
   and Curtin's defence policy, 101, 119, 122,
      124
   and Singapore strategy, 122, 383

Yamamoto Isoroku, Admiral, xvii, 282, 453
   plans for offensive, 268

Zhukov, Marshal Georgy, 180